UB $50.25
NO REFUNDS ON USED BOOKS
D0164169

WESTERN EUROPE IN THE MIDDLE AGES

300–1475

WESTERN EUROPE IN THE MIDDLE AGES 300–1475

Fifth Edition

BRIAN TIERNEY: Cornell University

SIDNEY PAINTER

McGraw-Hill, Inc.

New York St. Louis San Francisco Auckland Bogotá
Caracas Lisbon London Madrid Mexico Milan
Montreal New Delhi Paris San Juan Singapore
Sydney Tokyo Toronto

WESTERN EUROPE IN THE MIDDLE AGES, 300–1475

Copyright © 1992 by McGraw-Hill, Inc. All rights reserved. Copyright © 1983 by Alfred A. Knopf, Inc. All rights reserved. Previously published under the title of *A History of the Middle Ages, 284–1500.* Copyright © 1978, 1974, 1970 by Alfred A. Knopf, Inc. All rights reserved. Printed in the United States of America. Except as permitted under the United States Copyright Act of 1976, no part of this publication may be reproduced or distributed in any form or by any means, or stored in a data base or retrieval system, without the prior written permission of the publisher.

345678910 KPKP 99876543

ISBN 0-07-064613-9

This book was set in New Baskerville by Waldman Graphics, Inc.
The editors were David Follmer, Niels Aaboe, and Bernadette Boylan;
the production supervisor was Kathryn Porzio.
The cover was designed by Karen K. Quigley.
Arcata Graphics/Halliday was printer and binder.

Library of Congress Cataloging-in-Publication Data

Tierney, Brian.
Western Europe in the middle ages, 300–1475 / Brian Tierney, Sidney Painter.—5th ed.
p. cm.
"Formerly entitled: A History of the Middle Ages, 284–1500."
Includes index.
ISBN 0-07-064613-9
1. Middle Ages—History. I. Painter, Sydney, (date).
II. Title
D117.T6 1992 91-42799
940. 1—dc20

About the Authors

After serving in the Royal Air Force, **Brian Tierney** received his B.A. and Ph.D. from Cambridge University. He has taught at Catholic University, Washington, D.C., and at Cornell, where he is now Bryce and Edith M. Bowmar Professor in Humanistic Studies. He has been the recipient of Guggenheim Fellowships and of fellowships from the American Council of Learned Societies and the National Endowment for the Humanities. Professor Tierney has been awarded the honorary degrees of Doctor of Theology by Uppsala University, Sweden, and Doctor of Humane Letters by Catholic University. A specialist in medieval church history, he has published many articles and several books, among them *Foundations of the Conciliar Theory; Medieval Poor Law*; and *Origins of Papal Infallibility, 1150–1350.* He is coeditor with Donald Kagan and L. Pearce Williams of *Great Issues in Western Civilization.* His most recent work is *Religion, Law, and the Growth of Constitutional Thought, 1150–1650.*

Sidney Painter was chairman of the Department of History at The Johns Hopkins University from 1945 until his death in 1960. His academic degrees included a B.A. and Ph.D. from Yale and an LL.D. from Middlebury College. He taught at Yale from 1927 to 1931, when he joined the faculty at Johns Hopkins. Dr. Painter was a beloved teacher and a truly distinguished scholar. His books include *William Marshall; Scourge of the Clergy, Peter of Dreux, Duke of Brittany; French Chivalry; History of the English Feudal Barony; Reign of King John; Rise of the Feudal Monarchies;* and *Mediaeval Society.*

Contents

THE EMERGENCE OF EUROPE

EARLY MEDIEVAL EUROPE: A NEW SOCIETY

Maps

Note on the Fifth Edition

The various editions of this book have all been based on a few simple convictions about the writing of history. In the first place, historical discussion—even when it deals with complex themes—can almost always be presented in "the language of common sense," plain, uncluttered English. Also, clear narrative is an essential form of historical writing, a norm to which good historians return as other fashions come and go. Finally, the purpose of historical writing is not merely to entertain (though there is no reason why it should be painfully dull); the historian's task is to understand and to explain.

With this purpose in mind, a historian has to be sensitive to findings by scholars in other fields who, in different ways, deal with changing aspects of human society. For a medievalist, work in areas as diverse as comparative religion and historical geography is very important. Also relevant are studies in anthropology, archeology, demography, and other social sciences. The later editions of *Western Europe in the Middle Ages* have incorporated more material from these neighboring fields, but I have tried to include it unobtrusively, so as not to change the character of the work.

In recent years there has been a growing interest in the lifestyles of medieval women and in the "marginalized" classes of medieval society—heretics, Jews, the poor and oppressed. Besides substantial rewriting throughout the text, this fifth edition includes two new chapters, "The Jews in a Christian Society" and "Rural Life and Peasant Revolts." There is also new material on the activities of medieval women, on family structures, on heresy and inquisition, and on the "papal revolution" of the eleventh century. The bibliographies have been extensively revised.

Most teachers of medieval history like to supplement textbook narrative with samples of original source material and with interpretive studies by modern historians. Accordingly a revised two-volume paperback collection of medieval sources and modern readings has been prepared to accompany this book. References to *Sources* and *Readings* in the bibliographies at the ends of chapters in the following text refer to this work, *The Middle Ages*: Vol. I, *Sources of Medieval History*; Vol. II, *Readings in Medieval History* (New York, 1992).

Preface

Sidney Painter's history of the Middle Ages earned a great reputation as a vivid and vigorous account of medieval life. Professor Painter did not try to write a completely balanced textbook but concentrated on those aspects of medieval society that interested him most—and his pages were alive with the learning and wit of a great scholar.

In this new book I have tried to supplement Professor Painter's work. All his brilliant narrative and descriptive chapters on feudal politics, feudal warfare, and feudal society have been retained. The history of the early period from A.D. 300 to A.D. 800 has been written afresh. In the later chapters much of the material on church history, law, political theory, philosophy, art, and literature is also new. All the material has been rearranged to bring out more clearly the chronological structure of medieval history. I hope that, in this revised form, the book will serve the needs of a new generation of students.

The scope of the work is indicated in its title. Our central theme is the emergence of a distinctively Western civilization in medieval Europe, and we have tried to give the clearest possible account of this complex phenomenon. Accordingly, for the purposes of this book, medieval Byzantium and medieval Islam are considered primarily as formative influences on the Western world at certain crucial stages of its development. But no student of the medieval West should forget that Byzantium and the lands of Islam also nourished great civilizations which merit further study in their own right. They cannot be adequately understood as mere subtopics in a course devoted primarily to medieval Europe.

Brian Tierney

Introduction

There are two reasons for studying medieval history. The first is to learn to understand medieval civilization for its own sake, because it is intrinsically fascinating. The second is to learn to understand our modern world more deeply by exploring its medieval origins.

These are platitudes, but they were not always so. When Edward Gibbon wrote his great book, *The Decline and Fall of the Roman Empire,* in the eighteenth century, it seemed natural to him to present the history of the medieval period as a gloomy story of degeneration and decay. Similarly, when Jacob Burckhardt wrote *The Civilization of the Renaissance in Italy* a century later, he took it for granted that the emergence of the modern individual, the modern state, and modern civilization became possible only when Renaissance men turned their backs on the Middle Ages, which he saw as an era of "faith, illusion and childish prepossession." In these older views, the collapse of the Roman Empire in the West marked a disastrous setback in the progress of civilization and the revival of classical culture in the fifteenth century a dramatic resumption of that progress. In between stretched the stagnant Middle Ages, a thousand years of Gothic gloom, barbarism, violence, and monkish superstition.

This view of history involved two presuppositions. The first was that the culture of the Middle Ages was grossly inferior to that of the ancient world or the modern world. The second was that modern civilization grew directly from classical roots and that the life of the medieval world was essentially an aberration in the growth of modern society.

The first presupposition was rather naive, and the fact will seem self-evident to any twentieth-century person who has looked at a medieval cathedral or listened to medieval music or read the poetry of Dante and Chaucer. Fifty years ago, by way of reaction, a myth of a "golden Middle Age" grew up; but this was, if possible, even more of an oversimplification than the view it sought to correct. Perhaps, in the end, an evaluation of the esthetic achievements of medieval civilization in comparison with those of other cultures must be largely a matter of subjective taste. Some people will always prefer the cathedral at Chartres and some the Parthenon. The problem of historical periodization, on the other hand, is a matter for rational analysis, and the view that medieval civilization was merely an aberration in the development of the modern West has come to seem less and less tenable in the light of recent research.

Any student who seeks to understand the Middle Ages at all has to face this question of periodization. The problem is not merely a technical one for professional scholars. It involves the whole issue of how we orient ourselves in time, where we look for a tradition that will help to make the modern world intelligible. Many interrelated questions have to be considered. When did ancient civilization come to an end and the Middle Ages begin? And what are the criteria for answering such a question? When did the Western world begin to develop a distinctive religious tradition? When and how did Western people come to devise structures of government radically different from those of the ancient world and from the systems of Byzantium and Islam? When did the West begin to take the lead in technology? And what, if anything, persists of medieval achievements in all these spheres in the modern world? Such questions lead on inevitably to another problem of periodization. When did the Middle Ages end? Did the Reformation and the scientific revolution create a new world by abandoning medieval ways of thought or are such movements intelligible only as the endproducts of centuries of medieval development? Will the historians of some future civilization, looking on their past from a new perspective, perhaps think that twentieth-century people were still living in a ''Middle Age?''

Here we can only suggest an approach to such problems. From the standpoint of a medievalist, the ''fall of the Roman Empire'' can be seen not only as the end of an old civilization but as the beginning of a new one. The upsurge of Christianity and the settlement of barbaric peoples in the western provinces of the empire introduced a new dynamism into the Western world. To be sure, judged by almost all conventional standards, European culture stood at a far lower point in the centuries immediately after the fall of Rome than in the preceding period. For most people, life was brutish and short. Except for a few clergy, virtually all the people of Western Europe were illiterate. There was incessant warfare. And yet this tough, savage society, with all its faults, contained an immeasurably greater potential for growth and adaptation than the sterile late classical civilization that it replaced.

The slow, painful fusion of classical, Christian, and barbarian cultures in the early Middle Ages formed the seedbed of a new civilization. During the eleventh and twelfth centuries, a new distinctively Western culture emerged. Since then Western society has experienced a process of continuous change, and, indeed, the rate of change has continuously accelerated; but, since the twelfth century, there has been no sudden break, no universal relapse into barbarism, no inexplicable change of direction. The fifteenth and sixteenth centuries—the age of the Renaissance and the Reformation—were indeed a time of briliant achievement and bold innovation, but so were the twelfth and thirteenth centuries before them. The continuities between late medieval and early modern civilization are at least as striking as the discontinuities.

The whole point about studying the Middle Ages is that, in considering medieval civilization, we are not dealing with an alien culture that was "born" in some far-off era and then long ago "died." We are indeed far removed from our twelfth-century ancestors because eight centuries of accelerating change separate us from them. But our civilization has grown out of theirs. That is why medieval studies offer such a fascinating challenge to the historian. Medieval civilization is not so alien to us as to be merely irrelevant, but medieval people were so different from us that we must make a real effort of historical imagination to enter with sympathy into their ways of life and thought. Most students who make the effort find it well worthwhile.

READING SUGGESTIONS

Some general works dealing with medieval history are given below. Reading lists dealing with particular periods and particular topics are placed at the end of each chapter. These lists are necessarily selective. They include some of the older classics that students should know, but generally give preference to more recent works and to books published in paperback editions (marked with an asterisk). Citations to the accompanying paperback volumes of *Readings* and *Sources* will be found at the beginning of the Reading Suggestions list for each chapter.

Bibliographies. The standard bibliography of works on European medieval history is J. L. Paetow, *Guide to the Study of Medieval History,* rev. ed. (New York, 1931), continued by Gray C. Boyce, *Literature of Medieval History, 1930–1975,* 5 vols. (Millwood, NY, 1981). For current bibliography see the Leeds University series, *International Medieval Bibliography.*

Translations. For translations of medieval works, see C. P. Farrar and A. P. Evans, *Bibliography of English Translations from Medieval Sources* (New York, 1946), supplemented by M. A. Ferguson, *Bibliography of English Translations from Medieval Sources 1944*–1963 (New York, 1973). Two particularly useful series of translations are *Columbia Records of Civilization, Sources and Studies* and *Nelson's Medieval Classics.* Translations of the Church Fathers are available in the older *Select Library of Nicene and Post-Nicene Fathers* or in two current series, *Ancient Christian Writers* and *The Fathers of the Church.*

Atlases. W. R. Shepherd, *Historical Atlas,* 9th ed. (New York, 1964), and G. Barraclough, *The Times Atlas of World History* (London, 1979) are particularly useful. Other good atlases are * E. W. Fox, *Atlas of European History* (New York, 1957); * C. McEvedy, *Penguin Atlas of Medieval History* (Baltimore, 1961); * R. R. Palmer, *Historical Atlas of the World* (Chicago, 1958).

General Histories. The most massive, detailed account of the Middle Ages as a whole is J. B. Bury *et al.* (eds.), *The Cambridge Medieval History,* 8 vols. (Cambridge, 1911–1936). A more recent survey is * D. Hay (ed.), *A General History of Europe* (New York, 1966), which includes four volumes on the medieval period. A valuable reference source is J. R. Strayer (ed.), *Dictionary of the Middle Ages,* 13 vols. (New York, 1982–1989). On economic history, see *The*

Cambridge Economic History, J. Clapham *et al.* (eds.), vols. I–III (Cambridge, 1941–1961). Useful church histories are K. S. Latourette, *A History of Christianity* (New York, 1953); P. Hughes, *A History of the Church,* 3 vols. (New York, 1935–1947), and H. Jedin and J. Dolan, *Handbook of Church History,* vols. I–IV (New York, 1965–1980). Good encyclopedias for religious history are *The New Catholic Encyclopedia* (New York, 1967–1974), *Encyclopedia of Islam* (Leiden, 1960–1961), *The Jewish Encyclopedia* (New York, 1901–1906), and *Encyclopedia Judaica* (New York, 1971–1972). The standard large-scale work on political thought is R. W. and A. J. Carlyle, *A History of Medieval Political Theory in the West,* 6 vols. (London, 1903–1936). For a good one-volume survey see J. H. Burns (ed.), *The Cambridge History of Medieval Political Thought* (Cambridge, 1988). Detailed surveys of medieval philosophy and science are provided by M. de Wulf, *History of Medieval Philosophy,* 3 vols. (New York, 1925–1953), L. Thorndike, *History of Magic and Experimental Science,* 6 vols. (New York, 1923–1940), and A. C. Crombie, *Medieval and Early Modern Science,* 2 vols. (New York, 1959). For an introduction to research on medieval women see * S. M. Stuard (ed.), *Women in Medieval History and Historiography* (Philadelphia, 1987). Joan Evans, *The Flowering of the Middle Ages* (London, 1966) is a splendid pictorial introduction to medieval civilization.

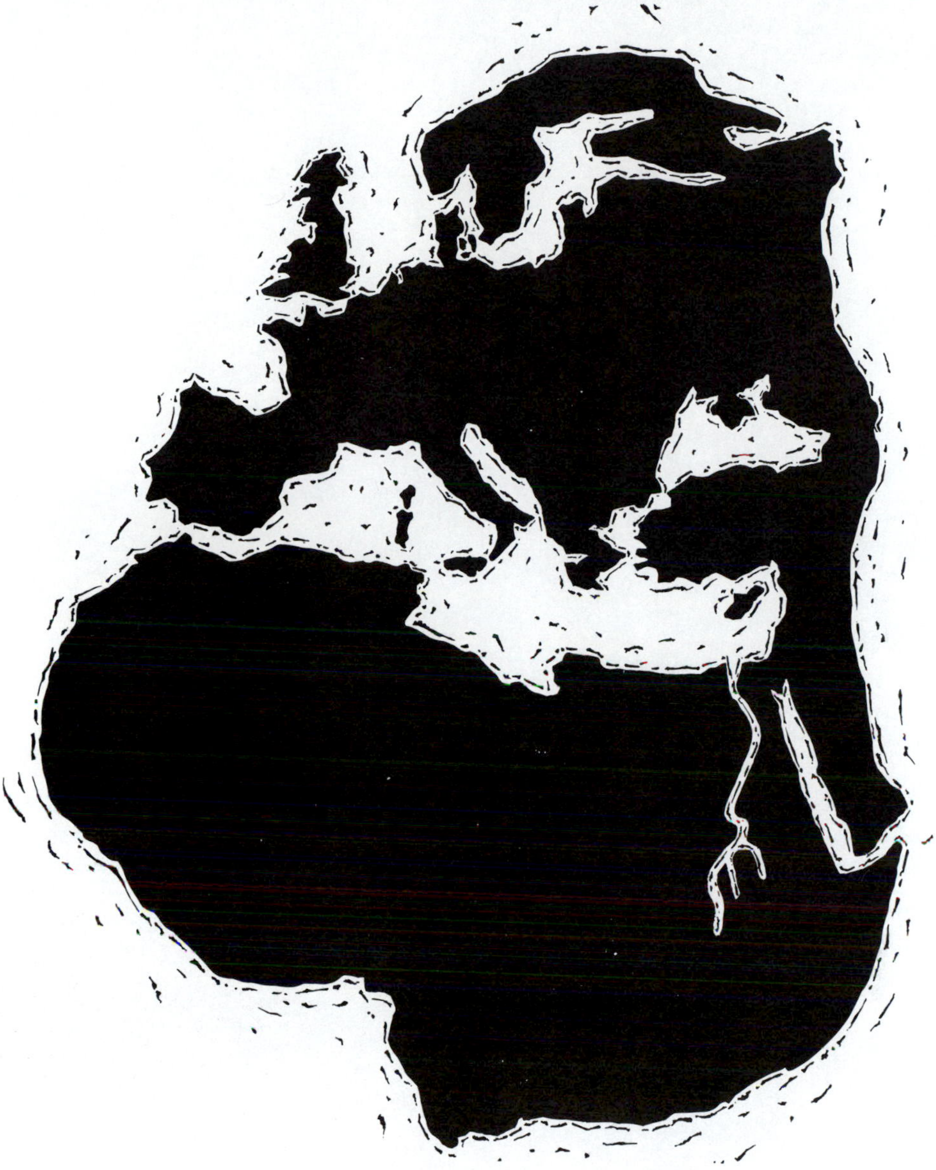

FOUNDATIONS OF WESTERN HISTORY

chapter

I

Europe: Land and People

On one level all history is a story of the interplay between peoples and their natural environments. When anthropologists deal with primitive, isolated societies, they can sometimes establish rather simple correlations between physical conditions and material culture, and then go on to show how material culture can shape complex patterns of social, religious, and political behavior. The task for historians of medieval Europe is rather different. They have to deal with many peoples, settled in a variety of terrains, living under different climatic conditions. For them a major problem is to explain how a single culture grew up from such diverse sources. Still, historians, like anthropologists, have to begin from the most basic realities—land and people.

1. *Land, Climate, Crops*

The whole of western Europe forms a peninsula, jutting out from the Eurasian land mass, bounded by the Mediterranean, the Atlantic, and the North Sea. No great physical barrier defines its eastern, landward borders; in prehistoric times (and for long afterwards), the entire region was open to settlement by successive waves of invaders moving westward from the steppes of south Russia and central Asia. The most obvious geographic division of Europe is between the Mediterranean basin and the lands of the north. The two regions are separated by high mountain ranges—the Pyrenees, the Alps, and, further east, the Carpathians. In southern France, however, a gap exists between the Pyrenees and the Alps; there the Rhone valley provides an obvious route for a Mediterranean power seeking to expand northward, or for northern invaders striking at the Mediterranean.

Around most of the Mediterranean, mountains or deserts press close to the shore, leaving a relatively narrow area of fertile coastland for settlement. Much of the coast is deeply indented, providing many good harbors. A typical form of early community that grew up in these conditions was the city-state, an urban settlement, usually on or near the sea, dominating the land for perhaps ten or twenty miles around. City inhabitants often owned land in the countryside and lived on its resources, supplemented by fishing and trade (or piracy).

Few great navigable rivers, opening up the hinterland to exploration, drain into the Mediterranean. (The Nile is a notable exception.) But the sea, calm in the summer months compared with the boisterous Atlantic, was easily traversed in ancient times by sailing ships or galleys. The coastal cities often found it easier to communicate and trade with one another over long distances than to deal with inland peoples who were relatively close at hand. Cities that grew rich as trading centers, or as administrative capitals, became sizable centers of population. Athens had over 100,000 people by the middle of the first millenium B.C., Rome perhaps a million at the height of its power.

The character of Mediterranean life has always been influenced by the climate and soil of the region. In classical times, as nowadays, the winters were moderately cool and wet, the summers hot and dry. Since virtually all the rainfall came in winter, much everyday life in the cities was carried on outdoors during the warm summer months; the marketplace was a center for social activities and political assemblies as well as for commercial transactions.

Mediterranean soil was mostly light and dry—though here again the rich alluvial land of the Nile delta was exceptional—and it supported a natural vegetation that included scrub pines, dwarf palms, shrubs, and a variety of grasses. (The cactus often encountered nowadays was a later import from America.) Hardwood trees suitable for building flourished only in mountainous areas, and there were already complaints of timber shortages in classical Greece. Hence, cities were built mainly of brick or stone.

The shortage of timber could have another effect. Pressure on limited resources of woodlands sometimes caused deforestation of mountain slopes; this in turn led to faster run-off of rainwater, creating a problem of soil erosion. Plato observed, with some exaggeration, that the Greece of his day was only a skeleton of mountains from which the soil had wasted away. In fact Greece was not very richly endowed with natural resources; other areas of the Mediterranean coastland offered greater reserves of arable land. The light soil was fertile and easily worked, well suited for growing the wheat and barley that provided the staple food of the region. Because of summer drought, winter and spring were the important growing seasons. Grain was sown in the fall and harvested in the early summer of the following year. Pastureland withered in the hot season, and animal stock had to be moved to mountain meadows where melting snow helped to maintain a supply of fresh grass. Sheep and goats could be reared more easily than cattle.

Mediterranean agirculture had its own specific problems and opportunities. The problems were to prevent soil erosion and conserve ground moisture; these aims could be achieved by irrigation, careful terracing, and frequent resting of the land. The opportunities were provided by an equable climate and reserves of fertile soil that proved adequate, until the days of the Late Roman Empire, to produce the large-scale grain crops needed to support growing urban populations. Apart from grain, the crops best suited to soil and climate were vines and olive trees, which put down deep roots to tap the scanty reserves of moisture, and flourished through the hot summers. Wine and olive oil were important items in the day-to-day diet of Mediterranean peoples.

North of the Alps very different conditions of landscape, soil, and climate existed, leading to different patterns of settlement and different kinds of agricultural activity. From the North Sea a great plain extended eastward across Germany to the steppes of Russia, and southward to the Pyrenees and the Mediterranean coast of France.

Physical Features of Europe and North Africa

The flat land was varied by limestone hills and upland plateaus with occasional outcroppings of relatively low mountain ranges. Between the hills flowed a series of great rivers, providing convenient routes for human migration—among them the Loire, Seine, Rhine, Elbe, and Oder.

Soil patterns were very varied. On the limestone uplands, light, easily worked soil was commonly found. In the low-lying regions heavy clays alternated with stretches of "loess," a light, loamy soil especially suitable for cultivation. The river valleys provided potentially rich alluvial land, but it required careful drainage to be suitable for crop-raising. The climate, generally much colder and wetter than that of the Mediterranean, differed especially in the pattern of rainfall; in the north, rain fell all the year round, and the relatively abundant summer rains influenced both natural vegetation and agricultural techniques.

During late prehistoric times, most of western Europe was covered with dense, deciduous forest—mainly oak, elm, and beech. In the more northerly and easterly regions, evergreens mixed with the broad-leaved trees, and the mixed forest extended to the tundra of north Sweden and the grasslands of Russia. Farming was practiced from Neolithic times, at first in forest glades, then, after the introduction of bronze and iron tools, on land cleared by a "slash-and-burn" technique. In such conditions, settlements were necessarily on a small scale—isolated farms or small villages of perhaps a dozen families living in houses built of timber and clay.

Wheat did not ripen so easily as in the Mediterranean lands and its cultivation required exceptionally favorable conditions. Subvarieties of wheat called spelt and emmer were grown, but barley was the most common cereal crop. Oats and rye were at first regarded as mere weeds of the grain fields but by 500 B.C. they had shown their value as hardy food crops, well suited to the northern climate, and were widely cultivated. The wet summers provided a longer growing season and it was possible to sow oats or barley in the spring to be harvested in the fall. Oats were used largely as fodder for animals but in the most northerly regions were also made into a gruel for human food. The widespread dependence on "coarse grains" in the north need not be regarded as a severe deprivation; the preference for wheat was largely a matter of taste—oats have more usable protein. Lacking the olive oil of the Mediterranean lands, northern people were more dependent on animal sources—mainly dairy produce—to provide the necessary fat in their diets, and stock-raising was always an important part of northern farming. Iron-Age chieftains counted their wealth in numbers of cattle as well as in quantities of gold treasure. In the most northern regions pastoralism predominated over agriculture; fishing was important in all coastal areas.

The cold, wet climate and dense forests at first made the northern lands a less hospitable area for human settlement than the Mediterranean, but eventually northern Europe would become a wealthy and prosperous region. The mountains proved rich in minerals; the plains offered vast areas of fertile, reclaimable land; the opportunity for a spring sowing eventually made possible an increased yield of crops. Full-scale exploitation of natural resources in the north began only in the early Middle Ages. From then onward, medieval peasants were able to produce a surplus of agricultural wealth that provided the foundation for a vigorous and sophisticated civilization. But, during the classical epoch, farming in northern Europe was limited to the light, easily worked soils and the northern world as a whole seemed to the richer, more advanced societies of the Mediterranean a barbarous, sparsely settled, relatively impoverished region, important mainly as a source of raw materials.

2. *Inhabitants: Early Europeans*

The earliest human inhabitants of Europe were Neanderthal people. Our human species, oddly called *homo sapiens,* appeared there some 30,000 years ago. The first settlers were hunter-gatherers, equipped with tools and weapons made of chipped stone. Their vivid, powerful wall-paintings of animal hunts, like the cave paintings that survive at Lascaux in southern France, are dated to about 25,000 B.C. After the glaciers of the last Ice Age receded (about 8,000 B.C.), Neolithic cultures, using beautifully crafted polished stone implements and decorated pottery, spread through western Europe. The first evidence of European farming comes from Greece and the Balkans (seventh millenium B.C.), and from there agriculture spread slowly westward. Fertility rites are a natural accompaniment of farming, and clay figurines from early Balkan sites suggest a cult of an earth-mother goddess. Much later, around 3,000 B.C., carefully oriented arrangements of great stone blocks (*menhirs*)—the most famous is at Stonehenge in England—indicate the spread of a solar cult. Archeologists trace the different waves of immigration into western Europe mainly by investigating the diffusion of specific types of pottery. Much is obscure, but it seems clear at least that the major movements of people came from central Asia with some additional immigration from North Africa into Spain, southern France, and Italy.

From about 2,000 B.C. onward, all of western Europe came to be dominated by Bronze-Age peoples speaking Indo-European languages. The affinities of language do not necessarily prove a single origin, but archeologists and linguists have most usually found a common homeland for these peoples in the Caucasus region of south Russia. (From there they also spread eastward and southward, carrying Indo-European language patterns to India and Iran.) The most northerly of the Indo-European peoples, the ancestors of the Germans, occupied south Sweden, Denmark, and the south Baltic coastal region by 1,000 B.C., and we shall encounter them in their later wanderings. Slavic-speaking people inhabited the plains of Poland and the Ukraine. But by far the most widespread of these early northern peoples were the Celts, a warlike folk who, earlier than their neighbors, became highly skilled in the working of bronze and then of iron. Nowadays Celtic languages and cultures survive only in the "western fringe" of Brittany, Wales, Ireland, and Scotland, but at the height of their power the Celts dominated a vast region extending from Britain to the Black Sea.

The Celtic peoples originated in southern Germany and began to expand during the Bronze Age in the second millenium B.C. Two early Iron-Age cultures associated with the Celts are known as the Hallstat culture (seventh century B.C.) from an archeological site in Austria, and the La Tène culture (fifth century B.C.), from a site in Switzerland. The last major waves of Celtic invasion carried the La Tène culture through France to Britain, Spain, and northern Italy.

At first the Celts ruled the earlier inhabitants of the lands they occupied as conquerors, then mingled with them and imposed their own language universally. In Spain, for instance, they blended with a pre-existing Iberian population to form a Celtic-speaking people known later to the Romans as Celtiberians. (The only surviving pocket of pre-Celtic speech in western Europe is in the Basque region of the Pyrenees.) The Celts usually lived in fortified hill villages, under local kings, supported by warrior aristocracies and subordinate populations of peasants and craftsmen. Their legends, set down only centuries later, tell stories of gods and heroes, of warrior prowess and personal honor, that may remind us of Homer's Greece. But Celtic visual art—preserved mainly as decoration on drinking vessels and weapons—developed differently from that of the Greeks. It derived its aesthetic appeal from abstract linear design rather than from the naturalistic representation that became typical of Mediterranean art.

While the Celts were extending their sway over northern Europe, other peoples moved into the Mediterranean area. Tribes speaking early forms of Latin and other Italic languages, the ancestors of the Romans, filtered through the Balkans and settled south of the Tiber. The Etruscans, a people with Near-Eastern affinities—perhaps invaders from Asia Minor—occupied the region of central Italy; their undeciphered language remains one of the great mysteries of classical archeology. North of the Etruscans, after about 400 B.C., were the ubiquitous Celts. (In 390 B.C. Celtic war bands sacked Rome.)

The Balkan area was occupied by Thracians and Illyrians (whose language was probably the ancestor of modern Albanian). Most important of all for the future of Western civilization, Hellenic peoples moved into Greece and settled all around the Aegean Sea, so that, during the first millenium B.C., the coast of Asia Minor became as thoroughly Greek in culture as mainland Greece itself. The first major surviving works in the Greek language, the epic poems of Homer, were probably written in the eighth century on the basis of earlier oral tradition. Subsequently the brilliant city-state civilization of classical Greece produced the superb works of literature, art, philosophy, and political theory which have remained a permanent part of the Western heritage.

The eastern and southern coasts of the Mediterranean were inhabited by peoples belonging to different language groups—semitic in the Levant and Arabia, hamitic in Egypt and North Africa. Great ancient civilizations existed in Egypt and the Near East long before the Hellenic peoples moved into Greece. Their arts, religions, and mathematical skills contributed to the formation of archaic Greek culture. Also, by the time the Homeric epics were composed, the Jews had found their promised land in Palestine; but at that time they probably seemed to their more powerful neighbors only a minor people with an eccentric taste in deities.

If we look only at geography and climate there seems no obvious reason why a single culture unit stretching from Scandinavia to Sicily (but excluding Africa and the Near East) should ever have grown into existence. A more obvious line of development might have been the emergence of a single Mediterranean civilization, separated from the cold, relatively barbarous northern world; and for many centuries events seemed to be moving in that direction. It is easy for us to think of the Mediterranean as a border, separating "Europe" from the very different continent of "Africa"; but in classical times the sea seemed more a highway, linking together peoples who had much in common with one another in spite of their diverse origins. Socrates once said, "We live around a sea like frogs round a pond," and even before his time the Mediterranean was surrounded by city-states that were in touch with one another through trading and cultural contacts. Before 500 B.C. the Greeks, pressed by population growth, had sent out colonies to establish new cities near the Black Sea and also along the north coast of the Mediterranean. Greek colonies were established in Sicily and south Italy, at Massilia (Marseilles) on the French Mediterranean coast, and as far away as western Spain. Meanwhile the Phoenicians, from their base in the Levant, were colonizing the south shore of the Mediterranean. After one of their early colonies, Carthage, became a great power in its own right, later settlements were established, either from Carthage or directly from the Levant, in North Africa and southern Spain.

In the fourth century B.C. the conquests of Alexander the Great (d. 323) absorbed the world of independent city-states in Greece and Asia Minor and carried Greek culture eastward as far as Afghanistan. When Alexander died his empire disintegrated into several separate kingdoms, but a veneer of cosmopolitan "Hellenistic" culture persisted, based on the widespread use of Greek as a common language among the rulers, scholars, and merchants of the Mediterranean world. Philosophers—Epicureans, Stoics, Neoplatonists—carrying on the Greek tradition of speculation, tried to provide guidance for people deprived of the comfortable, close-knit society of the city-state. Scholars studied the Greek classics and built up great libraries. Even the immemorial civilization of Egypt acquired a Greek ruling dynasty at this time, and the Egyptian city of Alexandria became a principal center of Hellenistic culture. However, the type of absolute monarchy established in Egypt and other parts of the eastern Mediterranean—usually called "Hellenistic kingship"—was not derived from Greece but from the ancient Near-Eastern civilizations that Alexander had conquered, where the ruler was commonly worshipped as a god.

Rome was the power that imposed ordered unity on this politically fragmented but culturally rather homogeneous society. The legendary date for the founding of Rome is 753 B.C., but any settlements that existed then on the site of the future city were only scattered villages, clusters of huts on the summits of the seven hills overlooking the Tiber. Rome was first formed into a unified city under Etruscan kings in the sixth century. Then around 500 B.C. the Romans expelled these first kings and established an aristocratic republic. At first it was just one more little city-state, like dozens of others scattered around the Mediterranean. The early Romans, however, displayed unusual qualities of discipline, prudence, stamina, and implacable ambition. Their expansion began in the fourth century with the conquest of Latium, the region south of the Tiber; by the end of the third century the Romans dominated the whole Italian peninsula. The principal rival of Rome at this time was the Phoenician city of Carthage in North Africa. After a series of bitterly fought campaigns against Carthage the Romans won a decisive victory in 202 B.C.; this victory ended the "Second Punic War" and established Rome as a major power. During the next two centuries, victorious armies extended Roman rule over all the lands of the Mediterranean. Finally, around the beginning of the Christian era (c. 50 B.C.–c. 50 A.D.), Roman legions moved northward from their bases in southern Gaul to conquer the Celtic lands of northern Gaul and Britain.

The Romans for the first time brought substantial territories of northern Europe under the rule of a Mediterranean power. The medieval world emerged from the disintegration of their empire. A survey of Roman civilization will provide some necessary background for understanding the course of early medieval history.

READING SUGGESTIONS

The best guide to historical geography is J. G. N. Pounds, *An Historical Geography of Europe, 450 B.C.–A.D. 1330* (Cambridge, 1973). See also C. T. Smith, *An Historical Geography of Western Europe before 1800* (London, 1967) and D. Whittlesey, *Environmental Foundations of European History* (New York, 1949). On prehistoric Europe see * V. G. Childe, *The Prehistory of European Society* (Baltimore, 1958); S. Piggott, *Ancient Europe* (Chicago, 1965); and G. Daniel, *The Idea of Prehistory* (Baltimore, 1965). For an introduction to Celtic culture see * N. Chadwick, *The Celts* (Baltimore, 1970). More detailed works are N. Chadwick and M. Dillon, *The Celtic Realms* (New York, 1967) and J. Hatt, *Celts and Gallo-Romans* (New York, 1970). A convenient survey of Hellenistic culture is provided by * W. W. Tarn, *Hellenistic Civilisation,* 3rd ed. (New York, 1952).

ROMAN, CHRISTIAN, BARBARIAN: THE ANCIENT WORLD TRANSFORMED

chapter

II

The Roman Empire

The civilization of western Europe in the period known as the Middle Ages grew out of a fusion between the institutions of the Roman Empire, the religion of the Christian church, and the cultures of various relatively primitive peoples whom the Romans called barbarians. The institutions of the Roman Empire as shaped by Augustus (31 B.C.–A.D. 14) had changed almost beyond recognition by the year 284, when Diocletian (284–305) became emperor. He and his successor, Constantine (306–337), created a new empire that bore little resemblance to the old. It was the civilization of this Late Roman Empire, increasingly permeated by Christian influence, that merged with the cultures of the barbarian peoples, chiefly Germans and Celts, to form the early medieval world. In the next three chapters, we shall examine these three cultures—classical, Christian, and barbarian—and try to explain some of the complicated ways in which they interacted with one another.

re: Constantine

3. *Rome: A Waning Civilization*

At the height of its power, in the second century of the Christian era, the Roman Empire stretched from the moors of northern Britain to the fringes of the Sahara Desert in Africa. Its northernmost permanent boundary was the great fortified wall built by the emperor Hadrian (117–138) to protect the people of Roman Britain against the Celtic tribesmen of Caledonia. From the North Sea to the Black Sea, the frontier followed roughly the lines of the rivers Rhine and Danube; then it swept in a great arc around the Mediterranean to include Asia Minor, Syria, Palestine, Egypt, and the coastal provinces of North Africa. The empire was essentially a Mediterranean state, with its richest provinces grouped around the Mediterranean Sea. The lands that

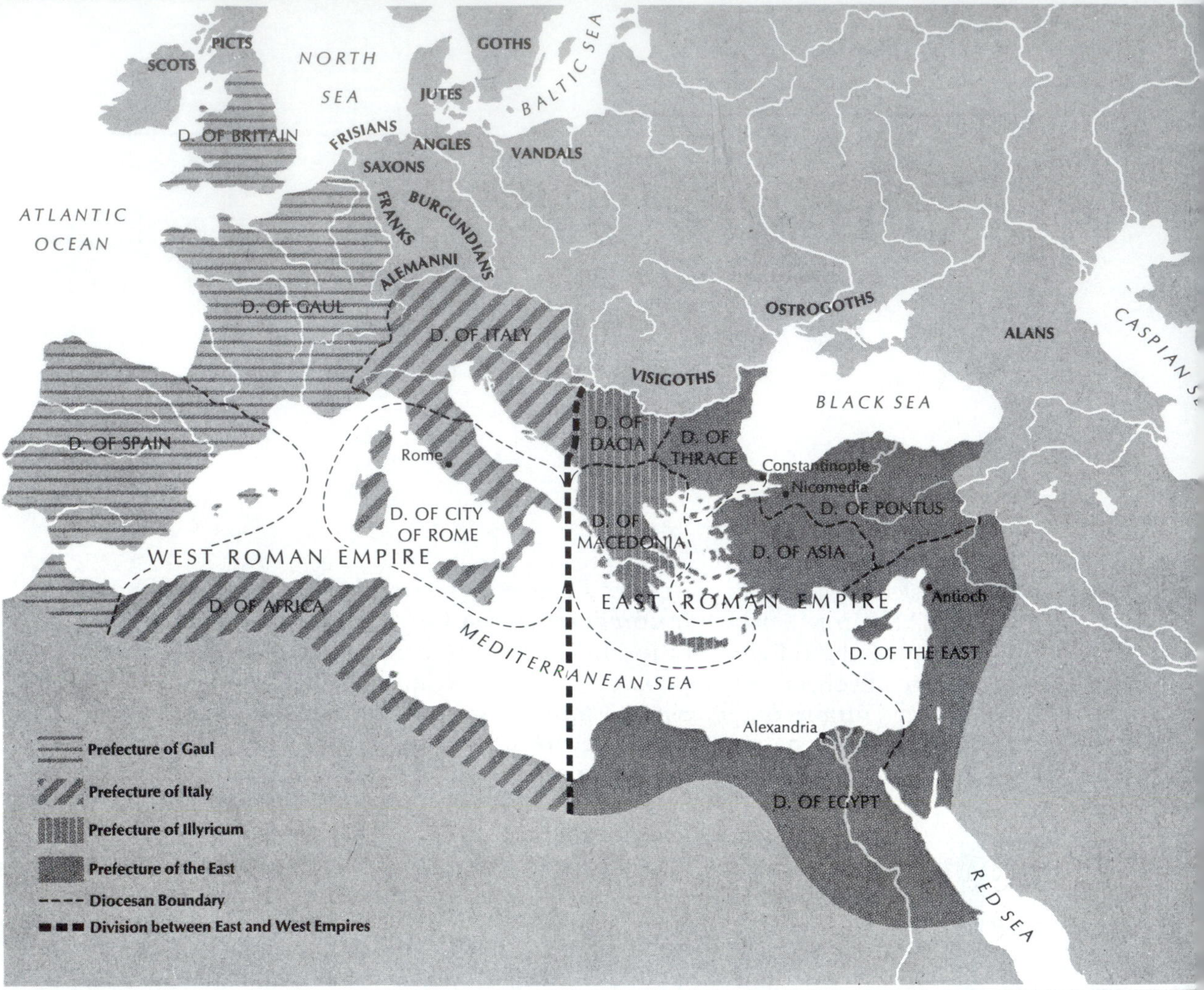

The Roman Empire, ca. 395 A.D.

The empire is at this point threatened by the barbarian peoples pressing westward and southward. Compare this map with the two following, which show the various waves of penetration and areas of settlement of the new rulers of the Mediterranean basin.

stretched away to the north were the last to be assimilated and were always relatively poor and thinly populated.

Evidently, this Roman Empire was by no means identical with the geographical region that we call Europe, the region that in later times would become the homeland of Western civilization. The empire included all the lands of the eastern and southern Mediterranean which have been dominated by Islam ever since the seventh century. It did not include Scandinavia or Ireland or most of modern Germany or the Slavic lands to the east of Germany. Hence a major problem for historians is to explain just how "Europe" emerged from the wreckage of the Roman Empire as a distinctive new culture unit.

We can note at the outset that the eastern and western halves of the empire always were markedly different from one another, even when they were held together under a common imperial government. The West was by far the most Latinized part of the empire, the region where Roman culture was most important and formative. In Gaul, Spain, and Britain, Rome established its rule in areas where no earlier pattern of high civilization existed. The Romans created centers of urban culture in these lands and reproduced the Roman pattern of life in the cities that they founded. These provincial cities were adorned with elegant temples dedicated to the Roman gods. They were often equipped with great stone amphitheaters for public games and with schools where Latin literature was taught. The leaders of the conquered peoples very commonly adopted Roman ways and came to look on the Latin culture as their own heritage. In Gaul and Spain, even the language of the conquerors was imitated; a coarsened form of Latin vernacular speech spread to the common people.

In the eastern half of the empire, by contrast, Rome expanded by conquering territories that had traditions of civilization older and more sophisticated than its own—areas like Egypt and the Greek city-states and the lands of the eastern Mediterranean that had become permeated with Hellenistic Greek culture in the centuries before the Roman conquest. In the eastern part of the empire, Greek, not Latin, was the common speech of the educated upper class. Rome imposed its culture on the barbarous West; it drew much of its own cultural tradition in turn from the East. Greek philosophy, Greek art, Greek literature all provided models for the Romans, and the religions of the Roman world nearly all had their origins in the eastern Mediterranean. There too were found the greatest centers of wealth and population. Apart from Rome itself, all the richest cities of the empire were in the East; and such cities were not mere administrative outposts (as was often the case in the West) but, more typically, thriving commercial centers. In the second century, the merchants of Antioch and Damascus carried on a trade that extended to the farthest borders of the empire and beyond the borders to India and even to China.

The whole complex of territories was governed by an emperor with autocratic powers assisted by a bureaucracy of professional administrators. For purposes of local administration, the empire was divided into provinces, which in the East often corresponded geographically to preexisting kingdoms or states that had been conquered and absorbed. Within the provinces, the basic unit of administration was the *civitas* or city. The *civitates* were allowed to exercise a substantial degree of self-government. They had their own senates, their own elected magistrates, often their own local deities. It was characteristic of the empire in the time of its greatest vitality that the local units displayed great vitality too. In all parts of the Roman world there were substantial citizens who were eager to rise to the rank of *curialis* from which local governing bodies were drawn and who were willing to undertake tasks of local administration for the sake of honor and prestige.

The cities were connected with one another by a network of excellent paved roads and, when necessary, were provided with a supply of water by great stone aqueducts. The Romans excelled in construction work of this kind. They were always inferior to the Greeks in the higher realms of aesthetic achievement and in the profundities of philosophical speculation, but they were good at practical things. Rome produced capable builders, excellent administrators, and superlatively good lawyers. Her success in establishing peace and order over such a vast area, in holding together so many peoples under a single government, was a triumph of practical administration; and the Roman law that regulated the life of the empire is one of the greatest bequests of classical civilization to the Middle Ages and to the modern world.

Historians have speculated endlessly about the reasons for the decay of this great imperial structure. The very magnificence of Rome's achievement has always challenged the imagination and understanding of those who seek to explain its downfall. Edward Gibbon, for instance, began his book on the fall of the Roman Empire with these words:

> In the second century of the Christian era, the empire of Rome comprehended the fairest part of the earth, and the most civilized portion of mankind. The frontiers of that extensive monarchy were guarded by ancient renown and disciplined valour. The gentle but powerful influence of laws and manners had gradually cemented the union of the provinces. Their peaceful inhabitants enjoyed and abused the advantages of wealth and luxury. The image of a free constitution was preserved with decent reverence.

Yet in spite of all this, even though the Roman state exemplified all the virtues that an eighteenth-century classicist could most readily admire, Gibbon saw the whole history of the Late Roman Empire as a process of "decline and fall."

Many modern historians have quarreled with this view; they prefer to write about a "transformation of the Roman world"; and such terminology is perhaps an improvement on Gibbon's, provided that we understand all that it implies. There were really two transformations. A crisis in the third century led to a period of civil war and near-collapse. Then a strong revival in the fourth century restored peace and order to the Roman world. But the empire had indeed undergone a transformation in this process of rebuilding; the changes included a new pattern of government, new ways or ordering economic life, and, most important of all, the adoption of a new religion, Christianity. The fifth century was again a period of radical disruptive change; by the end of it, all the provinces of the western Empire had been attacked and conquered by invading barbarian peoples. We can, if we choose, call this process too a "transformation" rather than just a "fall." Certainly, Roman influence did not simply disappear. The eastern Empire survived as a powerful independent state; in the West a new society slowly grew up which drew much of its culture, especially its religion, from the late Roman world. But such considerations should not lead us to minimize the catastrophic nature of the changes that occurred. The whole political fabric of the Roman empire in the West collapsed, and such a collapse calls for an explanation. (The Chinese had to cope with many of the same problems as the Romans, but their state did not disintegrate in the same way.) The breakdown of the Roman Empire in the West really does pose a serious problem that deserves all the attention historians have given to it.

Innumerable reasons have been advanced to explain the fall of Rome—moral decay, economic decline, civil wars, social injustice, even slow poisoning of the population from lead water pipes. Although the problem is a very real one, much of the argumentation about it is pseudoargument. That is, historians have often approached the question of Rome's decline by trying to identify one single, simple cause that would explain the whole process of disintegration, whereas the real problem is to show how the numerous causes of decay that were rooted in Roman society interacted with one another to produce the final breakdown of classical civilization.

Gibbon himself realized that the splendid civilization he had described was inherently unstable, and when he came to sum up his own views on the reasons for its decline, he wrote, "Instead of inquiring why the Roman empire was destroyed, we should rather be surprised that it subsisted so long." In fact, one can take every aspect of Roman civilization that Gibbon praised in the passage quoted above (p. 20) and find in it not a source of strength, but a cause of future weakness.

Even in the second century, it was becoming increasingly difficult to provide "disciplined valour" to guard the frontiers. At the beginning of the Christian era, the emperor Augustus had been able to recruit his armies mainly from Italy, for military service was then considered an honorable career. Every soldier became a Roman citizen and at the end of his period of service received a grant of land or money that enabled him to live decently as a respected veteran. During the second century, when the people of Italy became unwilling to volunteer in sufficient numbers for the rigors of army life, the large-scale forces needed to defend the borders came to be recruited principally from the Roman provincials of the frontier regions. By the mid-third century, even Romanized provincials could not be recruited in sufficient numbers; more and more the armies were coming to consist of barbarian warriors fighting under Roman commanders. Such troops had little instinctive attachment to a remote imperial government. They had never seen Rome or Italy. Because the emperor was often merely a name to them, their loyalties came to be concentrated on their immediate commanders.

Gibbon praised the unifying influence of common "laws and manners," and the extension of a veneer of common culture over the whole Roman Empire was indeed a remarkable achievement. But the common culture was only a veneer: it affected only an educated minority. An Egyptian peasant, a Celtic soldier, a Greek craftsman had no common world view, no common language, no common religion, no common ideals. In the end it proved that they had no common interests. For a time the provinces were knit together by a flourishing network of commerce, and the opening up of the mineral resources of Gaul and Britain at first stimulated the growth of trade. By the middle of the second century, however, the western provinces had developed their own manufactures and were becoming self-supporting. They produced a decreased surplus for export and required fewer imports. One immediate result was a marked recession in the economic life of Italy itself, which could no longer find easily profitable markets for its products. The different regions of the empire were becoming economically self-sufficient at the same time as they became militarily self-sufficient. There was still large-scale trading activity, but there was also a tendency toward economic stagnation that could easily turn into a disastrous depression if aggravated by labor difficulties or a currency crisis. In the third century, the empire suffered both problems.

We need to bear this in mind in considering Gibbon's remark about "the advantages of wealth and luxury." Of course, only a tiny minority in the Roman Empire enjoyed such advantages, and the reason was not just that the distribution of wealth was radically inequitable. That is true, after all, of most societies. In the Roman Empire maldistribution of wealth was complicated by deep-rooted problems of social structure and demographic change. During the early days of Roman expansion Italy had been a nation of free peasant farmers. The wars of conquest, however, brought in hordes of captive slaves, and the economy of the Roman world—agrarian and industrial—came to depend on the exploitation of their labor. Although small farms never ceased to exist, the typical unit of agricultural production in Italy became the great estate or "plantation." Such estates raised commercial crops (mainly vines and olives) for the Roman market. They were usually owned by absentee landlords and worked by gangs of slaves; displaced peasants drifted to the cities.

Although a slave system must offend our moral susceptibilities, dependence on such a system does not in itself explain the collapse of a whole civilization. Evidently it is not impossible to get the work of a society done by servile labor—provided that there are plenty of slaves. And during the period of Roman conquests, every victorious campaign brought in hordes of prisoners to replenish the slave markets. But after the frontiers had been stabilized in the second century, there were no more victorious campaigns to bring in a constant supply of new captives. Slave labor became more expensive. Moreoever the problem of labor supply was aggravated by a general falling off in population. Between 165 and 180, a major epidemic—perhaps smallpox—spread through the empire, carried by soldiers returning from the Persian frontier. Other epidemics followed in the third century—outbreaks of malaria, and of new illnesses brought in along the trade routes from Asia and Africa. Diseases like measles, which eventually became for the most part only passing ailments of childhood, were commonly fatal in a population that had built up no natural immunity to them. Roman population seems to have reached its height before the epidemic of 165 and declined thereafter. A falling population meant declining production of real wealth; in the third century, although there were many fabulously rich individuals who "enjoyed and abused the advantages of wealth and luxury," the empire as a whole was not really wealthy in relation to the demands made on its resources.

Gibbon tells us that "the image of a free constitution was preserved with decent reverence," but, in fact, a defective political structure was a major cause of instability in the Roman state. If one seeks to trace the actual process of breakdown in the third century, this political weakness provides the most convenient starting point. At the beginning of the first century B.C., the Roman form of government was republican. Real power rested with the Roman Senate, that is, with an aristocratic or oligarchic clique of the most wealthy and influential families. This system was disrupted by Julius Caesar, who staged a military coup d'état in 49 B.C. He was assassinated in 44 B.C., and a long-drawn-out struggle for power followed until Caesar's great-nephew Augustus Caesar emerged as sole ruler in 30 B.C. The official propaganda disseminated by Augustus presented him as a restorer of the Roman republic, and under his rule, the old republican magistracies were maintained and the Senate continued to function. But Augustus attached so many powers to his own person that, in fact, he commanded an overriding authority that no element in the state could resist. As *imperator* he was commander in chief of the Roman armies. As *consul* and *tribune* he held the highest civil magistracies. As *pontifex maximus* he was high priest of the state religion. From the time of Augustus onward, this whole complex of power was handed down from emperor to emperor.

The basic weakness in the system was the absence of any constitutional machinery to secure an orderly transfer of power at the death of an emperor. The imperial office was neither a hereditary monarchy nor a genuinely elective magistracy. From A.D. 96 to 180, from Nerva to Marcus Aurelius, each emperor selected his own successor, named him as coregent, and established him in a position of such unchallengeable power that his succession could not be disputed. In this way a series of great rulers came to the throne. But the system required both extraordinary discernment and extraordinary magnanimity in the reigning emperor, and, in the nature of things, it could hardly have lasted indefinitely. This system broke down in 180 when Marcus Aurelius secured the succession for his son Commodus, who proved thoroughly vicious and incompetent. Commodus was assassinated in 192, and from 193 to 211 Septimius Severus, a soldier from the province of Africa, maintained a despotic military rule. To him is attributed the cynical motto, "Look after the soldiers and scorn the rest."

After the death of Septimius Severus, the soldiers were indeed in charge of the situation. They made and unmade emperors capriciously, switching their support from candidate to candidate in return for promises of ever-greater rewards. Any frontier commander who was able to persuade his army to support him in an assault on Italy could aspire to be emperor. Over and over again, pretenders marched on Rome and either killed the reigning emperor or were themselves defeated and killed. The incessant civil wars naturally weakened the borders. Frankish tribes attacked the Rhineland, and Goths pressed on the Danube frontier. The wars also had the effect of undermining the financial structure of the Roman state. Each new emperor had to provide enormous bribes or "donations" demanded by the soldiers who had raised him to power—not unreasonably since their regular pay was usually in arrears. When the treasury became exhausted, he produced new supplies of money by debasing the coinage. Finally, an intrinsically worthless silver-washed copper coin was substituted for the old silver *solidus,* and this expedient was naturally followed by a ruinous inflation.

In the year 259 the imperial prestige suffered a major humiliation when the emperor Valerian was defeated in a campaign on the eastern frontier and captured by the Persians, who treated him with extreme contempt. When Valerian died, the Persian king preserved his stuffed skin as a grim trophy of war. The next emperor, Galienus, exercised effective power only in Italy. All the other parts of the empire were in the hands of rival pretenders. About this time there were some twenty would-be "emperors," each ruling some fragment of Roman territory. In 270 a horde of Germans broke through the Alpine passes into northern Italy and were narrowly defeated by the emperor Aurelian. During the middle years of the third century, the Roman Empire seemed to be sinking into a state of endemic civil war and permanent bankruptcy.

4. *The Reforms of Diocletian and Constantine*

The survival of the western empire for another hundred years was made possible by a sweeping series of reforms carried through by the emperors Diocletian (284–305) and Constantine (306–337). The most important features of these reforms were an increased emphasis on the absolute authority of the emperor, a sharp separation between the hierarchies of civil and military government, and the imposition on the empire of a new structure of taxation and economic regulation.

The most obvious weakness of the third-century empire was the absence of a stable central authority, universally respected and obeyed. Diocletian, a hard-headed and very successful soldier, saw this clearly enough and set himself to remedy the defect. He succeeded in this task, but in succeeding he premanently changed the nature of the Roman state. Under Diocletian the carefully concealed political dictatorship established by Augustus turned into an overt, divine-right monarchy. The powers and privileges once enjoyed by the Roman Senate either disappeared or became meaningless forms, and the Senate became in fact merely the local council of the city of Rome. The empire was governed by laws, but the emperor was the source of those laws. Hitherto the emperor had held power, at least in principle, as the first magistrate of the Roman people. It is true that, since the early days of the empire, the emperor had been revered as a semidivine being, but this divinity itself inhered in his role as a personification of Rome. From the time of Diocletian onward, a different, Oriental mystique of divine kingship was pressed into service to justify imperial absolutism. The emperor was presented as truly a god on earth or (after the acceptance of Christianity) as a divinely ordained representative of God—in any case, as a sacred figure set far above ordinary humanity. At the courts of Diocletian and Constantine, the emperor's person was surrounded by all the ceremonial trappings of an Eastern god-king. On state occasions the emperor appeared in splendid jeweled robes of blue and gold, wearing a tiara and carrying a scepter to symbolize his supreme authority. Courtiers prostrated themselves in his sacred presence.

Diocletian built himself a great palace in the eastern city of Nicomedia and made it the headquarters of a reconstituted bureaucracy. All power flowed from the emperor and was exercised at the highest levels by those who enjoyed his confidence. The three highest-ranking officers of the imperial administration were the Master of the Offices

Detail from the Ludovisi Battle Sarcophagus, ca. 250 A.D., showing Romans and barbarians in battle. The figure of a Roman general dominates the scene, but the struggles and sufferings of the barbarians are depicted with a vividness that contrasts sharply with the cold, impersonal battle scenes of earlier periods. *Marble, Museo delle Terme, Rome. Anderson-Art Reference Bureau.*

(a sort of senior Secretary of State), the Quaestor of the Sacred Palace (the highest legal officer whose duties included the drafting of imperial decrees), and the Count of the Sacred Largesse (the principal minister for finance). In practice, however, equally great authority was exercised by the chief official of the emperor's household, the Great Chamberlain, who enjoyed the real political power of close personal contact with a ruler who had become an almost unapproachable despot. In typical Oriental fashion, the Great Chamberlain was usually a eunuch.

Diocletian reorganized the local administration of the empire as well as its central government. In earlier times one single hierarchy of government had directed both civil and military affairs; the governor of a province was also the commander of the troops stationed there. This situation had tended to encourage the imperial ambitions of many local commanders, and Diocletian put an end to it. He divided the empire into four great *prefectures,* each presided over by a *Praetorian Prefect,* who was strictly a civil administrator with no military responsibilities. The boundaries of the prefectures ran roughly north and south. Thus the Prefecture of Gaul included Britain, Gaul, Spain, and the northwestern tip of Africa. The Prefecture of Italy stretched from Italy northward to the Danube and southward to include the central part of the African provinces. The Prefecture of Illyricum included most of the Balkan peninsula. The Prefecture of the East consisted of Thrace, the lands of the eastern Mediterranean, and Egypt. These great prefectures were divided into *dioceses* (twelve in all), each under an official called a *vicar.** The dioceses were subdivided into provinces and these in turn into *civitates,* the old basic units of the empire. The officials presiding over all these administrative divisions held no military command. The emperor could make appointments at will at any level of the hierarchy.

Supreme military command was vested in officers who bore the title *magister militum*—literally, "master of the soldiers" or, we might say, "general of the armies." Two such generals were permanently in attendance on the emperor. Three others commanded regions in the eastern half of the empire (one in Illyricum, one in Thrace, and one in the East). At first there were two *magistri* in the West, but by the end of the fourth century one supreme general stationed in Italy commanded all the troops of the western empire. Below the *magistri* were subordinate commanders called *duces.* The army was divided into three groups according to functions: There were two corps of imperial bodyguards whose duty it was to protect the person of the emperor; a mobile army ready to march to a threatened frontier or to combat a rebellion; and, finally, the troops who watched the frontiers of the empire. (These frontier troops, who often intermarried with the local populations, were regarded as inferior in quality to the mobile forces.) The various military commanders had no responsibility for civil administration. The emperor, who presided over both hierarchies of government, civil and military, was the sole link between them, the keystone holding together the whole state. New titles of nobility were

*See map, p. 18.

invented to dignify the high officials of the empire in the fourth century. At the top of the pyramid were *illustres*—illustrious ones—a rank held by Praetorian prefects and *magistri militum.* Then came *spectabiles,* then *clarissimi.* At the bottom of the scale were the high-sounding *perfectissimi.*

Diocletian attempted to solve the problem of succession to the throne by establishing a sort of imperial college. He appointed a coemperor, an old comrade in arms named Maximian, to rule over the western provinces and he and Maximian each appointed a deputy who bore the title "Caesar." It was intended that, when an emperor died or abdicated, he would be succeeded by his Caesar. Diocletian did abdicate in 305 (and lived placidly in retirement until 312). At Diocletian's insistence, Maximian reluctantly also abdicated in 305 and the two caesars, Constantius I in the West and Galerius in the East, were duly promoted. But at this point the succession scheme broke down, for Maximian, Constantius, and Galerius were all determined to press the claims of their own sons to be next in line of succession. In 306 the armies of Britain acclaimed Constantine, son of Constantius, as emperor, and a new round of civil wars broke out. Constantine made himself master of the western empire by winning a decisive battle at the Milvian Bridge near Rome in 313. By 323 he had also established his power in the East; after that he ruled for another fourteen years, during which time he was able to reimpose order and discipline throughout the empire. Constantine did not appoint a coemperor, but after his death the empire was divided between his sons. From this time onward, the more usual situation was that two emperors ruled together, one in the East and one in the West.

Besides continuing and intensifying the centralizing policies of Diocletian, Constantine made two personal innovations that were of the highest importance for the future. The first was his decision to embrace the Christian faith. The subsequent rise of Christianity and its acceptance as the official religion of the empire transformed the whole nature of late classical culture. (Its development, far too important a topic for a brief presentation here, will be discussed in a separate chapter.) The second major innovation of Constantine was his establishment of a new imperial capital in the old city of Byzantium, chosen for its splendid strategic location on the Bosporus. Diocletian had established an administrative headquarters in the East, but Constantine deliberately aimed at founding a new world capital there, a "New Rome" as he called it, complete with a great imperial palace, a vast amphitheater, a forum, even a senate house. His enterprise was enormously successful. For a thousand years after the fall of the West, Constantinople, as the city was later called, endured as one of the great cities of the world, the center of a magnificent civilization. But it was not really a "New Rome" that Constantine had created, even though the rulers of Constantinople always called themselves Roman emperors. The common speech of the city was Greek. Its characteristic styles of art, literature, and religious life, shaped by a mixture of Hellenic and Oriental influences, were sophisticated and fascinating but very different from those of ancient Rome. Eventually this Byzantine Greek culture came to exercise a formative influence on the civilization of Russia and eastern Europe, just as the Latin culture of old Rome influenced the lands of the West.

5. *Economic, Social, and Cultural Life*

Diocletian and Constantine coped very successfully with the short-term financial and administrative problems arising out of the civil wars of the mid-third century. They made the government solvent again. But neither emperor had any understanding of the underlying social and economic weaknesses of the empire, and in these spheres their policies of governmental centralization tended to exacerbate the existing difficulties rather than to alleviate them.

We have noted that Mediterranean agriculture sustained a growing urban population until the late classical period. In the Roman Empire, however, the balance between population and natural resources was always rather fragile. If there were too many people they pressed on the available reserves of food-producing land; if there were too few they were insufficient to support the expensive superstructure of the state. At the height of the Roman expansion, in the late second century, a contemporary observer, Tertullian, wrote, ''Cultivated fields have overcome the forests, the sands are being planted, the rocks hewn, the swamps drained. . . .'' In the fourth century, however, we encounter frequent references to *agri deserti,* ''deserted fields,'' land gone out of cultivation, with a consequent loss of agricultural production.

Some scholars have argued that the decline in output was due to erosion and exhaustion of topsoil caused by excessive exploitation of the land. No doubt this did happen here and there in particular cases. Deforestation, needed to extend agriculture, and intensive cropping of marginal land would tend to reduce fertility in a dry climate. And it would fit in very well with our modern concern over ecological problems if we simply assumed that the ancient Romans recklessly overworked their soil, turned fertile farmland into dustbowls, and suffered the natural consequence of ''decline and fall.'' In fact, though, there is no convincing evidence in classical times of soil erosion on a scale that would have seriously diminished agricultural activity as a whole. The ''dustbowls'' of the Mediterranean region were created many centuries later. All through the Middle Ages, for instance, southern Italy produced rich crops of grain.

The problem faced by the Late Roman Empire was not one of pressure by excessive population on limited resources, leading to their exhaustion. Instead, as we saw, population was declining from the late second century onward, so that usually when fields went out of cultivation, it was simply because there were not enough people to cultivate them. Still, reduced population does not in itself lead inevitably to economic crisis; we have to consider how a society responds to such a situation. From a modern point of view, the most obviously constructive response to a labor shortage would be to increase productivity by improved technology. But the Romans were notably ineffective in this whole area of activity. Surprisingly, in view of their remarkable achievements in other spheres of practical administration, they showed no creativity in developing new sources of power or even in organizing the available sources efficiently so as to maximize the production of material wealth. This fact is sometimes attributed to the tradition of classical education, which inculcated contempt for every kind of manual work. At any rate, compared with medieval people, the inhabitants of the Late Roman Empire made little use of wind power or water power. They did not even learn to harness draft animals with reasonable efficiency. The Romans preferred to use humans as animals by exploiting slave labor so long as ample supplies of slaves were available; and a society that had come to regard all mechanical labor as the proper business of slaves proved incapable of creative technological innovation when the need for it arose. No doubt the slaves and peasants who actually tilled the soil in the fourth century could easily have fed themselves. The basic economic problem of the Late Roman Empire was that their output was barely sufficient, even under the harshest state discipline, to support the unemployed populations of the cities, the large armies needed to defend the frontiers, and the extensive bureaucracy required to maintain ordered central government.

The only coherent policy that the emperors from Diocletian onward could devise to cope with this situation was to regulate the economic activity of the empire in such a fashion that the taxation needed to support the state would somehow be forthcoming. Under Diocletian a new survey of the land of the empire was carried out, and every district was assessed for taxes according to the fertility of the soil and the number of inhabitants. The basic unit of taxation was the *jugum,* a holding of land sufficient to support a single family; the tax levied on it was called the *annona.* This tax was collected in kind—in grain, oil, wine, cloth, and so on. Diocletian attempted to stabilize the currency, and he issued new gold and silver coins of good quality. But the imperial mints also circulated increasing amounts of copper coinage, which constituted the vast bulk of money in circulation for everyday purposes. The government had no desire to collect taxes in this intrinsically worthless currency. The *annona* constituted the basic source of imperial revenue, but it was supplemented by numerous indirect taxes and by frequent forced contributions from individuals and from associations of all kinds. In addition, forced labor was exacted to maintain roads and public buildings. The system of compulsory labor services called "liturgies," which had originated in the Egypt of the Pharaohs, was spread throughout the Roman Empire by the emperors of the fourth century.

In their attempts to maintain an adequate tax revenue, the emperors imposed an unprecedented degree of government control over all aspects of economic life. Taxes could be collected only from land that was occupied and cultivated. When small farmers tried to escape the tax burden by fleeing from their holdings, legislation was enacted that reduced them to a kind of serfdom by decreeing that they and their descendants were bound to the soil. They could not leave their family plots of land. In the cities, the various trades and crafts had been traditionally organized in guilds or *collegia.* When the *collegia* were assessed as units of taxation, the members tried to abandon them, and the principle of compulsion was again invoked. Membership in the appropriate guild became both compulsory and hereditary. When shipowners found that they could not afford to carry out their duty of bearing grain to Rome and Constantinople for the government and tried to enter other occupations, they in turn were forbidden to do so. One by one the chief occupations of the empire were made hereditary and those engaged in them were forbidden to change.

A similar system of compulsion was extended to even the prosperous upper classes of the provincial cities, the *curiales,* who had traditionally volunteered for the tasks of local government. In the fourth century, to be a *curialis* meant simply to be saddled with the task of returning an almost impossible burden of taxation to the imperial treasury. If the *curiales* failed to extort the taxes from the people, their own property could be confiscated. Naturally men ceased to offer themselves for the local *curia.* The government's answer was to make the position hereditary and to forbid anyone to withdraw from it. A *curialis* who tried to abandon his city could be apprehended and brought back like a runaway peasant. Thus the government's attempts to solve its problems led to a rigid stratification of society. Many men were bound forever to the position held by their fathers.* Another result was the gradual destruction of the middle class. As the demands of the government grew heavier and heavier, ruin overtook the groups on which the burden rested most heavily—the men with some property but with little political influence. The weight of taxation would not have been excessive if the empire had maintained its prosperity and if the taxes had been collected honestly and efficiently. In fact, under the system of state regulation, economic initiative was stifled, trade decayed, and the city populations came to consist more and more of idle mobs, supported by government doles. Moreover, it is clear that corruption was rampant and that even the most vigorous emperors were able to do little about it. The Master of the Offices maintained an elaborate network of secret agents, called *agentes in rebus,* to spy on all levels of the bureaucracy, but this did not stop large-scale peculation. The officials regularly extorted far more from the people than they passed on to the emperor.

The worst feature of the system was that the highest ranks of the aristocracy, the richest men in the empire, were exempted from taxation and those who were wealthy but not technically exempted simply evaded taxation by bribing the tax collectors. The rich had every op-

*Sources, no. 2

portunity to grow richer, and a crushing burden was laid on the poor. A writer of the early fifth century, Salvianus, recorded that, when the barbarian Visigoths invaded southern Gaul, the Roman peasants welcomed them as liberators. "The enemy is more lenient to them than the tax collectors. . . . They flee to the enemy in order to avoid the tax levies."*

The fiscal system of Diocletian and his successors was thus not only inefficient but also radically unjust. It would be easy to assert that there was a failure of virtue in the Late Roman Empire along with all its other failures. Some fourth-century writers, like the historian Ammianus Marcellinus, did indeed assert this.† But no one has ever invented an index for measuring moral corruption, and we cannot reasonably maintain that men of the fourth century were intrinsically more wicked than those of other periods. There always had been a certain moral obtuseness in Roman civilization, typified in the sickeningly sadistic spectacles staged by the public authorities to entertain the urban mobs. The government never had displayed sufficient regard for the peasants and slaves at the bottom of the social pyramid. But in the fourth century, attitudes that had always been morally questionable became a critical source of weakness to the state. In an age of economic decline, brought on in part by depopulation and labor shortages, the class that received least consideration from the government was the class whose productive labor supported the whole superstructure of the state.

The wealthy East suffered under the tax system, but it survived. In the West the structure of urban society began to change even before the barbarian invasions. The economic stagnation of the towns and the harsh pressures on their leading citizens contributed to an increasing "ruralization" of society. The laws specifying residence of *curiales* in their cities could not always be enforced, and the greater aristocrats could, of course, ignore such restrictions as they could ignore all obligations to the state. Wealthy Romans of the old senatorial class always had possessed great country estates and had commonly resided on them for part of the year as a pleasant way of recuperating from the sophisticated but demanding social life of the cities. During the fifth century, many of the aristocracy deserted the cities altogether and organized their rural estates into virtually self-supporting communities. The lord of such an estate could build himself a beautiful house, collect a fine library if he were so inclined, and live the life a country gentleman in the utmost luxury.‡ He usually maintained his own bodyguard and could defy any local imperial officials who tried to meddle with him if he did not choose to bribe them. Since slave labor had become uneconomical, the lord's lands were worked by men called *coloni*. Each *colonus* had a piece of land for which he paid rent in money, produce, or service. Some of the *coloni* were the descendants of slaves who had been technically freed but had remained as workers on their master's land; others were small free farmers who had given up their land to avoid the burden of taxation. Some of these great estates, precisely because they were autonomous self-sup-

*Sources, no. 3
†Sources, no. 1
‡Sources, no. 4

porting units, survived through all the chaos of the coming barbarian invasions. Thus, even before the invasions, some of the conditions we think of as characteristic of the early Middle Ages—ruralization and decentralization—were coming to exist in the western empire.

It has been said that Diocletian and Constantine turned the Roman Empire into a vast prison camp. We must remember that they did not take over a healthy, vigorous society and reduce it to slavery. Their measures were designed to hold together an empire that had seemed on the brink of complete disintegration, and those measures succeeded—for a time. The emperors gave peace to regions that would know nothing but war for centuries to come; later generations often looked back on this period as a golden age. Yet it remains true that, in the long run, the imperial policies could not stimulate the creativity and vitality that were needed to save the western empire. In the East, with its greater resources of wealth and administrative talent, Constantine's work provided the basis for an enduring civilization.

If we turn to the sphere of literature and thought, we find again a failure of originality and spontaneity among authors who continued to work in the old pagan classical tradition. It is symptomatic of the state of affairs that the only works of this sort which exercised continuing and significant influence on Western culture were textbooks. Two fourth-century books on Latin grammar by Donatus, the *Ars Minor* and *Ars Major,* and a more advanced treatise by Priscian, the *Institutes,* were used as standard school manuals throughout the Middle Ages. An encyclopedic work of the early fifth century, the *Nuptials of Mercury and Philology* by Martianus Capella, is also interesting to medievalists because it classified the various fields of knowledge into the "seven liberal arts"—grammar, rhetoric, dialectic, arithmetic, music, geometry, and astronomy—which formed the basic curriculum of the medieval schools.

There were still historians, poets, and playwrights in Rome but none to compare with the great figures of the golden age of Latin literature. Even the most attractive representatives of late classical culture seem nostalgic and unoriginal figures, men who were always looking to the past and trying unsuccessfully to imitate its achievements. We might consider as an example Quintus Aurelius Symmachus, a member of the senatorial aristocracy of Rome, who was born in 340. Symmachus attached the greatest importance to his membership in the Roman Senate, attended its meetings diligently, and considered it the highest of honors to be invited to deliver an oration. But this was all a kind of empty game, for the Senate was losing all its real power in the government of the state.

Symmachus had marked literary ambitions. Besides composing florid orations, he patronized poets, collected manuscripts, and engaged in endless sophisticated literary discussions. He wrote elegant letters that he carefully preserved for publication, although he sometimes found it necessary to complain that there was nothing interesting to write about—and this in an age when the last great civilization of the ancient world was sliding to ruin. Symmachus had no idea that he was living through such an epoch. The barbarian invasions that began during his lifetime seemed to him merely a tiresome interruption to a way of life that he assumed would go on forever. Certainly the idea never occurred to him that they called for any action or sacrifice on his part. It was not that Symmachus was unwilling to make sacrifices for Rome. On the contrary, he lavished enormous amounts of money and energy on a display of public games for the Roman people, which he provided in accordance with long-established tradition, during the year when his son assumed the office of praetor. Symmachus brought to Rome lions and crocodiles from Africa, dogs from Scotland, horses from Spain. He even succeeded in importing a band of Saxon captives to fight as gladiators in the arena. The Saxons, however, reluctant to fight to the death in order to provide an hour's entertainment for the Roman rabble, quietly committed suicide or strangled one another just before the day of the games. Symmachus was exasperated by their barbarous insensitivity to the grand traditions of Rome.

By far the most important development in the world of thought and culture during the lifetime of Symmachus was the rise of Christianity. Symmachus disliked novelties, and he had no sympathy with this newfangled fashion in religion. The one event in his whole career that stirred in him some depth of true feeling was the removal of the statue of Victory, a symbol of the old pagan religion, from the Roman Senate house. Symmachus protested over and over again to the imperial authorities, pleading with real eloquence that the old ways be at least tolerated. "Not by one path alone," he wrote, "can men come to so great a mystery." A Christian spokesman, Ambrose of Milan, replied: "What you know not, that we know by the voice of God. And what you seek by fancies we have found from the very wisdom and truth of God." The Christians, the new men, were not looking for truth. They believed they already possessed it.

READING SUGGESTIONS

* *B. Tierney,* The Middle Ages (New York, 1970), *vol. I,* Sources of Medieval History, *nos. 1–3; vol. II,* Readings in Medieval History, *nos. 1, 2. (Citations to the two paperback volumes that accompany this text.)*

Edward Gibbon, *The History of the Decline and Fall of the Roman Empire,* J. B. Bury (ed.), 7 vols. (London, 1896–1902) is a literary classic. Several abridged versions are available in paperback editions. Some problems raised by Gibbon's interpretations are considered in L. White (ed.), *The Transformation of the Roman World; Gibbon's Problem After Two Centuries* (Berkeley, 1966). A full-scale modern survey of the period is A. H. M. Jones, *The Later Roman Empire, 284–602,* 3 vols. (Oxford, 1964). See also M. Rostovtzeff, *The Social and Economic History of the Roman Empire,* 2nd ed., 2 vols. (Oxford, 1957); S. Dill, *Roman Society in the Last Century of the Western Empire* (London, 1899); H. I. Marrou, *A History of Education in Antiquity* (New York, 1956); H. F. Jolowicz, *Historical Introduction to the Study of Roman Law,* 2nd ed. (Cambridge, 1952). On the crisis of the third century see * R. MacMullen, *The Roman Government*

Response to Crisis, A.D. *257–357* (New Haven, 1976) and T. D. Barnes, *The New Empire of Diocletian and Constantine* (Cambridge, MA, 1982). The best contemporary account of life in fourth-century Rome is in Ammianus Marcellinus, *History,* J. C. Rolfe (trans.) (London, 1935–1939). The following works deal with the Late Roman Empire and also with the whole period of transition to the early medieval world: * W. E. Bark, *Origins of the Medieval World* (Stanford, 1958); * C. Dawson, *The Making of Europe* (London, 1934); * F. Lot, *The End of the Ancient World and the Beginnings of the Middle Ages* (New York, 1931); * H. St. L. B. Moss, *The Birth of the Middle Ages, 395–814* (Oxford, 1935).

chapter

III

The Christian Church

While in most respects the Late Roman Empire was a time of decline, in the field of religion it was a period of immense vitality. Perhaps there is truth in the generalization so frequently made that in times of political and economic confusion, men's minds turn to things spiritual. Be that as it may, the third and fourth centuries saw the rapid spread not only of Christianity but of many pagan cults. The eventual triumph of Christianity transformed the whole way of comprehending God and man and the universe for people of the late classical world.

To understand the religious life of the Late Roman Empire we have to appreciate both the uniqueness of Jesus as a religious teacher and the ways in which his teaching interacted with the pre-existing Hellenistic culture of the Empire. Jesus can only be understood as a Jew; his teaching was rooted in Judaic religion, with its worship of one supreme God (Yahweh or Jehova) and its prophetic tradition that foretold the coming of a Messiah to redeem Israel. But the message of Jesus was not addressed to the Jews alone; he told his followers to "make disciples of all nations." In carrying out this task, the first apostles had to address communities of gentiles and Jews scattered around the Mediterranean, people who share Greek as a common language and were influenced to a greater or less degree by the concepts of Hellenistic philosophies and religions. The books of the New Testament itself were not written in Hebrew or Aramaic, the semitic language that Jesus actually spoke, but in *koine* Greek (colloquial Greek), the everyday speech of the cities.

At first Christianity and Hellenism seemed inevitably hostile to one another. ("What has Athens to do with Jerusalem?" asked one church father.) Eventually Christian intellectuals came to realize that the message of Jesus was in many ways compatible with the teachings of the greatest Greek philosophers. The religious culture of the Late Roman Empire was shaped by this awareness.

6. *Hellenistic Culture and Christianity*

The ancient religion of Rome had little emotional content to inspire spiritual fervor; one performed the traditional services for the gods so that they would favor one's own projects; religion was largely a matter of scrupulously keeping a business bargain. Apart from the great gods of Olympus—borrowed from the Greeks and given Roman names like Jupiter, Mars, Venus—the Romans worshipped a host of lesser deities, including the deified emperors. Most of the gods were guardians of particular places or activities—a god of the household or city or state, a god who looked after seafaring, or sowing, or harvesting. It seemed a matter of common sense, when engaging in some activity, to placate the appropriate deity with ceremonies and sacrifices.

Roman religion was not at all exclusive. The gods of the conquered Gauls and Britons and of various Mediterranean peoples were identified with similar Roman ones or simply added to the heavenly pantheon. (The Jews' Yahweh was always a problem, though.) The cult of the old gods did not, and was not intended to, inspire people with a high moral ideal or teach them some ultimate meaning and purpose in life; religion was rather a series of formal transactions in which a god's favor was bought by appropriate tribute. Official worship was supplemented by recourse to magicians, soothsayers, astrologers, and compounders of love philters, all of whom also seemed useful in coping with the day-to-day contingencies of life.

Many people in the late Hellenistic world felt a yearning for truth and goodness that was left unsatisfied by the official cults; the fact is indicated by the widespread appeal of alternative philosophies and religions. Some of the philosophies that gained support were distinctly skeptical in tone. Epicureans taught that the whole universe was a random conglomeration of atoms and that the only sensible course for humans to pursue in an essentially meaningless world was to avoid pain and strife in order to achieve a life of quiet enjoyment. But other philosophers sought to combine the Greek concern for objective truth with a religious understanding of the world and man's place in it. Two of their systems of ideas—Stoicism and Neoplatonism—were especially important for later Christian thinkers.

Stoics taught that a single rational principle ruled the whole universe. Sometimes they called their ruling principle God, but they did not think of God as a creator, outside the material world; rather the divine principle was an intrinsic part of the cosmos, pervading all its parts and establishing a universal harmony among them. In every human person there was a spark of the divine; hence all people were essentially equal and all were bound by a universal natural law that human reason could discern. This natural law emphasized the virtues of justice, fidelity to duty, courage, self-control, and universal benevolence. By cultivating such virtues, by living in tune with the cosmic harmony, a person could maintain an inner life of tranquil peace, whatever external misfortunes might occur.

The idea of a natural law common to all peoples was attractive to the rulers of a universal empire, and one of its most eloquent exponents was the emperor Marcus Aurelius (121–180), himself a Stoic philosopher. The natural law of the Stoics could also be identified without too much trouble with the moral law handed down by Yahweh to the Jews. There is a trace of this already in St. Paul: "Gentiles who have not the law do by nature what the law requires. . . ." (Romans 2:14).

Neoplatonists also believed in a single, eternal being or God that they called "the One" or "the Good"; but for them "the One" was transcendent, rather than immanent in the universe as in the Stoic doctrine. Both Stoics and Neoplatonists used the term *logos* (which occurred also in Christian Scripture) to signify a creative principle emanating from God. For the Stoics, the *logos* was the indwelling law inherent in all things, for the Neoplatonists more a divine agent bringing created beings into existence. Neoplatonists held two other characteristic positions: they drew a sharp distinction between spirit and matter; and they saw the whole universe as a great hierarchy of being proceeding from the one God. Under God were immortal spirtual beings, below them were humans (with spiritual souls and material bodies), and below them the whole world of physical creation. This was the lowest kind of being but it still retained some imprint of the divine source.

Humans could remain wholly immersed in the world of matter; but they could also, by a great effort of intellectual and moral self-discipline, rise from the perception of material things to a contemplation of spirtual being and, ultimately, to mystical union with God. Later Christian and Jewish mystics found these ideas very congenial. Often they performed the considerable intellectual feat of identifying the abstract "One" of Neoplatonic philosophy with the very personal, willful Yahweh of Judaic religion.

There were many people in the Roman world who had no taste for abstract philosophy, but who were unsatisfied by the formalism of the official rites. Often they became devotees of various "mystery religions," cults which had usually originated in the eastern Mediterranean. Among the most popular deities worshipped in these religions were the Syrian goddess Cybele, Mythra from Persia, Dionysius from Greece, and the great mother-goddess Isis and her son Osiris from Egypt. The cult of *Sol Invicta* (the unconquered Sun) was especially popular in the army. Not uncommonly the myths associated with these divinities told of gods who died and were reborn; such stories reflected earlier cults of fertility gods who died in winter and whose rebirth brought new life to the fields in spring. All the mystery religions had rites that were participated in by all initiates. These rites were dramatic and calculated to arouse a religious enthusiasm bordering sometimes on actual hysteria. Moreoever, all the mystery religions promised their followers some sort of salvation by cleansing the soul of sin. Many of the ceremonies, such as being bathed in hot blood as it flowed from a slaughtered bull (a Mythraic rite), may seem to us horrible and disgusting. And such rites as those involving the enthusiastic use of a corps of temple prostitutes are immoral by Christian standards. But the general objects of these cults, cleansing from sin and encouraging a virtuous life, were worthy enough. The mystery religions were no more exclusive than the traditional religion of Rome. One could continue to worship the gods as one's ancestors had and still become an initiate of several mystery cults. We read of noble Romans who had entered almost all of them.

In some ways the primitive Christian church resembled the mystery religions, but it also had several striking characteristics of its own that help to explain its eventual success. In the first place, Christianity carried on the Jewish tradition of monotheism, and to most Westerners ever since the days of the Late Roman Empire it has seemed more reasonable (if one is to believe in a deity at all) to believe in a single supreme source of all being rather than in a whole pantheon full of feuding gods and goddesses. (Stoic and Neoplatonic philosophers were coming to see this, though without the Jewish concept of a personal God who revealed himself in history.) Again, the Christians could claim a much more immediate and concrete origin for their religion than the followers of other cults. Their divine founder was not just a figure in an old myth; he was a real man who had lived on earth and taught and sent out other men to teach in his name. Moreover, the doctrine that he taught was immensely appealing. On one level it was very simple; on another, exceedingly subtle. Christianity could appeal to humble and illiterate people, but it also came to attract the most sophisticated intelligences of the late classical world. There was inexhaustible material for meditation in phrases like "God is love" or "the Kingdom of Heaven is within you," with their implication that human love provided an analogue, perhaps the only possible analogue, for the unknowable essence of God himself. In later centuries that idea inspired some of the finest flights of medieval poetry and mystical literature.

Theologians have argued endlessly about how far, if at all, the Christian Scriptures present an accurate account of "the historical Jesus," the man who actually walked the earth and taught in Judea. The task of a medieval historian is fortunately simpler. For us it is enough that the Scriptures provide an excellent account of what the early Christians thought about Jesus. We can most easily explain their beliefs, therefore, by drawing on some passages of the New Testament to illustrate them.

Christians believed that there had existed for all eternity one single God whose divine power manifested itself in three *personae* or, we might say, in the fulfillment of three roles as God the Father, God the Son, and God the Holy Spirit. The human race had been created by God, but ever since the first man, Adam, had sinned by disobedience in the Garden of Eden, human nature had been flawed and corrupt. God promised to send a Messiah to his chosen people, the Jews, to redeem men from this heritage of sin. The redeemer appeared on earth in the reign of Caesar Augustus when God the Son became incarnate in the man Jesus Christ, who was miraculously born of the Virgin Mary.

> In the beginning was the Word (*logos*) and the Word was with God and the Word was God . . . and the Word became flesh and dwelt among us. (John 1: 1,14)

Jesus gave proof of his divinity by working miracles. He taught people how God wanted them to live and promised eternal life in heaven to those who believed in him and obeyed his commandments.

The message Jesus taught was one of love, love of God and love of one another. He picked out two precepts from the Old Testament to express this teaching:

> Thou shalt love the Lord thy God with thy whole heart, and with thy whole soul, and with thy whole mind and with thy whole strength. This is the first commandment. And the second is like it. Thou shalt love thy neighbor as thyself. There is no other commandment greater than these. (Mark 12: 30–31)

A Christian's faith was to express itself not so much in the external observation of the law but rather in an inward change of heart and in an overflowing charity toward others, most especially toward the weak and helpless:

> He who has the goods of this world and sees his brother in need and closes his heart to him, how does the love of God abide in him? My dear children, let us not love in word, either with the tongue, but in deed and in truth. (1 John 3: 17–18)

The Christian would also display an attitude of humility, forgiveness, and patience in the face of arrogance or oppression. "If someone strike thee on the right cheek turn to him the other also."

When Jesus' mission of teaching on earth was completed, the Christians believed, he gave a supreme example of loving humility by voluntarily undergoing a bitterly painful and shameful death. But then he gloriously fulfilled all his promises of eternal life in the world to come by rising from the dead and revealing himself to his disciples before he "ascended into heaven." Belief in Christ's resurrection was at the heart of early Christianity.

According to the Scriptures, Jesus personally chose certain followers to be his apostles, and various scriptural passages tell how he assigned to these apostles specific powers and duties. (Eventually the medieval church built up a whole structure of sacramental theology on the basis of these passages.) For instance, Jesus promised first to the Apostle Peter and then to all the apostles together the power of loosing men from their sins:

> Amen I say to you, whatever you bind on earth shall be bound also

> in heaven and whatever you loose on earth shall be loosed in heaven. (Matthew 16: 18 and 18: 18)

During his last meal with his disciples, Jesus gave them consecrated bread and wine to eat and told them to receive it as his body and blood:

> While they were at supper, Jesus took bread, and blessed and broke, and gave it to his disciples, and said, "Take and eat; this is my body." And, taking a cup, he gave thanks and gave it to them, saying, "All of you drink of this; for this is my blood of the new covenant, which is being shed for many unto the remission of sins." (Matthew 26: 26–28)

Finally, after the resurrection, Jesus sent out his disciples with a command to baptize and convert all the peoples of the world:

> Go, therefore, and make disciples of all nations, baptizing them in the name of the Father and of the Son, and of the Holy Spirit, teaching them to observe all that I have commanded you; and behold, I am with you all days, even unto the consummation of the world. (Matthew 27: 19–20)

These passages define the role of the first Christian missionaries. Their tasks were to offer forgiveness of sins, to convert unbelievers by preaching the gospel, to bring converts into the Christian community by the rite of baptism, and to celebrate the eucharist—the reenactment of the Last Supper—in memory of Christ.

During the first three centuries Christianity spread gradually through the Roman Empire. We know from the letters of St. Paul that, soon after the death of Jesus, Christian churches were established outside Palestine among Greek-speaking communities (sometimes groups of Hellenized Jews, sometimes of gentiles) from Rome to Asia Minor. Then, much more slowly, the new religion won converts in the Latin-speaking western half of the empire. By the third century, the Christians were numerous enough to be politically important and had begun to attract a number of members of the upper classes. Every substantial city had its little Christian community presided over by a bishop who was helped by priests and deacons. The bishops, who were regarded as successors of the first apostles, were chosen by the community and consecrated to their office by fellow bishops. When disputes about Christian doctrine began to arise, they were settled by local councils of bishops. The Christians were not just individual adherents of a new religion. They had a strong sense of themselves as an ordered community, a people set apart, a new Israel. They gave alms to their church to support members of the community who fell into want; a Christian author wrote with pride that during epidemics the Christians cared for their sick while sick pagans were abandoned. Above all, the Christians retained the Jewish sense of exclusiveness in religion. To become a Christian meant to give up all other forms of worship, including the official cult of the emperors.

As Christianity spread through the Greco-Roman world it encountered scornful hostility from many pagan intellectuals as well as eager acceptance among converts. Early Christian evangelists were faced by a problem that arises at the origin of many great religions. An inspired founder pours out a flood of new insights or revelations; some of those who hear him are utterly convinced and find their whole lives transformed. Then, after the founder has died, they have the task of explaining their new faith to nonbelievers who have not shared their experience and who are firmly set in other ways of thought. In the case of Christianity, the problem was complicated by the need to express an essentially semitic religion in language, institutions, and thought-forms that would be acceptable to minds formed by the Greek Hellenistic tradition. The task was not an easy one. Many leaders of the schools of pagan philosophy despised the new religion. The high-minded Stoic emperor, Marcus Aurelius, persecuted Christians; the greatest of Neoplatonic philosophers, Plotinus, bitterly attacked their teachings.

The difficulties that Christianity posed for educated pagans were not the ones that might occur most readily to a modern skeptic—miracles attributed to Jesus, for instance, or the story of his resurrection. People of the classical world expected divinities to intervene in human affairs and they were quite familiar with stories of gods who died and were reborn. The difficulty for the ancient pagan lay in the nature of this particular god—a shamefully executed criminal, disloyal to the state, claiming to displace all other gods, presenting his teaching in simple, forceful assertions rather than in reasoned argument or elegant myth. To many outsiders, Christianity seemed merely a perverse and irrational cult. Christian celebration of the eucharist gave rise to ugly rumors of ritual cannibalism and Christian love to accusations of unrestrained licentiousness. In the words of a pagan critic, "They know one another by secret marks and signs and they love one another almost before they know one another . . . there is a religion of lust among them . . . their vain and senseless superstition glories in crime."

In the second and third centuries, a group of Christian thinkers known as *Apologists* undertook to refute the pagan criticisms. The first major figure among them, Justin, was born about 100, and converted to Christianity when he was thirty-eight, after having been successively a Stoic and a Neoplatonist. Justin not only refuted the grosser libels against the Christians; he also argued that Christian doctrine was itself a reasonable philosophy, indeed the perfection of all past philosophies. According to Justin, Christian truth was known most securely because it was directly revealed by God, but there was an element of divine inspiration in all true philosophy. He thought that the divine *logos* which was finally manifested in Jesus had earlier inspired not only the Jewish patriarchs, but also the great pagan teachers. Socrates and Plato were forerunners of Christ just as Abraham and Moses were.

Christians could admire all that was true and valuable in the insights of the philosophers and then show how those insights were complemented and perfected by the teaching of Jesus.

Justin died a martyr, thrown to the beasts in 165, but his teaching was carried on by two great teachers of the school of Alexandria, Clement (c. 150–c. 210) and Origen (185–254). Clement taught that philosophy was to the Greeks what the law of Moses was to the Jews, a preparation for the full revelation of truth that they could find in the teaching of Jesus. Origen, a great systematic scholar, wrote influential commentaries on almost every book of the Bible and drew heavily on Greek thought in expounding Christian doctrine. The Christian philosophers of Alexandria were especially devoted to the work of Plato. Clement found there "a true Christian and orthodox philosophy"; he even thought he could discover the Christian doctrine of the Trinity in Plato's writings.

Writers like Clement were striving to defend Christian doctrine by showing that it was compatible with the truths of philosophy. This endeavor led on to the great syntheses of Christianity and classical culture achieved by the church fathers of the next century, and the task continued to engage Christian thinkers all through the Middle Ages. Another way of mingling religion and philosophy—more dangerous to orthodox Christianity—also appeared during the second century in the teachings of various Gnostic sects. Gnostics taught that all religions were only approaches to a higher truth which they, the Gnostics, possessed and could reveal to initiates. Their systems of thought drew on a variety of religious traditions. Some of them, for instance, found room in their teachings for a mother-goddess whom they named Charis (Grace). A Christian author, Irenaeus, writing in the second century, tells us that one Gnostic teacher called Marcus, who claimed to be filled with the spirit of Charis—and who was also an expert concocter of love potions—succeeded in seducing many Christian women.

A characteristic teaching that pervaded all the Gnostic sects was based on the supposed duality of matter and spirit. Gnostics taught that matter was intrinsically evil, only spirit good. This doctrine was formulated most systematically by Mani, a Persian prophet, whose religion (Manicheanism) spread both eastward to China and westward to the Mediterranean world. Mani taught that the universe was brought into being by two creator-gods, one good, one evil, one the creator of spirit, the other of matter. Such a teaching plainly contradicted the Old Testament account of creation and it was not really in keeping with the Christian idea of asceticism. Christians—like Neoplatonists in this—taught that the body should be tamed to maximize the spirit's liberty; but not that the body was intrinsically evil in itself. All the same, the Gnostic emphasis on superiority of the spirit appealed to some Christians. The Gnostics, for their part, were quite willing to spice their brew of religions with a little extract of Christianity, and various forms of Christian Gnosticism arose. The thing that prevented the main body of Christians from being drawn into any such religious syncretism was their strong sense of identity, their sense of themselves as a people set apart, living according to a faith handed down by the authority of the apostles.

7. *Christian Church and Roman State*

The sense of corporate identity and aloofness from the pagan world that helped the Christian churches to survive was also a major cause of conflict with the Roman imperial authorities. The attitude of the Roman state to the growing Christian church varied from grudging tolerance to fierce persecution. As a general rule, the imperial government tolerated with equanimity all the curious varieties of religious life that had grown up in the empire, and Christ had not commanded his followers to attack the authority of the state. Indeed, he had said, "Render to Caesar the things that are Caesar's." But the Christians, like the Jews, refused to worship the emperor as a divine being and hence seemed to threaten the unity of the state. There were other reasons for considering them dangerous: They met in secret to perform their rites, and no government likes secret meetings, particularly of the poor and the lowly. Moreover, the Christians were opposed to violence and sometimes refused to serve in the Roman army. To a government beset by enemies, the spread of such beliefs seemed dangerous. From the time of Nero (54–68) onward, the Christians were subjected to frequent persecutions. These persecutions failed in their intended effect, for although they were sometimes savagely cruel, they were never sustained long enough to wipe out the whole church, and the martyrs they created provided heroic examples to inspire the survivors.

The last great persecution was launched by Diocletian in 303. A dramatic change of fortune for the Christians came with the rise to power of the emperor Constantine. Under his rule, Christianity was transformed from a persecuted sect into the favored religion of the Roman state. The Christian bishop Eusebius has left a story about Constantine's conversion, which, he declared, was told to him by the emperor himself. According to this account, Constantine had a dream when he embarked on the campaign leading to the crucial battle of the Milvian Bridge. In the dream he was told to send his soldiers into battle led by a standard marked with Christian symbols. He obeyed this command and won a splendid victory.* There are other versions of the story, but they all mention a miraculous dream or vision as the cause of Constantine's conversion. Modern historians have evinced a natural skepticism about this tale and have looked for concrete political reasons to explain Constantine's eventual adoption of Christianity. But it is very hard to understand his motives. The Christians were not popular, they formed only a small minority in the whole population of the empire—perhaps twenty-five percent in the East, much less in the West—and they were particularly weak in the army on

*Sources, no. 6

which Constantine's power was based. On the other hand, the Christians had shown remarkable strength and resilience during the recent persecution, and they formed a coherent block of people whose support could be valuable to a new regime. We cannot be sure how much of all this Constantine appreciated. It seems at any rate clear that the emperor became genuinely convinced—possibly as the result of a dream followed by a successful battle—that the Christian God was a real god and a powerful one who needed to be placated. We may doubt whether at that time or later he had any real understanding of Christian doctrine or Christian ethics.

In 313 Constantine issued jointly with the eastern emperor Licinius a decree proclaiming tolerance for all the religions of the empire, including Christianity.* It was couched in terms of cautious neutrality: "To the Christians and to all men we decree that there be given free power to follow whatever religion each man chooses so that, whatever gods there be, they may be moved mercifully toward us." Later Constantine identified himself more openly with Christianity, declaring that he was "brought to the faith by God to be the means of the faith's triumph." All his successors were Christians except for the emperor Julian (361–363), who tried to promote a revival of paganism during his brief reign. Christianity quickly became the dominant religion of the empire. At first the old pagan state religion was permitted to exist alongside Christianity, but the emperor Gratian (375–383) confiscated the endowments of the pagan temples, and Theodosius I (379–395) finally forbade by law the practice of the old cult. During the following century, most of the inhabitants of the empire became at least nominally Christian.

As the official church of the empire, the Christian church received special privileges from the imperial government. It was given the right to receive legacies—an extremely important privilege for a perpetual corporation. Its clergy was exempt from taxation. When the Christians were a persecuted sect, they had tried to keep out of the imperial courts and settled their disputes by arbitration of the bishops. After the recognition of Christianity, the law allowed bishops to act as judges in all civil disputes to which a Christian was a party. In addition, the church was given the rights of sanctuary that the more important temples had possessed. In short, the church became a privileged corporation enjoying some governmental powers. After Constantine's conversion, the church also began to acquire a more organized hierarchy of government, and the units of ecclesiastical administration that developed corresponded quite closely to the units of civil government, especially on the lower levels. From the beginning, the Christian bishopric had usually coincided with the Roman *civitas*. During the fourth century, the bishoprics of each province were grouped together under an archbishop. Thus an ecclesiastical map of France in the Middle Ages shows quite accurately the old Roman provincial and city territories. Sometimes the bishoprics of a whole diocese were subordinated to a metropolitan. There was, however, no centralized

*Sources, no. 7

administration for the whole church comparable to the imperial bureaucracy, although a position of special dignity and prestige was conceded to the bishops of four great cities—Rome, Jerusalem, Alexandria, and Antioch. Constantinople joined this select group in the fourth century. The churches of these cities all claimed to have been founded by members of the original group of apostles sent out by Jesus. Among them the Roman church claimed a position of seniority both because it had been founded by the Apostle Peter and because Rome was the ancient capital of the empire.

The conversion of the emperors to Christianity obviously brought great new opportunities to the church, but it also brought new problems, including one that has persisted in Western society ever since the fourth century—the problem of the church and state. This issue had hardly arisen when the most that the church could hope for from the state was freedom from persecution. With a Christian emperor, the position was very different. Constantine and his successors were men of autocratic temperament; they made themselves champions of the church, but expected in return that the bishops would conduct themselves as loyal servants of the imperial government. The emperor would defend the true faith, but this implied that, if disputes arose among Christians, he would decide which faith to defend. It was hard to set any limit to "the things that are Caesar's" when Caesar had made himself the foremost friend of Christianity.

These problems came to the surface at once because the conversion of the Roman state to Christianity took place at a time when the Christian church was divided as never before over a basic issue of religious belief. The doctrine that gave rise to the controversy is called *Arianism* after its founder Arius, a priest of the church of Alexandria. Arius defined the position of the Son in the Christian Trinity in such a way as to deny his essential divinity. For Arius, the Son, the *logos,* had not existed from all eternity but had been created by the One God who alone was eternal. Christ was the highest of God's creatures, but still a creature. In the ensuing controversies, argumentation about this point became almost incomprehensibly complex, but it is not hard to understand in principle why Arius' doctrine created such an immense stir in the church. There could hardly have been a more fundamental issue of Christian theology. If the church had conceded in the fourth century that Christ was not truly divine, the whole Christian faith would necessarily have developed into something quite different from the historical religion that actually persisted down the centuries.

The teaching of Arius was promptly condemned by the bishop of Alexandria; but Arius was an eloquent, persuasive controversialist, and he began to win over many other bishops to his position. When Constantine became master of the eastern half of the empire in 324, he found his new provinces ablaze with religious controversy. Constantine decided to settle the dispute at once by calling all the Christian bishops together to discuss the matter. Until this time councils of bishops had met only on a local basis. By issuing a general invitation

Wall painting from the Catacomb of the Jordani, Rome, showing a Christian, perhaps the deceased, pleading for divine help. Depicting a figure with hands raised in prayer was originally a Greek motif which Christians adopted. Although catacombs were used for burial in many places and by many religious groups, those of the Christians at Rome are the most extensive. Outside the city are more than 60 miles of galleries, in which more than half a million tombs have been excavated. *Leonard von Matt from Photo Researchers*

to all bishops and making available to them the traveling facilities of the imperial postal service, Constantine brought into existence a new institution of church government, the *general council.*

The first such council, the Council of Nicea, met in 325 and produced a definition of doctrine that condemned Arianism and declared that the Son was "of one substance with the Father." This language was later incorporated into the Nicene Creed, which has been used as a touchstone of orthodoxy by most Christian denominations ever since the fourth century.* The decisions of Nicea were not, however, at once generally accepted. Many eastern bishops disapproved of the Nicene terminology and, after this initial setback, the followers of Arius again began to make converts. By 330 they had won over the imperial court; the greatest opponent of Arius, Bishop Athanasius of Alexandria, was sent into exile in Gaul.

Constantine's son, Constantius II (337–361) continued the Arian policy. Athanasius, who had been permitted to return to Alexandria after Constantine's death in 337, was again exiled from his see, and Arian bishops were imposed on churches throughout the East. Athanasium himself traveled to Italy, where he found a powerful ally in the Bishop of Rome, Pope Julius I (338–352). Constantius II, at first emperor only of the East, in 351 became master of the West also. And at this point the religious controversy took a new turn. Although the bishops of the West were almost unanimously opposed to Arianism, Constantius expected them to accept the imperial faith as a matter of course. He summoned church councils first at Arles and then at Milan and commanded all those present to subscribe to a condemnation of Athanasius. For the first time, the authority of Caesar was challenged: leading Christian bishops delivered sharp rebukes to a reigning Christian emperor. They suggested not merely that the emperor was erring in faith but that he had no right to intervene in matters of faith at all. Bishop Hosius of Cordoba wrote, "You have no power in the ministry of sacred things." Bishop Hilary of Poitiers called the emperor "Constantius the anti-Christ." Most of the bishops who were actually summoned to the emperor's presence, however, reluctantly acquiesced in the condemnation of Athanasius. A few who refused were sent into exile, among them Hosius, Hilary, and the Bishop of Rome, Liberius (352–366).

The issue of Arianism was finally settled under the emperor Theodosius I (379–395), who supported the Nicene faith. He summoned another assembly of bishops, the Council of Constantinople (381)—later recognized as a general council—which reaffirmed the doctrine of Nicea. Partly as a result of imperial coercion, this doctrine finally came to be accepted in the East as well as in the West. It was enormously important for the future of Western society that, in the course of this controversy, the principle of a distinction between the spheres of action of church and state had been vigorously asserted. It was also significant that the dispute was finally settled in the East according to the will of the emperor.

8. *The Age of the Fathers—Jerome, Ambrose, Augustine*

During the middle years of the fourth century, the new Christian and the old pagan cultures existed side by side in the Roman Empire,

*Sources, no. 5

constantly interacting with one another. The pagan Latin tradition had ceased to be creative. Its most attractive exponents were learned, tolerant, cultured men but profoundly dull writers. In comparison, the new Christian authors may seem fanatical, harsh, illiberal—but their works were filled with a fresh vision of life that would mold the mind of the Western world for the next thousand years. During the first three centuries, most of the greatest Christian thinkers had written in Greek, but in the second half of the fourth century, three great Latin authors appeared—Jerome, Ambrose, and Augustine—whose writings decisively shaped the tradition of Western Christianity that the medieval church inherited. During this same period, Latin replaced Greek as the ritual language of the Christian community in Rome.

The flood of converts who entered the church in the fourth century brought new responsibilities for the Christian leaders. One problem was to maintain the distinctiveness of the Christian tradition, to avoid being simply absorbed into the mass culture. This led to sharp attacks on pagan hedonism and to an increased emphasis on asceticism, voluntary mortification of the body, as an essential element in the Christian life. Monasticism—the abandonment of the world to seek a life of perfection in the wilderness—became an important movement in the life of the church. Also, during the fourth century the discipline of celibacy was adopted in the western church to set bishops and priests apart from the everyday life of the world.

But, while some aspects of the pagan tradition were rejected, others were adapted to serve the needs of the church. The work of the old Apologists now had to be continued among a mass of new Christians, many of them sophisticated intellectuals. If they were to be instructed persuasively, it was necessary to absorb into Christian culture all that was valuable from classical literature, from classical law, and above all from classical philosophy.

For a long time, Christian thinkers found it harder to accept the traditions of pagan Latin literature than the speculations of pagan Greek philosophers. This problem—the adaptation of Latin literary studies to serve the purposes of Christianity—was a special concern of St. Jerome (345–420). After studying literature in Rome, Jerome lived in Antioch for a time and became fluent in both Greek and Hebrew. He made himself one of the most learned men of his age. He was also a brilliant stylist, a master of satirical Latin prose. He was, however, distrustful of his own literary skill and in this way was typical of many early Christian writers. Jerome once had a dream in which he was rebuked by God for being "more a Ciceronian than a Christian." A little later on, St. Augustine lamented that he had wasted his youth in studying the "lascivious fables" of the pagan poets. In 580 Pope Gregory the Great bitterly reproached the Bishop of Vienne for daring to open a school of Latin letters. Even as late as the tenth century, Abbot Odo of Cluny compared the poetry of Vergil to an exquisite vase filled with hideous writhing serpents. For a thousand years, men could not rid themselves of the fear that the study of pagan literature, with its seductive beauties, might constitute a temptation to the faith of a Christian. Fortunately, they often allowed themselves to be tempted.

Jerome resolved the issue for himself by adapting a text of the Old Testament. The book of Deuteronomy decreed that an Israelite could marry an alien woman after she had undergone appropriate rites of purification. So too, Jerome declared, the arts of pagan eloquence could be purified by a Christian scholar and then used in the service of the true Christian faith.* Jerome was much given to this kind of allegorical interpretation of Biblical texts, and his writings helped to popularize the technique among later authors.

In 382 Jerome returned to Rome as secretary to Pope Damasus and soon made a reputation for himself as an eloquent critic of the abuses that were creeping into contemporary Christian society. Jerome preached a fierce asceticism to the Romans. He himself lived as a celibate and regarded marriage as a radically inferior way of life, just barely tolerable for a Christian. Women were the targets for some of his most savage and bitter invective; but almost the whole Christian society of Rome seemed to Jerome infected with a growing worldliness. He wrote in one of his letters:

> I say nothing of the heavy meals which crush such mental faculties as we possess. I am ashamed to speak of our numerous calls, going ourselves every day to other peoples' houses, or waiting for others to come to us. The guests arrive and talk begins: a brisk conversation is engaged: we tear to pieces those who are not there: other peoples' lives are described in detail: we bite and are ourselves bitten in turn. . . . we remember not the words of the gospel: "thou fool, this night thy soul shall be required of thee.". . . we buy clothes, not solely for use, but for display. When we see a chance of making money, we quicken our steps, we talk fast, we strain our ears.

Writing like this made Jerome highly unpopular in Rome. When his patron Pope Damasus died in 385, he found it expedient to leave the capital and traveled to the Holy Land, where he settled at Bethlehem. Even in Bethlehem Jerome could not give up his taste for acrimonious theological controversy and for exercising his mordant wit at the expense of his fellow Christians. But for more than thirty years he devoted himself primarily to the great constructive task of interpreting and translating the text of the Scriptures. Existing Latin translations of the Old and New Testaments were imperfect, and Jerome therefore set himself to produce a new Latin version of the whole Bible based on the best Greek and Hebrew manuscripts that were available.

Jerome's translation was a masterpiece, and it became universally accepted in the Western church as the standard version of the Scriptures. Hence it was known as the "Vulgate," or common, text. The poetry of Jerome's Bible was not imitation Vergil nor its prose imitation Cicero, though no one would have been better qualified than Jerome to indulge in such academic exercises. His achievement was much greater: he took the living language of the Roman Christian

*Sources, no. 8

community of his own day and showed how it could be used to create great literature. His Vulgate Bible influenced medieval Latin authors at least as much as the King James Bible influenced English writing of the seventeenth century.

Jerome showed how the Latin literary tradition could be adpated for effective use by Christian writers. His contemporary, Ambrose (ca. 340–397), was more immersed in the juridical tradition of Rome. Ambrose's father had been Praetorian Prefect of Gaul, and, following in his father's footsteps, Ambrose entered the imperial service and rose to become governor of the province of Emilia in northern Italy. In 370 the bishopric of Milan became vacant and the people clamored for Ambrose, their governor, to become their bishop. After some hestitation he accepted. Ambrose had been a good practical Christian before his election as bishop, but it was only after his ordination that he turned seriously to the study of theology. Although he became a very able theologian, he was not a strikingly original one. Ambrose's interests were pastoral rather than speculative. Many of his theological treatises grew out of the sermons he preached to the people of Milan. He interested himself greatly in church music too, and composed both words and melodies for hymns to be sung at divine service. Ambrose also introduced into the church of Milan a pattern of antiphonal chanting—the singing of short stanzas alternatively by choir and congregation—that came to be adopted throughout the Western church.

It is typical of Ambrose's down-to-earth temperament that one of the most influential books he wrote was a practical treatise on diocesan administration. Cicero had written a book on moral duty, called *De Officiis.* Ambrose produced a work with a similar title, *De Officiis Ministrorum,* which incorporated some of Cicero's Stoic ethics into a treatment of ecclesiastical offices and their duties. Much of the work consisted of moral exhortation, but there was also much about practical questions such as the right use of diocesan revenues. Ambrose considered in some detail, for instance, the problems of urban poverty. A bishop had to concern himself to feed the poor, he wrote. It would be a shameful thing if any Christian were allowed to die through neglect. But it was not enough just to hand out indiscriminate doles; individual cases had to be investigated. The deacons charged with administering poor relief were to distinguish between the old and sick who needed permanent support and the young and strong who could normally fend for themselves. Orphans had to be educated. Poor girls needed dowries. The deacons had to look out for cases of concealed poverty, for people who had once been well-to-do and had fallen into want might be ashamed of their condition and prefer to endure destitution rather than ask for the help they needed. Such cases were to receive especially sympathetic consideration. Ambrose's humane and sensible precepts were copied into the canon law of the twelfth century and formed the foundation of the medieval law of poor relief.

At the end of the fourth century the city of Milan was the seat of the imperial government in the West, and so its bishop was often brought into contact with the imperial authorities. In dealing with them, Ambrose continued the tradition of Hilary and Hosius, the bishops who had stood out against Constantius II. A Roman administrator to his fingertips, Ambrose had a strong sense of the church as a community with its own intrinsic principles of right order and its own structure of offices to give effect to those principles. In accord with these convictions he vigorously defended the church's right to independence in matters of religion and persistently resisted imperial attempts to dictate ecclesiastical policy. "Palaces belong to the emperors," he wrote, "churches to the priesthood." Again, in a striking phrase, "The emperor is within the church, not above the church." On one occasion the emperor Theodosius I commanded a massacre to be carried out in the city of Thessalonica. Theodosius was a powerful ruler and a noted defender of the Catholic faith, but Ambrose considered the massacre cruel and sinful. He rebuked the emperor sharply: "Thou art a man. Temptation has come upon thee. Conquer it." Theodosius at first resented Ambrose's intervention in what he considered a purely political matter, but in the end he accepted the rebuke and did public penance in the cathedral of Milan. The incident was often remembered in later conflicts of church and state.*

The greatest Christian philosopher of the Western church in this age—one of the greatest of all ages—was St. Augustine of Hippo (354–430). He was born in the African province of Numidia, the son of a pagan father and a Christian mother. As a young man, Augustine studied rhetoric in the schools of Carthage; many years later he wrote in his *Confessions* that there he gave himself over to a life of vice and self-indulgence. "To Carthage then I came . . . a cauldron of unholy loves." Augustine could find no lasting satisfaction in such a way of living. Through all his years as a student he was distressed by his failure to discern any sort of ultimate meaning or purpose in life. The problem that above all tormented him was the problem of evil. How could belief in a divinely ordered universe be reconciled with the evident wickedness and cruelty that he saw all around him? Christianity seemed to Augustine merely a barbarous superstition. For a time he flirted with Manicheanism, the Oriental doctrine which asserted that there were two supreme creative principles in the universe, one good and one evil.† Augustine moved on from his belief to the Neoplatonic doctrine that there existed one eternal light which was the source of all being. According to this doctrine, evil was not a positive force but mere absence of light or good.

Augustine's mind was still not at rest, but his career prospered; he became a professor of rhetoric. His profession took him first to Rome and then, in 384, to Milan. There he heard Ambrose preaching, and for the first time, apparently, the idea occurred to him that Christianity might be intellectually respectable. While he was reflecting on this new insight, he experienced a sudden dramatic conversion that seemed to him an immediate personal call from God.‡ From then on he saw the doctrines of Christianity as living truths, compared with

*Sources, no. 7

†See p. 42.

‡Sources, no. 6

which the insights of the Platonists were mere intellectual abstractions. "The Platonists saw the truth," he wrote, "but they saw it from afar." For Augustine, after his conversion, the Christian God was a vivid reality. In the beginning God had made the whole universe and saw that it was good. Apparent evil was the effect of man's turning away from God by misusing his free will, as Augustine himself had done in his youth.

Augustine's experience of life thus led him to a belief in the omnipotence and goodness of God, to an intense revulsion against human sin as the source of all evil, and to a very urgent sense of God's grace and mercy in redeeming the sinner. He returned to Africa, where he became bishop of the city of Hippo in 390, and poured out these insights in a flood of writings—sermons, letters, treatises on all kinds of theological and moral problems. These works were studied all through the Middle Ages. Augustine's conviction that philosophy could bring a man to a partial understanding of the truth but that it needed to be complemented by divine revelation became the standard teaching of the medieval schools. His teachings on predestination, grace, free will, and the origin of evil shaped the whole central tradition of medieval theology and exercised a profound influence on Luther and Calvin at the time of the Reformation.

As a controversialist, Augustine engaged in three major disputes. Because all of them were concerned with heresies that, in different forms, kept recurring throughout the Middle Ages, it is easy to understand why Augustine's writings never lost their relevance. In the first place, he attacked the Manicheans, opposing to their dualism the Christian doctrine of a single God. Second, Augustine wrote against the Pelagians, who taught that man could achieve salvation through the unaided exercise of his own free will. Augustine's personal experiences had convinced him that the human will was powerless without the help of God's grace. Third, Augustine engaged in a vigorous controversy with the Donatists. They were a sect of Christians who maintained that the sacraments of the church could not be administered by priests who had fallen into mortal sin. At the time of Diocletian's persecution, many bishops and priests had fallen away from the faith rather than undergo martyrdom. The Donatists were descended from Christians who refused to accept the ministrations of such men after their return to the church. They formed only a small minority in the church as a whole, but they were strongly entrenched in Africa. Augustine regarded them as narrow fanatics who were setting themselves in stiff-necked fashion against the authority of the whole Catholic church and who were denying God's absolute power to distribute divine grace through any instruments he chose, even imperfect ones. (The word *catholic,* meaning universal, was used to distinguish the main body of Christian bishops and believers, who maintained communion with one another, from various dissident sects.) Disputes between Donatists and Catholics led to frequent riots and street fighting in the cities of Africa. Finally the emperor Honorius (395–423) confiscated the property of the churches held by the Donatists and made the practice of their religion illegal. Augustine vigorously supported this act of imperial coercion. His attitude is understandable, perhaps, but nonetheless unfortunate. His writings on the Donatist controversy provided the first defense of religious persecution by a major Christian theologian.

These polemical writings do not reflect adequately Augustine's mature thought on the problems of Christianity and the state. Certainly he was very far from regarding the church as subordinate to secular government or man as made for the state. Apart from the autobiographical *Confessions,* his most famous work was the *City of God.* It was addressed to precisely these questions. The immediate occasion that led Augustine to begin writing the *City of God* was an unprecedented disaster, the sack of Rome by the Goths in 410. Adherents of the old pagan cults naturally maintained that the disaster was due to the abandonment of the ancient gods. Many Christians were dismayed too because, after the conversion of the empire to Christianity, they had come to see the Roman state as a necessary complement to the Catholic church in the divine ordering of the world. Since, in fact, the Roman Empire was about to crumble away, this was a dangerous fallacy for Christians. In considering these issues, Augustine created not just a theory of church and state but a whole philosophy of history in which he saw the saving grace of God working in the hearts of men through all the vicissitudes of transient human empires. Augustine saw two societies competing through the centuries for the allegiance of men, the City of God and the City of the World. The City of God was the community of those who loved God and would find their final home in heaven. The City of the World was the community of those whose minds and hearts were set only on wordly things. Augustine did not precisely identify the City of God with the organized church or the City of the World with the Roman state; nor did he condemn secular government as such. He held that no worldly state could be an embodiment of pure justice but that, because men were corrupt, even imperfect states served a useful purpose. Coercive government had to exist precisely because so many men gave their allegiance to the City of the World, because they would rob and fight and kill if they were not restrained by force. Christians could properly take advantage of the civil order imposed by the state to live out their lives in tranquillity, but their own conduct was not determined by the state's coercive regulations. Their only necessary permanent allegiance was to the City of God.* Augustine was arguing, in effect, that Christianity could go on, whatever happened to the Roman Empire. It was a perceptive insight. Augustine lived to see the destruction of Roman civilization in North Africa. At the time of his death in 430, his own city of Hippo was enduring a seige by an army of invading Vandals.

*Sources, no. 7

9. *Papal Leadership: Sylvester to Leo the Great*

The claim of Rome to a position of primacy among the other Christian churches is very ancient. There are vague references to Roman pre-eminance in letters of St. Ignatius (A.D. 110) and St. Irenaeus (ca. A.D. 185). On the other hand, the claim of the medieval popes to exercise a direct centralized jurisdiction over all Christians on the basis of their primacy was formulated only very slowly in a long process of historical evolution. The last century of the western empire, the age of the great Latin Fathers, was a period of crucial importance in this development.

Various arguments could be used to support the Roman claims, for example, that the Roman church had been founded by Peter, the leader of the apostles; that it was the church of the capital city of the empire; that it was sanctified by the blood of many martyrs; that it preserved the apostolic faith uncontaminated by the heresies that arose in other churches. In practice, the influence exercised by individual popes in the controversies of the early Christian centuries varied greatly with the personalities of particular pontiffs. Sylvester I, for instance, the pope at the time of Constantine's conversion, was a negligible figure in spite of all the myths that grew up about him in the Middle Ages. His successor, Julius I, on the other hand, played an active role in the Arian controversy as a supporter of Athanasius.

The first explicit acknowledgment by a church council of Rome's primacy of jurisdiction came in 344. The Council of Sardica (Sofia) decreed that any bishop who had been deposed by a local council could appeal to Rome for a final judgment in his case.* The Council of Constantinople (381) affirmed Rome's primacy but added that the bishop of Constantinople held second place after the pope "because Constantinople is the New Rome." This idea that ecclesiastical dignity should be based on the civil importance of a bishop's city was unwelcome in Rome. On that basis, the bishop of Constantinople might well come to consider himself equal to or even greater than the Roman pontiff. During the next century, therefore, a series of able popes insisted that their headship over the whole church was based essentially on their role as successors of St. Peter. They also gave an increasingly juridical meaning to the concept of ecclesiastical headship.

The *Petrine* doctrine of papal power was based primarily on three Scriptural texts. The first is Matthew 16: 18–19, which records that Peter acknowledged Christ as the Messiah with the words, "Thou art the Christ, the son of the living God," and that Christ replied:

> And I say to thee, thou art Peter and upon this rock I will build my church and the gates of Hell shall not prevail against it. And I will give thee the keys of the kingdom of heaven and whatsoever thou shalt bind on earth it shall be bound in Heaven and whatsoever thou shalt loose on earth it shall be loosed in heaven.

*Sources, no. 17

The other two important texts are Luke 22: 32, where Christ said to

Peter, "I have prayed for thee that thy faith may not fail," and John 21: 15–17, where Christ gave Peter the threefold command, "Feed my lambs. . . . Feed my lambs. . . . Feed my sheep."

Pope Damasus (366–384) reacted to the Council of Constantinople by asserting that the Roman primacy was not based on any synodal constitutions but on the words that Christ himself had spoken to Peter. Damasus was also the first pope to refer to the Roman church as "the Apostolic See." His successor, Pope Siricius (384–389), declared that the spirit of Peter lived on in the Roman bishops and wrote extensively to the bishops of Gaul, Spain, and Africa seeking to impose uniformity in religious rites. The first papal decretal that survives is from his reign. Pope Innocent I (402–417) repeated the doctrine of Siricius and attempted to exercise the papal jurisdiction in a case involving the bishop of Constantinople himself. The bishop in question, St. John Chrysostom (ca. 347–407), was deposed by a council of bishops and exiled by the emperor Arcadius (395–408). Innocent declared the sentence unjust, excommunicated John's successor, and refused to resume communion with the church of Constantinople until John's name was restored to honor. (The saint himself had meanwhile died in exile.)

The greatest pope of the fifth century was Leo I (440–461). He was important both for his influence on contemporary events and for his exceptionally clear and systematic formulation of the Petrine theory of papal authority.* Like many of the greater popes of this age, he was descended from an old Roman aristocratic house and brought to the papacy the instinct for orderly administration that had once characterized the leaders of the Roman state. During Leo's pontificate the imperial authority in Italy was weakening and the Roman bishop was emerging as an important figure in the civil affairs of Rome. This is shown especially by the fact that twice, when barbarian armies invaded Italy, Leo I played a major role in the negotiations with their leaders. He bargained effectively with the Huns to avert an attack on Rome in 453 and less successfully with the Vandals in 455.

Leo also intervened decisively in the greatest theological controversy of the fifth century. No sooner had the Arian heresy been suppressed than new disputes arose. The Council of Nicea (325) had decided that Christ was truly God. Now questions were raised asking whether he was truly a man and how a divine and human nature could coexist in one individual. Nestorius, a priest of Antioch who became bishop of Constantinople in 428, insisted on a clear separation between the two natures of Christ and was inclined to emphasize the human element. His characteristic teaching was that Mary, the mother of Jesus, was mother of the man Jesus but not of the God Jesus. This doctrine was bitterly attacked by St. Cyril of Alexandria (ca. 376–444), who was supported by the contemporary popes, and it was condemned at the Council of Ephesus (431). The traditional formula that called Mary "mother of God" was reaffirmed, and Nestorius was sent into exile. Many Nestorians left the empire at this time to settle in

*Sources, no. 16

Persia; eventually they spread all over Asia, even establishing Nestorian churches in China.

In the empire itself, the deposition of Nestorius did not end the controversies he had stirred up. Cyril's successor as bishop of Alexandria, Dioscoros, developed Cyril's doctrine in a fashion that seemed to the popes just as heretical as the condemned teaching of Nestorius. Dioscoros deemphasized the human element in Christ to the point of maintaining that Christ possessed only a single nature, that is to say, a divine nature (this doctrine is called *Monophysitism* from the Greek words for "one nature"). Leo condemned Dioscoros' teaching in a theological treatise known as the *Tome,* which set out in lucid and succint Latin the Roman belief that Christ was a person who possessed two natures, divine and human. He was, as the later formula put it, true God and true man. A second council was held at Ephesus in 449, but it was thinly attended and packed with Alexandrians. This council upheld Dioscoros, and the emperor Theodosius II (408–450) supported its decisions. Pope Leo was furious and called the assembly "not a council but a den of robbers." It is still known as the "Robber Synod."

The situation was saved for the pope by a change of emperors. Theodosius II died in 450 and was succeeded by Marcian (450–457), who happened to be strongly Catholic in religion. In agreement with the pope, Marcian summoned a new general council, which met at Chalcedon in 451. Here Leo's *Tome* was approved as a definitive explanation of the orthodox faith, the fathers of the council declaring that "Peter has spoken through Leo." The Council of Chalcedon thus achieved a great work of reconciliation; the Greek and Latin churches again shared a common faith. But, seen from another point of view, the council introduced irreversible schisms into the Christian world. The church of Egypt remained staunchly monophysite, and, as noted earlier, many Nestorians, refusing to accept the official version of Christianity, followed their leader into exile. They first settled in Persia, then spread all through central Asia, eventually establishing churches as far away as China. The story of the Western church that we shall be pursuing is only one part of the whole history of Christianity.

The decision of Chalcedon was a considerable triumph for the papacy, but Leo's success should not be exaggerated. The eastern bishops had approved the pope's doctrine partly because the emperor wanted them to do so. If the emperor's policy were to change, many of the bishops would be prepared to change too. Moreover, having settled the issue of doctrine, they proceeded to enact a disciplinary canon conferring on the church of Constantinople the same juridical supremacy in the Orient that Rome possessed in the West. Leo refused to approve this decree.

As to the basis of his authority, Leo insisted that he was the "heir" of St. Peter and that Christ had appointed Peter to be head of the whole universal church. Leo believed that all bishops were successors of the apostles and possessed the powers that Christ had originally conferred on them. This was the common belief of the time. But Leo also held that all the other apostles had been subordinated to Peter and that, accordingly, all bishops were subordinated to the popes who succeeded to Peter's See of Rome. (He wrote that the bishop of Alexandria was only a successor of the Apostle Mark and that he must therefore defer to the successor of Peter.) In Leo's theory the authority of the papacy did not depend on any individual pope's personal qualities. He realized that the popes could not claim to inherit the personal merits of Peter, but he maintained that as his heirs they could and did inherit an office of supreme government that Peter had received from Christ.

This is obviously a highly controversial proposition. Since the papacy became one of the most vital formative influences in the growth of medieval civilization, it may be useful to indicate at the outset how far it was generally accepted in the Middle Ages. Virtually all Western Christians came to agree that the pope was indeed the successor of St. Peter and, as such, head of the whole church. They disagreed profoundly, however, about the actual powers of government that were implied by this headship. The disagreements arose most obviously when the popes tried to assert for themselves an overriding authority in temporal affairs. Such claims were always strongly resisted. Even in internal matters of church government, there were differences of opinion as to how much centralized authority could properly be exercised by the papacy. It is sometimes supposed that, throughout the Middle Ages, the Western church accepted all the claims that the papcy put forward on its own behalf. This is not really true, and, indeed, the presupposition renders large tracts of medieval history unintelligible.

In the world of the Late Roman Empire, the rise of the papacy and the simultaneous growth of a vigorous Latin theology had important implications for the spheres of culture and religion. The Greek language lent itself to almost infinite subtleties of philosophic discourse in arguments about the doctrines of Christian faith. The Latin language, reflecting the whole tradition of Rome, was better adapted to discuss law, ethics, and practical problems of administration and government. After the initial controversies over Arianism and Monophysitism, the eastern churches continued to produce innumerable refinements of doctrine, seeking always to define the basic articles of Christian faith with increased philosophic precision. The Roman church usually championed a staunch adherence to traditional formulations, even when those formulations were not readily defensible in philosophic terms. To the Greeks it seemed (sometimes correctly) that the bishops of Rome were trying to impose solutions for complicated theological problems without having really understood what the arguments were all about. To the Romans it seemed that the Greeks were willing to endanger the most basic truths of Christian faith in order to indulge a perverse taste for philosophic hairsplitting. In the course of these disputes, the Greek church usually showed itself willing to accept the rulings of the imperial authority in matters of religion as it did in other matters. The Roman church often resisted imperially sponsored doctrines as being departures from the traditional faith. The churches of the West came more and more to look upon the bishop of Rome as their natural champion and leader. In the East the claims of Rome to a primacy of jurisdiction were sometimes denied and at best accepted grudgingly. It is important to remember that, while there was only one great apostolic see in the West, Rome, in the East there were four—Antioch, Alexandria, Jerusalem, and Constantinople. The tradition of the eastern church was always more polyarchal, multicentered, than that of the West.

The rise of the papacy in the West and the slow growing apart of the Greek and Latin churches were of decisive importance in the emergence of medieval Europe. We have seen that the eastern and western halves of the empire differed in their political and economic structure. At the time of the barbarian invasions, they were beginning to drift apart in religion also.

READING SUGGESTIONS

* *B. Tierny,* Sources *and* Readings; *vol. I, nos. 5–8, 13, 16–17; vol. II, no. 3.*

The most important reading on early Christianity is, of course, the New Testament. The historicity of the Gospel narratives was discussed in a classical work by Albert Schweitzer, originally published in 1906, *The Quest of the Historical Jesus,* 3rd ed. (New York, 1961). More recently the question has been reconsidered by J. Robinson, *A New Quest of the Historical Jesus* (London, 1959), and by M. Grant, *Jesus: An Historian's Review of the Gospels* (New York, 1977). * M. Burrows, *The Dead Sea Scrolls* (New York, 1955) provides a good introduction to its subject. On the two greatest apostles, see * O. Cullmann, *Peter* (New York, 1958), and * A. D. Nock, *St. Paul* (New York, 1963). On Christianity and Roman paganism see R. A. Markus, *Christianity in the Roman World* (London, 1974); R. L. Fox, *Pagans and Christians* (New York, 1986); * R. MacMullen, *Christianizing the Roman Empire, A.D. 100–400* (New Haven, 1984).

The best general history of the early church is J. Danielou and H. I. Marrou (eds.), *The Christian Centuries,* vol. I, *The First Six Hundred Years* (London, 1964). For a briefer survey, see * H. Chadwick, *The Early Church* (Harmondsworth, 1967). Outstanding among the numerous works on Constantine's religious policy are A. Alföldi, *The Conversion of Constantine and Pagan Rome* (Oxford, 1948); H. Dörries, *Constantine and Religoius Liberty* (New Haven, 1960); * A. H. M. Jones, *Constantine and the Conversion of Europe* (London, 1948). E. G. Weltin, *The Ancient Popes* (Westminster, MD, 1964) provides a brief account of the first popes, while J. T. Shotwell and R. Loomis, *The See of Peter* (New York, 1927) presents valuable source material.

On early Christian thought and culture, see * H. O. Taylor, *The Emergence of Christian Culture in the West; The Classical Heritage of the Middle Ages* (New York, 1958), originally published in 1901; * C. N. Cochrane, *Christianity and Classical Culture* (New York, 1957); H. A. Wolfson, *The Philosophy of the Church Fathers* (Cambridge, MA, 1956); R. A. Markus, *Christianity in the Roman World* (London, 1974). P. Brown provides a stimulating survey in * *The World of*

Late Antiquity (New York, 1970). Other important studies by the same author are * *Society and the Holy in Late Antiquity* (Berkeley and Los Angeles, 1982); *Religion and Society in the Age of Saint Augustine* (New York, 1972); * *Augustine of Hippo* (Berkeley and Los Angeles, 1967). On Augustine see also * R. A. Markus, *Saeculum. History and Society in the Theology of St. Augustine* (Cambridge, England, 1970) and * F. Van der Meer, *Augustine the Bishop* (New York, 1961). On Jerome, see J. N. D. Kelly, *Jerome: His Life, Writings, and Controversies* (New York, 1975) and on Ambrose, F. H. Dudden, *The Life and Times of St. Ambrose,* 2 vols. (Oxford, 1935). All three of the great Western Fathers are discussed in * E. K. Rand, *Founders of the Middle Ages* (Cambridge, MA, 1928). Among the many editions of Augustine's works are his * *City of God,* V. J. Bourke (trans.) (New York, 1950), and * *Confessions,* E. B. Pusey (trans.) (London, 1907). The *Letters* of Jerome have been translated by F. A. Wright (London, 1933), and the *Letters* of Ambrose by M. M. Beyenka (New York, 1954).

chapter

IV

The Barbarians

We have examined two of the basic elements that went into the making of the medieval world, the civilization of the Roman Empire and the religion of the Christian church. We can now turn to the third important factor, the barbarian cultures of the Celts and Germans. These cultures were "primitive" in the sense that they lacked many of the refinements of classical civilization. But primitive societies often produce vigorous art and literature, and primitive customary law, although it may seem unreasonable to us, can provide effective principles for maintaining the stability and cohesion of a society. In all these spheres, the vitality of the barbarian peoples made major contributions to the later growth of medieval civilization.

10. *The Germanic Peoples*

Julius Caesar.

Around 500 B.C. Germanic peoples began to migrate from their northern homelands; by the first century B.C. they had occupied the region we call Germany, formerly the land of the Celts, and were settled along the western border of the Roman Empire. (Julius Caesar encountered German tribes there during his campaigns in the Rhineland and wrote an account of them in about 50 B.C.) Other German peoples subsequently moved eastward and established a kingdom in the steppes of south Russia. After the Germans had settled in the lands of the Roman Empire, from the fourth century onward, their attitudes and institutions profoundly influenced the culture of early medieval Europe. It is important, therefore, to understand their way of life as fully as possible. The evidence is sparser than one would wish. But, from Caesar's account, supplemented by archeological finds and information derived from studies of later German laws and languages (which often preserve archaic elements), we can construct a reasonably adequate picture of Germanic society in the age of the migrations.

As regards material culture, the early Germans were primarily a pastoral people living on the produce of their flocks and herds—meat, butter, and cheese. They knew how to work iron but had only very scanty supplies of this metal. They used iron principally for weapons; other utensils were made of bronze, wood, or leather. The Germans practiced agriculture (with the help of ox-drawn plows) but it was a secondary activity for them. Their supply of meat was augmented by hunting, a pursuit that German men engaged in with avidity. Their other favorite pursuit was fighting, either in organized campaigns to seize the land of some neighboring people or, often, in individual forays in search of plunder—cattle, slaves, precious ornaments, weapons.

Like other primitive peoples the Germans knew no political relationship of the individual citizen to an ordered state; instead, the fabric of German society was woven together by ties of personal loyalty. The two principal bonds, which existed in prehistoric times and persisted long into the Middle Ages, were those of *kinship* and *lordship*. The kinship group or clan was the most primitive unit. A group of associated clans formed a tribe, which often maintained its cohesion by fabricating a story of common descent from some legendary god or hero.

German kindred groupings do not fall neatly into the categories that anthropologists commonly use in describing other primitive peoples. Their system was not strictly patrilinear or matrilinear; we can find examples of succession through both male and female lines. Similarly, although we are dealing with a male-dominated warrior society, in which ties between males were stressed—Anglo-Saxon for instance has more words for male relatives than female ones—still kinship was not traced through the male line alone. A person's kin group included the mother's kindred as well as the father's.

The Germanic system tends to produce in a few generations a very widespread kin whose members are only distantly related to one another. Every marriage creates a new web of relationships. We do not know how far the ties of kinship extended in practice; no doubt a person's "effective kin" was the circle of relatives actually willing to lend support in time of need. An essential function of the kin group was mutual protection. If a person was killed or injured the members of the injured party's kin were expected to exact vengeance from the offender or the offender's kin. Blood feuds were a common feature of life in primitive Germanic society.

The other major bond of loyalty, the relation of lordship between a leader and his retinue of warriors, also arose from the warlike proclivities of the early Germans. Unlike kinship this was a voluntary relationship. One was born into a kin; one chose a lord. When one of the leading men proposed to undertake some raid or foray he would issue a call to brave youths in search of adventure. Those who volunteered to follow him swore to serve the leader faithfully in return for his protection and a share of the booty. Individual members of different clans would join such bands, without obligating other members of their kin to support the venture. They formed groups of sworn companions bound to one another and to their leader in a chosen relationship, outside the traditional ties of kinship.

The institutions we have considered so far existed among all the Germanic peoples as far back as our evidence can take us. Presumably, before they started migrating from their homeland in northern Europe, the Germans differed little from one another in either language or customs; but individual groups became isolated from their fellows during their wanderings and developed linguistic and cultural peculiarities. Moreoever, each group was obliged to adjust its ways of life to the environment in which it found itself. Thus decided differences developed among them. By the fourth century the most striking differences were not between individual Germanic peoples but rather between the two major groups of West Germans and East Germans. The West Germans—Saxons, Suevi, Franks, and Alemann—had simply moved south from their homeland into regions of essentially the same general nature, until their expansion was halted at the borders of the Roman Empire. There they formed permanent settlements and supported themselves by farming.

But the East Germans—Goths, Vandals, and Lombards—had moved into regions far different from northwestern Europe. The Hungarian plain and the steppes north of the Black Sea offered vast areas of open grazing land. There the German conquerors lived as nomadic horsemen and herders. Moreover, the southern Russian steppes had long been a frontier land between Slavic farmers to the north, Greek colonists on the Black Sea coast, and fierce nomads of the Asian grasslands. The region had been dominated for centuries by nomadic peoples who moved in as invaders, stayed as conquerors, and were in turn absorbed by new invaders. The group in control at the time of the Gothic invasion was the Sarmations, a nomadic Iranian people from whom the Goths learned the art of fighting on horseback. In southern Russia the Goths succeeded in defeating all rivals and setting themselves up as the dominant group. Like previous conquerors, they were a military minority ruling over a strange agglomeration of different subject peoples. The Goths themselves were divided into two groups. The Visigoths lived along the lower reaches of the Danube, while the vast Ostrogoth state stretched from the Dniester to the Don. In the course of the conquests, the Gothic peoples had developed a rather more advanced political organization than the other Germans; they were united under strong kings.

During the fourth century, the Goths were in close contact with the eastern Empire. There were periods of hostility, but there was also cultural interchange in times of peace. Gothic nobles visited Constantinople, and their people learned much of Roman ways. The most important result of this intercourse was the spread of Christianity among the Gothic peoples. The process was initiated by St. Ulfilas, a Roman citizen of Gothic descent, who began to preach to the Visigoths about the middle of the fourth century. Ulfilas devised a Gothic alphabet and translated much of the Bible into the Gothic language. As happened over and over again in the history of the barbarian peoples, conversion to Christianity meant not just the adoption of a new religion, but the opening up of the whole world of literacy. The surviving fragments of Ulfilas's Gothic Bible represent the earliest written literature in any Teutonic language. Ulfilas's work of conversion was continued by other missionaries from Constantinople. But (like Ulfilas himself) they were Arian missionaries, sent out during the reign of the Arian emperor Constans II (337–361). Hence the Visigoths, and subsequently the other East German peoples, adopted the Arian form of Christianity; this had major repercussions after they migrated into the Roman Empire.

For the East German peoples we have a detailed description written by the Roman historian Tacitus at the end of the first century.* Some of his passages, especially his remarks on the unassailable virtue of the German ladies, have seemed to modern historians mere exercises of the imagination, intended to satirize or rebuke the weaknesses of his own society. But much of Tacitus' account is obviously based on eyewitness information and is amply confirmed by other sources. The Roman historian describes the Germans as huge men with red hair and fierce blue eyes, fond of warfare and of feasts and wild drinking bouts in the interludes of peace. They lived in villages of primitive wooden huts and wore cloaks of skins or woven cloth. The German peoples Tacitus describes adhered to the old Teutonic pagan religion (and they continued to do so until after they had settled in the Empire). They had no temples, we are told, but offered sacrifices to their gods in sacred groves of trees. Tacitus describes the Teutonic deities by the Roman names Mars, Mercury, and Hercules, which probably corespond to the Teutonic Tiu, Wodan, and Thor (whose names survive in our days of the week, Tuesday, Wednesday, Thursday).

Barbarian leaders are often referred to by the title *rex,* or "king," in Roman sources, but the political institutions of the West German peoples were, in fact, very primitive and the real status of the German leaders is better conveyed by our word "chieftain" than by "king." As late as the fourth century, terms like *Franks* and *Saxons* do not refer to organized nations but to groups of tribes similar in speech and customs. There was typically no central government for such a people. A single war leader might be chosen in time of emergency to wage a major campaign, but for the most part the different tribes lived under their own chieftains who led their people in religious rites as well as in military adventures. A permanent kingship for all the Frankish peoples, for instance, was established only after the invasion of Gaul in the fifth century. There was still no sense of allegiance to a common state. Such cohesion as existed was maintained by the old personal loyalties—ties of kinship and the devotion of warriors to the chieftains who led them in battle.

Tacitus mentions kinship groups but he specially emphasizes the role of lordship. At the time when Caesar wrote, about a hundred and

*Sources, no. 9

fifty years earlier, bands of young warriors gathered under their leaders for some particular foray and then often dissolved. By the time of Tacitus the relation between a lord and his retinue had become a permanent one, and the lords formed an established nobility. Tacitus describes a variety of social classes among the Germans—nobles, free men, freedmen, and slaves. He notes that the leading warriors disdained to take part in agricultural labor; they left farm work to the women, the old, and the weak. Such warriors maintained permanent retinues whom they provided with food, clothes, and expensive weapons—partly from the produce of lands worked by their dependents, partly from the profits of plundering raids. In return the lords expected complete loyalty from their followers. In the case of a mere plundering foray, a chief might take only his retinue as his main fighting force. In larger expeditions it served as his bodyguard. Tacitus has a famous passage describing the relationship of a group of companions to their chief:

> As for leaving a battle alive after your chief has fallen, that means lifelong infamy and shame. To defend and protect him, to put down one's own acts of heroism to his credit—that is what they really mean by "allegiance." The chiefs fight for victory, the companions for their chief.

This loyalty of a fighting man to his leader, transmuted into the feudal relationship of vassalage, remained a basic bond of society all through the Middle Ages.

Justice was administered in popular courts, assemblies of free warriors presided over by their chiefs. Germanic law was primarily devoted to supplying alternatives to the private vengeance of the kin. If one man injured another, the latter brought a complaint before the court. The accused was then summoned to appear and his kin was expected to ensure that he did so. If he did not come, he was declared an outlaw. If the accused did appear, his guilt or innocence was established by an appeal to the supernatural. The judgment of the gods was ascertained either by compurgation, an oath-taking ceremony, or by various forms of ordeal.* These rites of compurgation and ordeal are not peculiar to the Germans, nor are they common to all primitive peoples. They are found predominantly in Europe and in Africa. Anthropologists have surmised that they may have spread from a common center in the Middle East.

A hundred years ago (and for long before that), historians were much impressed by the role of the popular tribal assembly in German government, and they commonly assumed that the whole structure of Western constitutional democracy evolved almost inevitably from primitive Germanic institutions, which were widely admired and misunderstood. (Thomas Jefferson spoke of "the Saxon chiefs from whom we claim the honor of being descended and whose political principles and form of government we have assumed.") In part this view was based on mere racist prejudice, often unconscious; in part it

*See pp. 101–102.

reflects confusion between two things—democratic government and individual freedom. Democracy means the rule of the people; a democratic government can restrict the liberty of the individual just as severely as can an autocracy. At the same time, a government that is not a democracy can believe that its rights over individuals are limited. The German system of dispensing justice in popular courts seems democratic, but the tribesmen assembled essentially to witness a religious rite, not to debate and vote on the cases brought before them. The distinctions made between men of different rank were plainly undemocratic. It seems clear that the warriors had some part in the choice of a chief, but there is little evidence of democratic control over the chief once he was chosen. Tacitus tells us that assemblies of free warriors were held to approve plans for a coming campaign and to stir up enthusiasm for it. But a Teutonic tribal council was more like a primitive pep rally than a session of a legislative assembly. (Tacitus describes the war cries which roused the warriors' fighting spirit as "not so much an articulate sound as a general cry of valor.") The democratic elements in German society must therefore not be taken too seriously. On the other hand, it is clear that the functions of government among the Germans were extremely limited. Government provided leadership in war and a means of settling quarrels without a bloody feud. For the rest, it left the people to their own devices. Hence the Germans did have a tradition of personal freedom—of having a very small amount of government. They were wild, fierce warriors, impatient of restraint of any kind. Their love of freedom, one may even say of license, was to play an important part in the development of Western civilization.

11. *The Barbarian Invasions*

During the fourth century, the frontiers of the empire did not separate a purely Roman world from a purely barbarian one. Ever since the last century before Christ, Roman and barbarian had been influencing each other. Two Roman provinces, Gaul and Britain, had been from the beginning combinations of Roman and Celtic civilizations. The Romans had also brought in numerous Germans, both as slaves and as *coloni* on their estates. Many other Germans had enlisted in the Roman armies. Some joined the legions as individuals; others formed the units known as *foederati,* or "allies." These were bands of German warriors who fought in the service of Rome under their own chieftains. They were often rewarded with grants of land in the border regions of the empire. Then the civilization of Rome was bound to spread to some extent beyond its political frontiers. The barbarians outside these frontiers had been Romanized in varying degrees, according to their receptivity and their proximity to the border. The Goths, as we saw, received Christianity from the eastern empire. In the West an active trade was carried on across the Rhine frontier. The Germans supplied slaves and cattle in exchange for various manufactured goods—glass and bronze vessels, ornaments, weapons, textiles. Such Roman artifacts have been found at archeological digs in many parts of Germany.

The gradual Germanization of the western provinces of the empire and the corresponding Romanization of the Germanic peoples went on throughout the third and fourth centuries. Peaceful trading was varied by frontier warfare. The Germans constantly pressed against the empire's borders. At times they would defeat the frontier guards and raid an imperial province, but eventually fresh troops would arrive and the Germans would be driven back. In the far northwest, the Angles and Saxons took to their ships and raided the coasts of Britain. On the lower Rhine, the Franks occupied both sides of the frontier—those in Roman territory, the *foederati,* holding the border against the others. Frankish troops were heavily relied on to help control the Alemanni on the upper Rhine. The same general policy was used along the upper Danube, bands of Germans being hired to reinforce the Roman border garrisons. By the end of the fourth century, when we read of a Roman army, the words really mean an army of barbarians fighting under Roman command. Many of these barbarian soldiers rose to high rank in the imperial forces. Even the office of *magister militum* of the West, which carried command over all the western armies, was often held by a man of Germanic origin.

Perhaps the process of slow infiltration by itself would have led in the end to the establishment of Germanic states in the territories of the empire. In fact, the process was radically accelerated in the years around 400 by a new set of circumstances. Instead of launching mere raids, whole Germanic peoples began to migrate into the empire and to make permanent settlements there, living under their own leaders, in accordance with their own laws. As the Germans occupied whole provinces of the empire, centralized imperial government ceased to exist in the West.

To understand how all this came about, we must remember the situation of western Europe as a peninsula of the Eurasian land mass, always open to pressures from the east. The collapse of the western empire as a political entity was not brought about by new developments within the empire itself (though deep-rooted economic and political weaknesses made it vulnerable to attack). Nor were there major internal changes among the German tribes on the borders. The fresh factor in the situation was the rise of a new power in central Asia, the Huns, "a race savage beyond all parallel," as a Roman author wrote. Ethnologists have not had much success in tracing the remoter origins of the Huns. They were mainly Mongolian in appearance and spoke a language of the Altaic group (to which modern Turkish belongs). The Huns were expert horsemen and fought as lightly armed mounted archers. Having been defeated on the borders of China, hordes of them turned westward, ranged across the Russian steppes, and began to terrorize the Germanic peoples settled along the frontiers of the Roman Empire. Their attacks set in motion a whole new wave of migrations.

In 375 the Visigothic people petitioned the emperor Valens (364–378) for permission to cross the Danubian border and settle in imperial territory. This was the first migration of a whole Germanic nation into the empire, and the immigrants came as suppliants, not as conquerors. In 378, however, the Visigoths complained of mistreatment by Roman provincial officials and rebelled against the imperial authority. They won a major victory at the battle of Adrianople, where Valens himself was killed. It seemed for a few months that the whole Balkan peninsula and perhaps even Constantinople lay open to their attack. The situation was saved by the next emperor, Theodosius I (379–395), who was a very able general. He restored order, and as long as he lived, the Visigoths were content to revert to the status of *foederati.* In 396 they rose again under their greatest king, Alaric I, and ravaged Greece. Alaric was pacified for a time by being given the office of *magister militum* of Illyricum, but in 402 he led his Goths in an attack on Italy. He was repelled by the commander of the western armies, Stilicho, a Vandal. It is symptomatic of the whole situation that the defense of Rome itself now depended on the skill and courage of a Vandal general.

The year 406 brought a sudden deterioration in the situation. In order to defend Italy, Stilicho had had to weaken the Rhine frontier, and in the last days of 406 the border defenses gave way and a mixed horde of Germanic peoples, predominantly Vandals, surged into the empire. After ravaging their way through Gaul, they moved on to Spain with the intention of establishing a Vandal kingdom there. Stilicho fell out of favor with the imperial court, and in 408 he was executed by order of the emperor Honorius (395–423), himself an incompetent weakling. Alaric seized the opportunity to attack Italy again. In 409 he was bought off with an enormous bribe, but in 410 he attacked Rome itself, captured the city, and looted it. The news of this unprecedented disaster sent a shock wave of startled dismay to the ends of the empire. Far off in Bethlehem, Jerome wrote, "Who would believe that Rome fights no longer for glory but for her very existence, and no longer even fights but purchases her life with gold?"

Alaric apparently intended to lead the Visigoths into the rich province of Africa, but he died a few months after the sack of Rome, and his successor, Ataulph, reverted to the traditional Visigothic policy of using his armies, at least nominally, as *foederati* in the service of the imperial government. Ataulph married Galla Placidia, the sister of the emperor Honorius, and led the Visigoths into southern Gaul and then to an attack on the Vandals in Spain. His successors built up a great Visigothic kingdom that stretched from the Straits of Gibraltar to the river Loire. Meanwhile, the Burgundians, who had settled in the region of Lake Geneva, were extending their kingdom along the Rhone River into southeastern Gaul. The territory to the north of them was held by the Alemanni.

The Vandals were pressed by the Visigoths in Spain and migrated from there into North Africa in 429. The Roman province of Africa was on the brink of civil war because of dissensions arising out of the Donatist controversies, and the Vandal king Gaiseric was an exceptionally able warrior. After a number of hard-fought sieges, he succeeded in subduing the whole province. This was a major blow to Rome, for Italy had come to rely heavily on imports of grain from Africa. Moreover, Gaiseric was the only one of the East German rulers who set himself up as an avowed enemy of Roman government. He built a powerful fleet and harassed Sicily and southern Italy so effectively that in 442 the Roman authorities were compelled to recognize him as an independent ruler, not even nominally subject to the emperor. This did not stop the Vandal attacks, and in 455 Gaiseric's Vandals looted the city of Rome even more thoroughly than the Visigoths had done.

During this period imperial authority in Italy was exercised by Gala Placidia, the widow of the Visigoth Ataulph. After her first husband's death, she married a Roman general, Constantius, and ruled for nearly twenty years as regent for their infant son, the Emperor Valentinian III (425–455). The principal headquarters of the imperial government had now been moved to Ravenna, a marsh-girded city on the Adriatic. Galla Placidia's splendid mausoleum, adorned with translucent marble and jeweled with mosaics, can still be seen there. The empress' greatest general was Aetius, the last man of Roman stock who effectively filled the office of *magister militum* in the West. He is renowned especially for a major victory over the Huns. After terrorizing the Germanic and Slavic peoples outside the imperial borders for a century, the Huns, led by their king Attila (433–453), finally broke across the Rhine into the empire itself in 452. Aetius succeeded in making an alliance with the Visigothic king, and at the head of a mixed army of Gallo-Romans, Visigoths, and other Germans, he decisively defeated the Huns in a battle near Chalons. The Huns attacked again during the following year, penetrated into Italy, and threatened Rome; but their armies were weakened by pestilence, and they were persuaded to withdraw without attacking the city. Later in 453 Attila died, his power was divided among several successors, and the Hunnish threat to the western provinces of the empire passed away.

Nevertheless, the situation in Italy continued to deteriorate. Aetius was stabbed to death in 454 by the emperor Valentinian III, but Valentinian, in turn, was assassinated in the following year. The next emperor, Maximian, lasted only a few months. He was lynched by the Roman mob for failing to protect the city against the Vandals, who sacked it thoroughly under the leadership of Gaiseric. In 456 the German *magister militum,* Ricimer, seized power in Italy and ruled until his death in 475. The emperors he appointed during the last ten years of his life were mere puppets whom he set up and deposed at will—there were five of them in the period 466–476. Ricimer's successor, Odoacar, deposed the last of the emperors, Romulus Augustulus, in

476 and did not trouble to apoint another puppet in his place. In that casual way the Roman line of emperors in the West came to an end.

There were two further invasions of Gaul and Italy still to come during the disastrous fifth century, and these led to the establishment of the two most powerful and successful of the German "successor states"—the kingdoms of the Franks and of the Ostrogoths. When the last western emperor was deposed, there was still one surviving region in Gaul that had resisted barbarian occupation, the lands between the Seine and the Loire commanded by the Roman general Syagrius. (The Germans called him "king of the Romans.") This territory was seized by the Frankish chief Clovis in 486. The Ostrogoths had crossed the Danube at the time of the breakup of the Hun kingdom in 453. When they threatened the Balkan provinces of the eastern empire, the emperor Zeno was only too happy to confer the title of patrician on their king Theodoric and dispatch him to Italy, nominally as an imperial officer appointed to expel the usurper Odoacar. Theodoric led the whole Ostrogothic nation over the Alps in 489, defeated and killed Odoacar, and established himself as ruler of Italy.

The one region of the western empire that we have not so far considered is the outlying province of Britain. Here too major Germanic invasions occurred during the fifth century. It is not clear when the last Roman troops were permanently withdrawn from Britain: A.D. 407 is the date usually given, and it is as likely as any other. After the legions had left, the Angles and Saxons from Denmark and northern Germany who had been harrying the coasts of Britain for a century past began to come not only as plunderers but as settlers. In general, the people of Roman Britain had lived on the high country with its light soils and had avoided the heavy soils of the river valleys. To the Germans, who were used to swamps and deep forest, these valleys were the ideal place to settle. Hence they ran their boats up the rivers of the south and east coasts and settled along the banks of these rivers.

In some regions, at least, the Celtic Britons and the Germans seem to have lived together in comparative peace for a long time, the Britons on the high ground and the Germans in the valleys. But as the Germans expanded their settlements, conflict was inevitable. We know little of the struggle between the Britons and their German foes except that it was long and stubbornly fought. If there is a historical basis for the legendary King Arthur, he was one of the leaders of the Britons in their defense of their lands. Bit by bit the Germans triumphed, until at the beginning of the seventh century, the Celts held only the western fringe regions of Cornwall, Wales, and Cumberland. There they preserved the tradition of Christianity that had become established in Britain during the last century of Roman rule. The Germans dominated all the rest of what is now England.

By A.D. 500 every part of the old western empire was ruled by barbarian kings. It is difficult to summarize the effects of the invasions. Before the Germans entered the empire in mass, the material prosperity and civilization of the western provinces had already declined; they simply accelerated the process. But this acceleration must have

An Anglo-Saxon buckle from the Sutton Hoo Treasure in East Anglia, buried ca. A.D. 660. Made of gold and niello, the design of the surface, in the so-called animal style, shows the combination of abstract and organic shapes that became an important element in Celtic and Germanic art of the early Middle Ages. The tails, legs, and jaws of fighting animals are elongated into bands forming a complex interlacing pattern. *Trustees of the British Museum*

been very decided. The Roman government in its strongest periods found it difficult to control piracy on the sea and robbery on the roads. These obstacles to trade must have been greatly aggravated in the disorder attending the migrations. The lowering of standards of civilization was probably equally pronounced. Throughout the fifth century, there remained in the western provinces great Roman nobles whose houses were centers of classical culture, but they were few in number, and their associates were wild Germanic chieftains. (One of them, Sidonius Apollinaris, left a collection of letters that vividly portray both the elegant luxury of country house life in eastern Gaul and the uneasy relations between the Roman landowners and the barbarians who were filtering into the region, first as *foederati,* then as conquerors.*) Rome, the ancient capital of the empire and the center of the Roman world, had been twice plundered by barbarian hosts. And by the end of the fifth century the Roman Empire in the West had ceased to exist as a political entity.

12. *The German Successor States: Gaul, Italy, and Spain*

In the course of their invasions, the Germanic peoples had made several different kinds of settlement in the lands of the Roman Empire. In Britain, the Angles and Saxons drove off most of the preexisting population and extinguished virtually all traces of Roman civi-

*Sources, no. 4

lization. In the kingdoms established by the Ostrogoths and Visigoths, East Germans formed an army of occupation living on the tribute of conquered Roman populations, who outnumbered the invaders many times over. Moreoever, at the time of the invasions the East Germans were separated from their subject peoples not only by race and culture but also by religion; for they were all Arians, while the Roman populations were overwhelmingly Catholic. In the kingdom of the Franks we find yet another kind of Teutonic invasion. The Franks did not migrate; they expanded. They never lost touch with their original German homeland beyond the Rhine. In addition, when they were converted to Christianity, they accepted the Catholic religion from the beginning, not Arianism. Only in Gaul did the Roman and Germanic cultures meet on something like equal terms. In this section we shall consider in turn the three major "successor states" that were established in western Europe—the kingdoms of the Franks, the Ostrogoths, and the Visigoths.

Clovis' occupation of the "kingdom of Syragrius" in 486 raised his status dramatically. From being merely a petty kinglet of one group of Franks, he became at once one of the most powerful Germanic rulers in the West. Clovis was, morever, a man of overwhelming ambition, and this initial victory proved to be only the beginning of an extraordinary career of conquest. In 496 and again in 501 he waged campaigns against the Alemanni, which led to the conquest of the region that is now southwestern Germany. During the course of the first campaign he was converted to Christianity, the Catholic Christianity of his Gallo-Roman subjects. This was a crucial event. We are perhaps inclined to take the survival of the Roman Catholic Church too much for granted. The fact is that in 495 there was no major ruler anywhere in the Christian world who was in communion with the pope. All the East German kings were Arians, the Franks were still heathens, and the Byzantine emperor was separated from the papacy by a schism arising out of a theological dispute concerning the nature of Christ's incarnation. In these circumstances, the conversion of Clovis marked a turning of the tide.

Clovis

The story told of Clovis' conversion is similar to the one about Constantine. He prayed to the Christian god during a crucial battle, won a striking victory, and promptly announced his acceptance of Christianity together with three thousand of his warriors. All the evidence we have of Clovis' subsequent behavior suggests that his conversion was even more nominal than that of the first Christian emperor. The long-range importance of the event is that it opened the way for the whole Frankish people to be genuinely converted by Christian bishops and missionaries during the next century. As for the immediate consequences, the acceptance of Catholicism brought Clovis obvious political advantages, and he was certainly shrewd enough to be aware of them. The whole south of Gaul was occupied by a Catholic people subjected to Arian Visigothic rulers. The people and their bishops could be expected to welcome and cooperate with a Catholic king who could present himself as a liberator. Accordingly, in 507 Clovis

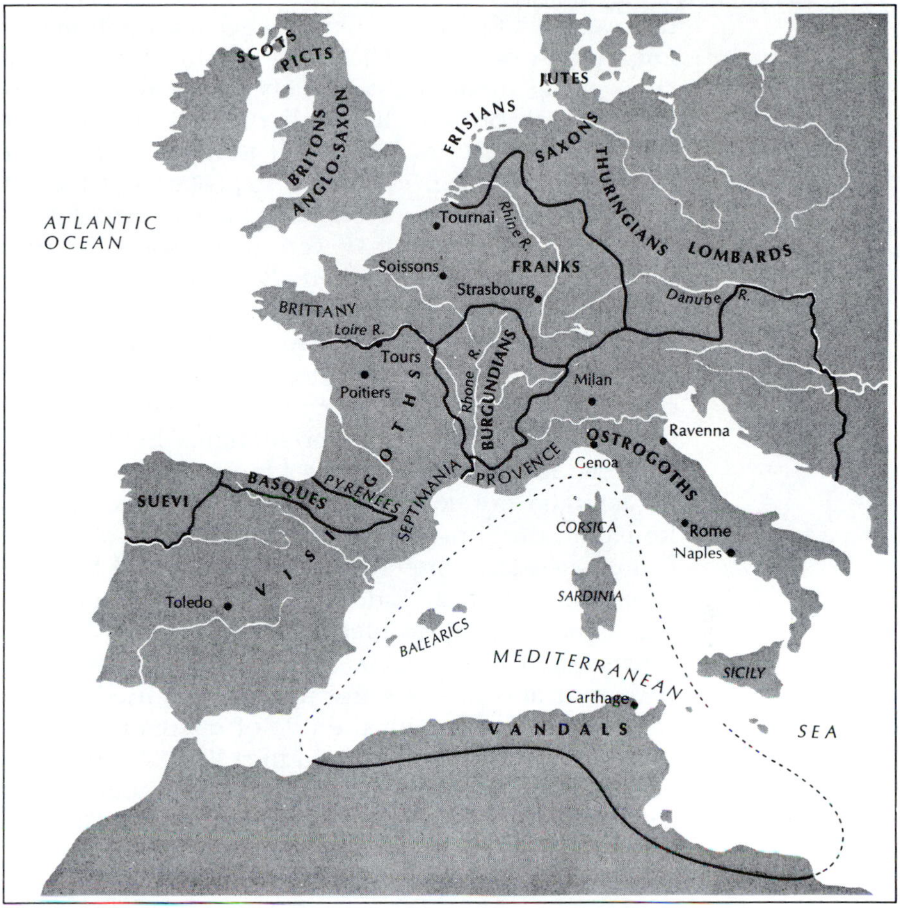

The Barbarian Kingdoms, ca. 500 A.D.

The old provinces of the western Roman Empire have by this time become independent kingdoms. The kingdom of the Franks was the only one that combined substantial German provinces east of the Rhine with conquered provinces of the empire.

declared, "I take it very hard that these Arians hold part of Gaul. Let us go with God's help and conquer them." He won a great victory a few miles south of Poitiers, and the Visigoths were driven out of Gaul into Spain. Clovis was prevented from reaching the Mediterranean by Theodoric of Italy, who took the Visigoths of Provence under his protection, but he had made himself the ruler of a vast kingdom stretching from the Pyrenees to the old Frankish homeland beyond the Rhine.

Clovis spent the last years of his life in industriously killing off various relatives who bore the title of king over different groups of Frankish tribes so that he and his descendants would be left as undoubted kings over the whole Frankish people. He displayed considerable ingenuity in this task. On one occasion, Clovis successfully urged a young prince to kill his own father; then he promptly sent his men to murder the prince and presented himself to the father's subjects as the avenger of their dead king. They gratefully accepted Clovis' rule. On another occasion, Clovis bribed the warriors of a certain Ragnachar, giving them gold bracelets to betray their king in battle. The warriors duly brought Ragnachar's skull with his battle ax. Then the treacherous warriors discovered that the "gold" they had received was only gilded bronze. When they protested, Clovis said grimly, "This is the kind of gold deserved by a man who lures his lord to his death," and told the warriors they were lucky not to be put to death themselves. When he had killed off all his close relations, Clovis was heard to complain, "Woe unto me who am left as a traveller among strangers and have no kin left to help me." "But," the account goes on, "he did not thus allude to their death out of grief but craftily, to see if he could bring to light any new relative to kill." Clovis was an authentic hero and, in his way, an important figure in the history of the Western Church, but he was not really a model of a Christian gentleman.*

Clovis did not consciously intend to destroy Roman civilization or Roman institutions. Indeed, he was proud to accept the title of consul from the eastern emperor Anastasius. But all the higher levels of Roman administration had collapsed before Clovis' conquest and the Franks had almost no idea how to preserve what still did exist. The *civitates* survived as viable units, partly because they coincided with ecclesiastical bishoprics, and Clovis appointed a Frankish follower to rule in each *civitas* with the title of *comes*, or "count." For a time, at least, these officials continued to collect the old land tax; and with a titular consul as head of state and the Roman *civitates* functioning as units of local government, it might seem that Clovis was simply a German successor to the Roman rulers of Gaul. The apparent political continuity was, however, largely an illusion. The state ruled by Clovis and his successors was in essence a primitive Germanic monarchy. The Merovingian family was believed to have been descended from a god, and the royal office was elective within the family (the name Merovingian comes from Merovech, the half-legendary founder of Clovis' dynasty). The king's real power was based on the loyalty of his Frankish counts, illiterate warriors for the most part who knew nothing of the traditions of Roman law or the techniques of Roman government. Such taxes as were collected went to swell the king's private treasure. The kingdom itself was treated as if it were the private property of the royal family; when a king died it was divided among his sons.

The Roman tradition of public order maintained by an efficient corps of trained administrators could not survive in these conditions. On the other hand, ecclesiastical institutions did survive. Often Gallo-Roman bishops shared power with Frankish counts in the cities. And, as the Franks obliterated the Roman political order, they themselves were gradually assimilated into the church of the late Roman Empire. The slow fusion of Latin and Germanic cultures made possible by the conversion of the Franks was of decisive importance for the future of medieval civilization.

Theodoric the Ostrogoth, Clovis' contemporary, was a much more

*Sources, no. 11

sophisticated and civilized ruler than the Frankish king. Only one treacherous murder is laid to his account, that of his rival Odoacar, and in Theodoric's Italy, more than in any other barbarian kingdom, the Roman tradition of orderly government was successfully maintained. Theodoric had spent several years while a young man as a hostage at the court of Constantinople. He was not only a most effective warrior leader of his own Ostrogothic people but also an intelligent administrator who understood the Roman imperial tradition; so much so that in 507 he could write to the emperor at Constantinople, "My kingdom is an imitation of yours, the one true pattern of government." At the time of the Ostrogothic invasion, the whole apparatus of bureaucratic Roman administration by provinces and *civitates* survived in Italy. Theodoric retained this whole structure. He did not entrust the work of civil administration to his Gothic warriors; rather, there was a sharp separation of functions. Theodoric relied on Roman administrators to direct the preexisting machinery of civil government, and the Italian population continued to live under Roman law administered by Roman officials. The functions of the Goths were purely military. The great landowners of Italy were required to set aside a portion of their estates—up to a third—for the use of the invaders, and the revenues from these estates supported the Gothic people. In return, the Goths provided armies that, so long as Theodoric lived, proved entirely adequate for the defense of Italy against any futher attacks. The Goths lived apart from the Romans under counts of their own race, governed according to their own customs, and practicing their own religion. Although Theodoric, like all his people, was an Arian, he displayed an exemplary tolerance toward the Catholic faith of the Italian population. "We cannot command the religion of our subjects," he declared, "since no one can be forced to believe against his will."

This system of dual responsibility worked remarkably well for a time. Italy was better governed by its Ostrogothic king than it had been by any Roman emperor of the fifth century. Theodoric coped successfully with the task of provisioning Rome, turning to Sicily as a source of grain supply now that Africa was lost to the Vandals. The people continued to receive doles of grain and wine; the aqueducts that brought water to the capital were repaired; in cities like Milan, Ravenna, and Rome, schools of law and rhetoric still flourished. The wealthy landowning classes enjoyed a new security, and the poorer people, too, benefited from the Ostrogothic rule. Theodoric gave them a generation of peace and order, strictly controlled food prices, and even changed the tax system so that the wealthy would pay more and the poor less.*

Besides all this, Theodoric conducted a successful foreign policy based on an intricate structure of marriage alliances. He achieved a settlement with the Vandals, the people that threatened Italy most of all, by marrying his sister to the king. One of his daughters married the king of the Visigoths, another the king of the Burgundians. Theodoric himself married the sister of Clovis. Thus he brought together

*Sources, no. 10

all the Germanic peoples of the West in a structure of interwoven alliances centering around his own kingdom.

On the face of it, the success of Theodoric's government seems to suggest that, even as late as A.D. 500, there still existed the possibility of a great revival of Roman civilization in the West. In truth, the whole system was inherently unstable, and it did not survive Theodoric's death by more than a few years. Theodoric ruled Italy, in theory, as a viceroy of the eastern emperor; in fact, he was an independent king who took no orders from Constantinople. Theodoric understood this well enough. So did his Goths. So did the eastern emperor. In such a situation, everything depended on the personality of the ruler. The system worked at all only because of the rare accident that, in Theodoric, a king had appeared who could command both the enthusiastic allegiance of the Gothic warriors and the effective cooperation of the Roman aristocracy. But although the Romans did cooperate, their loyalty was always suspect; they would always prefer a Catholic ruler to an Arian heretic, even though the Arian was treating them with admirable tolerance. Through most of Theodoric's reign, the danger of a pro-imperial movement against him was minimized by the ecclesiastical schism between Rome and Constantinople. When the schism ended in 518, however, there followed an exchange of emissaries between Rome and the eastern capital. Soon afterward Theodoric accused a group of eminent Roman aristocrats of plotting against him. Among them was the philosopher Boethius, whom Theodoric executed in 524.

When Theodoric died in 526, his system was already showing signs of strain. He left as successor only an infant son, and soon a succession dispute broke out. Meanwhile, Byzantium was experiencing a notable revival of power under the emperor Justinian (527–565),* who was lucky to have in his service the greatest general of the Late Roman world, Belisarius. Justinian first sent Belisarius against the Vandal kingdom of Africa in 533. Belisarius shattered the Vandal power in two major battles, and the Vandals as a separate nation disappeared from history at this point. Justinian next turned his attention to Italy. Belisarius landed in Sicily in 535, occupied the island, and then invaded the mainland and quickly captured Rome. The Ostrogoths brought up their main forces to besiege him there, and through 536 and 537 Belisarius was hard-pressed. But then he was able to move over to the offensive, and by 540 he had conquered virtually all Italy, though the Ostrogothic armies were still not destroyed.

Given another year of campaigning, Belisarius might well have pacified the whole country, but he was suddenly withdrawn from Italy to defend the eastern provinces of the Byzantine empire against a massive Persian incursion. This gave the Ostrogoths an opportunity to recover. They abandoned the house of Theodoric and chose for themselves a new war leader, Witigis. Under him and his successor, Totila, they maintained a vigorous resistance against the Byzantines for another twelve years until they were finally subjugated in 552. At that point the Ostrogoths disappeared as a separate people. Some

*See pp. 85–88.

were enslaved, others took service in the Roman armies, and the rest were absorbed into the Italian population. The Gothic wars of Justinian devastated the country far more than any of the preceding barbarian invasions. The whole peninsula was fought over time and time again; most of the major cities had to stand repeated sieges; and Rome itself changed hands several times in the fighting. This period, in fact, marks the end of ancient Rome as one of the great metropolises of the Mediterranean world. The population was scattered; the great aqueducts were destroyed; palaces fell into ruin. The Roman Senate, which had maintained a ghostly existence up to this time, finally disappeared. In 549 the Gothic king Totila staged a performance of circus games in the Colosseum of Rome. It is the last recorded instance of such a performance. At the end of the wars, only a fraction of the original population lived on in the ruins of the great city.

Moreover, the Byzantines were not even able to defend effectively the province they had won back at such a great price. It is usually said that Justinian "overstrained" the resources of the Byzantine Empire by an overambitious policy of expansion. This may be partly true; but it is also true that the Mediterranean world suffered severe epidemics of bubonic plague from 542 onward—the same Black Death that returned with devastating effects in the fourteenth century—and, as a consequence, we find frequent complaints of lack of manpower in the last years of Justinian's reign. There were just not enough men available to fill the armies or to garrison the frontier forts that the emperor had built, and after Justinian's death, the weakened defenses of Italy proved incapable of stemming the last major Germanic invasion, that of the Lombards. The Lombard people swarmed over the Alps in 568 and established a kingdom in northern Italy under their king Alboin. Two Lombard leaders broke away from the main force and struck further south to establish the independent duchies of Spoleto and Beneventum. The Lombards were far more savage and destructive and far less interested in preserving the institutions of the Roman state than the Ostrogoths had been. But their disunity and fondness for fighting one another prevented complete destruction of the imperial power in Italy.

At the end of the sixth century, the Byzantines were still in control of Sicily and southern Italy. They also held a number of strips of coastal territory that included several major cities, notably Ravenna, Naples, Rome, and Genoa. A powerful center of imperial government was maintained at Ravenna. The other cities tended to become autonomous in local government even though they acknowledged imperial suzerainty.

The Visigothic kingdom in Spain survived longer than the Ostrogothic one in Italy—until the Muslim invasion of 711. In Spain we find yet another type of coexistence between a Roman and a German population. The Visigothic state was at first more similar to Theodoric's Italy than to Clovis' Gaul but it soon developed distinctive characteristics of its own. In 554 the Visigoths were threatened by a Byzantine invasion, a part of Justinian's general program of reconquest, but their kingdom was preserved by Leovigild (568–586), a strong and successful king, who established a permanent capital at Toledo. A major obstacle to any further consolidation of a united kingdom was the difference in religion between Visigoths and Hispano-Romans. As in Italy the Goths formed a warrior aristocracy outnumbered many times over by the Roman population; and, again as in Italy, the Goths were Arian, the masses of the people Catholic. Leovigild tried to convert the Catholic bishops to Arianism, but this only provoked a rebellion. His son Recared (568–601) took the opposite course. He adopted the Catholic religion of his Roman subjects and persuaded the Arian bishops to follow suit. This removed a tension that was always a source of instability in Ostrogothic Italy.

The conversion of Recared inaugurated a period of close cooperation between church and state. The kings appointed the bishops and protected them. They in turn supported the royal authority. National councils of the Spanish church, summoned by the king, met frequently at Toledo. (Eighteen councils were held there between 589 and 701.) Sometimes lay nobles attended as well as bishops and clergy, and then the council could function as a kind of national assembly advising the king on civil as well as ecclesiastical affairs.

Much of the preexisting structure of Roman society and government survived under the Visigoths. In the countryside wealthy Roman aristocrats still lived on vast estates worked by slaves or *coloni*; also the Roman provinces and *civitates* survived as administrative units. The Visigothic kings appointed a duke to rule over each province and a count for each *civitas*, choosing both Visigoths and Romans for these offices. The work of actually apportioning and collecting taxes in the cities was still carried out by municipal councils as in the Late Roman Empire.

From the middle of the sixth century onward the Visigothic and Roman populations began to merge together. Leovigild repealed an old law which had forbidden intermarriage between the two peoples and, after the conversion of Recared, there was no religious obstacle to their fusion. At first the two peoples kept their own separate laws, but, at least from the time of Leovigild onward, Visigothic kings promulgated legislation that was binding on all their subjects. A new body of law common to Goths and Romans grew up. King Receswinth (649–672), drawing on both Gothic and Roman traditions, produced a major codification known as the *Book of Judgements,* which provided a common law for all the people of Spain. This work was translated into Castilian in the thirteenth century as the *Fuero Juzgo.* It remained a living part of the law of Spain all through the Middle Ages.

In spite of the considerable achievements of the Visigothic state, there was one major weakness in its structure. All legitimate authority was centered in the king; but the Visigoths had neither a law of hereditary succession nor any settled procedure for electing a new ruler. When a king died, any Gothic noble with a sufficient retinue of warriors might try to seize the throne. Often there was a period of warfare before a new king established himself. Often too an ambitious noble was not patient enough to wait for a king to die and resorted to assassination. Four kings were murdered between 531 and 555. A modern historian observes, "The assassination of Visigothic rulers by their subjects was almost a matter of course." A sixth-century Frankish chronicler called assassination "the Gothic sickness" and added, "If any of their kings displeases them, they go after him with their swords and then make king whomever they wish."

The church tried to remedy this situation by emphasizing the sacred authority of the royal office. The king was hailed by the bishops as a "new Constantine" wielding a divinely ordained authority, and at his accession he was anointed with holy oil in the manner of Old Testament rulers. (This rite of anointing later spread to the Anglo-Saxons and the Franks.) At the fourth council of Toledo (633) the church tried to establish an orderly procedure for regulating succession to the throne.

> No one of us shall dare to seize the kingdom; no one shall arouse sedition among the citizenry; no one shall think of killing the king; but when the king has died in peace, the chief men of all the people, together with the priests, shall, by common consent, constitute a successor for the kingdom. . . .

Unfortunately the references to sedition, seizing the throne, and killing the king represent the realities of the situation more accurately than the pious hopes for common consent and peaceful successions.

The close union between church and state in Visigothic Spain had one unhappy result—frequent persecution of the Jews who formed the only significant religious minority. The same council of Toledo that sought to regulate the royal succession enacted a series of harsh anti-Jewish measures, though the bishops drew the line at actual forced conversion, a policy that the king wanted to adopt. It has often been suggested that the oppressed Jews contributed to the downfall of the Visigothic kingdom by cooperating with the Muslim invaders who eventually destroyed it, but there is no contemporary evidence for this.

The Visigothic state had a more obvious defect than the resentment of a persecuted religious minority. At the time of the Muslim onslaught in 711 the Visigoths were feuding among themselves in yet another dispute over succession to the kingship. The instability of the monarchy was the fatal weakness in the Visigothic kingdom. After the Muslim conquest of nearly all Spain the Visigoths, like the Vandals and Ostrogoths before them, ceased to exist as a separate, identifiable people. Of all the Germanic peoples who settled in the western lands of the Roman Empire, only the Franks survived to found an enduring nation.

Although all the East German kingdoms we have mentioned eventually passed away, leaving almost no traces of their existence except for archeologists and philologists, their preservation of some elements of Roman civilization for a time in Italy and Spain made possible the

Gilded copper plaque with hammered reliefs that may have been part of a helmet, depicting Agilulf, king of the Lombards, surrounded by warriors and spirits of victory. The style reveals the transformation and debasement of classical art as the culture of the Late Roman Empire was engulfed by that of the barbarian tribes. Museo del Bargello, Florence. *Alinari–Art Reference Bureau*

appearance of a number of literary works that were to be of importance for the future. Two figures in Theodoric's Italy, Boethius (480–524) and Cassiodorus (ca. 490–580), and Isidore of Sevile (ca. 570–636) in Visigothic Spain produced works that were widely read in the Middle Ages. To be sure, there was no brilliant new ''Age of the Fathers'' under the Ostrogoths and the Visigoths. We have noted that the tradition of classical literature had become sterile and backward-looking by the fourth century. The same can be said of the Christian writers of the sixth century. Their task was just to preserve the heritage of the past; but that was a work of some importance for the future.

Perhaps the only book from the period that still seems a piece of living literature is Boethius' *Consolation of Philosophy,* written while he was in prison awaiting execution. The author first describes his miserable plight. Then, in a dialogue with an allegorical lady, Philosophia, he is led from despair to resignation and finally to the perception that a man who lives his life virtuously carries his own happiness within himself and need fear no external misfortune. Although Boethius was a sincere Christian, the teaching of his most famous book was essentially old-fashioned Stoicism; but the circumstances of the book's composition inspired the author to infuse a new life and urgency into the old doctrine and to present it in language of rare eloquence. Boethius was also important as a translator. He set himself the task of rendering into Latin all the philosophic works of Plato and Aristotle with explanatory commentaries. Unfortunately, he was able to complete only the more elementary logical treatises of Aristotle and an introduction to them by Porphyry, and these translations were all the West was to know of Aristotelian thought for several centuries.

Cassiodorus was a Roman aristocrat who rose to high rank in Theodoric's government. The letters he wrote as secretary to the Gothic king provide a major source of information about this period.* As a

*Sources, no. 10

young man, Cassiodorus dreamed of founding a Christian Academy in Rome that would give a Christian education as effectively as the old pagan academies had taught classical literature and philosophy. The wars that swept Italy after Theodoric's death made this plan impracticable, and Cassiodorus retired to his family estates in southern Italy. There he founded a monastic community which aimed to put into practice Jerome's advice that Christians should use literary studies in the service of religion. Great emphasis was placed on the collection and preservation of classical and Christian writings. Cassiodorus also produced a curriculum of studies for a Christian scholar in his *Introduction to Divine and Human Readings,* a work of practical bibliography covering both theology and the liberal arts. It was widely copied and much used in monastic schools during the following centuries.

Isidore of Seville was the most distinguished scholar of Visigothic Spain. Isidore wrote on theology, history, and natural science. He also supervised the preparation of an extremely influential collection of canon law, the *Collectio Hispana.* He was a quite unoriginal thinker but an indefatigable compiler. Isidore's best known work is the *Etymologiae,* an attempt at compiling in twenty volumes an encyclopedia of all human knowledge—science, law, history, theology, and the liberal arts. The exposition took the form of explaining the origin and meaning of Latin words. These "etymologies" are often highly imaginative. Thus, "Man (*homo*) is so called because he was made out of earth (*ex humo*) as is recounted in Genesis." Isidore's linguistic methods seem to modern scholars almost comically inaccurate, merely a kind of wild punning. The medieval mind apparently found a deep symbolic significance in his fanciful parallels. Despite its errors, his work preserved in conveniently accessible form a great mass of valuable information from the ancient world.

Many older historians placed the "end of the ancient world" and the beginning of a new era in the late fifth and early sixth centuries, whose history we have surveyed. More recently this view has been challenged in various ways. Henri Pirenne argued that the economic unit of the Mediterranean world survived the Germanic invasions and was shattered only by the rise of Islam in the seventh century. Other economic historians, like Dopsch and Latouche, have called attention to important continuities between late classical and early medieval civilization. For example, many Roman cities survived as inhabited places throughout the Middle Ages (and, indeed, down to the present day) even though they suffered so greatly in the crises of the fifth century. But perhaps the older point of view is after all the most defensible one, at least as regards western Europe. (In the eastern Mediterranean, Byzantine civilization survived and, in that region, it was indeed the Islamic invasions that caused sudden, irreversible changes.) Evidently, there can be no absolute break in the history of a society whose people survive at all, for parents always pass on something of the old ways to their children. The fact that may justify our regarding the fifth century as truly the end of an era is that radical changes occurred simultaneously on so many different levels. The slave economy of the ancient world gave way to a system based on the labor of half-free peasants; the peoples of the empire were swept by a religious revolution; the governmental system of the Roman state disintegrated in the West. Moreover, all these changes proved irreversible. Neither the economy, nor the pagan religion, nor the political structure of the ancient Roman Empire was ever successfully revived.

READING SUGGESTIONS

**B. Tierney,* Sources *and* Readings, *vol. I, nos. 4, 9–11.*

E. A. Thompson, *The Early Germans* (Oxford, 1965) is a convenient introductory sketch. On particular peoples see J. O. Maenchen-Helfen, *The World of the Huns* (Berkeley and Los Angeles, 1973); B. S. Bacharach, *A History of the Alans in the West* (Minneapolis, 1973); *H. Wolfram, *History of the Goths* (Berkeley and Los Angeles, 1988); E. A. Thompson, *The Visigoths at the Time of Ulfila* (Oxford, 1966) and *The Goths in Spain* (Oxford, 1969); *P. H. Blair, *Introduction to Anglo-Saxon England* (Cambridge, 1956); *E. James, *The Franks* (Oxford, 1988); O. M. Dalton, *The History of the Franks by Gregory of Tours,* 2 vols. (Oxford, 1927) [vol. I is an introductory essay on Frankish Gaul and vol. II a translation of Gregory's *History*]. T. Hodgkin, *Italy and Her Invaders,* 8 vols. (Oxford, 1892–1916) provides an elaborately detailed account of the invasions. *J. B. Bury, *The Invasion of Europe by the Barbarians* (London, 1928) is a good but much slighter work. Other good surveys are *J. M. Wallace-Hadrill, *The Barbarian West* (New York, 1962); L. Musset, *The Germanic Invasions* (State College, PA, 1975); and W. Goffart, *Barbarians and Romans, A.D. 418–584: The Techniques of Accomodation* (Princeton, 1980).

Two fine books on the mingling of classical, Christian, and Germanic influences in early medieval literature are *W. P. Ker, *The Dark Ages* (New York, 1904), and *M. L. W. Laistner, *Thought and Letters in Western Europe, A.D. 500–900* (London, 1931). The impact of the invasions on the Western economy is considered by A. Dopsch, *The Economic and Social Foundations of European Civilization* (New York, 1937), and *R. Latouche, *The Birth of the Western Economy* (London, 1961).

The *Poems and Letters* of Sidonius Apollinaris, W. B. Anderson (trans.), 2 vols. (London, 1936–1965), and *The Governance of God* by Salvianus, J. O'Sullivan (trans.) in *The Writings of Salvian the Presbyter* (New York, 1947) provide sharply contrasting pictures of life in fifth-century Gaul. *The Letters of Cassiodorus,* T. Hodgkin (trans.) (London, 1886), describes conditions in Theodoric's Italy.

THE EMERGENCE OF EUROPE

chapter

V

Byzantium, Frankish Gaul, and Rome

Three major institutions emerged from the ruin of the Roman world: the Byzantine Empire, the Frankish kingdom, and the Roman church. In different ways each preserved some elements of Roman classical civilization and blended them with other cultural traditions—Oriental, Greek, or barbarian.

The ways in which they interacted with one another in the centuries after the downfall of Rome determined the future course of history in eastern and western Europe.

13. *Byzantine Civilization*

Justinian

The great Germanic migrations that, during the course of the fifth century, brought the western provinces of the Roman Empire under the control of Anglo-Saxons, Franks, Burgundians, Visigoths, Ostrogoths, and Vandals had comparatively little effect on the eastern provinces. Although the provinces south of the Danube were fearfully ravaged, the Germans made no permanent settlements there, and Asia Minor, Syria, Palestine, and Egypt were essentially untouched. When Romulus Augustulus (475–476), the last emperor resident in the West, was deposed, his colleague Zeno (474–491) continued to rule in Constantinople. Zeno and his successor were barely able to hold their own in the East and could do nothing to recover the western provinces. But Byzantine civilization displayed an enormous capacity for survival. The eastern provinces of the Empire had always been the richest and most populous; the demographic and economic resources to sustain a great civilization persisted there. And at times of great crisis the Byzantine state always produced able rulers who defended Constantinople successfully for the next thousand years. In 518 control of the empire passed into the hands of Justinian (527–565), who, first as the deputy of his uncle and later as emperor, ruled for forty-seven years. Justinian's campaigns of reconquest in the West, which we have already mentioned, were only one aspect of a far-ranging policy that aimed at a complete restoration of Roman institutions and Roman civilization in the Mediterranean world.

Justinian's personality is difficult to grasp. Historians have perhaps been too much inclined to dismiss him as a mediocrity because he did not achieve all that he set out to do. But his ambitions were such that no man could have achieved them all, and some of the things that Justinian did accomplish were of great and lasting importance. He reorganized the Byzantine state. He carried through an epoch-making codification of Roman law. He enriched Byzantium with splendid new buildings, among them the cathedral of Hagia Sophia, which still survives and is renowned as one of the most magnificent Christian churches ever built.*

Justinian's greatest successes were all achieved at second-hand. He launched great campaigns, but he himself never led an army in battle. He always worked behind a screen of brilliant generals, jurists, and artists. It was Justinian, however, who was responsible for choosing those men. He also displayed considerable discernment in his choice of a wife. With all the ladies of Byzantium to pick from, he selected Theodora, a low-born actress and prostitute. For an emperor to want to marry a prostitute is not so remarkable perhaps; the unusual thing about Justinian is that he succeeded in finding one who made a splendid empress. Theodora was an intelligent, proud, courageous woman, and for more than twenty years she was virtually coruler of the empire with her husband. In the early years of the reign she even saved his throne for him. A sudden rebellion arose in Constantinople in 532. Mobs filled the streets and Justinian was besieged in his palace, uncertain of the loyalty of his troops. At the imperial conference held to decide on a course of action, he considered fleeing from the city. Then Theodora rallied his courage with a bold speech reported by the Greek historian Procopius:

> For one who has been an emperor it is unendurable to be a fugitive. May I never be separated from this purple, and may I not live that day on which those who meet me shall not address me as mistress. If now it is your wish to save yourself, O emperor, there is no difficulty for we have much money, and there is the sea, here are the boats. . . . For myself I approve a certain ancient saying that royalty is a good burial shroud.

Justinian commanded his troops to attack the rebels, and the insurrection was quickly suppressed.

So far as the civilization of the Western world is concerned, Justinian's most influential work was his codification of Roman law. Since the earliest days of the Roman Republic, this law had been growing and changing to meet new conditions. It consisted of legislation by such authorities as the Senate and the emperors, decisions made by judges, and comments of distinguished jurists. The mass of law that

*Sources, no. 22

The Empire After Justinian and the Western Kingdoms

Note the contrast between the western and eastern portion of the empire: the West was divided into Germanic kingdoms, whereas the East survived as a political unit until the onslaught of Islam.

had accumulated by the third century was known as the *jus vetus* (old law). From the fourth century onward, nearly all legislation was by imperial edict. This later body of law was known as the *jus novum* (new law). Roman law dealt in subtle detail with all the problems that arose when great multitudes of people lived a civilized life together in a vast empire. It was to be many centuries before questions arose for which it had no answer. On the other hand, since Roman law had grown up in a haphazard fashion over such a long period of time, it was full of obscurities and internal contradictions. Justinian decided to eliminate them all.*

*Sources, no. 12

In 528 he put his jurists to work on the more manageable task of codifying the *jus novum,* and they quickly produced the *Codex Justinianus.* In 530 the emperor appointed a new commission to cope with the vast mass of the *jus vetus.* This was a more formidable project, but the work was finally completed in the fifty books of the *Digest.* Justinian rounded off his work by publishing the *Institutes,* a terse summary of the main principles of Roman law intended for use as a textbook. It was of the highest importance for the future that he had taken such pains to preserve the law of ancient Rome. Justinian himself was an autocratic ruler, and all the legislation of the later emperors was absolutist in tone. But the legal texts of the earlier period declared that the power of the emperor was derived from the people and that even an emperor was expected to rule in accordance with the law. Thus, in later centuries, Roman law could be used (and was used) to support both absolutist and democratic theories of the state. Justinian's codification was made too late to become widely known in the barbarian West, but when it was rediscovered at the end of the eleventh century, it exercised a profound influence on medieval law and political theory.

Justinian himself was a transitional figure. He was the last of the Byzantine emperors who spoke Latin as his native tongue and who cared deeply about the revival of Latin culture and the recovery of the Latin-speaking provinces of the West. His jurists used the Latin language in codifying Roman law, but the fact that Constantinople was a Greek city and that Greek was the basic language of the major part of the empire is clearly demonstrated by the Greek abridgments of the *Codex* and *Digest* that appeared almost immediately. Moreover, within fifty years of his death, the court and government of the empire had become Greek. A famous treatise on military science from about 580, usually attributed to the emperor Maurice, gave transliterations of Latin military terms into Greek in order to make them intelligible. In architecture Justinian made use of both classical and oriental motifs. His greatest monument is the church of Hagia Sophia, a vast domed structure designed by Greek architects using ideas developed in Syria. Roman architects knew how to build a dome (as in the surviving Pantheon) but they never made one the central feature of such a huge edifice. Hagia Sophia inspired future Byzantine architects to further experimentation with domed structures, but they never again built anything on the scale of Justinian's "Great Church."

As far as the emperors after Justinian were concerned, the European provinces of the empire already ravaged by German invaders were of comparatively little importance. They centered their attention on the protection of their rich Asiatic lands. Here they faced a truly formidable enemy—the great Persian state. A period of civil war and general confusion in the empire during the reign of the utterly incompetent emperor Phocas (602–610) gave the Persians an excellent opportunity. In 611 they swept into Syria. In 613 Damascus fell and in 614 Jerusalem. During the following year they overran Asia Minor and reached Chalcedon, just across the Sea of Marmora from Constantinople. In 619 their armies conquered Egypt, while a great horde of Avars and Slavs besieged Constantinople. But Phocas' successor, Heraclius (610–641), was a determined and able soldier. In a series of campaigns, he drove the Persians from the empire and invaded their country. In 627 a great victory near the site of ancient Nineveh crushed forever the Persian power. On the eve of the seventh-century Islamic invasions, Byzantium still seemed a formidable, almost unvanquishable power.

By the end of Heraclius' reign the East Roman empire had already acquired many of the distinguishing features that would continue to characterize it as long as Byzantium endured. Byzantine culture was founded essentially on the Hellenic and Oriental elements in late Roman civilization, without the admixture of Germanic and Celtic influences that would be so important in the medieval West. This is evident in many spheres, for example, Byzantine economic organization, institutional structure, religion, art, and literature.

The Byzantine emperors continued the Late Roman policy of governmental regulation of economic activity. They were fully aware that the empire's survival depended to a large extent on its economic resources. Most important of all was agriculture, for it supplied not only the food needed by the people but manpower for the army as well. The emperors were extremely active in colonizing waste and uncultivated lands. Slavic peoples were settling in the European provinces of the empire at this time. Some came as invaders, but others were brought in as colonists. All of them, when settled on the land, increased the agricultural production. Although there were many great estates tilled by *coloni,* there were also villages of free farmers and individual homesteads. Fields of grain, orchards, olive groves, and vineyards covered the land. In the reign of Justinian silkworms were introduced, and this valuable material was produced in considerable quantity.

The numerous cities of the empire were centers of industry and commerce. Constantinople held a population approaching one million people during this period; Thessalonica, 500,000. While the other towns were smaller, there were many of them. The more important industries were carried on by guilds or corporations strictly controlled by the state. The state regulated the purchasing of raw materials, the marketing of the finished product, the methods of manufacturing, prices, and profits. Everything was carefully watched by government inspectors. Actually, the crafts workers were employees of the state working under its direction. The result was a high degree of industrial stability but little or no technological progress. Except for arms and armor, the chief manufactures were of luxury goods: silks, fine woolens, tapestry, jewelry, and ornamental articles of enamel and ivory. Particular care was lavished on articles connected with religion, such as chalices and reliquaries. The products of the Byzantine workshops were valued and copied throughout Europe.

Commerce was as closely controlled as industry. The two most profitable trades, those in grain and silk, were government monopolies, but all merchants were rigidly regulated. This did not prevent them from building up a flourishing network of commerce. Constantinople was the greatest market of the world. To it came the products of the East: silks, cotton, sugar, and spices. To it also came many products of the West, carried in the ships of its Italian subject cities, such as Venice, Ravenna, and Amalfi. The merchants who came from distant lands to sell their goods in the markets of Constantinople bore back with them the products of the empire. The official imperial coin, the *bezant*, was carefully maintained in value. Although few Byzantine merchants achieved great wealth, they and the artisans formed an active, vigorous middle class.

In a state surrounded with foes, the most important institution is bound to be the army. The Byzantine army was well paid, carefully organized, diligently drilled, and thoroughly equipped. Its backbone was its heavy cavalry, which accounted for about half the total force. The Byzantine cavalryman wore a steel cap, a mail shirt reaching to his thighs, and metal gauntlets and shoes. His arms were the sword, lance, and bow. He was thus a heavily armed mounted archer, capable of harassing a foe with arrows and overwhelming him by a charge. The infantry was of two sorts, light and heavy. The light infantry were archers who wore no protective armor but carried bows that could outrange those borne by horsemen. The heavy infantry wore helmets, shirts of mail, and often gauntlets. They also carried shields and were armed with swords, lances, and battle-axes. The Byzantine generals were professional soldiers, not dashing amateurs like the warriors of Western Europe. They did not believe in taking unnecessary chances and never risked a battle unless they felt fairly certain of victory.

From the time of Heraclius onward a new system of military organization grew up, based on regions called *themes*. Historians still argue about the origins and development of this system, but its essential feature was that a military commander assumed responsibility for the civil administration of a district and commanded an army drawn from the local population. Most of the thematic soldiers did not serve on a full-time basis but were allowed to spend part of the year cultivating agricultural smallholdings that were assigned to them. They provided a valuable, mainly defensive force to supplement the elite professional troops stationed in and around Constantinople.

The government of the empire was a complex bureaucracy. Although it was large and extremely expensive, it was also comparatively efficient. Under weak emperors who neglected the business of state, it tended to grow corrupt, but the strong emperors carried out vigorous reforms. At the head of the government stood the emperor or, at times, emperors. During the first period of Byzantine history the imperial dignity was in theory elective. One became emperor by being proclaimed by the Senate, the people, or the army, or by any combination of these groups. Actually, the son of the late emperor usually succeeded, but if he proved weak and incompetent he was likely to be overthrown and replaced by the leader of the revolt. As time went on the hereditary principle grew stronger. After the eighth century, when an incompetent emperor was removed from power, he was likely to be left with the imperial title, and the leader of the revolt ruled as an associate emperor. The hereditary principle also made it possible for women to play an important role in Byzantine government from time to time. If an emperor died leaving a minor son to succeed him, the child's mother would rule as regent until the boy became of age. Two such empresses who decisively shaped Byzantine policy, especially in religious affairs were Irene (d. 803) and Theodora (d. 867).* Theodora

The Byzantine emperor was a sacred person appointed by God to rule over his subjects. He was crowned and anointed in solemn ceremonies, and everything connected with him was holy. The emperor Heraclius recognized that he was a ruler in the tradition of the semidivine Hellenistic kings by taking the title *basileus.* The emperor's subjects prostrated themselves before him as their ancestors had before the pagan god-kings. The emperor lived in magnificent state: his residence was a splendid palace, which was actually a number of luxurious buildings, surrounded by gardens, on the shore of the Bosporus. His life was a continuous solemn ceremony, and at all times he was surrounded by a horde of officials, servants, and guards. This incredibly expensive and luxurious court was no mere extravagance. The traditions of the lands that composed the Byzantine Empire demanded that the king should be set apart from other individuals, and the court made this fact apparent.

The emperor was an absolute monarch whose power was limited only by the danger of deposition or assassination. As long as he was in power, the civil government and the army were absolutely at his disposal. Byzantine civilization was essentially religious in inspiration, and the emperor was also to a great extent the ruler of the church. He controlled the appointment of the patriarch of Constantinople, who was the head of the ecclesiastical organization. He summoned the councils of the church and issued their decrees. Byzantium possessed what Rome had always lacked in the days of its greatest power—a common religion, deeply rooted and shared by all classes. A single faith inspired the devotions of the common people, the dominant forms of art and architecture, and the professed aims of the government. Christianity could obviously serve as an integrative element, binding the state together, but it could also be a cause of discord in an age of constant theological controversy. Usually, however, the emperor could have his way in matters of religion. While he might not claim the right actually to determine questions of dogma, by choosing the patriarch he could direct the course of orthodoxy. But even in Byzantium the emperor's power over the church was not quite absolute. The people of the empire were deeply religious and had a lively interest in religious questions. The emperor could not with impunity attack a patriarch on an issue on which the latter had popular support. Thus we occasionally find strong emperors submitting to the patriarch, especially in questions involving the ruler's personal life.

Byzantine civilization showed great originality in its art. In the Late Roman Empire, two more or less distinct forms of Christian art had developed. One of these was essentially Greek in inspiration and was

*See p. 131.

imbued with the earthly beauty and gaiety that marked Greek culture. For the artists of this school, Christ was a handsome, beardless young man, who was usually shown naked. The other type was developed in Palestine and Syria. Its basic feature was awesome dignity. Christ was a bearded figure in long, flowing Oriental robes. Both these schools had a profound effect on medieval art in western and eastern Europe.

In the Byzantine Empire, these two trends were quickly merged to form the art we know as Byzantine. This art found expression in two ways—in mosaics and in the illumination of manuscripts. The Byzantine church was essentially built to house mosaics. Outside it was impressive with its great towering dome, but it was also plain and grim with no attempt at decoration. Inside it was a mass of marvelous mo-

saics. These depended for their effect almost entirely on the use of color—rich gold, blue, red, and purple. There was no attempt at what we call realism. The figures were not intended to look natural; they were essentially symbols that fitted into the design and spirit of the decoration. But the impressive dignity of these symbolic figures and the rich beauty of the color achieved a result unequaled by any other art. (Splendid examples of such work can be seen at Ravenna in the churches of S. Vitale and S. Apollinare in Classe.) These same characteristics appeared in the miniatures that illuminated the Byzantine manuscripts. There again the charm of symbolic figures carefully fitted into a design and rich color combine to produce rare beauty. But the love of beauty was not confined to makers of mosaics and illuminators of manuscripts. The Byzantine crafts workers who made ornaments for both secular and religious use displayed the same skill in decorative art. Mosaics in enamel and beautiful carved ivories embellished such articles as reliquaries, chalices, and crucifixes.

(Left) Ninth-century mosaic in Hagia Sophia. The Byzantine Christ is a majestic, dominating figure. *Courtesy of Dumbarton Oaks, Center for Byzantine Studies, Washington, DC*

(Right) Christ as Teacher. This classical statue, from the third or fourth century, presents Christ as a handsome young man. *Hirmer Fotoarchiv*

The Byzantines made little progress in pure science, though they produced various practical inventions like the famous Greek fire. But Byzantium nourished a great literary tradition. Its scholars and writers both preserved and added to the heritage of the classical past. Byzantine scholars industriously read, copied, and annotated the literary works of ancient Greece, while dictionaries, grammars, and encyclopedias increased the usefulness of the accumulated learning. The new, distinctively Byzantine works of literature were commonly based on classical models, but they were also influenced by the changing forms of the Greek vernacular language. Byzantine writers produced a variety of practical treatises on law, geography, the art of warfare, and the techniques of government administration. Apart from such utilitarian works, Byzantine literary achievement was greatest in two spheres: writings on history and writings on religion.

The greatest historian of Justinian's reign, Procopius, was secretary to the general Belisarius; thus he provides first-hand evidence for many of the events that he describes. He wrote in a lively and vigorous style in the tradition of great classical historians like Thucydides. Nevertheless, Procopius makes an ambiguous witness. The works he published in his lifetime contain conventional praise of the emperor and the great figures of the day. But he also left a *Secret History* filled with scurrilous and obscene gossip about Justinian, Theodora, and other court notables.* The emperor Maurice (582–602) was a great patron of art and literature, and under him Menander, called "the Protector," wrote a history of the years 558 to 582. At the end of the sixth century Evagrius of Syria composed an *Ecclesiastical History,* which recounts the story of the church from the Council of Ephesus (431) down to 593. The tradition of historical writing continued throughout the course of Byzantine civilization; almost every epoch of Byzantine history is illuminated for us by the work of perceptive historians.

*Sources, no. 22

The subtlety and power so evident in ancient Greek philosophical thought survived among the Byzantines, but their intellectual endeavor was directed primarily to theological issues. Every new religious controversy produced a spate of treatises and sermons. There was also an enormous literature of hymns, lives of saints, and speculative and mystical theology. The greatest religious poet of Justinian's age, the hymn-writer Romanus Melodus, is noteworthy for his use of accentual rhythm in place of the classical Greek quantitative metre. (The same change appeared later in medieval Latin poetry.*) For the Western world the most influential of the mystical theologians was a Syrian Neoplatonist, later known as Dionysius. (He was confused in medieval times with the Dionysius of Athens mentioned by St. Paul in the *Acts of the Apostles.*) This "Dionysius" taught that man was led to God through a long ascent of the spirit culminating in a divine illumination of the soul. His works *On the Celestial Hierarchy* and *On the Ecclesiastical Hierarchy* describe how a hierarchy of angels in heaven is mirrored by the hierarchy of the church on earth, which leads men toward the final illumination. This idea of earthly society as a permanent, ideally unchanging image of the heavenly order was a central motif of Byzantine civilization. Compared with the incessant changes that would occur in the West, Byzantine culture presents a picture of extraordinary continuity and stability. This was not mere accident. Stability was precisely what the Byzantines were aiming for.

Although the cultural traditions of East and West diverged after the barbarian invasions, Byzantine influence on the growth of medieval civilization was very considerable. The basic creeds of the Christian faith were hammered out mainly by Greek theologians at councils summoned by eastern emperors. Italian art was dominated by Byzantine models down to the thirteenth century. Repeated attempts during the Middle Ages to create a new Roman Empire in the West were inspired not only by memories of old Rome but by the living reality of Byzantine imperial government; and Justinian's great legal codification profoundly influenced the legal traditions of the Western world from the time of its rediscovery in Italy around 1100.

To sum up: Byzantium remained for centuries the center of a brilliant culture, but it was a culture in many ways different from that of the medieval West with which we are mainly concerned. The two civilizations continued to influence one another throughout the Middle Ages, and their relationship constitutes an important theme of medieval history. In later chapters, we shall deal with Byzantine political and religious affairs at the points where they influenced the course of events in the West.

14. *The Kingdom of the Franks*

When we turn from the sophisticated civilization of Byzantium to consider the Frankish kingdom in sixth-century Gaul, it is as though we step into a different world. Judged by the standards of classical civilization, the Franks were in every way more backward and barbarous than the Byzantines. Any intelligent observer, looking at the state of

*See p. 454.

the west Roman Empire in 500 A.D., might have supposed that the future lay with the relatively advanced Ostrogothic and Visigothic peoples. Yet, although the Frankish king Clovis was a merely crafty and bloodthirsty savage compared with the more civilized of the Gothic rulers, it was the kingdom of the Franks that survived. The vital difference between the Frankish state and the states of the East German peoples was that the Frankish kingdom contained a great reservoir of Germanic labor power in the Frankish lands beyond the Rhine. Also, from the early days of the conquest, there was no religious cleavage between the Franks and the Roman population. A new society could grow up that rested on both Gallo-Roman and German foundations. Moreover, the center of Frankish power was too remote from the Mediterranean to be subjugated by either Byzantine or Muslim invasions.

We shall have to analyze in some detail the social, religious, and political structure of Merovingian Gaul. But perhaps, to begin with, we can convey the realities of the time more vividly by a bald narrative of events than by an abstract analysis of institutions. Much of our knowledge about the history of the Franks under the sons and grandsons of Clovis comes from a chronicle written by Gregory of Tours in the second half of the sixth century. Gregory was a bishop and proud of his Roman ancestry. Yet he wrote bad Latin by classical standards and was conscious of the fact the he did so. His defective style is symptomatic of a general decay in standards of civilization in Frankish Gaul. So is the story that he had to tell—a wild, barbaric tale of treachery, violence, and lust, which seems more like a turgid historical novel than sober factual history.

When Clovis died in 511, his kingdom was divided among four sons. In spite of frequent feuds against one another, the brothers cooperated in conquering the Thuringians in 531 and the Burgundians in 534. Finally, the Franks occupied Provence in 536 and so extended their kingdom down to the Mediterranean coast. This whole expanded realm fell into the hands of Clothar I, who was the last of Clovis' sons to survive. When he died in 562, there was again a fourfold division of the kingdom. The simplified genealogy on the following page will illustrate the relationships between the leading figures of the Frankish royal house after Clothar.

From this time on, there were four generally accepted major divisions of the Frankish state. The ancient Frankish lands on both sides of the Rhine formed the kingdom of Austrasia, while northern Gaul was known as Neustria (the new territories). The former kingdom of Burgundy in the valleys of the Rhone and Saone formed a third Merovingian state. Southwestern Gaul, usually called Aquitaine, was at times independent and at times attached to one of the other kingdoms.* In the division of 562, Charibert received Aquitaine; Chilperic, Neustria; Guntram, Burgundy; and Sigibert, Austrasia. However, Charibert died in 567 and his kingdom was divided among his three brothers. Of these, Guntram appears in Gregory's chronicle mainly as a peacemaker between the other two. He was, for those times, quite

*See map, p. 87.

a good king. As the nineteenth-century historian Michelet wrote, "No one had anything against him except a few murders." Sigibert is presented by Gregory as an honorable if bellicose leader. Chilperic was apparently the most downright wicked of the three brothers, and he was encouraged in his wickedness by a fascinating but startlingly depraved wife named Fredegund. (Gregory wrote that she "bewitched" men—but he meant the word to be taken literally.) As for Chilperic, Gregory calls him "the Nero and Herod of our times." Like Nero, Chilperic had literary and intellectual pretensions. He argued about theology with his bishops; he tried to write Latin verses; he even had the original idea of adding four new letters to the alphabet.

Sigibert greatly deplored a habit that had grown up among the Frankish princes of marrying base-born serving women (like Fredegund). Only a real princess would do for Sigibert, and accordingly he imported one from Visigothic Spain. His wife, Brunhilde, proved to be a striking and talented woman. Chilperic was at once jealous and decided the he too must has a Spanish princess, "although he already had many wives," according to Gregory. After negotiations with the Visigothic king, Brunhilde's sister, Galswintha, came from Spain to marry Chilperic. He was at first delighted with the arrangement "because she brought much treasure"; however, after a few months, he tired of his new bride, had her strangled, and married his favorite mistress, Fredegund. From this point on, a bitter blood feud broke out between the families of Sigibert and Chilperic. Sigibert invaded Neustria in 575 and defeated his brother. The Neustrian Franks were willing to accept Sigibert as their king and prepared a ceremony of acclamation at Vitry. Fredegund, however, was equal to the situation. She sent an assassin with a poisoned dagger who stabbed Sigibert to death as he was being raised on the shields of the warriors. Deprived of their king, the Austrasians streamed back to their own land, taking with them Sigibert's infant son, Childebert. Brunhilde was captured by Chilperic but, surprisingly, she was not killed. Instead she was sent into exile at Rouen.

The story now takes an improbable turn. Chilperic had a rebellious son named Merovech. At this point he fell in love with his aunt Brunhilde, or, at any rate, he married her. Chilperic sent an army against them, but Brunhilde managed to escape to Austrasia. Merovech, after a series of improbable adventures, was hunted down by Chilperic's warriors and, to avoid capture, had himself killed by a faithful slave. At least this was the story that was put about, and the slave was savagely tortured to death to lend credibility to it. Many believed, however, that Merovech's death had been arranged by Queen Fredegund.

For the next few years there were no major changes in the situation. Guntram of Burgundy took the young prince Childebert under his protection and also made the boy his heir. Brunhilde, as regent for her son, was the real ruler of Austrasia, and she never willingly gave up this power as long as she lived. Fredegund continued to assassinate old enemies and to make new ones. Chilperic devoted himself to op-

Frankish Royal House

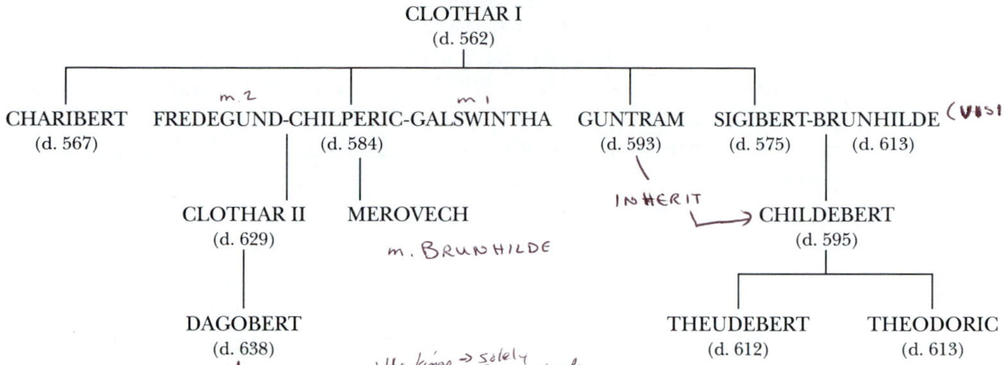

pressing his subjects and to building a great amphitheater at Soisson, where he hoped to revive the old spectacles of the Roman circus. Unfortunately, he was assassinated before completing the project.

When Guntram died in 593, Childebert inherited his kingdom of Burgundy and united it with Austrasia, but he died two years later, apparently poisoned. Fredegund died in the same year. Brunhilde was thus left in triumph as ruler of Austrasia and Burgundy on behalf of her two grandsons, Theudebert and Theodoric. The Austrasian nobles, however, were growing increasingly resentful of their alien, imperious old queen. In 612 Theudebert led a faction of nobility against Theodoric, who supported his grandmother. Theudebert was defeated and killed, but Theodoric also died in 613. The Austrasians refused to recognize his infant sons as kings, because to have done so would have simply perpetuated the rule of Brunhilde. Instead, they turned to Clothar II of Neustria and offered him the kingship. The aged Brunhilde was captured and handed over to the new king, the son of Fredegund and Chilperic. He had her tortured for three days and then tied to the tail of a wild horse and dragged to death. That was the end of the feud. Clothar II ruled over the whole kingdom of the Franks.

The bloody story of Clovis' sons and grandsons conveys clearly enough the pervasive violence of life in Merovingian Gaul. But that is not quite the whole picture. Gregory of Tours gives us occasional glimpses of another world, of poets and scholars who still cared for Latin literature and of saints who, in various quiet backwaters, were still maintaining high standards of Christian piety. The most attractive saint of the period was the ex-queen Radegund, and the most considerable poet was Venantius Fortunatus. Radegund was a Thuringian princess who was captured by Clothar I in the campaign of 531 and carried off to become his wife, or one of his wives. When Clothar murdered her young brother, she ran away to Poitiers, where the bishop consecrated her as a nun and somehow persuaded Clothar to leave her in peace. A group of religious ladies gathered around Radegund, and they founded a convent. Radegund, an educated, cultured woman, always refused to accept any superior office in the community but undertook the most humble and servile tasks and devoted herself especially to the care of the poor and sick.

Venantius Fortunatus, the poet, was born in Italy and educated at the schools of Ravenna. In 565 he made a pilgrimage to Gaul to visit the shrine of St. Martin of Tours and then settled down to spend the rest of his life in the northern kingdom as a sort of unofficial court poet. At Tours, Fortunatus met Bishop Gregory, the chronicler, and they became friends. He was present at the marriage of Sigibert and Brunhilde and wrote a poem for the occasion in which Brunhilde figures as a "jewel of Spain" and a "newborn Venus." A little later on he performed a similar service for Fredegund. Fortunatus had a great gift for turning out elaborate eulogies and pretty compliments, a talent that made him welcome wherever he went. Most of his verse seems tedious enough nowadays, so that modern historians have been surprised that he found an audience at all. We have to remember, however, that among the Frankish kings, Chilperic at least was a man with literary interests who fancied himself a versifier. Gregory of Tours wrote that Chilperic's poems were hopelessly bad, but Fortunatus characteristically observed that they were rather pleasing.

In 567 Fortunatus visited Poitiers and was captivated by the personality of Radegund. Finally, he became a priest and chaplain to her convent. There are many poems from this period, slight but sometimes charming. Fortunatus was deeply impressed by Radegund's humility, especially since she had once been a queen, and in one verse, sent with a gift of flowers, he played on the royal colors that she would not deign to wear:

O Queen that art so high
Purple and gold thou passest by . . .
Wilt thou not hold
The violet's purple and the crocus' gold?

The disconcerting thing about Fortunatus is that, along with all the light verse and facile flattery, he struck out two powerful, moving hymns—*Pange lingua gloriosi* and *Vexilla regis prodeunt*—which have lived through the centuries in the liturgy of the Catholic Church. He ended his career as bishop of Poitiers.

The story of Fortunatus and Radegund makes a sort of counterpoint to the history of the warring Frankish princes. When we read the chronicle of Gregory of Tours or the numerous lives of saints that were written in the sixth and seventh centuries, we always receive this twofold impression of Merovingian Gaul. There were occasional islands of peace and piety standing in sharp contrast to a surrounding sea of savage violence. But, for a historian, the most important aspect of Merovingian life was something else, something that no contemporary chronicler described and analyzed for us; that is, the slow growing together of Franks and Gallo-Romans in sixth-century Gaul that eventually produced a new nation and a new culture. The fusion took

This bronze buckle, ornamented with incised patterns and applied motifs, is Frankish work contemporary with the buckle from the Sutton Hoo Treasure shown in Chapter III. *The Walters Art Gallery, Baltimore*

place on all levels. In some spheres—religion, language, certain aspects of economic organization—the Roman tradition was dominant. But in the sphere of law and government, Frankish institutions almost totally replaced Roman ones; and since these institutions formed the basis of early medieval government, we must consider them in some detail.

Frankish conceptions of law and political organization differed from Roman ones in almost every possible way. The Roman idea of the state had been essentially similar to the modern one. A sovereign authority existed, charged with the duty of upholding the public welfare. To fulfill this task, the imperial authority enacted such legislation as was necessary and collected heavy taxes. The taxes were used to maintain a large army and a professional civil service and to finance an extensive program of public works. The citizen was expected to feel a sense of loyalty to the state, to the *res publica.* None of this existed in the Frankish system. Insofar as the kingdom held together at all this was achieved through the personal loyalty of warrior nobles to their king and through the ability of the nobles, in turn, to command the loyalty of their own followers. There was no idea of the king as a public official charged with maintaining the public welfare. He was essentially a war leader. Though Clovis held the dignity of consul and his court swarmed with officials bearing high-sounding Roman titles, they were not really carrying out the specialized functions of their Roman counterparts. They had no bureaucracy to direct. They were really a group of personal friends who were bound to the king by a special bond of loyalty, a Frankish version of the old German *comitatus.* (The Franks called this body the *truste* and its members *antrustiones.*) Similarly, the Frankish counts in the *civitates* bore little resemblance to the Roman administrators whom they replaced. They held a court and maintained order, but they were not paid officials of the state. They lived from the income of private lands that had been granted to them by the king at the Frankish conquest. Their relationship to the king was again one of personal loyalty, and when weak or unpopular kings were unable to retain that loyalty, the counts tended to become independent.

Above all, the law that the counts administered to the Franks was radically different from Roman law. Roman law was based on a jurisprudence that regarded reason and justice as the necessary foundations of legal order. Particular rules were exemplifications of universal principles of justice. Such principles could be discovered by conscious reflection and the appropriate rules promulgated as law by command of a legislator. All the presuppositions of Germanic law were different. None of the Germanic peoples conceived of laws as either exemplifications of abstract justice or as rules promulgated by a sovereign legislator. To them, law was the ancient custom of the tribe, unwritten, assumed always to have existed, handed down from generation to generation by word of mouth. Each people had its own law. Even among the Franks themselves, the two main branches of the nation, the Salian Franks and the Ripuarian Franks, had different customs. All the separate Germanic peoples who were assimilated into the Frankish kingdom, like the Burgundians and the Alemanni, continued to use their own laws. There was no idea that the law of a conqueror should be imposed on a defeated enemy or that any one set of customs was superior to the others and so deserving of universal recognition. A person's law was a part of that individual's inheritance, part of the person's very identity.

The content of Frankish law was very primitive. We can open the Code of Justinian at random and come upon complex legislation dealing with commerce and contracts and partnerships, with forms of tenure, rules of evidence, court procedure—the same kinds of things we would expect to find in a modern law book. When we turn to the Salic law of the Franks, we encounter passages like these:

> If any person strike another on the head so that the brain appears, and the three bones which lie under the brain shall project, he shall be sentenced to 1,200 denars which makes 30 shillings. . . . If anyone shall have called a woman harlot, and shall not have been able to prove it, he shall be sentenced to 1,800 denars which makes 45 shillings. . . . If anyone shall have killed a free Frank, or a barbarian living under the Salic law, and it have been proved on him, he shall be sentenced to 8,000 denars. . . . But if anyone has slain a man who is in the service of the king, he shall be sentenced to 24,000 denars, which make 600 shillings.

But although primitive Teutonic law was crude and savage, it preserved one valuable feature that had almost disappeared from late Roman law, the implicit assumption that law was and ought to be a natural outgrowth of the whole life of a people, not merely a set of rules imposed from above.

The earliest Teutonic codes that have survived reflect a state of society in which a primitive pattern of blood feuds was giving way to a system of organized fines.* In Roman law, a criminal was individually responsible for his or her offense, and the public authorities were responsible for punishment. In Teutonic society, a crime against an individual involved the whole kin of the criminal and the victim. If a

*Sources, no. 14

man was murdered, his kin had the right and duty of inflicting vengeance on the murderer and his kin. Since feuds of this kind could weaken the fighting strength of a whole tribe, the fines were devised to provide an honorable alternative. Any offense could be atoned for by an appropriate penalty to "buy off the spear." A portion of these fines went to the king, the rest to the injured man (or his heirs) and to his kin. The king's share perhaps originated as a payment for his service in presiding over the court personally or through a deputy.

Every person had a *wergild,* the price that had to be paid for taking his or her life. This varied according to rank. A noble in the king's service was "worth" 600 shillings, a free Frankish warrior 200 shillings, a Roman 100 shillings. Women were highly valued in Frankish law. The fine for killing a woman of child-bearing age was 600 shillings; it increased to 700 shillings if she was pregnant. When she could no longer have children a woman's price was the same as a man's, 200 shillings. The penalty for rape was 63 shillings.

According to Germanic law a girl was subject to the guardianship of her father until she married and then similarly subject to her husband. In the form of marriage called *Muntehe,* from the word *Munt* referring to guardianship, the marriage was arranged by the girl's father and the bridegroom's family. The future husband was required to provide a substantial payment for his bride, rather than the bride bringing him a dowry. At first this was a brideprice, a sort of purchase price for the woman, paid to her father, but by the sixth century it had become an endowment for the bride hersef, which she kept if her husband died. In addition, on the morning after the wedding night, the husband gave the bride a "morning gift" confirming her status as his lawful wife. There was apparently another sort of marriage called *Friedelehe* (from *Fridela,* a friend or beloved), though the sources are very confused in referring to it. This was a marriage based on free choice in which the bride did not pass out of the guardianship of her kin or receive an endowment; but the husband still gave her a "morning gift," as a sign that he had really taken her as his wife. Inheritance customs varied from people to people but generally favored male heirs. Usually daughters could inherit if there were no sons, though in a famous provision of the law of the Salian Franks women were excluded altogether from inheriting Salic land.

Germanic codes of law insisted that wives must be faithful to their husbands, but there was no comparable standard for men. Frankish kings and nobles commonly practiced polygyny. A man might have one wife from a *Munt*-marriage, several more from *Friedel*-marriages, and concubines as well. There was no very sharp distinction between lawful wives and concubines or between legitimate and illegitimate children. Gregory of Tours often referred to the many wives of the Frankish kings whose deeds he recorded.

In the administration of justice, the presiding officer of a court—usually a count in Frankish Gaul—did not hear evidence and then reach a verdict on the basis of it; the only way of establishing guilt or innocence was by an appeal to the supernatural. The most primitive form of proof was *compurgation.* A man of exceptional standing, like a bishop, might be permitted to clear himself by his own oath, but all others needed a group of "oath-helpers"—perhaps twelve or twenty-five men—who would swear that they held the accused person worthy of belief. The assumption was that a guilty man would not find so many honest supporters and that the compurgators for their part would not risk divine wrath by committing perjury. Moreover, the oath to be taken was an elaborate ritual formula, and any stumbling over a word or phrase meant that the divine judge was dissatisfied and that the oath had failed.

The alternative to compurgation was *ordeal,* which took various unpleasant forms.* In the ordeal of hot iron the accused was required to pick up a weight of red-hot iron and carry it a set number of paces. Then his burned hand was bound up. Three days later the wound was examined. If it was healing cleanly, the man was held innocent; if it was festering, he was held guilty. A variant was the ordeal of hot water. The accused was required to pick a stone from a cauldron of boiling water, and again the scald was bound up and examined after three days. In the ordeal of cold water, the accused was flung into a pool of water that was previously blessed. If the holy water rejected the man so that he floated to the surface, he was considered guilty. If he sank into the water, he was held innocent and was pulled out before he drowned. A very simple form of ordeal, popular in the later Middle Ages, was trial by battle. The accused and the accuser fought to the death; the survivor was held innocent. The two litigants could fight in person or through appointed champions.

The kind of legal institutions we have been describing were not peculiar to the Franks. The Anglo-Saxons in England and the various Germanic peoples to the east of the Frankish kingdom lived according to similar laws. Throughout the north of Europe, legal cases were decided by the barbaric rites of compurgation and ordeal up until the beginning of the thirteenth century. Then the church forbade priests to participate in the ordeals, and alternative methods of proof had to be devised.

In the Frankish kingdom, the Gallo-Roman population continued at first to live according to their own Roman law. (The last codification of Roman law in the West, the *Brevarium Alarici,* was prepared in 506 by order of the Visigothic king Alaric II. It was intended for the use of his Roman subjects in southern Gaul.) But there were no schools to train new generations of jurists, and when the supply of competent judges died out, Roman law survived only in a debased form as another customary law, with compurgation and ordeal used to establish guilt.

It was the same with the Roman system of taxation. The first Frankish kings greedily collected all the taxes they could extract from their subjects and added the receipts to their own private treasure-hoards. But the Roman system required a trained body of clerks and accountants for its operation, and the Frankish kings after Clovis possessed no such staffs. They had only a few priests at court to write their letters

*Sources, no. 15

for them. Moreover, at the bottom of their hearts they knew very well, as any decent Frankish warrior would, that the whole system of extorting tax payments from subjects was intrinsically wicked. Gregory of Tours tells a story involving Queen Fredegund that illustrates the point. Two of Fredegund's children became desperately ill, and she decided that a really striking act of atonement for her past sins was necessary in order to ward off the wrath of God. She therefore said to King Chilperic, "Let us burn the wicked tax registers"—which they proceeded to do. It is difficult to run a sophisticated fiscal system on such a basis. Gradually the Roman land tax dwindled to a customary tribute from certain estates. Indirect taxes, tolls, and market dues could be collected more easily, but they were often retained by the local count. The great bulk of a Frankish king's revenue came from his own private estates.

In the sphere of religion, Frankish paganism slowly gave way to Roman Christianity, but in the process there were important changes in the structure of the church. Clovis and his successors fully realized the value of their alliance with the church and were determined to make the most of it. They were extremely generous in making gifts of property and privileges to both secular and regular clergy. The bishops became great landholders, and rich monasteries sprang up. The special rights enjoyed by the church under the Roman government were greatly enlarged. The ecclesiastics, accustomed to the sophisticated Roman judicial system, had no enthusiasm for what seemed to them very primitive German law. Hence they persuaded the kings to grant them jurisdiction over the clergy. Moreover, the great prelates did not want wild Frankish counts wandering over their lands and pleaded for "immunity." This privilege meant that no royal officer could enter the lands of the church. Officers of the church arrested criminals and turned them over to the count in cases where the church lacked the right to try the criminal.

But, although the Merovingian church was well endowed with privileges, church appointments became increasingly subject to secular control. In Roman law, the church had been regarded as a legal corporation within which the bishop exercised administrative control of property and personnel. The Franks knew nothing of such subtleties. When a Frankish landowner built a church on his country estate, he regarded it as his own and the priest as his servant to be appointed and dismissed at will. The same system grew up in other Teutonic countries as they accepted Christianity. Most of the rural churches that became the parish churches of medieval Europe had a patron, usually the local landowner, who enjoyed the right of appointing the village priest. (In the church of England, the practice persisted from Anglo-Saxon times down to the twentieth century.) The consent of the bishop was required in principle, but it was often a mere formality. The bishops themselves were appointed by the kings, and the canon law requiring them to be elected by clergy and people fell into disuse. As the episcopate became largely Germanic, there was a rapid decline in both literacy and ecclesiastical discipline.

The complex economic organization of the Roman Empire was equally subject to deterioration by neglect. The Roman villa system survived, but not much else. The gradual decline of commercial activity in Gaul, which had been in progress since the third century, became more rapid in the Merovingian period. The Franks were essentially warriors rather than traders and had no interest in urban life. Moreover, their kings did not consider the encouragement of trade and commerce by keeping roads and bridges in repair, policing the trade routes, and protecting merchants and their goods as part of their royal function. Although the ancient cities on the Mediterranean coast continued some seaborne commerce, trade almost disappeared in the interior. By the end of the Merovingian era, Gaul was essentially an agricultural region with a localized agrarian economy. There was little money in circulation, and few traders moved along the roads. If one is to call any period the "Dark Ages," the later Merovingian period is the one to choose.

During the last century of the Merovingian age, the power of the kings declined greatly. The last of Clovis' dynasty who ruled vigorously and effectively was Dagobert (629–638). After his death, the kingdoms of Austrasia and Neustria were again divided, and in the middle years of the seventh century, their rulers were often at war with one another. The Merovingian monarchs of this period are usually portrayed as pathetic degenerates, but this information is based mainly on writings by authors favorable to the next dynasty, the Carolingians. What is certain is that the last Merovingians were remarkably short-lived. Under a succession of minor kings, real power passed to the chief officer of the king's household, called the *mayor of the palace,* who exercised the royal authority on their behalf. Under King Dagobert, the mayor of the palace was a certain Pepin of Landen, and the office subsequently became hereditary in his house. This Pepin was the ancestor of Charlemagne and the later Carolingian dynasty. Pepin's grandson in the male line tried to make himself king but was defeated and killed in 656. His daughter's son, Pepin of Heristal, became mayor of the palace in Austrasia, and this second Pepin succeeded in bringing to an end the wars between Austrasia and Neustria. In 687 he invaded Neustria, won a decisive victory at the battle of Tertry, and made his king, Theodoric III, ruler of all Gaul. From then until his death in 714, Pepin was the real ruler of the whole kingdom of the Franks. He was succeeded by his illegitimate son Charles, known as Martel or the Hammer, after another interlude of civil war.

In Charles Martel, something of the old savage ambition and warlike ability of the first Frankish kings was reborn. He succeeded in uniting the turbulent nobility under his leadership and led them in frequent attacks against the Frisians to the north and Bavarians to the east. Moreover, he changed the Frankish style of waging war. The Frankish warriors had always been foot soldiers; only the kings and great nobles fought on horseback. The new style of fighting was based on an apparently simple little invention, the stirrup. We do not know with certainty where the stirrup was first used or precisely when it was introduced into Western Europe, but it seems clear that Charles Martel's forces were the first to exploit its potentialities in warfare. With the stirrup, a mounted man could use his lance for striking as well as for throwing, and by rising in the stirrups he could deliver highly effective strokes with his sword. Charles Martel built up a substantial force of such cavalrymen to supplement the traditional Frankish army of foot soldiers and bound them to himself by personal oaths of loyalty. This change in the art of war had important implications for the future growth of feudalism, and we shall consider it again in that context.

If we try to sum up the state of Gaul in the sixth and seventh centuries, it is evident that an intricate mingling of Roman and Frankish cultures was taking place, but that this mingling was accompanied by a great decay in standards of civilization. Teutonic kingship and primitive customary law replaced the institutions of the Roman state. Roman order gave way to frequent internal warfare. Christianity, the religion of the Late Roman Empire, was generally accepted but often in a debased form. The Roman villa system persisted, and the tendencies toward local self-sufficiency and a primitive agrarian economy that had existed in the last days of the Roman Empire were greatly accentuated. Finally, we may note that in language the Latin tradition survived. The Franks continued to speak German only in their old homeland along the Rhine. In the region we call France (with the exception of Celtic Brittany) a vulgar Latin speech, now on its way to becoming French, was universally adopted.

15. *The Roman Church*

Between Gaul and Byzantium lay an Italy facing a very uncertain future in the sixth century. Rome was no longer the capital of a secular empire, but if her bishops could make good all their claims, she would still hold a position of importance in the Christian world. However, the realization of papal claims was impeded both by the undisciplined barbarism of the western provinces and by the sophisticated theocracy of the East. Once the Roman Empire had passed away, it was not easy for the Roman church to survive.

The Byzantine emperors regarded themselves as sacred rulers, divinely appointed to govern the Christian world. The Roman popes considered themselves to be direct successors of St. Peter and, as such, commissioned by Christ himself to rule the whole church. Given these claims, there was an inherent probability of friction between Rome and Byzantium. New disagreements over points of doctrine made further conflicts inevitable. At the root of all the doctrinal problems of the sixth and seventh centuries was the fact that virtually the whole Egyptian church remained passionately attached to the Monophysite faith, which had been rejected at Chalcedon and condemned by Rome.* Religious dissent led to civil disorders in Alexandria. The im-

*See p. 56.

perial authorities, naturally wanting to maintain peace, were constantly casting around for some compromise formula which would satisfy the Monophysites without outraging the Catholics.

The first such attempt was made by the emperor Zeno, who promulgated a statement of faith called the *Henotikon* in 482. Like many would-be compromisers, he did not succeed in pleasing anyone. The patriarch of Constantinople, Acacius, was excommunicated by the pope, and new riots broke out in Egypt. The ensuing breach between Rome and Byzantium, known as the Acacian schism, helped the Ostrogothic king Theodoric to establish his rule in Italy at this time. The schism is important in church history because it led Pope Gelasius I (492–496) to formulate a trenchant declaration about the respective roles of priests and kings in the government of the Christian world. He wrote to the Byzantine emperor Anastasius in 492:

> Two there are, august emperor, by which this world is chiefly ruled, the sacred authority of the priesthood and the royal power. Of these the responsibility of the priests is more weighty insofar as they will answer for the kings of men themselves at the divine judgment.

The text clearly emphasized a duality of functions, but it also indicated that the priestly role was of greater dignity than the royal one. In later centuries, the words were used to support both theories of church-state separation and theories of papal supremacy.

When Justinian assumed power in 518 as aide to his uncle, the emperor Justin, he quickly opened up negotiations with Rome and ended the schism on terms laid down by Pope Hormisdas (514–523). Justinian needed a reconciliation with Rome as part of his grand design for the reconquest of Italy, but he had not the slightest intention of obeying the Roman pontiffs in matters of religion if it became politically inconvenient for him to do so. And meanwhile the strength of the Monophysites in Egypt had not diminished. When Pope Silverius (536–537) displeased the emperor, he was accused of treason and summarily exiled to the island of Palmeria where he quickly died, allegedly of starvation. Silverius is the last pope who is revered as a martyr in the liturgy of the Roman church. The next pope, Vigilius (537–555), was a protege of the empress Theodora, but even he balked when Justinian attempted yet another compromise with the Monophysites. Vigilius was carried off to Constantinople, imprisoned, subjected to frequent indignities, and prevented from returning to Rome for several years until finally he agreed to accept the imperial policy. His successor, Pelagius I (555–560), was again an imperial nominee.

The mid-sixth century was a low point in papal history. At the end of Justinian's reign, there seemed a strong probability that the pope of Rome would become a mere tool of Byzantine imperial policy. The Lombard invasion of Italy in 568 prevented this from happening, but after the invasion it seemed probable that Rome could survive only as a remote, ineffectual outpost of Catholic Christianity, dominated by the barbarians. (One pope of this period, Pelagius II, was an Ostrogoth.) This second possibility was averted by the emergence of one of the greatest pontiffs in the history of the Roman church, Gregory I, known as Gregory the Great, who is often called the father of the medieval papacy.

Gregory was born in 540 of a wealthy noble Roman family. As a boy, he lived through the Gothic wars of Justinian and saw the ruin of Italian civilization that they brought about. He would have been twenty-eight when the Lombards invaded Italy. By then he had entered the imperial civil service and had risen to become prefect of the city of Rome. In 574 Gregory abandoned his secular career and entered a monastery, but in 579 Pope Benedict I persuaded him to go to Constantinople as papal ambassador to the imperial court. In 685 he returned to Rome to help the pope in his administration of the Roman church. Finally, in 590 Gregory himself was elected pope. He profoundly influenced the future history of the church by his ability and activity as both a ruler and a teacher.*

As a ruler, he took upon himself the direction of all the affairs of the city of Rome. By the end of the sixth century, there had been a complete breakdown of civil administration. Starving people clamored for food and there was no one to help them. Lombards threatened the city and there was no one to organize its defense. Wronged men wanted justice and there were no adequate secular courts to hear their cases. Gregory himself described the state of the city in a sermon preached to the people of Rome in 593. He took as his text the words of the prophet Ezekiel, "The meat is boiled away and the bones in the midst thereof."

Pope Gregory the Great

> What Rome herself, once deemed the Mistress of the World, has now become, we see—wasted away with afflictions grievous and many, with the loss of citizens, the assaults of enemies, the frequent fall of ruined buildings. . . . Where is the Senate? Where is the people? The bones are all dissolved, the flesh is consumed, all the pomp of the dignities of this world is gone.

Gregory negotiated a truce with the Lombards in 592 and directed the defense of the city when war broke out again in 593. To feed the people, he undertook a major reorganization of the vast estates in southern Italy that the Roman church had acquired through the accumulated endowments of past centuries. The lands in each province were grouped under a clerical official called a rector, and a lay bailiff supervised each estate. Gregory himself took a personal interest in the management of the whole complex of lands. His letters dealing with their administration reveal him as a hard-headed, very successful man of business. He looked for favorable markets. He arranged to export timber to Egypt and grain to Constantinople. The result of his efforts was an enormous increase in the revenues of the Roman church at a time when the demands on the pope were heavier than ever before. The increased revenues were used to relieve famine, to ransom captives, and to provide endowments for churches, hospitals, and schools.

*Sources, no. 18

Outside Rome, Gregory exercised a firm control over all the churches of Italy, often intervening in their affairs to settle disputes and helping them financially from his own resources. His influence also spread beyond Italy. He maintained a considerable correspondence with the rulers of the Franks, especially with Brunhilde, whom he urged, not very successfully, to undertake the reform of the Frankish church. The leading bishop of Spain, Leander, sought Gregory's advice and support. The bishop of Constantinople received a papal rebuke for presuming to use the title "universal patriarch." (Gregory also refused the honorific title for himself, preferring the humbler appellation "servant of the servants of God.")

By far the most important of Gregory's interventions in affairs outside Italy was his dispatch of the mission that undertook the conversion of England in 597.* A legend set down by the Anglo-Saxon historian Bede and familiar to many generations of English schoolchildren tells that Gregory first learned about conditions in England from a group of fair-haired, blue-eyed slave boys who were offered for sale in the Roman market. He was struck by their beauty and distressed to learn that they were heathens. "Who are they?" he asked, and was told that they were Angles. "They should be angels," Gregory replied. Then he continued the word-play. Where did they come from? From Deira (a province of Northumberland), he was told. "They shall be saved *de ira dei* (from the wrath of God)," the pope promised. Who was their king? It was a certain Aelle. "His people shall sing alleluia," said Gregory. The story has no doubt grown somewhat in the telling, but it is likely enough that Gregory encountered English slaves in Rome. It is certain that he sent a mission to England that profoundly influenced the religious history of Northern Europe—an act of striking courage and imagination when one remembers the state of his own shattered city.

As a teacher, Gregory was ranked by medieval men as the fourth great Doctor of the Church along with Jerome, Augustine, and Ambrose. Most modern scholars would hardly agree with this estimate. Gregory was not a profoundly original thinker; his theological works are important mainly because they transmitted to the medieval schools the central doctrines of St. Augustine in a somewhat simplified and popularized form. Gregory's major exegetical work, a commentary on the Book of Job, consisted mostly of farfetched allegories. Another work, usually known as the *Dialogues,* is also hard going for a modern reader. The book is better described by its alternative title, the *Miracles of the Italian Fathers.* It is a remarkable compilation of anecdotes about saints and sinners, filled with accounts of highly improbable miracles. Gregory displayed a hard, clear intellect in all matters of practical administration but a naive credibility concerning tales of divine or diabolical interventions in human affairs. He was a man of his own time. People took for granted the frequent intervention of supernatural forces in day-to-day life, an attitude that persisted throughout the Middle Ages. Gregory's use of anecdotes to enliven

*See p. 119.

his homilies was a new departure in the development of preaching, much imitated in later sermons.

Perhaps the most influential of all the pope's works was his *Book of Pastoral Care,* a treatise on the episcopal office that reflected the pope's high idealism in the way of life he laid down for a good bishop and his profound understanding of ordinary human nature in the advice he gave on the care of the bishop's flock. The title of the last section gives the flavor of the whole work and a good characterization of the author too: "How the Preacher, When He Has Done Everything That Is Required of Him, Should Take Care Lest His Life or Preaching Make Him Proud." Centuries later, the *Pastoral Care* was translated into the West Saxon dialect by King Alfred of England. It was one of the first major books to be set down in any form of English. Besides all these writings, more than eight hundred of Gregory's letters survived, preserving for future generations the image of papacy confidently presiding over all the western churches. Another major achievement of this age, often associated with Gregory's name, was the growth of the great tradition of liturgical music commonly called Gregorian chant—but there is no evidence that the pope personally played any significant role in this particular sphere.

Gregory's pontificate effectively reasserted for Rome a position of primacy among the churches. Some historians have maintained that, more than this, Gregory was also the true founder of the temporal power of the papacy in Italy. But this is only partly true. Legislation of the emperor Justinian had conceded substantial authority in civil affairs to the bishops, and Gregory certainly exercised that authority to the full; no doubt he even went beyond what had been conceded. There was a vacuum of power in Rome, and Gregory stepped in to fill it. He undertook the tasks of an imperial governor because there was no one else to undertake them, and subsequent popes continued the tradition he had established. But it never occurred to Gregory to set himself up as an independent prince, to repudiate the sovereignty of the emperor at Byzantium. He was prepared to rebuke emperors when he thought they were behaving sinfully, but he always addressed them respectfully as the legitimate sovereigns of Italy. The idea that Rome might secede from the Romen Empire was quite alien to his thought.

A historian can hardly help treating Gregory as a great builder for the future. But that was not the pope's intention at all. Gregory was quite convinced that he was living in the last days of the world, that the end of all things was at hand. In the little time that was left, he did the tasks that came to hand. He preached to the people, fed the hungry, instructed his clergy, and converted heathens; and in doing all this superlatively well, he was unconsciously shaping an institution that would endure through all the medieval centuries and beyond. Gregory left to the papacy greatly increased wealth and greatly enhanced prestige. Above all, he left the memory of his own dominant personality, which lived on in his letters and other writings. A later pope wrote him a fitting epitaph: "In a straitened age . . . he disdained to be cast down though the world failed."

READING SUGGESTIONS

B. Tierney, Sources *and* Readings, *vol. I, nos. 12, 14–15, 18, 22.*

The fourth volume of the *Cambridge Mediaeval History,* dealing with Byzantium, has been rewritten and published in a new edition edited by J. M. Hussey, 2 vols. (Cambridge, 1966–1967). Those volumes provide the most comprehensive account of Byzantine civilization as a whole. Good one-volume surveys are * N. H. Baynes and H. St. L. B. Moss, *Byzantium: An Introduction to East Roman Civilization* (Oxford, 1948); G. Ostrogorsky, *History of the Byzantine State* (Oxford, 1956); * A. A. Vasiliev, *History of the Byzantine Empire, 324–1453,* 2nd ed. (Madison, WI, 1952); * S. Runciman, *Byzantine Civilization* (London, 1933); C. Mango, *Byzantium: The Empire of New Rome* (New York, 1980). On Justinian, see * P. N. Ure, *Justinian and His Age* (Harmondsworth, 1951), R. Browning, *Justinian and Theodora,* 2nd ed. (London, 1987); and J. W. Barker, *Justinian and the Later Roman Empire* (Madison, WI, 1966). Among the best works on Byzantine art are C. R Morey, *Early Christian Art,* 2nd ed. (Princeton, 1953); O. Demos, *Byzantine Mosaic Decoration* (London, 1949); O. von Simson, *Sacred Fortress: Byzantine Art and Statecraft in Ravenna* (Chicago, 1948). For source material, Procopius' * *Secret History,* R. Atwater (trans.) (Ann Arbor, MI, 1961) and *History of the Wars,* H. B. Dewing (trans.) (London, 1914–1935) make lively reading.

On Merovingian Gaul, besides the works of Dalton, Ker, and Laistner cited above (Chapter III), see S. Dill, *Roman Society in Gaul in the Merovingian Age* (London, 1926); * K. F. Drew, *The Burgundian Code* (Philadelphia, 1949), and *The Laws of the Salian Franks* (Philadelphia, 1991). An excellent recent study is * P. J. Geary, *Before France and Germany. The Creation and Transformation of the Merovingian World* (New York, 1988). See also J. M. Wallace-Hadrill, *The Long-Haired Kings* (New York, 1962); and * P. Riché, *Education and Culture in the Barbarian West* (Columbia, SC, 1976). On the Lombards see * K. F. Drew, *The Lombard Laws* (Philadelphia, 1973).

Walter Ullmann, *The Growth of Papal Government,* 2nd ed. (London, 1962) is a complex study on the ideology of papal power. G. Barraclough provides a brief overview in * *The Medieval Papacy* (New York, 1968). Two substantial biographies are T. Jallard, *The Life and Times of Saint Leo the Great* (London, 1941), and F. H. Dudden, *Gregory the Great: His Place in History and Thought* (New York, 1905). For a more recent study of Gregory see J. Richards, *Consul of God* (Boston, 1980). Among the translations of the popes' writings are Leo's *Letters and Sermons,* C. L. Feltoe (trans.) (New York, 1895); Gregory's *Dialogues,* O. J. Zimmermann (trans.) (New York, 1959); and *Pastoral Care,* H. Davis (trans.) (Westminster, MD, 1950).

chapter

VI

The Crisis of the Eighth Century

No one thinks of the seventh and eighth centuries as a great age in the history of Europe—but if the events of that period had turned out differently, there might never have been a Europe at all. In this chapter we have to consider three sequences of events which occurred independently of one another but which all contributed to a radical new alignment of forces in the middle of the eighth century. As a result of them, three separate cultures emerged in the old lands of the Roman Empire—Latin Christendom, Byzantium, and Islam. In the north the British Isles improbably flared up into a vital center of Christian culture while a new order of monks spread papal authority through northern Europe. At the other end of the Roman world the followers of a new prophet, Mohammed, snatched away from the Byzantine Empire the ancient Christian lands of the eastern Mediterranean and North Africa. Finally, new quarrels broke out between the popes and the Byzantine emperors. The popes were left hesitating between the old, sophisticated, half-Oriental civilization of Byzantium and the raw, new powers of the north. In the middle of the eighth century a number of important men—popes, Frankish kings, Byzantine emperors—with various choices open to them elected certain courses of action. Their decisions influenced the religious and political structure of the Western world for the rest of the Middle Ages.

16. Monasteries and Missions: Roman Christianity in the North

Monastic institutions played a major role in early medieval civilization. In the first place, the monks took a leading part in converting the pagan peoples of northern Europe to Christianity; subsequently, they were instrumental in preserving the heritage of classical and early

Christian culture during a new period of pagan invasions. The first forms of monastic life appeared in the lands of the eastern Mediterranean. Very early in the history of the church, enthusiastic Christians began to leave their fellows and go off to lonely places to lead the lives of hermits. Alone, with the absolute minimum of food and clothes, they passed their time in prayer and contemplation. All lived lives of frugality and celibacy. Some endured rigorous fasts and self-inflicted scourgings. Others developed more ingenious forms of asceticism, as did the well-known St. Simon the Stylite, who lived on top of a pillar for many years. When the recognition of Christianity as the state religion moved many Christians to compromise to some extent with the standards of the Roman world, extreme enthusiasts turned more and more to the ascetic life of the hermit.

In the early fourth century, two influential leaders appeared among the many hermits who lived in Egypt: St. Anthony (d. 356) and St. Pachomius (ca. 290–346). Anthony won a great reputation for holiness through his fervent asceticism and attracted followers who settled in the desert to live near him. They still led solitary lives, coming together only occasionally to pray or to listen to Anthony's teaching. Pachomius was the founder of cenobitic monasticism, that is, of ordered community life for monks. He organized thousands of Egyptian Christians in large-scale monastic communities and wrote a Rule for them which strongly emphasized the virtue of obedience. The monks were all required to obey their superiors; the monastic superiors in turn were subject to the local bishop. Pachomius also believed that manual labor should be an essential element of the monastic life. His followers were organized into work groups and encouraged to produce as much as possible. Any surplus beyond their simple needs went to the poor.

About 360 A.D., St. Basil developed the ideas of Pachomius further. He believed that both work and fellowship were essentials of the perfect Christian life, but did not emphasize individual acts of asceticism so much as the Egyptian monks. His monks lived together, ate together, worked together, and worshiped together. By establishing this ideal of a simple, chaste, frugal life devoted to hard work and lived in common with others, St. Basil became the true founder of Christian monasticism in the Eastern church.

Monasticism was carried to the Western church by St. Athanasius, the great opponent of the Arians, during his years of exile in Gaul (ca. 340).* Athanasius was bishop of Alexandria, and so it was the Egyptian ideal of extreme asceticism and bodily mortification that he spread to the western part of the empire. The two principal founders of monasticism in Gaul, St. Martin of Tours (ca. 316–397) and St. John Cassian (ca. 360–432), were also influenced by Egyptian models, especially by the example of Pachomius. Like the Egyptian monks, the followers of Martin and John Cassian left the cities to live in the wilderness. But conditions were different in Gaul. The Egyptian monks were heroes to the Christian population; St. Simon the Stylite does not seem to have lacked for admirers on his pillar. Moreover,

*See p. 47.

the desert places of Egypt were solitary except for occasional crowds of Christians who made excursions from the cities to watch some favorite saint performing his picturesque penances. But the countryside of Gaul was populated by peasants, and by heathen peasants at that. In Gaul, therefore, the monks first began to undertake the conversion of pagans as a normal part of their religious duties.

The form of monastic life that eventually became dominant in the Western church was established in Italy at the beginning of the sixth century by St. Benedict of Nursia (ca. 480–543). Benedict was a contemporary of Boethius and Cassiodorus in the Italian kingdom of Theodoric. He established a monastic community at Monte Cassino between Rome and Naples and there, probably about 520, composed his *Holy Rule* for monks.* In contrast to the Egyptian pattern of monasticism, Benedict's Rule was inspired by the classical ideals of moderation and stability. The Benedictine monk was not required to indulge in heroic fasts or ingenious self-inflicted torments, but he was expected to lead a hard and highly disciplined life in accordance with the ideals of poverty, chastity, and obedience. His meals were sufficient to maintain health but were very simple and frugal. The spirit of moderation implicit in the Rule is conveyed in some of its dietary provisions:

> It is with some hesitation that the amount of daily sustenance for others is fixed by us. Nevertheless, in view of the weakness of the infirm we believe that a half liter of wine a day is enough for each one. Those moreover to whom God gives the ability of bearing abstinence shall know that they will have their own reward. But the prior shall judge if either the needs of the place, or labor or the heat of summer, requires more; considering in all things lest satiety or drunkenness creep in. Indeed we read that wine is not suitable for monks at all. But because, in our day, it is not possible to persuade the monks of this, let us agree at least as to the fact that we should not drink till we are sated, but sparingly.

The monk was required to sink his own individual will and desires in a corporate life of unvarying routine under the close supervision of a superior. Government was entrusted to an abbot, "the father of the monastery." He was elected by the monks but thereafter exercised full patriarchal authority over them. Each abbey was endowed with enough land to support the monastic community. The Benedictine abbey was thus a self-sufficient, autonomous community capable of sustaining its own orderly life however much the surrounding society might disintegrate.

Benedict's Rule required the monk to divide each day into periods of work and periods of prayer. To guard against idleness, the monk was required to perform several hours of manual labor each day, but it is clear that, from the beginning, most of the heavy field work was done by serfs. "Prayer" meant either private meditation and spiritual reading or corporate community worship, which was especially emphasized in the Rule. At regular intervals throughout the day and

*Sources, no. 20

h generatio

night, seven times in each twenty-four hours, the monks met together for a service of psalms and prayers. Benedict regarded this liturgical worship—the *opus dei,* or "work of God"—as the very raison d'être of the community. "Let nothing be preferred to the service of God," he wrote in reference to it. The monks slept in a common dormitory; ate in a common refectory; and worked, studied, and performed the services of the church together. The Benedictine could not leave his monastery without permission; he lived and died within its walls.

During the sixth and seventh centuries, very important developments in the history of monasticism occurred in Ireland and England. One might expect that after their conversion to Christianity, such remote islands would be mere outlying backward provinces of the church. But, in fact, the Celts of Ireland and the Anglo-Saxons of England embraced their new religion with unusual fervor and formed important new syntheses of barbarian and Christian culture. Then, through extensive missionary work, they spread their forms of religious life to many parts of Europe. Thus the churches of Ireland and England came to influence the whole future of medieval Christianity. We need to consider them in some detail.

The familiar story of the conversion of Ireland by St. Patrick (ca. 390–461) is probably substantially true, although it offers great difficulties of chronology. According to the traditional account, Patrick was born among the Christian population of western Britain toward the end of the fourth century. As a young man, he was captured by Irish raiders and carried off to Ireland, where he lived as a slave for several years. Then he escaped to Gaul and spent nearly twenty years studying in various monastic centers that had been influenced by the ascetic tradition of Egyptian monasticism. Finally, in about 432, he returned to Ireland as a bishop and spent the next thirty years preaching and teaching there. It is clear that some Christians already lived in Ireland before Patrick's mission, but the mass conversion of the whole people was brought about through his efforts.

The monogram of Christ from the *Book of Kells,* one of the finest of Irish illuminated manuscripts. In the years around 800, Irish monks combined geometric and animal forms, Christian themes and Oriental motifs, to produce masterpieces of ornamental design in a unique style. *The Board of Trinity College, Dublin*

Ireland had never been a part of the Roman Empire, and shortly after its conversion, the barbarian invasions impeded communications with the continent of Europe. Irish Christianity therefore developed apart from the Western church as a whole and acquired many distinctive characteristics of its own. The most important one was a different pattern of ecclesiastical organization. The Western church was divided into administrative districts corresponding to the old Roman *civitates,* with a bishop presiding over each one. No such administrative units existed in Ireland, and there were no cities to provide centers for them. In these circumstances, monasteries rather than bishoprics became the basic units of ecclesiastical organization. Each clan had its own tribal monastery, normally founded by the chief of the clan and ruled by an *abbot,* who was a member of the chief's immediate family. Bishops continued to be ordained, but they performed purely sacramental functions; the abbots were the real governors of the church, and the Irish could conveive of no other form of church authority. When they wanted to refer to the pope, they called him the Abbot of Rome. Other differences between Irish and Roman Christianity were relatively minor. They included a different form of tonsure, a different rite for the administration of baptism, and a different way of calculating the date of Easter.

The Irish monasteries are not to be thought of as great, imposing stone buildings like the abbeys of the Middle Ages. An Irish monastery was usually just a cluster of thatched huts surrounding a small church and guarded by a stockade. The monks who inhabited these monasteries followed a fiercely ascetic way of life.* They spent most of the day in silence, endured frequent fasts, and prayed for hours immersed in icy water or with the arms outstretched in the form of a crucifix. They were attempting to live a life of perfection and were deeply concerned with searching out any flaws in their daily behavior. This led to a constant scrutiny of the individual conscience and to frequent confessions of sins to a superior. The practice of making such confessions eventually spread to the whole Western church. More surprisingly, the monks also dedicated themselves enthusiastically to learning. As a modern author noted (remembering the conquests of the ancient Celts), "That fierce and restless quality which had made the pagan Irish the terror of Western Europe, seems to have emptied itself into the love of learning and the love of God." A man could become a perfect Christian only by meditating on the Bible and the writings of the great Fathers, but the Scriptures and the Fathers came to Ireland in Greek and Latin texts. These were completely foreign languages for the Irish. They studied them from classical grammars and learned them in a pure classical form. At this time, all over Europe, spoken Latin was being corrupted into a variety of Romance dialects. Through a strange combination of circumstances, pure classical Latin survived best in a remote island which had never been a part of the old empire, and from Ireland it was eventually carried back to the continent of Europe.

The Irish developed not only new forms of religious life but also a whole new style of Christian art, exemplified most finely in their illuminated manuscripts. The primitive art of all the northern peoples tended to take the form of geometrical, abstract patterns in contrast to the humanistic, naturalistic art forms of the Greek and Roman world. In Irish art, the typical pattern was one of interlacing lines. A whole page of a manuscript would be given to a capital letter decorated with intricately interwoven and brilliantly colored spirals and circles. The work was enlivened by Oriental elements derived from the stories of Scripture and from imported manuscripts. Vine leaves and bunches of grapes were represented. Human faces and symbolic animals peered out from the abstract tracery. Often the animals were conventionalized versions of Eastern creatures—lions, birds of paradise, or fantastic reptiles. In contrast to the fantasy of the decoration, the actual lettering of Irish manuscripts was beautifully clear and legible. The distinctive Irish script was carried to England and then, with some modifications, to Gaul.

Irish influence began to spread to other lands in the sixth century

*Sources, no. 19

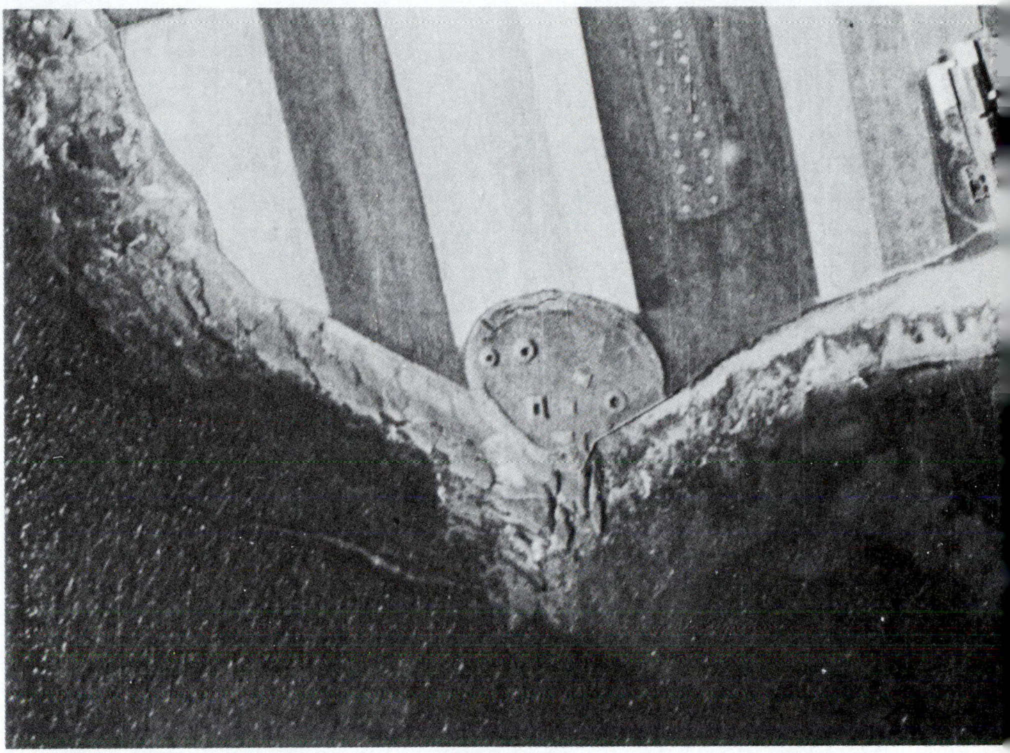

Irish monastery on Illauntannig Island, Co. Kerry. The circular wall encloses a small church and a group of huts. The surviving ruins are of stone buildings from the seventh and eighth centuries. (It was unusual for stone to be used so early.) *Courtesy Department of Defence, Ireland*

because of another characteristic of Irish monasticism, an inclination to adopt a life of voluntary exile as a particularly demanding form of ascetism. In 563 St. Columba (521–597), "desirous to be a wanderer for Christ," established a monastery on the island of Iona off the coast of Scotland and from there traveled all through Scotland converting the Pictish inhabitants. St. Columbanus (ca. 530–615) traveled much farther. About 590 he made his way, with twelve companions, to the court of the Merovingian king Guntram of Burgundy and subsequently established several monasteries in that region. After Guntram's death, Columbanus quarreled with Queen Brunhilde and wandered on into Italy where he founded the abbey of Bobbio. Many of the abbeys that Columbanus and his followers founded survived as major centers of learning throughout the Middle Ages, but their most important immediate role was to serve as centers of evangelization for the surrounding countryside. Even after the cities had become predominantly Christian in the Late Roman Empire, the peasants of the rural districts remained obstinately pagan. The Irish were countrymen themselves, and they knew how to preach to peasants. Their work led to the mass conversion of the rural population of Western Europe.

Moreover the Irish monks penetrated to areas of Germany that had never been part of the Roman Empire and that had never received Christianity. Their missionary work in those regions began a process that would be of immense importance for the future of medieval civ-

A page from the *Gospels of St. Gall.* In this Irish work of the eighth century there is no attempt at realistic portrayal. The artist is interested rather in creating an intricate ornamental pattern. *Stiftsbibliothek, St. Gallen, Switzerland*

ilization, the assimilation of Germany into the common religious culture of western Europe.

In the process of conversion many of the more harmless practices of the old nature religions were assimilated into the life of the medieval church. Old feasts continued to be celebrated under new names, and sacred places continued to be venerated. (Pope Gregory the Great explicitly encouraged such practices.) A grove of trees consecrated to Wodan would be rededicated to a Christian saint and emerge as "Holywood." The home of the local water sprite became St. Mary's Well or St. Bridget's Spring. The persistence of pagan practices, especially at the seasons of New Year, Midsummer, and Halloween, remained an important element in the subculture of the common people throughout the Middle Ages. Some of these practices, in fact, have never died out in the Western world.

The conversion of the Anglo-Saxons to Christianity was achieved partly by Irish monks and partly by the mission sent out from Rome by Pope Gregory the Great. The leader of the Roman mission was a monk named Augustine (not to be confused with the great bishop of Hippo). Augustine set out in 596 but hesitated for a time in Gaul, apparently discouraged by the stories he heard about the savagery of the English. Urged on by Gregory, he finally reached England in 597.*

Augustine found in England a primitive Germanic society almost untouched by the traditions of Roman civilization. The people worshipped the old Teutonic gods and lived in petty states under the rule of kings and nobles who were essentially warrior leaders. Customary law was administered through the old rites of compurgation and ordeal in popular assemblies of freemen. At the time of Augustine's mission, seven important kingdoms were beginning to emerge from the chaos of little states established during the Anglo-Saxon invasions. These were Kent, Wessex, Sussex, Essex, East Anglia, Mercia, and Northumbria. The three most powerful were Northumbria, Mercia, and Wessex, and each of these in turn tried to dominate all England. Eventually, but not until the tenth century, it was the royal house of Wessex that provided a national monarchy for the whole country.

The kingdom of Kent, where Augustine landed, was ruled by a king, Ethelbert, who had married a Christian Frankish princess, a niece of Brunhilde. He gave Augustine permission to preach and soon became converted along with all his people. Augustine built a monastery at Canterbury to serve as headquarters for the evangelization of England and was named archbishop of Canterbury by the pope. He also sought to obtain the cooperation of the Celtic bishops of western Britain and to assert his authority over them, but here he met with complete failure. The Welsh prelates who met with Augustine had no great enthusiasm for converting the bitter enemies of their people. Why should they want to save the Anglo-Saxons from the fires of hell? Augustine was more successful among the English. In 604 the East Saxons became converted and were given a bishop with his seat at London. When Augustine died in 605, Kent and Essex seemed securely Christian. However, such rapid conversions as those achieved by Augustine

*Sources, no. 18

were unlikely to be very deep. After King Ethelbert died in 616, the rulers of Kent and Essex both reverted for a time to paganism, and it seemed that the Roman mission might end in ignominious failure. Fortunately, Ethelbert's successor changed his mind and decided after all to accept Christianity, so the continuity of the church in Kent was preserved.

The next major developments took place in the north of England. King Edwin of Northumbria married a daughter of Ethelbert, and one of the Roman monks, Paulinus, traveled north with the new queen. In 625 King Edwin accepted baptism, and for the next eight years Paulinus was highly successful in converting the inhabitants of the province of Deira. Then his work was cut short by the temporary conquest of Northumbria by the pagan Penda of Mercia, which forced Paulinus and his fellow missionaries to flee to the south. Penda was soon driven out of Northumbria by the head of a rival branch of the royal house, Oswald. This prince had spent several years in exile near Iona and there had been converted to Christianity by the Irish monks. Once he was secure on the Northumbrian throne, Oswald sent for a Celtic monk, Aidan, to preach to his people. Aidan founded as his seat a monastery on the island of Lindisfarne near Oswald's capital of Bamborough. Working under the protection of Oswald, Aidan continued the work of converting the Northumbrians to Christianity.

Oswald's successor, Oswy, also married a princess who had been brought up according to the Roman Christian tradition in Kent. She took her own priests to Northumbria, and hence, during the middle decades of the seventh century, Irish and Roman missionaries were working there side by side. Inevitably disputes arose because of their differing religious practices. No great theological issues were involved, but the differences of ritual and discipline seemed highly important to the people concerned. The Romans insisted that the Irish ought to conform to the common practices of the Western church; the Irish would not give up the traditions handed down by their own saints. In 664 King Oswy called a meeting at Whitby of the great men of Northumbria, both laymen and clerics, to decide between the two systems. The two groups argued learnedly for days. Finally, the Roman spokesman made a remark that decided the issue for Oswy; he said that the pope was the successor of St. Peter, who had been appointed by Christ to rule his church. The king asked the Celtic clergy if this were true; when they conceded that it was, he gave the decision to the Roman party.* At this point, many of the Irish monks left Northumbria, but others accepted the Roman usages and continued to play a major part in converting the peoples of northern and central England. From this time on, the English church was united in doctrine and practice and closely allied to Rome.

Up to the time of the Synod of Whitby, the English church was essentially a missionary organization. Most bishops had no definitely marked dioceses and wandered about wherever the need for evangelization called them. Then in 669 Pope Vitalian sent to England a new archbishop of Canterbury, Theodore of Tarsus, who set up new,

*Sources, no. 21

clearly defined dioceses and persuaded the kings to grant lands as permanent endowments for cathedral churches. In 673 he was able to summon the first national synod of the English church, which met at Hertford.

Theodore of Tarsus came from the eastern Roman Empire, where there was still a living tradition of classical studies. An erudite man himself, he brought with him two great scholars, the abbot Hadrian, an African, and Benedict Biscop, an Anglo-Saxon noble turned monk, who had been studying in Rome. This strangely assorted trio stimulated a great growth of learning in Anglo-Saxon England. Hadrian established a school at Canterbury, and Benedict Biscop founded two famous Benedictine monasteries in the north of England at Wearmouth and Jarrow. He also journeyed several times to Rome and on each occasion returned with a supply of manuscripts to bolster the resources of his monastic libraries. Northumbrian Christianity was influenced by both the Irish and Roman traditions of learning, and under Biscop's leadership, the monasteries of the region developed into centers of Christian culture superior to any others west of Italy. The continuing Irish influence was especially evident in the beautiful illuminated manuscripts produced by the monks, such as the famous Lindisfarne Gospels.

Biscop's pupil, the Venerable Bede, was probably the greatest scholar produced by western Europe between the decline of Roman civilization and the age of Charlemagne. He became the complete master of all the learning available to him and in his writings interpreted it and made it available to his contemporaries. Perhaps Bede's most valuable work is his *Ecclesiastical History of the English People.* Bede had a true historical sense, a realization of the distinction between knowledge and hearsay, fact and legend. Using some older sources now lost for the period before his own day and his own knowledge for the events of his lifetime, he gives us our chief fund of information about early Anglo-Saxon England. Bede wrote his scholarly works in Latin, of course, but the development of literacy in England stimulated a considerable growth of vernacular literature too. The great Anglo-Saxon epic *Beowulf* was written in its present form around 700. The first collection of Teutonic law to be set down in writing was made in the kingdom of Kent shortly after its conversion to Christianity. Two writers of religious verse, Caedmon and Cynewulf, produced a large number of devotional poems in Anglo-Saxon.

Women played an important role in English monastic life. There were many houses of nuns and some "double monasteries" in which a community of monks and a community of nuns lived together under a single head—usually an abbess. Bede tells us that one such house, ruled by the abbess Hilda, was renowned for learning and that five future bishops were educated there.

By the early eighth century, Christian culture in England had become so well established that the English could take the place of the Irish as the most effective missionaries to the still heathen parts of Europe. The greatest leader in this work was the Benedictine monk

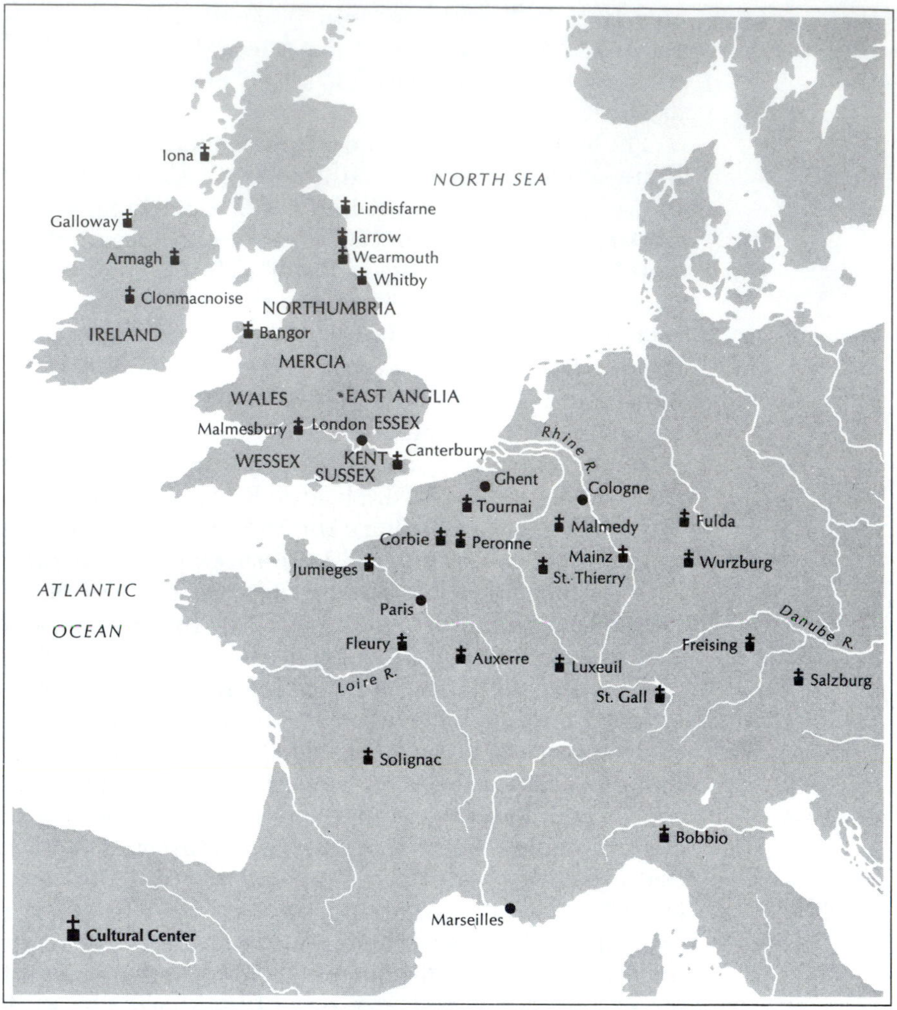

Anglo-Saxon England and Irish and Anglo-Saxon Cultural Centers

This map shows graphically the widespread influence exercised by the small bands of Irish and Anglo-Saxon monks who migrated to the Continent and carried with them the skills of literacy and scholarship—the writing of Latin, the preservation and illumination of manuscripts—as well as a strong and vibrant Christian faith. The monasteries they founded became centers of learning and religious life throughout the Middle Ages.

St. Boniface (ca. 680–755), sometimes called "the Apostle of the Germans." The great difference between his work and that of the individualistic Irish saints lay in the fact that Boniface was not only a zealous missionary but also a great ecclesiastical organizer who worked in close cooperation with the papacy. He first visited Rome in 718 and was sent to work in Frisia. In 722 Pope Gregory II recalled Boniface to Rome, consecrated him as bishop, and sent him to preach in the German lands beyond the Rhine. Boniface labored there for the next twenty years, founding numerous Benedictine monasteries. He maintained close contacts with the Anglo-Saxon church as well as with

Rome and was able to bring over to Germany a steady supply of trained English monks to help staff his new foundations. (Also many Irish monasteries in Europe adopted the Benedictine Rule through the influence of the English missionaries.) Boniface also brought from England a learned nun, St. Leoba, who established a convent at Bischofsheim; from there other religious houses for women were founded in central Germany.* In 742 Boniface was named archbishop by the pope, and subsequently he organized the lands he had converted into eight permanent episcopal dioceses stretching from Salzburg in modern Austria to Erfurt in Germany.*

As a papal legate, Boniface also played a major role in reforming the church of Gaul. This work could begin only after the death of Charles Martel in 741. Charles had given Boniface letters of protection that helped him in his missionary work, but the Frankish leader had no intention of tolerating any papal interference with his own Frankish church—and Charles' government of the church was particularly scandalous. He habitually used church revenues to support his soldiers and awarded bishoprics to highly unsuitable friends and supporters. (Boniface wrote of such prelates, "Those who can boast that they are not adulterers or fornicators are drunkards and soldiers who do not shrink from shedding Christian blood.") Charles Martel's son Pepin (741–768) was more amenable to Boniface's influence and, between 741 and 747, the legate held a series of councils to enact reform legislation. In the hope of establishing discipline, archbishops were directed to hold provincial councils, and bishops diocesan councils every year. In addition, the monasteries of the Frankish state were ordered to adopt the Benedictine Rule.

The Irish and English monks made Europe a Christian continent by converting the humble, primitive, peasant folk of the countryside to their faith. The work of St. Boniface in particular influenced the development of the Western church in two ways. His missionary labors brought a great part of the Germanic peoples into the framework of a Christian Europe for the first time. And his activities in Gaul established closer ties than had ever existed before between the Frankish church and the papacy.

17. Islam: A New Civilization

While papal influence was growing in the north of Europe, the Christian provinces of the Mediterranean world fell under devastating attack from a new enemy. The onslaught came from an unlikely region, the peninsula of Arabia, which before the seventh century had exercised no significant influence on the history of the Roman world. Arabia was a sort of no-man's land between the Byzantine and Persian empires. Both of the great powers tried to exercise some degree of suzerainty there, but without much success. The arid interior, inhabited by fierce nomadic tribesmen, was in a constant state of anarchy.

*Sources, no. 21

The Expansion of
Islam to 750

A religious movement rivaling in strength and influence that of Christianity, Islam in the space of a single century united the diverse peoples of the Middle East and North Africa to form a new civilization.

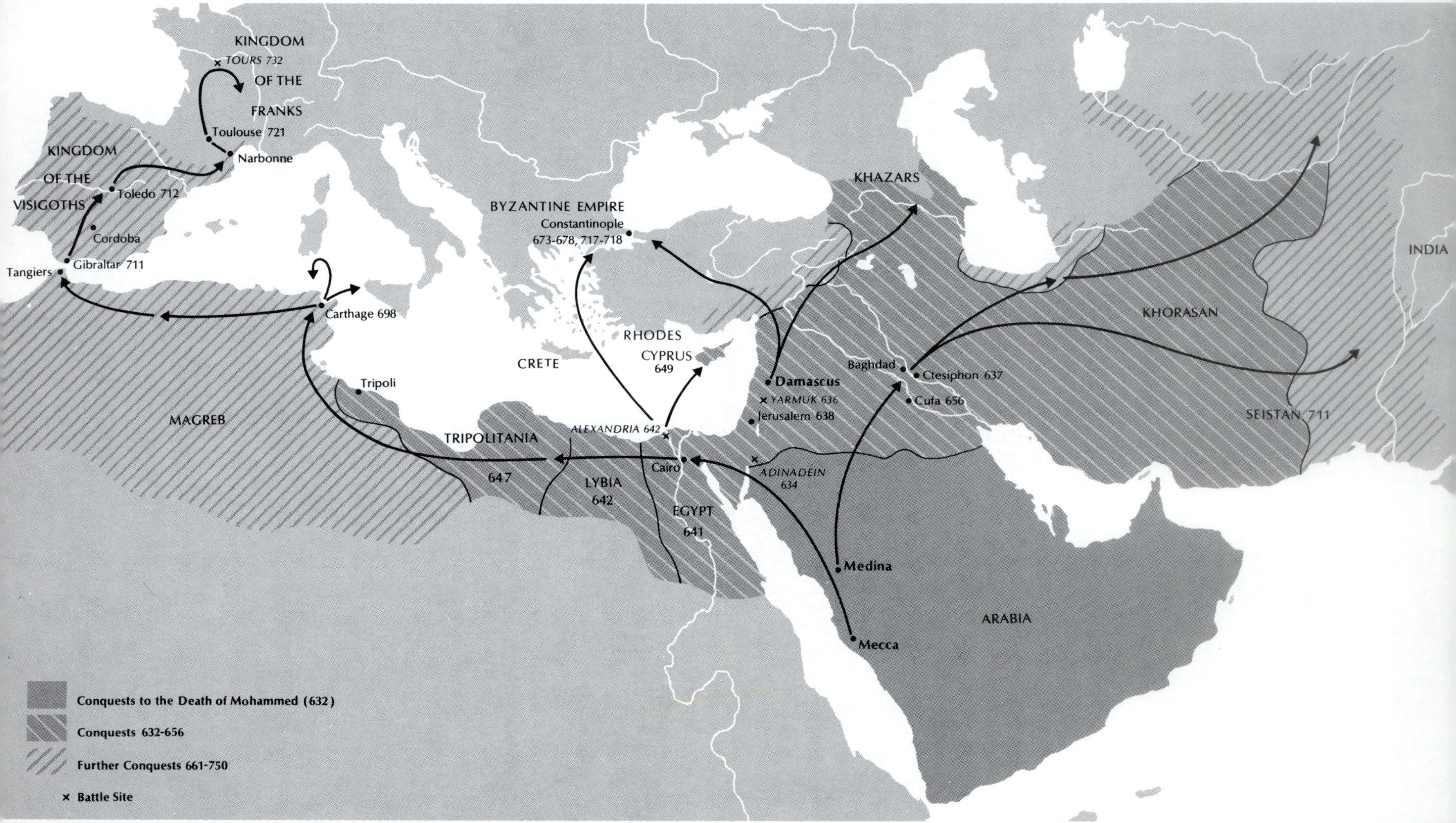

In the more fertile fringe districts, there were trading cities whose merchants acted as middlemen in the traffic between Syria and the Far East. Some Christian and Jewish communities existed, but the dominant religion was primitive, pagan idol worship.

The prophet Mohammed (ca. 570–632), who transformed the whole situation, was born in the city of Mecca. In middle life he experienced a series of revelations that he accepted as direct communications from God and that were subsequently set down in the holy book of the Muslim faith, the Koran. His teachings formed the last of the three great world religions that have grown out of Old Testament monotheism. Mohammed's God, Allah, was an omniscient being of infinite power and inexorable will. For Mohammed there was no Trinity and no Incarnation to complicate the doctrines of God's oneness and transcendence. God had revealed himself to man through a series of prophets—Abraham, Moses, Jesus Christ (whose teachings the Christians misunderstood), and last of all through his prophet Mohammed—who could then present divine revelation in its most complete and perfect form. The uncompromising monotheism of Mohammed's doctrine obviously reflects the influence of Judaism, but Mohammed borrowed from the Christians an intense preoccupation with personal immortality in a world to come. The duty of man was to carry out the will of God. Those who failed to do so went to hell, but the true servants of Allah entered an eternal heaven, whose sensuous delights Mohammed portrayed in winning detail.*

Mohammed

Mohammed's ethical teaching was simple and severe. The believers in Allah formed a united fellowship that transcended divisions of tribe and class. They were all to treat each other with justice and mercy. As in Christianity, the duty of charity to the poor and weak was strongly emphasized. There were detailed regulations concerning ceremonial purity and dietary practices, borrowed in part from Judaism, though the Muslims were forbidden wine as well as pork. Muslims were required to observe a routine of prayer five times a day. They were also required to fight for the faith, and death in a Holy War (*jihad*) was regarded as a sure road to heaven.

Mohammed's attack on the local idol worship aroused hostility among the people of Mecca, and in 622 they drove him out of the city. The date of this flight (the Hegira) is the first year in Muslim chronology. Mohammed found refuge in the rival city of Medina, soon converted the people there, and became their leader. In early Mohammedanism there was no distinction between civil and religious authority; to submit to Allah meant to submit to his prophet in all things. And Mohammed soon proved himself a brilliant political organizer and military tactician. From Medina he launched a series of attacks on the caravans of Mecca until, by 630, he was strong enough to conquer the city that had rejected him and to win over its people to his new faith. Mohammed's religion was simple enough to be readily grasped by the primitive tribesmen of the interior, but it was far more sophisticated and satisfying than their own local cults; and Mohammed's military prowess impressed them as perhaps nothing else

*Sources, no. 23

could have done. The last two years of the prophet's life saw all the warring tribes of central Arabia accept a common religion and submit to a single political center.

Mohammed left no ordered scheme of succession, but his followers chose a capable leader, Abu Bakr (632–634) as *caliph* (that is, "deputy" or "successor"). Abu Bakr was succeeded by the caliph Umar (634–644). His successor in turn was Uthman (644–655), the first caliph from the great Umayyad family. The Umayyads subsequently established a dynasty that ruled the Muslim word until 750. The Umayyads were challenged by a son-in-law of Mohammed, Ali, but he was assassinated in 661 and his son Husain in 681. The power of the Umayyads was preserved, though the followers of Ali formed dissident religious groups in the Muslim world that still persist in the Shi'ite sects of modern Islam.

Mohammed himself launched the first attacks against the Byzantine borders in 629. The major expansion of Muslim power from Arabia began immediately after the prophet's death. Under the caliph Umar, Syria was invaded in 634. The Byzantine emperor Heraclius, who only a few years earlier had decisively routed the Persians, realized that this was no mere border raid of the traditional type and mobilized a large army for the defense of the threatened province. But the Byzantines were crushingly defeated in the battle of the Yarmuk (636), and in the following two years, the fortified cities surrendered one by one. Jerusalem fell in 638. By 640 the Arabs had completed their conquest of Syria. Immediately afterward, they invaded Egypt, which was overrun by 641. Meanwhile, other Arab forces had struck eastward. In 637 they decisively defeated the armies of Persia, and by 650 they had conquered the whole Persian Empire. Then they pressed still farther eastward across the Indus River and on into Central Asia. In the Mediterranean world, Muslim conquests continued throughout the second half of the seventh century as the Arabs pushed on from Egypt westward through the provinces of North Africa. At first they met strong resistance from the Berber tribesmen of the region, but by the end of the century, the Berbers were themselves for the most part converted and provided new reserves of manpower for still further campaigns. In 674 a powerful Arab fleet besieged Constantinople itself and was narrowly defeated. By 700 the Umayyad caliphs, who had made Damascus their capital city, ruled a vast empire stretching from the borders of China to the Atlantic Ocean.

Historians have found it difficult to explain such a dramatic expansion. No doubt the diminution of internal warfare in Arabia produced a surplus of military energy that could be used for foreign conquests. Certainly the Arab leaders were brilliant generals, and their soldiers were often inspired by a fervent faith in their new religion. But, beyond all this, the Arabs were lucky because their attacks came at a time when both the Byzantine and Persian states had been gravely weakened by their long war against one another. After the defeat of the Persians, civil wars broke out in their empire. Byzantium had ended the war victoriously, but the provinces of Syria and Egypt showed no enthusiasm for the restoration of imperial rule. When Heraclius won them back from the Persians, he had to impose heavy, unpopular taxes to pay for his campaigns. Moreover, many of his subjects were disaffected in religion. The Jews of Syria and the Monophysite Christians of Egypt had suffered persecution from the imperial government and saw no reason to defend it with enthusiasm. The Islamic rulers, on the other hand, did not persecute other religions or convert their subject peoples at the point of the sword but merely compelled them to pay tribute.

During the first quarter of the eighth century, the Arabs launched new assaults at both ends of the Mediterranean world. In 711 they invaded Spain from North Africa and again found a land divided by dynastic dissensions and civil wars. The Visigothic kingdom collapsed after a short campaign, and the invading army of Arabs and Berbers established a Muslim state in Spain with its capital at Cordoba. The Christians continued to hold only the kingdom of Asturias, a mountainous region of the northwest. In 720 the Muslims crossed the Pyrenees, captured the fortified city of Narbonne, and occupied much of Provence. In 732 they struck northward from there but were defeated near Tours by Charles Martel. Some Western historians have been inclined to minimize the significance of the battle of Tours, pointing out that the Arab lines of communication had become too extended for them to have seriously attempted the conquest of Europe. Other historians, noting that in spite of all logistical problems the tide of Islamic conquest had carried Arab arms from the Indus to the Loire, think it was just as well that such a formidable warrior as Charles Martel commanded the Frankish armies in 732. In a series of subsequent campaigns, the Frankish leader drove the Muslims from most of their conquests in southern Gaul.

Meanwhile, in 718 the Byzantine emperor Leo III had won a victory over the forces of Islam that is generally regarded as one of the decisive battles of the world. The last emperor of the Heraclian dynasty, Justinian II, was a cruel and highly unpopular tyrant. He was deposed and executed in 711, but no capable successor emerged until Leo, a military commander of the Anatolian province, seized the throne in 717. He came just in time to save the city. In the year of Leo's accession, the caliph Suleiman launched an attack on Constantinople that was intended to extinguish the Christian empire once and for all. An army of eighty thousand warriors besieged the city by land, while a strong naval force attacked from the sea. Leo beat off the attacks launched in the summer of 717, and the besieging armies, inadequately housed in camps around the city, suffered severely in the unusually cold winter that followed. In the spring of 718, Greek fireships destroyed the Muslim fleet. In the summer, Suleiman gave up his siege and retreated with heavy losses. Leo subsequently reconquered the Byzantine provinces in Asia Minor that Suleiman had occupied. His work reestablished Byzantium as a powerful state that would survive, unconquered, for another five hundred years.

The victories of Leo III and Charles Martel ensured that the forces of Islam would not overrun the whole Christian world in their first great wave of expansion. Circumstances that developed within the Islamic world also tended to check further advances after the early eighth century. During the middle years of the century, a series of rebellions against the Umayyad house broke out, partly inspired by the Shi'ite sects; and in 750 a new dynasty, the Abbasids, seized the caliphate and transferred the capital of the Arab empire from Damascus to Bagdad. The Abbasids were not able to maintain effective control over the whole vast complex of conquered territories. A branch of the Umayyad house retained power in Spain, and subsequently new dynasties of emirs owing only nominal allegiance to the Abbasid caliphs appeared in North Africa and Egypt.

In spite of this political decentralization, the Islamic world retained a unity of religion and culture. Arabic became an international language and the vehicle of a great literature. At first the Arab conquerors lived as a military aristocracy separated from the subject peoples and living on their tribute, but gradually a process of amalgamation took place. Although Christian communities survived in the Arab world (and have survived down to the present day), the great majority of the conquered peoples came to accept the Islamic religion. At the same time, the originally barbarous Arabs assimilated the higher culture of the lands they occupied. The caliphs adopted Byzantine or Persian systems of administration. The whole body of Greek philosophic and scientific writing was translated into Arabic, mostly by Nestorian Christians. Muslim philosophers and theologians began to wrestle with the problems of reconciling rational philosophy and divine revelation. New forms of art and architecture grew up, based more on Oriental than on Hellenistic models. Great schools of medicine were founded, inspired by the writings of Hippocrates and Galen (though the physicians of the Islamic world went far beyond their Greek mentors in developing medical science). From China and India the Arabs learned sophisticated mathematical techniques, particularly the Indian decimal system and the use of the zero. They themselves developed the sense of algebra. All this Arabic learning was eventually, at a much later date, transmitted to the Western world and profoundly influenced the development of medieval thought.* In the centuries immediately after the Islamic invasions, however, Western scholars were hard put to preserve the bare rudiments of their own classical and Christian culture in isolated monastic centers, and they lacked the intellectual vitality to learn from a civilization that seemed to them alien and heretical.

The material prosperity of the Islamic world also stood at a very high level. The Mediterranean provinces that the Muslims had conquered were the richest ones of the old Roman Empire, and their wealth was increased by the vigorous activity of Arab traders. Great cities were built with magnificent mosques, splended palaces, libraries, schools, hospitals—all at a time when, in northern Europe, a "city" was usually only a cluster of wood huts built around some sheltering fortress. Up until the twelfth century, medieval Europe must

*See pp. 418–420.

be seen as a very backward and underdeveloped region compared with the world of Islam.

18. *Byzantine Iconoclasm: The Frankish-Papal Alliance*

The Islamic invasions destroyed any possibility of a common religion continuing to dominate all the lands of the old Roman Empire. At the beginning of the eighth century, the future grouping and organization of the Christian lands that remained was highly unpredictable. Conversion of large areas of northern Europe through missionary work directed from Rome created the possibility of a fusion between Latin civilization (which now found its principal focus in the papacy) and the culture of the Teutons and Celts. The more obvious line of development, given the resurgence of Byzantine power, was the emergence of a truncated Greek empire based on Constantinople that would have included Asia Minor, the Balkan countries, and Italy. Byzantine influences dominated the cultural and religious life of Italy in the eighth century. If Byzantium had also been able to hold Italy as a province of the eastern empire, the distinctive Western civilization of the Middle Ages could never have grown into existence. But, in the middle years of the eighth century, the Roman pontiffs decided to seek an alliance with the barbarian forces of northern Europe. This was a decisive event in "the emergence of Europe."

Two factors influenced the papal decision—the inability of the emperors to defend Rome against renewed Lombard attacks and, perhaps still more important, the outbreak of further embittered theological disputes between Rome and Constantinople. The middle years of the seventh century saw a dreary epilogue to the Monophysite controversy. The Council of Chalcedon had declared that Christ possessed two natures, human and divine. The Monophysites of Egypt preferred to believe that there was only one (divine) nature in Christ. In an attempt to conciliate the Egyptian church, the patriarch of Constantinople, Sergius, devised yet another ingenious theological formula, which was promulgated as official doctrine by the emperor. It might be held, Sergius suggested, that the natures of Christ were activiated by a single will, and this would safeguard the unity that the Monophysites insisted on. (This doctrine is called Monothelitism from the Greek words for "one will.") The contemporary pope, Honorius (625–638), was evidently incapable of understanding the issues involved in the controversy and acquiesced in the new doctrine, but a later pope, Martin I (649–655), vigorously denounced it as a radical departure from the orthodoxy of Chalcedon. The emperor of the time, Constans II (641–668), who had his hands full trying to cope with the Muslim invasions, was not prepared to accept any insubordination from Rome. A force of Byzantine troops seized Pope Martin in the Lateran basilica and carried him off to Constantinople. There he was condemned as a traitor by the Byzantine senate and shortly

A view of the interior of the sanctuary, the mosque at Cordoba, looking east. Begun by the Muslims in 786, the mosque was converted into a church after the Christian reconquest in 1236. The shape of the arches and the treatment of space show the combination of North African and Spanish influences that became the distinctive Moorish style. *GEKS*

afterward died in exile. However, the Monothelite doctrine ceased to serve any useful purpose from the emperor's point of view once it became clear that there was no hope of recovering Egypt from the Muslims. It was condemned as heretical by a council held at Constantinople in 681, but this did not bring any enduring harmony between the Roman and Greek churches. In 692 the pope refused to approve the decrees of another Byzantine synod, and at the beginning of the eighth century, the two churches were still in a state of simmering hostility.

The emperor Leo III, who saved Constantinople from the Muslims, brought about the next crisis. In Leo's view there were two grave dangers to the welfare of the state—one religious and the other social and economic. From very early times, the Christian church had made extensive use of images, paintings, mosaics, and sculptures of Christ and the saints. They were of obvious value for the religious education of the illiterate and supplied concrete inspiration to worship. But there was a strong inclination to worship the images instead of the saints they represented, especially in the regions where conversion from paganism had been recent. This had long been deplored by many earnest men, and in the Asiatic provinces especially there was a strong movement against images. Leo, who was extremely devout, came from a district where this feeling ran strong.

The second problem that troubled Leo was the increasing transfer of land out of lay control into the hands of the church. The monasteries especially, through accumulated endowments, had acquired vast estates. Moreover, they were exempt from taxation and had very extensive rights of jurisdiction. Thus large amounts of land were removed from the tax rolls with serious effects on the hard-pressed imperial treasury. As the monks were in general firm supporters of images, a policy of *iconoclasm*—an attack on the use of images in worship—would serve the purposes of both religious and land reform. Although it seems certain that the religious issue was the chief consideration in Leo's mind in attacking the images, he undoubtedly welcomed the double effect of his policy.

The first iconoclastic decree was issued in 726, and it led to revolts in Greece and Italy which were suppressed only with extreme difficulty. Leo's opponents thought that to deny the possibility of representing Christ by a material image was to cast doubt on the possibility of Christ being incarnated in a material body. This of course had been the whole point of the great theological controversies that had divided the church before the Council of Chalcedon. To its opponents, iconoclasm seemed a reversion to the old Oriental way of thinking which saw material creation as intrinsically evil, a doctrine that St. Augustine had fought. The extreme passions aroused by the iconoclastic controversy are intelligible only when we understand the doctrinal issues involved in it. If the crudest "image-worshippers" were mere fetishists, the most extreme iconoclasts were almost Manicheans. The dispute continued in Byzantium for more than a century. The empress Irene abandoned the iconoclastic decrees in 787, but Leo V restored them in 815. Not until 843, when another empress, Theodora, finally restored the images, did the iconoclastic controversy come to an end. Here again, in the Byzantine tradition of caesaropapism, a complex theological dispute was finally settled by imperial authority.

The first iconoclastic decree of 726 produced a decisive breach between Rome and Constantinople. Up until this time, in spite of all the doctrinal disputes, the popes had always regarded themselves as loyal subjects of the empire and had treated the emperor with the deference and respect due to their sovereign lord. Pope Gregory II (715–731), however, not only refused to obey Leo's iconoclastic decree but addressed the emperor in harsh, upbraiding, defiant language. The whole Western world was loyal to St. Peter's successor, wrote Gregory, and if the emperor tried to tear down the image of St. Peter at Rome, the pope would turn to the Western barbarians for help.* Leo thereupon commanded the exarch of Ravenna to march on Rome and take Gregory prisoner, but the exarch's army was attacked and defeated by a force of Lombards, while the troops in Rome remained loyal to the pope. The emperor then confiscated all the vast papal estates in the Byzantine territories of South Italy. He also transferred the episcopal dioceses of South Italy and of Illyricum from the jurisdiction of the pope to that of the patriarch of Constantinople.

The final factor that influenced the course of events in Italy was a great resurgence of Lombard power under two warlike kings, Liutprand (712–744) and Aistulf (749–757). We saw in Chapter III that the Lombards had established a kingdom in northern Italy and two independent duchies further south. As time went on, they abandoned Arianism, became Catholics, and on the whole lived amicably with the papacy. But in the early eighth century, Liutprand began to expand his power and showed his intention of making himself true king of Italy. He first absorbed the independent Lombard duchies and then commenced attacks on the remnants of Byzantine power. The Lombards would not have injured the See of St. Peter; in fact, they would undoubtedly have made it the chief ecclesiastical seat of their realm. But the pope had no desire to give up his authority over Rome and its environs and become simply the chief ecclesiastic of the Lombard kingdom. Hence he looked about for a military power that could protect him from the Lombards. In 739 Pope Gregory III (731–741) appealed to Charles Martel for help. As Charles believed he might some day need Lombard aid against the Muslims, he refused to intervene. Nevertheless, the Frankish state was the only power strong enough to aid the papacy, and the pope was anxious for its good will. The despatch of St. Boniface as papal legate to Gaul in 741 had political as well as religious significance.

The alliance between the papacy and the Franks was brought about a few years later by the mutual necessities of the popes and Charles Martel's successor, Pepin. Pepin faced a serious political problem. When King Theuderich IV (720–737) died, Charles Martel had not bothered to find a new king but had simply continued to rule as mayor of the palace and duke of the Franks. The illegality of this situation troubled Pepin, and he found a distant relative of the late king whom he placed on the throne as King Childeric. It seemed essentially silly, however, to have one man reigning while another ruled, and Pepin was inclined to declare himself king of the Franks. The difficulty was that the Merovingian house was by tradition divinely appointed to rule; moreover, the leading men of the Franks, prelates and warriors alike, had sworn oaths of fidelity to Childeric. Pepin therefore felt that the transfer of the crown to a new line could be secure only if that line obtained divine sanction. In 751 two envoys of Pepin made their way to Rome to ask Pope Zachary (741–752) whether it was proper for one man to be called king while another actually ruled. Here was the pope's opportunity to gain a powerful friend, and he at once replied that "it was better for the man who had power to be called king rather than one who remained without royal power." Per-

*Sources, no. 24

haps in sending this answer the pope was not unmindful of his own condition. He too wielded an independent authority in Rome and the surrounding countryside without any legitimate title to do so. On receiving the pope's reply, Pepin deposed King Childeric, and then St. Boniface solemnly anointed him with holy oil and crowned him as king. The new royal Frankish house had obtained its divine sanction.

The pope soon had need of his new ally. In 752 Aistulf captured the city of Ravenna and began to threaten Rome. Pope Stephen II (752–757) urged Pepin to intervene, and the king sent an escort of Frankish warriors to conduct the pope over the Alps for a personal conference. At the same time, an embassy from Byzantium arrived commanding the pope to open new negotiations with the Lombards. Stephen complied to the extent of putting the imperial demands before Aistulf, who promptly rejected them. Then the pope turned his back on Constantinople and journeyed over the Alpine passes into the kingdom of the Franks. Pepin greeted him with appropriate enthusiasm and was again anointed as king, this time by the pope himself. Stephen also bestowed on Pepin the title Patrician of the Romans, which had normally been borne by the imperial governor of Ravenna. For his part, the Frankish king promised to help the papacy against the Lombards. In 755 Pepin invaded Italy and forced King Aistulf to beg for peace and to promise to surrender Ravenna and its hinterland to the pope. When Aistulf failed to keep his agreement and actually attacked Rome, Pepin returned with his Frankish army and defeated him once more. This time Pepin stayed in Italy until the pope was firmly in possession of the exarchate of Ravenna. The Byzantines demanded, of course, that the territory reconquered from the Lombards be returned to the eastern empire, but Pepin angrily refused. He had fought his war for St. Peter, he declared, and it was to "St. Peter," that is, to the papacy, that he handed over his conquests.* From this time onward, the pope claimed to rule in central Italy as an independent monarch. Pepin's donation marked the beginning of the Papal States that would endure until 1870.

Donation of Constantine

It was probably also about this time that some enterprising cleric in the Roman curia produced the famous forgery known as the Donation of Constantine.* Ever since the fifth century, there had been a legend that, when the emperor Constantine founded his new capital in the East, he relinquished the secular government of Rome and the western empire to Pope Sylvester. The forged Donation purported to be the original imperial charter setting out the terms of the grant. It was probably intended to provide additional evidence for the legitimacy of the pope's rule in central Italy, and it was widely accepted as genuine down to the fifteenth century. The forged Donation, however, played a lesser part in the development of later papal claims than one might expect. Most of the great popes of the Middle Ages were reluctant to admit that any of their power had been bestowed on them by the emperor; they preferred to maintain that all their authority came from God alone.

*Sources, no. 25

In mid-eighth century the popes were far from formulating all the grandiose claims of later medieval pontiffs. They were only too happy to have found a powerful warrior-king on whose protection they could rely. Indeed, all the participants in the events of the 750s that we have described acted from short-term motives of mutual convenience. But their actions had long-range results that no eighth-century man could have foreseen. Above all, the Frankish-papal alliance consolidated the links between Rome and northern Europe that missionaries like Boniface had established; and by doing so, it helped to shape the whole cultural and religious future of medieval Europe.

READING SUGGESTIONS

* *B. Tierney,* Sources *and* Readings, *vol. I, nos. 19–21, 23–25; vol. II, nos. 4, 5, 7.*

On pre-Benedictine monasticism, see * H. Waddell, *The Desert Fathers,* and for Benedict and his order, E. C. Butler, *Benedictine Monachism* (London, 1919); J. Chapman, *St. Benedict* (New York, 1937); L. von Matt, *Saint Benedict* (London, 1961). The spread of monasticism in the north is discussed by J. Décarreaux, *Monks and Civilization* (London, 1964), and by * E. S. Duckett, *The Gateway to the Middle Ages* (New York, 1938), and * *The Wandering Saints of the Early Middle Ages* (New York, 1959). The following works deal with Celtic Christian culture: L. Bieler, *The Life and Legend of St. Patrick* (Dublin, 1949); J. Ryan, *Irish Monasticism* (London, 1931); L. Gougaud, *Christianity in Celtic Lands* (London, 1932); K. Hughes, *The Church in Early Irish Society* (Ithaca, NY, 1968); F. Henry, *Irish Art in the Early Christian Period* (Ithaca, NY, 1965). On the Anglo-Saxon church see P. H. Blair, *The World of Bede* (London, 1970). For source material, see *The Rule of St. Benedict,* J. McCann (trans.) (Westminster, MD, 1952); * Bede, *History of the English Church and People,* L. Sherley-Price (trans.) (Harmondsworth, 1955); *The Life of St. Columba,* W. Huyshe (trans.) (London, 1908); *The Life of Bishop Wilfrid by Eddius Stephanus,* B. Colgrave (trans.) (Cambridge, 1927); *The Life of St. Boniface by Willibald,* G. W. Robinson (trans.) (Cambridge, MA, 1916); *The Letters of St. Boniface,* E. Emerton (trans.) (New York, 1940).

Two good introductions to Muslim religious concepts are * Tor Andrae, *Mohammed, the Man and His Faith* (London, 1936) and * W. Montgomery Watt, *Mohammad, Prophet and Stateman.* On the history of Islam, see * H. A. R. Gibb, *Mohammedanism: An Historical Survey,* 2nd ed. (London, 1953); * A. Guillaume, *Islam,* 2nd ed. (Harmondsworth, 1956); R. Levy, *The Social Structure of Islam* (Cambridge, 1957); F. Donner, *The Early Islamic Conquests* (Princeton, NJ, 1981); and H. Kennedy, *The Prophet and the Age of the Caliphates* (London, 1986). Standard histories of the Arabs are * B. Lewis, *The Arabs in History,* 4th ed. (London, 1958), * P. K. Hitti, *History of the Arabs from Earliest Times to the Present,* 7th ed. (London, 1960); and A. Hourani, *A History of the Arab Peoples* (Cambridge, MA, 1991). On Islamic culture, see * G. von Grunebaum, *Medieval Islam: A Study in Cultural Orientation,* 2nd ed. (Chicago, 1961); H. A. R. Gibb, *Arabic Literature* (London, 1926); T. W. Arnold, *Painting in Islam* (London, 1928); K. A. C. Creswell, *Early Muslim Architecture* (Oxford, 1932). B. Lewis (ed.), *The World of Islam* is a beautifully illustrated survey. M. Pickthall, *The Meaning of the Glorious Koran* (New York, 1930) provides a good translation of the Koran. Other documents are collected in * B. Lewis,

Islam from the Prophet Muhammad to the Capture of Constantinople (New York, 1974).

* H. Pirenne, *Mohammad and Charlemagne* (London, 1939) is a seminal, provocative study dealing with the impact of the rise of Islam on the economy of the West. The problems raised by Pirenne are discussed in * A. F. Havighurst, *The Pirenne Thesis* (Boston, 1958).

The complex relationship between Byzantium, Rome, and the Frankish monarchy in the eighth century is well treated in the books of Dawson and Moss cited in Chapter I. See also * T. F. X. Noble, *The Birth of the Papal State, 680–825* (Philadelphia, 1984).

chapter

VII

The First Europe

The alliance between the popes and the Frankish kings was consolidated under Pepin's son Charles. His conquests made him lord of all western Europe, and his coronation as Roman emperor by Pope Leo III established a new, close relationship between the imperial and papal offices that persisted throughout the Middle Ages. Charlemagne's reign may be considered a "false start" in the history of Europe in the sense that the political unity of his empire did not endure. But, searching on a deeper level, a historian can see that the fusion of Roman, Christian, and German cultures, which was symbolized in Charlemagne's coronation, had become an irreversible process by the time the emperor died.

19. *The Empire of Charlemagne*

When Pepin died in 768, he was succeeded by his two sons, Charles (768–814) and Carloman (768–771). As the two brothers could not agree, it was fortunate for the state that Carloman died three years after his father. Charles ignored Carloman's infant son and promptly took possession of the entire Frankish kingdom. Physically Charles was a moderately tall, powerfully built man with red hair, a bull neck, and a fine large belly. He loved both hunting and feasting well on the game brought in. His biographer, Einhard, assures us that he drank with great moderation, rarely taking more than three cups of wine with a meal.* One who has seen the cups of the time will not worry too much over Charles' temperance.

In character Charles was aggressive, ambitious, determined, and utterly ruthless in attaining his ends. He had a keen, inquiring mind. He was soldier, statesman, and patron of scholars. But no process of adding up his known characteristics can give us an explanation of Charles' capacity. His achievements remain almost incredible, and to

*Sources, no. 26

explain them one must resort to such vague phrases as force of character. He was the dominant figure of the Western world in his own day, a legendary hero to the men of the Middle Ages, and historians still call him Charlemagne, or Charles the Great.

Soon after Charlemagne ascended the throne, it became clear that Pepin's settlement in Italy could not be permanent. As long as able and ambitious kings ruled the Lombard state, they were going to try to conquer all Italy. The papal state could never be safe while the Lombard kingdom existed. Moreover, Charlemagne had a personal quarrel with the Lombard king Desiderius. He and Carloman had married two of Desiderius' daughters, but Charlemagne soon repudiated his own wife and then usurped the inheritance of her sister's children. Stung by these insults, Desiderius began to intrigue with groups of Frankish nobility hostile to Charlemagne. Hence in 773 Charlemagne led his warriors into Italy, besieged and captured the Lombard capital of Pavia, put the Lombard king in a monastery, and himself assumed the Lombard crown. Although for administrative convenience he had his son Pepin crowned as king of Italy in 780, Charlemagne remained for the rest of his life the effective ruler of the Lombard state.

Even before he marched south to crush the Lombards, Charlemagne had set out to complete the work of his father and grandfather in northern Germany—the conquest of Saxony and the conversion of its people to Christianity. In 772 he marched through southwest Saxony as far as the river Weser, receiving the submission of the local chiefs. But as soon as the king left for Italy, the conquered Saxons rose and raided the Frankish frontier. In 775 Charlemagne returned to Saxony and subdued the same region once more. The Saxons were a stubborn, hardy, and warlike people. They fought bitterly until they were obliged to surrender and then rose in revolt as soon as the Frankish army had gone home. They were true to their own gods, and Charlemagne was able to make them convert to Christianity only by using brutal coercion. In 782 the Saxons wiped out a Frankish invading force, and Charlemagne responded with a punitive campaign that culminated in a major victory followed by a massacre of several thousand Saxon warriors. In 785 the Saxon leader Widukind surrendered to Charlemagne and accepted Christianity. This marked the end of large-scale resistance, though Charlemagne had to suppress lesser revolts in Saxony several times during the next twenty years.

In his efforts to stabilize his Saxon conquests, Charlemagne used all the ordinary devices. He built great fortresses and garrisoned them with Frankish troops. He brought in Frankish counts and gave lands to Frankish followers. He even moved large masses of Saxons into his western domains and replaced them in Saxony with Frankish colonists. His chief reliance, however, rested on close cooperation with the church. Charlemagne not only forced the Saxons to accept Christianity but also established episcopal sees in the conquered lands and endowed monastic foundations there that served as missionary centers. His decrees made relapses into paganism and disobedience to the church fully as serious as revolt against his rule. In short, Charlemagne expected his armies and fortresses to keep the Saxons in order for a time, but relied on the church to make them into obedient and reliable subjects. His hopes were not in vain. After some thirty years of coercion and evangelization, Saxony became an integral part of the Carolingian state.*

Although Pepin had obliged the duke of Bavaria to recognize him as overlord and St. Boniface had reorganized the Bavarian church, this duchy had remained essentially independent. Charlemagne resolved to incorporate it in his kingdom. Using various disagreements with the duke as his excuse, he invaded Bavaria in 787, and the following year the duke was removed and Bavaria divided into counties. The addition of Bavaria to his domains brought Charlemagne into direct contact with the fierce Avar horsemen, who had long harassed the Byzantines and who held the Hungarian plain and the region now known as Austria. Charlemagne led a great army against them in 791 and pressed them back in the Danube valley. His son Pepin, king of Italy, at the head of his Lombard cavalry waged a series of campaigns against the Avars and cleaned them out of Carinthia (now a region of southern Austria). This completed Charlemagne's eastern conquests. Although he conducted several campaigns against the Slavs between the Weser and the upper Elbe, they were essentially punitive expeditions and did not result in the permanent occupation of new territory.

While he was conquering the Saxons, Charlemagne was also at war with another foe at the opposite end of his kingdom. In 778 he led a large army into northern Spain. This expedition was not a great success. He spent most of his time fighting the Christian Basques, and as he returned home across the Pyrenees, they ambushed and destroyed his rear guard. This disaster was the original basis for the famous *Song of Roland,* one of the finest of the legends that grew up about Charlemagne.† The great king's persistence, however, eventually led to success. In a long series of campaigns, he and his generals conquered a strip of territory south of the Pyrenees that was called the Spanish March. By granting benefices in this territory to many of his warriors, Charlemagne turned it into an effective buffer between the Frankish kingdom and the Muslims of Spain.

A mere systematic account of Charlemagne's conquests does not give a full picture of his astounding military achievements. This can only be gained by glancing briefly at the chronology of his campaigns. In 772 he invaded Saxony; in 773 and 774 he conquered the Lombard kingdom; in 775 and 776 he renewed his attacks on the Saxons; in 778 he invaded Spain. The year 779 saw him back in Saxony. The mustering almost every year of the military resources of the Frankish kingdom and the moving of them to distant frontiers was a stupendous task. Even though his armies were probably comparatively small in numbers, the problem of supplying them must have been ex-

*Sources, no. 27

†See p. 462.

tremely hard to solve. The fact that Charlemagne was able to do this is all the evidence one should need of his unusual ability and unshakable determination.

Fully as difficult as the conquest of new territory was the administration of so vast a realm. The peaceful interior parts of the kingdom were ruled by counts. In the border regions, where defense was important, larger territorial units were administered by *margraves*—from *mark graf,* "mark" meaning a border district and "graf" meaning count. Above these officials was a small group of lieutenants of the king who watched over his interests. Finally there were Charlemagne's sons, who were the titular kings of various parts of the state. The great difficulty was to be sure of the loyalty of these numerous officers, and Charlemagne had to suppress a number of dangerous plots. It was in the hope of securing adequate information about the behavior of his local officials that Charlemagne created the officials known as *missi dominici.* Two men, a prelate and a lay noble, were sent out together to survey a section of the realm and bear the king's orders to the counts and margraves. Each year the pairs were shifted about so that the same men should not repeatedly visit the same region. This device was valuable as a means of supervision, but its actual effectiveness depended on the power and prestige of the monarch. As long as Charlemagne's sword loomed behind his *missi,* the administrative system worked fairly well. But Charlemagne did not succeed in devising any institutions that could make it possible for a weaker monarch to manage his vast state.

All the different peoples of his empire continued to live according to their own national laws. Charlemagne had no intention of abolishing this diversity; indeed, he commanded that the different codes of customary law should be set down in writing to preserve them more effectively. But he supplemented these local laws with a substantial body of new decrees that were imposed on all his peoples alike. These imperial decrees are known as *capitularies.* They dealt with such matters as the obligation of military service and the system of *missi* that we have described. Other capitularies regulated the conduct of the clergy and defined the duties of the bishops. Charles was a theocratic monarch, convinced that he ruled "by the grace of God," and he took for granted the right and duty to govern ecclesiastical as well as secular affairs. He was fond of listening to readings from St. Augustine's *City of God,* and it has often been said that his aim was to establish a city of God on earth. If so, he had certainly misunderstood St. Augustine, and the result necessarily fell far short of the objective. In considering Charlemagne's government, we are still dealing with a primitive Germanic monarchy—but a primitive Germanic monarchy presided over by a political genius.

The economy of Charlemagne's empire was primitive too. There was no ordered system of public taxation. The emperor lived mainly on the produce of his own vast estates scattered throughout his territories and, until late in life, he spent much of his time journeying from one to another of them, taking his whole court with him. This

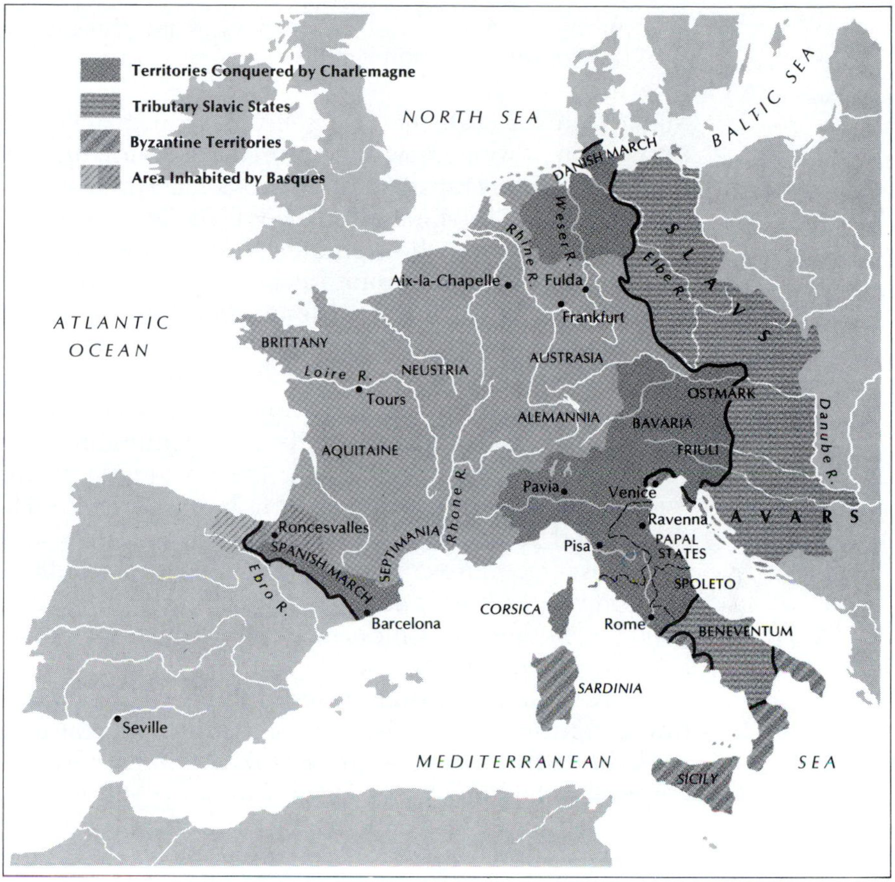

The Carolingian Empire

The evolution of the Frankish kingdom into an empire whose cohesion, such as it was, stood out in marked contrast to the chaos on its borders was symbolized by the imperial coronation of Charlemagne in 800.

was partly for economic reasons, to consume the produce of each estate in turn; but the constant traveling also gave Charlemagne an opportunity to supervise the administration of the local counts, to hear appeals from their judgments, and to ensure that they were carrying out the instructions of his *missi.* A capitulary, *De Villis,* from Charlemagne's reign gives a detailed picture of one of the great royal estates and the kinds of activities that went on there*:

> We desire that each steward shall make an annual statement of all our income from the lands cultivated by the oxen which our own plowmen drive and from the holdings which owe us plowing services; also from pigs, rents, obligations and fines for taking game in our forests without permission . . . from mills, forest, fields, bridges and boats . . . from markets, vineyards . . . hay, firewood, torches, planks and other kinds of lumber . . . from vegetables . . . from wool, flax and hemp . . . from fruit trees and nut trees . . . from gardens, turnips and fishponds . . . from hides, skins and horns,

*Sources, no. 27

> from honey and wax . . . from wine, mead, vinegar, beer . . . from chickens and eggs and geese. . . .

Many kinds of craftsmen were listed, from blacksmiths to bakers to net makers, "who know how to make nets for hunting, fishing, and fowling." The steward was also to keep supplies on hand for the "women's work"—linen, wool, wool combs, teasels, soap, and various dyestuffs. Evidently the women's work consisted of textile manufacture in a workshop set aside for them. The capitulary added that the women's area was to be guarded by good fences and stout doors.

Commercial activity had dwindled since the days of the late Roman empire but trading never ceased altogether. Traders carried salt from coastal regions to inland areas and wines to northern districts where the vine did not flourish, while Jewish merchants in the south of France maintained a trickle of trade with Egypt. Charlemagne interested himself in these activities as in everything else. He put out edicts that aimed to standardize weights and measures and issued a new coin, the silver penny or denier which, he said, would be "pure money of good weight." Archeologists' finds of coin hoards show that Charlemagne's denier was indeed 25 percent heavier than the ones that had circulated earlier.

There remains to be considered the incident which symbolized for future centuries the unity of western Europe that Charlemagne had brought into existence—the Frankish king's coronation as Roman emperor in St. Peter's basilica on Christmas Day in the year 800. Charlemagne traveled to Rome at the end of that year in order to settle the affairs of the papacy. In 799 a rebellion had broken out in Rome against Pope Leo III (795–816). The pope was attacked while he walked through the streets in a procession. He was brutally beaten and then imprisoned for a time, but he succeeded in escaping from Rome and made his way over the Alps to Charlemagne's court. The king heard his story with sympathy and sent him back to Rome with a force of Frankish warriors strong enough to reestablish him in the city. The faction that had attacked Leo then sought to justify its action by bringing a series of criminal charges against him, and since there was no authority in Rome competent to judge the pope, the case remained unsettled until Charlemagne himself arrived in Rome. On December 23, 800, the king called together in St. Peter's a council of prelates and nobles. The pope appeared before the council and took a solemn oath affirming his innocence, which the council accepted. On December 25 the king returned to St. Peter's for the mass of Christmas Day. Just as he rose from prayer, the pope, who was officiating, produced a crown and set it on Charlemagne's head. Thereupon the people in the church, evidently well-drilled beforehand, cried out the ritual acclamations that greeted the inauguration of a new emperor, "To Charles Augustus, crowned by God, great and peace-giving emperor, life and victory."

It is very hard to determine whether the papal court or Charlemagne's Frankish advisers initiated the idea of the imperial coronation. The pope had an obvious motive—he needed a permanent protector. Moreover, only a friendly Roman emperor could legitimize papal rule over the former Byzantine territories in central Italy that Pepin had snatched away from the eastern empire. At the same time, we find the term "Christian empire" used to describe the king's realm among Charlemagne's court circle in the years just before the coronation. Charlemagne himself never displayed any overwhelming enthusiasm for the imperial title; the most likely reason why he was persuaded to assume it at all was in order to assert a position of equality with the Byzantine emperor. Charlemagne was the greatest conqueror of his age. He wrote as an equal to the great caliph Harun al-Rashid of Bagdad. But in his dealings with the eastern emperor, he was always addressed as a mere subking, while the ruler of Constantinople was emperor and *basileus.* The situation must have been highly exasperating.

Modern disputes about the imperial coronation are complicated by the fact that two of the most important primary sources give diametrically opposed accounts of what happened. The *Frankish Royal Annals* record that, after the pope's case had been disposed of at the council of December 23, the assembled nobles and prelates went on to consider the state of the empire and persuaded Charlemagne to accept the imperial dignity. On the other hand, according to Charlemagne's biographer, Einhard, the king was so angry after the coronation that he declared he would never have entered the church on that day, even though it was a great feast, had he known of the pope's intention.*

Certainly the coronation added nothing to Charlemagne's real power, which continued to rest solely on the support of his Frankish warriors. Some scholars have suggested that Charlemagne agreed to accept the imperial title but was angered by the introduction of a ceremony of papal coronation into the ritual of acclamation by the Roman people. At any rate, once he was reconciled to his new title (and he did not use it for several months after the coronation), Charlemagne was determined that the Byzantine government should acknowledge him as a true emperor. He waged a series of campaigns against the Greek possessions in Italy until, in 813, the emperor Michael I gave way and sent emissaries who formally greeted Charles as emperor and *basileus.* Shortly thereafter Charlemagne crowned his son Louis a coemperor.

In discussing Charlemagne's coronation, the nineteenth-century historian of the Holy Roman Empire, Lord Bryce, wrote that the shout of acclamation in St. Peter's "pronounced the union, so long in preparation, so mighty in its consequences, of the Roman and the Teuton, of the memories and the civilization of the South with the fresh energies of the North." And, he added, "From that moment modern history begins." Even if this seems exaggerated, it remains true that the imperial coronation was a momentous event. Many later controversies of church and state turned on the precise significance attributed to the pope's action in crowning Charles. Above all, the coronation sym-

*Sources, no. 26

bolized the emergence, for the first time, of an ordered western Christian society, with its religious capital in Rome and its military center of gravity north of the Alps, a society clearly distinguishable from the Byzantine civilization to the east and the Islamic civilization to the south.

20. *Carolingian Culture*

One of Charlemagne's prime ambitions was to revive the light of learning in his vast barbarous realm. He was probably moved to some extent by purely practical considerations: an effective government required some literate officials. But it seems clear that he had also a real curiosity and enthusiasm for the knowledge stored in books written by the scholars of previous ages. At any rate, Charlemagne gathered about him in his palace learned men drawn from all Europe—some by quiet abduction, others by honest hiring. The chief of them was the Saxon Alcuin, from the famous school at York that had inherited the Northumbrian tradition of learning. From Italy Charlemagne drew Peter of Pisa, a grammarian, and Paul the Deacon, who wrote a history of the Lombards. Einhard (ca. 770–840), the royal biographer, was a Frank. Theodulf, a Visigoth from Spain, was trained in the tradition established there by Isidore of Seville. Other learned men were drawn from Ireland and Germany. For fifteen years Alcuin conducted a school in Charlemagne's palace. The king himself studied industriously and is said to have understood both Latin and Greek. The scholars brought together by Charlemagne began the long, slow task of making the learning of the past available for the men of the Middle Ages. The first steps were necessarily simple. The rules of classical Latin grammar were studied and taught; the elements of logic were slowly absorbed. Alcuin adopted from Cassiodorus the late classical division of knowledge into seven liberal arts and himself introduced the division into *trivium* and *quadrivium* that was used in the medieval schools.*

The foundation of nearly all the learning of Charlemagne's age was the network of monastic communities established by Irish or English missionaries during the preceding two centuries. Many of the scholars at the palace school had been trained as monks, and some of them, including Alcuin himself, returned to monasteries when they left the court. Most of the literary and theological studies of the Carolingian age were carried on away from the court in the greater abbeys, though still with the active encouragement and support of Charlemagne himself. About 796, for instance, the king wrote to the abbot of Fulda in central Germany urging him to further the development of education and learning in the abbey and the surrounding region; and, in fact, Fulda became a great center of learning with a school that produced some of the most distinguished scholars of the Carolingian era. Einhard was trained there; his contemporary, the abbot Hrabanus Mau-

*See p. 416.

rus of Fulda, compiled a massive commentary on the Bible made up for the most part of selected texts from the four great Latin Fathers, supplemented by quotations from Isidore and Bede. Hrabanus' pupil Walafrid Strabo, who went from Fulda to become abbot of Reichenau, was a sensitive poet and learned scholar.* He produced a shorter work of biblical exegesis, mostly excerpted from Hrabanus, that greatly influenced the standard biblical commentary of the high Middle Ages, the *Glossa Ordinaria.* Indeed, these works of Hrabanus Maurus and Walafrid Strabo influenced the whole Western tradition of biblical exegesis throughout the Middle Ages and into later times.

We must bear in mind that, in spite of Charlemagne's efforts, the vast majority of the population of his empire remained barbarous and illiterate. Charlemagne tried to establish schools outside the monasteries in cathedrals and other churches so as to provide teaching for the secular clergy and layfolk, but one lifetime was not enough for the task of educating a whole continent. When we speak of Carolingian culture, therefore, we are dealing with the work of only a few dozen significant writers, scattered in monasteries all over Europe. There was no educated society to support a broader movement of culture.

Despite such limitations, scholars have sometimes dignified the civilization of the ninth century with the name "Carolingian Renaissance." If the term is to be meaningful at all, we must distinguish between the actual cultural achievement of the era and the significance of that achievement for later times. The original creative work of the ninth century is of relatively little value. Carolingian scholars produced a substantial mass of Latin verse, competent enough but for the most part unexciting. The monasteries often kept annals, recording the major events of each year. They are very useful to modern historians but have no pretension to literary value in their own right. A few biographies were written, the most notable being Einhard's life of Charlemagne. The age produced one original philosopher, John Scotus Erigena, but he had no successors.

Erigena, who understood Greek, attempted to construct a new synthesis of Neoplatonism and Christianity. The Platonic element predominated so much that the work veered off into heresy at many points, but, fortunately for Erigena, none of his contemporaries could understand his arguments and the Church did not get around to condemning his work for another four centuries. In other areas of thought some stirrings of theological controversy did arise during the Carolingian period. Charlemagne interested himself in the iconoclastic dispute and had his scholars produce a series of works, the *Libri Carolini,* that sought to find a middle road between the extremes of iconoclasm and image-worship. The monk Gottschalk raised the thorny theological issue of predestination and was condemned and imprisoned for his trouble. But such enterprise was exceptional. More typically, Carolingian theologians limited themselves to making compilations of patristic texts in the manner of Hrabanus Maurus. In the sphere of visual art, the best Carolingian illuminated manuscripts

*Sources, no 28

were significant and original achievements that interwove Byzantine themes with Celtic, Anglo-Saxon, and classical motifs. Little Carolingian architecture survives. An outstanding exception is Charlemagne's splendid chapel at Aachen, modeled on the Byzantine church of San Vitale at Ravenna.

All this is not negligible, but the total achievement was extremely limited when compared with the greatest epochs of European culture. A handful of readable poems, a few useful encyclopedic compilations, some well-painted books—it seems hardly enough to make a Renaissance. And yet there was a Renaissance in the most limited, technical sense of the term. That is, there was a notable revival of classical studies and humane learning. By the middle of the ninth century, not only in the Celtic and Byzantine fringes of Europe but in monasteries scattered all through Gaul and Germany, there existed communities of learned men who could read and write Latin and who could appreciate classical literature and understand patristic theology. The monks of the Carolingian age set themselves to assimilate and preserve the whole heritage of ancient Latin and early Christian culture, and in this task they succeeded admirably. From the ninth century onward, it was taken for granted that the "work" which a monk was required to perform for several hours each day according to the Benedictine Rule would normally consist of copying books. This multiplication of manuscripts was very important for the future. Although many classical writings disappeared altogether between the age of the barbarian invasions and the time of Charlemagne, almost nothing that survived up to 800 has subsequently been lost. To put the same point in a different way, more than 90 percent of the works of ancient Rome that we know nowadays exist in their earliest form in a Carolingian manuscript. These manuscripts form the basis of nearly all modern editions.

A major reform of handwriting accompanied this large-scale production of manuscripts. Late Merovingian scripts had become almost illegible. The letters ran into one another in a scrawled, almost indecipherable mass, and books written in such script suffered corruptions at every fresh copying. A new form of writing known as Carolingian minuscle was developed mainly at the abbey of Corbie; the letters were exquisitely formed and the words neatly separated from one another. This form of writing was popularized through the influence of Alcuin. He spent his last years as abbot of the monastery of St. Martin at Tours and there founded a *scriptorium,* or writing office, which produced carefully edited texts of the Bible and of various liturgical works in the new handwriting. Characteristically, Charlemagne interested himself in this activity as in everything else. One of his capitularies bears the title, *On Scribes—That They Should Not Write Corruptly.* The Carolingian minuscule script was revived by the Renaissance humanists of the fifteenth century, and our modern lowercase letters are derived from it.

The light kindled by Charlemagne's efforts was not very bright, and it shone flickeringly in a vast sea of darkness, but it was never to go

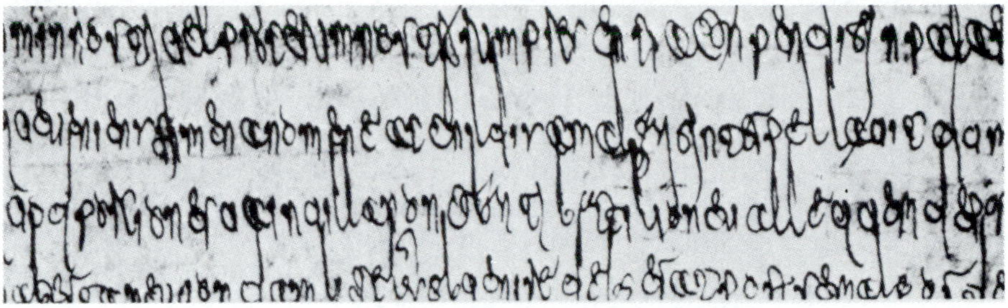

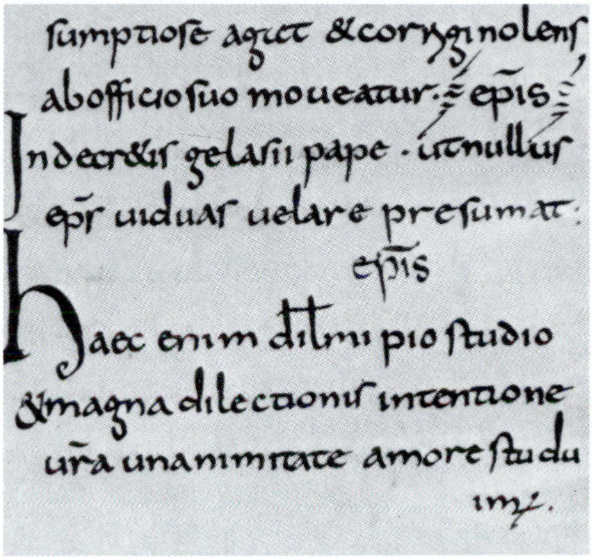

The contrast between Merovingian writing in its most debased form and the reformed script, Carolingian minuscule, is clearly shown in these two samples. Above: Merovingian cursive from a royal diploma of Theodoric III, ca. 680. *Archives Nationales, Paris.* Below: Carolingian minuscule, from a manuscript of Carolingian capitularies, ca. 825. *Stiftsbibliothek, St. Gallen, Switzerland*

out completely. Although the creative literary achievement of the ninth century was slight, the work of the monks was of decisive importance for the future. Without the texts that they copied in the monastic *scriptoria,* there could simply not have been any medieval civilization as we know it or any later Renaissance.

21. *The West Besieged: Magyar, Muslim, and Viking Invasions*

A brief summary glance at western Europe about 800 A.D. shows a Christian civilization surrounded by foes. The emperor Charlemagne was king of the Franks and the Lombards. Except for the peninsula of Brittany, he ruled the coast of the Atlantic Ocean and the North Sea from the Spanish March, below the Pyrenees, to the base of the Danish peninsula. The eastern frontier of his domains ran along the river Elbe to the Bohemian Forest. He was master of Italy north of Rome. In England, the Anglo-Saxons, under the vague overlordship of Egbert of Wessex, held the east coast as far north as the Forth and the west coast except for Cornwall and Wales to the Solway Firth. This was German Christian Europe. To its west lay a fringe of Christian Celtic lands: Britanny, Cornwall, Wales, Ireland, and Scotland. Italy south of Rome and Sicily were still nominally under the rule of the Byzantine emperors. Around the borders of these Christian lands of western Europe were the non-Christian peoples. In Scandinavia lived Germanic pagans. East of the Elbe and the Bohemian Forest were the Slavs, and remnants of the Avars occupied the Hungarian plain. Spain and North Africa were held by the Muslims, whose fleets had taken command of the Mediterranean.

Charlemagne's empire began to disintegrate soon after the death of the emperor himself, a process that was probably inevitable. The empire contained a medley of peoples, each with its own language, its own law, and its own traditions. There never had been anything to hold them together as a political unit except the personality of Charlemagne himself. The various peoples of the empire did share a common religion, and the ideal of a united and ordered Christendom was cherished by a few educated clerics, but such men were unable to impose their ideals on the savage Frankish nobility. Moreover, the natural tendencies to disintegration were intensified by internal civil wars and by attacks from external enemies.

When Charlemagne died, he left only one surviving son, who is known as Louis the Pious (814–840).* Louis was an educated, civilized man, but he was no warrior, and he proved incapable of controlling his own sons, let alone the wild Frankish nobles. The new emperor wanted to preserve the unity of the empire and tried to arrange a plan of succession that would have given the imperial title and the bulk of the royal estates to his eldest son, Lothair, while the younger sons would have received only minor subkingdoms. This arrangement was highly unsatisfactory to Lothair's brothers; from 829 onward, they fought incessantly in a variety of permutations and com-

*See chart, this page; for more detailed Carolingian genealogy, see Appendix, Table 1.

The Descendants of Charlemagne

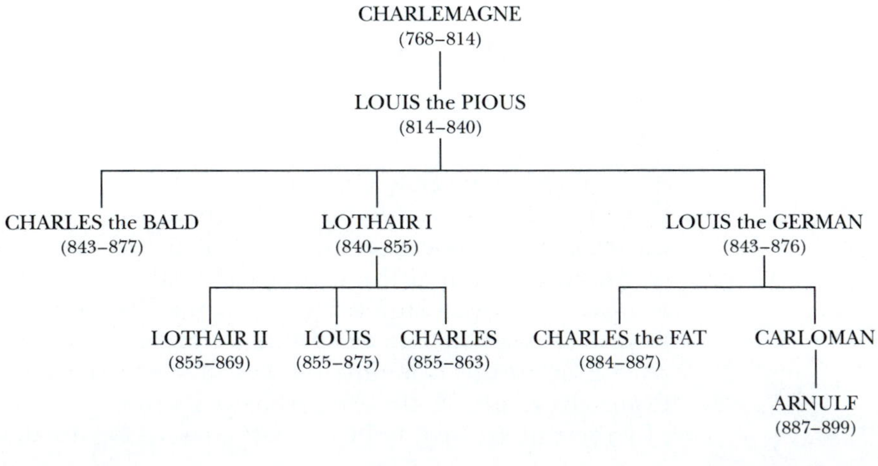

binations against Lothair and his father. After Louis' death in 840, his two surviving younger sons, Charles the Bald (843–877) and Louis the German (843–876), united against Lothair, and a climactic battle was fought at Fontenoy. Although the slaughter was very great, the result was indecisive, and in 843 the brothers agreed to divide the empire into three equal shares. Charles took the West Frankish territories that later became the kingdom of France; Louis, the Germanic lands to the east. Lothair (840–855) received the imperial title together with a "Middle Kingdom," consisting of a strip of land running from the North Sea to Italy. It included the Netherlands, the Rhineland, the Rhone valley, and northern Italy.

This division was certainly not made for nationalistic reasons, but it anticipated some of the most important permanent national divisions of Europe. For the first time, a Romance-speaking West Frankish kingdom emerged as a political entity separate from the Teutonic-speaking East Frankish realm. The clear-cut linguistic division that had emerged is illustrated in the Strasbourg Oaths, which Charles the Bald and Louis the German took in 842 to pledge mutual support to one another. Charles spoke in German so as to be understood by Louis' warriors, and Louis spoke in the Romance tongue in order to be intelligible to Charles' men. The Romance version of the oath was set down by a contemporary chronicler, Nithard, and it provides the earliest surviving record of any Romance language. Carolingian dynasties continued to rule in Germany until 911 and in France until 887, after which Carolingians and Capetians alternated on the French throne for another century.

The "Middle Kingdom" of Lothair proved the most unstable of the three realms. On Lothair's death in 855, it was divided among his three sons.* Lotharingia (later Lorraine) went to Lothair II (855–869); Provence, to Charles (855–863); and Italy, to Louis (855–875). The imperial title passed first to Louis of Italy, then to Charles the Bald of the West Frankish kingdom, and after his death in 877, to Charles the Fat of the East Frankish line and to his successor, Arnulf. The title was subsequently held by a series of petty Italian kinglets down to 924, after which the imperial office remained vacant for nearly forty years. When Lothair II died in 869, the West Frankish and East Frankish kings each tried to seize his northern territories. The disputes between them continued into the tenth century. Indeed, France and Germany have been squabbling about Lorraine ever since.

While the descendants of Charlemagne were industriously making war on each other, their kingdoms were exposed to a series of destructive incursions launched by the non-Christian peoples who surrounded the lands of the old Carolingian Empire. In 895 a new people, the Magyar (an Altaic people who had originated in Central Asia), arrived on the plains of Hungary, where they joined the remnants of the Avars. Five years later, they swept up the Danube and ravaged Bavaria. In 906 they plundered Saxony, and two years later, Thuringia. During the next twenty years, they raided all Germany and the border regions such as Alsace and the Rhine valley. In 937 they reached

*See chart, p. 148, and Appendix, Table 1.

Reims in France. Their ravages continued until they were crushingly defeated at the battle of the Lechfeld by Otto I, king of Germany, in 955.*

The ninth century also saw a new wave of Muslim attacks in the Mediterranean world. In 827 the Muslims invaded Sicily and subsequently conquered the whole island in a series of campaigns lasting through the middle decades of the century. In the year 843 they threatened the city of Rome itself. The Muslims also occupied Corsica, Sardinia, and the delta of the Rhone in southern France. Although the Muslim forces made no regular settlement on the Italian mainland, they occupied bases there until 915, when they were finally expelled by a Byzantine army and fleet. During this entire period they ravaged the country brutally. Sicily remained in their hands for over a century more and was the seat of a flourishing Muslim culture.

The most important of all the new incursions came from Scandinavia. In the last years of the eighth century, the people of that region started the last great wave of Germanic migration. The causes of this movement are far from clear. In all probability, the basic explanation was a rapid increase of population in a land of very limited resources. Peasants who had no farms to till and nobles without lands to rule were inclined to take to the sea in search of adventure and a living. The era of migration also coincided with the period in which a semblance of orderly government was established in Scandinavia, as the numerous small groups that had been independent before the ninth century were gradually unified under the kings of Denmark, Norway, and Sweden. It has been suggested that, as these kings began to establish internal order, the more turbulent of their peoples migrated to other lands. Neither of these explanations seems completely satisfactory. The historian can only say that some combination of circumstances induced great numbers of Scandinavians, both nobles and peasants, to take to their ships and sail forth in search of booty. The Scandinavians called these warrior-seamen Vikings, and modern historians have adopted that term; but to the people of Christian Europe they were the Northmen.

Although all three of the Scandinavian peoples took part in these migrations, only those of Norway and Denmark operated in western Europe. The Swedish Vikings ruled the Baltic Sea and invaded the Slavic lands to the east. In the middle of the ninth century, they established a post at Novgorod to the southeast of the Gulf of Finland and soon spread southward to establish themselves at Kiev, on the Dnieper. These Swedish Vikings, or Varangians as they are often called, founded fortified posts throughout the Slavic lands. From these centers they conquered the rural Slavic population and made the people accept their rule. Like the Vikings of the West, the Varangians were merchants as well as warriors. At Kiev and other points on the rivers they loaded boats with the products of the Russian forests (furs and honey) and also with captured slaves and carried them to the Black Sea and along its shores to Constantinople. Sometimes they visited the Byzantine capital as simple traders, but at other times they

*See p. 211.

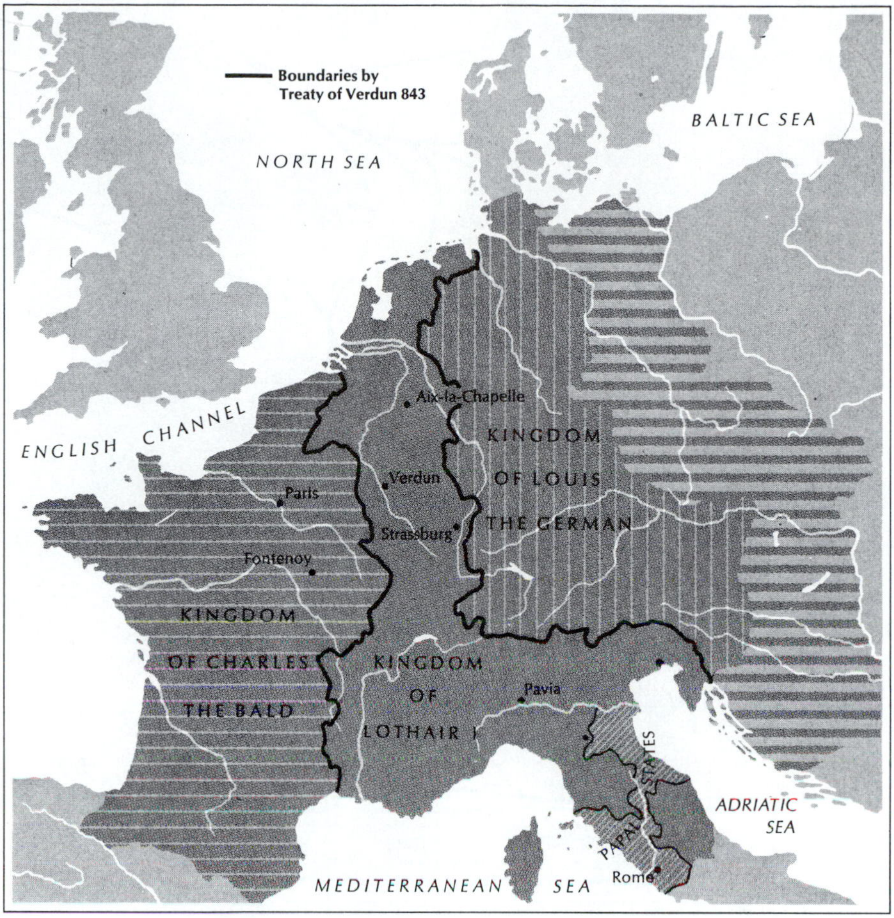

The Treaty of Verdun, 843 A.D.

The division of the Carolingian Empire into these three kingdoms shows the beginnings of modern France and Germany; the Middle Kingdom (the kingdom of Lothair) was until the twentieth century an area whose possession was in dispute.

were invading enemies. Several times they launched large-scale attacks on the great city. Although they never succeeded in making much progress against its mighty walls, they did obtain commercial privileges from the emperor. During the tenth century, the Varangians made themselves masters of what is now western Russia and welded this vast territory into a state—the first Russian state—ruled by the prince of Kiev.

Although an occasional Swedish adventurer appeared in the North Sea and the Atlantic Ocean, in general these were the highways for the Vikings of Norway and Denmark. The Viking raiders first struck England in the summer of 787, and within seven years the monasteries of Lindisfarne and Jarrow were plundered and burned. In 814 the Northmen burned the monastery on the island of Noirmoutier, off the mouth of the Loire River. For about half a century, almost every summer brought forth Viking bands ravaging the coasts and the lower

Invasions of the Ninth and Tenth Centuries

The wave of Viking invasions and migration is startling not because of the numbers of Vikings but because of the huge geographical area they roamed; from Scandinavia south to the Mediterranean and from the Britsh Isles east to Russia, the Black Sea, and Constantinople, the Northmen penetrated the coastal areas of every part of Europe. Their only permanent settlements on the Continent were Normandy in France and the area of European Russia that became the Kievan kingdom.

were small and confined their activities to plundering isolated monasteries and the open countryside. But in 841 a large fleet ran into the mouth of the Seine and plundered the city of Rouen. Two years later another strong Viking force sailed up the Loire to Nantes, took the town by storm, slaughtered the inhabitants, and plundered and burned the city. Then, instead of returning home for the winter as they always had before, the Northmen landed on the island of Noirmoutier and spent the winter there. In 851 a Danish fleet established its winter quarters on the isle of Thanet in the estuary of the Thames. Thus began a new phase of the Viking invasions: they were no longer mere summer raiders, but permanent scourges with well-established bases.

From their base off the mouth of the Loire, the Vikings intensified their operations in France. In 844 they ravaged the valley of the Garonne, moved on south to the coast of Spain, and eventually sacked Seville. The next year they plundered the valley of the Loire. By 857 Bordeaux, Tours, Blois, Orleans, Poiters, and Paris had been sacked one or more times. Then in 859 a Viking fleet sailed south, plundered the coasts of Spain, passed through the straits of Gibraltar, raided Morocco and the Balearic Islands, and finally camped for the winter in the delta of the Rhone, in southern France. From there they ravaged the Rhone valley as far north as Valence. By 862 this fleet had returned to its base in the Loire. In 872 the Loire Vikings captured Angers and for some years used it as their headquarters. By 880 the western part of France had been thoroughly ravaged many times, and the Vikings were looking for fresh regions to plunder. In 885 a great fleet sailed up the Seine bound for eastern France. When it arrived before Paris, it offered to spare the city if the garrison would allow it free passage up the river. But the count of Paris refused the offer, and the result was a two-year siege of the city that ended only with the arrival of the emperor Charles the Fat (884–887) with a strong German army. Unfortunately, the emperor was at odds with the Burgundians and cheerfully allowed the Vikings to plunder that region.

Even if the successors of Charlemagne had been united and had devoted all their energy and resources to the defense of the realm, it seems unlikely that they could have checked the Vikings effectively. The Norse bands were highly mobile, and one place was just as satisfactory to plunder as another. When they found a town well garrisoned, they usually simply went around it, and they rarely risked battle with strong armed forces. An invader who seeks to conquer and hold a region can be met by defending key strategic points, but mere plunderers are almost impossible to cope with. Not until the early tenth century did the Franks discover an effective device—meeting Vikings with Vikings.

In 911 Charles the Simple, king of the West Franks (893–923), granted to the Viking leader Rollo the land around the mouth of the Seine. Later this grant was enlarged until it included all the region since known as Normandy. In return, Rollo became a Christian and nominally the king's vassal.* The establishment of Rollo in Normandy effectively protected France from Viking raids along the Channel coast and gave the West Frankish kings valuable allies to help them in the Loire valley. Although raids on the Loire and southern France continued for some twenty years after 911, the Viking invasions came to an end then.

During the second half of the ninth century, England had suffered even more severely than France. In 870 the Danes had conquered East Anglia. In 876 they occupied Northumbria, and in 877, most of Mercia. While the Vikings plundered according to their custom, these were no mere raids, but serious attempts to conquer the country. The

*Sources, no. 31

Anglo-Saxon resistance was organized and led by Alfred (871–899), king of Wessex. For a time it looked as if Alfred's cause was hopeless, but by 885 he had checked the Danes so successfully that they were willing to make peace. The lands south of the Thames remained directly under Alfred's rule, while western Mercia became an Anglo-Saxon duchy allied to Wessex. The Danes retained East Anglia, eastern Mercia, and the region now embraced in the counties of Lincolnshire and Yorkshire. This region was known as the Danelaw. As part of the peace settlement, Alfred insisted that the Danes accept Christianity, and this made possible the eventual assimilation of the Danish settlers into a united kingdom ruled by Anglo-Saxon kings.

The Vikings also swept the northern seas from shore to shore. Early in the ninth century, they attacked Ireland. For some years they were in control of most of the island, but eventually they were forced to retire to the eastern ports—Dublin, Wexford, and Waterford, which were essentially Norse settlements. The isles of the northern seas—the Orkneys, Hebrides, and Shetlands—and the Isle of Man were occupied by Viking colonists. In 874 they made their first settlement on Iceland. Later, adventurers from Iceland went on to Greenland and even to the North American coast. Greenland is still ruled by the king of Denmark and Iceland was until 1944. Until the middle of the thirteenth century, Viking kings ruled Man and the Scottish isles.

The civilization that had been slowly and painfully developed in western Europe during the eighth and early ninth centuries was almost wiped out in the great era of invasions. In the West Frankish state few monasteries had escaped destruction, and most towns had been sacked and burned several times. Great numbers of people had been slaughtered, leaving much land untilled and rapidly turning to forest and waste. The Muslims in Provence harassed communications between France and Italy. Although the Magyar raids in the East Frankish state did not extend over so long a period as those of the Norsemen in the west, they were extremely destructive. It was in the process of recovery from this deep slough that the medieval civilization of western Europe was developed.

READING SUGGESTIONS

* *B. Tierney,* Sources *and* Readings, *vol. I, nos. 26, 27–29; vol. II, no. 6.*

Several of the works already cited are especially useful for the Carolingian period. On the general historical background, see the books of * Moss and * Dawson cited in Chapter I, and of * Wallace-Hadrill cited in Chapter III. On economic conditions see the works of Dopsch and Latouche cited in Chapter II; and on literature, those of * Laistner and * Kerr cited in Chapter III.

* R. Winston, *Charlemagne: From the Hammer to the Cross* (Indianapolis, 1954) is a popular biography. The classic account of Charlemagne as founder of a new empire is * J. Bryce. *The Holy Roman Empire* (London, 1904). More recent interpretations of Charlemagne's coronation are presented in * R. E. Sullivan (ed.), *The Coronation of Charlemagne: What Did It Signify?* (Boston, 1959).

Two good surveys are * H. Fichtenau, *The Carolingian Empire* (Oxford, 1957), and F. L. Ganshof, *Frankish Institutions Under Charlemagne* (Providence, RI, 1968). On Carolingian culture, see W. Levison, *England and the Continent in the Eighth Century* (Oxford, 1946); E. S. Duckett, *Alcuin, Friend of Charlemagne* (New York, 1951), and *Carolingian Portraits: A Study in the Ninth Century* (Ann Arbor, MI, 1962); * Helen Waddell, *The Wandering Scholars* (London, 1927); L. Wallach, *Alcuin and Charlemagne* (Ithaca, NY, 1959), a more technical study than Duckett's; * R. Hinks, *Carolingian Art* (Ann Arbor, MI, 1962); E. A. Lowe in *The Legacy of the Middle Ages,* C. G. Crump and E. F. Jacob (eds.) (Oxford, 1926). W. Horn, *The Plan of St. Gall* (Berkeley, 1979) is a splendidly illustrated work on monastic life and culture. For social history see * P. Riché, *Daily Life in the World of Charlemagne* (Philadelphia, 1978) and S. F. Wemple, * *Women in Frankish Society: Marriage and the Cloister* (Philadelphia, 1981). Economic issues are discussed in R. Hodges and D. Whitehouse, *Mohammed, Charlemagne, and the Origins of Europe: Archeology and the Pirenne Thesis* (Ithaca, NY, 1983). W. Ullmann, cited in Chapter IV, and K. Morrison, *The Two Kingdoms: Ecclesiology in Carolingian Political Thought* (Princeton, 1964) discuss ecclesiastical institutions. See also R. McKitterick, *The Frankish Church and the Carolingian Reforms, 789–895* (London, 1977). * Einhard's *Life of Charlemagne* has been well translated by S. E. Turner (New York, 1880). See also * *Carolingian Chronicles,* B. W. Scholz (trans.) (Ann Arbor, MI, 1970).

On the Vikings, see P. Sawyer, *the Age of the Vikings* (London, 1962) and * *Kings and Vikings: Scandinavia and Europe, A.D. 700–1100* (London, 1982); * J. Brøndsted, *The Vikings* (Harmondsworth, 1960); D. M. Wilson and O. Klindt-Jensen, *Viking Art* (Ithaca, NY, 1966). Their trading activities are discussed in A. Lewis, *The Northern Seas, A.D. 300–1100* (Princeton, 1958), and their settlement in Russia in S. Vernadsky, *Kievan Russia* (New Haven, CT, 1948). For the Magyar invasions, see C. A. Macartney, *The Magyars in the Ninth Century* (Cambridge, 1930).

EARLY MEDIEVAL EUROPE: A NEW SOCIETY

chapter

VIII

The Feudal World

The era of the Norse, Muslim, and Magyar invasions brought to an end the period of transition from Roman to medieval civilization. The ruins of Charlemagne's empire served as a seedbed for medieval institutions. When driven to the edge of bare survival, the people of western Europe displayed an extraordinary resilience. Under the threat of external invasions, they built up a new kind of political and military system that could beat off future attacks. Under the threat of starvation, they found new ways of working the land that greatly increased agricultural production. When their religion seemed sunk in corruption, they engendered a powerful new movement of reform. Through these achievements the men of the ninth, tenth, and eleventh centuries created the material and spiritual foundations for a new civilization. We shall consider first their reordering of political and military institutions.

22. *Origins of Feudalism*

Feudalism is a vague word invented by modern historians to describe a complicated pattern of social, military, and political arrangements that grew into existence in the early Middle Ages. The best way to define it is to start out from its etymological origin. Our word "feudalism" is derived from the medieval Latin *feudum,* meaning a fief. In the Middle Ages the word normally designated an estate of land held from a lord in return for military service. A feudal society is one in which nearly all land is held in the form of fiefs or, more generally, a society in which the basic social and political structure is determined by the practice of fief holding. Feudal tenure of land could have these broad implications for the structure of society as a whole because, in a primitive agrarian society, virtually all wealth consisted of land and the immediate produce of the land. Moreover, the relationship between the lord and his tenant was not simply an economic one. The tenant was a *vassal* of the lord; that is, he was bound to the lord by a special oath of loyalty. Moreover, a vassal normally exercised rights of jurisdiction in the lands that he held as a fief. He was a governor as well as a tenant.

In discussing the emergence of feudalism, the problem is not just to account for the origins of the different elements of the system. That is not too difficult; all the relevant practices can be traced back to the time of the barbarian invasions of the western empire, and it seems clear that some came from the Germans, some from the Romans. Thus the relationship of sworn loyalty binding a vassal to his lord is most obviously derived from the German *comitatus.* On the other hand, the conditional tenure of land in return for specified services came from late Roman land law. In Frankish Gaul, land so held was called a *benefice* and, although the word *feudum* became more common after the ninth century, the older word *beneficium* continued to be used throughout the Middle Ages to mean a fief. The different elements of feudalism existed then at a very early period. But they existed separately from one another. A warrior who had sworn to fight for a lord did not necessarily hold a benefice from him. Most holders of benefices were not sworn vassals. Rights of jurisdiction were not linked to tenure of land. The main problem for a historian of feudalism is to explain how all these different elements fused together to form a new kind of society in which a vassal as a matter of course held a fief and exercised rights of jurisdiction over it.

One important period in this development was the reign of Charles Martel in the early eighth century, when the Franks first began to use cavalry on a large scale. Infantry were at a disadvantage before horsemen using the stirrup, protected by armor and a shield, and armed with sword and lance. But this equipment was extremely costly, and its effective use required continual practice. To handle a shield, sword, and lance while managing a horse was a feat that could only be achieved by long experience and rigid training. Soldiers of this type had to be rich enough to buy horse and arms and free from the need of working for their living. By the eighth century, the Frankish state had little or no money revenue; the kings and nobles supported themselves, their families, and their households from the produce of their estates. If Charles was to have an army of mounted soldiers, he would have to supply each one with land and labor to cultivate it.

The system devised by Charles was the natural product of the customs and conditions of the time. He enlisted able warriors and had them swear absolute fidelity to him. They became his *vassi dominici,* vassals of the lord. To each one he granted a *beneficium,* an estate large enough to support him, which he could hold as long as he served Charles well as a soldier. But it was difficult to find enough land to supply as many benefices as were needed. Charles undoubtedly used the royal estates for this purpose, but to do so too extensively would seriously weaken the resources of the government. Soon Charles was looking with a greedy eye on the vast lands of the church. The church was accustomed to grant out its land in benefices. Why should it not do so to his soldiers? Charles obliged the prelates to grant benefices to men on condition that they serve him as soldiers. Although in theory these benefices were held from the church and remained church land, they actually passed into the control of Charles. When the soldier to whom such a benefice had been given died, Charles granted it to another capable warrior. Thus Charles solved his military problems. He obtained a large force of mounted soldiers who were bound to him by oath and held their lands at his pleasure. In the process the association of vassalage with benefice holding became much more common.

A second decisive phase in the evolution of feudalism came during the breakdown to Charlemagne's empire in the ninth and tenth centuries. The savage civil wars between Louis the Pious and his sons, continued after Louis' death between the brothers Lothair, Louis the German, and Charles the Bald, were in themselves enough to create a period of near anarchy in which armed force was the only effective law. The intensification of this internal confusion by Viking, Muslim, and Magyar raids produced an era that was the heyday of the warrior. No village, cathedral city, or monastic establishment was safe unless adequately protected by armed men. The peasant could not till his fields nor the priest say mass in his church without the aid of the soldier. Moreover, the soldier most in demand was the armored cavalryman. Although the armor of the ninth century was comparatively light—usually rings of metal sewn on a long shirt of leather or cloth—it could usually turn any strokes inflicted by an infantryman. And the tremendous striking power of the horseman rising in his stirrups placed the foot soldier almost completely at his mercy. In the Latin writings of the ninth century, the mounted warrior was called simply *miles,* or soldier. Later, in French, he was designated *chevalier,* or horseman. We shall use the equivalent English term, *knight.*

During the confusion of the ninth century, two processes contributed to the emergence of a new powerful class of feudal lords. On the one hand, there was constant alienation of royal rights from above; on the other, a process of voluntary submission by lesser folk from below. In the civil wars, rival kings had to bargain for the support of the most effective warriors and frequently bribed them with grants of royal land, which were held as fiefs in return for specified services. If a lord undertook to provide, say, fifty knights for the king's armies, he would probably create subfiefs out of his own great holding to support the knights. In the process, the lord often acquired rights of government over his lands. This could happen in various ways. In the Frankish state, political and judicial power had been wielded by counts, but the Frankish kings had often granted "immunity" to the greater ecclesiastical establishments. This meant that the count and his officers could not enter the church's lands. At first, in all probability, the arrangement was simply that the landholder arrested criminals and turned them over to the count, but by the ninth century, most possessors of immunity were judging and punishing their own men. When, as commonly happened in the ninth century, feudal lords took over the protection of church lands, they took over these rights too.* Again, the political powers of a count were sometimes granted by kings to their greater vassals along with the grant of land. Finally, it was hard to prevent any powerful lord from usurping these powers whether he had any real right to them or not. By the end of the tenth century, the rights of government were widely dispersed among the landholding class. An important lord would have full rights of jurisdiction over the men who lived on his lands; a less important one, partial rights. The distinction lay in whether or not a lord could inflict capital punishment. If he could, he had what was later called "high justice." The possession of a gallows was considered an important symbol of rank and prestige.

The second process that we mentioned, voluntary submission to great feudal lords by lesser men, was stimulated by the general disorder of the times and especially by the Viking raids. The old Frankish military system was singularly ill-adapted to cope with such attacks. Traditionally, a great host assembled from all parts of the kingdom on a fixed day in early summer and then moved off to wage the regular summer campaign. By the time such an army had assembled, the Vikings would have completed their raids and be out to sea again in their longboats. If there were to be any effective protection against them, it had to be locally improvised. This was an important factor in stimulating political decentralization. The ordinary freeman in these circumstances had little choice. He could accept the protection of a knight and sink to the status of a serf, or he might strive to become a knight himself. But even the more substantial freeman who was capable of fighting and had enough property to support himself as a knight still could not hope to defend his property alone. Very commonly he would surrender his land to a more powerful man, receive it back from him as a fief, and become his vassal.

Thus, during the ninth century, there developed a hierarchy of lords and vassals. The simple knight who had just enough land and peasant labor to support him and his family was the vassal of a larger landholder, who in turn would be the vassal of a still mightier man—perhaps of a count. The count might be the vassal of a greater count, of a duke, or of the king. In short, a great pyramid was formed with the king at the top and the ordinary knight at the bottom. In the ninth century, this structure was not complete, nor did it cover all the Carolingian realm. It developed most rapidly in the West Frankish state—the France of today—and in Lorraine and Franconia. But even in these regions it was not all-embracing. Lands held in full ownership, called *allods* in contemporary records, were numerous until the twelfth century and persisted in some regions throughout the Middle Ages. Nevertheless, in northern France at least, allods were rare by the end of the eleventh century, and the dictum dear to feudal lawyers, "no land without a lord," was in general accurate. In later chapters we shall see how feudal patterns of tenure spread to England, Spain, Germany, Sicily, and the eastern Mediterranean.

*Sources, no. 32

23. *Feudal Obligations and Feudal Politics*

During the period in which the feudal hierarchy was taking form, the relationships between lords and vassals underwent profound changes. The most important of these was the transformation of the benefice from a revocable or at best a lifetime grant into a hereditary one. The basic reason for this development must have been the extreme difficulty of preventing an adult son of a vassal from taking over the family benefice. When Charles the Bald was about to set out for Rome to assume the imperial crown, he decreed that if a royal vassal died during his absence, the vassal's son should hold the benefice until his return.* While lack of material makes it impossible to follow the process in detail, it is clear that, by the tenth century, most benefices were hereditary. The prevailing system of inheritance was *primogeniture;* that is, the eldest son inherited his father's fief. As long as the benefice was a revocable grant, the obligations of the vassal must have been essentially determined by the lord's will; but when the benefice became transformed into the hereditary fief, these obligations were governed by a mutual contract. No longer could a lord take back a benefice whenever he saw fit; he could do so only if the vassal violated the contract. It became customary for the relationship between lord and vassals to be determined by the assembled vassals sitting under the presidency of the lord. As a result, each fief had its own customs.

Historians often write of a "feudal system," and we need some such expression to describe a whole set of relationships, centering on the fief, which were characteristic of medieval society. But it is important to bear in mind that real-life feudalism was anything but systematic. Feudalism grew up in a haphazard fashion. Feudal practices varied from time to time and from place to place. Commonly used phrases like "feudal law," "feudal custom," or "the feudal system" can give a false impression if they are taken to refer to a uniform pattern of organization existing all over Europe all through the Middle Ages. What really existed was the custom of a particular fief at a particular time, and rarely were the customs of two fiefs exactly alike, even in France. The precise degree of jurisdiction possessed by a vassal, the particular services owed to a lord, the detailed rules of inheritance—these things varied from fief to fief. Moreover, when feudalism spread to other regions, its workings were complicated by preexisting local conditions, for example, by the survival of Anglo-Saxon institutions in England and of Byzantine administrative traditions in Sicily. Modern research has been much concerned with the investigation of these regional variations.

But, when all this is understood, it remains true that certain feudal practices, which originated mainly in northern France, had spread through much of the medieval world by the twelfth century. The description of feudal obligations in the next few paragraphs is simply an account of these more common practices of feudal society.

*Sources, no. 32

The basic purpose of the feudal relationship was cooperation in war. The chief function of the lord was to protect his vassals and their lands, and theirs was to serve in his army. In the early days when Viking raids harassed the land and general anarchy reigned, there was probably no limit to the military service owed by the vassal to his lord. He joined his lord's army whenever he was summoned. But as time went on, the vassals began to distinguish between two types of war—offensive and defensive. When the lord's fief was being invaded, his vassals were obliged to serve him until the enemy was driven off. On the other hand, when the lord was engaged in plundering his neighbors' lands or trying to add another castle or village to his possessions, the vassals were inclined to limit their obligations. As a rule, forty days a year became the maximum time that a vassal had to serve in an offensive operation. It is interesting to notice that this period just about covers the time of pleasant summer weather between spring planting and the harvest. In some fiefs, the vassal had to serve forty days at his own cost and another forty if the lord fed him and his horse. In others, the period of service was thirty days or even less. But everywhere there was the distinction between the defense of the fief and raids on neighbors.

Closely related to the obligation to serve in the lord's army in the field was the duty of acting as a member of the garrison of the lord's castle. In the tenth century, most castles were motte and bailey fortresses. These were made by digging a ditch, usually about ten feet deep and thirty feet wide, and piling the dirt into an artificial mound. The edge of the ditch and the top of the mound were fortified with wooden palisades. On the summit of the mound inside the stockade stood a wooden tower. Usually shallower and narrower ditches with stockades would enclose one or two areas at the foot of the mound. The mound was the *motte*, and the other enclosed areas, the *baileys*. The lord and his household lived in the tower on the motte. The baileys held the stables and other outbuildings and served as a place of refuge for the peasants, their families, and stock, in case of danger. By the eleventh century, every lord of any importance had at least one of these castles, and his vassals were expected to supply the garrison. This duty, call *castle-guard*, differed greatly from fief to fief. A petty lord with only a few vassals might arrange to have one of them always on duty in the castle to command the household knights and peasants in its defense. A great lord with many vassals could provide a strong permanent garrison. Thus the lord of the great barony of Richmond in England divided his 186 knights into six groups, each of which served two months in the castle. This was probably an unusually heavy castle-guard service. It seems likely that as a rule the vassal's garrison duty was limited to thirty or forty days.

Next to military service, the most important obligation of a vassal to his lord was to attend the latter's court when summoned. Such attendance could be for a number of purposes. The necessity of taking counsel before taking any significant step was deeply inbedded in the ideas of the Middle Ages. It is particularly noticeable in the monastic rules, where the abbot was directed to ask the advice of his monks before doing anything of interest to the congregation as a whole. It was also a basic feature of feudal custom. The lord and his vassals were partners in the fief, and what affected its welfare was of interest to all. Before the lord chose a wife for himself or his son or a husband for his daughter, he was expected to seek the counsel of his vassals. If he planned to go on a crusade or to wage war on a neighbor, he first asked his vassals' advice. In short, it was customary for a lord to seek counsel on any question of interest to the fief as a whole and it was practically necessary if he had in mind a project that required his men's assistance. Hence the obligation to give honest advice to his lord was an important duty of the vassal.

The assembled vassals in the lord's court decided any disputes that arose between lord and vassal or between two vassals. If the lord charged a vassal with failing to fulfill his obligations to him, the question was heard in the lord's court. The same procedure applied when a vassal accused his lord of an offense against him. When such questions as who was the rightful heir to a fief arose, they came before this same court. It was the lord's court that gradually built up the feudal custom of the fief. But even if the lord needed no advice and had no cases to try, he could summon his vassals "to do him honor." The status of a member of the feudal hierarchy was determined chiefly by the number of men who were ready to follow him to battle. When the writers of romances wanted to indicate a man's importance, they told how many vassals stood behind him on a state occasion. It was the duty of the vassals to bolster their lord's prestige by attending him when he summoned them.

Although military and court service were the two active obligations of vassals in general, a lord might grant a fief in return for other types of service. The chief officers of the lord's household, his seneschal, constable, marshal, and sometimes the chamberlain and butler, held fiefs as compensation. The constable of a castle might have a fief to support him. Such officers as foresters were usually holders of fiefs. The king of England granted a fief to a man as compensation for being "marshal of the prostitutes who follow the court." There are many cases of grants to a cook. In short, in the early days of feudalism, a lord had but two means of paying his officials and servants. He could feed and clothe a man in his household or grant him a fief for his support. The feudal lawyers of the thirteenth century were inclined to make a distinction between those fiefs granted officials and servants and those given for the normal feudal services. The fief given to the official or servant was called a *serjeanty.* There is, however, no evidence that this distinction existed in the early times; such fiefs were a vital part of feudal organization.

In addition to the basic feudal services, the vassal had other obligations to his lord. One of these was called *relief.* In all probability, relief originated in payments made to secure the renewal of the grant at the death of either lord or vassal, before benefices became hereditary. When the hereditary fief developed, relief became a feudal obligation. There is evidence that orginally relief was due when either lord or vassal died, but by the eleventh century it was usually demanded only when an heir succeeded to a fief. Apparently it was most often paid in military equipment—the arms and armor of the late vassal. By the twelfth century, it was paid in money. No general rule laid down the amount that could be demanded, but there is evidence that a sum equal to the revenue of the fief for a year was commonly considered about right.

Another obligation of the vassal was known as *aid.* When a lord needed extra resources, he naturally sought them from his vassals. If the lord was captured by his foes, it was the duty of his vassals to raise his ransom. The knighting of the lord's eldest son and the wedding of his eldest daughter were occasions for expensive festivities. The vassals were required to contribute to the cost of these affairs. Perhaps at first the vassals simply supplied food and wine, but later a money payment was customary. Then if a lord planned to go on a crusade, build a new castle, or do anything that cost more than he could afford, he was inclined to ask his vassals to contribute.

Although relief and aid were the only economic services that were common to the vassals of all fiefs, the duty of offering hospitality to the lord was widely prevalent. At first this was probably unrestricted—the vassal was expected to entertain his lord and the lord's followers whenever the lord chose to visit him. But, as time went on, this obligation tended to be strictly limited. The lord could visit a vassal a certain number of times a year, for a certain length of time, with a fixed number of followers mounted on a fixed number of horses. In some cases the menus for both men and beasts were set by agreement, or by custom.

In addition to the feudal services, the lord had certain rights over the vassal and his fief that grew out of the basic nature of the feudal relationship. When the daughter of a vassal married, she carried to her husband as her marriage portion some part of her father's fief, and thus gave him an interest and a foothold in the lord's lands. No lord could be expected to permit an enemy to secure such a position. Hence the vassal was bound to secure the lord's approval of his future son-in-law. If a vassal died leaving a son too young to fight or an unmarried daughter, there was no one to perform the service due from the fief. The lord then had the right to demand that some male have custody of the fief and perform the service. Often the lord himself would take custody of the heir and his lands. In the case of a male heir, he held the fief until the boy came of age. In the case of a female, it was the lord's duty to find her a husband who could perform the service owed him from the fief. This, as a matter of fact, was one of a feudal lord's most cherished privileges. He always had young knights in his household who were eager for fiefs, and from the lord's point of view the easiest way to satisfy such a desire was to grant his knights an heiress in marriage. This was almost the only way a landless knight could hope to become a man of importance.

When a vassal died leaving no one whom the lord and his court would recognize as his heir, the fief passed into the lord's possession by what was called *escheat.* If a vassal were condemned in the lord's court for violating his obligations, the fief could be declared forfeit. This did not happen very frequently, for the assembled vassals were reluctant to condemn anyone to forfeit his fief. Each vassal realized that he might some day find himself in a similar difficulty.

So far we have been discussing the material obligations of a vassal to his lord, but it is important to remember that personal duties played a vital part in the feudal relationship. A vassal was bound to be completely loyal to his lord, to do everything possible for his benefit and nothing that might harm him.* The most serious crime a vassal could commit was to wound or slay his lord. To seduce the lord's wife or eldest daughter was almost equally grave an offense. While younger daughters were rarely mentioned by feudal lawyers, it was probably considered bad taste for a vassal to seduce them. The vassal was expected to guard his lord and his lord's family as carefully as he did his own.

The relationship between a lord and his vassals was a mutual one; each had obligations to the other. On the material side, the lord had one all-important duty to his vassal. He was obliged to protect the vassal and his fief from all foes outside the lord's own fief. The lord was also bound to "do justice" to his vassal in his court. If a vassal believed his lord was mistreating him and demanded a hearing before his fellow vassals, it was his lord's duty to grant it. The lord was also bound to respect the family and personal interests of his vassals. If a lord failed to fulfill his obligations to a vassal, the vassal could *defy* him—that is, declare that he was no longer his vassal. It was quite common for a vassal to renounce his lord because his lord had failed to protect him or his fief, and defiance for denial of justice was reasonably frequent. The lord would then declare the fief forfeit; the vassal would maintain that he had every right to retain it since it was the lord who had defaulted on his obligations; and the issue would be settled by war. Since the defiance of a lord by his vassal meant war, as a rule a vassal made sure of the support of some enemy of his lord before he risked formal defiance.

The relationship between lord and vassal was inaugurated in a solemn ceremony known as swearing *fidelity* and doing *homage.* The vassal knelt before the lord, placed his hands between the lord's, and swore to be a faithful vassal and to perform the services due from the fief. The rite might be concluded with a ceremonial kiss. Often the lord gave the vassal a clod of earth as a symbol of the granting of the fief. Historians have tried to distinguish between fidelity and homage, but without any great success. The most common hypothesis is that fidelity established the personal relationship, whereas homage was done for the fief and involved the promise to perform the customary services. This view is supported by the fact that prelates who could not with propriety do military service admitted their obligation to swear fidelity but usually refused to do homage. On the other hand, it seems clear that homage was performed at times when no fief was involved. When a knight joined the household of a lord to serve him in return for

*Sources, no. 33

food and clothing, he commonly swore fidelity and did homage. In short, swearing fidelity and doing homage ordinarily went together. When they were separated, the significance of each was probably interpreted according to the tastes of the parties involved and the custom of the fief in question.

Although it is conceivable that in the early days of the feudal system a vassal was expected to have only one lord, this situation cannot have endured very long. If a man received land as a marriage portion with his wife, he became the vassal of the head of his wife's family. A younger son might go forth, take service with a lord other than his father's, receive a fief from him, and eventually inherit the original family fief. Then a lord was inclined to buy the friendship and aid of powerful neighbors by granting them fiefs. Open conquest was often politely covered by the performance of homage. Thus, when the count of Anjou drove the count of Blois from Touraine, he did homage to the count of Blois for the conquered territory. He continued to hold his county of Anjou from the king.

By the twelfth century, most important landholders were vassals of several lords. The count of Champagne was vassal to the king of France, the duke of Burgundy, the Holy Roman Emperor, the archbishops of Reims and Sens, and the bishops of Langres, Chalons, Autun, and Auxerre because he held fiefs from all of them. Among his vassals were men who held fiefs of the king and some eighty other lords. These complexities in the feudal system could obviously be a source of considerable confusion, especially when two of a man's lords were at war with each other. Hence, as time went on, a new conception was developed: that of *liege* homage. A man did liege homage to one lord and his personal services were due to him. To his other lords he simply rendered the services owed by his fief. Thus the count of Anjou was the liege vassal of the king of France. If the king and the count of Blois were at war, he was expected to serve the king in person and to send a suitable contingent to serve the count of Blois.

The feudal relationship was probably the most important one among members of the warrior class, but there was another tie which requires mention. We have seen how early Germanic society was united by bonds of kinship and lordship. In the feudal age, although lordship became so important, kinship never ceased to be significant. Family connections played a vital part in medieval politics. When a lord went to war, he relied fully as much on his *lignage,* his relatives, as upon his vassals. Alliances among lords who had no feudal relations were commonly based on family connections. Members of a family often united to procure the advancement of the whole group. Thus the members of the house of Clare, high in favor with King Henry I, obtained a dominant position in England early in the twelfth century; and a hundred years later this same family formed the backbone of the resistance to King John. In short, a comparatively minor baron whose resources in lands and vassals were slight might be a man of great power through his relatives. Brothers and cousins might quarrel bitterly and wage war against one another enthusiastically, but they could usually be relied on to combine against the outside world.

There is one further aspect of feudal society that must be considered here. Feudalism was not merely a cluster of institutions with quaint names. It was a way of organizing the political life of a region; it actually functioned as a structure of government. Feudal institutions first grew up in France at a time when the country faced almost complete anarchy. The question naturally arises as to how effective they were as a means for keeping order. Certainly feudalism had grievous imperfections when considered as a system for keeping the peace. The most obvious one is that the whole point of the system was to maintain a large class of professional warriors who thoroughly enjoyed fighting. Also, in early feudal society there was commonly a lack of effective centralized power. In theory, the whole pyramid of loyalties culminated in the king; in practice, the king of France, for example, was an almost powerless figurehead in the tenth century. At what stage in the hierarchy was a man most independent of those above him and most fully able to rule as he saw fit? Until the latter part of the twelfth century, this position was occupied by the lowest man in the scale able to build and garrison a strong castle. Even a motte and bailey castle was expensive in terms of labor and could only be built by a lord with adequate resources. Then only the lord of a fair number of knights could garrison a stronghold through the castle-guard obligations of his vassals. The lord who could have a strong and adequately garrisoned castle was in an excellent position. If such a stronghold was defended with any resolution, it was impossible to capture it during the forty days that a feudal host could ordinarily be kept in the field. Thus the holder of a castle who defied his lord could usually escape any serious consequences by shutting himself up in his fortress. At the same time, his vassals who did not possess castles were largely at his mercy. In eleventh-century France, the term *baron* usually marked the owner of a castle, and high justice and possession of a castle were likely to go together. The virtually independent feudal states that were emerging in tenth-century France usually corresponded in size to the area that could be dominated by mounted men operating out of such fortified strongholds.

At first glance, it is the disorder, the near anarchy of early feudal society that most impresses a historian. But there is another way of looking at the situation. If we consider the state of France at the time when Charlemagne's empire was disintegrating and the Viking attacks were multiplying, then the growth of the major fiefs can be seen as a process of constructive state building. The feudal principalities provided effective units for defense against the Vikings. Their emergence prevented a total collapse of society into a condition of "war of all against all." They established small-scale but relatively ordered, disciplined units of government, which could eventually be welded into a broader unity.

The growth of feudal monarchies that were strong enough to exercise real, effective control over the great vassals of a kingdom was a slow and difficult process. The fact that fiefs were hereditary meant that a king could not choose whom he wanted to govern the provinces of his kingdom. The concentration of military, political, and economic power in the hands of a single lord encouraged the development of autonomous feudal states. In case of conflict, the average knight was likely to feel more loyalty to the lord immediately above him in the feudal hierarchy than to a remote king. These problems were formidable but not insuperable, given a succession of able and strong-willed rulers. A feudal king who wanted to be an effective monarch had to have at his own immediate command enough power and wealth to coerce the greatest of his vassals or any likely combination of them. He had to build up structures of government based on appointed officials rather than on hereditary fief holders. He had to insist that loyalty to the king took precedence over all other loyalties. We shall see in later chapters how some medieval kings succeeded in achieving all these things while others failed.

24. *Feudal Families*

Between the time of the Germanic invasions and the emergence of a feudal society in the tenth and eleventh centuries major changes occurred in the family structures and inheritance practices of the aristocratic classes. Some of them were due to ecclesiastical influences, some to secular ones.

Through the centuries the church persistently opposed the polygyny and concubinage common among the Frankish lords,* upholding instead a Christian idea of life-long monogamous marriage with fidelity of *both* partners to the marriage vows. The church also tried to restrict the choice of spouses severely by forbidding marriage within seven degrees of consanguinity. That is to say, if a man and woman had a common ancestor in the past seven generations, they could not legally marry. (Eventually, the rule was changed by the Fourth Lateran Council to a more practicable four degrees.) Various reasons have been put forward to explain these policies of the church. According to one argument, the pattern of monogamy and exogamy (marriage outside the kin) prevented the consolidation of vast estates within one family; and the greater diffusion of property, it is suggested, increased the probability that land would be bequeathed to the church. Another suggestion is that the church's regulations encouraged a more equitable distribution of women in the society; if elite males retained numerous women in their households then obviously other men would have less chance of finding a wife. From still another point of view it has been argued that the church's hostility to concubinage reduced the chances of lower-class women improving their status by becoming members of a royal or noble household.

Probably all these changes occurred to some extent. But it would

*See p. 101.

be fanciful to suppose that any church leaders deliberately planned such far-reaching economic and sociological consequences of their decrees. The policy of the church regarding marriage can be more simply explained as an ongoing attempt to impose its own severe sexual morality on a rather unreceptive society. The medieval church was inclined to regard all sexual activity as a kind of impurity, something to be restrained as far as possible. So celibacy was prescribed for the higher clergy and monogamy for lay people; and celibacy was always presented as the more perfect way of life. The licitness of sexual activity in marriage was accepted, but rather grudgingly. One of the church fathers, St. Jerome, wrote that a man who was too ardent a lover of his own wife was like an adulterer. In the ninth century Bishop Jonas of Orleans was asked at what times married couples should abstain from sexual relations. He suggested, among other restrictions, forty days before Christmas, forty days before Easter, eight days after Pentecost, every Sunday, Wednesday, and Friday, the eve of all great feasts, and five days before taking communion. This did not leave the married couple a great deal of opportunity; there are only 365 days in the year.

Evidently a great gap existed between the ideal of the church and the realities of medieval society. Around 800, Charlemagne still had acknowledged concubines and illegitimate children from them, for all of whom he made handsome provision. And there is no reason to suppose that many married couples even tried to follow the regimen of bishop Jonas. But gradually, over the course of centuries, the church's teaching did modify standards of behavior, at least as regards what was publicly acceptable. In the feudal era, a lord might have casual affairs with prostitutes or other women. If he had illegitimate children he would probably acknowledge them without any particular embarrassment. But he had only one lawful wife, and he did not keep a group of concubines in his castle on a more or less equal footing with the wife.

Other changes in family relationships grew out of the feudal ethos itself, especially the desire to safeguard the unity of the fief and to pass it on intact from generation to generation. This led to the system of inheritance already mentioned, called *primogeniture;* that is, the eldest son inherited all of his father's estate. (Earlier codes of law, both Roman and Germanic, had taken it for granted that all the children, or at least all the sons, would share in the inheritance.) Also, in place of the old, widespread, loose kindred traced through male and female relatives there grew up an emphasis on patrilinear or *agnatic* lineage. When a feudal lord thought of his family connections he thought primarily of his male ancestors who had held the fief before him and passed it on from father to son.

We know, for instance, of a twelfth-century Count Fulk Rechlin of Anjou who traced his ancestry back to the ninth century through a whole series of earlier Fulks. The first count was Fulk the Red (d. 960), who brought substantial new lands to the family through his marriage. He was followed by Fulk the Good (d. 960), a man famed for his piety. Then came Geoffrey Greymantle (d. 987) who acquired a legendary reputation in the *Song of Roland* as a supposed companion of Charlemagne. The next count was Fulk the Black (d. 1040), Fulk Rechlin's grandfather. Of him it is recorded that he built thirteen castles and two monasteries and twice went on crusades to Jerusalem. The story of the counts of Anjou is a typical one of the rise of a great feudal family through acquisition of land, alliance with the church, and extensive castle building. But the immediate point is that when Fulk Rechlin wanted to trace his lineage he was interested only in the patrilinear line of descent. He did not trouble to inquire into his mother's kin or her mother's.

Recent historians have laid great stress on the emergence of the patrilinear lineage. Still, we should remember that the old kinship ties through female relatives did not simply cease to exist even though they were less emphasized. The church still traced kinship through male and female lines in reckoning degrees of consanguinity. If a lord's wife had relations who were rich and powerful, he would probably want to cultivate the kinship ties and perhaps form political alliances with them. But still his central concern was the male line of descent in his own family.

The custom of primogeniture, which preserved the fief intact by passing on all of a lord's estate or nearly all of it to his eldest son, obviously influenced all the other members of the family. A great lord might be able to assign some small properties to his younger sons, sometimes to be held as fiefs from the eldest son. But typically daughters and younger sons were excluded from the inheritance. The daughters were usually provided for by an arranged marriage, or they might enter a convent. By the eleventh century the terms of the "marriage market" had changed, for in feudal society there seem to have been always more marriageable young women than suitable husbands. There were several reasons for this. Young men were often killed in battle; there was a substantial class of celibate clergy, not available as husbands; and, probably most important, younger sons were often not in a position to marry or at least not until late in life. In earlier times a husband had been expected to pay a brideprice for his wife,* but by the eleventh century a bride was expected to take a dowry to her husband. The custom persisted that a wife should be endowed with a part of her husband's estate at the time of the wedding, and if she became a widow she could hold it for life. But to make a suitable marriage, the bride now had to have a dowry of her own. Twelfth-century law books suggested that the husband's marriage settlement and the bride's dowry should be about equal.

Although feudal inheritance practices favored male heirs, women were not altogether excluded. If a man died without leaving a son, his daughter inherited the fief or it was divided among several daughters. A young woman could therefore be a rich heiress, much sought after as a marriage partner. If a lord died leaving unmarried daughters, the right of giving them in marriage passed to his feudal overlord. Similarly if he left a minor son as heir, the overlord became the son's

*See p. 101.

guardian until he was old enough to take over his fief and do homage for it.

A younger son who grew up without an inheritance of his own often entered the service of the king or some great noble, hoping to win fame in battle and eventually be granted a fief. If a boy showed any taste for acquiring the esoteric skills of reading and writing, he might be sent to school, perhaps at the local cathedral, and destined for a career in the church. (Most of the higher clergy came from the noble class.) The happiest outcome of all for a landless knight was to marry an heiress; but only a few lucky ones could achieve that ambition. The desirability of heiresses, and their unattainability most of the time, perhaps contributed to the later cult of chivalry and courtly love, in which the lover adored a noble lady from afar, without much hope of tangible reward.

There was not much courtesy and chivalry about the behavior of a feudal male in the eleventh century. He had one primary function: fighting. His education and his way of life were aimed at fitting him for this occupation. At the age of seven or eight he was sent away from home lest the indulgence of his parents, especially his mother, might soften him. He received his education at some friendly feudal court, usually that of his father's lord or of a relative. For some years he was a page serving the lady of the castle. Any nonmilitary talent he acquired, such as playing a musical instrument or singing, was likely to be gained in these years. At fourteen or fifteen he became a squire and served the lord. He cared for the horses, polished armor, and served his lord at table. He was hardened to the wearing of armor and trained in the use of knightly equipment. When he was considered old enough and adequately prepared, usually when he was about twenty, he was given arms, armor, and horse of his own, and solemnly made a knight. In its simplest form, before the development of chivalric ideas, this ceremony consisted of putting on his new armor, kneeling before a knight—usually the lord who had trained him—and receiving a terrific blow from the knight's fist or the flat of his sword. Once the feudal male had been knighted, he became of age. He could do homage and rule his fief.

The knight's principal occupation and favorite amusement was fighting. If he were a baron, he fought to keep his vassals in hand and to gain what he could from his neighbors. The simple knight who held a fief followed his lord to battle because it was his duty and in the hopes of sharing in the booty. The landless knight fought for his living. War could be extremely profitable. Although plundering peasant villages could rarely have yielded much booty, there was always the chance of capturing another knight and ransoming him. But entirely apart from the chance of profit, it is important to remember that fighting was considered a delightful sport.

When he was living peacefully at home, a feudal lord rose well before dawn, heard mass in his chapel, and got the business of the day out of the way. He consulted with his officials, judged cases, and generally saw to the business of his fief. By dawn he was ready for the really important occupation of the day—hunting. This could take many forms. The most highly esteemed—because it was most like war—was the pursuit on horseback of a stag or wild boar and the slaying of the quarry when the chase was over. Deer, wolves, and wild-cats were hunted in the same manner. A more gentle form of hunting, considered peculiarly suitable for ladies but practiced avidly by their lords as well, was hawking. Here one rode through the green meadows beside a stream with a trained hawk on one's wrist and sent it in pursuit of any game bird that appeared. Hunting formed an extremely important part of a noble's life, and he kept great packs of hunting dogs and many trained hawks, or more properly falcons.

About two or three o'clock in the afternoon, the knight settled down to a good solid meal consisting of course after course of meat and poultry, well reinforced with bread and pastry and washed down with incredible quantities of ale or wine, according to the custom of the country. When he finished this repast, he was in the mood to be entertained. Here tastes differed. King John of England considered a hanging a suitable after-dinner entertainment, but others preferred less gruesome forms. Wandering minstrels came by, ready to display their varied talents. Some were merely storytellers, with a magnificent supply of the types of tales that have amused men of all epochs. Others had with them tumblers, dancing bears, or dancing girls. A few had learned long narrative poems, which they recited.* As the only artificial light available was smoky torches, the knight was likely to go to bed soon after darkness set in.

Needless to say, the knight of the eleventh and early twelfth centuries was no model of gentleness and refinement. He drank himself into a stupor with considerable regularity. If he became annoyed with his opponent during a chess game, he was inclined to brain him with one of the massive chessmen of the day. When a servent was slow in bringing his wine, he threw a javelin at him to speed his steps. If his wife annoyed him, he beat her savagely. In one contemporary tale, there is a scene where a wife suggests to her husband that it is not quite the thing to murder a guest while he is taking a bath. She is promptly knocked down for her trouble.

There was little or no legal restraint on the personal behavior of a member of the feudal class. While he was bound not to injure his lord, his lord's immediate family, his vassal, or his vassal's family, and might have to answer in his lord's court for an offense against a fellow vassal, the feudal system left him entirely free in regard to all other persons. Before the thirteenth century, only feudal custom had any vitality in France; public law was practically nonexistent insofar as nobles were concerned. In an attempt to reduce the disorder in Normandy in 1091, William Rufus and his brother Robert issued a decree directing that if a man wanted to slay his enemy, he should give him fair warning by blowing his horn before attacking him. In England there was an effective public law before which all freemen were equal in theory. In practice, however, the royal officials often ignored

*See p. 462.

Manuscript illumination of a knight receiving a sword from his lord, in this case a king. This illustration, an initial from a Latin bible of the early 14th century, shows the costume and artistic conventions of the later period. *Dean and Chapter of Durham Cathedral, England*

offenses committed by men of importance unless someone equally important complained.

The knight was religious in the sense that he accepted without question the basic teachings of the church and followed the prescribed forms of observance. He heard mass regularly. According to his means, he gave alms and made donations to religious corporations. In general, he was inclined to feel that repentance and atonement were far easier than virtue. He did much as he pleased and make generous gifts to the church. Perhaps he even went on a long pilgrimage or a crusade. There were few feudal families of any importance that did not found a religious house, and a great baron might have four or five such houses endowed by his family and its vassals. It is impossible to question the knightly zeal for religion and devotion to the church and its teachings, but faith does not seem to have interfered with personal conduct to any extent.

The women of the feudal class shared the characteristics of the men. If we are to believe preachers and storytellers, they were far too fond of drink. In fact, a not uncommon description of a lady in contemporary tales is "the fairest woman who ever drained a bottle." They beat their maidservants, sometimes to the point of death. Of course, their ordinary daily life was less violent. Their work was spinning, sewing (often fine embroidery), and supervision of their households. This last was no light task. In a large castle it meant provisioning and managing all the domestic arrangements of an establishment that could contain hundreds of persons. It was more like managing a large, noisy, boisterous hotel than looking after a modern household.

The status of women in feudal society was extremely complex. Since a woman could not fight, she was always treated as a minor by early feudal custom. She was always in the custody of some man. Before she was married she was in the care of her father. Afterwards, she passed under the authority of her husband. When her husband died, she was in the custody of his lord or her eldest son. She had no rights whatever against her husband, and her person and property were completely under his control. But before bemoaning too much the status of woman in the early feudal epoch, one should compare it with her position in other contemporary societies. The Muslim women were confined in a harem under the supervision of servants, and the Byzantine noble-women were little freer. The feudal lady was completely at the mercy of her husband, but against all others she enjoyed his rank. When a knight was away, his wife ruled his household and his fief. Despite their handicaps, women could and did play an important part in feudal society.

The life of a knight in the eleventh century was simple and crude; he enjoyed little more luxury than the peasants who tilled his fields. A knight had at his disposal a plentiful supply of whatever his lands produced. He could have all the bread and game he could eat and all the ale or wine he could drink. But although his food was unlimited in quantity, it was far from varied. He could also have all the woolen clothes he could wear, but they were fashioned by the comparatively unskilled hands of his wife and her maids. In short, he had more food and clothing than a peasant, but they were of the same general quality.

The knight's castle was extremely simple and must have been most uncomfortable. There were usually two rooms: the hall and the chamber. In the hall the knight did his business with his officials, his vassals, and his peasants. There he ate, on tables made of planks laid across sawhorses. The hall must have been a scene of wild confusion, filled with servants, men-at-arms, guests, and the lord and his family. At night the servants slept in the hall, either on the tables or the floor. The chamber was the private room of the lord and his family. There he entertained guests of high rank. At night the lord, his lady, and their children slept in beds, while their personal servants slept on the chamber floor. Sometimes a great lord had a chapel in his castle. By the twelfth century, a few were so luxurious as to have a dressing room, called a *wardrobe,* attached to the chamber. The castles were cold and drafty. The windows were covered by boards or open. If the castle was of wood—as most were before the thirteenth century—the knight could not have a fire. In a stone castle one could have fire, but as chimneys did not appear until the late twelfth century, the smoke must have been almost unbearable. It seems likely that if we were offered the choice between spending a winter night with the lord or his serf, we might choose the comparatively tight mud hut with the nice warm pigs on the floor.

READING SUGGESTIONS

* *B. Tierney,* Sources *and* Readings, *vol. I, nos. 31–34; vol. II, nos. 8–11.*

* Carl Stephenson, *Mediaeval Feudalism* (Ithaca, NY, 1942) provides a brief, clear introduction. More advanced is * F. L. Ganshof, *Feudalism* (London, 1952), while * Marc Bloch's *Feudal Society* (London, 1961) is a work of fundamental importance. C. Odegaard, *Vassi and Fideles in the Carolingian Empire* (Cambridge, MA, 1945) discusses the origins of feudal lordship, and R. Coulborn (ed.) *Feudalism in History* (Princeton, NJ, 1956) compares Western institutions with those of other feudal societies. On military aspects see J. Beeler, *Warfare in Feudal Europe* (Ithaca, NY, 1971). Important studies on early feudalism will be found in the following collections of essays: C. Stephenson, *Medieval Institutions* (Ithaca, NY, 1954); * S. Thrupp (ed.), *Early Medieval Society* (New York, 1967); R. S. Hoyt (ed.), *Life and Thought in the Early Middle Ages* (Minneapolis, 1965); F. L. Cheyette, *Lordship and Community in Medieval Europe* (New York, 1968). See also * G. Duby, *Warriors and Peasants from the Seventh to the Twelfth Centuries* (Ithaca, NY, 1974) and *The Three Orders, Feudal Society Imagined* (Chicago, 1980). * R. W. Southern, in his very perceptive and far-ranging book, *The Making of the Middle Ages* (London, 1953), treats feudalism as both a social and a political system. * J. R. Strayer, *Feudalism* (New York, 1965) and D. Herlihy, *The History of Feudalism* (New York, 1971) provide good collections of documents. Works dealing with feudal institutions in later periods and in particular countries are given in subsequent reading lists.

chapter

IX

Agriculture and Rural Society

Early medieval society was almost entirely rural and agricultural. The urban life and extensive commerce that had marked the early Roman Empire had been severely damaged by the civil wars of the third century and reduced still further by the Germanic invasions. The Carolingian empire had little trade and probably few, if any, real towns. While there were clusters of houses around cathedrals and royal palaces, the inhabitants lived from the produce of the adjacent fields rather than from industry or commerce. Very little money circulated and, given the state of the economy, little need for it was felt. Men lived directly from the land: food, clothes, and shelter had to be produced in the immediate neighborhood. If there was ever to be a revival of European civilization, it had to start out from this simple agrarian basis.

25. *Peasant Life and Rural Economy*

The rural workers of medieval Europe were a type of peasantry, a form of society that occurs in many cultures at a stage of development between primitive and modern. Peasants are by definition small-scale rural cultivators, living mainly by subsistence agriculture. A peasant society differs from more primitive ones in that the peasants' labor produces a surplus which is used to support a ruling class. It may also support an organized church and a whole superstructure of advanced civilization; but everything depends at bottom on the peasants' labor and the means by which a portion of their output is diverted to support a ruling elite. Peasant societies have some features in common but they also differ from one another in various ways. When we seek to define the characteristics of a particular society, questions like these arise: How did the peasants exploit the land? How did the rulers exploit the peasants? And how did the peasants order their own lives so as to cope with the demands made on them?

Exploitation of the land can be carried on in various ways, each of which has its own advantages and disadvantages. The soil may be worked with hoes by purely human labor, or by draft animals drawing plows. Use of animals obviously multiplies the available power, but it requires that a portion of the produce be set aside to feed the plow teams. Land may be worked very intensively as in the rice paddies of China, with a relatively huge amount of labor devoted to the work of irrigating, fertilizing, and weeding. In such systems we typically find a very high yield per acre but a very small holding of land for each family. Alternatively, cultivation can be carried on less intensively, with lower yields and larger holdings. The system adopted will depend on soil, climate, terrain, density of population, and available technology.

Exploitation of the peasant—the diversion of a part of his produce to support a ruling elite—also takes various forms. Income can be extracted from a peasant population in cash or crops or forced labor. It may go to an administrator of a central government, an official who lives on the tribute of the peasants he rules, or to a local lord who holds a village as a hereditary family estate. In some societies peasant income is appropriated largely by moneylenders.

Beyond the specifically economic relationships, a variety of social arrangements can be found in different peasant cultures. The peasants may live on scattered farms or in organized villages. They may be more or less equal in status or divided into castes so rigorously separated that intermarriage is impossible. They may live in "nuclear families" (a married man and woman with their children) or—this is much more common—in "extended families" (several related nuclear families living together in one household). The land of the village may be held by all the peasants in common (as in the early Russian *mir* system), by large clans, or by individuals. When we discuss the medieval peasants of western Europe in particular, it is useful to consider where they fit into this whole spectrum of possibilities.

Let us begin with the most fundamental features—the patterns of settlement and the ways in which the land was exploited. Western Europe knew two settlement patterns: substantial villages and dispersed settlements where the peasants lived in tiny hamlets or isolated family farms. The "nucleated villages" were more easily defensible, but only the more fertile regions could support such concentrated settlements. Hence the dispersed pattern was widely established in regions of poor soils, such as Scotland, Wales, Cornwall, Brittany, western Normandy, and the central highlands of France. The more fertile lands formed a country of villages.

In the regions of dispersed settlement, the cultivation of the soil was extremely primitive. Each household had a small plot of land close at hand (the *in-field*), which was fertilized with manure from the farm's stock and so could be cultivated continuously. In addition, a section of open land (the *out-field*) was cultivated for a year or two until it became exhausted; then it was abandoned and another plot substituted for it. Wasteland surrounding the arable field was used for grazing. This type of agriculture is usually called *in-field and out-field exploitation.* It is suited to a sparsely populated region of poor soils.

The region where people most commonly lived in villages fell into two great divisions. In the time of Charlemagne, most of England, France north of the river Loire and east of the mouth of the Seine, and the fertile parts of Germany were ordinarily cultivated by what we call *open-field* farming. Each village was surrounded by an unfenced tract of arable land usually divided into two approximately equal parts; one lay fallow each year, while the other was planted. Each field was divided into long, narrow strips by "balks" made with the plow. Typically, each house in the village held a number of scattered strips in each field. South of the river Loire in France and in the Mediterranean region in general, the lands of the village were commonly divided into enclosed rectangular plots, which were nearly square. Each house had several of these plots, and again there was a biennial rotation between fallow and crops.

These patterns of land exploitation were related to the basic climatic conditions of Europe and to the primitive resources of early medieval agricultural technology. In the Mediterranean regions, where rain fell mainly in winter, and the summers were long and dry, a major problem for the farmer was to retain ground moisture throughout the summer. Deep plowing would have increased the rate of evaporation, and so a light scratch plow that merely broke up the surface of the soil was commonly employed. Such plows could be used for repeated criss-cross plowing, and the squarish fields of the south were of a convenient shape for this kind of agriculture. In the north, where rain fell throughout the year, a ridge-and-furrow pattern was desirable to drain off the often excessive summer rainfall. This was achieved by the great, heavy, deep-cutting plow of the Germanic settlers. The use of these plows made possible the cultivation of rich, wet bottom lands, which had been generally neglected by the Romans and Celts. However, the heavy plow needed a team of four to eight oxen to draw it. These cumbersome teams were extremely difficult to turn, and the long, narrow strips characteristic of northern agriculture seem to have been adopted to reduce such turns to a minimum. The need for several oxen to draw the plow also led peasants to pool their animals and so helped to establish the pattern of cooperative village agriculture common in northern Europe. In the south, independently worked family farms formed the basic units of cultivation.

In all parts of Europe medieval farmers encountered one common problem—a shortage of fertilizers. Men knew nothing of crop rotations that could restore nitrogen to the soil. The only fertilizer available was animal manure, and there was never enough of that to keep the land productive if it was repeatedly cropped. The only solution medieval men could find was to "rest" the land periodically. This is why, in both the northern and southern patterns of agriculture that we have described, only half the arable land was cultivated each year, while the other half lay fallow.

An important feature of medieval agriculture was its low yield per acre and per bushel of seed in comparison with results achieved in modern times. By the thirteenth century, when methods of cultivation had improved somewhat over those of earlier times, only the best farmers could harvest ten bushels of wheat from an acre that had been planted with two bushels of seed. In 1850 England was producing twenty-six bushels per acre, and parts of France and Germany were obtaining even better yields. The low yield of medieval times was particularly serious because the grain produced supplied not only the chief food, bread, but in many parts of Europe—such as England—the standard drink. It is estimated that bread and ale shared about equally the English crop. Hence it was necessary to put every possible acre under grain if the population was to be supported. But the growing of good hay requires land as fertile as that used for grain, and in all northern Europe the stock had to be fed during long winter months. As a result, a perpetual problem was the shortage of hay. If the fields were to be cultivated, the plow teams had to be fed, and the teams of from four to eight oxen consumed a large amount of hay. Shortage of hay strictly limited the number of stock other than plow animals that could be kept over the winter, and this, in turn, kept down the amount of manure available.

When one remembers that in addition to lack of fertilization of the land, all sowing was done broadcast to the great benefit of the birds, the low yields per acre are easily understood. On the other hand, holdings of land in early medieval Europe were often large compared with those found in other peasant societies. Medieval peasant agriculture, then, stands at the opposite extreme from the oriental, rice-paddy, type of cultivation. It reflects a situation where a society with a primitive agricultural technology had access to ample resources of raw land because population was very thinly distributed. (In the early twentieth century, Chinese peasant agriculture supported 250 people per square mile; England had about 40 per square mile at the beginning of the twelfth century.)

Let us glance for a moment at the pattern of village life in the region of open-field strip farming. Each house had its garden with a few fruit trees. It also had its strips in the fields and its share of the hay crop. The tenant could turn his stock loose to graze in the common pasture that occupied village lands unfit for the plow. In the village woods, he could pasture his pigs and gather dead wood to burn. If there was a stream, he could fish in it. In short, the economic resources of the peasant were of two sorts: his own garden and his strips in the fields, and his share in the other resources of the village. The village was essentially an agricultural partnership. The villagers plowed together, reaped together, and threshed together. The narrow strips in the open fields made cultivation on an individual basis practically impossible. One person could not sow grain while another pastured his beast on an adjoining, unenclosed strip. Pasture and woods were shared by all under rules established by common consent. The village herdsman looked after the stock of his neighbors as well

A detail from the Luttrell Psalter, ca. 1340, showing broadcast sowing. A dog chases one bird, but another is helping itself from the sack. English, Add. MS. 42130, fol. 170V. *Reproduced by permission of the British Library Board*

as his own. The system was thus thoroughly cooperative, but it was not completely communal. The strips of arable land were held by individual households, and each peasant kept for his own family the produce of his own land.

The peasant's life centered in his village, and he had few, if any, contacts with the world beyond its borders. The lands of the village supplied his food, clothing, and shelter. All these were extremely simple. He lived in a hut made largely of mud with a thatched roof. His clothes were the crude products of unskilled village women. His food was chiefly bread, and his drink ale or wine. The garden behind the hut produced some fruit and vegetables in season, and the woods occasionally supplied nuts and berries. If he was lucky, he had a few chickens. In the autumn when he slaughtered the animals that he could not keep over the winter, he got a little very tough beef. In general, however, the only meat regularly available to him was pork. Pigs could fend for themselves in the woods and pastures in winter and summer. They were thin and tough, but they were edible and cheap to keep. So important was the pig in the village economy that, in the great Domesday survey of England in 1086, the size of a village's woods is expressed by saying how many pigs it could support.

26. *Lords and Peasants: The Medieval Manor*

The agrarian practices of a village community were much the same in England, northern France, and most of Germany; but the political, legal, and social status of its inhabitants differed from region to re-

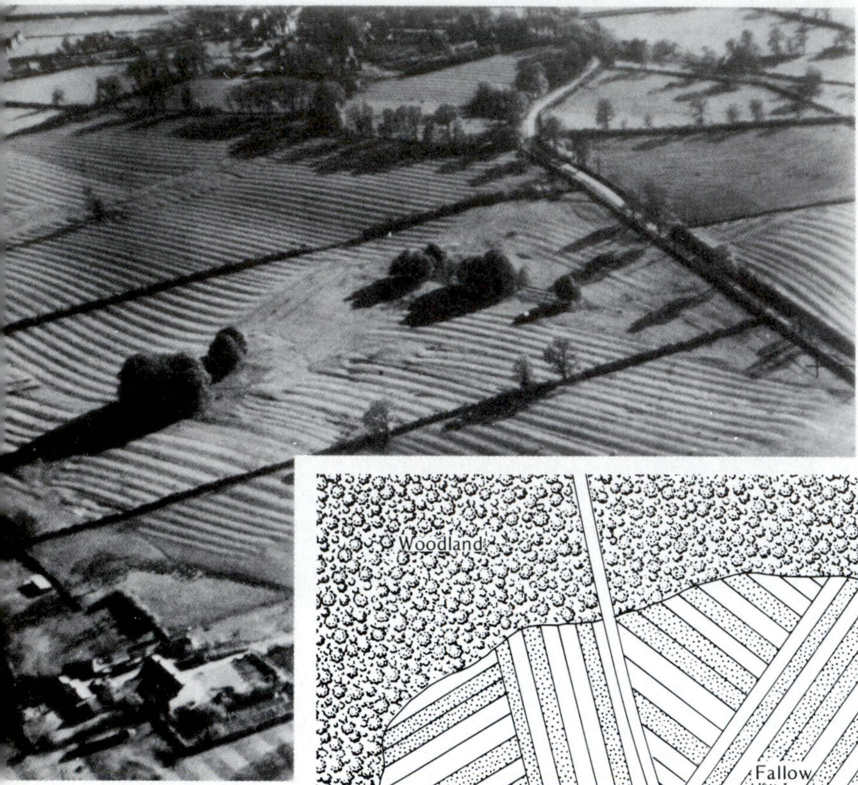

Village of Padbury. The medieval open fields were enclosed in 1796. This aerial photograph shows the old pattern of open-field strips running through the boundaries of the modern fields. *Courtesy Selwyn College, Cambridge University*

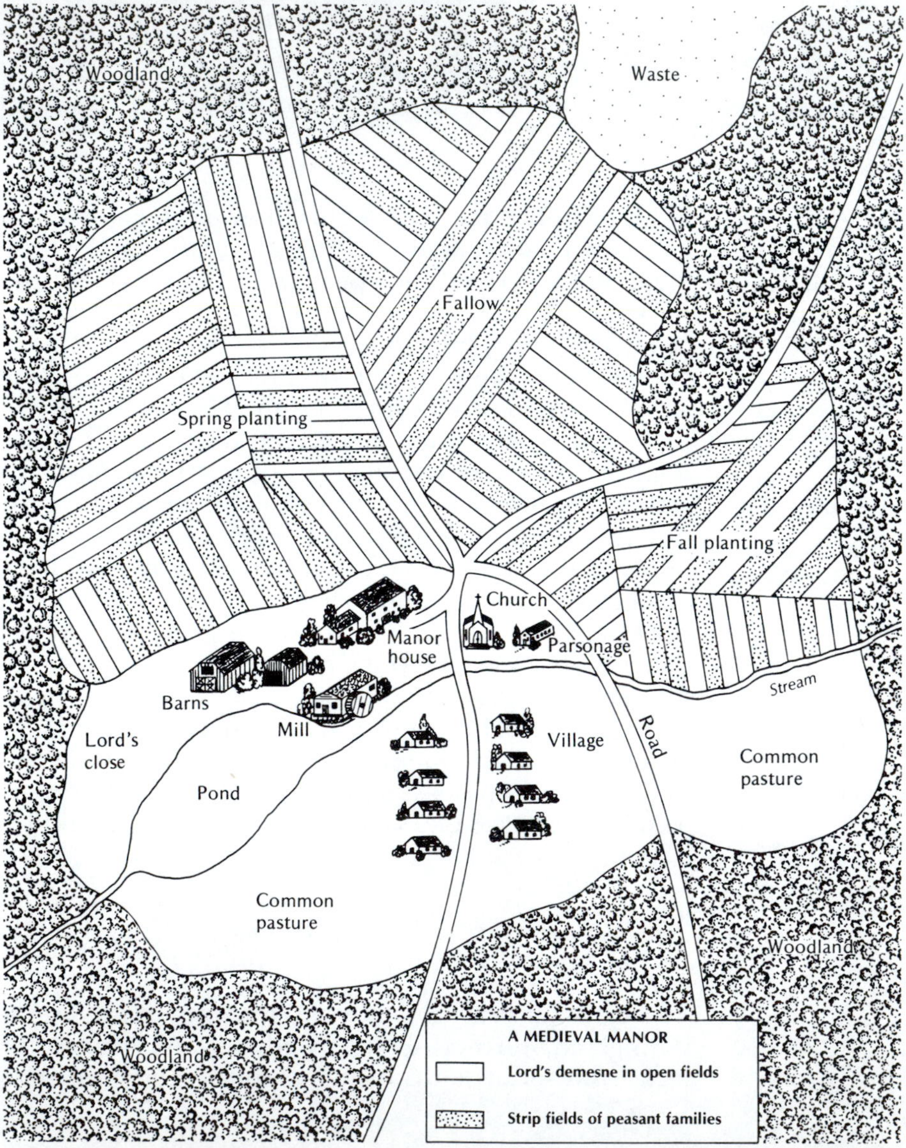

A medieval manor. The lord's holdings in the open fields are shown as light strips.

gion, from village to village, and even among individuals in the same village. In the tenth century, the part of England that had been conquered and settled by the Danes was a land of free villages.* The people worked their fields in common and enjoyed all their produce. The same situation existed in parts of Germany. But most villages were subject to a lord, and the inhabitants were his tenants who supported him in return for his protection. The whole caste of feudal lords, whose life we have described, was supported by the surplus produce exacted from a subordinated peasantry. The agricultural estates in a particular locality under the control of a single lord are called a *manor*. Often the village and manor coincided; that is to say, one settlement of peasants formed the estate of a particular lord. But sometimes a manor could contain two or more villages, and sometimes a large village was divided into two or more manors.

The arrangement by which a lord exploited his tenants is usually called the *manorial*, or *seignorial*, system. (The term "feudal system" is used to describe relationships among the knightly upper classes.) The origins and early development of the manorial system are far from clear. In France some great estates that had been worked by slaves or *coloni* in Roman times may have survived under new lords into the medieval period. In England, in the parts of France settled by the Franks, and in western Germany, the farmers of villages founded by a chieftain and his followers may have been subject to the chieftain and have owed him services from the beginning. Then it seems clear that villages that originally had no lords were brought into subjection by powerful men. In the disorders that marked the ninth and tenth centuries, no man was safe unless he had a soldier to protect him. As we have seen, some villages made voluntary submission to a mounted warrior, while others were forced to do so. Also, through the grants of kings and great lords, many villages became subject to ecclesiastical lords—to monasteries or cathedral churches.

When the lord was a single knight he might live on his estate and manage it himself. Very commonly (because a great feudal lord would have many widely scattered manors) a steward or bailiff supervised village affairs and collected the lord's revenues. A lord controlled the lives of his villagers in several ways. As a landlord he collected rents and services from them. Also, he had rights over the persons of his tenants. That is to say, they were his slaves or, much more commonly, half-free serfs. (Outright slavery was becoming rare by the tenth century.) Finally, a lord commonly exercised rights of jurisdiction over his peasants, rights that had formerly belonged to the king and his officials. We can look at each aspect of a lord's power in turn.

As a landlord he extracted rent from the peasants for the plots of land they held, principally in the form of labor services. A part of the arable land of the village, usually between a third and a half, was reserved for the lord. It usually consisted of strips in the fields and was called the *demesne*. The peasants worked the demesne for their lord. The lord also had a share of the meadow where his tenants harvested the hay. The lord's stock grazed on the village pasture un-

*See pp. 153–154 and 200–201.

der the care of the village herders. If the lord wanted a ditch dug or a barn built, the peasants supplied the labor. The amount of labor demanded from the tenants for the lord's benefit varied greatly; it was often as much as three days' work in a week. Wives of unfree peasants were expected to work in the lord's house at tasks like spinning, weaving, or combing wool. In addition to performing these services, the tenants also owed the lord a variety of rents in kind. In return for grazing his cow in the common pasture, the tenant paid a rent in cheese. If he had pigs feeding in the woods, he paid the lord a rent in pork for the privilege. When the tenant fished in the stream or pond, he gave the lord part of the catch. In return for gathering dead wood in the woods, he kept the lord supplied with firewood. The list could be extended almost indefinitely. There were rents in chickens, in fruit, in vegetables, and in wool. In short, the lord received a share of every type of produce raised by his tenants. Besides all this the peasant was required to pay *tithe* (a tenth of his produce) to the local parish church.

In addition to the rents and services he received as possessor of the land, the lord had profitable rights that sprang from his control over the persons of his tenants. These rights varied greatly according to the position of the lord and the legal status of his tenants. The descendants of the Roman *coloni* and slaves on the great estates of the Frankish period often became what we call *serfs* or *villeins;* and during the long era of disorder, many peasants who had been freemen were slowly depressed in status by their lords until they too became serfs. There was no absolute rigidity of status, even among the serfs. The dues they owed to the lord varied considerably. And, over the course of generations, some landholding serfs sank into the class of landless laborers, while others built up considerable holdings and became individuals of substance in the village. But, typically, all serfs lacked some of the rights of freemen. The basic restriction on their freedom was that they were not allowed to leave the manor where they were born. The serfs were "bound to the soil"; they were the labor that went with it. The church insisted on their right to make Christian marriages but, although the serf could marry, he could not marry anyone outside his village without his lord's leave.

As the seignorial system developed, the serf also became subject to the lord's jurisdiction. The right to hold a court and exercise police power gave the lord a firm hold over his tenants. Also the possession of rights of jurisdiction permitted him to establish profitable monopolies. He could refuse to allow his peasants to own or operate hand mills to grind grain into flour, thus forcing them to bring their grain to his mill and pay a fee for having it ground. He could also oblige them to bake their bread in his ovens and pay a fee for that privilege. In short, the lord with rights of jurisdiction controlled both the persons and the property of his tenants, and all lords had at least some such rights. In most of France and western Germany, the lord might well have the power of life and death; in Normandy and England, "high justice" was normally reserved to the duke and the king.

Much of our information about village life in the early Middle Ages comes from surveys of manorial estates made by the greater monasteries. (Monks were more likely than lay lords to set down in writing the details of their holdings, and documents stored away in a monastery were more likely to survive.) Those surveys often list by name all the inhabitants of a village, giving their status and their obligations to the lord. From such documents we can construct a kind of elementary sociology of rural life. The most informative of the surveys was one made in the first half of the ninth century for the great abbey of Saint-Germain near Paris. The compilers of this inventory carefully distinguished the personal ranks of the subject peasantry on each of the abbey's estates. A *servus* was a slave (though perhaps by this time serf would be a better translation), normally settled on his own plot of land. A *colonus* was personally free though he owed labor services to the lord in return for his holding of land. A *lidus* held a semi-free status in between the other two classes.

Although the peasants differed in status, they were not divided into rigid castes. The different ranks commonly intermarried. Thus in the little village of Neuillay, one of the manors of Saint-Germain, we can read of "Electeus, a *servus* and his wife a *colona,* by name Landina."* Electeus had a holding of about twenty acres. He and his wife had no children. Another *servus,* Hildeboldus, and his wife Bertenildis (a *lida*) had a similar holding of land but nine children to support, by far the largest family in the village. The poorest peasant was a certain Gautmarus. The entry about him runs like this: "Gautmarus, a *servus* and his wife a *lida* by name Sigalsis. These are their children: Siclevoldus and Sicleardus. He lives in Neuillay. He holds a fourth part of a farm which has in arable land one and one-half bunaria [about five acres] and in meadow one arpent [less than half an acre]. He pays the fourth part of a full farm." Gautmarus probably eked out a living by working as a laborer for the lord or for a richer peasant. A group of three peasant families, who hold about forty-eight acres between them, owed the following services and rents: "They do carting to Anjou and in the month of May to Paris. They pay for the army tax 2 muttons, 8 chickens, 30 eggs, 100 planks and as many shingles, 12 staves, 6 hoops and 12 torches. They bring 2 loads of wood to Sutre. They inclose, in the lord's court, 4 perches with a palisade, in the meadow 4 perches with a fence, and at the harvest as much as is necessary. They plow in the winter field 8 perches and in the spring field 26 perches. Along with their corvées and labor services, they cart manure into the lord's field. Each pays a head tax of 4 pennies."

Neuillay was only a small settlement. Nineteen families were listed there. Five of the families were childless and the other fourteen had forty-two children between them (all listed by name). We can be sure that many more children were born who did not survive infancy. Bertenildis with her nine surviving progeny was quite exceptional. There is little evidence of "extended families" living together in medieval villages. The typical peasant household consisted of a man and wife with two or three children. At Neuillay nineteen adult men were listed

*Sources, no. 29

but only fourteen women. (Several families were headed by men without wives, presumably widowers.) The figures from Neuillay alone would not be statistically significant, but they are confirmed by the surveys of other villages. Among the several thousand serfs of Saint-Germain, males outnumbered females by 132 to 100. Evidently girl children had less chance of surviving than boys. We do not understand the reasons for this. Female infanticide has been suggested but there is no real evidence, and certainly the church would have condemned such a practice if it had existed. Moreover the traditional codes of Germanic law did not discriminate against women, but rather the reverse. In the law of the Salic Franks a woman of childbearing age was protected by three times the wergild of a free warrior and by the same wergild after she ceased to have children. But, in a society living at a bare subsistence level, even a marginal discrimination against girl babies in care and feeding could have influenced their survival rate. Whatever the cause, whether girl children were more neglected, or women were more prone to suffer violence, or less able to endure the harsh rigors of peasant life, it remains true that in the early Middle Ages female serfs did not survive as well as males. In the later Middle Ages conditions changed and the sex ratio became more nearly equal. In the earlier period, the available evidence suggests that there must have been a shortage of women of marriageable age, but this did not prevent a substantial growth of population (discussed below) which occurred from the tenth century onward. The whole situation presents an interesting problem for demographers which is still not adequately resolved.

A few further remarks seem in order in regard to the position of the unfree peasant. In theory—the lords' theory—he was economically at the complete mercy of his *seigneur*. The lord could demand any rents and services he saw fit. But there was obviously a practical limit to the use of this right. Dead peasants were of no use to the lord, and so he had to leave them enough to keep alive. Similarly, the lord's arbitrary power of jurisdiction was tempered to some degree by the need to maintain a viable village community. Disputes among villagers and disputes about services due to the lord were settled in the manorial court. The court was presided over by the lord's bailiff, but cases were judged according to the custom of the manor, a structure of community regulations handed down among the peasants from generation to generation. These customs varied from village to village, but they always protected the serf's holding of his own land in hereditary right so long as he rendered the services due from it. The Middle Ages was a period in which the authority of custom was very great, and men were inclined to do what their predecessors had done. A lord might seek to increase the rents and services due from his tenants, and many undoubtedly did so; but there was always at least a presumption that change was evil, and this must have protected the peasants to some extent.

For all that, the lot of the unfree peasant was far from enviable. His village was a little settlement hacked out from the surrounding forest.

There he lived a life of harsh, grinding labor, cut off from the world in an isolated self-supporting community. The peasant's only knowledge of the world of ideas came from the village priest. The priest cared for his soul—baptized him and married him and tried to teach him the rudiments of religion. But the priest himself was probably a barely literate peasant, only a little more educated than the serfs themselves. The feasts of the church provided the villagers' only recreation. These were often survivals from pagan times carefully assigned to some day devoted to a Christian saint. They at any rate provided an excuse for the peasants to get drunk on the local wine or beer, one recreation that they enjoyed as much as their lords. If a peasant had a substantial holding of twenty or thirty acres he and his family could count on enough to eat in good seasons. In bad seasons they all came close to starvation, and the weaker and poorer peasants did starve. A peasant's lord could sometimes hang him and could usually mete out lesser punishments at will. Compared with the position of a modern free workman, the status of a medieval serf was appalling. On the other hand, compared with the chattel slavery of the ancient world, serfdom represented an advance in status. The serf's day-to-day life was regulated by the custom of a village community in which he had a voice. Most important of all, that custom guaranteed to him the right to hold his own land and to pass it on to his heirs.

This discussion of the position of the peasantry of the early Middle Ages has been centered in the condition of the unfree inhabitants of the villages because, in the tenth and eleventh centuries, they formed the major part of the agricultural population of England, France, and western Germany. By the twelfth century, the seignorial system had spread into central Germany. Later it moved on into eastern Germany and eventually into Russia. But it is important to remember that, in the tenth and eleventh centuries, there were many free peasants. Anglo-Saxon England held many small freemen, especially in the Danish districts, and although the Norman conquest reduced many of them to the status of unfree villeins, others kept their freedom. Throughout this period, there were in eastern England free farmers who paid money rents for their lands. Certain parts of France, notably the region around Bordeaux, continued to have numerous small farmers. And Saxony was a land of free farmers too. In general, the manorial system did not become established in regions of dispersed upland farming. The historians are obliged to concentrate on the dominant features of the society they are describing, but their readers should always remember that what is dominant is rarely universal.

27. Population Growth and Agrarian Expansion

Although he lived an impoverished and often brutish life, the medieval peasant was tough and tenacious. (No doubt it was only the tough ones who survived.) He could improve his economic status by increasing his holding of land or by working it more efficiently, and the ways in which medieval peasants seized these opportunities shaped the economic future of Europe. During the tenth and eleventh centuries, they laid the foundation for the future political and economic dominance of that region by enormously increasing its population and productivity. The process has been described as an "agricultural revolution" comparable in importance to that of the eighteenth century. In fact, changes took place much more slowly in the medieval period than in the later "revolution"; all the same their cumulative effect was very great.

The centuries of highest medieval achievement, from the tenth century through the thirteenth, were marked by a steadily rising population. The evidence of it is found in the establishment of many new agricultural settlements, in the growth of cities, and in the steady expansion of arable land around existing villages. Everything else achieved in that age—splendid architecture, ordered institutions of government, feudal chivalry, great universities—all depended on an increasing output of agricultural wealth by a vigorous, expanding peasant society.

We cannot be certain how the demographic change of the tenth century was "triggered." Obviously, for a population to increase, the gross birth rate has to exceed the gross death rate; but population changes depend on many other factors—distribution of population by age and sex, average age of marriage, fertility rates, proportion of live births to pregnancies, infant mortality. This last is especially important in a medieval context. An evident feature of medieval life was the very high number of children who died at birth or in early infancy; if a slight improvement in standards of nutrition permitted only a few more to survive in each generation, this would have markedly affected the population trend. Alternatively, the opening up of new land could have created conditions in which earlier marriage was possible, with a consequent increase in births. We must remember also the unusually high ratio of men to women in the ninth century. Any amelioration of conditions that enabled parents to rear more infant girls to maturity would have significantly increased the number of births in the next generation. Any or all of these factors may have been at work. The one certain point is that the increase in population, however initiated, could not have been sustained for three centuries without a corresponding increase in food production.

All historians agree that a great expansion of agricultural output occurred from the tenth century onward; there is less agreement about the importance of the various factors that contributed to it. Some economic historians maintain that the growth of production is adequately explained by the somewhat higher level of peace and order that prevailed as the Viking and Magyar attacks were gradually beaten off. In times that were less anarchic, even if only slightly less anarchic, there was more security of tenure, and more secure tenure encouraged more careful and efficient farming. Other scholars have emphasized the importance of a gradual transition, beginning in Carolingian times, from the two-field system that we have described to a three-field system of agriculture. In the tenth and eleventh centuries, more and more villages in northern Europe adopted this three-field system. (It was not well suited to the climatic conditions of the south.) The change was simple, but its results could be substantial. In the two-field system, one field lay fallow each year, while the other was planted with a cereal crop sown in the fall and harvested at the end of the following summer. In the three-field system, one field again lay fallow each year and one was planted with winter grain (sown in the fall), but a third was sown in spring with another crop—often oats or legumes. A community of peasants with 600 acres of arable land to cultivate would be able to plant 400 acres of crops every year under the new system, instead of 300 under the old. Productivity could at once increase by a third. Moreover, less plowing was needed since it was necessary to plow the fallow land twice each year to keep down weeds. Under the old system, 900 acres had to be plowed each year; under the new system, only 800 acres. No doubt innumerable local vicissitudes prevented such mathematically tidy results being achieved in all cases, and some villages in the north were still using the ancient two-field system at the end of the Middle Ages. But the changeover to the three-field system that took place in many northern regions could have greatly increased the total food production of Europe. The essential innovation was the spring sowing (though not all villages that introduced it changed to a three-field pattern). This practice had never been widely adopted in the old Mediterranean civilizations because the spring grain needed the relatively wet summers of the north.

The changeover to a three-field system was accompanied by major improvements in the use of animal power. We owe much of our information about these developments not to professional historians but to a French cavalryman named Lefebvre des Nöettes, who devoted his retirement to studying the history of horses. He did not know as much about the Middle Ages as the economic historians, but he knew a lot more about horses, and the knowledge proved invaluable. Lefebvre des Nöettes found that the methods of using draft animals in the ancient world were extremely inefficient. Nailed horseshoes were not generally used, and it is probable that they were not known at all, so that the animals were often incapacitated by broken hooves. Above all, the ancient system of harnessing was almost incredibly inept. A yoke rested on the horse's withers, and a strap attached to this passed around the beast's neck. When the horse strained forward to pull a load, the strap pressed into its windpipe and began to choke it. The modern rigid horse collar rests on the horse's shoulders, so that the whole bodyweight of the animal can be used in drawing a load. A horse so equipped can do three or four times as much work as one harnessed in the ancient fashion.

Lefebvre des Nöettes thought that the horse collar was a European invention of the ninth century. Other scholars have argued that it was imported into Europe from the Mongoloid peoples of Central Asia or even from the Lapps of the far north. What is certain is that it came to be widely adopted in northern Europe from the tenth century onward. The advantage of the horse as a draft animal was that it could work far more quickly than the slow-moving oxen. A disadvantage was that the horse had to be fed relatively expensive grain as well as hay. But in the more fertile parts of northern Europe, the three-field system produced large enough grain crops for oats to be used as horse fodder. At about the same time that the rigid horse collar was adopted, nailed horseshoes came into use, and a more efficient method of harnessing horses in tandem (instead of side by side) was devised. Simultaneously, there was an increase in the use of water wheels for grinding grain. Taken together, these innovations greatly increased the available sources of nonhuman productive power.

The adoption of a three-field system created the opportunity for some rudimentary experimentation in crop rotation. Previously, the only major field crops had been grain—wheat, barley, oats, or rye, depending on soil and climate. The peasant's diet consisted basically of carbohydrates eked out with a little meat and cheese. In the ninth and tenth centuries, it became a usual practice to plant legumes at the spring sowing. The important point is that the new field crops—mainly peas, lentils, and broad beans—were relatively rich in proteins. Hence the tenth-century peasant probably enjoyed a more protein-rich diet than the proletarians of the old Roman Empire.

The rise in population from the tenth century onward was accompanied by an increase in the total amount of land under cultivation. The earliest efforts at reclamation were directed toward the land that had been deserted during the period of confusion in the ninth and early tenth centuries. Bit by bit, land that had grown up in brush and light woods was cleared and plowed. Then the peasants started nibbling at the edges of the great forests. Since draining marshes was technically far more difficult than clearing forests, it was less common, but in some regions it was carried on with great energy and some success.

Unfortunately, this vast work of reclamation was of little interest to contemporary writers, and they tell us little about it in detail. Some of our knowledge comes from place names. The word for a clearing was *assart,* and such names as Assart-le-Roi, the king's clearing, indicate a village founded on cleared land. La Foret-le-Roi has a similar meaning. Sometimes it was a matter of clearing a large tract and founding new villages, but more often it was simply the extension of the arable land of villages bordering on a forest—the creation of little assarts along the edge of the woods. Whatever the effects of changing agricultural technology may have been—and experts argue about this—there can be no doubt that this extension of cultivated land at the expense of forest, marsh, and wasteland was the most important of all the factors involved in bringing about an increase in the total agricultural production of Western Europe during the early Middle Ages.

READING SUGGESTIONS

* *B. Tierney.* Sources *and* Readings, *vol. I, no. 29; vol. II, nos. 11, 12.*

Any short account of medieval agricultural systems is necessarily an oversimplification. The subject is surveyed in all its complexity in *The Cambridge Economic History,* M. M. Postan (ed.), *The Agrarian Life of the Middle Ages,* vol. I, 2nd ed. (Cambridge, 1966). * G. Duby, *Rural Economy and Country Life in the Medieval West* (London, 1968) is a fine synthesis of recent scholarship, while H. Heaton, *Economic History of Europe,* rev. ed. (New York, 1948) provides a briefer introduction. Heaton properly emphasizes the diversity in the patterns of manorial organization. The same point is made in the more specialized studies of H. L. Gray, *English Field Systems* (Cambridge, MA, 1915), and F. G. Emmison, *Types of Open Field Parishes in the Midlands* (London, 1937). See also Marc Bloch, *Land and Work in Medieval Europe* (Berkeley and Los Angeles, 1967), and B. H. Slicher van Bath, *Agrarian History of Europe* (London, 1963). C. S. and C. S. Orwin, *The Open Fields,* 2nd ed. (New York, 1954) describes the open-field system of strip farming, and early field systems are illustrated in M. W. Beresford and J. K. S. St. Joseph, *Medieval England, An Aerial Survey* (Cambridge, 1958). * W. E. Bark, cited in Chapter I, and * L. White, *Medieval Technology and Social Change* (New York, 1966) emphasize the improvements in agricultural technology during the early Middle Ages. On peasant life, see the essays collected in J. A. Raftis (ed.), *Pathways to Medieval Peasants* (Toronto, 1981).

chapter

X

Early Medieval Government

The close of the era of invasions saw the major part of western Europe divided into three stages—those of the Anglo-Saxons, the West Franks, and the East Franks. The only well-populated and productive part of Christian Europe that lay outside the boundaries of these three great states was the Indian peninsula.

To the north, in Scandinavia, the kingdoms of Norway, Sweden, and Denmark were beginning to take form. In Eastern Europe, Poland, Bohemia, and Hungary were growing into permanent states. Farther south, the Balkan peninsula lay mainly within the Byzantine sphere of influence. The military dominance of western Europe lay in the lands of England, France, and Germany. Between 850 and 1100 their political structures were vitally changed by the development and spread of feudal institutions and by the appearance of rival power, the papal monarchy. In this chapter we shall see how feudal and ecclesiastical influences shaped the political forms of Western Europe and its northern and eastern borderlands. The state of Italy and the papacy will be considered in the next chapter.

28. *France: The First Capetian Kings*

The two chief fragments of the Carolingian Empire, the West and East Frankish kingdoms that eventually became France and Germany, were essentially different in political structure and made different adjustments to the needs of the era of confusion. All the territory of the West Franks had been part of the Roman Empire and had been ruled since the fifth century by the Merovingian and Carolingian dynasties. Except for Brittany and to some extent Aquitaine, there were no groups who thought of themselves as a separate people with their own culture and traditions. The land was divided into counties based on the dioceses, which in turn reflected the Roman *civitates*. The counts were the key figures in the political structure of the West Frankish state. Nominally vassals of the king, they became increasingly independent with the growth of feudal institutions. Sometimes a powerful noble would gain possession of a number of counties. One family in particular was extremely adept at the art of collecting counties. Charles the Bald appointed a very able warrior known as Robert the Strong as *missus* in the Loire valley to hold the region against the Vikings. Although Robert and his successors were only moderately successful at repelling Vikings, they were experts at extending their own power. Soon they were counts of Angers, Tours, Blois, Orleans, Chartres, Paris, and other places. The descendants of Robert the Strong, the future Capetians, were the most powerful nobles of the West Frankish state, but there were other similar dynasties well entrenched in several counties.

Although the early Carolingian kings had passed the crown from father to son, in theory the royal office had remained elective, and the great feudal lords were inclined to make this theory a reality. It was difficult for a monarch who gained the throne by election to act very strongly against those who chose him. In a purely elective system, moreover, each great lord felt that he himself might achieve the royal dignity. At first the nobles simply used the elective principle to choose among the various Carolingian claimants, but in 887 they elected as king Odo (888–898), marquis of Neustria, son of Robert the Strong. The next century was marked by bitter rivalry between the Carolingian princes and the descendants of Robert. At times a Carolingian would hold the crown, at other times a member of the rival house. Frequently, the head of each family claimed to be king and waged fierce war on his opponent. From the point of view of the feudal lords, whose chief desire was freedom from effective control, this was an excellent situation. Each lord could sell his support to whoever offered the highest price in fiefs and offices. The noble class, bred and trained for warfare, thrived on continued anarchy.

At the death of Louis V (986–987), the last West Frankish Carolingian king, the nobles and prelates of the West Frankish kingdom chose to succeed him the head of the house founded by Robert the Strong, Hugh Capet (987–996), who bore the title duke of France. Hugh thus became the founder of the dynasty that was to rule France for centuries. His direct heir in the male line is the present claimant to the French throne.

The nobles who chose Hugh Capet to be their king had no intention of establishing a new dynasty on the throne. They fully expected to continue their established practice of giving the crown now to one family and now to another. But Hugh was determined to make the crown hereditary in his family. Hence, shortly after his accession, he announced that the royal duties were too heavy for one man and asked the nobles to elect his eldest son as his crowned and anointed associate. It was difficult to refuse such a request; the nobles grumbled but complied. This practice started by Hugh Capet was continued by his successors. Not until 1227 did a king of France die before he had seen his successor safely crowned. This scheme, combined with the Capetian ability to produce male heirs, succeeded in making the French crown hereditary.

In order to understand the position of Hugh Capet, it is necessary to think of him in three distinct capacities. He was the crowned and anointed king of the West Frankish state, the successor to the Carolingian monarchs. He was also the feudal overlord or suzerain of the great lords of the realm. Finally, he was the ruler of his own duchy. Although, for purposes of convenience, the West Frankish kingdom after Hugh's accession to the throne will be referred to here as France, this term does not represent the contemporary usage. Hugh called himself king of the Franks, as had the Carolingians. France was the present Ile de France, that is, Paris and the country around it. This region was the center of Hugh's power and comprised the bulk of his fief, the duchy of France. It was no greater in wealth and power than the fiefs of many other French counts.

As king, Hugh had in theory all the traditional authority of the Carolingian monarchs. He could issue decrees that had the force of law throughout his realm. He could summon every able-bodied man to follow him to battle. The counts were his officers, exercising jurisdiction as his agents. It was his duty to defend the country from outside foes, maintain internal order, and support and protect the church. His anointment gave him a special sanctity. Most of these royal prerogatives were of little practical use to Hugh. If he issued decrees, his counts enforced them or not as they saw fit. The counts might be his officers, but they were hereditary officials whom he could not remove or control. And the warriors of the realm were all vassals of the feudal lords and bound to follow them to battle. Being an anointed monarch did have at least two decided advantages, however, The person of the monarch was sacred, and the wildest lord would hesitate long before violating it. Then he had the firm support of the church. The bishops, commonly appointed by the king, preferred a strong monarchy to feudal anarchy and their support was by no means restricted to spiritual weapons. The prelates of France held vast lands and had enfeoffed many knights.

As suzerain of the great lords of France, Hugh Capet stood at the apex of the feudal hierarchy. A small group of dukes, counts, archbishops, and bishops were his vassals, the men later called peers of France. In theory at least, these great lords owed the king all the regular feudal services. Actually, this did not mean very much. The duke of Aquitaine did not recognize the Capetian dynasty for several generations. Not until the twelfth century did either of the great potentates of southern France, the duke of Aquitaine and the count of Toulouse, bother to do homage to the Capetian king. The duke of Normandy admitted that it was his duty to do homage and attend the royal court, but he insisted that the king was obliged to come to the frontier of his duchy when these services were to be performed. The great lords of northern France also acknowledged their suzerain's right to demand military service. They had been skillful bargainers, however, and the contingents they owed to the royal host were ridiculously small compared to their actual resources in knightly vassals. Thus the count of Champagne, who had at his disposal some two thousand knights, owed but ten to the royal host.

The real power of Hugh Capet rested on his duchy of France, which became the royal demesne at his accession to the throne. There, in his own counties, he exercised full powers of government and collected fines for criminal offenses, tolls at bridges, and other customary dues. There lay the demesne manors that supplied food and clothing for Hugh and his court. The men who held fiefs in the demesne, the vassals of the duke of France, owed him feudal services and were less able to ignore their obligations than were the great vassals of the crown. The power of the Capetian king depended chiefly on the size and resources of his demesne and the effectiveness of his control over it.

In reality, the France of the late tenth century should not be thought of as a unified state but rather as a loose alliance of great feudal princes. These princes were bound together by their common vassalage to the Capetian king. In practical politics, however, they treated the king as one of themselves—as duke of France. When it suited a prince's purpose, he allied with the king against other great lords, but he was just as willing to join a coalition against his suzerain when that seemed the most profitable course.

During the century following the accession of Hugh Capet to the French throne, it was impossible to check the further fragmentation of political authority. Not only were Hugh and his immediate successors completely unable to curb the independence of their great vassals, but they could not retain their original power in the royal demesne. The greater vassals of the Paris region, such as the lords of Puiset, Coucy, and Montmorency, built strong fortresses and cheerfully defied the authority of their duke and king. The successors of Hugh Capet could not travel in safety from Paris to Orleans without the leave of the lord of Puiset, whose great castle at Etampes dominated the road between the two cities. Moreover, feudal ideas of hereditary office were so strong that they were bound to affect the relations between the king and his agents in the demesne. Officials called *provosts* superintended the king's demesne manors and collected his dues. These positions were farmed; that is, the holders bargained with the king for a fixed amount to be rendered to him each year. In addition, the office of provost became hereditary, and its holders were almost as hard to control as the feudal vassals.

It would be difficult to exaggerate the simplicity of the court, household, and way of life of the early Capetian kings. The *chaplain* heard confessions and said mass in the chapel. Since the chaplain, as a clerk, was literate, he wrote the king's letters. In time he was called a *chancellor* and had other clerks under him who served as chaplains and secretaries. The other household officers who controlled the royal government (such as it was) were great secular nobles. The *chamberlain* looked after the bedchamber. He watched over the king's valuables that were stored there, were they jewels, clothes, or charters, and generally controlled access to the king. The *constable* and the *marshal* saw to the horses. The *steward* was responsible for the provisioning of the household and was assisted by such officials as the *butler,* who procured the wines, and the *dispenser,* who supervised their issuance. These same officers who ministered to the domestic needs of the royal household conducted the business of the realm. Thus the constable and the marshal were the king's deputies in commanding his troops. By far the most powerful of these officers was the steward. As it was his duty to procure supplies, he was in charge of the provosts who held the manors that yielded the supplies; for all practical purposes, he was the head of the administration. So powerful did the steward become that the kings left the office vacant after the twelfth century.

Hugh Capet, his son, and his grandson were all tough and vigorous soldiers. It was a considerable achievement that, in a chaotic age, they established an undisputed claim to the title of king. They also succeeded in holding on to the strategically placed royal lands around Paris. But, still, these early Capetians were far from mighty figures. They wandered about among their estates in the vicinity of Paris and waged fierce wars against their rebellious vassals of the duchy of France. Occasionally, they became involved in warfare between the great lords, but as many of these lords had greater resources than they, the kings could not play a very vital part in such major affairs. One may well ask why, under such circumstances, the monarchy was able to survive. Probably the chief factor was the unflagging support of the church. Moreover, the kings were so weak that they could not annoy the great lords seriously, and their demesne was too small to be an extremely tempting prize. To attempt to crush the anointed of God, the sacrosanct king of France, was a serious matter. The possible profits did not seem worth the risk. Finally, feudal theory required a suzerain; and what suzerain could be more harmless than the Capetian king?

The power of the Capetian monarchy had reached its lowest point by the beginning of the reign of Philip I (1060–1108). Ever since the accession of Hugh Capet, Philip's great-grandfather, the royal demesne had been shrinking. Philip, however, managed to stop the decline and even added to the royal lands. When the viscount of Bourges wanted money to go on the First Crusade, Philip bought his fief. Then in return for recognizing a count of Anjou who had captured and imprisoned his elder brother, the king received some Angevin lands south of the royal forest of Fontainebleau. But still Philip was no great king. He was unable to discipline effectively the barons of his own duchy of France and, even with his additions to the royal demesne, he commanded fewer resources than his greatest vassals. By this time the great feudal states had become fairly stable, thus limiting the king's opportunities to take advantage of quarrels among the feudal princes. In the north, the county of Flanders covered what is now western Belgium and extreme northern France. Next to it on the coast stood the duchy of Normandy, the fief of the descendants of Rollo the Viking. The Celtic inhabitants of the Breton peninsula and a band of French-speaking people along its eastern border from below Nantes to Mt.-St.-Michel formed the duchy of Brittany. East of Brittany and south of western Normandy lay the counties of Maine and Anjou. To the east of these feudal states lay the vast possessions of the house of Blois, whose leaders styled themselves counts of Champagne from the twelfth century onward.

South of the county of Champagne lay the duchy of Burgundy. Then south of the river Loire was the vast duchy of Aquitaine. Finally, the Mediterranean coast of the kingdom and a broad belt of land running westward to Toulouse comprised the county of Toulouse.

While the feudal princes of France differed greatly in power, most of them were stronger and none of them much weaker than the ruler of the tiny duchy of France who was their king. It was the most powerful of these princes, the duke of Normandy and the counts of Flanders and Champagne, whose lands lay adjacent to the royal demesne. King Philip was completely hedged about by vassals far mightier than he. Early in his reign this situation was made still worse by the Norman conquest of England.* The future history of the medieval French monarchy is a story of the rebuilding of royal power from the highly unpromising situation of the late eleventh century.

29. *Saxons and Normans in England*

The long struggle against the Danes that marked the ninth and tenth centuries made England a unified kingdom. The true founder of the English national monarchy was Alfred the Great (871–899), even though he himself never ruled all England. After making peace with the Danes in 885,‡ Alfred devoted the second half of his reign to a great program of reconstruction. He reorganized the Anglo-Saxon system of military levies, established a navy, and built a chain of fortified bases as strong points against any future Viking attacks. Alfred also tried to remedy the decay of literacy and learning that resulted from the Viking destruction of many major monasteries and urged even laymen to learn to read and write. The king himself knew Latin and translated or helped to translate a number of important works into the West Saxon dialect. Among them were Pope Gregory's *Pastoral Care,* Bede's *Ecclesiastical History,* and Boethius' *Consolation of Philosophy.* In addition to all this, Alfred promulgated a code of laws that was not, like earlier codes, merely a record of the customs of his own people but one that borrowed eclectically from the laws of the other Saxon tribes.

Alfred's son, Edward the Elder (899–925), and his grandson Aethelstan (925–939) conquered the regions occupied by the Danes, and their successors were masters of the entire English realm. In fact, they ruled rather more than the England of today, for their kingdom included eastern Scotland as far as Edinburgh. But the unification of

*See pp. 205–206.

‡See pp. 153–154.

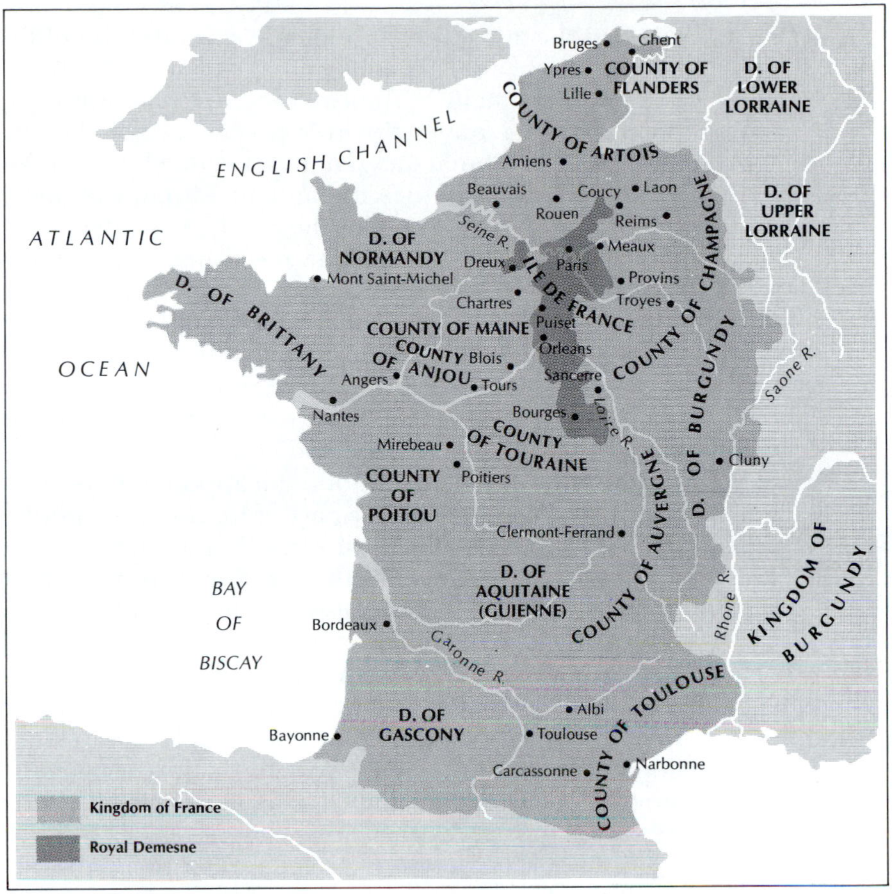

France in the Reign of Philip I, 1060–1108

The Capetian kings, at this time exceedingly weak, had actual control over very little of the area of France. In the reign of Philip, however, the size of the royal demesne, which had been shrinking, was stabilized and enlarged by the addition of Bourges and some Angevin lands south of Fontainebleau. From this time on, French kings were able to continue the steady expansion of the area under their control.

England under one king did not mean the wiping out of the difference between the Anglo-Saxons and the Danes. The Danish settlers remained on the land with their own laws, traditions, and customs. While the old Anglo-Saxon regions had long been largely organized in manors, the Danelaw was a land of independent farmers, where manors with their demesnes were almost unknown. Another result of the Danish occupation was the reorganized political geography of a large part of central England. The first English *shires* or counties had been administrative regions of the kingdom of Wessex, or lesser kingdoms that were absorbed by Wessex (for example, Kent, Sussex, Essex). In the lands reconquered from the Danes, new counties were created around the fortified boroughs, and each county was given the name of its chief borough—Nottinghamshire and Nottingham, Lincolnshire and Lincoln, Bedfordshire and Bedford, and so on. These units sometimes corresponded to divisions that the invading Danish armies had made in portioning out their conquests. Only in East Anglia and the ancient kingdom of Wessex did the old counties remain intact.

The government of the Anglo-Saxon state was far more effectively organized than any other in Western Europe. The monarchy was in theory elective, but it was generally assumed that eligibility for election was confined to the descendants of Alfred, the members of the ancient royal house. The king held estates scattered all over England. Every able-bodied Englishman owed him military service at his summons. He received a portion of the penalties inflicted by the local courts for criminal offenses in general and probably the entire penalty in the case of certain serious crimes. He thus had an army, ample land to support himself and his court, and a regular if small money revenue. Moreover, in every county or shire he had an agent appointed by him, removable by him, and completely under his authority—the *shire-revee*, or *sheriff*. In addition, he appointed bishops and abbots and considered them a regular part of his administration. Because of the unchallenged supremacy of Alfred's line, there was much less feudal disintegration in England than in France during the tenth century.

The Anglo-Saxon state also had an assembly known as the *Witangemot*, an assembly of the great men of the realm—officials, landowners, and prelates. It went through the form of electing the king, and he apparently was expected to seek its advice on important matters such as new legislation. Finally, the Anglo-Saxon kings had an exceptionally efficient *chancery*, or writing office, which issued *writs* (royal letters), composed in Anglo-Saxon, to convey the king's wishes to his subordinates.

It is important, however, to remember that only a small part of what we think of as the work of government was carried on by the king and Witan. The king was the military leader of his people. He probably set the penalties for certain serious crimes, such as rape, murder, and arson. But the general enforcement of the law was left to the local courts. At set times the freemen of each shire met together in the shire court under the presidency of the *ealdorman* (the chief local military official), sheriff, and bishop. Each court had its own body of custom. This custom was carried out by the people themselves under the guidance of the presiding officials. Guilt and innocence were established by the old Teutonic rites of compurgation and ordeal. But although ancient Anglo-Saxon law provided only money penalties for offenses—payments to the injured or family—by the tenth century royal decrees had made certain crimes punishable at the king's pleasure, and he may well have used corporal punishments.

Early in the eleventh century, England was once more invaded by the Danes. This time it was not a matter of plundering raiders but a great fleet led by King Swein of Denmark and his son Canute. In the summer of 1016, the Anglo-Saxon king, Edmund Ironside (1016), came to an agreement with Canute. England was to be divided between them, and if one died, the survivor was to rule the whole realm. Edmund lived only a few months after this treaty, and Canute (1016–1035) became king of all England. He proved to be a just and

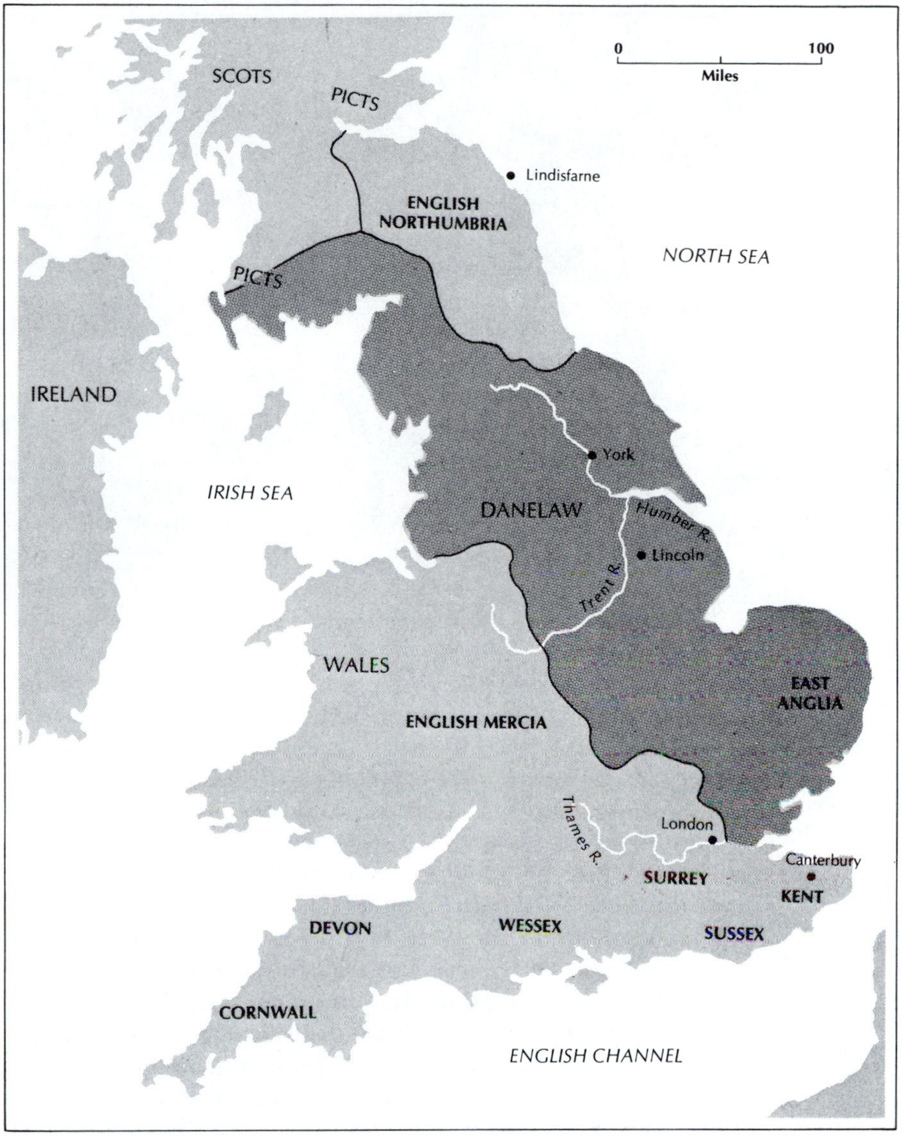

Saxon England, ca. 885

able ruler who maintained the laws and customs of his predecessors. Canute also protected and even fostered the Church. He safeguarded his authority in England by maintaining a small standing army of Danish troops, which he supported by collecting the *danegeld,* a tax originally levied to buy off Viking raiders—a bit of irony that may well have pleased him. When Canute died in 1035, his sons, who were quarreling fiercely over the Danish throne, were unable to maintain themselves in England. The Witan elected as king the younger brother of Edmund Ironside, Edward the Confessor (1042–1066).

The event that transformed the history of England in mid-eleventh century, the Norman conquest of 1066, came about like this: Edward's

Detail from a portion of the Bayeux Tapestry showing the death of King Harold in the Battle of Hastings, 1066. It is not certain whether Harold is the man struck by an arrow, at left, or the man being attacked by the knight on horseback. *Treasury of the Cathedral, City of Bayeux; Giraudon*

mother was a sister of Richard II, duke of Normandy, and during Canute's reign Edward lived at the Norman court. When he returned to England, a number of his Norman friends accompanied him and received lands and offices. Other Norman lords were frequent visitors at Edward's court. The king's favor to his foreign friends and relatives annoyed the most powerful family in England, Godwin, whom Canute had made *jarl*, or earl, of Wessex, and his sons. Godwin had played a large part in securing Edward's election by the Witan, and the king had married his daughter. As Edward had no children, Godwin dreamed of the day when he or one of his sons might be elected king. But there was another man with the same ambition. Edward's cousin William, duke of Normandy, felt that he was the logical successor to his childless relative. In 1051 William found an opportunity to move toward his goal as the result of an open break between Godwin and Edward's Norman friends. The count of Boulogne and his followers were attacked in Dover by the inhabitants. Since Dover was part of Wessex, Edward ordered Godwin to punish his men, but the earl, who sympathized with them, refused. As a result, Godwin and his sons were exiled. William took advantage of the situation to visit England, and he later maintained that, on this occasion, Edward had promised him the succession to the throne.

King Edward and the house of Godwin were soon reconciled, and when Godwin died the ablest of his sons, Harold, became earl of Wessex. Then in 1064, while sailing in the English Channel, Harold was shipwrecked on the Norman coast and captured by a vassal of Duke William. According to later Norman chronicles, Harold swore, as the price of his freedom, to aid William to become king of England when Edward died. Harold was to be chief man of the realm under the king and was to marry William's sister. In fact, when Edward died in 1066, the Witan elected Harold king. But Duke William had no intention of abandoning his hopes. He promptly despatched messengers to the pope accusing Harold of breaking his oath. Whether or not the pope took this charge seriously, he had good reason to support William. The papacy was trying to unify the church under its control and to enforce uniform laws and practices. William had in general proved cooperative. And the English church was but slightly under Roman influence; it was firmly controlled by the king. Hence the pope blessed William's idea of enforcing his claim to the throne. The duke summoned his vassals to follow him to England, but here he met a check. With some few exceptions, the Norman lords refused to go, on the ground that they did not owe military service for adventures over the sea. William then issued a general invitation to adventurers who hoped to gain booty and fiefs. This was most successful. From Flanders, Brittany, Maine, Anjou, and Poitou, men flocked to his banner. A few great Norman lords who were William's close personal friends and many younger sons of noble Norman houses also joined the host. A great fleet was collected, and William poised his invading force of about five thousand to await favorable winds.

King Harold was in an extremely difficult position. His elder brother, Tostig, jealous of Harold's success, had formed an alliance with Harold, king of Norway, for an invasion of England. Edwin and Morcar, joint earls of Northumbria, had no great love for Harold. He was only sure of the earldoms ruled by his own brothers and his old earldom of Wessex. Harold gathered his army, consisting of his house earls, or professional bodyguard, and the pick of his Wessex fighting men, near the coast to wait for William. But suddenly he learned that Tostig and Harold of Norway had landed in the north and routed Edwin and Morcar. Harold hastened north, destroyed the invading army at Stamford Bridge in Yorkshire, and turned south once more.

But, just three days after Harold had won his great victory, Duke William made good his landing on the south coast. On October 14, 1066, Harold's exhausted army, reinforced by hasty levies from Wessex and East Anglia, met William's force near Hastings. Just what happened is far from clear. The raw levies broke fairly quickly, but the Norman cavalry could make no impression on the house carls and other regular fighting men drawn up in a solid line of spears on a rise of ground. In some way, perhaps by a feigned retreat, William got the Saxons to break ranks. Then his heavily armed knights plunged into the gaps and cut the Saxon infantry to pieces. Harold and his brothers died with their men. For all practical purposes, England had been won by Duke William. Although it was some five years before the last stubborn Saxon rebels were routed out of their retreat in the fenland, the new king's position was never seriously threatened by them.

The conquest of England was a stroke of good luck. Had Harold not been called north to meet the Norwegian host and been able to oppose Duke William's landing with a fresh army, he might well have

England after the Norman Conquest

been successful. If instead of offering battle at Hastings he had retired to the midlands to await the reorganized musters of Northumbria under Edwin and Morcar, he would have had an excellent chance of victory. And if he had refused to offer battle and simply drawn William's army farther and farther into England, his eventual victory would have been almost certain. For the best Saxon troops were good fighting men, and no one realized it better than the Norman duke. As William moved through the country, he erected a castle in each borough to watch the burghers. The most famous surviving one is the central keep of the Tower of London. Another noticeable feature of his military arrangements in England was the care with which he assured himself of a safe retreat to the Continent in case of need. At Dover he built a great castle, and all Kent was placed under his half-brother, the bishop of Bayeux. Along the Sussex coast was built a line of fortresses: Bramber, Lewes, Hastings, Pevensea, and Arundel. Each was the seat of a compact fief granted to one of the duke's most reliable followers. If the Saxons rose successfully, the Normans would have strong, well-garrisoned castles in which to take refuge until their fleet could take them off.

The military organization of his conquest was William's first concern, for it appeared to be menaced by foes on every side. To the north lay Scotland, whose king was a relative of the house of Wessex. To the west was Wales. It had not been many years since a Danish king had ruled England, and a Norwegian host had been defeated just before his arrival. To William, the Scandinavian powers were a permanent threat. Finally, there was always the possibility of a Saxon rising. As William was the lord of a feudal state, the duchy of Normandy, he naturally conceived the new military organization in feudal terms, in terms of fiefs and knightly service. The low, comparatively level country on the east coast just below the Scots border, the county of Northumberland, was given as a centralized fief to a great Norman lord, who bore the title of earl of Northumberland. The neighboring county of Durham was given as a block to the bishop of Durham. Then, along the Welsh border, William created three other centralized fiefs—the earldoms of Chester, Shrewsbury, and Hereford. Thus facing the Scots and the Welsh were a string of fiefs, each under the unified command of a single lord.

In dividing the rest of England into fiefs, Duke William simply followed the most easy and natural course. Since he did not consider himself a conqueror in the usual sense but rather the rightful heir of Edward the Confessor, he naturally took the royal lands for himself. The Anglo-Saxon landholders who had not borne arms against him were left in possession of their lands and became his vassals. Then each of the chief men of his army was given the lands of one or more Saxons who had resisted the conquest. As the Saxon landholders had not held compact blocks of territory but had had estates scattered over a wide territory, the fiefs of William's followers were similarly dispersed. Each holder of a fief, whether Saxon or Norman, was assigned a quota of knights that he was obliged to supply to the royal army. As William knew little of the size or productivity of the fiefs he was granting, these quotas were merely rough guesses as to how many knights the fiefs would support. William also assigned quotas of knights to the bishops and to abbots of the Benedictine monasteries. The total service provided for came to some five thousand knights. The great fief holders who held directly from the king were left to divide their holdings among subvassals at their own discretion. The emergence of a stable pattern of individual knights' fiefs was a slow process that took more than a century to complete.

Historians have argued at great length—and the argument still continues—about the impact of the Norman conquest on Anglo-Saxon society. Some maintain that the conquest marked a radical break in the continuity of English history. Others have held that "William conquered neither to destroy nor to found but to continue." The truth seems to be that after 1066 much was preserved from the Anglo-Saxon past, but much was changed too. The new English state that grew up in the twelfth century was neither Saxon nor Norman but an Anglo-Norman synthesis.

As we have seen, William considered himself the rightful heir to Edward the Confessor. He promised to maintain the ancient customs of England and to recognize the laws of the Anglo-Saxon kings. The popular courts continued to administer the customary law. The Anglo-Saxon sheriffs were replaced by Normans, usually the most powerful baron in the shire, but the office remained unchanged. On the other hand, William did separate the lay and ecclesiastical jurisdictions to conform with Continental custom. The bishop no longer sat with the sheriff in the shire court but had his own court for ecclesiastical cases. Apart from that, the most important changes that William made in the English political structure arose from his introduction of Norman feudal practices. William's feudal *curia,* the assembly of his vassals, took the place of the Witan. Every Norman of any position was given *sac* and *soc,* or police court jurisdiction over his own men—essentially the privilege to which they were accustomed. More important men received the right of *infangentheof,* or the privilege of hanging one of their tenants caught on their land red-handed in theft. This was an important right from the point of view of the Norman lord; it enabled him to have a gallows, which was one of the chief symbols of rank in the seignorial world. Finally, the bishops and abbots of Anglo-Saxon England had possessed the right of immunity on at least part of their lands—the right of forbidding the entrance of royal officials. William extended this privilege to a few of the greatest of the lay lords.

The statement has frequently been made that the Norman conquest depressed the political, social, and economic status of the English people. This is unquestionably true to a certain extent. The few great Anglo-Saxon landowners who were not dispossessed were burdened with feudal services. Lesser Saxon landholders became vassals of the barons. The lower classes also suffered. In Anglo-Saxon England, there were many gradations of rank in the peasant population. Between the fully free farmers and the villeins who were bound to the soil and owed heavy labor services, there were many tenants who owed various services to a lord but were regarded as personally free. The Norman conquerors tended to treat such intermediate classes as villeins and to apply to them the customs of the seignorial system. Thus many small farmers who had enjoyed free status in Anglo-Saxon England found themselves subjected to the arbitrary will of a lord under the Normans.

Although King William had been brought up in a feudal environment and held political ideas that were essentially feudal, he was also fully aware of the deficiencies in the structure of the ordinary feudal state. He himself had spent the early years of his rule as duke in a series of bitter struggles with his Normal vassals, and he well knew the weakness of the Capetian monarchy. He had no intention of allowing his English barons to become as independent as the great Norman lords, to say nothing of the great vassals of the French crown. In fact,

William was the first ruler in Europe who showed how feudal principles could be used as the foundation for a strong, centralized monarchy. The feudal knight-service that was owed to the king gave him formidable military power. He was able to extract the service because his control of the lands of the old Anglo-Saxon royal house made him enormously more wealthy and powerful than any of his vassals. He also inherited from the Anglo-Saxon monarchy an efficient chancery and a right to levy occasional taxes in the form of the Danegeld. Except on the Welsh and Scottish borders, his vassals did not control contiguous blocks of territory but only scattered fiefs, and the royal right to appoint sheriffs gave William an opportunity to control local legal and administrative affairs through nonfeudal officials. In 1086 he held a great assembly of subvassals who were required to take an oath of loyalty to him as king, an oath overriding their loyalty to their immediate lords. From the beginning, the king was able to forbid private warfare among his barons. For an eleventh-century kingdom, England was exceptionally peaceful and disciplined once William had formally established his power.

The efficiency of William's government is illustrated especially by the compilation of the vast survey known as *Domesday Book* in 1086. Royal commissioners were sent out to hold sessions in each county court, at which a jury, summoned from each village in the county, gave detailed information about the resources of its district. The information was carefully recorded and then reorganized into a form convenient for use by the royal administration. In *Domesday Book,* all the lands of England were listed by counties and, within the counties, by baronies held of the crown. We have the name of the estate, the name of the baron who held it, and the name of the subtenant if there was one. Then we are told how many hides or assessment units the estate held. In addition, we are given the arable land, the size of the labor force, the number of the plow teams, any extra item of value such as woods, mills, and fisheries, and, finally, the estimated annual value of the estate in King Edward's time and in 1086 when the survey was made.* Obviously, *Domesday Book* is a mine of information for the historian, but King William wanted it for more practical purposes. No other contemporary monarch in western Europe had at his disposal such an accurate, large-scale account of the taxable resources of his subjects.

William and his barons had been partners in a great and hazardous adventure. They worked closely together to secure and hold the kingdom of England. At first, they were strangers in a strange land surrounded by foes. But this situation soon changed, and none of the things William feared ever came to pass. Danish raiders killed several of his earls, but no serious invasion ever came from Scandinavia. The strong fiefs established on the frontiers were more than able to handle the Welsh and the Scots; in fact, Norman lords were soon taking over the lowlands of South Wales and pressing their conquests up the river valleys into the hills. After the liquidation of the rebels in the fens, the Saxons gave no trouble. As William's position grew stronger, ten-

*Sources, no. 74

sions built up between him and his barons. William was resolved to maintain intact the powers of the Anglo-Saxon monarchy. The barons of England, on the other hand, wanted all the independence they could gain—certainly as much as their Norman peers enjoyed. Thus, while William strove to maintain and, if possible, increase the power of the crown and its agents—the sheriffs—the barons tried to infringe on that power. As long as William lived, he was able to dominate the baronage. Later kings of England, however, were not always so successful.

30. *The Medieval Empire*

The political structure and traditions of the East Frankish state were different from those of England and France, and its rulers had different problems to contend with. Except for Lorraine and western Franconia, none of its territory had formed part of the Roman Empire. Lorraine and Franconia were also the only sections of the East Frankish state that had been an integral part of the Merovingian lands. In the tenth century, Lorraine was still wavering in allegiance between the West Frankish and the East Frankish kingdoms. Although Bavaria had for a time been subject to the Merovingian kings, it had been little affected by that experience, and its actual incorporation in the Frankish state was the work of Charlemagne's father, King Pepin. The conquest of Saxony was a purely Carolingian enterprise, started by Charles Martel and completed by Charlemagne. Although Charlemagne had established a few *vassi dominici* along the Slavic frontier, in general feudal institutions had not spread beyond Lorraine and Franconia. In most of the East Frankish state there were no organized counties. The counts were simply royal agents with powers of supervision over the local popular courts. Finally, the seignorial system had not penetrated far into the German lands and was practically unknown in Saxony. This was a land of noble and nonnoble free farmers.

When the power of the Carolingian kings began to crumble in the middle of the ninth century, the peoples of the East Frankish state had not had time to forget their independent past. In particular, the Saxons and Bavarians thought of themselves as distinct peoples. When their kings failed to defend the land from Vikings and Magyars, they sought local leadership that recalled their ancient traditions. Thus, in each of the chief districts of the kingdom—*Saxony, Franconia, Lorraine, Swabia,* and *Bavaria*—an important local landholder became the military leader of the people. These leaders took the title duke, and historians have called them tribal, or *stem,* dukes. The power of these dukes rested on their own landed possessions and on their personal influence over their peoples. At first, they had no authority over the counts and no rights in respect to the bishoprics and abbeys in their duchies. Naturally, however, each duke was ambitious to gain full power in his duchy by usurping the royal demesne, making the counts dependent on him, and obtaining the rights of patronage over the churches. During the feeble reign of the last East Frankish Carolingian king, Louis the Child (899–911), they made decided progress in this direction and were well on the way to becoming kings in their own duchies. They were inclined to leave the throne vacant and to consolidate their own power.

Two forces were chiefly responsible for the failure of the dukes to achieve their purpose—the church and the Magyars. In Germany, as in France, the church wanted a strong monarchy and for similar reasons. The prelates vastly preferred to deal with one king rather than with five dukes. They felt the need for a powerful ruler, who would be able to maintain peace and order throughout the land, and many of them cherished a theocratic ideal of sacred monarchy. But the church might not have been able to persuade the dukes to choose a king had it not been for the Magyars. Their raids were at their height, yet no duke could be convinced of the need for action against them until they entered his own duchy. It was clear even to the dukes that the Magyars could be curbed only by unified leadership. Hence they attempted a compromise. They chose as king the weakest of the dukes, Conrad of Franconia (911–918). This experiment was not successful. Conrad permitted Lorraine to fall under the control of the French king, Charles the Simple (893–923), but in the other regions of his kingdom, Conrad constantly intrigued with the dukes' subjects, especially with the clergy, aiming to undermine ducal power; and he made no serious attempts to organize resistance to the Magyars. Very reluctantly the great lords of Germany came to the conclusion that they would have to elect as king the most powerful of the dukes, Henry, called the Fowler, duke of Saxony. On his deathbed, Conrad I named Henry his successor, and he was elected without difficulty.

Henry I (919–936), the founder of the Saxon dynasty,* adopted a policy sharply different from that of Conrad. He exacted from all the dukes an explicit acknowledgment of his status as king but then left them to control the internal affairs of their duchies as almost autonomous rulers. Henry devoted himself to building up his own power in the north. He reannexed Lorraine and made an alliance with its duke. He built frontier fortifications on his eastern border and used them as bases for attacks on the Slavic peoples beyond the Elbe. Finally, Henry raised a large force of cavalry which proved effective in curbing the Magyar raids. He left a formidable base of power to his son.

Henry's son and successor, Otto I (936–973), often called Otto the Great, was one of the dominant figures of the early Middle Ages. He established a strong kingship in Germany and founded the medieval empire, later called the Holy Roman Empire, that in one form or another continued down to the days of Napoleon. He also, in 955, inflicted a final devastating defeat on the Magyars at the battle of the Lechfeld and so created the climate for the growth of an orderly civilization in eastern Europe. After their defeat at the Lechfeld, the

*See Appendix, Table 3.

The Ottonian Empire, ca. 960

The expansionist policies of Otto I, vigorously executed, created a new empire, which now included the German kingdom and parts of Italy as well as some areas of the old Middle Kingdom of Lothair that had been under French control. Saxon power was also expanding across the Elbe into Slav territory.

Magyars never again invaded Germany on a large scale but withdrew to Hungary and established a permanent Magyar kingdom there.

From the outset of his reign, Otto made it clear that he would not be content, like his father, to be a mere "first among equals" in relation to the other dukes. He deliberately revived the Carolingian

This ivory panel illustrates the Ottonian theory of divine sanction of secular kingship; Christ in Majesty between the Virgin and St. Maurice is worshiped by Otto II, his empress Theophano, and their son, the future Otto III. Done at Milan ca. 980. Museo del Castello Sforzesco, Milan. *Art Reference Bureau*

tradition by traveling to Aachen, Charlemagne's old capital, to be solemnly crowned and anointed as king. The dukes rendered ceremonial homage to Otto at his coronation, but when they realized that he was determined to be a king in fact as well as in name, they commenced a wave of rebellion against him. Otto crushed them all by 938 and, in doing so, greatly strengthened his own power. The duke of

Franconia died during the fighting, and Otto left the office vacant and himself ruled Franconia directly. In Saxony he gave extensive lands to one of his favorites, Magnus Billung, but carefully withheld the ducal title. Thus he had complete control of two of the four stem duchies. The annexation of the ducal lands of Franconia permanently strengthened and enriched the German crown.

Above all, Otto relied on the support of the church in building up his power against the dukes. In the tenth century, a king was often regarded as a sacred figure, consecrated to a spiritual office much as priests were consecrated at their ordination, and Otto played this theocratic role to the full. He chose the great bishops and abbots of the realm at his own will and greatly increased their wealth and power, but he insisted on their complete allegiance and support in return for his protection. The kings of France and England also relied on the support of their clergy, but in Germany more than anywhere else, the church became the chief bulwark of the monarchy. Bishops normally held rights of government over their own lands and were often given count's rights over neighboring districts that did not belong to their churches. They were obliged to send strong bodies of soldiers to the royal armies whenever they were needed. In this way Otto made sure of having a reliable army and established powerful supporters of the crown in all the duchies. If a duke rebelled, he found the forces of the church within his lands arrayed against him. Otto had no capital city and few officials except the counts. His only army was his Saxon levy and the men supplied by the churches. But as long as his Saxons followed him and he retained his control of the church, his monarchy was very strong and effective.

In the early years of his reign, Otto was essentially a northern potentate whose power lay in Saxony and Franconia. In southern Germany his power was limited to control of some of the counts and the church. This situation was not alarming so long as there was no strong power in the south. But the dukes of Swabia and Bavaria were ambitious men, anxious to extend their authority. Both looked greedily at Lombardy across the Alps in northern Italy, and the duke of Swabia had ambitions to secure the kingdom of Burgundy. Any such addition to one of the southern duchies would destroy the balance of power in Germany. Moreover, a combination of Italy and Burgundy under a strong ruler would form a menace to the German kingdom, since such a ruler was bound to want to regain the rest of the ancient realm of Lothair. When Rudolph II of Burgundy died in 937, this threat to Otto's position seemed imminent. Hugh of Arles, king of Italy, seized Burgundy. Otto acted quickly. He drove Hugh from Burgundy and placed the son of the late king on its throne under his protection. Fourteen years later he himself invaded Lombardy. In organizing this new province, he followed the system that had been so successful in Germany. The bishops were given control of the secular as well as the ecclesiastical affairs in their dioceses and so were bound closely to Otto's interests.

Historians have accused Otto of allowing greed and love of conquest to divert his attention from Germany to Italy to the detriment of the German monarchy, but it seems clear that, in his case at least, expansion to the south was purely defensive. As long as there was no strong ruler in Lombardy, the region lay open to any adventurer, and Otto could not risk having it fall into the hands of a south German prince.

When Otto conquered Lombardy in 951, he planned to assume the imperial crown at once. The reasons that lay behind this intention were probably quite simple. Any great Germanic conqueror would have been proud to assume the title of Charlemagne. Moreover, the ancient Middle Kingdom ruled by the emperor Lothair had consisted of Italy, Burgundy, and Lorraine. All these regions were subject to Otto, and by becoming emperor he would secure the traditional title to them. But the Roman nobles who controlled the papacy were not anxious to have the imperial authority revived. Their opposition combined with troubles in Germany—a revolt of great nobles and fresh Hungarian raids—to delay Otto's plans, and it was not until 962 that he led an army to Rome and was solemnly crowned emperor. The pope of the time, John XII, a singularly depraved character, at first welcomed Otto as an ally against the groups of Roman nobility opposed to his own faction, but he soon found the emperor's rule oppressive and fomented a rebellion against him. Otto thereupon convoked a synod that deposed the pope. From then on, Otto and his successors took it for granted that, as emperors, they could appoint popes in Rome just as they appointed bishops in Germany.

Otto's assumption of the imperial title brought him into conflict with the Byzantines who still held the major cities of southern Italy, although they were subject to frequent harassment by Saracens raiding from Sicily. After a series of indecisive campaigns, Otto was able to negotiate a peace settlement. His title was duly acknowledged and his son, the future Otto II, married a Byzantine princess, Theophano.

Otto II (973–983) had a less successful and less fortunate reign than his father. He managed to beat down a major rebellion led by the duke of Bavaria in 978, and in 980 he received the imperial coronation in Rome. Two years later he led a major campaign against a new Saracen invasion of southern Italy but suffered a devastating defeat in which he lost a great part of his army. Otto himself returned to Rome, where he died a few months later. When the news of his death and humiliating defeat reached Saxony, there was a sudden uprising of the Slavic peoples between the Elbe and the Odor who had been conquered by Otto I. The German colonists and missionaries were wiped out, and the Saxons barely succeeded in holding the old Elbe frontier. The process of German colonization was halted for two centuries.

Otto left as his heir a three-year-old child who was brought up in the custody of his mother, Theophano. This Otto III (983–1002) was essentially a Byzantine prince and planned to make Rome the capital of his empire. He built himself a palace on the Aventine Hill and appointed the greatest scholar of the age, the Frenchman Gerbert, to be his pope. Gerbert significantly called himself Sylvester II; the first Sylvester had been pope in the days of the great emperor Constantine. This whole policy was a young man's romantic dream, probably shaped by his mother's influence. It could never have succeeded, for Otto had no real basis of power in Rome. His only strength lay in the support of a Saxon army, and the Roman aristocratic factions never voluntarily accepted his rule. In any case, Otto died when he was only twenty-one years old. He had no son and was succeeded by the head of a younger branch of the Saxon house, Henry II (1002–1024). Although Henry belonged to the Saxon dynasty, his lands and interests were largely in Bavaria, and he could not command the loyalty of the Saxons. Throughout his reign he was fully occupied maintaining his position in Germany.

Henry II was the last king of the Saxon dynasty. When he died in 1024, the nobles and prelates of Germany elected as their king Conrad II of Franconia, a descendant of a daughter of Otto the Great. He inaugurated the dynasty called *Salian* (because Franconia was the homeland of the Salian Franks). The problems that faced a German king had changed somewhat since the days of Otto the Great, and at this point it seems well to pause for a moment to glance at a group that was to play a vital part in German politics: the great nobles called *Fürsten* by German historians, "princes" by English writers. Although the chief method used by the Saxon kings to curb the power of the stem dukes was to strengthen the ecclesiastical lords, they also employed the device of establishing favored laymen within the various duchies as rivals to the dukes. Thus, by the end of the Saxon period, there were in Germany many powerful lords who were neither dukes nor prelates. The nature of their positions varied widely. A man might hold extensive lands in allodial (that is, nonfeudal) tenure, be a count, and also hold fiefs granted him by the emperor or one of the dukes. Perhaps the most striking of the princely families of this period was the house of Billung. Magnus Billung, the first of the line, was an important Saxon landholder who had been a favorite of Otto I and had received extensive property as fiefs from the crown. Bit by bit the Billungs extended their holdings, until by the end of the Saxon period they considered themselves dukes of Saxony; it is not quite clear whether they were ever recognized as such by a Saxon king. But the Billungs were only one of many such families. Each was striving to build up its possessions and to obtain privileges and rights of jurisdiction. While these men represented the same social and political group as the great feudal lords of France, they were not in this early period in so strong a position. Their allodial lands were theirs to pass on to whom they pleased; but offices such as that of count, which gave rights of jurisdiction, were not hereditary in Germany, and the hereditability of fiefs held from the crown was not fully recognized by the kings. In fact, one of the chief aims of the princes was to make their offices and fiefs hereditary, if possible without giving the same rights to their subordinates.

Conrad II (1024–1039), the first king of the new Salian line, was no paragon of Christian kingship. He was a hard, tough, illiterate soldier, but he showed himself well able to cope with the problems of upholding royal authority. In 1033 the throne of Burgundy fell vacant, and relying on a rather tenuous claim through his wife, Conrad was able to seize the kingship for himself and so annex Burgundy to the German crown. He also won major victories over the Poles and compelled them to acknowledge his overlordship. In his internal policy, Conrad realized that control of ecclesiastical fiefs in itself was not a sufficient foundation for a strong monarchy, and he began to build up a class of lay servants called *ministeriales.* These men were peasants, usually serfs, chosen from the royal demesne and trained to be either warriors or administrators. Such men could provide a corps of civil servants and an army of knights who were not linked by family ties or community of interest with either the nobles or the clergy.

Conrad's son, Henry III (1039–1056), continued his father's policies. Like all his predecessors, he relied heavily on the support of the great prelates of Germany, but he also saw that there was need for a firm center of royal power, such as Otto the Great had had in Saxony. A truly effective government also needed loyal lay officials and an adequate money revenue. The Salian house were dukes of Franconia and had extensive possessions in Swabia. If to these lands could be added southern Saxony and Thuringia, the crown would control the heart of Germany. Henry began to build castles in Thuringia and southern Saxony and to garrison them with *ministeriales* from his Swabian lands. These men were completely dependent on him, devoted to his interests, and had no sympathy for the Saxon nobles, who objected to this extension of the king's authority. With their aid, Henry started to take into his own hands the ducal rights in southern Saxony. Naturally, this gravely annoyed the Billungs, who considered themselves dukes of Saxony, and troubled all the Saxon nobles, who had for years been almost completely independent of royal control.

Henry III was an able monarch with a high conception of his function as king and emperor. While he thought of the church as an important element in the political structure of his realm, he was also interested in its capacity to perform its spiritual obligations. He supported monastic reform movements in his own lands and also encouraged the members of the papal curia who were imbued with similar ideas and who wished to make the papacy the instrument for a reform of the church as a whole.* Henry's policies rested on two presuppositions: the first was that the princes would acquiesce in a steady growth of royal power; the second was that the church would remain unwaveringly loyal to the monarchy. Both presuppositions proved disastrously mistaken in the generation after Henry's death, but as long as he lived the system worked. By 1046 he had pacified all Germany. When, in that year, he traveled to Italy to establish his power there and to be crowned as emperor in Rome, the theocratic monarchy of Germany stood at an apogee of power and prestige.

*See p. 232.

31. Borderlands of Europe: The Spread of Christianity

During the two centuries from 850 to 1050 important changes occurred in the religious and political structures of the borderlands surrounding Christian Europe. The major development was a spread of Christianity to pagan peoples and their gradual assimilation into the culture of an expanded Christendom. These changes affected the Scandinavian countries; Poland, Bohemia, and Hungary in eastern Europe; and the Slavic peoples of Russia and the Balkan peninsula. Often the process of Christianization was accompanied by the establishment of permanent kingdoms or dukedoms which would survive as political units into the modern age. The overall effect of these sometimes aparently obscure events was very great. They shaped for the future the boundaries of Latin Christendom, the region in which a distinctively western European culture would develop.

During the major part of the great era of Viking activities, the ninth and tenth centuries, the Scandinavian countries had little political organization. There were local popular courts corresponding to the Anglo-Saxon hundred courts and regional assemblies called *things.* There were also regional chieftains who waged continual war against one another when they were not leading raids against the coasts of Christian Europe. Occasionally one of these chieftains would achieve a fairly wide dominance, but until the time of Harold Fairhair, who subdued all Norway in about the year 900, no one could be called the king of a Scandinavian state. Despite their lack of unity, however, the Scandinavian peoples occupied a vast empire in northern Europe. In addition to the Scandinavian peninsula and Denmark, they held the Russian states of Novgorod and Kiev; Frisia; Normandy; eastern England; the western English kingdom of Strathclyde; a large part of Ireland; the Faroe, Hebrides, Orkney, and Shetland islands; Iceland; and some settlements in Greenland. This was at the height of their expansion.

The first substantial groups of Scandinavian people to accept Christianity (around 900) were the Danes who settled in eastern England and the Vikings of Normandy. Even before that, in 826, King Louis the Pious had sent the monk Ansgar as missionary to Scandinavia. Ansgar preached in Denmark and Sweden with little success and subsequently became archbishop of Bremen. His succesors in the see carried on the work of conversion, helped by missionaries from England. In the last half of the tenth and first half of the eleventh centuries, three great kings—Harold Bluetooth of Denmark, Olaf Trygvesson of Norway, and Olaf, called the Taxgatherer, of Sweden—firmly established the three Scandinavian kingdoms and made Christianity their official religion. In all probability, the purpose of these monarchs in renouncing paganism was as much political as religious: they believed that church organization was necessary to an orderly state. Harold Bluetooth of Denmark was converted about 960. Olaf Trygvesson accepted Christianity while living in England and estab-

The Spread of Christianity

lished his new religion in Norway after he had seized the throne there in 995—partly by encouraging the work of English missionaries, partly by brutal coercion of reluctant pagans. At about the same time Olaf the Taxgatherer of Sweden became a Christian; but the old heathen religion survived most tenaciously in his country and conflict between paganism and Christianity continued throughout the eleventh century. The greatest center of the old religion was at Uppsala. The chronicler Adam of Bremen left a lurid account of the rites of human and animal sacrifice which, he stated, were still practiced there in the 1070s. "Dogs and horses may be seen hanging close by human beings. A Christian told me he had seen seventy-two bodies hanging together." Before 1100 the temple at Uppsala had been torn down. By the early twelfth century Christianity was generally accepted. Iceland accepted Christianity at about the year 1000 and the episcopal see of Gardar was established for Greenland in 1050.

For more than a century the archbishop of Bremen was considered the metropolitan of all the dioceses in the three northern kingdoms. But in 1104 Lund in Denmark, in 1152 Nidaros in Norway, and in 1164 Uppsala in Sweden became seats of archbishops. Although there were at times fierce quarrels between the Scandinavian kings and the church, in general the ecclesiastical hierarchy supported the royal authority and aided in the unification of the three kingdoms.

Throughout the eleventh and twelfth centuries, the political history of the Scandinavian states was a tale of war and revolt. The three kingdoms fought one another and rival families struggled for the throne in each state. Internally, the period was marked by the rise to dominance of a landowning noble class. In the eleventh century, there were large and small landowners, but all held the same general status and were required to answer the king's summons to war. By the thirteenth century, however, only the nobles were expected to perform military service and were exempted from taxation, while the ordinary free peasant paid taxes instead of serving. Naturally, there was a tendency for the peasants to give up their land to the nobles and become their tenants. Although the kings tried to prevent this conversion, the noble lands continually increased. The development of the noble class was hastened by the introduction of feudal practices. Late in the twelfth century, the kings of Denmark began to grant fiefs in return for military service, and later this custom spread to Norway and Sweden. Although the fiefs were not hereditary and the chief bases of the power of the nobles lay in their allodial lands, the fiefs added to the resources of favored individuals. The nobles in all three states met in great councils and worked to limit the authority of the kings.

On the whole, it seems clear, however, that the feudal system never was dominant in the Scandinavian countries. There were nobles who held fiefs, but the noble class as a whole drew its power from allodial lands. The military service owed by the nobles and the use of imported titles such as baron, knight, and squire give a false feudal front to what was essentially a nonfeudal society. The seignorial system was even more strikingly absent. Fief holders and nobles had no rights of jurisdiction unless they happened, as was common in Norway, to hold a royal office; but the jurisdiction was recognized as a public function and did not go with the possession of the land. Although the church enjoyed with the nobles the right of exemption from taxation, the prelates did not hold their lands as fiefs.

During the tenth century important developments also occurred in the religious and political structure of eastern Europe. Beyond the eastern borders of the German kingdom three permanent states emerged—Poland, Bohemia, and Hungary. All these lands were converted to Christianity in the tenth and early eleventh centuries, mainly by German missionaries. Otto I regarded the spread of Christianity as a duty of a Christian emperor, and also as a way of extending his own influence. Accordingly, in 968 he established an archbishopric at Magdeburg without any fixed eastern border, intending it to serve as a center from which German Christianity would be carried to the Slavs of Poland. Regensburg, in Bavaria, was the principal center for the conversion of Bohemia. The dukes of Bohemia accepted Christianity as early as 894 and by the 920s the Czechs had produced their first martyr, St. Ludmila. An episcopal see established at Prague was at first held by German bishops but a Czech, St. Adalbert, was appointed in 982. Adalbert subsequently traveled to Rome and became a close friend of Emperor Otto III. He died as a missionary to the heathens of the Baltic region.

The short reign of Otto III was important for the spread of Christianity in eastern Europe. Influenced perhaps by Adalbert, the young Otto (or his advisers) was more willing than his predecessors to approve the founding of national churches, independent of the German bishops. In Poland the decisive period was the reign of Prince Mieszko (c. 960–992). Mieszko married a Czech Christian princess and willingly accepted baptism. He was quite unwilling, though, to accept the jurisdiction of the German see of Magdeburg over his church. In 990 he put his land under the direct protection of the Roman church, holding it from then onward as a vassal of the pope. In the year 1000 an independent Polish archbishopric of Gniezno was established by the pope with approval of Otto III.

At about the same time Roman Christianity was established in Hungary. After their defeat by Otto I at Lechfeld the Magyars settled down to form a permanent state. Their leaders accepted German missionaries, mainly from Regensburg and Salzburg, in the second half of the tenth century and Christianity was firmly established by St. Stephen, king from 997 to 1038. In 1000 he received a royal crown from the pope and subsequently established a Hungarian hierarchy directly dependent on Rome. Thus by about 1000 Bohemia, Poland, and Hungary had all accepted western Christianity and had established direct contacts with the Roman church. Only in the north, between Poland and Russia, were there still large populations of pagan Slavs.

South of Hungary, the peoples of the Balkan peninsula had been converted a century earlier, but here the process of conversion was complicated by the rivalry between the two great churches of Rome and Constantinople. In 863 the Byzantine emperor Michael III sent two brothers, Cyril and Methodius, as missionaries to the Slavs. Before setting out, the brothers invented a Slavonic alphabet and translated the Gospels into Slavonic. When they had made a substantial number of converts they went further and created a Slavonic liturgy. In 867 they journeyed to Rome and obtained the pope's approval for this innovation. (It was a considerable achievement of Cyril and Methodius that they succeeded in remaining loyal to both Rome and Constantinople at a time of growing tension between the two sees.) Soon, through the efforts of Cyril and Methodius and the disciples whom they trained, all the south Slav peoples accepted Christianity.

The pope and the patriarch of Constantinople were both eager to win the allegiance of the new converts. Eventually the Croats, settled along the Dalmatian coast, became attached to Rome, but the Serbs accepted Greek Christianity.

A major dispute between Rome and Constantinople that broke out at this time requires more detailed treatment. The dispute concerned the religious allegiance of Bulgaria. It was complicated by an attempt of the pope to judge between two rival claimants to the patriarchate of Constantinople, Ignatius and Photius. The sequence of events was complex, but the affair is an important one because it forms a significant chapter in the history of the gradual estrangement between Greek Orthodox and Roman Catholic Christianity.

The Bulgars, originally a Turko-Mongol people, had conquered the Slavs in the region of modern Bulgaria in the seventh century and had then been assimilated by the much more numerous Slav population. During the ninth century they created a powerful state which dominated almost the entire Balkan peninsula and at times threatened Constantinople itself. Toward 860 it became clear that the adventurous and opportunistic Khan Boris of Bulgaria was willing to convert to Christianity. At this point the dispute between Rome and Constantinople about the Byzantine patriarchate broke out. It began in 858 with a quarrel at Constantinople involving the patriarch Ignatius and the powerful regent Bardas (who ruled on behalf of the young emperor, Michael III). Ignatius publicly condemned Bardas for carrying on an adulterous affair with his daughter-in-law. The emperor then summoned a synod which deposed Ignatius and chose in his place Photius, a friend of Bardas. Photius was an urbane, learned aristocrat, well-fitted for the role of patriarch, though he was still a layman when his elevation was announced. The usual letters proclaiming his accession were sent out to other patriarchs, including the pope at Rome.

It happened that the pope at this time, Nicholas I (858–867), was one of the most strong-willed and assertive figures in the whole line of Roman pontiffs. He wrote back that he could not accept Photius until his legates had investigated the whole affair. Also, he wrote, it would be fitting for the emperor to return to the jurisdiction of the Roman church the lands in South Italy and Illyricum which had been snatched away by Leo III more than a century earlier.* (Illyricum now included Boris' Bulgaria.) Some historians maintain that the dominant motive of the pope in the whole subsequent dispute was simply to extend the jurisdiction of the Roman church in these regions.

The Byzantines reacted with typical subtlety and finesse. They welcomed the papal legates, treated them with every possible honor, and loaded them with lavish gifts or bribes. Understandably the legates confirmed the elevation of Photius without pressing for the concessions the pope wanted in Italy and Illyricum. Exasperated by the performance of his legates, Nicholas summoned a council at Rome in 863 which repudiated their work; it rejected Photius and reinstated Ignatius.

*See p. 132.

The Byzantines had no intention of permitting Rome to meddle in their affairs. Moreover their position was strengthened at this point by events in Bulgaria. Threatened by a powerful Byzantine army, Boris decided to adopt orthodox Christianity. He was baptized by Photius in 864 and the sponsor at his baptism was the emperor Michael himself. Michael also wrote to the pope coldly rejecting his judgment in the case of Photius. This letter provoked a rejoinder from Nicholas which set out in a most intransigent form the Roman claim to jurisdiction over all the churches, including the church of Constantinople. The pope's authority, Nicholas wrote, extended "over the whole earth, that is over the whole church."

These were mere words. The pope had no way of enforcing his claims. But once again the situation was complicated by the ambitious Boris of Bulgaria. Although he had accepted eastern orthodoxy Boris did not want to be dependent on the Byzantine patriarchate. He asked for a patriarch of his own and also for the right to continue various Bulgarian customs which conflicted with Greek orthodox practices. Photius, making a diplomatic blunder for once, contemptuously brushed aside these requests. Boris thereupon turned to Rome again. Nicholas dispatched to him a long, sympathetic letter promising to send an archbishop to Bulgaria and approving those Bulgarian practices which, if barbarous, were not actually heretical. (The pope drew the line at polygamy, but conceded that it was permissible for women to wear trousers.) Most importantly, Nicholas introduced into Bulgaria theological doctrine which, from this time onward, would cause endless trouble between the Greek and Roman churches. It concerned an obscure point of theology concerning the Trinity. The ancient council of Constantinople (381) had issued a creed including the words "The Holy Spirit, who proceeds from the Father." In the western churches (beginning in Spain) it had become customary to vary the formula and declare that the Holy Spirit proceeded "from the Father and the Son" (*patre filioque*). Pope Nicholas' legates approved this formula in their negotiations with Boris. It is not clear whether a profound point of theology was involved or merely a technicality of language which both sides seized upon as an excuse to condemn the other. At any rate a synod of eastern bishops excommunicated Pope Nicholas in 867 and so initiated the so-called Photian schism.

In the same year a palace revolution brought to power a new emperor, Basil I (867–886), and under him the outstanding issues were settled. Ignatius was restored to the patriarchate, but after he died in 877 Photius succeeded him, this time with the pope's approval. Communion between the churches of Rome and Constantinople was reestablished in 879, but without any real agreement being reached concerning the *filioque* dispute or the Roman claim to universal jurisdiction. As for the Bulgarians, Boris soon became disenchanted with the papacy which, after all, did not send him a distinguished prelate as archbishop. In 870 he turned to the eastern church again and accepted from Constantinople an archbishop and twelve bishops who established an orthodox hierarchy for his country. From then onward the Bulgarians remained firmly attached to eastern orthodoxy. In the 890s they adopted the Slavonic liturgy spread by the disciples of Cyril and Methodius.

A century later the Byzantine church achieved its last great missionary conquest among the Slav peoples, the conversion of Russia. The emperor Basil II (976–1025) was to become a very powerful ruler, but in the early part of his reign he was embarrassed by a series of rebellions and unsuccessful wars. In 987 he appealed for help to Vladimir, prince of Kiev. (The principality had been originally established by Swedish Vikings. From the mid-tenth century onward its rulers took Slavic rather than Scandinavian names.) Vladimir agreed to provide help and also to accept orthodox Christianity on one condition: Basil was to send his own sister Anna, a Byzantine princess of the highest rank, "born in the purple," to be Vladimir's bride. This Vladimir by all accounts was a monster of vice and cruelty. One wonders why such a man should have accepted Christianity at all. The reason was probably at least partly political as with the Scandinavian kings. Vladimir wanted to build a strong principality, and an organized church could help to establish an organized state. When he asked for a Byzantine princess to marry he already had several wives and more than eight hundred concubines. But Basil had little choice in the matter. The wretched Anna was dispatched to Kiev and Vladimir kept his part of the bargain. Soon there was a Russian church, organized on the Byzantine model, housed in buildings of Byzantine style, and acknowledging the patriarch of Constantinople as its supreme head.

The religious changes of the ninth and tenth centuries in eastern Europe had lasting consequences. As we have seen, the Poles, Bohemians, Hungarians, and Croats adopted western, Latin Christianity. The Serbs, Bulgarians, and Russians accepted eastern orthodoxy. The religious loyalties established in this early period have continued to affect the politics and culture of eastern Europe down to the twentieth century.

So far we have considered the influence of Byzantium on the Slavic peoples of eastern Europe. If we discuss briefly the Byzantine empire itself among the "borderlands of Europe" it must be understood that the phrase is used only in a geographic sense. Constantinople was still the capital of a great empire, more powerful and far more civilized than any of the western kingdoms at this time. Moreover the empire was not entirely or even predominantly a European power. The major sources of wealth and labor power lay in the provinces of Anatolia (modern Turkey). Constantinople was a great port, the hub of a network of commerce that stretched through central Asia as far as China.

Successive emperors were served by three enduring institutions, all essential to the stability of the state—the civil service, the army, and the church. At Constantinople an intricate bureaucracy, recruited from the most educated and intelligent citizens, supervised taxation, foreign affairs, and all matters of domestic administration. The army drew its strength from the provinces of the empire. The provinces were ruled by a military aristocracy and populated by sturdy free farmers who provided the rank and file of the Byzantine cavalry forces. The church offered a common religion for the people and enacted the splendid liturgical ceremonies which attracted all classes of Byzantine society. The church also provided an ideology of empire. Although individual emperors were often deposed and sometimes assassinated, no one doubted that the imperial office was established by God to direct all the affairs of the Christian world. The Byzantines were fully conscious of the continuity of their state with the Christian Roman Empire of late antiquity. Even though they sometimes found it diplomatically convenient to recognize the imperial title of a Charlemagne or an Otto I, they never ceased to regard the western emperors as mere barbarian upstarts. A Lombard bishop, Liudprand, who was sent as an ambassador to Constantinople by Otto I, wrote a lively account of his experiences there. His pages illustrate vividly how the gap between Byzantine and Western culture had widened since the time of the late Roman Empire. Liudprand was half-fascinated by the magnificence of the imperial court and wholly exasperated by the arrogance of the Byzantines and by their silky sophistication which constantly frustrated his attempts to bargain on behalf of Otto I.*

During the tenth century the Byzantine empire entered on a new period of growth and vitality. The period has been called a "golden age" of Byzantine art and letters. Certainly it was a time of vigorous military expansion. In 971 eastern Bulgaria was conquered and by 1018 the western regions of Bulgaria had been occupied and assimilated into the empire. These victories reestablished the ancient imperial frontier along the Danube. Still more important was the conquest of Muslim-held territory in the east. Crete fell to the Byzantines in 961 and Cyprus in 965. In a series of campaigns from the early 960s onward two great soldier-emperors, Nicephorus II (963–969), and John I (969–976), conquered almost all of Syria and Palestine, including the great city of Antioch. Basil II (976–1025) extended Byzantine power to Armenia. By the end of his reign the Byzantine state formed a great empire stretching from Azerbaijan to the Adriatic.

READING SUGGESTIONS

* *B. Tierney,* Sources *and* Readings, *vol. I, no. 30.*

* Sidney Painter, *The Rise of the Feudal Monarchies* (Ithaca, NY, 1951) provides a brief introduction, while * C. Petit-Dutaillis, *The Feudal Monarchy in France and England from the Tenth to the Thirteenth Century* is a substantial comparative study. France, England, and Germany are all discussed in * C. Brooke, *Europe in the Central Middle Ages 987–1125* (New York, 1964). For France, see also * R. Fawtier, *The Capetian Kings of France* (New York, 1966) and E. H. Hallam, *Capetian France, 987–1328* (New York, 1980). Good books on Anglo-Saxon England are F. M. Stenton, *Anglo-Saxon England* (Oxford, 1943), and * D. Whitelock, *The Beginnings of English Society* (Harmondsworth, 1952). See also T. J. Oleson, *The Witangemot in the Reign of Edward the Confessor*

*Sources, no. 30

(Toronto, 1955). The effects of the Norman conquest are considered in * D. C. Douglas, *William the Conqueror: The Norman Impact upon England* (Berkeley, 1964); F. M. Stenton, *The First Century of English Feudalism, 1066–1166,* 2nd ed. (Oxford, 1965). Briefer surveys are H. R. Loyn, *The Norman Conquest* (London, 1964), and F. Barlow, *William I and the Norman Conquest* (London, 1964). * G. O. Sayles, *The Medieval Foundations of England,* rev. ed. (London, 1950) discusses both the Saxon and Norman periods, as does H. R. Loyn, *The Governance of Anglo-Saxon England, 500–1087* (Stanford, CA, 1984). D. Whitelock, *English Historical Documents c. 500–1042* (London, 1955) is a massive collection which includes the whole of the Anglo-Saxon Chronicle and a reproduction of the Bayeux tapestry. On Germany and the Empire, see * G. Barraclough, *Origins of Modern Germany* (New York, 1946) and *Medieval Germany,* 2 vols. (Oxford, 1938). The second volume is a collection of essays by German historians. An older, detailed work is J. H. Thompson, *Feudal Germany* (Chicago, 1928). See also K. J. Leyser, *Rule and Conflict in an Early Medieval Society: Ottonian Saxony* (Bloomington, IL, 1979). E. Kantorowicz, *The King's Two Bodies* (Princeton, 1957) discusses the theocratic ideology of the early empire. *The Works of Liudprand of Cremona,* F. A. Wright (trans.) (London, 1932) provides a vivid picture of conditions in Italy and of Byzantine civilization as seen by a Western bishop. For Byzantine history in this period see * R. Jenkins, *Byzantium: The Imperial Centuries, 610–1071* (New York, 1969). On central and eastern Europe see F. Dvornik, *The Making of Central and Eastern Europe* (London, 1949) and *The Slavs in European History and Civilization* (New Brunswick, NJ, 1962); A. P. Vlasto, *The Entry of the Slavs into Christendom* (Cambridge, 1970). F. Dvornik, *The Photian Schism* (Cambridge, 1948) is an important study on the origins of the schism between the Greek and Latin churches. The conversion of Scandinavia is discussed in the works on the Vikings cited in Chapter VI and in C. Dawson, *The Making of Europe,* cited in Chapter I. A good contemporary source is Adam of Bremen, *History of the Archbishops of Hamburg-Bremen,* T. J. Tschan (trans.) (New York, 1959).

chapter

XI

The Reform of the Church

In the ninth and tenth centuries, while a few zealous missionaries were spreading Christianity to new peoples, church institutions in the heartland of western Europe were often falling into decay. During the tenth century the western church reached a nadir of corruption and indiscipline. Then a widespread burst of religious enthusiasm revitalized the structure of ecclesiastical institutions and raised the church to a higher spiritual and moral level. The reforms of this period made possible the dominant role that the church was to play in the culture of the twelfth and thirteenth centuries.

These reforms also led to a struggle between empire and papacy that helped to shape the whole future history of Germany and Italy. In the eleventh century, the papacy decisively rejected the tradition of royal theocracy that had become established in imperial Germany and that was also characteristic of the neighboring civilizations of Byzantium and Islam. A certain tension between church and state and a continuing concern of many religious leaders to reform and renew the structure of Christian society would remain characteristic features of Western civilization throughout the Middle Ages and for long afterward. In these ways the church reform movement of the eleventh century marks a turning point in the history of Western society.

32. *Disintegration and Reform*

For a brief period during the disintegration of Charlemagne's empire in the middle of the ninth century, the leaders of the church tried to maintain some degree of order and discipline in the lands of western Europe. The archbishops of France, led by Hincmar, metropolitan archbishop of Reims, tried with some success to control the policies of the French kings and to establish themselves as the final arbiters in political disputes. And the papacy at this time produced one of its most powerful pontiffs in Nicholas I (858–867). In the dispute with the Byzantine church concerning the election of the patriarch Photius, he vigorously reasserted the primacy of the Roman See.* He also strongly emphasized the right of the papacy to judge the moral conduct of secular rulers in a conflict with Lothair II, king of Lotharingia (855–869). Nicholas violently rebuked Lothair for making an illegal second marriage, compelled him to take his first wife back, and deposed two high-ranking German bishops who had condoned the king's offense. The letters recording these actions give an exaggerated impression of the real power of the papacy in the ninth century, but they provided important precedents for later popes in future conflicts.

Another valuable collection of precedents—this time forged—was concocted in France during this same period. The bishops of France found themselves under intense pressure from the great metropolitans like Hincmar, who were inclined to treat them as mere servants, and also from the local feudal nobility. They needed a collection of church law which would affirm unambiguously that bishops could be deposed only by the pope and that their lands were immune from secular control. Since no such collection could be found in the libraries of Gaul, an industrious cleric in northern France decided to manufacture one. His method was to forge letters and attribute them to the half-legendary popes of the earliest Christian centuries. The forgeries were then intermixed with genuine papal decretals and the whole collection ascribed to the seventh-century saint Isidore of Seville. The primary intention of the forger was to safeguard episcopal independence against the encroachments of local lay and ecclesiastical princes. The principal effect of his work was to provide a series of alleged papal claims to sovereignty in the church that apparently far antedated the real claims of Pope Leo I (440–461). The "False Decretals" were universally accepted as genuine during the Middle Ages and were incorporated into many later collections of canon law.

The strong pontificate of Nicholas I provided only a temporary rally of papal power. After his death, the papacy and indeed the whole western church were dragged down to a squalid state of corruption by the violence and anarchy of the times. Italy was politically fragmented at this time. Sicily and southwestern Italy were ruled by the Muslims. On the Adriatic lay the remnants of Byzantine possessions in Italy—a few actual Byzantine posts and some petty independent states under Byzantine influence. The popes ruled central Italy, and to the north lay an independent kingdom made up of virtually autonomous cities and duchies. The nominal "kings of Italy" rarely ruled more than the valley of the Po.

The papacy was in a particularly vulnerable situation. Rome and the Papal States were continually threatened by Muslim incursions from Sicily, and there was no strong king or emperor to defend them. The pope was the civil ruler of Rome at a time when only a powerful local noble could offer protection to the city. In these circumstances, the papacy came to be regarded primarily as a secular office, a prize that the parties of the Roman nobility fought for. The popes of the early

*See pp. 222–223.

tenth century were merely chiefs of aristocratic factions—and often disreputable chiefs at that. For half a century the noble house of Theophylact dominated Rome and appointed a series of incompetent pontiffs culminating in the scandalously immoral and sacrilegious John XII. John became pope in 956 at the age of sixteen and reigned until 963, when the emperor Otto I had him accused of a lurid series of crimes and deposed. For the next century the German emperors appointed popes (for the most part reasonably good ones) during the relatively short intervals when they dominated Rome. The Roman nobility chose the popes (usually very bad ones) during the much longer periods when they controlled the city. The papacy at this time reached its lowest ebb in dignity and spiritual prestige.

Meanwhile, all over Europe, the church was suffering grievously from the effects of Viking, Magyar, and Saracen invasions. In Ireland and along the western coasts of Britain, the great Celtic monasteries were almost completely wiped out by the Viking raids. In France many monasteries survived, but they had suffered heavily; and with a few notable exceptions, they had little discipline and less learning. The prelates were hardly different in point of view and way of life from their knightly relatives. In Germany the situation was much the same until the rise of the Ottonian dynasty. Moreover, throughout the Frankish kingdom, lay lords took advantage of the confusion to usurp church lands.

In order to survive, the church was obliged to enter into close relations with the lay rulers, the only power able to offer protection. Many bishops were appointed by the kings. Others fell under the control of feudal princes. As vassals they were obligated to perform the usual feudal services. But as a prelate could not kill or sentence to death, he could not with propriety lead his contingent of knights to battle or carry out the functions of a secular judge. Although there were warrior bishops—some used a mace in battle on the ground that dashing out a man's brains was not shedding blood—the majority sought some other solution. Usually, a prelate chose a lay lord to act as his *advocate.* The advocate led the prelate's knights in battle and performed his secular judicial duties in return for a fief or some other consideration, such as the chief share of the penalties imposed in the courts. Sometimes the lay advocate came to dominate the church. Also, the great lords expected to appoint whom they pleased as bishops and abbots without interference from any source. In a parallel to the secularization of the papacy, the high spiritual functions of the episcopacy became mere adjuncts to fief holding.

A similar process went on at the parochial level. Originally, the bishop and his priests had lived in the cathedral city and from there served the country round about. In the early days of the Frankish invasion of Roman Gaul, village churches began to be established, and the process accelerated as Europe broke down into small semi-independent fiefs. A lord wanted to control the religious side of his fief as well as the secular. He built a church, collected the tithes and the revenues from the land assigned to it, appointed a priest, and paid him the minimum sum necessary to enable him to live. (The tithe was a tenth part of all agricultural produce owed to the church according to canon law.) Thus the income from tithes and parish lands became an important source of the lord's revenue. Another result, however, was the creation of the network of rural parishes that was so important a part of the ecclesiastical structure.

Monasteries also fell under lay control. Since each Benedictine monastery was independent, its discipline depended almost entirely on the abbot, who was likely to be an appointee of a lay lord, chosen for reasons that were essentially political. In fact, in tenth-century France, it was common for the lord to be the titular abbot and enjoy his revenues while an ecclesiastical deputy cared for the spiritual function of the office. In theory, the bishops were responsible for the monasteries in their dioceses and had the authority to inspect them, but this was not an effective control.

Bishops and abbots who were primarily feudal nobles or priests who were hired servants of lay lords were not likely to be zealous religious leaders. The early feudal period saw a general collapse in standards of clerical discipline. According to Western ecclesiastical law, priests were supposed to remain unmarried and to live chastely, but the requirement was not taken very seriously anywhere in Europe. In Anglo-Saxon England it was common for parish priests and even higher church officers to be married and to pass their offices to their sons by inheritance. Although on the Continent the female companions of priests were rarely recognized as their wives, their existence was pretty much taken for granted. The issue was not purely a moral one. A clergyman who had a family was extremely likely to use church property to endow his children, whether or not they were considered legitimate by their neighbors. Another common offense of the time was *simony*—trafficking in church offices. As ecclesiastical appointments came to be regarded primarily as sources of revenue, they were flagrantly put on sale, often to the most unsuitable candidates. To ecclesiastical reformers, these two offenses, clerical marriage and simony, typified all that was wrong in the existing situation. They seemed to symbolize the subordination of spiritual values to material interests that was corrupting the whole life of the church.

For despite the generally low level of religious zeal, there were always some devoted churchmen who saw clearly the evils of the age and were determined to remedy them. Early in the tenth century, a group of such men succeeded in inaugurating a major movement of monastic reform. In 910 they prevailed on Duke William of Aquitaine to found the abbey of Cluny. Various provisions were made in the foundation charter in the hope that Cluny could avoid the difficulties of other houses and act as a spearhead for general monastic reform. Cluny did not hold land in return for feudal services. All gifts made to it were in free alms, that is, owing no service except masses and prayers for the donor. The foundation charter also confirmed the right of the monks to elect their own abbot and exempted the abbey from all local ecclesiastical control. Cluny was directly subordinate to the pope; given the state of the papacy, this meant that the community was effectively independent.*

These measures created a framework that made reform possible. Then an attempt was made to remove the chief sources of evil in monastic life. One of them was idleness. Work on manuscript copying and illumination provided a partial substitute for the manual labor prescribed in the old rule, but it did not keep the whole community adequately occupied. The solution of the founders of Cluny was to increase greatly the amount of time devoted to corporate liturgical worship, while the other two traditional elements of the Benedictine life, private prayer and productive work, were correspondingly de-emphasized.

The founders of Cluny naturally hoped that other monasteries would be founded on the same bases and that established houses would embrace the Cluniac rule. Here they planned to avoid another evil of contemporary monasticism—lack of effective supervision over the houses. The Cluniac order was to have only one abbot, the abbot of Cluny. All the other houses were to be ruled by priors. The abbot had general responsibility for the discipline of all the houses and was expected to make frequent inspections of them. The order spread with amazing rapidity under a succession of great abbots. Many Cluniac houses were founded, and a number of the proudest Benedictine monasteries of France accepted its rule. Moreover, the order maintained a very high level of discipline. The abbot of Cluny became the head of an ecclesiastical empire comprising hundreds of monastic houses spread over most of western Europe.

Although the Cluniac revival of monastic life was the most widespread reform movement of the tenth century, it was by no means the only one. In England an independent movement of monastic reform was carried through by St. Dunstan with the support of King Edgar (959–975). Many monasteries in France were reformed on the pattern of Cluny without joining the order. In the cities of northern Italy, there were growing movements of lay piety, whose members were violently critical of clerical corruption. Another very important center of reform was Lotharingia (Lorraine). There the initiative was taken by both bishops and abbots, supported by the kings of the Ottonian dynasty, and the reformers sought to raise standards of Christian life among the diocesan clergy as well as in the monasteries. The great Lotharingian abbey of Gorze was second only to Cluny in its influence as a center of reformed monasticism.

All these movements flowed together in a great international movement of reform led by the papacy from the mid-eleventh century onward. This papal reform movement can be called epoch-making in the most literal sense of the word. It transformed the structure of the medieval church and, in doing so, profoundly influenced the whole future history of Western institutions. We have seen that the papacy had fallen into a dismal state by the beginning of the eleventh century. But, in spite of the failings of individual pontiffs, Rome was still revered in the Christian world as the city of St. Peter. Papal headship

*Sources, no. 35

in the church had become quite ineffective in fact, but no one disputed it in theory. The letters of great pontiffs like Leo I and Gregory I, with their high claims for the Roman See, survived in the papal archives. Rome would be the natural center of a universal reform movement if ever a line of popes emerged who were capable of reviving the tradition of their great predecessors.

The establishment of such a line of popes was made possible by the emperor Henry III of Germany. When he traveled to Rome for his imperial coronation in 1046, he found a situation that was unusually scandalous even for those times. There were three candidates all claiming to be the rightful pope. One of them, Gregory VI, was a zealous reformer; the other two, mere faction leaders. Henry made little attempt to unravel the intricacies of their respective claims, but deposed all three of them and installed one of his own German bishops as pope. This pontiff and his successor, another German, each reigned for only a few months. But Henry's third pope, Leo IX, ruled from 1049 to 1054, and in those five years, he succeeded in establishing the papacy as the head of a new reform movement. Unlike the Cluniac movement, it did not aim merely at creating bands of monks who could live tranquil Christian lives by cutting themselves off from the world. The papal objective was rather to reform the world. Bishops and diocesan clergy were to be purified by a rigorous insistence on the law of celibacy and by a systemic elimination of all simony. Then the clergy, reconstituted as a true spiritual elite, was to lead and inspire the masses of laity.

Leo IX was a cousin of the emperor and had been the bishop of a diocese that was a center of the Lotharingian reform movement. As pope, he showed himself to be primarily a brilliant ecclesiastical organizer. His major achievement in this role was the creation of a body of *cardinals* who, from this time onward, played a major role in the government of the Roman church. The title of cardinal had existed earlier, but it was a mere honorific dignity held by some of the Roman prelates who performed liturgical functions in the great basilicas of the city. Leo transformed the nature of the office by naming outstanding reformers from various parts of Europe as cardinals of the Roman church and then using these men as his most trusted counselors and administrators. Three of Leo's cardinals were of especial importance. Hildebrand, who later became Pope Gregory VII, had been secretary to the Gregory VI deposed by the emperor in 1046. Humbert, a monk from Lotharingia, became the leading theoretician of the reform movement and an ardent defender of papal power. Peter Damian was an Italian monk who had won a great reputation as an ascetic and a fiery preacher. He was violently opposed to contemporary abuses in the church but conservative in his political outlook.

Helped by such men, Leo IX held a series of synods at Rome that framed new legislation directed against simony and clerical marriage. Moreover, the pope was not content merely to promulgate such decrees in Rome and leave them unenforced. His second great innovation, along with his reorganization of the Roman See, was to travel throughout Europe, holding councils in major ecclesiastical centers in order to publicize and put into practice the new reform decrees. In one year alone, 1049, the pope presided over assemblies at Rome, Pavia, Mainz, and Reims. Later journeys took him to councils at Augsburg, Regensburg, and Trier. All the neighboring bishops and clergy were summoned to these meetings. On each occasion, reform decrees were promulgated and accusations were heard against prelates alleged to have acquired their offices by simony. Sometimes bishops were deposed on the spot, sometimes summoned to Rome for further hearings. The pope's legislative and judicial power was seen working effectively in the lands north of the Alps as it had not been seen for centuries. When Leo died in 1054, he had effectively reasserted the headship of the papacy in the western church and had established an able group of reformers at Rome who were well equipped to carry on his work.

33. *From Reform to Revolution*

The harmony between empire and papacy did not last for long. The conflict between them that soon broke out used to be called the Investiture Contest. More recently it has become fashionable to describe the affair as a Papal Revolution. It did indeed involve a radical challenge to the existing structure of Western institutions.

The "revolution" began when the reformers at Rome turned against the imperial authority that had nurtured their movement in its earlier stages. The emperor Henry III died in 1056, leaving an infant son, Henry IV, to succeed him. During the long minority of this young prince, the first signs of dissatisfaction with the imperial government began to appear among the reformers, and soon their dissatisfaction turned to bitter hostility. To understand the issues involved in the ensuing conflict, we must recall the way in which the imperial government was organized in mid-eleventh century. Henry III gave great temporal power and wealth to his bishops, but he chose them himself and used them as royal servants. Their support was essential to the stability of his government. Similar conditions existed to a lesser degree in France and England. There was little idea of any separation between the spheres of spiritual and temporal government. Kings appointed bishops, but bishops ruled secular provinces. A kingdom was a sort of unified church-state over which the king presided. Royal appointment of prelates was not regarded as an abuse but was justified by a widely held doctrine of royal theocracy, which had been formulated by the churchmen themselves during the troubles of the ninth and tenth centuries, when stronger kings seemed the only possible alternative to sheer anarchy. The coronation ritual of England compared the Anglo-Saxon king to Moses, Joshua, David, and Solomon. The emperors of the Ottonian and Salian dynasties were acclaimed as vicars of God on earth. Eleventh-century kings did not merely designate bishops but actually conferred ecclesiastical office upon the men of their choice by "investing" them with ring and staff, the symbols of episcopal power. The reformers came to challenge this practice of lay investiture; in doing so, they challenged the whole basis of royal authority.

It was almost inevitable that the challenge would be made. The reformers, who were interested in returning to the discipline of the early church, devoted much energy to making collections of ancient canons to serve as a guide for their own programs. They found plenty of texts (genuine and forged) to uphold the supreme power of the pope in the church but few to support the claims of the kings. According to early church law, a bishop was supposed to be canonically elected and then consecrated to his office by fellow bishops. The prevailing practice of lay investiture had no canonical basis, as Cardinal Humbert pointed out in a treatise written about 1055. "How does it pertain to lay persons," he wrote, "to distribute ecclesiastical sacraments and episcopal grace, that is to say, the crozier staffs and rings with which episcopal consecration is principally effected?" The objection of lay investiture was not, however, merely a matter of canonical theory. There could be no permanent, effective reform movement directed from Rome if appointments to all major ecclesiastical offices, including the papacy itself, were to be made at the whim of secular kings who might or might not be reasonably responsible Christian rulers. Henry III had made scrupulously good appointments. His predecessor, Conrad II, had made notoriously bad ones. No one knew what line Henry IV might take when he became old enough to govern his kingdom.

For the reformers, the most important thing of all was that they should retain control of the papal office. Accordingly, in 1059, during the short pontificate of Nicholas II (1059–1061), a council at Rome promulgated a decree regulating the conduct of papal elections. It included both the lay Roman aristocratic factions and the imperial government from effective participation in the choice of future popes and entrusted papal elections to the cardinals of the Roman church.* This system, with various procedural modifications, has existed ever since. In case such a bold innovation should meet with violent resistance, Nicholas II made an alliance at this point with the Norman warriors who had been settling in southern Italy during the preceding half century.†

The same council that promulgated the papal election decree also declared vaguely that in future no priest should receive any church from a layman, but there was no attempt to enforce this decree or to spell out its precise meaning. The decree concerning the papacy, on the other hand, was put into effect as soon as the next vacancy arose in 1061. The cardinals chose a Lombard reformer who took the name Alexander II, and with the support of the Normans, he was installed at Rome. After two years of hesitation, the German bishops and the imperial regents recognized him as pope. Alexander had a rather long

*Sources, no. 35

†See p. 254.

reign of twelve years, which provided an important period of consolidation for the gains that the reformers had so far achieved.

One of their main objectives was to extend the authority of the papacy over the whole church. This applied to the East as well as to the West, and Leo IX had sent Cardinal Humbert on a mission to Constantinople in 1054. However, his intransigent defense of papal prerogatives offended the Greeks and served only to precipitate a new schism. In western lands papal legates had more success. They were active not only in Germany and France but also in the border lands of Christendom, such as Scandinavia, Hungary, and Spain. In all these countries, papal legates presided over local church councils at which the new reform decrees were promulgated. During this period, it also became customary for the pope to hold a council at Rome in the spring of each year. Such councils were attended by the local Italian bishops and by any prelates from other lands who happened to be in Rome at the time.

During the relatively peaceful reign of Alexander II (1061–1073), two important developments were taking place. Hildebrand, the most radical and vehement of the reformers, was becoming the dominant figure in Rome, and the young Henry IV (1056–1106) was growing up in Germany. There would probably have been a dispute between the reformed papacy and the imperial government in any case, but the bitterness and violence of the conflict that actually broke out was determined in part by the personalities of these two antagonists. Henry IV found his royal authority gravely weakened through usurpations of power made by the German princes during his long minority. He needed the support of his bishops and had no intention of letting a foreign pope meddle with his free choice of the men he wanted to serve him. Henry had no sympathy whatsoever with the cause of ecclesiastical reform. He did not want to disturb his comfortably married priests with fanatical ideas about clerical celibacy. His objective was to rebuild the royal power, and he subordinated everything else to that purpose.

On the other hand, Hildebrand, who became pope in 1073 as Gregory VII, was a passionate reformer, convinced that he was God's chosen instrument to purify the church, and also convinced that enduring reform could be carried out only if royal control over ecclesiastical appointments was broken once and for all. Hildebrand seems to have been utterly heedless of the political implications of this demand. He was God's vicar, so he thought. If a king dared to resist his divine mission, so much the worse for the king. The most obvious criticism that has been made of Hildebrand is that, not content with the spiritual authority of a priest, he tried to make himself temporal overlord of Europe as well. But this seems an oversimplification. He did not value the authority of temporal rulers so highly as to want it for himself; rather, he despised worldly power and refused to recognize in it any intrinsic dignity or real right to consideration. Kings and feudal princes were to him essentially police chiefs who had the duty of using coercive force to achieve objectives laid down by the church. When Hildebrand was accused by contemporaries of seeking to usurp royal power, he seems to have been genuinely puzzled and indignant at the charge. He did not covet the policeman's office. He regarded it as beneath his dignity.

When Alexander II died in 1073, Hildebrand was first acclaimed by the Roman people as their choice for the papacy and then duly elected by the cardinals. Already, before his election, relations between the papacy and King Henry had become very strained. Even under the moderate Alexander, five of Henry's chief ministers had been excommunicated for flagrant simony. Also, a dispute had broken out concerning an election in Milan in which pope and king supported rival candidates for the bishopric. Milan was of the highest importance to both sides. Its bishop was the civil ruler of the city, and if imperial authority was ever to be reestablished in northern Italy, the emperor had to control the governor of the greatest city of the Lombard plain. But Milan, the See of St. Ambrose, was also the most distinguished bishopric in Italy after Rome itself. If the reformers' principle of canonical election of bishops was to be meaningful, it had to be applied there of all places.

Shortly after his election, Hildebrand, now Pope Gregory VII, wrote to King Henry sternly commanding him to mend his ways in Germany and cease intervening in Milan. At the time, Henry was embarrassed by a major rebellion in Saxony and sent a conciliatory reply. In February 1075, Gregory presided over a synod in Rome, which decreed that henceforth no bishop or abbot should receive investiture from a lay ruler. Immediately after this, Gregory set down in his official register a series of a propositions concerning the power of the pope, which are usually known as the *Dictatus Papae.* They included assertions such as these:

> That all princes shall kiss the feet of the pope.
> That he may be permitted to depose cmperors.
> That he himself may be judged by no one.*

Such assertions, together with the decree on lay investiture, constituted a decisive challenge to the whole existing theory and practice of imperial government. Henry had no intention of complying with the new decree. In the summer of 1075 he won a major victory over the Saxons and, in the autumn, he resumed his support for the imperial candidate in Milan. Events quickly moved to a crisis. Gregory wrote to Henry threatening to excommunicate and depose him. The king replied by summoning a synod of German bishops, which declared that Gregory was a usurper who had seized the papacy by force and had further shown himself unworthy of the papal office by encroaching on Henry's royal authority. The news of this action came to Rome in February 1076. Gregory promptly carried out his threat. Solemnly invoking the authority to "bind and loose" conferred by Christ on Peter, the pope declared Henry to be both excommunicated

*Sources, no. 36

The Investiture Controversy: Henry IV at Canossa pleading with Abbot Hugh of Cluny and Countess Matilda of Tuscany for their help in obtaining his pardon from Pope Gregory VII. Ms. Lat. 4922, fol. 49r. *Vatican Library, Rome*

and deposed from his office of kingship. This was a revolutionary application of the old Petrine text.*

The pope's action produced an immediate and striking effect in Germany. The princes were always reluctant to accept the rule of a strong centralized monarchy, and Henry IV's victory in Saxony had made him far too powerful for their liking. They were delighted to have a pretext for rebellion. Even the bishops who had at first supported Henry were shocked and dismayed by the solemn sentence of excommunication pronounced by the pope himself. The king found himself abandoned by all his supporters and was obliged to give way to the demands of the princes. It was agreed that a *Diet* of nobles and bishops should be held at Augsburg in 1077 under the presidency of the pope. Henry would there make his submission to the papacy, and the Diet would then decide whether he was fit to be restored to the office of king. This was a delightful prospect from Gregory's point of

*Sources, no. 37

view. Henry, however, upset the arrangement by an action that was personally humiliating but politically advantageous.

As the pope journeyed northward in December 1076 for the projected Diet, Henry traveled over the Alps and met the papal party at Canossa. There the king presented himself barefoot as a humble penitent, meekly confessed his sins, and begged absolution. Gregory gave himself the satisfaction of keeping the king waiting for three days but then granted his request. To grant absolution was the proper course of conduct for a priest faced with a penitent sinner, but it turned out to be a tactical blunder nonetheless. Once he was released from the papal sentence of excommunication, Henry succeeded in again building up a faction of supporters in Germany. The princes who continued to oppose the king felt that the pope had betrayed them by coming to a private agreement with Henry. Without consulting Gregory, they elected a rival king, Rudolph. The Diet at Augsburg never took place, and for the next three years Germany was ravaged by a bitterly fought civil war.

At the beginning of his reign, Gregory tried to apply his reform program in France and England as well as in Germany. King Philip I of France was a thoroughly corrupt monarch and a notorious simonist. A typical illustration of his methods is the story of the good abbot, a close friend of Philip's, who asked him to support his candidacy for a vacant bishopric. Philip replied that he loved the abbot and that he would make an excellent bishop. But the abbot had little money and would be unwilling to commit simony anyway. Moreover, Philip had already allowed the queen to sell the bishopric for money to buy jewels. The king, however, had a solution. The new bishop had promised to pay for his see within a year. Once the queen had her money, Philip would accuse the bishop of simony, have him removed, and make sure that the worthy abbot got the see. Stories of behavior like this of course infuriated Gregory, and in 1075 he threatened to excommunicate Philip. But, as the pope became caught up in the struggle with Henry IV, he found it expedient to postpone action against the French king.

The situation was rather different in England. As duke of Normandy, William I had been known as a friend of the reform movement. He was determined to go on appointing bishops in his kingdom of England, but on the whole he appointed good ones. When Gregory issued his decree against lay investiture, William refused to let it be promulgated in his territories. Gregory in turn reproached William but did not excommunicate him.

In 1080, after three years of indecision, Pope Gregory finally decided to support Henry IV's rival Rudolph in the German civil war and for the second time excommunicated and deposed King Henry. On this occasion, however, Gregory had timed his move badly. Henry was beginning to gain the upper hand in the fighting just at the time when the pope declared in favor of Rudolph. During the course of 1080, he defeated and killed his rival. With Rudolph disposed of, Henry could turn to an offensive against the pope. He again denounced Gregory as a usurper and then appointed an antipope and invaded Italy. After repeated sieges, the imperial armies occupied Rome in 1084. Henry was crowned emperor by his antipope in St. Peter's, while Gregory took refuge in the impregnable fortress of St. Angelo a few hundred yards away. From there the pope appealed for help to his allies, the Normans of southern Italy. The Normans advanced on Rome, and the imperial forces withdrew from the city. Gregory was duly rescued, but the Normans had a reputation for ferocious savagery, and they fully lived up to it on this occasion. Finding Rome completely at their mercy, they looted the city before withdrawing to the south, taking the pope along with them. Gregory died a few months later, convinced that he had failed in all his endeavors.

In fact, the fight was far from over. For the rest of his reign, Henry was harassed by outbreaks of revolt among the German princes. He never did succeed in reestablishing the strong, stable monarchy of his father, and when he died in 1106, his own son, Henry V, was leading a rebellion against him. Meanwhile, the popes, with Norman support, were able to reoccupy Rome. Urban II (1088–1099) vigorously reasserted all the main points of Gregory's reform program, including the condemnation of lay investiture. Philip of France received a long-overdue and well-deserved sentence of excommunication at this point, and St. Anselm, archbishop of Canterbury, carried the struggle over lay investiture in England. In 1100, twenty-five years after Gregory VII's initial decree, the issue he had raised remained quite undecided.

By the early years of the twelfth century, the Investiture Contest had stimulated a considerable body of writing about the problems of royal and papal power, in effect a rebirth of Western political theory. The most extreme statement of the royalist case came from an unidentified Anglo-Norman cleric, usually known as the "Anonymous of York." He argued that kings and priests were both, in their different ways, representatives of Christ. But the king represented Christ's divine nature, while the priest represented merely his human nature. The king was therefore immeasurably greater than the priest, just as God was immeasurably greater than man. At the other extreme, the propapal German writer Manegold of Lautenbach declared that the papacy "excelled all the principalities and powers of this world," but that a king was merely an administrator, appointed by his people and removable by them "like a swineherd" if he failed to discharge his duties properly. Extreme views like these contributed nothing to a practical solution of the contest. After twenty years of conflict, however, moderate men in both the papal and imperial camps began to make serious attempts at compromise. The essential interest of the church was that lay rulers should not confer spiritual office. The essential interest of the kings was that bishops who were going to be secular rulers should acknowledge that they held their temporal power from the king. The two claims did not have to be mutually exclusive, as the French canonist Ivo of Chartres pointed out in 1097. There could be no objection to the king investing a properly chosen candidate after a canonical election had been held, Ivo suggested, since then everyone would understand that the king was conferring only temporal power. Another French writer, Hugh of Fleury, added that the king ought not to use the ring and staff in making the royal investiture since these symbols had become closely identified with the spiritual office of bishop.

These suggestions pointed the way to a possible solution of the conflict. The first agreements between the papacy and secular kings on the subject of lay investiture were arrived at soon afterward, during the pontificate of Pope Pascal II (1099–1118). In 1107 St. Anselm of Canterbury and Henry I worked out a solution for England, which was subsequently approved by the pope. The agreement was that a bishop should first be canonically elected. Then, after the election but before his consecration as bishop, the candidate would do homage to the king as a feudal vassal and receive from him the feudal lands and secular jurisdiction attached to his office. The king abandoned the use of the ring and staff, but since he could refuse the homage of any candidate who was not acceptable to him, he retained a decisive say in the choice of bishops. About the same time a similar arrangement was worked out in France with the successor of King Philip, Louis VI (1108–1137).

There remained the problem of Germany. In 1111 King Henry V (1106–1125) occupied Rome with an imperial army, intending to reach a final solution of the investiture question as a preliminary to his imperial coronation. Pascal II, who regarded the agreements already made with England and France as mere temporary concessions, now revealed his own preferred solution to the problem. It was an extremely radical one. The king claimed the right to appoint bishops because they held royal lands and exercised secular jurisdiction. The pope proposed, therefore, that the bishops renounce all their feudal lands and worldly power. They would again become simply pastors of souls, and thus the king would have no reason to interfere in their appointments. The historian Arnold Toynbee has suggested that, if the church had taken this course, it might well have united all Christendom in a strong spiritual empire and thus changed the whole future of Western civilization. But, appealing as Pascal's proposal may seem to a modern historian, there was never the slightest chance of it being put into practice. The imperial bishops had no intention of giving up their wealth and power. Some of them no doubt were moved by merely worldly considerations, but even the best of them were unpersuaded. In a feudal society, it seemed that the only way the bishops could avoid subservience to the lay nobility was to rule as feudal lords themselves. As soon as the pope's plan was made public, both the German bishops and the Roman cardinals rejected it. Henry V thereupon carried the pope away from Rome as a captive, and a few months later, this time clearly acting under duress, Pascal conceded to Henry the right of investing with ring and staff. But once again the pope's action was repudiated by the cardinals. The situation had now become so embittered and confused that no solution could be achieved in Pascal's reign. The agreement that ended the contest, known as the

Concordat of Worms, was made between Henry V and Pope Calixtus II (1119–1124) in 1122. The solution adopted was similar to the one worked out for England except that in Germany the king had the right to be present at the election of bishops.*

34. *The Aftermath*

So far as the technical issue of lay investiture was concerned, the outcome of the struggle was a compromise. Kings gave up the theocratic claim that they could actually confer spiritual office as vicars of God but in practice continued to nominate bishops. However, it became much more difficult for them to impose flagrantly unsuitable candidates on the church. Even if they coerced the electors into choosing such a man, an appeal to the pope could often prevent him from taking possession of his see. Certainly, the standard of episcopal appointments improved notably in the twelfth century.

All the major participants in the conflict were affected differently. The results were least important in England and France, since at the crucial point of the conflict, the king of England was strong enough to command the support of his barons, while the king of France was so weak that his barons saw no reason to rise in rebellion against him. The situation was strikingly different in Germany. There the challenge of Pope Gregory VII came at a time when a rising class of feudal princes was eager to resist the authority of a powerful and ambitious monarch. There would no doubt have been rebellions in Germany without the investiture issue, but Henry IV might well have succeeded in suppressing them and consolidating a strong monarchy if he had not become involved in a conflict with the papacy. Instead, the princes took advantage of the general confusion of his reign to increase their power. When Henry V died in 1125 without an heir, the princes then passed over the most powerful of the dukes, Frederick of Hohenstaufen, to elect as king the heir to the house of Billung, Lothair of Supplinburg, duke of Saxony.

Since he owed his throne to the princes and not to any hereditary claim, Lothair (1125–1137) was powerless before them. In every part of the realm the princes consolidated their power. They usurped offices and fiefs and passed them on from father to son. They strewed their lands with castles garrisoned by loyal *ministeriales.* This spirit of usurpation naturally spread downward in the political structure. Petty lords and knights forced the small freemen to become serfs, and the seignorial system became firmly saddled on most of Germany. By the end of the period of confusion, the countships and the jurisdiction that went with them had been swallowed up by the princes. Finally, feudal institutions spread over the land. The lesser lords became vassals of the princes, and the princes maintained that their offices and possessions were hereditary fiefs. Henry IV had been well on the way

*Sources, no. 38

to establishing a strong, centralized national monarchy. Lothair of Supplinburg was as much a figurehead as had been Hugh Capet.

The papacy emerged from the conflict with greatly enhanced prestige. Although the political claims of Gregory VII did not find general acceptance, the position of the pope as supreme ruler of Christendom in ecclesiastical affairs had been vigorously reasserted and was universally acknowledged. A major problem for the popes during the next century was to build up a structure of law and administration that would enable them to function more effectively in the role they had marked out for themselves. At the beginning of the twelfth century, there was no uniform code of ecclesiastical law applicable over the whole of Europe. Again, it was very difficult for the pope to obtain adequate information about local conditions outside Italy, and any action he took was likely to be both ill-informed and tardy. The reformers tried to overcome this problem by the use of *papal legates.* Some legates had general commissions to reform any abuses they might find, while others were sent to deal with a specific problem. The reformers also encouraged visits by bishops and other high prelates to Rome. Especially important were the visits traditionally made by archbishops at the time of their election. From very early times, the popes had been accustomed to honor a particularly eminent archbishop by giving him a *pallium,* a band of white wool embroidered with four purple crosses. In this custom, the reformers saw an opportunity to give the pope a veto power over archiepiscopal elections and an opportunity to personally instruct newly elected prelates. They declared that an archbishop could not perform his functions until he received the *pallium* and that only extremely strong reasons were to be allowed to free him from the necessity of visiting Rome for the purpose. These first centralizing measures of the reformed papacy proved useful but inadequate. The next century saw a further great growth of papal law and papal governmental machinery.

Since the church was to play such an important role in medieval history, it will be useful to survey briefly its organization at the end of the Investiture Contest. Below the pope and cardinals, the key figure in the ecclesiastical hierarchy was the bishop. The archbishop was more powerful than his suffragans to the extent that his own episcopal see was larger and richer than theirs, and he could hear appeals from the suffragan bishops' courts. But he did not exercise any effective control over the internal affairs of their dioceses. The bishop possessed the full spiritual authority of the church. He could perform all the sacraments and could, by the sacrament of ordination, pass on this power to others. He alone could perform the sacrament of confirmation. In theory at least, he appointed all the lesser clergy in his diocese, though in practice this usually meant approving the choices of the local patrons. The bishop was responsible for clerical discipline. He had control of the lands of his church. In short, he was the master of the personnel and property of the church in his diocese and was practically independent of any higher spiritual authority except the pope. According to canon law, the bishop was to be elected by the clergy and people of his diocese, but in practice, only the higher clergy attached to the cathedral church, known as the cathedral *canons*, participated in the election.

The canons not only formed an electoral college but provided the principal officers who helped the bishop in administering his diocese and serving the cathedral church. The *dean* was the head of the canons and the chief dignitary in the diocese after the bishop. A *chancellor* supervised the cathedral school and issued licenses to teach. A *treasurer* was responsible for financial administration. A *precentor* supervised the choir and arranged the musical services of the cathedral. Each diocese was divided into administrative districts called *archdeaconries*, usually four in each diocese. The *archdeacons* who supervised these districts were the bishops' principal officers for enforcing discipline among the lower clergy, and because of this disciplinary role, they were often highly unpopular. (Medieval students used to debate the delicate problem, "Whether it is possible for an archdeacon to save his soul.") The archdeacon's office was much coveted nonetheless, since it was often a stepping stone to higher preferment in the church. The archdeacons were assisted by rural deans, and below them came the mass of ordinary, village priests. Socially, the clergy were divided as was secular society. The bishops, their officers, and the canons were usually members of the feudal class. The parish priests were ordinarily drawn from the ranks of the peasants. It was not impossible for a man of the humblest birth to rise to high office in the church, but it was naturally very difficult.

It is important to remember that, apart from the higher orders of clergy, there was a host of clerics in "minor orders." These were men who had accepted the tonsure and put themselves under ecclesiastical jurisdiction but who were not ordained as priests and who often had no intention of becoming priests. From them were drawn the clerks who served both lay and ecclesiastical princes as secretaries and in any other capacity in which literacy was required. Eventually, the administrative methods of the secular governments of Europe were to a great extent developed by ecclesiastics who used the papal government as a model.

After considering some results of the Investiture Contest, we can ask finally: Was there really a papal revolution? Certainly a radical ideology of papal power was asserted; and the attempt to implement the ideology led to rebellions that changed the history of Germany. Pope Gregory VII not only encouraged nobles to rise against their kings but also urged common layfolk to reject the priests and prelates who would not accept his reforms. As happens with most revolutions, this one did not achieve all of its objectives; much of the old order persisted in the postrevolutionary era. But some things would never be the same.

On the political level, the most important result of the conflict was that it ended the drift toward a general acceptance of royal theocracy as the normal pattern of government in the Western world. But it did not succeed in imposing the rival doctrine of papal theocracy.

Gregory VII's assertion that he could depose kings was never accepted by the kings themselves and remained, at best, highly controversial. The investiture contest thus ensured that henceforth there would be a sort of duality in medieval government, a persistent tension between church and state. This decisively influenced the future course of Western constitutional development. Henceforth, there was never just one hierarchy of government, commanding obedience by divine right, but always two hierarchies, each limiting the power of the other. Moreover, another effect of the controversy was to stimulate the growth of doctrines upholding the right of resistance against rulers who abused their authority. This is most obvious in the writings directed against Henry IV of Germany; but the opposition of the cardinals to Pascal II indicates that similar ideas could also find a foothold in the church.

Whether we use the word revolution or not, it is clear that the direction of Western history changed in the age of the papal reform movement. The significance of the movement can best be understood when it is set in this broader context of change. In the years before 1100 the demographic curve had turned upward. With the increasing population, trade and trading cities began to expand after centuries of stagnation. New wealth made possible the rise of a more sophisticated civilization. And in every sphere of life and thought the reformed church made vital contributions. The greatest change associated with the "papal revolution" was a change in the attitude of the church to the world. In the preceding centuries of violence and chaos, there was a natural impulse for devout Christians to retreat behind the high secure walls of an abbey and turn their backs on the savagery outside. The reformers of the late eleventh century were inspired by a different ideal. They wanted to go out into the world and reshape it, to make a harmonious Christian commonwealth out of the turbulent society of early medieval Europe. In the following chapters we shall see how far they succeeded.

READING SUGGESTIONS

* *B. Tierney,* Sources *and* Readings, *vol. I, nos. 35–38; vol. II, nos. 23–24.*

On the reform movements before the Investiture Contest, see J. B. Russell, *Dissent and Reform in the Early Middle Ages* (Berkeley and Los Angeles, 1965); B. Rosenwein, *Rhinocerous Bound: Cluny in the Tenth Century* (Philadelphia, 1982); H. E. J. Cowdrey, *The Cluniacs and the Gregorian Reform* (Oxford, 1970). On the contest itself, there are valuable discussions in works already cited: R. W. and A. J. Carlyle (Introduction), W. Ullmann (Chapter IV), R. W. Southern (Chapter VII), C. Brooke (Chapter IX), and G. Barraclough (Chapter IX). For a general survey of church life see * R. W. Southern, *Western Society and the Church in the Middle Ages* (Baltimore, 1970). * S. Williams (ed.), *The Gregorian Epoch* (Boston, 1964) is a useful collection of excerpts from modern scholars. See also * B. Tierney, *The Crisis of Church and State, 1050–1300,* repr. (Toronto, 1988); G. Tellenbach, *Church, State and Christian Society at the Time of the Investiture Contest* (Oxford, 1940); U. Blumenthal, *The Investiture Contest* (Philadelphia, 1988). * H. Berman stresses the revolutionary implications of the Gregorian Movement in *Law and Revolution: The Formation of the Western Legal Tradition* (Cambridge, MA, 1983). See also I. S. Robinson, *Authority and Resistance in the Investiture Contest* (New York, 1978). For England, see N. Cantor, *Church, Kingship and Lay Investiture in England 1089–1135* (Princeton, 1958), and Z. N. Brooke, *The English Church and the Papacy*, 2nd ed. (Cambridge, England, 1952). Two valuable collections of source material are * *The Correspondence of Gregory VII*, E. Emerton (trans.) (New York, 1932), and *Imperial Lives and Letters of the Eleventh Century*, T. E. Mommsen and K. F. Morrison (trans.) (New York, 1962).

THE FLOWERING OF THE TWELFTH CENTURY

chapter

XII

Expansion of Europe: The First Crusades

The last four chapters have described the social, economic, political, and religious development of medieval culture in western Europe from the ninth century to the eleventh. In the ninth century it seemed doubtful that a western European civilization could survive at all. In the tenth century western religion and western institutions began to spread to the borderlands of northern and eastern Europe. From about 1050 onward this slow expansion was followed by a movement of overt conquest in the Mediterranean region directed against the Muslim-held lands of Spain, Sicily, and Palestine.

The great wave of expansion during this period was the result of many circumstances. As we have seen, the period was one of vigor and vitality in many fields. The population, productivity, and wealth of the central regions of western Europe increased with great rapidity. There was surplus labor power and wealth to be used for expansion. In the new movement of conquest the papacy is found in close alliance with the feudal class and, in the Mediterranean, the populations of the Italian cities joined with them. Above all, we must remember that this was an age of church reform and popular religious revivalism. Among all the circumstances that contributed to the launching of the crusades, simple religious enthusiasm must be counted as one of the most important.

35. *Spain and Sicily*

At the beginning of the eleventh century, the Muslims held the southern two-thirds of Spain, the Balearic Islands, Corsica, Sardinia, Sicily, the entire coast of North Africa, Palestine, and part of Syria. Religious enthusiasm and political and economic ambition moved the people of western Europe to attack these Muslim lands. The feudal class, especially its cadets, or younger sons, saw unlimited opportunities to acquire both spiritual and temporal rewards, salvation and rich fiefs, through engaging in their favorite occupation. The rising Italian towns, especially Genoa and Pisa, were anxious to free themselves from the continuous danger of Muslim naval raids and to conduct their trade peacefully along the shores of the western Mediterranean. The papacy may have had more complicated motives. Certainly, the popes desired to spread the Christian faith and their own authority, but it also likely that they thought it an excellent idea to turn the turbulent belligerency of the feudal class into worthy channels. The church was trying desperately to reduce feudal warfare by means of the Peace of God and the Truce of God*; finding a new outlet for the military energy of the nobles might aid the good cause.

The Muslim conquest of Spain had never been complete. When the Saracen hosts overran the country in the eighth century, the remnants of the Visigoth army retired to the northwestern corner, where they established the kingdom of the Asturias. By the year 1000, this kingdom had been divided into two states, Leon and Castile. To the east of these lands, along the southern fringes of the Pyrenees, Charlemagne had established the Spanish March. Before the end of the ninth century, the western portion of the Spanish March became the independent kingdom of Navarre, which included the land of the Basques with its capital at Pamplona and the region later known as Aragon. Then in 1035 Aragon became an independent kingdom. The eastern part of the old Spanish March was known as the county of Barcelona. These lands—Leon, Castile, Navarre, Aragon, and Barcelona—comprised Christian Spain in the middle of the eleventh century.

As long as the Muslim power remained reasonably united under the emirs and later the caliphs of Cordoba, the Christian states could do little more than hold their own. That they succeeded in doing so was as much the result of dissension among the Muslims as of their own valor and military capacity. Then in 1034 the quarrels among the Muslim chieftains came to a climax in the complete disruption of the caliphate of Cordoba and the appearance of more than a score of independent Muslim kingdoms. This gave the Christian states their great opportunity, at a time when the forces of expansion were strong in western Europe.

By the beginning of the eleventh century, the monks of Cluny were establishing houses south of the Pyrenees. Soon the monks began to encourage the nobles of France to undertake expeditions against the Spanish Muslims. In 1018 Roger de Tony, a great Norman lord, led a force to Spain to war against the infidel and from then onward there were frequent harassing attacks on the Muslims by expeditions from the north, usually led by French counts. In the second half of the eleventh century, most of Christian Spain came under the rule of two monarchs, Alfonso VI (1065–1109), king of Leon and Castile, and Sancho Ramirez (1063–1094), king of Aragon and Navarre.† Aided by strong bodies of French knights, especially Normans and Burgundians, these two kings took the offensive against the Muslims, and in

*Sources, no. 34

†See Appendix, Table 9, for genealogical chart.

1085 Alfonso captured the important city of Toledo. Although this was the most substantial permanent gain made during his reign, the long series of wars waged by him and by Sancho Ramirez seriously weakened all the Muslim states. This was the era of the mighty warrior and semilegendary Spanish national hero Rodrigo Diaz de Vivar, usually called the Cid. While the French knights who came to Spain might be crusaders for the faith, that was not the attitude of the Spanish nobles. The Muslims were their neighbors—one day their enemies and the next their friends. They had no objection to calling for Muslim aid in wars between two of the Christian states. The Cid fought valiantly and successfully for his lord, Alfonso VI, when the two were on good terms, but during their frequent quarrels he cheerfully served Muslim princes. Once, at the head of a Muslim army, he defeated the count of Barcelona, took him captive, and became the governor of the land in dispute, the region around Lerida; but he treated the count so kindly that the latter married his son and heir to the Cid's daughter.

The successful campaigns of Alfonso VI and Sancho Ramirez quickly convinced the petty Muslim princes of Spain that they could not resist the Christian power without aid, and they appealed for help to the ruler of the Almoravides, a Berber people who were masters of northwest Africa. The Almoravides arrived in Spain in 1086. Their army forced Alfonso VI to evacuate the extensive conquests made by the Cid in Lerida and Valencia. Fortunately for the Christians, the Almoravides soon began to quarrel with the Spanish Muslim princes, and the Muslim power soon began to lose its unity. In 1118 Aragon conquered the Muslim principality of Saragossa, and in 1137 was united with Barcelona to form a greatly enlarged state. Meanwhile, Alfonso VII (1126–1157), king of Castile and Leon, raided deep into Muslim territory, even occupying for a time the southern city of Cordoba.

In the course of the campaigning of the early twelfth century, Portugal emerged for the first time as a separate kingdom. Earlier it had been a dependent county of the kingdom of Leon comprising the northern third of the modern state of Portugal. The count of this region, Alfonso Henriques (1112–1185), waged war against both the Muslims and his cousin and overlord the king. In 1139 the pope intervened in the latter quarrel and arranged a treaty of peace. Alfonso Henriques took the title king of Portugal, as a vassal of the papacy. Four years later, a fortunate accident enabled the new king to extend his territory southward. A fleet bearing English, Flemish, and northern German crusaders on their way to join the Second Crusade to Palestine stopped at Oporto and listened to Alfonso Henriques' plea for aid. They captured Lisbon and turned it over to the king of Portugal before proceeding on their way. Thus, by the middle years of the twelfth century, Spain was half Christian and half Muslim. The most important Christian kingdoms that had emerged were Castile, Aragon, and Portugal.

During the eleventh century, while the territory of Christian Spain

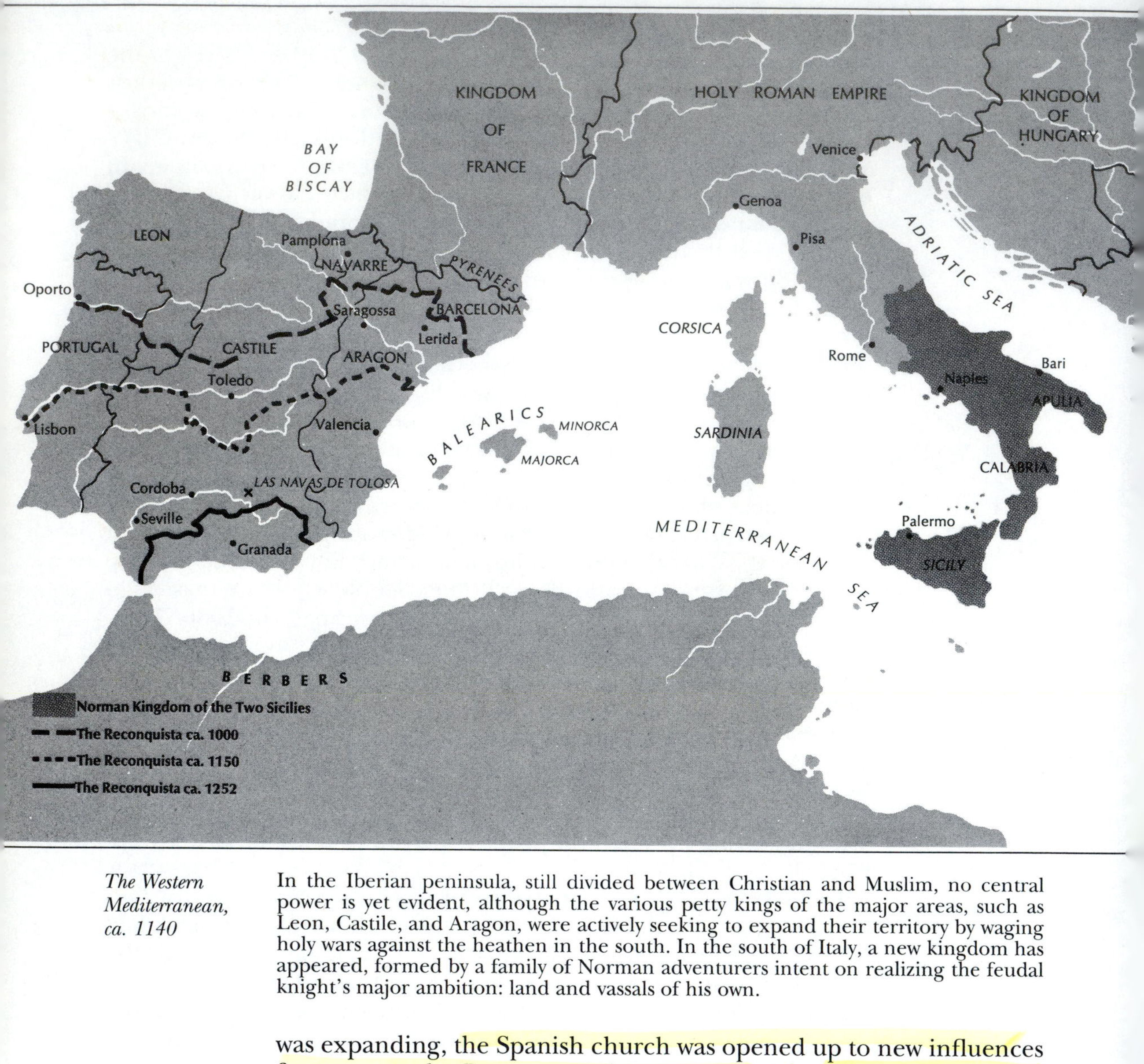

The Western Mediterranean, ca. 1140

In the Iberian peninsula, still divided between Christian and Muslim, no central power is yet evident, although the various petty kings of the major areas, such as Leon, Castile, and Aragon, were actively seeking to expand their territory by waging holy wars against the heathen in the south. In the south of Italy, a new kingdom has appeared, formed by a family of Norman adventurers intent on realizing the feudal knight's major ambition: land and vassals of his own.

was expanding, the Spanish church was opened up to new influences from across the Pyrenees and from Rome. The city of Compostela, where, according to an old legend, the body of the apostle James was buried, became one of the great pilgrimage centers of the medieval world. French pilgrims as well as French knights poured into northern Spain throughout the eleventh century. Meanwhile, the monks of Cluny introduced into Spain the ritual practices of the Roman church. During the centuries since the original Muslim invasion of Spain, the Spanish Christians had clung to their ancient, Visigothic form of liturgy. At first there was resistance to the new rite of the Cluniacs. But Pope Gregory VII (1073–1085), as part of his campaign for reform and centralization in the church, insisted on the adoption of the Roman usages. Alfonso VI supported the papal policy, and the Roman liturgy was accepted at the Council of Burgos in 1080. Alfonso VI also permitted Gregory's legates to hold reforming councils, but he drew the line at a suggestion that he should hold his kingdom of Castile as a fief from the pope.

A fresh chapter of Spanish history began in 1146 with the arrival of a new, vigorous Muslim people—the Almohades. In 1125 the Almohades had overthrown the Almoravides' power in North Africa, and the Muslims of Spain, alarmed by the recent Christian successes, turned to them for aid. The Almohades spent nearly twenty years in consolidating their power over the Muslim principalities. They then began a vigorous campaign against the Christians, which soon recovered most of the territory conquered by Alfonso VII. Soon, however, they found themselves facing one of the ablest warrior kings in the history of Spain, Alfonso VIII (1158–1214), king of Castile. Both sides prepared for a decisive campaign. The Almohades mustered all the forces of Moorish Spain and brought over more troops from North Africa. The pope declared a crusade against the Muslims, and many knights of Europe led by the Spanish-born archbishop of Narbonne joined Alfonso's host, as did the forces of all the Christian states except Leon. On July 16, 1212, the two armies met at Las Navas de Tolosa. The result was an overwhelming victory for Christian arms and the end of the power of the Almohades.

The chief weakness of the Spanish kingdoms lay in the fact that, whenever they won a victory over the Muslims, they heaved a sigh of relief and turned to fighting among themselves. Thus it was not until 1230, when the grandson of Alfonso VIII, Ferdinand III (1217–1252), became king of both Leon and Castile, that the war against the Muslims was renewed with any vigor. In 1236 Ferdinand captured Cordoba and in 1248 Seville. Meanwhile, King James I (1213–1276) of Aragon had conquered Majorca and Minorca. In 1238 James took Valencia. When Ferdinand III died in 1252, the Muslims had lost all the Spanish peninsula except the province of Granada, which they were to hold until it was wrested from them by Ferdinand the Catholic (1479–1516) in the fifteenth century.

The institutions of Christian Spain in the Middle Ages were by no means uniform over the whole land. The county of Barcelona had been part of the Spanish March, and its counts were deeply involved in the feudal politics of southern France. Hence this region had a fully developed feudal system on the French model. The same was true to a lesser extent of Aragon. There the nobles seem to have held their lands by feudal tenure, but there was no highly developed hierarchy, and a large proportion of the nobles were the king's direct vassals. The western states—Castile, Leon, and Portugal—can hardly be called feudal. There were men who held land in return for military service, but most nobles and churchmen seem to have had allodial holdings. There was no feudal hierarchy, and the fief-holding vassals fought side by side with peasant warriors similarly armed and equipped. Serfdom of the European type was pretty well confined to the lands that had never been occupied by the Moors. In the newly conquered territories, the land was more commonly worked by free peasant farmers or by slaves.

Outside Spain, the most direct contact between the Muslims and the peoples of western Europe was in southern Italy. In the ninth century, the Muslims had conquered Sicily and sent strong raiding parties to the mainland of Italy. They captured a number of towns, fearfully ravaged the countryside, and even threatened Rome itself. They were eventually expelled by a papal army aided by a Byzantine fleet. But southern Italy remained in a state of great political confusion. There were districts ruled by the officers of the Byzantine Empire and others that were in the hands of Lombard chieftains. Between these groups there raged a continuous series of petty wars.

Early in the eleventh century, a band of Norman knights returning from a pilgrimage to Jerusalem passed through southern Italy and immediately realized that there was an environment that would give full scope to their talents. Among these adventurers were three brothers, sons of a petty Norman lord named Tancred de Hauteville. At first the Norman knights were simply mercenary soldiers fighting for whoever offered the best pay, but soon they were seizing lands for themselves. When the eldest brother, William, died in 1046, he was master of Apulia. Meanwhile, the brothers had apparently sent home some enthusiastic reports of the opportunities open in southern Italy for good knights, for soon several younger sons of Tancred came to join in the family adventure. Among them were two outstanding leaders—Robert, called the Guiscard (the cunning), and Roger.

In 1059 the pope recognized Robert as duke of Apulia and Calabria and took his homage for these fiefs. Robert (1057–1085) then set to work to conquer the country held by the Byzantine emperor and sent his brother Roger (1061–1101) to invade Sicily. Both brothers were successful. In 1071 the fall of Bari gave Robert the last Byzantine possession in southern Italy, and in 1072 the two brothers combined their forces to take Palermo. During the next twenty years Roger completed the conquest of Muslim Sicily. The next great figure of the Hauteville house was Roger's son, Roger II (1103–1154), who became count of Sicily in 1103. When Robert Guiscard's grandson died in 1127, Roger seized his lands in south Italy; then three years later the pope gave him the title of king of Sicily to hold as a vassal of the pope. This Norman kingdom of Sicily passed in turn to Roger's son, William I (1154–1166), and then to his grandson, William II (1166–1189).

Roger I and Roger II built a strong state with a highly centralized government. They tried to give equal treatment to the various peoples under their rule. Their chancery issued documents in Latin, Greek, and Arabic; and Norman feudal custom, Roman law, and Muslim law were enforced in their appropriate realms by professional judges appointed by the crown and supervised by itinerant justices. Financial affairs were handled by two bodies, the names of which aptly illustrate the complex nature of this strange state: the *Duana de Secretis* saw to the ordinary royal revenues, while the *Duana Baronum* collected the feudal income. *Duana* derives from the Arabic *divan, secretis* was a common Greek term, and *baronum* was good feudal Latin. The barons and knights of the kingdom were organized in a regular feudal hierarchy, and their obligations to the crown were carefully registered in a *catologus baronum.* The kings of Sicily had one great advantage over other monarchs of western Europe. As vassals of the papacy and the conquerors of Sicily from the infidel, they had been created by the pope permanent papal legates. Hence they had absolute control over the prelates of the realm and could settle themselves all appeals from their ecclesiastical courts. Not even Norman England was a greater triumph of the political genius of the Norman people than this kingdom of Sicily.

The general offensive conducted during the eleventh, twelfth, and thirteenth centuries by the knights and townsmen of western Europe against the Muslim masters of the Mediterranean had important and permanent results. All the Spanish peninsula except the province of Granada, the Balearic Islands, Corsica, Sardinia, and Sicily were recovered from the Saracens and assimilated into Christian Europe. We must now turn to the far more spectacular, but in the end far less successful, expeditions against the Muslims in the Middle East.

36. *Byzantium, Islam, and the First Crusade*

During the second half of the eleventh century, while the Christians were pressing back the Muslims in the West, the situation was far different in the eastern Mediterranean region. At Constantinople, the great emperor Basil II (976–1025) was succeeded by a series of weak and incompetent rulers. They failed to maintain adequate frontier defenses while straining the resources of the imperial treasury to support a lavish court life that was extravagant even by Byzantine standards. The pomp of the imperial court was never more ostentatious; the provinces were neglected. There had always been a tendency for the provincial aristocracy to absorb into their own great estates the small holdings of lesser individuals, thus reducing to the status of dependent peasants the free farmers who had been the backbone of the Byzantine armed forces. Basil II had seen the danger of this development and had restrained it by legislation and vigorous administration. Under his feebler successors it went on unchecked. Something akin to western feudalism developed in the provinces of the empire; the more powerful the provincial aristocrats became, the less reliable was their loyalty to the central government. In 1081 a new, more vigorous dynasty was inaugurated by the emperor Alexius Comnenus (1081–1118). But by then the situation of the empire had grown desperate.

The Byzantine empire had passed through periods of feeble government before and had always survived them. The new danger in the eleventh century arose from the fact that, just when the empire was at its weakest, a powerful, aggressive new power arose in the Islamic world, the Seljuk Turks. Late in the tenth century, a band of Turks from Central Asia, led by a chieftain named Seljuk ibn Takah and his sons, had entered the eastern part of the Muslim empire and taken service under one of the local sultans. There they were converted and became enthusiastic Muslims. During the third decade of the eleventh century, the Seljuk princes became masters of the eastern provinces of the caliphate, and in 1055 a grandson of Seljuk seized Baghdad and was solemnly proclaimed sultan by the caliph. Soon he was in complete control of the caliph and his capital. In 1071 the emperor Romanus IV (1067–1071) had the temerity to advance against the Turks. They met him at Manzikert in Armenia, wiped out the imperial army, and captured the emperor. The sultan himself then turned to a campaign in Turkestan, leaving his second cousin, Suleiman, to carry on the war with the Byzantines. Soon Suleiman had a sultanate embracing all Asia Minor, with its capital at the great city of Nicea. The Byzantine empire had lost all its Asiatic territory. The loss was devastating because the provinces that had fallen to the Turks had been among the richest of the empire and especially valuable as a source of military personnel.

The First Crusade was launched in response to appeals from the Byzantine emperors for help in recovering their lost lands. For two centuries before the battle of Manzikert, relations between Byzantium and Rome had been uneasy and at times overtly hostile. There were always two sources of friction, the Greeks' reluctance to accept the papal claims to effective headship of the church and their desire to maintain a position of political power in southern Italy. As we have seen, a dispute broke out in the reign of Pope Nicholas I (859–867) between the pope and the Byzantine patriarch Photius.* Then, in the middle years of the tenth century, there was renewed bickering concerning Otto I's claim to the imperial title. The most recent dispute between Rome and Byzantium had taken place in 1054. It began with political disagreements in southern Italy. Then Pope Leo IX unfortunately chose as his legate to Constantinople the impetuous Cardinal Humbert. Humbert did not attempt any serious negotiations but presented an intransigent statement of the papal claims; when they were not fully accepted, he flung a sentence of excommunication at the patriarch. An angry mob thereupon chased the legate out of the city. The growing estrangement between the Greek and Roman churches, strikingly symbolized in this incident, gradually hardened into a formal schism that has still not been healed.

In spite of all this background of dissension, there still existed in the West a feeling that the Greeks were fellow Christians who deserved support, at any rate when they were fighting against a common enemy, the forces of Islam. When the emperor Michael VII (1071–1078) asked Pope Gregory VII for aid against the Turks after the battle of Manzikert, the pope was inclined to accede to his request. Only twenty years had passed since the dispute of 1054, and effective assistance against the Turks might well heal the schism. But before he had time

*See pp. 222–223.

to take any effective action, Gregory became embroiled in his bitter quarrel with the emperor Henry IV, and subsequently he was in no position to embark on other ventures. Then, in 1094, Emperor Alexius Comnenus (1081–1118), the founder of the Comneni dynasty, made a similar appeal to Gregory's successor, Urban II (1088–1099).

The idea of the papacy inspiring and directing a great expedition against the Turks appealed to Urban, but in his mind it took a form far different from that envisaged by Alexius. The emperor wanted a body of knights to aid him in recovering his Asiatic provinces. This clearly did not greatly interest Pope Urban. He conceived the idea of an attack on the Turkish power in Syria and Palestine intended to recover for Christendom the holy places of the Faith. Despite the Muslim possession of Jerusalem, Christian pilgrims had been journeying there in considerable numbers. Perhaps their tales of ill treatment had had some influence on the pope. But there is no need to seek any particular source for Urban's idea. Toledo had just been taken by Alfonso VI, and Roger de Hauteville had completed his conquest of Sicily. What was more natural than for the head of Christendom to turn the eyes of the knights of Europe toward another Muslim land, one that was held sacred by all Christians?

On November 27, 1095, Pope Urban preached the crusade before a council assembled at Clermont in the hills of Auvergne. The Muslim victories were a disgrace to Christendom. The nobles of Europe should give up their continuous strife among themselves and turn their swords against the enemies of the Faith to aid the churches of the East and to recover the Holy Land. This would be a Holy War, and all who died in it would gain a reward in heaven.* After the council was over, Urban toured about France preaching the crusade. Other enthusiastic preachers moved through the various lands calling on Christians to undertake the holy enterprise.

While Urban II probably had no knowledge whatever about the topography and climate of Asia Minor, Syria, and Palestine and the military tactics of the Turks, he was no dreamy idealist who thought anyone could defeat the infidel with the aid of God. He was determined to send forth an army of the best troops he knew of—the heavily armed knights of western Europe. As he fully realized that no one baron was inclined to obey another, he appointed as leader for the host, Adhemar, bishop of Le Puy. The baronial leaders formed a notable group. There were the brothers of the kings of England and France—Robert, duke of Normandy, and Hugh, count of Vermandois. The Flemings and the crusaders from the northwestern fiefs of the empire were led by Count Baldwin of Flanders and his brother Godfrey de Bouillon, duke of Lower Lorraine. The crusaders from southern France followed the banner of Raymond de St. Gilles, count of Toulouse, a veteran of the wars against the Spanish Muslims. Finally, Bohemond, son of Robert Guiscard, gave up a fierce war he had been waging with his brother Roger Borsa over their Apulian inheritance to take part in the crusade. It is noteworthy that no great king

*Sources, no. 39

took part in the First Crusade, but both Philip I of France and Henry IV of Germany were embroiled in disputes with the papacy and were excommunicated at the time when the crusade was proclaimed.

Unfortunately, Pope Urban conveyed to those who preached the crusade throughout the countryside his enthusiasm but not his good sense. Although Urban had contemplated the enlistment of no one but responsible lords who could equip and finance their bands, the preachers gave the cross to penniless knights and adventurous peasants. Since these individuals had no preparations to make, they started for the Holy Land in the spring of 1096. This was the so-called Peasants' Crusade. Its principal leaders were Peter the Hermit, the most successful of the preachers, and a poor French knight named Walter Sansavoir. In southern Germany Peter was joined by a mass of German crusaders, which included a few nobles. As the crusaders had neither supplies nor money, they could support themselves only by receiving gifts or by plundering. Some of them began the plundering in Hungary and were destroyed by the irate Hungarians. One group was routed by the king of Hungary at the border of his kingdom. Other crusaders passed through Hungary peacefully but were harassed on their march through Bulgaria. In the end a large contingent did succeed in reaching Constantinople. But, after one look at the half-armed and completely undisciplined mob that had come to his aid, Alexius hastily shipped them across the straits to Asia Minor. There the Turks quickly cut them to pieces. A few managed to find refuge with Byzantine garrisons and awaited the arrival of the baronial host.

The Peasants' Crusade was a futile endeavor; but still it remains a remarkable manifestation of faith. Thousands of sincere Christians faced with confidence the terrors of a long journey and a savage foe. They believed very literally that God willed it and that he would nourish them on the journey and give them victory over the Turks.

The main force of crusading barons and their followers who started in the late summer of 1096 followed three different routes to Constantinople. Godfrey de Bouillon took the most obvious all-land route—that down the Danube through Hungary and Bulgaria. The count of Toulouse invented a route of his own, which no one else was silly enough to use. He marched across Italy, through the territory of Venice, and down the Adriatic coast to Durazzo. Passing through this land of wild mountains and still wilder peoples cost him many of his followers. The Normans and northern French went down the Italian peninsula to Apulia and from there crossed to Durazzo. In Apulia they were joined by Bohemond, his nephew Tancred, and several other members of the house of Hauteville. While many of the crusaders were genuinely moved by religious zeal, it seems fairly clear that Bohemond was not one of them. His sole purpose was to win in Palestine or Syria the fief that he had failed to acquire in Italy.

The emperor Alexius was considerably perturbed when he learned of the composition of the crusading host. He had hoped for a body of knights who would serve under him for pay. Instead of that, he was getting an army well, if not over-well, supplied with baronial leaders whose primary purpose was to recover the Holy Land and only incidentally to aid him. The policy Alexius adopted was both simple and wise: he would supply the crusaders with food and transportation to Asia Minor and exact in return an oath of allegiance from the leaders. But nothing Alexius could do was likely to avoid all trouble with his dangerous allies. To the western barons and their men, the Greeks were degenerate, soft, luxury-loving, and completely untrustworthy. At the same time, the emperor and his subjects could only think of the Westerners as wild barbarians. They were not entirely wrong. Godfrey de Bouillon and his men plundered and burned a suburb of Constantinople where they were quartered before Godfrey was finally induced to take the oath of allegiance to the emperor. Once all the crusaders were safely in Asia Minor, the emperor must have breathed a sigh of relief. In May 1097 the crusading host laid siege to Nicea, once the Turkish capital and a fortress dangerously near to Constantinople. When it fell about a month later, it was occupied by imperial troops. Alexius then set to work to clear the Turks out of the vicinity, while the crusading host began its long march to Palestine.

By good luck rather than by calculation, the crusaders had chosen an excellent time to attack the western fringes of the Abbasid Empire. The Muslim chieftains of the region had broken away from the control of the sultan in Baghdad and were quarreling fiercely among themselves. Most of Asia Minor belonged to the sultan of Rum, and petty princes ruled in Aleppo, Antioch, and Damascus. As soon as he learned that his capital of Nicea was under seige, the sultan of Rum began to muster his troops, but he was not ready for battle until the crusaders had captured the city and commenced their march across his realm. Considering that they were in hostile territory, the crusaders marched in a magnificently casual fashion. The army split into two columns; the northern one was commanded by Robert of Normandy and Bohemond, while the southern was headed by Godfrey of Bouillon and Raymond of Toulouse. According to some accounts, this division was accidental, but others say it was made because of a shortage of forage for the horses. Be that as it may, the two columns made no serious effort to keep in touch with each other, and neither had more than a faint idea where the other was.

Unfortunately, there is little evidence that can be used to determine the size of the crusading host. Contemporary figures that set it at 100,000 knights and 600,000 infantry are utterly fantastic. It seems likely that there were 2,000–3,000 knights and 8,000–12,000 infantry. In addition, the army was followed by a horde of noncombatants, both men and women. Many pilgrims went along with the crusaders, and no medieval army could be expected to get along without its servants and prostitutes. The countryside had been severely ravaged in the wars between the Turks and the Greeks, and the Turks carefully destroyed whatever lay in the path of the crusaders. Hence the army was soon suffering severely from lack of food for both men and horses.

On July 1 Bohemond, who was in command of the northern column, learned from his scouts that a strong body of Turks was approaching. He immediately placed his baggage and noncombatants by a small swamp and ordered his infantry to guard them. He then despatched messengers to notify the other column and drew up his knights in line of battle. The Turkish host was composed entirely of mounted archers and was greatly superior to the crusaders in numbers. The Turks quickly surrounded the knights and rode around their position, showering them with arrows without coming within reach of their weapons. A few groups of knights tried charging the Turks, but the lightly armed horsemen kept out of their reach until they were far from the main body of the crusaders and then cut them to pieces. Seeing that such attacks were useless, Bohemond ordered his men to stand together on the defensive. But knights were never intended to sit passively under a rain of arrows, and the line began to waver. Meanwhile, the Turks had charged the ill-armed infantry and were plundering the camp and slaughtering the noncombatants. Although the Turkish arrows had little effect on the heavily armored knights except to annoy and exasperate them, many of the horses were killed and their riders left helpless. The situation of the crusaders looked completely hopeless when suddenly Godfrey de Bouillon and his knights appeared at the top of a nearby ridge and immediately charged the Turks. This completely disrupted the Turkish tactics. Caught between two bodies of knights, they were helpless before the swords and lances of the heavy horsemen. Many were killed, and the rest fled in disorder.

This great victory, called the Battle of Dorylaeum, broke the spirit of the Turks for the time being, and they dared not attack the crusaders again on their march to Antioch. The crusaders' success was, of course, the result of pure good luck. The camp of Godfrey de Bouillon was only six miles from the scene of the battle, yet it took Bohemond's messengers five hours to find it. Obviously, they had no notion where to look and could easily have failed to find it in time.

After their victory, the only peril that faced the crusaders was an acute shortage of supplies. Many of the infantry died of want, and the army lost a large proportion of its horses. Fortunately, the army reached the friendly Christian Armenian states before it was completely destroyed by the rigors of the journey. Then Godfrey's brother Baldwin left the host with a small band of followers to establish a fief for himself around Edessa. The rest of the army marched south to Antioch. There they settled down to what the Middle Ages called a *siege.* The army was not nearly large enough to invest the city, and it had no siege engines. All it could do was camp near the walls and keep scouting parties out to make it difficult for the garrison to communicate with the outside country. Obviously, the city could stand a siege indefinitely. But after the crusaders had defeated two Turkish forces that sought to relieve Antioch, some of the garrison got discouraged. Bohemond succeeded in persuading the commander of a tower to surrender it to him. He then proposed to his fellow barons that they should make an assault. The first one to get inside the city should have it for his own. Bohemond himself was first, of course.

Antioch was taken, and Bohemond as its ruler took the title prince of Antioch. Within a few days, fresh Turkish troops arrived and besieged the crusaders in the city. At this point, the crusaders were heartened by the supposed discovery of a marvelous relic, the very lance that had pierced the side of Christ at the Crucifixion. On June 28, 1098, they sallied out to offer battle. This time the Turks made a mistake. They allowed the crusaders to catch them in a confined space with water behind them, and were thus forced to fight at close quarters. The result was another Christian victory.

Leaving Bohemond in his dubiously won stronghold to carve out a fief for himself in northern Syria, the crusading host marched on down the coast, ignoring the Turkish garrisons in the coastal cities. In June 1099 the army reached Jerusalem and laid seige to it. On July 13 they succeeded in entering the city. There followed a frightful massacre of the inhabitants. According to contemporary accounts, ten thousand were slain in the Temple of Solomon, and the floor was ankle-deep in blood. Even granting room for enthusiastic exaggeration, the "judgment of God" hailed by the chroniclers was a horrible one.*

37. The Crusaders and Their States, 1099–1204

As soon as they were firmly established in Jerusalem, the crusaders proceeded to elect a king to govern the state they were founding. During the siege of Antioch and the march to Jerusalem, Raymond of Toulouse had quarreled continually with Bohemond. There was no chance that either of these parties would allow the other to hold the crown. The only important leader who was neutral was Godfrey de Bouillon; he was promptly elected. Shortly afterward Godfrey did homage to Daimbert, archbishop of Pisa and patriarch of Jerusalem, thus admitting that his kingdom was held from the church—Godfrey actually took the title "Defender of the Holy Sepulcher" rather than "king." The organization of the new state was influenced by the pattern of the original conquests. Baldwin retained the county of Edessa and Bohemond kept Antioch. Raymond of Toulouse was awarded the county of Tripoli.

Within a month of their capture of Jerusalem, the crusaders were forced to defend their conquest. Jerusalem had not been a part of the Turkish lands when it fell to the crusaders but had been under the rule of an officer of the Fatimid caliph of Egypt, who promptly despatched an army to recover it. Godfrey mustered his men and met the Egyptians near Ascalon, in the extreme south of Palestine. The caliph's forces consisted largely of lightly armed cavalry without bows, and they were no match for the European knights. Godfrey easily won a complete victory, and the First Crusade was over.

*Sources, no. 40

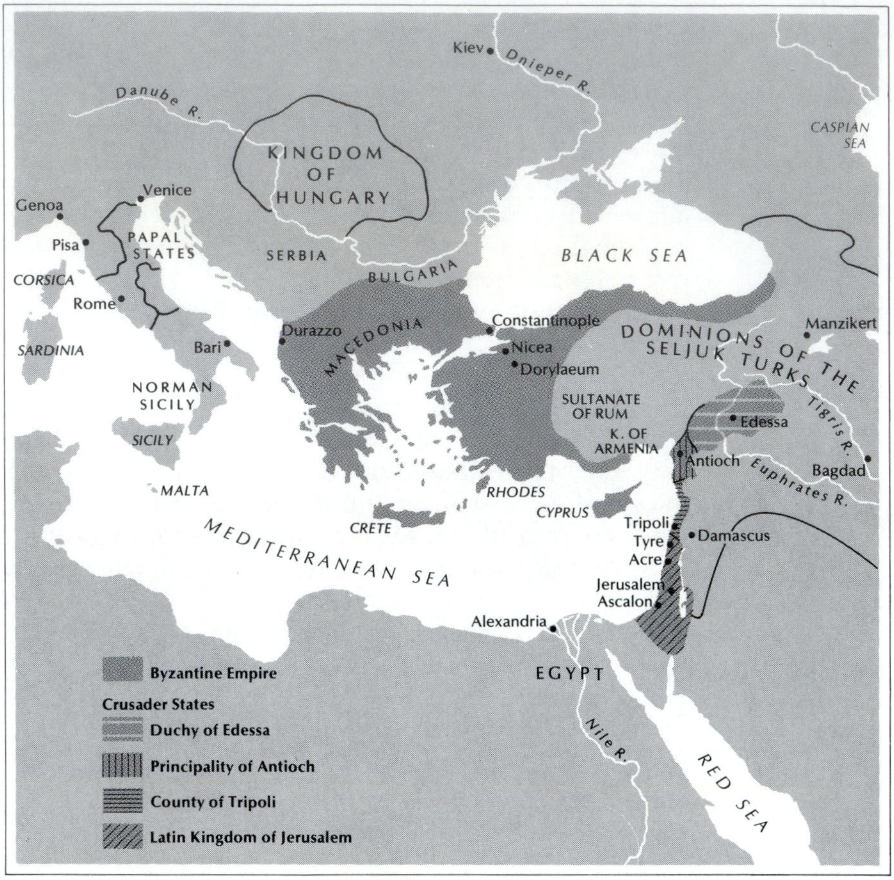

The First Crusade and Byzantium

The plight of the Byzantine Empire, engaged in a struggle with the Muslims to maintain its existence, was the original impetus for the crusades. As is evident from the map, however, the crusaders were intent on realizing their own ambitions and spent their energies not in protecting the empire but in creating new kingdoms of their own.

Godfrey de Bouillon lived less than a year after the capture of Jerusalem. He was succeeded by his brother Baldwin, count of Edessa, who became the real founder of the Latin kingdom of Jerusalem. With the assistance of Italian naval squadrons, Baldwin (1100–1118) conquered the coastal towns that had been bypassed by the crusaders in their march on Jerusalem. He also crossed into Jordan and established fortresses there. Godfrey had begun to distribute the conquered lands, as well as many of those still to be conquered, as fiefs. Baldwin I continued the process. Jerusalem and the ports of Tyre and Acre formed the royal demesne. The great barons who held fiefs directly of the king in turn gave fiefs to their men, and a fully developed feudal hierarchy was established. In the two most completely feudal states of Europe, England and France, the monarchs retained, in theory at least, the powers of the Anglo-Saxon and Frankish kings in addition to the prerogatives of a feudal suzerain. In Jerusalem, however, there had been no kingdom, and there was no royal tradition. Hence the king was simply a feudal suzerain. The real power in the realm lay in the *High Court,* the assembly of the tenants-in-chief. This body chose the king, and he could do nothing without its approval. It acted as the chief court of justice in all matters involving the barons, as executive council, and as the legislative body. Each baron had his own feudal court that performed the same functions within his fief. The barons owed feudal services to the king, but the nature and extent of these services were determined by the High Court. One might say that the Latin kingdom of Jerusalem was the perfect feudal state, where the king enjoyed no powers except those given the suzerain by feudal custom.

The High Court and the feudal courts of the barons dispensed justice to the noble fief holders. Another set of courts, called *courts of the bourgeoisie,* had jurisdiction over the nonnoble population. Each lord had a court of the bourgeoisie for his own demesne. The lord's agent, the viscount, presided over the court, but its decisions were rendered by twelve jurors appointed by the lord from the bourgeoisie of his lands. Subordinate courts under native judges cared for the needs of the native population. Thus, in the kingdom of Jerusalem, feudal and seignorial jurisdiction were clearly separated.

The relationship between the kingdom of Jerusalem and the three crusading states of Syria—the principality of Antioch and the counties of Tripoli and Edessa—was never very clearly established. The lords of these states did homage to the king of Jerusalem, and the king usually exercised the right of custody in case of a minority, but the lords were not subject to the High Court. Each of these fiefs had its own feudal custom and its own court. Each was, like the kingdom of Jerusalem, a highly organized feudal state.

The military power of the kingdom of Jerusalem was drawn from a number of sources. There were, of course, the barons of the realm and their vassals who owed regular military service. As the productive land available for fiefs was very limited and the king and his barons drew large revenues from trade, money fiefs became extremely common and supplied a large proportion of the feudal levy of the kingdom. Then an important part of the permanent garrison of the kingdom was supplied by the two great military orders—the Knights of the Temple and the Knights of the Hospital of St. John of Jerusalem.

In the reign of Baldwin I, a French knight, Hugh de Payen, and eight companions took the oaths of regular canons and began serving as police escorts for pilgrims on the road from the coast to the Holy City. Soon they were given a house near the Temple of Solomon and became known as Knights of the Temples. In 1128 the pope and a church council formally established the Knights of the Temple as a military religious order, and St. Bernard of Clairvaux drew up a rule for them based on that of the Cistercians.* They thus became a monastic order, the chief function of which was to fight the Muslims. The Templars provided a model for three Spanish military orders—the Orders of Calatrava, Alcantara, and Santiago—that were formed to carry on the struggle against the Saracens in Spain. Their example

*See pp. 300–302.

was also followed by the men serving the Hospital of St. John in Jerusalem, which had been founded early in the eleventh century to care for Christian pilgrims. Although they continued to operate their hospital, they became a military order as well. Some years later, in 1198, another order, the Teutonic Knights, was founded. The two senior orders in the Holy Land received vast tracts of land, preferably in the most exposed regions, from the kings of Jerusalem. These lands they protected with great fortresses supplied with strong permanent garrisons. Perhaps the most famous of these was Crac des Chevaliers, which held the frontier between the Turks and the county of Tripoli.

At their height, the Hospitalers could supply five hundred knights for service in the field; the Templars, three hundred. These enormous military establishments were only to a slight degree supported by local resources. The two orders acquired extensive and valuable properties throughout Europe to support their activities in the Holy Land. They thus furnished the kingdom of Jerusalem with a permanent military force maintained by endowments beyond the reach of Turkish arms. Although the usefulness of the two orders would have been greater if they had not quarreled fiercely with each other, together they were one of the chief mainstays of the Latin kingdom.

The permanent military forces of the Latin kingdom were reinforced by widely varying numbers of temporary visitors—crusaders and armed pilgrims. A special emergency in the Holy Land might bring to its aid a large crusading army. In between such major expeditions, there was a steady flow of crusaders coming as individuals or in small bands. There was probably never a time when there were not in the Holy Land some knights who planned to fight the Muslims for a year or so, visit the tomb of Christ, and then return home. Some of these men stayed to become vassals of the king of Jerusalem, but most of them went back to Europe or died on the crusade. Thus, when the young king Henry, eldest son of Henry II of England, lay on his deathbed, he asked his friend and mentor, William Marshal, to bear his cross to Jerusalem. William went to Palestine, did some fighting, and returned with a rich silk cloth to be used to cover his coffin. Such visiting knights from the West were not invariably helpful to the established authorities. The Arab noble Ousama observed in his autobiography, written toward the end of the twelfth century, that it was possible for Muslims to live on easy terms with Frankish crusaders who had been settled for a long time in Palestine. They had grown tolerant of the Muslim religion, he wrote, and understood Eastern ways, but the bellicose newcomers from Europe were always stirring up trouble.*

Finally, it is extremely important to remember that the Latin kingdom could not have come into existence, much less survived, without the fleets of the Italian cities. They maintained control of the sea and kept the Muslim fleet at bay. The army of the First crusade was furnished the supplies needed for the march on Jerusalem by an Italian fleet, and troops from the fleet participated in the capture of the Holy City. Baldwin I could not have reduced the coastal towns without naval

*Sources, no. 41

aid. It was the ships of the Italian towns that carried supplies and pilgrims to the Holy Land throughout the existence of the Latin kingdom. At best, the crusaders' states were frontier posts that needed continuous aid from Europe, and the communications vital to their existence were supplied by the Italian towns.

In 1144 the ruler of Mosul conquered the county of Edessa. This Muslim victory horrified Christendom and moved the pope to preach a second crusade to recover the lost territory. The success of this plea was largely the result of the unusual persuasive powers of St. Bernard of Clairvaux, who devoted all his enthusiasm, energy, and oratorical capacity to encouraging the nobles of Europe to take the cross. The two chief potentates of western Europe, Louis VII of France, and Conrad III of Germany,* took the cross; but of the great lords of France, only the count of Flanders joined the king, and Conrad was at bitter feud with most of the German princes. Hence, though the rank of the leaders was imposing, their armies were probably not very large. King Roger II of Sicily offered them passage to the Holy Land aboard his fleet, but they preferred to proceed by land.

Ten days after leaving Nicea, Conrad's army was attacked by the Turks and almost destroyed. Conrad himself and about a tenth of his men managed to retreat to Nicea and there take ship for Palestine. Louis, who reached Nicea just as the defeated Conrad returned to it, marched on through Asia Minor. In a mountain defile, he was attacked by the Turks and lost his baggage, many of his horses, and most of his camp followers. This persuaded the king that he did not like the land route. He marched to the coast and took ship for Antioch with all his knights and part of his infantry. As there were not enough ships for all, the rest of the infantry were ordered to proceed by land and were promptly massacred by the Turks. Once arrived at Antioch, Louis was urged by its prince, Raymond, to aid him in recovering Edessa, but the king insisted that he was going to go to Jerusalem. One cannot say whether his motive was a burning desire to visit the Holy Sepulcher or determination to get his queen, Eleanor, away from her too-affectionate uncle, Raymond, prince of Antioch. At Jerusalem he met Conrad, and the two monarchs decided to attack Damascus. At first the siege went well, but then the two kings quarreled violently. Conrad abandoned the struggle and returned home. Louis was unable to continue alone. The Second Crusade had accomplished exactly nothing.

Toward the end of the twelfth century, Jerusalem itself was threatened by a new Muslim power. The great Kurdish general known to history as Saladin (1137–1193) had made himself master of Egypt in 1169 and in 1174 had taken over Damascus. By 1186 Saladin was master of both Egypt and Muslim Syria, and the crusading states were faced by the same power on two frontiers. In June 1187, Saladin mustered all the forces of his extensive lands for an invasion of the kingdom of Jerusalem, marched up the western shore of the Sea of Galilee, and laid siege to Tiberias. The town fell easily, but its lady—wife of Raymond, count of Tripoli—retired into the castle with her troops

*See pp. 334, 338

and was besieged there by a detachment of Saladin's army. Guy de Lusignan, king of Jerusalem, decided to throw all his resources into a supreme effort to defeat Saladin's host. He summoned his feudal levy and the troops of the military orders. The garrisons of the fortresses of the kingdom were drained of almost all their men. It is possible that Guy collected as many as twelve hundred knights and fifteen thousand footmen.

The army mustered at Saffaria, a village lying in a well-watered valley some sixteen miles from Tiberias. But the sixteen miles between Saffaria and Tiberias ran through wild desert country almost totally devoid of water. Despite the fact that his wife and children were being besieged in Tiberias, Raymond of Tripoli advised the king to wait for Saladin at Saffaria, where there was plenty of water and fodder for the horses. The other lords, however, insisted on going to seek the Muslim host. It was a fatal mistake. No sooner had the army entered the desert country than it was surrounded by Turkish mounted bowmen. Finally, in a state of almost complete exhaustion, the army reached Hattin, a point six miles from Tiberias, and halted to take counsel. It was faced by a range of high hills covered with Turks. Raymond insisted that the only course was to push on at any cost in order to reach water, but once more Guy spurned his advice and ordered the army to pitch camp. All night the Turks harassed the camp, and in the morning King Guy drew his troops up in line of battle. It was, however, a hopeless situation. Neither men nor horses had had water since the day before, and they were completely surrounded by a superior Turkish force. Count Raymond and a small body of followers cut their way through the Muslim host and escaped. The rest of the army was killed or captured. Saladin treated King Guy and the other lay prisoners with great courtesy, but he slaughtered every Templar or Hospitaler who fell into his hands. The battle of Hattin completely destroyed the military power of the Latin kingdom, and Saladin had little difficulty in conquering the whole interior of Palestine and Syria, including the city of Jerusalem.

When the news of the disaster at Hattin reached Europe, the pope preached a crusade to rescue the Holy Land from Saladin. For the Third Crusade, Henry II (1154–1189) of England, Philip Augustus (1180–1223) of France, and the emperor Frederick I (1152–1190) took the cross,* but the kings of France and England were too intent on their own quarrels to get started promptly, and Frederick departed without them in 1189. He followed the well-worn land route through the Balkans and Asia Minor, where so many armies had met their end. Frederick, however, was an extremely able captain. He had mastered the art of using infantry bowmen whose bows could outrange those of the Turkish mounted archers to hold the enemy at a distance, and he knew when to use his cavalry to best advantage. Again and again the Turks attacked the crusading host, but they were always beaten off with heavy losses. When he reached Iconium, the capital of the sultanate of Rum, he took the town by storm and found it full of provisions as well as plunder. This capture of his capital so discour-

*See pp. 326–327, p. 335, and p. 338.

Battle miniature from an Old Testament, showing the armor and weapons used by knights in the mid-thirteenth century. Note the script at left: in 1507 a Polish cardinal presented the manuscript to the Shah of Persia, who had the illustrations captioned in Persian. Enlarged. French, ca. 1240, Ms. 638, fol. 23V. *Pierpont Morgan Library, New York*

aged the sultan that he offered Frederick free passage through his lands if he would move on quickly. Unfortunately, the great emperor was drowned while bathing in the Calycadnus River. Although his army arrived in safety at Antioch, many of its members went home from there.

Henry II died before his crusading preparations were complete, but his successor, Richard I (1189–1199), known as the Lionhearted,* started with Philip Augustus from Vézelay, in central France, in the summer of 1190. After quarreling furiously all winter in Sicily, the two kings sailed from Messina in the spring of 1191. During the summer of 1189, the surviving Christian forces of the kingdom of Jerusalem had laid siege to the port of Acre. They were joined by the remnants of the army of Frederick I a year later, and in the early summer of 1191 Philip Augustus and Richard arrived. As Richard and Philip continued to quarrel, it was difficult to arrange a general assault on the city, but eventually the garrison ran short of food and surrendered. King Philip then went home. Richard marched to within sight of Jerusalem but did not feel strong enough to start a siege. He marched to southern Palestine and built a strong castle at Ascalon. Then he made a truce with Saladin. Christian pilgrims were to be allowed free access to Jerusalem, and Jaffa and several other coastal towns were returned to their Latin lords. It was a rather meager accomplishment for a great crusade led by the rulers of the three chief states of western Europe.

The Fourth Crusade, launched by the great pope Innocent III

*See p. 396.

(1198–1216),* ended in the worst debacle of all. In 1204 Innocent succeeded in getting an army underway abroad a Venetian fleet, but the Venetians were far more interested in their own commercial enterprises than in the recovery of the Holy Land, and especially in securing for themselves a monopoly of the lucrative trade with Constantinople. From the beginning the Venetians perverted the Crusade. First they persuaded the crusaders—who were heavily in debt to them—to capture for Venice the city of Zara on the Dalmatian coast. Innocent III excommunicated the whole army for attacking a Christian city, but then relented and allowed them to continue the crusade to the Holy Land. The Venetians, however, had other plans. A succession dispute had broken out between two would-be emperors of Constantinople. The Venetians decided to support one of them in return for an enormous bribe in gold, a promise of Byzantine troops to defend the Holy Land, and an understanding that the emperor would reunite the Greek and Latin churches.

The leaders of the crusade agreed to use their army to install the Venetian candidate in Constantinople. They succeeded in doing this but then the people of the city rebelled against the ruler who had been imposed on them. At that, the crusaders seized the city for themselves and indulged in a three-day orgy of unrestrained pillaging. They plundered and desecrated Greek Christian churches; a prostitute was enthroned in the patriarch's chair of Hagia Sophia. In the end, a major result of the "crusade" was the disintegration of the ancient Byzantine empire, which for centuries had guarded the eastern approaches to Europe against Muslim attacks.

A Latin empire of Constantinople was established, and Count Baldwin of Flanders took the title of emperor; but he exercised direct control only over the capital and over Adrianople, the lands between these two cities, and the adjacent coast of Asia Minor. The kingdom of Thessalonica, the duchy of Athens, the principality of Achaea, and several other states were formed for the benefit of crusading barons. While these states were in theory fiefs held of the emperor, they were in fact independent. The Venetians obtained a large section of Constantinople, all Euboea, Crete, Corfu, and a number of valuable ports such as Durazzo. In addition, Venetian nobles were allowed to set up a number of island states that were held from the doge as fiefs. Meanwhile, several Byzantine princes created states in regions not reached by the crusaders. Theodore Lascaris, whose wife was a daughter of a Byzantine emperor, estabished his capital at Nicea and proclaimed himself emperor. In the wild mountains of Albania, a bastard of the imperial house set up the despotate of Epirus. Finally, two Comneni princes founded the empire of Trebizond, which comprised the southern shore of the Black Sea.

Until the final onslaught on Constantinople, Innocent III persistently resisted the diversion of his crusade away from the Holy Land. But, after the event, he welcomed the establishment of the Latin Empire as an evident work of God. He was appalled when, belatedly, he learned of the savage pillaging that had accompanied the conquest.

*See p. 349.

But he soon became reconciled to the *fait accompli*; it did, after all, add another realm to Latin Christendom.

A great deal of good printer's ink has been used in discussing the effects of the crusades on western Europe. Actually, these effects seem to have been rather slight—insignificant, indeed, when one considers the enormous cost of the expeditions in both material and human resources. The capture of naval control of the Mediterranean by the Italian cities was hastened by the demands of the crusaders. The returning warriors undoubtedly brought home some knowledge of the East and a taste for its products. But one cannot claim that without the crusades the Italian cities would not have sought the markets of the East or that they could not have taught the peoples of Europe to like sugar and spices. The crusades remain, however, of extreme interest to the historian of the Middle Ages because of the evidence they provide about the motives and attitudes of medieval people.

Although some individuals undoubtedly went crusading in search of fiefs and plunder, because they found their native land too hot for them, or simply from love of adventure, it seems clear that the majority were moved by genuine religious enthusiasm and complete confidence that the crusade was the path to salvation. Innumerable men mortgaged or even sold their lands, left their wives and families, and faced all the terrors of a long journey through inhospitable lands or over fearsome seas to serve God against His foes. The general assumption was that a crusader would never return home. Although many did return, usually worn and bankrupt, far more found their graves in distant lands. The crusades are a proof of the tremendous vitality and expansive power of medieval civilization. But the savageries of the crusaders illustrate the terrible difficulty of wedding the ideals of the Christian religion to the ethos of a warrior aristocracy. In many ways—good and bad—the crusades provide the most striking example of the meaning of the common expression, "an age of faith."

READING SUGGESTIONS

* *B. Tierney,* Sources *and* Readings, *vol. I, nos. 39–41.*

On Spain the best general history is J. F. O'Callaghan, *A History of Medieval Spain* (Ithaca, NY, 1975). The older work of R. Merriman, *The Rise of the Spanish Empire,* vol. I (New York, 1918) is still valuable. For a more recent detailed study, see R. I. Burns, *The Crusader Kingdom of Valencia* (Cambridge, MA, 1967), and for a brief survey, * G. Jackson, *The Making of Medieval Spain* (London, 1972). A classical account of the Normans' expansion is C. H. Haskins, *The Normans in European History* (Boston, 1915). For their settlement in Sicily, see J. J. C. Norwich, *The Normans in the South, 1016–1130* (London, 1967).

There is a vast literature on the crusades; R. A. Newhall, *The Crusades,* rev. ed. (New York, 1963) is an introductory sketch. The two outstanding large-scale historians are * S. Runciman, *A History of the Crusades,* 3 vols. (New York, 1964–1967), and K. M. Setton (ed.), *A History of the Crusades,* 2nd ed., 6 vols.

(Philadelphia, 1969–1989). The one-volume survey of * J. Riley-Smith, *The Crusades: A Short History* (New Haven, CT, 1987) contains a substantial bibliography. See also J. Richard, *The Latin Kingdom of Jerusalem,* 2 vols. (New York, 1979); R. C. Smail, *Crusading Warfare* (Cambridge, England, 1956); * A. S. Atiya, *Crusade, Commerce and Culture* (New York, 1966); also, on the Fourth Crusade, see E. Bradford, *The Great Betrayal* (London, 1967); and * D. E. Queller, *The Fourth Crusade* (Philadelphia, 1977). See also * J. Powell, *The Anatomy of a Crusade, 1213–1221* (Philadelphia, 1986) and E. Siberry, *Criticism of Crusading, 1095–1274* (Oxford, 1985). On relations between the Greek and Latin churches, see G. Every, *The Byzantine Patriarchate* (London, 1962). Among the translations of crusading chronicles are *Fulcher of Chartres: Chronicle of the First Crusade,* M. E. McGinty (trans.) (Philadelphia, 1941); *The Deeds of the Franks,* R. Hill (trans.) (London, 1962); * *The Journey of Louis VII to the East,* F. Marzials (trans.) (London, 1908). Of particular interest are the *Alexiad,* E. A. S. Dawes (trans.) (London, 1928), and *The Autobiography of Ousama,* G. R. Potter (trans.) (London, 1929), which present Byzantine and Muslim points of view. A useful guide to medieval and modern literature on the crusades is * J. Brundage, *The Crusades: A Documentary Survey* (Milwaukee, 1962). W. P. Topping's translation of the *Assizes of Romania* (Philadelphia, 1949) is a good source for studying the feudal structure of the crusader states. On the theory of the Crusade see F. H. Russell, *The Just War in the Middle Ages* (Cambridge, England, 1975).

chapter

XIII

Economic Revival and Social Change

During the eleventh and twelfth centuries, a fundamental change was taking place in the economic system on which the civilization of western Europe rested. The basic feature of this change was the gradual reappearance of an economy based on vigorous exchange of goods and a simultaneous increase in the amount of money in circulation. By 1200 one could sell one's surplus production and buy what one could not produce. Closely related causally to this increase in trade was a revival of specialized craftsmanship and the development of towns. Into a society of priests, knights, and peasants were introduced merchants, tradesmen, and artisans. These new phenomena had a profound effect on every phase of medieval civilization—political, cultural, social, and economic. This chapter will trace the revival of trade and commerce, the growth of towns, and the reappearance of a money economy, and show the general effect of these developments on medieval society.

38. *The Revival of Commerce*

The general decline of trade in western Europe, which began with the civil wars of the second and third centuries and was aggravated by the Germanic invasions, probably reached its nadir in the ninth century. The Mediterranean routes that had served as the chief arteries of commerce for the Roman Empire were for the most part dominated by the Muslims, who held the coasts of Africa and Spain and the islands of the western Mediterranean. The problem was not that Muslim lands refused to trade with Christians. It was rather that the Christian West had little to export to them. In addition, Muslim corsairs made sea voyages hazardous.

But gradually new trading systems became established. After the Vikings had made permanent settlements in England, France, and

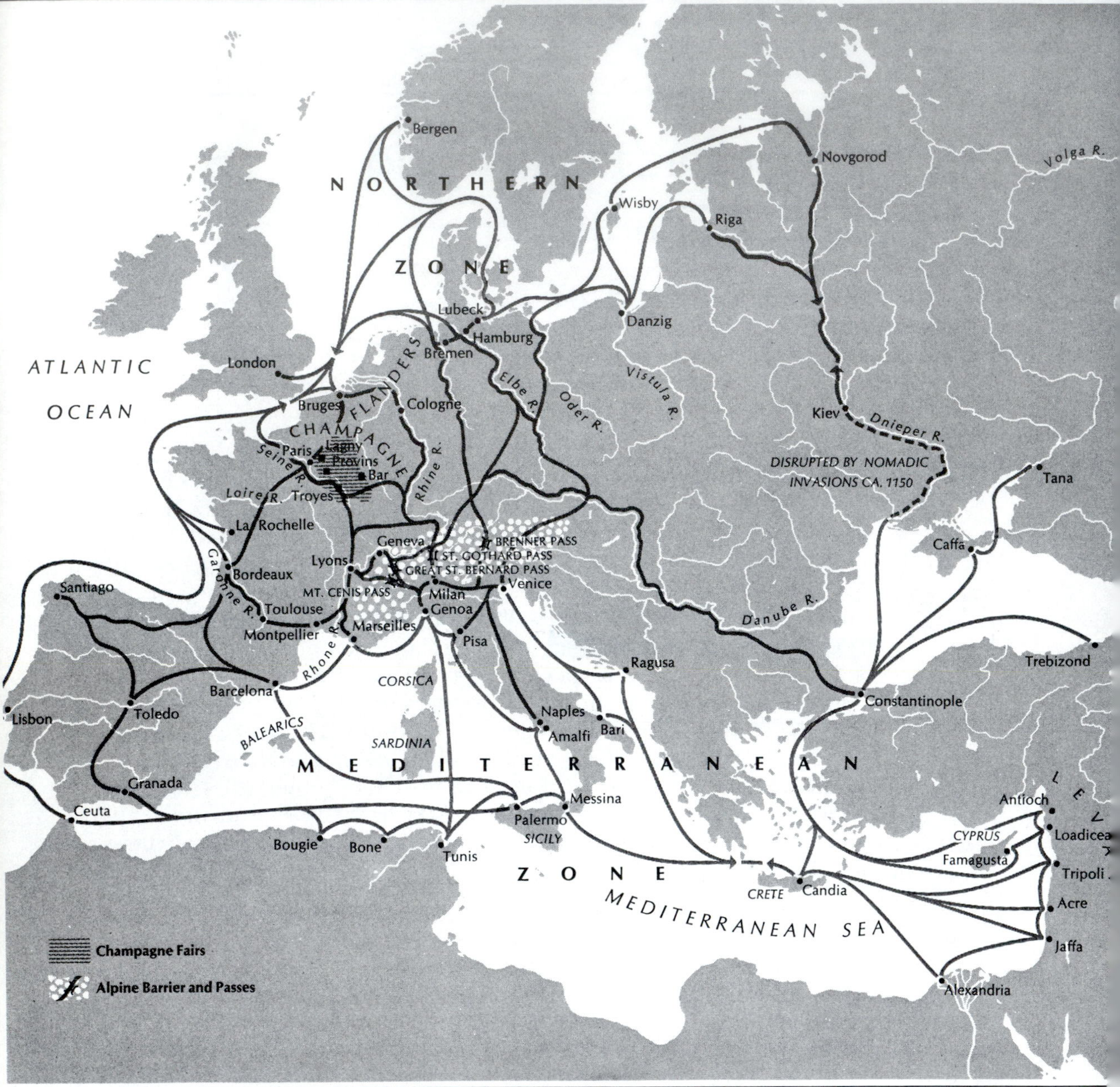

Kiev, they continued their great tradition of voyaging but turned more to trade and less to plundering, with furs and slaves as principal items of export. In return they took manufactured goods, such as cloth and Frankish swords and armour, and of course gold and silver too to supplement the great hoards already acquired as booty. The Scandinavians gradually built up a network of commerce ranging along the northern coasts of Europe and down the Russian river systems as far as the Black Sea and Constantinople.

Meanwhile, in the Mediterranean region, the marsh-girt city of Venice was emerging as a major trading center. Venice was unique among Italian towns in that it had no substantial agricultural land surrounding it, so from the first its inhabitants had had to live from the sea, first by fishing, then by commerce. By the end of the tenth century Venice was shipping grain, wine, and lumber to Constantinople and receiving in return fine silken cloth that it sold to its northern Italian neighbors. Also by that time merchants from Amalfi had established extensive trading contacts with Cairo. The inland towns of northern Italy began to have some industry of their own, notably the weaving of woolen cloth, but the markets for this cloth were very limited at first. The opening of new routes to new markets was largely the work of the coastal settlements of western Italy. In the tenth century, the men of Genoa and Pisa began to sail along the coast toward France on trading ventures, despite the ever-present threat of Muslim raiders. As late as the early years of the eleventh century, Genoa and Pisa were periodically plundered by Muslim squadrons, but in 1016 their combined fleets drove the Muslims from Sardinia. While Genoa and Pisa conquered Corsica and Sardinia and raided the Muslim ports in Africa, Norman adventurers from southern Italy occupied Sicily. When the Norman conquest was completed in 1092, the western Mediterranean was essentially free for Christian commerce.

Trade Routes, Twelfth and Thirteenth Centuries

The wealth and influence of the rulers of the County of Champagne is easily understood geographically: the most convenient overland route for all the trade and commerce of Western Europe was through France, and the Fairs of Champagne were the major market centers for importers and exporters from all over the Continent.

The development of Genoa and Pisa was greatly accelerated by the crusades. In 1097 a Genoese fleet made its way to Antioch. Soon Genoese and Pisan vessels were sailing regularly to the newly established Latin kingdom of Jerusalem with crusaders, pilgrims, and supplies, while the war fleets of the two cities gradually wrested from the Muslims the control of the eastern Mediterranean. The kings of Jerusalem and their barons were duly grateful to their allies. Genoa and Pisa received free access to the markets of the Latin kingdom and made highly profitable use of it. They were allowed to establish mercantile settlements in the principal ports where the Italian merchants could live together under their own laws. From Baghdad, one of the world's greatest emporiums, the goods of the East flowed to Damascus and from there to the Italian merchants in the ports of Syria and Palestine. Silks, sugar, and spices that had trickled into western Europe from Venice and other Adriatic ports began to flow in large quantities along the new routes. From Genoa and Pisa these products of the East were carried along the coast to Marseilles, Narbonne, and Barcelona. Another major commercial activity of the period was traffic in slaves, with the major trade routes leading from the Slavic lands to the ports of Italy or southern France and thence to the Muslim lands of Spain, Syria, and Egypt; but this trade was dwindling in the eleventh and twelfth centuries.

While northern Italy was becoming the center of a revived Mediterranean commerce, Flanders was playing the same part in northern Europe. From before the Roman conquest of Gaul, the country along the coast of what is now Belgium and northwestern France had been famous for its woolen cloth. In the Carolingian period, this cloth had been one of the few products in which there was an active trade. Flanders suffered severely from the Viking raids, but by the second half of the tenth century strong counts had established order in the region. Soon it was producing cloth more vigorously than ever. The location of Flanders gave it easy access to markets for what it produced. When Scandinavian merchants came down from the north with the valuable products of their homelands—furs and hunting hawks—Flanders was close at hand and could supply cloth in exchange for their wares. Then the Flemings had at their disposal the Rhine with its tributaries to serve as convenient routes into France and Germany.

By the middle of the eleventh century, the Flemings were selling their cloth throughout northern Europe, and their chief towns, Bruges, Ghent, Lille, Ypres, and Arras, were flourishing centers of both trade and production. Before long, the salt marshes of Flanders could not produce enough raw wool for the spinners and weavers. Flemish merchants carried cloth to wool-producing regions and returned with raw wool. Southern England was one of their chief sources of supply in the eleventh century; and in the twelfth, when the Cistercians began raising sheep on the moors of northern England and in Wales, England became the chief wool-producing region of western Europe. Thus Flanders became a great center of commerce. Merchants carried raw wool and all the products of the north to Flanders and returned home with cloth.

Although the trade in cloth was the chief impetus to the revival of commerce in northern Europe, at least one other such impetus deserves mention. The Anglo-Saxons drank ale made from the grain they grew themselves. But when Edward the confessor became king, his Norman friends could not become accustomed to so rude a drink and wanted the wine they were used to. Boatmen who lived along the Seine in Paris went up the river, loaded their boats with wine in Gatinais, and carried it down the Seine to Rouen. Merchants of Rouen transported it to London. The Norman conquest greatly stimulated this trade by placing in England many more wine-craving gullets. Soon the wine trade between Rouen and England was flourishing. When Henry II, count of Anjou and duke of Aquitaine, became king of England in 1154, the valley of the Loire and the region around Bordeaux became the chief sources of wine for England.

Although both Flanders and northern Italy were active centers of commerce by the end of the eleventh century, trade between these centers was comparatively slight. This was primarily the result of the difficulty of transportation. The sea route from Italy to Flanders was extremely dangerous. The Straits of Gibraltar and its vicinity were still dominated by Muslim pirates, and the Bay of Biscay was noted for its storms. Only strong war fleets, such as that which carried the army of Richard I of England to the Third Crusade, could risk the journey. Not until the fourteenth century did Italian merchants use this route and then only in the great galley fleets sent out by Venice and Genoa. The easiest and most practical route from Italy to Flanders was to sail to Marseilles, cross Provence to the Rhone valley, and follow the valleys of the Rhone and Saone to east-central France. From there a short journey would bring one to the Rhine, the Moselle, the Seine and its tributaries, or the Loire. But such overland trade was both dangerous and costly. Entirely apart from the actual costs of transportation was the expense of satisfying the feudal lords along the way. Every baron claimed the right to charge tolls to merchants passing through his lands. If he wanted a lot of money in a hurry, he rarely had any objection to plundering the merchants of all their goods.

Early in the twelfth century, a powerful feudal dynasty saw in this situation a chance to obtain a large revenue. The key region, the lands between the upper Saone and the tributaries of the Rhine, Seine, and Loire, was dominated by the counts of Champagne. These counts set to work to turn their lands into a vast marketplace. At a number of their chief towns, such as Troyes, Provins, and Lagny-sur-Marne, they founded fairs. The counts set aside a place for the fair, erected booths, provided police to keep order and judges to settle disputes, and set up money-changers to handle the wide variety of coins brought in by merchants from many lands. The fairs were spaced so that there was usually one being held somewhere in their lands. Moreover, the fairs were carefully organized. Each day was set aside for trade in a different product or group of products. No money changed hands during the days of trade, but careful accounts were kept. Then, on the last day, all the merchants took their money to the exchange; secured the official money of the fair, the pound of Troyes; and settled their accounts. The count collected a sales tax on all goods sold at the fair, rented the booths at good prices, received the money penalties paid for offenses against the rules of the fair, and, finally, enjoyed the profits of the exchange. This revenue he used to extend his own power and to develop the business of the fairs. The barons who lived along the chief routes by which merchants traveled on the way to the fairs were offered money fiefs—annual incomes in return for homage and service. Their chief function was to protect the merchants bound for the count's fairs.

The fairs of Champagne become the meeting place of the merchants from Italy and those of the north. There the Italians brought products of Italy such as cloth, fine swords, and magnificent Lombard war horses. They also bore the silks, sugar, and spices they had obtained in Syria. The men of the far north brought furs, honey, and other products of the great forests. From Flanders came Flemish cloth, and from England its invaluable tin. For about two hundred years, these fairs were the most important marketplaces in western Europe. Every great lord, both lay and ecclesiastical, wanted a fair at his chief town or manor. Many of these were, of course, little more than annual cattle markets, where a few peddlers appeared with goods from afar. Some, however, were extremely important. The bishop of Winchester had the fair of St. Gilles just outside his cathedral city. While the fair was in progress, all business was stopped in Winchester, so that all buying and selling had to be done at the fair. Merchants who landed at Southampton just before the fair had to take their goods to Winchester or wait until the fair was over before selling them. In eastern England, Boston fair was a great wool market. There the Flemish merchants came with the products of the East bought from the Italians and sold them to obtain money for purchasing raw wool. In fact, by the late twelfth century, there were Italian merchants in England seeking raw wool for Italian spinners and weavers.

The great fairs were essentially what we call wholesale markets. Foreign merchants would bring their goods and sell them to local merchants who would distribute them through the country around. But princes and great lords did much of their buying at these fairs. When William Marshal, then a young knight-errant, wanted a new war-horse, he went to the fair of Lagny-sur-Marne to buy it. When Boston fair was about to open, the sheriff of Lincolnshire would receive a long shopping list from the king's steward of the household. In the early thirteenth century, Robert Grosseteste, bishop of Lincoln, wrote a letter advising a young noblewoman how to manage her affairs. He told her that once a year she and her steward should figure out what she and her household would need for the year and at what fairs the goods could best be bought.

The revival of commerce naturally increased the need for coined money. Western Europe had no gold mines, and this precious metal was not widely available for coinage until the fourteenth century. Italy accumulated gold earlier through its trading contacts with Muslim lands. Genoa and Florence struck gold coins in 1252, and even before that, Emperor Frederick II had issued strikingly beautiful gold pieces called *augustales*. But for the most part, the money of western Europe in the Middle Ages was of silver. The basic coin was the silver *denarius*, or penny. Twelve of them made a *solidus*, or shilling; and twenty solidi, a *libra*, or pound. There was also a *mark*, worth thirteen shillings and four pence. In England there was only one money, the pound sterling, but on the Continent every lord of any importance had the right to coin. In the thirteenth century, King Louis IX decreed that his money, the pound of Paris, should be accepted everywhere in his lands, but that did not end the local circulation of other coinages. And the temptation was always strong for a lord, or for that matter a king, who was deeply in debt to depreciate his coinage in order to pay off his obligations more cheaply.

In the twelfth and early thirteenth centuries, the chief institutions dealing in foreign exchange were the two great military orders, the Templars and the Hospitalers. They held large properties in every part of western Europe, and the fact that they combined religious sanctity with military power made anything in their possession peculiarly safe. They would accept money in one country and pay it out in another. King John of England kept large balances with both orders to use in ransoming his men who were captured in war and in paying subsidies to his Continental allies. But, by the thirteenth century, there were merchants, whose activities were widespread enough to enable them to take part in foreign exchange operations. When a western monarch sent an embassy to the papal court, he gave the members letters stating that any sum up to a certain amount furnished them would be repaid by him at his treasury. Thus Italian merchants would advance money to English envoys, and their agents would collect the debts in London.

39. *Cities and Guilds*

The revival of commerce played an important part in stimulating a new growth of urban life from the eleventh century onward. Towns in the economic sense, places where merchants and artisans supported themselves by plying their trades and buying their food with their profits, largely disappeared from western Europe with the Germanic invasions. There were, however, places where a fairly large number of people lived together. In France the ancient Roman *civitates* were still the seats of bishops and usually of counts, and they were likely to be the sites of important monasteries. Thus in Rouen there stood the Tower of Rouen belonging to the Norman duke, the cathedral, and the great monastery of St. Ouen. Each of these was a center of a manor that embraced agricultural lands outside the town. In the tower were ducal officials and a garrison. Around the cathedral, in addition to the clergy who served it, were always some specialized artisans who cared for the fabric of the church, fashioned its ornaments, and performed other necessary functions. In Paris the Ile de la Cité held the cathedral, the bishop's palace, the dwellings of the clergy, and a royal residence. Across the river, on the left bank, were the monasteries of St. Genevieve and St. Germain des Prés. On the other side of the Seine, some distance to the north, was the abbey of St. Denis. In short, although the ancient towns lacked real urban life, they were centers of both lay and ecclesiastical administration.

Some medieval trading cities grew up through a gradual resettlement of craftsmen and merchants in these ancient centers. Kings, counts, bishops, and other great lords were very likely to encourage their tenants to become skilled workers. It seems probable that every manor where a lord resided had a few specialized craftsmen, such as a blacksmith and armorer. When the manor was the chief seat of a great baron or prelate, there might be many such individuals. Where several such seats were in close juxtaposition, as in Rouen, there could be a large settlement of craftsmen. These, in turn, might attract merchants to buy and sell the craftsmen's surplus produce.

In other cases, new cities were founded, usually outside the boundaries of the old Roman Empire, by colonies of merchants who settled around some fortified stronghold—a castle or monastery—which was strategically located on a major trade route or at the intersection of two or more routes. The merchants could take refuge within the walls of the stronghold in case of attack. Then, if the colony became permanently established and prosperous, the merchant settlement would

Town of Corfe. The pattern of a small medieval borough, dominated by castle and church, survives in this photograph of Corfe in southwestern England. Fairs were held within the protection of the castle walls from the thirteenth century onward, and a population of craftworkers grew up around this center. *Courtesy, Selwyn College, Cambridge University*

be surrounded by a new wall. Sometimes population expanded beyond this first fortified boundary, and yet another wall would be built to protect the suburban settlements. The economic historian Pirenne was able to demonstrate that many cities of the Low Countries grew up in precisely this fashion. Other historians have emphasized the importance of the old administrative centers in the pattern of medieval urban life.

All medieval cities were very small in comparison with the great metropolises of the ancient world or the modern world. A substantial trading city, with a permanent settlement of merchants and a fair important enough to attract traders from foreign countries, would typically have only about 5,000 inhabitants. Many of the people who lived in such places would still farm land in the surrounding countryside or would pasture animals in the common fields surrounding the city. In northern Europe, only a few of the greatest centers of commerce, places like London, Bruges, and Ghent, had as many as 40,000 inhabitants. The great cities of Italy—Venice, Florence, Genoa, Milan, Naples—had populations of the order of 100,000. Throughout the Middle Ages (and for long afterward), the population of Europe remained predominantly rural. But, because of their wealth, the cities came to exercise an influence on economic and political life out of all proportion to the total number of their inhabitants.

The craftsmen and laborers who worked in medieval cities were normally recruited from the peasants of the surrounding countryside. The origin of the merchant class is more complicated and controversial. Sometimes a runaway serf might scratch together a little stock of goods that enabled him to set up as a wandering peddler, and a few of the most successful of such peddlers became prosperous merchants. But it seems that, more typically, merchants' businesses were founded by younger sons of knights or well-to-do farmers who could bring some capital to their enterprise as well as skill and hardihood.*

The inhabitants of a medieval city had certain important interests in common. Whatever their origins might have been, they all needed freedom from servile obligations if they were to conduct their affairs with reasonable efficiency. Since everything possessed by a villein was liable to arbitrary taxation, there was little incentive for an unfree craftsman to produce to the full limit of his capacity. The disability resulting from unfree status was even more serious for one who wanted to live as a merchant. In order to trade one had to move from place to place, and villeins had no right to leave this lords' land. Beyond this basic requirement of personal freedom, the inhabitants of towns found it advantageous to obtain as much autonomy as possible in managing their own fiscal and judicial affairs.

By the end of the eleventh century, many groups of artisans, merchants, and prospective merchants were obtaining from their lords the privileges they needed. At first the initiative probably came from the artisans and merchants. They approached the lord and offered to supply him with a tempting money revenue if he would grant them the privileges they wanted. Often they were able to produce a large lump sum to whet his appetite. Later the initiative often came from the lord. When a baron saw his neighbor profiting from the revenues of a flourishing town, he wanted one himself. Sometimes a lord would grant privileges to a few people living near his castle in the hope that others would be attracted there.

Usually the charter granted by the lord provided that everyone living in the town created by the charter should be free and that anyone who lived there for a year and a day should become free. Thus if runaway serfs went to town and escaped capture for a year and a day, they were free. Often the lord stipulated that his own serfs could not take advantage of this right, but he was always delighted to receive the serfs of other lords. Then merchants or artisans had to be able to pay the rent for their houses or warehouses in the product of their business—money. They could not be effective in their trade if they had to perform labor services for their lords. Hence the charter usually stated that the inhabitants of the town should hold their lands and buildings by *burgage tenure;* that is, for a money rent. The rent for a *tenement* was often fixed in the charter. Finally, the townsman had to be secured from arbitrary seizure of their property. No one was likely to strive hard to make money if the lord could take it at will. This security was difficult to arrange because of the numerous ways a lord could extort money from his tenants. The charter usually provided that tallage could not exceed a certain sum. Often the money

*Sources, no. 49

penalties for crimes were also fixed. In some cases, the lord's right to debase his money was limited. In short, the lord's opportunities to raise money at will were restricted as much as possible.

The three basic privileges discussed in the last paragraph were found in practically all town charters. Also, it was quite common to provide that a burgher could be neither tried for a crime committed in the town nor sued for property located in the town except in the town courts. Traders needed quick decisions in commercial disputes, and many lords gave the townsmen jurisdiction over such cases—the right to hold a *pied-powder,* dusty-foot, or merchants' court. The grant of such a privilege automatically involved the right to some sort of political organization. When such an organization existed, the lord commonly gave it low justice, or the right to handle what we would call police-court cases. Town government was likely to take the form of a provost or mayor and a council of aldermen. In England a town frequently bought from the king the right to have its own government represent him within the town. The burghers' officers collected the king's dues and performed the sheriff's functions within the town. Sometimes the chief official of the town was appointed by the lord; sometimes he was elected by the burghers.

Many town charters stated specifically that the inhabitants could form a *guild.* In others it was taken for granted that a guild already existed. Among the Germanic peoples, the term "guild" had long been used to designate a social and especially a drinking club, but it is clear that the guilds of the town charters were something different. They were, in fact, organizations created by the burghers to serve their common interests. On one hand, they were organized for security of all sorts. When merchants lost their stock in a wreck or at the hands of a robber baron, other guild members aided them to start again. If a person in another town refused to pay his or her debts to a guildsman, the guild would seize the next inhabitant of the same town who came its way. When members died, other members would bury him and care for widows and children. Often the guild maintained a school to train the members' sons. The guild usually also acted as a religious fraternity to sponsor religious festivals and to aid the local church. On the economic side, the guild secured a monopoly of the town's business for its members. No non-member could sell at retail in the town. If foreign merchants brought goods to the town, they had to sell them to a member of the guild or at least pay a very heavy sales tax.* Often the guild was the agent for its members in dealing with the lord. In fact, as a rule, the officers of the guild and the officials of the town were the same individuals operating in the two capacities.

At first, in most towns, there was just one guild to which both artisans and merchants belonged. But as time went on these two groups were likely to draw apart. The merchant could make far more money than the artisan and become much richer. Then there was likely to be a conflict of interest. The merchants who brought goods of all sorts into the town wanted high prices to enhance their profits, while the

*Sources, no. 47

artisans who consumed the goods wanted lower prices. The common result was for the craftsmen to leave the guild and form their own craft guilds. Thus the original guild became the merchant guild. There were craft guilds in the more important industries of most towns by the end of the twelfth century, and they grew with astonishing rapidity in the thirteenth. Every conceivable occupation had its guild—there were even guilds of prostitutes. In a complex industry a different guild represented each process of manufacture. In cloth making, for example, there were guilds of spinners, weavers, fullers, and dyers. As a rule the members of a guild lived together on the same street.

The basic functions of the craft guild were the same as those of the merchant guild. The guild buried its members and cared for widows and orphans. It formed a religious fraternity to conduct the religious side of guild life. The marvelous stained-glass windows in the nave of Chartres Cathedral were contributed by the guilds of the town. The guild also rigidly controlled the economic activities of its members. It prescribed the price and the quality that had to be maintained and also the methods of manufacture. Then, to make sure that the supply of goods did not exceed the demand, the guild controlled the number of men who could enter the trade. Artisans started their careers by becoming *apprentices* and serving as such until they learned the trade. The number of apprentices and their length of service were settled by the guild. When apprentices had finished their service, they showed their ability by producing a "masterpiece"; that is, a product that proved them worthy to be accepted as a *master* and a guildsman. Sometimes they were required to serve a further number of years as *journeyman,* a paid craftsman, before they could open their own shop and have their own apprentices.

The wife of a craftsman often worked alongside her husband at his trade. Sometimes a woman practiced a craft on her own and was admitted as a full-fledged member of the appropriate guild; this was common, for instance, when a widow continued to carry on the business of her former husband. Some guilds, especially those connected with textile-making, were dominated by female workers. In thirteenth-century Paris there were five guilds concerned with different aspects of silk manufacture, all composed mainly of women.

The guilds protected their members from many of the ordinary hazards of life and from competition both from other members and from outside the guild. They played an extremely important part in the development of urban life, industry, and commerce. Yet it is necessary to realize that they had certain disadvantages from the point of view of society. As each guild had a monopoly of its craft in a town, it was always tempted to raise prices and lower its standards of quality. In England, where the royal government was strong, the quality, measure, and price of necessities such as bread and ale were strictly regulated; but where the only government consisted of town officials controlled by the guilds, they were able to abuse their monopoly. And even when there was no flagrant abuse, guild regulations tended to reduce competition and also, perhaps, to discourage technological innovation.

So far we have been discussing towns as economic and social entities and assuming that the essential political powers, such as high justice, were retained by the lord. As a matter of fact, many towns in the north never achieved extensive political authority. In Paris, for instance, the burghers had an elected head, the provost of the merchants, who held commercial courts and exercised low justice; but high justice remained in the hands of the royal provost of Paris. Feudal princes and great barons could fairly easily be persuaded to grant economic privileges and low justice, but they were likely to be most unwilling to abandon more of their authority. When a town gained extensive political powers, it often did so by force rather than by persuasion. This force was commonly exercised by means of a sworn alliance of the townsmen—by what was called a *commune.*

Communes first appeared in Italy, where urban life had never declined to the same extent as in the north. In Lombardy and Tuscany in particular, the basic conception of the city-state—that is, of the essential unity of the town and the country around it—had been preserved. The town was usually ruled by its bishop, and the nobles whose lands lay about it were his vassals. Whether they lived in the town or on their rural estates, the nobles were interested in the affairs of the town. The political authority of the bishops was strengthened by the power of the emperors, who relied on them as the bulwark of the imperial authority. But toward the end of the eleventh century, the chief inhabitants of the towns grew restive under episcopal rule. The merchants and artisans formed sworn alliances or communes with the bishops' noble vassals to destroy their authority. The alliances between wealthy merchants and rural nobility—which were common in Italy but quite uncharacteristic of northern Europe—proved extremely formidable. We hear of independent communes in Lucca and Pisa by 1080. During the next century, bishops were generally deprived of their political authority, and the communes set up their own governments. This led, in the twelfth and thirteenth centuries, to long and bitter struggles with the emperors, which will be discussed in a later chapter; but in the end the communes were victorious, and the major towns grew into independent city-states.

In the late eleventh century, communes also began to appear in France and Flanders, but in these regions they were formed by townsmen alone. When these sworn associations rose in armed revolt against a lay lord, they had little chance of success, for the lord could usually muster sufficient force to suppress them; but the bishops could rarely do so. The first recorded communal rebellion in the north came in 1077, when the people of Cambrai rose against their episcopal overlord. In 1111 the townsfolk of Laon purchased the right to form a commune from their bishop, and when he tried to revoke the privilege a few years later, a bloody riot broke out, in the course of which the bishop himself was murdered.* Communes also seized

*Sources, no. 45

power in other northern cities, such as Beauvais, Noyons, and St. Quentin, at about the same time. Later in the century, many towns acquired a degree of political independence by persuasion and bribery rather than by force. Conditions varied from place to place, but certain generalizations can be made. A commune elected its own officials, and no agent of the lord had authority within its territory. Its obligations to the lord were definitely fixed—usually a definite annual payment and a certain amount of military service. The town officers had high justice and full rights of government in the town. But in France and England, all the towns remained subject to the ultimate political authority of the king and did not develop into independent city-states like the Italian communes.*

Something should be said in conclusion about the general physical appearance of medieval towns. Since walls were extremely expensive to build, the space within them was always used to the utmost. This meant extremely narrow streets with the second stories of the houses built out over them. In fact, the houses were often crowded so close against the wall of the town that many had to be destroyed in case of a siege. Before the fourteenth century, almost all the houses were built of wood, and hence a town could burn with great ease and rapidity—and be rebuilt rather quickly as well. The chief architectural feature of a town was its churches, of which there were an incredible number; London in 1200 had as many as 120. When the town adjoined an episcopal city, the cathedral towered far above the other buildings and was the pride and glory of the citizens. In addition to the cathedral, there would be a number of collegiate and monastic churches and a crowd of parish churches. Church towers and spires were the chief feature of the town as seen from a distance.

Next to the churches in prominence would be one or more castles. In Italian towns numerous fortified towers marked the residences of the nobles who lived there. In the north the nobles did not live in towns, and fortified residences were less numerous. Paris held two great royal castles, the Louvre and the Bastille, and a smaller fortress that served as the seat of the king's provost. In London, in addition to the royal castle, the Tower of London, there were two baronial strongholds, and in Winchester, both the king and bishop had castles. As a rule, the castle belonging to the lord of the town straddled the walls so that it could be supplied and reinforced from outside. This was desirable because the castle was intended as much to keep the citizens in order as to aid in their defense. Other than churches and castles, the chief buildings in the towns were the guildhalls, which showed to all the wealth and prosperity of the community. By the fourteenth and fifteenth centuries, a few rich merchants were building palatial stone houses such as the house of Jacques Coeur at Bourges. That magnificent mansion was erected on sloping ground so that one side looked like a large and ornamental merchant's house while the other had the appearance of a baronial stronghold.

*Sources, no. 46

40. *Social and Economic Attitudes*

The revival of commerce and the reapparance of an exchange economy had profound effects on medieval society. One of the most striking of these was the creation of the middle class—the *bourgeoisie,* or men of the towns. Within this class there were, of course, wide differences. The rich merchant was far removed both socially and economically from the struggling journeyman. But all had common characteristics. They were all legally free. All kept a substantial part of their wealth in movable goods—money or stock in trade. All lived together in the towns under the town governments. As a rule, there was no love lost between the townsmen and the nobles of the coun-

tryside of the north. (The situation was different in Italy, as we have seen.) The merchant considered the noble an idle waster who was ready to plunder him if an opportunity arose, while the nobles saw in the merchants rivals for their exclusive position at the head of society. Merchants were likely to have more ready money than nobles. They could often dress as well and live as luxuriously. Yet they were inclined to be careful with their money, since they needed it to use as capital in their trading ventures. The nobles considered the merchants incredibly stingy because they spent with care. The nobles' wealth was in land and their money represented income. Hence they could and did spend it recklessly.

Medieval commentators liked to divide society into three classes, "those who prayed, those who fought, and those who worked." The highest class, the clergy, served God and labored for the salvation of their fellow-men. The second class, the nobles, defended the church and society as a whole from its foes. The third class supplied the material needs of the other two by productive labor. The merchants did not fit neatly into this picture at all, and it was hard for them to find an accepted and respected role in medieval society. To be sure, there always had been some slight degree of social mobility. Throughout the Middle Ages, men of poor birth but exceptional ability rose to high positions in the church, and some of the German peasant *ministeriales* managed to found knightly families. As late as the middle of the twelfth century, it was considered conceivable that the son of peasant parents might be given the qualities of a noble and aspire to become one. As long as society consisted essentially of clerics, nobles, and peasants, this theory was tenable from the noble point of view; few peasants were going to be able to rival the nobles and seek admission to their ranks. But the rise of the townsmen changed this situation. A whole numerous class could and did achieve economic equality with the nobles. The doctrine of nobility by birth developed rather slowly and was clearly intended to keep the bourgeoisie in their place. Nevertheless, a continuous seepage from the merchant into the noble class did occur, often through service to the crown.

Royal officers collect taxes in money rather than in services or produce. Note the balance for weighing coins. Enlarged detail of a drawing from the Canterbury Psalter, English, ca. 1148, Ms. R 17 1, fol. 230r. *The Master and Fellows, Trinity College, Cambridge, England*

The rise of a more vigorous economy challenged some of the most deeply held ideas of twelfth-century men as well as modifying the structure of their society. In the early Middle Ages, men were inclined to believe that God had made the world as He wanted it to be and that it was essentially stable and unchanging. The possibility that a certain sum of money would purchase less sometime in the future or that prices would rise and hence the same product would be worth more does not seem to have occurred to them. Kings and nobles blithely rented lands and rights in perpetuity for a fixed money rent. Even when they were caught by inflation, they appear not to have had any clear idea of what had happened. This belief in economic stability led to the doctrine in the field of public finance that a king should be able to support his government and court on his ancient traditional revenues and that any increase in his sources of income except to meet some immediate emergency was essentially immoral. Similarly, the whole rural society of the early Middle Ages presupposed a fixed, unchanging social order. There were permanent, stable obligations rooted in fixed plots of land. Serfs were bound to the soil and the lord was bound to protect them. But commerce was the very negation of such a fixed scheme of things. The right to come and go at will was the very essence of the merchants' way of life. The wealthy bourgeoisie thus constituted a new, progressive, potentially disruptive element in the pattern of feudal life.

The attitude of medieval kings to the new merchant class might be described as one of instinctive hostility, tempered by greed. Whatever the prevailing theory said, kings did in fact need larger revenues, and they found the cities very useful as sources of taxes. There was a marked change in royal attitudes to the rise of towns during the course of the twelfth century. Louis VI of France, at the beginning of the century, tried hard to suppress new communes; his grandson Philip Augustus went out of his way to encourage them. The large cash revenues that cities could provide eventually made it possible for kings to escape from reliance on feudal loyalties in ruling their realms and so transformed the practice of medieval government.

The church at first regarded all commercial activity with suspicion. After all, the whole objective of trade was to make money, and avarice was a deadly sin according to Christian morality. But once trading activity had become common enough to be taken for granted as a normal way of life, there was little in church doctrine to prevent its development. Medieval moralists concentrated on three aspects of economic ethics—poor relief, fair prices, and usury. Their teachings were influenced by Christian doctrine, prevailing custom, and humanity's natural inclinations. In the first area, the attitude toward the poor and the sick, the Christian element was dominant. Few other civilizations have accorded the unfortunate more respect and given them better care in relation to the available resources than did that of the Middle Ages. The poor and sick were regarded as a blessing rather than a curse, for they gave people an opportunity to practice the most important of Christian virtues—charity. Every person of means was expected to give alms to the poor. Princes and nobles had almoners and dispensed alms in generous fashion. Lords, both lay and ecclesiastical, and rich merchants, too, founded hospitals for the care of the sick. There was nothing in medieval principles of poor relief to discourage commerce, providing the merchants were prepared to show some generosity to the needy in disposing of their profits.

The church's doctrine of the just price also offered no bar to commerce. Medieval views on fair prices were much less rigid than is often supposed. Several different theories were advanced that tried to fix the value of the commodity in terms of its utility, scarcity, or cost of production; but the most commonly accepted doctrine, that of Thomas Aquinas, held simply that a "just price" was one fixed by fair bargaining on an open market. That is, merchants were asking a "just price" for their goods as long as they did not misrepresent their quality and had not distorted the market by creating an artificial scarcity through hoarding.

The attitude of the medieval church toward usury did constitute a hindrance to large-scale commerce, especially by impeding the development of banking operations. According to medieval doctrine, any interest charged for the loan of money to fellow Christians was sinful. Moneylending was left largely to the Jews.* The medieval doctrine was derived from the classical idea that money was inherently barren, supplemented by the Scriptural text, "Give and expect nothing." If a neighbor was in need, a Christian's obvious duty was to help. To take advantage of the neighbor's plight in order to extract interest charges seemed evidently perverse. This way of thinking made sense in the rural, peasant society of the early Middle Ages, and the church's prohibition of loans at interest saved the medieval peasantry from the corrosive influence of village moneylenders, who play such an important role in some Oriental peasant societies nowadays. But the medieval doctrine did not discriminate between loans for consumption and loans for investment. From the thirteenth century onward, however, major modifications were made based principally on the idea that a lender was entitled to payment for the risk of capital losses involved in making a loan.

41. *Peasant Life*

The growth of the towns and the consequent development of a market for agricultural produce significantly changed the organization of rural society, largely to the advantage of the peasant. As this change was extremely gradual, with many of its phases going on simultaneously, it is difficult to describe it in orderly fashion. One aspect was a great increase in the number of serfs being freed. The church had always preached that it was a pious act for a lord to free a serf. Piety and gratitude for good service moved many lords to free individual serfs, but large-scale enfranchisement had to await the appearance of stronger motives. This came with the growth of towns, which made it possible for peasants to sell their surplus if they cared to work hard enough to have one. The serfs of a village could offer their lord a tempting money revenue in return for freedom. Moreover, the existence of towns made freedom more attractive. In them lay opportunities of which a freeman could take advantage. At the same time, by offering temptation to serfs to run away, the towns increased the lords' problems.

Another factor working to the advantage of the peasantry was a great increase in new agricultural settlements during the twelfth century. During the agrarian expansion of the tenth and eleventh centuries, new land was brought under cultivation by disorganized "squatting" or by assarting (that is, by extending the arable land of an existing village).* In the twelfth century, kings and great lords

*See p. 373.

often took the initiative in inviting peasants to settle on their land and establish new villages. The advantages for the lord were obvious. He derived no income at all from a tract of wasteland. Once the land was cultivated, he could begin to collect rents. In order to attract settlers, the lord had to offer favorable terms, which usually included personal freedom, exemption from most labor services, and a considerable degree of autonomy for the community in handling its own affairs. The new settlements commonly received a charter similar to the city charters we have already discussed. A widely imitated model was a royal grant to the little town of Lorris in the Loire country made by Louis VI (1108–1137). It guaranteed to every inhabitant a house and land at a fixed rent, personal freedom after a year and a day, and exemption from arbitary taxes and arbitrary punishments.† These "Liberties of Lorris" proved extremely popular and were imitated in the charters granted to dozens of other French communities. The newly founded settlements were known as *ville neuves* in France, and Villeneuve remains a very common place-name in modern France.

The attractions of the *ville neuves* probably stimulated lords of neighboring, established villages to offer more favorable terms to their peasants in order to discourage them from running away. Thus, in the twelfth and thirteenth centuries, mass freeing of serfs became fairly common. The freed peasants still owed rents and services to his lord, but they were now fixed by charter; he was no longer subject to the lord's arbitrary will.

Whether people remained serfs or became free villeins, the development of a market for agricultural produce modified their position. As soon as it was possible for the peasant to sell part of their produce and pay the lord a rent in money, there was an inclination on both sides to make this change. The traditional labor services were heartily disliked by the peasants. When the weather was just right for planting, harvesting, or cutting hay, they were obliged to work in the lord's land and let their own wait. These services were also unattractive from the lord's point of view. Unwilling labor is inefficient labor. Contemporary books on estate management devote a large amount of space to describing methods for supervising the peasant workers and making them do an adequate amount of labor each day. If the lord took money instead of service, he could hire labor to work his demesne and pay it what it earned. Sometimes a lord went further. He divided the demesne into farms and rented them out to tenants. Then all the lord needed was a rent collector. This process, sometimes called "the distintegration of the manor," began in the twelfth century. It seems to have halted in the thirteenth century, when rising prices made demesne farming very profitable. Then it resumed again on a much wider scale at the end of the Middle Ages.‡

When commutation of rents first took place, it was simply a convenience for both parties, lord and tenants. But once tenants held their land for a fixed rent in money, any increase in prices or depreciation in the value of money improved their situation. Prices rose slowly but steadily during the thirteenth century under the stimulus

*See p. 185.
†Sources, no. 46
‡See p. 557.

of an expanding market. As a result, the real value of fixed rents declined, to the profit of the peasants and the loss of the lords. But, although the developments we have discussed were generally advantageous for the peasantry, it must be added that change for the better was generally slow and by no means uniform. At the end of the twelfth century a village population still commonly contained various grades of peasants, free and unfree. For many villagers the conditions that we described in an earlier chapter continued to hold—forced labor services, immediate subjection to a lord, and a diet that was barely adequate at best.*

Let us turn from generalities about economic change to some details of peasant life and peasant culture. In a pioneering study on the sociology of thirteenth-century English villagers, George Homans reconstructed a typical year's round of activities for a peasant family on the older type of manor. With minor changes his account would be valid for most of the peasant population of northern Europe. The story is not simply one of day-to-day drudgery, though that certainly filled a major part of every villein's existence. The peasant's life was shaped most obviously by the changing seasons of the year and the labors that they imposed. But this round of work was interrupted by the greater and lesser feasts of the church. Also, the peasant's life was given some color and variety by the persistence of ancient practices deriving from the pre-Christian world of nature worship and fertility rituals. Such practices were woven inextricably into the pattern of village life, even though the peasants may have been unaware of the original religious significance of their folk customs.

The three great feasts of the church were Christmas, Easter, and Pentecost (celebrating the birth of Christ, his resurrection, and the descent of the Holy Spirit on the apostles fifty days after the resurrection). But the number of days set aside as holidays to honor popular saints or special feasts of the Virgin steadily increased until there were often fifty of them in a year and in some dioceses as many as a hundred (and every Sunday was a holiday too). There is plenty of evidence that the holidays were celebrated with enthusiasm. A twelfth-century author wrote, "On feast days . . . the youths exercise themselves with leaping, dancing, wrestling, casting the stone, and throwing the javelin . . . and Cytherea leads the dance of the maidens until moonrise."

The cycle of the farming year began at the end of September after the old year's harvest was safely gathered in. It was marked by the feast of St. Michael and All Angels (September 29), and "Michaelmas" was a common day for beginning leases, rendering accounts, and paying annual dues. In October the work of preparing for the next year's harvest began with plowing and harrowing and the sowing of winter grain crops, usually wheat or rye. Then came the celebration of Hallowe'en, a typical mixture of paganism and Christianity. Many religions have celebrated a feast of the dead toward the end of the year and November 1 was such a festival in ancient northern Europe. (It formed one of a cycle of four feasts; the other three came at the beginning of February, May, and August. All of these were still cele-

*Sources, nos. 74–76

brated in one way or another in the Middle Ages.) Since the peasants were going to celebrate a feast of the dead anyway, the medieval church designated November 1 as All Saints' Day (or All Hallows) and November 2 as All Souls' Day. The peasants dutifully went to mass to celebrate the glory of the saints on November 1 and to pray for the souls in purgatory on November 2. But the really exciting activities came on All Hallows' eve. Men knew that the spirits of the dead were abroad then and took steps to ward them off. Church bells were rung all night, or great bonfires were lit and people danced round them, sometimes disguised in masks. This was a favorite night too for divination, foretelling the future. (There were many games whose outcome could predict whether a girl or youth would be married in the coming year.)

In November there might be more plowing, and the grain from the preceding harvest had to be threshed and stored away. But the most characteristic activity of this month was the slaughter of livestock. There was never enough fodder to keep alive through the winter all the animals that had grazed out of doors in the summer. The surplus animals were slaughtered in November and the meat salted away for the winter.

December was dominated by preparation for the Christmas festivities which began on December 25. Christmas, an old feast of the winter solstice, celebrated as the feast of Christ's birth ever since the fourth century, was the greatest holiday of the peasant's year. It was an ideal time for celebration. There was still plenty of food stored away and little work to do on the land. On Christmas Day, after mass, the peasants usually feasted together in the lord's hall. Then the next twelve days were all holidays, culminating in the feast of the Epiphany on January 6. This was a time of feasting, drinking, and general relaxation of normal standards. A "Lord of Misrule" was chosen to preside over the revels (or a "Boy-Bishop" in the cities). This was the time too when the mysterious mummers' plays were performed. The action varied from village to village but there was always a common theme. One or more of the characters was killed and then miraculously brought back to life. Perhaps this was a survival of an old rite celebrating the death and rebirth of the year.

February 2 was celebrated as Candlemas, a feast of the Virgin when the people carried lighted candles in church. During February the pace of agricultural work began to quicken. In a three-field village, the field that had grown wheat the year before had to be plowed now and prepared for a spring sowing—probably oats and barley, together with peas and beans. (And whenever the peasants plowed and sowed their own land, the lord's land had to be worked too.) The church calendar in this season was dominated by the coming of Easter, a movable feast that could fall on any Sunday from March 22 to April 25. The forty days before Easter were observed as Lent, a time of fast and penance in preparation for the coming feast. Probably the peasants had little enough to eat in any case at that time of the year.

Our word Easter is derived from *Eostre,* the name of an Anglo-Saxon fertility goddess. But the feast as the peasants observed it was filled with the powerful symbolism of medieval Christianity. All through Lent a veil was hung before the altar of the church and the crucifix was shrouded in cloth. On Good Friday the veil was torn aside and the crucifix revealed. The people shuffled forward on their knees to kiss the cross laid at the foot of the altar, a rite called "creeping to the cross." On Easter Eve there was a ceremony of "new fire." In a darkened church a flame was kindled and used to light a huge Paschal candle, a symbol of Christ as "the true light." Finally on Easter morning came the most joyous celebration of the Christian year, the mass of the resurrection.

The week after Easter was a time of holiday. The next great church feast, Pentecost, came fifty days after Easter and again it was followed by a week's holiday. In between came Mayday. This was not a church festival at all but it was celebrated with great gusto by the peasants. Mayday was a feast of young people, of flowers and garlands and lovemaking. The young men and girls of the village went out into the country to collect hawthorn blossom (called "may" in England). A May Queen was chosen. There was dancing around a maypole or in the churchyard. We know that medieval peasants liked to dance in the village churchyard on feast days because the ecclesiastical authorities were always rebuking them for doing so. Indeed the authorities were inclined to disapprove of dancing altogether, especially on church holidays. One medieval moralist wrote, "If servile works such as plowing are a mortal sin upon holy days, then it is far more sinful to dance than to plow." The peasants seem to have taken no notice of such admonitions.

To describe the peasant year in terms of its high points, its festivals, gives a misleading impression unless we remember the background of incessant labor on a medieval manor. The early summer months were relatively easy ones but they were filled with necessary tasks—more plowing after Easter, endless weeding in the fields of corn and vegetables, sheep-shearing, carting and spreading manure. Then there were always cows to be milked and other animals to be fed and tended. The villagers found time to celebrate Midsummer which was kept on June 24, a feast of John the Baptist, though again the celebration was really a pre-Christian survival. On St. John's Eve youths ran through the fields with flaming torches and rolled burning wheels down the hills. But after this almost every hour of the long summer days was filled with urgent, demanding labor. July was the month of the hay harvest which was vitally important to the village economy. Unless at least enough hay was gathered to feed the plow animals through the winter the village would be in a sorry plight.

The last major feast day was Lammas, from the Anglo-Saxon half-mass (loaf-mass). This fell on August 1 and traditionally marked the beginning of the corn harvest. Now every available man, woman, and child in the village would be pressed into service. The peasants' staple food was bread and his survival through the coming winter depended on an adequate harvest of wheat or rye. And just when they needed most to work on their own land the lord's steward would be pressing them for labor to harvest the demesne crop. There were hard, hectic weeks of work. Then at last, some time in September, the last sheaves were cut and the whole village could relax at a harvest-home supper in the lord's hall. Then it was Michaelmas again and the whole cycle started once more.

Peasant women shared in the seasonal routine of village labor. The work of plowing was left to the men but women would help to gather the harvest, and gleaning, picking up grains of corn that the harvesters had left behind, was commonly a woman's task. Women carried baskets of animal dung to help manure the fields. They looked after the animals that the family would keep on the patch of land around its house—hens, pigs, perhaps a cow. Medieval sources often mention milkmaids and shepherdesses. At home, women cooked and baked and sewed and cared for young children. The spinning of thread was a traditional occupation of women—hence our word spinster. Brewing beer was also women's work. A peasant household might brew its own drink but a substantial village usually also had a "brewster," a woman who made beer for sale. Workers at other village crafts—carpenters, wheelwrights, thatchers, smiths—were nearly always men.

We should not think of rural society as either uniform or static in the twelfth and thirteenth centuries. In any village community there were great variations of economic status among the peasants. Some were prosperous small farmers; others barely managed to survive. A thirteenth-century survey of an English manor lists fifty-three villeins by name.* Eighteen of them, including two women, each held a full virgate of land, that is, about thirty acres, a substantial holding. Five held half-a-virgate each. Thirty were listed as cotters, holding only a cottage and a patch of land around it. These people probably practiced village crafts or hired themselves out as servants to the lord or to their wealthier peasant neighbors. Sometimes the fortunes of peasant families would change greatly over two or three generations. A capable man who made a good marriage and had strong sons to help him could increase his holding by clearing waste land, and might eventually build up a substantial estate. Weak or sick peasants might have to sell their land and have little or nothing to leave their heirs. If an estate were divided between several heirs, each of them might receive a portion too small to support a family; they would have to supplement their income by wage labor. Occasionally a boy from a family of villeins might acquire some rudimentary education and become a village priest, a person of importance in the community. Sometimes peasants ran away from the village to seek their fortune in a nearby town; some of them prospered and some starved.

Inheritance practices varied greatly from region to region and between villages within the same region. One universal custom was that, when a man died before his wife, some part of the estate, often a third, was set aside to support the widow. Apart from that, a peasant's estate was sometimes divided among his surviving sons and sometimes the eldest son took the bulk of it. In the county of Kent in England,

*Sources, no. 74.

by way of exception, the youngest son was the principal heir. Daughters were often assigned a dowry during their father's lifetime and this excluded them from any further claim on the inheritance.

As in the earlier period, a peasant household typically consisted of a small nuclear family; married children did not stay with either set of parents to form an extended family group but instead set up their own households. A village wedding was typically preceded by a carefully negotiated marriage contract in which the parents of each party specified what they would contribute to the young couple—it might be money, or a farm animal, or household chattels, or a patch of land. After the wedding all the property that husband and wife had brought to the marriage fell under control of the husband. Although he was usually forbidden to alienate his wife's portion without her consent, this was often not a meaningful restraint since she was required to obey him in all things.

The condition of medieval villagers improved from the tenth century to the thirteenth. It is important, however, not to form an exaggerated idea of their material well-being. Life was always precarious. The seasons of feasting were followed by seasons of hunger at times when one crop had been consumed and the next one not yet gathered. The great economic historian, Marc Bloch, describing rural life in medieval France, pointed to some realities that remained constant through the whole medieval era. (He divided the medieval centuries into two "feudal ages," the periods before and after c. 1050.) "The men of the two feudal ages were close to nature—much closer than we are; and nature as they knew it was much less tamed and softened than we see it today. . . . The wild animals that now only haunt our nursery tales—bears and, above all, wolves—prowled in every wilderness and even in the cultivated fields . . . . The nights, owing to the wretched lighting, were darker; the cold was more intense. In short, behind all social life there was a background of the primitive, of submission to uncontrollable forces, of unrelieved physical contrasts."

We must always remember that medieval conditions were essentially similar to those of an "underdeveloped" society nowadays and that medieval people had no outside sources of capital to draw on. In the very best medieval periods, the incidence of hunger, disease, and infant mortality was appalling by modern standards. The expectation of life at birth rose to thirty-five years in mid-thirteenth-century England, about the same as in China during the 1930s. It is a lamentably low figure judged by the standards of the modern West. On the other hand, it is extraordinarily high compared with the figures for most other pre-industrial societies.

42. *Chivalry: A New Social Code*

The first effects on the knightly class of the development of a money economy were thoroughly pleasant and greatly changed its mode of living. The knight could sell the surplus from the production of his demesne and the rents received from his tenants. With the money he got he could buy luxuries that he had never before enjoyed. He no longer had to be satisfied with rough clothes made from his own wool by unskilled peasant women but could buy high-quality woolens from the looms of Flanders. Sugar and spices became a regular part of his diet. For state occasions he had a gown of silk from the East. His armor was made by skilled artisans. Soon he was living far more luxuriously than had his ancestors. The change was even more striking for the baron with many manors. No longer was it necessary for him to journey from demesne manor to demesne manor, eating the supplies from each one. He could fix his residence in one place, sell the produce of the other manors, and use the money to live on. Instead of four of five wooden castles on earthen mounds, he could build a fine stone castle at his chief seat, and he could make it more comfortable. He moved out of the grim donjon and built a pleasant house surrounded by high stone walls flanked with massive towers. There would be a handsome hall with a great open fireplace where the lord and his retinue could feast and also smaller private rooms for the lord and his family. The walls were at first decorated with mural paintings and later hung with tapestries. All this was a vast improvement over the grim conditions of the tenth and eleventh centuries. To us, no doubt, even the finest medieval stone castle would seem cold, drafty, uncomfortable, and unsanitary. But so were the great baroque and rococo palaces of later rulers. All ages have known luxury of a sort. Comfort is a modern invention.

The revival of commerce greatly widened the gap between the mass of the nobles—the knights and petty barons—and the feudal princes. While the former might receive some income from small fairs or by charging passing merchants tolls at bridges, the bulk of their revenue came from agriculture. But the big profits lay in controlling the great fairs and in owning large and prosperous towns, and these were in the hands of the princes. While the fairs of Champagne were at their height, the counts of Champagne were among the richest lords in France, and the count of Flanders drew immense revenues from his flourishing towns. Although all the nobles benefited from the revival of trade, the greater ones gained far more than the lesser.

During the twelfth and thirteenth centuries, a number of forces combined to civilize to some extent at least the knights' code of ethics and their way of life. The reappearance of a money economy certainly played some part in this change by allowing the knights to live a more easy and luxurious life and by strengthening the power of the feudal princes. The princes were able to maintain a greater degree of order in their territories, and greater ease of living is perhaps likely to make a man less savage. The earliest signs of the new and more civilized knightly ethics—what we usually call *chivalry*—appeared, as one would expect, in connection with warfare and seem to have been primarily calculated to make it more pleasant for the participants. When one knight captured another, he no longer put him in chains and threw him in a dungeon until his family and vassals ransomed him. Instead, the captive was treated as an honored guest. In fact, it soon became the custom to let him go free to seek his ransom on his promise to return if he could not raise it. Then, knightly armor was extremely hot, heavy, and generally uncomfortable. To travel in it on a warm day must have been pure misery. Yet a knight never knew when he might meet a foe and dared not ride unarmed. By the middle of the twelfth century, it became improper, in fact disgraceful, to attack an unarmed knight. Any decent knight would give his foe a chance to put on his armor before he attacked him. This permitted a knight to travel in comfort, with his armor loaded on a pack-horse to be put on in case of need.

The underlying idea behind this more civilized code of conduct was that of knightly honor. To take a fellow knight at a disadvantge cast doubt on the attacker's own bravery and prowess and hence was dishonorable. By the end of the twelfth century, many knights would no longer admit they fought for profit. In theory, they fought merely for glory—for prestige among their fellows and for reputation with future generations. In practice, most knights retained a keen interest in possible profits. The biographer of William Marshal continually insists that his hero fought only for glory, yet his story shows clearly that William kept his eye very closely on all chances to take prisoners or horses. And the author himself quotes with pride an estimate of William's profits during a season of tourneys.

Another major factor affecting knightly conduct was the gradual civilizing influence of the church. From the time of the conversion of the German warriors, the church had been trying patiently and consistently to impose its ethics upon them. The church had always opposed and tried to curb feudal warfare. It had preached the sinfulness of fighting for booty. In the eleventh century, church councils had proclaimed the Truce and Peace of God. The Truce of God provided that there should be no fighting on holy days—Sundays and the chief feasts. The Peace of God forbade attacks on noncombatants such as women, merchants, peasants, and priests. While neither of these could be completely enforced, they played a part in reducing and ameliorating feudal warfare. Still, there remained throughout the Middle Ages a tension between the ideals of the church, preaching a religion of peace, and the instinctive attitudes of the feudal upper classes, whose whole ethos was rooted in a love of war. The influence of the church on the knightly class is shown most clearly in the crusades. While many motives moved people to go against the foes of Christendom, religious enthusiasm was clearly a most important element. The church found it extremely difficult to persuade knights not to fight, but comparatively easy to direct their warlike energy toward its enemies.

Yet another important influence on knightly behavior in the twelfth century came from a new emphasis on the role of ladies in feudal society. This was partly due to the influence of the church, partly to the new cult of courtly love. Although the church taught that women should be subject to their husbands, it steadily preached respect for them and gentleness toward them. The steady pressure of the clergy during the twelfth and thirteenth centuries probably wrought an improvement in the status of women in society, but the only definite evidence of this is in the field of matrimony.* In the early medieval period, no member of the feudal class had any compunctions about abandoning a wife of whom he was tired and marrying another. By the twelfth century, matrimony was securely established under the rule of canon law. If both parties were willing, a fairly feeble pretext could bring annulment; but if the lady protested, the church stood ready to protect her interests, and its right to do so was generally accepted.

Courtly love was a highly unecclesiastical influence on medieval society. Its central tenet was that a knight could most effectively win honor by dedicating himself to the service of a lady—normally someone else's wife—whom he served with faithful adoration. This odd notion was invented by the troubadours of southern France and was propagated in the north by great ladies like Eleanor of Aquitaine and Marie of Champagne who, understandably, found the new theory irresistibly attractive. The literature of courtly love and the ideas it conveyed will be discussed in another chapter. Here we are interested only in knightly behavior. The influence wielded by the ladies either directly or through the literature imbued with their ideas is hard to estimate. While the knights were willing to devote long evenings to listening to romantic tales of courtly love, it is difficult to discover how much their actual conduct was affected. There was certainly some improvement, at least superficially. Most knights tried to acquire some art pleasing to ladies such as singing, playing a musical instrument, or reciting lyric love poems. Women were treated with greater consideration. There seems little doubt that the seduction of a noblewoman in the thirteenth century was a far more delicate and refined process than it was in the eleventh century. Evidence of the general improvement in the status of women is fairly extensive. Thus, in the eleventh century, a woman could seldom do homage for her lands and rule them; if she had no husband, she had to be in some male's custody. But, early in the thirteenth century, it was common for a lord to accept the homage of a widow for the lands of her own inheritance.

All the factors that influenced knightly conduct during the Middle Ages can be seen at work in the development of the tournament, a favorite entertainment of the feudal aristocracy. As the feudal princes succeeded in reducing the warfare among their vassals and began to impose comparative peace in their fiefs, the knights grew bored. Fighting was not only their function in life but also their chief amusement. Hence they began to arrange semifriendly battles called *tournaments.* Some great lord would send messengers through the countryside announcing that on a certain day at a certain place the knights of Normandy would tourney with those of the Ile de France. On the appointed day, the knights would form two parties and these groups would charge each other as in a regular battle. In fact, these early

*See pp. 170–171.

tournaments differed but little from battles. Usually two places were roped off as safety zones where knights could put on or repair their armor, and men who were captured were always allowed to go free to collect their ransoms. For the rest, the tourney differed from the battle only in that there was no purpose beyond amusement and personal profit.

Naturally, hot-blooded knights were prone to lose their tempers in such engagements, and men were often killed. This was simply homicide for sport and profit and it was obviously sinful from the church's point of view. The popes therefore forbade tournaments and thundered excommunications against all who took part in them. This did not greatly affect the popularity of tourneying among the knights. On the other hand, partly because of the church's influence, the tournament became a much gentler affair. By the late twelfth century, the mass attack of the two parties, the *melée,* was often preceded by a series of single combats. Soon these combats, called *jousts,* became the chief, then the only, part of the tournament. In the second half of the thirteenth century, we hear of tournaments being fought with blunted lances and swords made of whalebone. Then ladies began to attend as spectators, and after the tourney there would be a great banquet at which the ranking lady present would give a prize to the knight who fought best. Thus tournaments became great social affairs where knights fought for glory and the praise of ladies—and no one expected them to get hurt.

One must be careful not to exaggerate the change in the status of women and the morality and manners of knights. The Victorian age was not born in the thirteenth century, and few knights would recognize themselves in the *Idylls of the King.* Wives were still brutally beaten by their husbands. A woman's testimony was unacceptable in court except in regard to the rape of herself or the murder of her husband in her presence. The mode of living in a crowded castle made what we might consider female modesty out of the question. In the fourteenth century, the knight of La Tour Landry, a very rigid moralist, suggested to his daughters that they should not undress in the hall if too many strangers were present. Prostitutes were still found in the castles, and no noble blushed because of his bastards. In short, the change in both morals and manners was important but still only comparative.

READING SUGGESTIONS

* *B. Tierney,* Sources *and* Readings, *vol. I, nos. 45–48, 72–74; vol. II, nos. 14–15, 19–20.*

The most detailed account of the revival of commerce and city life is *The Cambridge Economic History,* vol. II, M. M. Postan and E. E. Rich (eds.), *Trade and Industry in the Middle Ages* (Cambridge, England, 1952). See also H. Heaton's *Economic History,* cited in Chapter VIII; * C. M. Cipolla (ed.), *The Fontana Economic History of Europe: The Middle Ages* (London, 1972); G. Luzzatte,

An Economic History of Italy (to 1500) (New York, 1961); * R. S. Lopez, *The Commercial Revolution of the Middle Ages, 950–1350* (Englewood Cliffs, NJ, 1971); E. Ennen, *The Medieval Town* (Amsterdam, 1979); M. Beresford, *New Towns of the Middle Ages* (New York, 1967); and S. Reynolds, *An Introduction to the History of Medieval English Towns* (Oxford, England, 1977). For a recent discussion on the role of guilds, see S. A. Epstein, *Wage Labour and Guilds in Medieval Europe* (Chapel Hill, NC, 1991). Two outstanding shorter works by H. Pirenne are * *Economic and Social History of Medieval Europe* (London, 1937), and * *Medieval Cities* (Princeton, 1925). M. V. Clarke, *The Medieval City-State* (London, 1926) is also valuable. On medieval social and economic theories, see J. W. Baldwin, *Medieval Theories of the Just Price* (Philadelphia, 1959) and *Masters, Merchants and Princes*, 2 vols. (Princeton, 1970); B. N. Nelson, *The Ideal of Usury* (Princeton, 1949); J. T. Noonan, *The Scholastic Analysis of Usury* (Cambridge, MA, 1957); B. Tierney, *Medieval Poor Law* (Berkeley and Los Angeles, 1959); John Gilchrist, *The Church and Economic Activity in the Middle Ages* (New York, 1969). Among the best studies on social life in town and country are * A. Luchaire, *Social France in the Age of Philip Augustus* (New York, 1912); * U. T. Holmes, *Daily Living in the Twelfth Century* (Madison, WI, 1952); * H. S. Bennett, *Life on the English Manor* (Cambridge, England, 1937); G. C. Homans, *English Villages of the Thirteenth Century* (Cambridge, MA, 1941); * M. Bloch, *French Rural History* (Berkeley and Los Angeles, 1970); R. Fossier, *Peasant Life in the Medieval West* (Oxford, England, 1988); and G. Duby, *Rural Economy*, cited in Chapter VIII. See also B. Hanawalt, *The Ties that Bound: Peasant Life in Medieval England* (Oxford, England, 1988) and *Crime and Conflict in English Communities, 1300–1348* (Cambridge, MA, 1979). For the theories and practices of chivalry, see * S. Painter, *French Chivalry* (Baltimore, 1940) and *William Marshal* (Baltimore, 1933); L. Gautier, *Chivalry* (London, 1965); * G. Duby, *The Chivalrous Society* (Berkeley and Los Angeles, 1977); and * C. S. Jaeger, *The Origins of Courtliness* (Philadelphia, 1985). On women's activities, see * D. Herlihy, *Opera Muliebra: Women's Work in Medieval Europe* (New York, 1990) and * *Medieval Households* (Cambridge, MA, 1985). Several recent collections of essays also discuss the roles of medieval women. See * J. Kirshner and S. F. Wemple (eds.), *Women of the Medieval World* (New York, 1985); R. T. Morewedge (ed.), *The Role of Women in the Middle Ages* (Albany, NY, 1975) and S. M. Stuard (ed.), *Women in Medieval Society* (Philadelphia, 1976). See also J. and F. Gies, *Women in the Middle Ages* (New York, 1978), and, for an overall survey, * S. Shahar, *The Fourth Estate: A History of Women in the Middle Ages* (London, 1983).

chapter

XIV

Religion and Learning

The twelfth century saw a brilliant flowering of cultural activity as well as a major expansion of the medieval economy. This period has been called an age of "humanism," and it was so in many senses of that vague word. The famous description of a later Renaissance—"the discovery of the world and of man"—applies to this age also. The writers of the twelfth century reveal themselves to us as living personalities more vividly than those of the earlier Middle Ages. There was a revival of "humane" studies, that is, of classical literature. Above all, medieval culture from the twelfth century onward was pervaded by a new, more confident attitude toward the natural world.

We find a vivid feeling for nature in twelfth-century lyric poetry and a new naturalism in Gothic art. For a time, intellectuals and artists were convinced that they could explore all the mysteries and beauties of the physical universe while still holding fast to belief in a transcendent God and a divinely revealed religion. Leaders of church reform movements tried to reshape natural human society into an ordered unity that would reflect the universal government of God. Jurists revived Stoic and early Christian ideas of natural law as a guide to human conduct. Philosophers sought to reconcile Aristotle's natural science with Christian revelation.

Some of these aspects of medieval civilization will be considered in later chapters*; here we shall discuss the basic ecclesiastical and intellectual developments of the twelfth century. In these spheres we find new movements of monastic reform with, again, a strong humanist or personalist element in the forms of religious devotion they encouraged, and new ways of thought in theology and philosophy, together with a great revival of legal studies.

43. *New Religious Orders: Bernard of Clairvaux*

The great wave of religious enthusiasm that marked the second half of the eleventh century and the first half of the twelfth influenced

*See Chs. XVI, XVIII.

every sphere of medieval life. Some people were so carried away by the need they felt for a more pure, unworldly form of religion that they broke with the institutional church altogether and formed heretical groups.* More typically new ways of life grew up within the established church, especially in the form of new religious orders. Thus in 1066 England contained 48 Benedictine houses—36 of monks and 12 of nuns. By 1154 the realm possessed 245 houses of monks and 72 of nuns distributed among six orders. These new orders were of different types and served varied purposes in religious life and in society as a whole. In Italy there was a revival of the eremetical way of life during the eleventh century; the leaders of the movement were inspired by the stories of the Desert Fathers from the early centuries of the church. By the end of the eleventh century similar movements had appeared in France. The order of Citeaux, which became the most influential of the new movements, was purely monastic in character and represented an attempt to observe the Benedictine Rule with great strictness. Yet another pattern of religious life was represented by the regular canons, groups of priests who came together to live a life in common. We will consider these different types of organization in turn.

The most important of the new hermit-like religious groups was the Carthusian order. Its founder, Bruno, master of the cathedral school at Reims, after spending some years as a hermit, wandered into the diocese of Grenoble with a small group of followers, and settled in a barren mountain valley. There in 1084 he established the mother house of the order, La Grande Chartreuse. The monks spent almost their entire time in individual cells and gathered together only to attend certain church services and to eat in the refectory on Sundays and feast days. They never ate meat. Three days a week they fasted on bread and water, while on the other four they had vegetables, milk, or cheese, and wine mixed with water. Since the house refused to accept any property outside its wild valley, the poverty of monks was assured. In its early days, the Carthusian order spread very slowly, as the severity of its rule appealed only to the extremely enthusiastic. Its great expansion and considerable importance in Christian monasticism was a development of the later Middle Ages.

The order of Citeaux was inspired by one of the greatest religious leaders of the twelfth century, St. Bernard, though Bernard was not the actual founder of the order. In 1098 Robert, abbot of Molesme, grew discouraged in his efforts to improve the observance of the Benedictine Rule in that abbey. Followed by a group of his monks, he migrated to a new site at Citeaux and there founded a monastery where the rule was to be strictly observed. Robert soon returned to Molesme, but Citeaux continued a rather tenuous existence until 1109, when a man of both energy and imagination, Stephen Harding, became abbot. Shortly after, in 1113, a young Burgundian nobleman named Bernard entered the monastery with some thirty companions. Three years later, Bernard became abbot of the daughter house of

*See pp. 358–362.

Clairvaux. From then until his death in 1153, St. Bernard of Clairvaux (1090–1153) was a dominant figure in the western church.

Bernard was a religious enthusiast, a mystic, in many ways a fanatic, who had no doubt that his views were right and no inclination to avoid combat with those who disagreed with him. He waged bitter verbal battle against the scholar and theologian Peter Abelard*; the monk and statesman Suger, abbot of St. Denis; and the whole order of Cluny, rebuking them all for lack of religious zeal. At the same time, he showed flashes of tolerance and practical good sense. He was gentle and kindly toward his monks, even the erring ones. When the duke of Burgundy asked to be accepted as a monk, Bernard told him to stay where he was. There were plenty of virtuous monks but few pious dukes. Because of his great reputation for holiness and eloquence, Bernard was often asked to intervene in the public affairs of his age—and his dynamic personality led him sometimes to intervene without being asked. He was an advisor to the French king, Louis VII. He helped to found the new military order of Knights Templars. He exercised a decisive influence during a disputed papal election of the 1130s by swinging public support to Pope Innocent II (1130–1143). He took a leading part in preaching the Second Crusade, and its dismal outcome was one of the few setbacks Bernard encountered in his public career. He was also horrified that his preaching of the crusade led to massacres of the Jews, and he used all his great influence to check this unhappy byproduct of crusading zeal.

Bernard possessed a striking capacity to lead and inspire. His preaching and influence brought about an incredibly rapid expansion of the Cistercian order. In 1115 there were five Cistercian houses, Citeaux, la Ferté, Pontigny, Clairvaux, and Morimond. When St. Bernard died in 1153, there were 343, and by the end of the thirteenth century this number was doubled. In their heyday the Cistercian houses were large as well as numerous. Rievaulx in England contained 650 monks in 1142, at a time when the largest of English Benedictine houses, Christ Church Canterbury, could muster no more than 150.

The basic purpose of the founders of the Cistercian order was implicit obedience to the Benedictine Rule in its strictest interpretation. They insisted on the single simple garment and meager ascetic diet provided by the rule. The churches and other buildings were to be simple and undecorated. The accessories of the altar such as crucifixes and candelabra were to be simple and of cheap, plain materials. Banished was the profusion of gold and silver ornaments that embellished other monastic churches. The long hours of liturgical worship that characterized the Cluniac houses were curtailed so as to leave more time for private prayer and manual work. Moreover, the Cistercians were not to be supported by the labor of a peasant population. Their monasteries were to be located on uninhabited land, and they were to refuse gifts of manors with their peasant labor.

All the Cistercian monks worked for a part of the day in the fields or shops; monastic life again provided an example of men from

*See pp. 309–311.

wealthy, aristocratic families laboring like peasants for the love of God. But, since the Cistercians accepted only wasteland to cultivate, and the monks also had to spend several hours a day in prayer and study, their work was not sufficient for all the necessary tasks. Hence the Cistercians adopted the device of lay brothers. These lay brothers, recruited from the peasant population, took monastic vows and joined the monks at prayer twice a day, but they remained illiterate. Their function was to perform the bulk of the manual labor needed to support the community. In this way a great religious order for the first time provided a monastic vocation open to the masses of uneducated peasants.

The refusal of Cistercians to accept inhabited lands had important results. For one, it undoubtedly played a part in the rapid expansion of the order. To found an old-style Benedictine monastery was a very expensive proposition, demanding the donation of valuable manors. But a Cistercian abbey could be endowed with a tract of wasteland of no value to the lord. The spiritual prestige of the Cistercians and the spiritual benefits conferred by such endowment combined with the cheapness of a foundation to make a great appeal to any lord interested in his welfare in both this world and the next. Then, in making productive the wastelands they occupied, the Cistercians performed a great service to society at large. In England they turned the wild moors of Yorkshire into vast sheep pastures and made England into a great wool-growing center. In eastern Europe Cistercian abbeys opened up great new areas of rich grain-producing land. In fact, so successful were the Cistercians at agriculture that they did not long remain in the poverty they so eagerly sought.

The organization of the Cistercian order was an effective compromise between the completely autonomous Benedictine abbeys and the highly centralized Cluniac system. The Cistercian system was essentially hierarchical and reminds one of the feudal political structure. When a new Cistercian house was founded, the nucleus of the new establishment was a band of monks from an older house. Thus Citeaux itself had daughter houses such as Clairvaux and Pontigny; they, in turn, had daughter houses of their own, and these too could colonize new monasteries. The mother house retained rights over its daughters. The abbot of the mother house was expected to visit the daughter houses regularly and oversee their compliance with the rule. Thus the responsibilities that in the Cluniac order rested solely on the abbot of Cluny were divided among many Cistercian abbots. Once a year all the Cistercian abbots gathered at Citeaux to consider the problems of the order as a whole. This assembly could remove abbots who seemed unworthy of their high office. Finally, the abbots of the four senior daughter houses—la Ferté, Pontigny, Clairvaux, and Morimond—were given the authority to visit Citeaux and remove the abbot if it seemed necessary. Thus the Cistercians provided for effective supervision and control while leaving a fair amount of independence to the individual houses and preventing the abbot of Citeaux from acquiring too much power.

One more significant feature of the Cistercian rule requires mention. The Benedictine and Cluniac houses had always accepted young boys as *oblates* to be trained in the monastic life. While they were allowed to decide between the monastic life and the secular world when they reached maturity, most of them naturally remained in the career they had become accustomed to. As a result, comparatively few monks in these houses were there because of genuine religious enthusiasm. The Cistercians, however, would accept no one under sixteen and rigidly enforced the rule that all newcomers had to serve a year as a novice before taking permanent vows. The Cistercians were all volunteers. For each of them the monastic life was a freely chosen vocation.

The Cistercian was by far the most successful of the new monastic orders. Although as time went on it relaxed some of the provisions of its original rule, it retained a comparatively high standard of discipline. And while the passing of the wave of religious enthusiasm that brought it into being reduced the number of its monks, its houses remained well populated. For centuries, it continued to serve society by keeping inhospitable lands productive and to serve the church by preserving an example of Christian life. Although the Cistercians had a high reputation for sanctity and immense spiritual prestige, they were not always beloved by their contemporaries. The other orders and the secular clergy resented the existence of men living more strictly than they were willing to. Moreover, the nobles and higher clergy were inclined to view the monasteries as convenient hotels, and, from this point of view, the Cistercian houses were most unsatisfactory. They refused to admit women guests, and all guests had to share the meager fare of the monks. To Walter Map, archdeacon of Oxford, the Cistercians appeared simply stingy. And, asked Walter, what must be the depravity of men who need such a strict life to keep them from sin?

Alongside the new orders that were strictly monastic in character, the twelfth-century church also produced numerous new communities of *regular canons.* From very early times ecclesiastical reformers had attempted to improve the discipline of secular priests serving collegiate churches by imposing on them a semimonastic rule. Such reformers as St. Peter Damian and Pope Gregory VII were vigorous supporters of this policy and the groups of regular canons became more and more numerous. (They were called "regular" from the Latin *regula,* meaning a rule.) By 1100 a majority of these groups had adopted a single rule—called the Rule of St. Augustine because it was based on one of his letters. The Augustinians spread with remarkable rapidity during the twelfth and thirteenth centuries. Although the rules followed by these canons were not unlike the regular monastic rules, there were essential differences. In an ordinary monastery, many of the monks were not priests, but all canons had to be ordained to the priesthood. The canons were not so completely cloistered as the monks and hence could perform services that monks could not. The canons could serve as parish priests. They were particularly useful in conducting hospitals and almshouses.

Among the other orders of regular canons established during this same period the most important one was the Premonstratensian order. (The Augustinians were often called "black" canons and the Premonstratensians "white" canons from the color of their habits.) The Premonstratensian canons were founded by Norbert, a friend of St. Bernard's, in 1120. They were clearly intended to bear the same relation to the Augustinian canons as the Cistercian monasteries did to the ordinary Benedictine houses. The Premonstratensians followed a strict rule based on the Cistercian and formed a definite order organized on Cistercian lines. In the early days of the order, the white cannons served parish churches and performed similar secular functions, but as time went on its houses tended to become more and more purely monastic.

The new religious orders represent more than just changing patterns of ecclesiastical organization. They also exemplify new kinds of spirituality that were coming to characterize twelfth-century Christianity, that is to say new ways of perceiving and expressing the relationship between God and humanity. In the older Benedictine and Cluniac houses a monk gave honor to God by serving him faithfully in endless hours of ritual prayer. His attitude was rather like that of a vassal faithfully serving his lord. The new hermit-like movements aspired to a more immediate experience of God through solitary contemplation. Bernard of Clairvaux, in this as in other spheres the most influential leader of his age, inspired in the Cistercian order a new way of piety that was both more mystical and more personalist than the religion of the earlier Middle Ages.

In his treatises and letters on the religious life written for his fellow monks, Bernard described a way of "ascent to God," four stages of love by which a soul could attain to ecstatic, mystical union with the Divinity. These works are classics of religious literature.* But often Bernard's sermons dealt with more homely themes. He would recreate the familiar Gospel stories with vivid word pictures. The central figures of the Christian story, Jesus, Mary, and the Apostles, had always been revered but as remote hieratic figures. Bernard presented them as living, breathing personalities. He wanted to inspire in his audiences not just awe for a remote godhead but ardent, emotional love for the person of Jesus, and he emphasized the role of Mary as an intercessor who could lead men to her Son. A hardened sinner might feel too terrified by his own guilt to approach a stern, just God directly. But Bernard drew for him or her the picture of a tender, gracious, infinitely merciful lady to whom anyone could turn for help. It was about this time that collections of stories about Mary, known as *Miracles of the Virgin*, began to be popular.† Bernard's preaching gave a powerful stimulus to the cult.

Women participated actively in the new religious movements of the twelfth century, though the attitude of the medieval church toward them was always ambivalent. When medieval moralists remembered the sin of Eve in the Garden of Eden they thought of women as weak, sinful, easily tempted creatures. But they also knew that Mary, the

*Sources, no. 44

†Sources, no. 53

mother of Jesus, was the most perfect of all human beings. During the twelfth century the status of women was in fact becoming more important in both religious and secular thought. At the same time that devotion to the Virgin Mary was increasing, the troubadour movement and the cult of courtly love made woman an important subject of secular literature. In this environment many new houses for religious women were founded during the twelfth century. Some followed the old Benedictine Rule. Others adopted the Cistercian reforms. Also houses of canonesses often grew up in association with the new orders of canons. Perhaps the greatest of the new foundations for women was the monastery of Fontevrault established by Robert de Arbrissel. Robert was a priest who had become a hermit in the border lands of Brittany, Maine, and Anjou. As a preacher and religious leader, Robert had appealed greatly to women and had a strong following among the great ladies of the countryside. At Fontevrault the chief element was a group of nuns who led a severely ascetic, contemplative life. Then there was a band of priests who served as chaplains to the nuns and lay sisters who acted as servants. The nuns included many women of noble birth. They were the dominant part of the house, and the abbess ruled over all the groups—nuns, monks, and lay sisters. While there were many nunneries in western Europe, few, if any, were as large and rich as Fontevrault and carried as great prestige in both religious and secular society.

The new orders of canons had their own distinctive contribution to make to the spirituality of the twelfth century. Sometimes monks, like Bernard, engaged in activities outside the cloister, but this was seen as a departure from their true, central vocation. The canons were more routinely engaged in outside activities in parishes, schools, or hospitals as an essential part of their way of life. This activity was reflected in their spiritual writings. In the older styles of monastic piety a monk aimed to serve God and he hoped, by serving God, to perfect himself. The canons did not abandon these ideals, but they added a new emphasis. For them an essential purpose of self-perfection was to serve as an example for others. A recurring theme in their writings was the need for people to serve God by serving other individuals. Eventually all the characteristic elements of twelfth-century spirituality—personal devotion to Jesus, mystical experiences, service to others—flowed together in the new orders of friars that arose in the thirteenth century.*

It would be difficult to overestimate the importance of monasticism in the development of western European civilization during the tenth, eleventh, and twelfth centuries. Moreover, all the religious orders we have mentioned survived throughout the Middle Ages and for long afterwards (most of them to the present day). During the later Middle Ages standards of observance often became looser and there were many complaints of lax conduct among the monks. One may doubt whether the services to society of the monasteries in the later Middle Ages justified the vast wealth dedicated to their support. If one refuses to accept spiritual services as valuable, they certainly did not.

*See pp. 366–373.

But the people of the Middle Ages valued these spiritual services above all others. Benefactors of monasteries had their rewards in the unending stream of prayers that the monks offered to God for the benefit of all humanity and especially for the souls of the benefactors. By purely materialistic standards the upkeep of the monasteries perhaps represented a prodigious waste of productive resources; but the Middle Ages was not a materialistic era.

44. *The Cathedral Schools: Anselm, Abelard, Peter Lombard*

In spite of the great vitality of monastic reform movements at the beginning of the twelfth century, monasteries did not continue to provide the greatest centers of cultural and intellectual activity in the succeeding period. The Cistercian order represents the last great movement of revival and renewal within the old Benedictine framework. Already in the twelfth century, cultural leadership was beginning to pass from monks to secular clerics, from monasteries to cathedral schools, although there were inevitably a few exceptions. For example, the monastery of St. Victor in Paris produced a notable school of mystical theologians during the twelfth century. The shift in the cultural center of gravity was due to several factors. Monastic life followed an age-old conservative routine, but the twelfth century was a period of rapid growth and change. The monasteries were often out of touch and out of sympathy with the new commercial life in the cities. They were unsympathetic, too, to the new movements of thought that were emerging in the twelfth century. The finest minds of the age gave themselves increasingly to speculative theology, to logic, and to legal studies. They were forming rival schools of thought and eagerly attacking one another. All this was out of tune with the traditional liturgical piety of the monasteries.

Besides all this, the papal reform movement had asserted a more activist role for the church in medieval society. The reformers wanted to reshape the world, not just withdraw from it. Bernard of Clairvaux was always torn between the old ideal and the new one. After him nearly all the most active leaders of the church devoted themselves to tasks of administration and reform in the world outside the great abbeys, and the most brilliant scholars wanted to be engaged in teaching such individuals. Hence there was a rapid growth of new schools outside the old monastic centers.

In Italy, ever since the days of the Late Roman Empire, there had been private tutors giving lessons to fee-paying students. North of the Alps, the foremost scholars usually attached themselves to a cathedral or other wealthy church that could provide a regular stipend. During the eleventh and twelfth centuries, many cathedral cities, especially in northern France, became famous as centers of learning where a

Daily life in the monastery: the bell ringer, in the doorway at bottom, signals the time for prayer; in the *scriptorium,* monks and a young helper are at work. Spanish manuscript illumination, Ms. 429, fol. 183. *Pierpont Morgan Library, New York*

student could find instruction in all the "seven liberal arts" (although most of the emphasis fell on the literary and philosophical subjects of the *trivium*).* Already at the beginning of the eleventh century, Bishop Fulbert had established a distinguished school of literary studies at Chartres. Laon became famous for theology, and Orleans for law. Reims and Nevers and Tournai all had well-known schools. Most important of all, Paris was emerging as the greatest center of scholarship north of the Alps.

*See pp. 32 and pp. 416–417.

The growth of so many new centers of learning was accompanied by a ferment in the world of thought. Old problems that had puzzled the subtlest pagan and Christian minds of antiquity—and that had been happily ignored in the intervening period—suddenly resurfaced in the twelfth century. Two such problems in particular began to be discussed in the years around 1100, and they continued to be debated all through the Middle Ages. Each of them engaged the attention of one of the great creative thinkers of the age. The problems were to prove the existence of God and to define the nature of the universals. The thinkers were St. Anselm (ca. 1034–1109) and Peter Abelard (1079–1142).

The first problem is easy to state though hard to solve. Can we prove by rational argumentation that God exists? If not, can we be sure that there is a God? The thinker who addressed himself to this problem, St. Anselm, was typical of his age in that he began his career as a monk, but left the cloister to become a bishop. (As archbishop of Canterbury, he played a major role in negotiating the settlement of the Investiture Contest in England.) Anselm, of course, never really doubted the existence of God. He thought that Christian faith was the beginning of all true wisdom. "I believe in order that I may understand," he wrote. But he also believed that the process of understanding was important and that by intellectual effort Christians could both deepen their knowledge of the faith and learn how to persuade unbelievers. In undertaking to prove the existence of God, Anselm took as his starting point the words of the Psalmist, "The fool hath said in his heart, 'There is no God.'" Anselm's "proof" was an attempt to demonstrate that the statement "There is no God" was inherently self-contradictory. By definition, Anselm argued, God is a being "than which nothing greater can be conceived." But a being endowed with actual existence is greater than a being which exists merely in man's subjective imagination. Therefore, our very idea of God implies his existence, and the statement "God does not exist" is self-contradictory.* In its first form, the argument was easily vulnerable to attack, and a monk named Gaunilo won for himself a little niche in the history of philosophy by promptly producing a derisive pamphlet, *On Behalf of the Fool.* One might just as well argue, wrote Gaunilo, that because we can conceive of an island endowed with all possible perfections, such an island must therefore necessarily exist. Anselm replied, in effect, that his argument applied only to God and not to any created things. He was not maintaining that every perfect thing we could imagine necessarily existed but that this argument did apply in one case of perfect Being as such. To conceive of such Being and simultaneously to deny its existence was self-contradictory. In this form, the argument has been wrangled over by philosophers ever since the twelfth century. They are still disagreeing about it.

The second major philosophical problem of the early twelfth century concerned the general terms, the "universals," that are used to describe whole classes of individuals. Such terms can be either concrete or abstract, words like *rose* or words like *beauty*. The problem is to decide whether there exists in nature anything corresponding to

*Sources, no. 42

these general terms. Sense experience informs us only of the existence of innumerable individual objects. It would seem a matter of common sense, therefore, to affirm that only individual things exist. But, when we apply one common term, rose, to countless thousands of separate, individual flowers, we feel that we are using the term meaningfully. How can it be meaningful unless all the separate roses have some real quality in common? Plato, who raised this problem in ancient Greece, thought that there existed a world of "forms" or "ideas" beyond the world of sense experience and that every individual object apparent to our senses was merely an imperfect exemplification of an archetypal "idea" stored up in this other world. This doctrine is called philosophical "realism" because it asserts that universal ideas have real existence. The opposing doctrine is called "nominalism" because it maintains that universals are mere names invented by people. The whole problem is abstruse and may seem pointless, but an approach to it can determine a philosopher's attitude to many obviously important questions. In politics: Is the collectivity, the state, more real than the individuals who compose it? In ethics: Are there unchanging principles of virtue or only a flux of individual actions which the observer judges according to their own particular prejudices? In theology: Is there a divine essence more real than the three individual persons of the Christian Trinity?

At the end of the eleventh century, a certain Roscellinus began to teach a doctrine of extreme nominalism, and a certain William of Champeaux, one of extreme Platonic realism. Between them stood Peter Abelard, the man whose agile mind and arrogant personality came to dominate the schools of Paris in the first half of the twelfth century. Abelard taught that universals have a real existence but they do not exist separately from the individual things in which they inhere. When we use the term "beauty," we are referring to something that really exists; but it exists only in actual individual things. It does not exist independently in an "ideal" world of its own. The universal conceived of separately from individuals is an abstraction of the human intellect. This point of view was generally accepted until the early fourteenth century.

ABELARD

Abelard himself had a stormy career. He was born in 1079, the son of a Breton knight, and he studied under William of Champeaux. Abelard was dissatisfied with William's teaching and, according to his own account, defeated his teacher in a public debate. After a period of teaching philosophy, he went on to study the higher subject of theology under Anselm of Laon (not the great Anselm). Again he quarreled with his teacher. Anselm had a great flow of words, Abelard wrote, but they did not have much meaning. Abelard announced that he could do better himself and, to make good the boast, began to give a series of lectures on the Book of Ezekiel. The lectures were well received, and in 1113 Abelard settled in Paris as a teacher of theology. He was now at the height of his career, handsome, formidable in argument, and—according to one of his enemies—"sublime in eloquence." Yet when he came to write the story of his life, he called it

A History of Calamities; and from this point on, the calamities began to overwhelm him. First there came a tragic love affair. Abelard lodged in the house of a canon of Notre Dame cathedral named Fulbert, who had living with him a young niece, Heloise. Abelard and Heloise fell in love, and Heloise had a child. At this point, Abelard insisted on marrying her, although Heloise protested that she would rather live as Abelard's mistress than upset his future career (which might have led to high office in the church) by an imprudent marriage alliance. For the time being, the marriage was kept secret, but news of the affair had apparently spread through the schools and taverns of Paris. Fulbert felt dishonored and, to revenge himself, hired a gang of hoodlums who attacked Abelard and castrated him. The affair ended with Abelard entering the abbey of St. Denis near Paris and Heloise taking the veil as a nun. They corresponded with one another after the separation, Heloise always passionately in love, Abelard more impersonal and formal in his writing. The self-revelation of their letters is another symptom of the new "humanism" of the twelfth century.*

Peter Abelard found no peace at St. Denis. He first quarreled with the monks by arguing that their founder was not, as legend held, the famous Dionysius the Areopagite mentioned in the New Testament. Then certain of his doctrines were attacked as heretical. He was condemned by a local church council and compelled to burn the book that had given offense. For a time Abelard tried to live as a hermit outside Paris, but his students followed him out of the city and insisted that he teach them. Abelard next became abbot of a monastery in his native Brittany. It was a wild and undisciplined place, however, and after several miserable years Abelard fled from it in 1133. He resumed a career of teaching, first at Reims, then again at Paris, and it seemed that once again he would establish himself as a dominant leader in the schools. He was a compelling teacher who always fascinated young people, though he often exasperated their elders. Unfortunately for Abelard, at this stage of his career he attracted the attention and hostility of the great Bernard of Clairvaux. Bernard was convinced that Abelard was corrupting the minds of the young by false teaching and used all his influence to have Abelard accused of heresy for a second time. Abelard was again condemned, but on this occasion he decided to appeal to the papacy and set off for Rome. On the way through Burgundy he fell grievously sick and took refuge at the abbey of Cluny. The abbot, Peter the Venerable, a great scholar in his own right, persuaded Abelard to stay there, and he died at a priory of Cluny a few months later. Toward the end of Abelard's life, Bernard went to visit him, and Peter the Venerable wrote that, at this last meeting, "their ancient enmities were appeased" and they parted in charity.

Abelard's solution to the problem of universals was his major contribution to formal metaphysics. He also wrote an important treatise on ethics, arguing that the moral value of any action depended solely on the intention of the actor. But he was famous above all for his whole style of philosophizing. It was this that aroused the hostility of

*Sources, no. 43

Abelard + Heloise

heresies

ethics

St. Bernard. On the two occasions when Abelard was condemned, the issues involved were highly abstruse points of theology concerning the Trinity and divine grace. But everyone must have understood that what was really on trial was Abelard's whole method of applying critical reason to the interpretation of sacred texts. This method was exemplified in Abelard's most famous work, called simply *Sic et Non (Yes and No)*. The book consisted of a long series of disputed propositions, some of them touching the very foundations of the Christian faith. Abelard first posed a problem; for instance, "That God can do all things—and the contrary." Then he cited a series of texts from the most revered Fathers of the Church proving definitively that the affirmative point of view was correct. Next he produced another series of texts from the same authorities proving equally decisively that the negative view was correct. Then he went on to the next question. Abelard did not seek to reconcile the conflicting texts. He left that to his students. The exercise would "sharpen their minds," he wrote. But he did provide an introduction to his work that pointed out the kind of analysis that had to be applied. The same word could have different meanings; sentences taken out of context were often misleading; even the texts of sacred Scripture could be corrupted by scribal errors; the early Fathers had sometimes changed their minds on particular points so that even genuine quotations from their writings did not necessarily express their mature opinions.*

heresies

Abelard summed up his attitude in the words, "By doubting we come to enquiry, through enquiry to the truth." It seems the very opposite of Anselm's "I believe in order that I may understand." And yet Abelard was not a skeptic seeking to undermine the faith; he was rather a believer pointing out that new logical techniques were needed to defend it. The whole point of his book was to show that one could not settle theological issues by rejecting reason and relying solely on authority because, by an ingenious selection of texts, one could prove almost anything out of the accepted authorities. The citing of authoritative texts was not an end in itself but the starting point of a necessary process of rational inquiry. Abelard made the point in a willfully provocative way and suffered for his rashness, but his argument was irrefutable and the "dialectical method" that he proposed for theological inquiry came to be generally adopted in the school soon after his death. The first completely successful application of Abelard's method was made at Paris by Peter Lombard who, about 1150, produced a compilation of texts called the *Book of Sentences.* It was a much more ample collection than Abelard's and it was equipped with a commentary designed to show how all the texts cited could be interpreted in accordance with the traditional faith.

The *Book of Sentences* was soon adopted as a standard textbook for teaching theology, and it continued to be so used throughout the Middle Ages. Innumerable commentaries on it were written, their contents ranging over the whole field of Christian theology. Among the most important successors of Peter Lombard in the theology schools of Paris during the second half of the twelfth century were

*Sources, no. 43

Ralph Ardent, Robert of Courçon, Stephen Langton, and the pleasantly named Peter Comestor (that is, Peter the Eater—but it was books that he was supposed to devour). Perhaps the most important achievement of Peter Lombard's followers was the final clear definition of the church's sacramental doctrine. A brief survey of this doctrine will serve to remind us that the rationalizing tendencies of twelfth century thought were very much at the service of a supernatural religion. A sacrament was defined as an "outward sign of inward grace." It was generally accepted that Christ himself had established certain rites and practices through which divine grace was conferred on believers. The essential function of the Christian priesthood was to administer these sacraments to the faithful. But there had never been complete agreement on just how many sacraments Christ had instituted. In the eleventh century, the question was disputed whether the consecration of a king was a sacrament. After the Investiture Contest, the theologians understandably decided it was not. The followers of Peter Lombard produced a final list of seven sacraments: the mass, baptism, confirmation, extreme unction, penance, marriage, and ordination. The mass was, of course, the supreme sacrament. To one who believed, as all men did, that the priest changed bread and wine into the flesh and blood of Christ, the mass was a majestic miracle and the true symbol of the spiritual powers of the church. Baptism, confirmation, and extreme unction were steps on the path of every Christian from birth to death. Ordination provided for the passing on from generation to generation of the spiritual authority given by Christ to his apostles. Penance permitted people to avoid the penalties for sins for which he was truly repentant. Marriage was recognized as a sacrament to solve a serious dilemma. The church had consistently preached the superiority of the celibate life, in accord with its ascetic tradition. Yet if all men and women were celibate, the race would quickly disappear: hence marriage was regarded as a sacrament to dignify intercourse engaged in with the purpose of begetting children.

One of these sacraments, penance, requires rather detailed comment because of its prime importance and the fact that the methods of administering it were rapidly changing. The basic ideas behind the penitential system were relatively simple. The sacrifice of Christ had procured God's mercy for humanity. When one was sincerely penitent for sin and confessed to a priest, one was saved in the sense that one avoided hell. But a stain remained on the soul that had to be erased by a sojourn in purgatory. This could be shortened or even avoided altogether by doing some act or acts pleasing to God. These acts were called *penance*. Before the eleventh century, confession was made only rarely and was for the graver, so-called mortal sins. But about this time the Irish practice of making frequent confessions that included all sins, grave and light, came to be widely adopted.* Obviously, this change enormously increased the influence of the church on people's lives. At each confession, the ethical teachings of the church on every conceivable subject that was pertinent were brought to one's atten-

*See p. 116.

tion. Penitentials, or lists of sins and the penance suitable to them, had always been an important part of ecclesiastical literature. With the change in the conception of confession and penance, these became far more complicated and detailed. They were, in fact, digests of the canon law as it applied to human ethics.

45. *The Revival of Law*

Medieval intellectuals had a passion for order. It was a natural reaction against the chaos and violence from which their civilization was emerging. When we read the sophisticated philosophical speculations of an Anselm or an Abelard, we must remember that these men were born into a society in which endemic warfare was taken for granted and in which the only known legal procedures were comparable to those of some savage and primitive tribal society in the modern world. Every fief had its own set of customs. There was no common law that was applied over a whole kingdom. Ideas about the nature of law had not changed much from those that the barbarians had brought with them when they invaded the Roman Empire. Thus law was not thought of as a structure of regulations promulgated and, when necessary, reformed by a competent legislator; it was conceived of rather as ancient custom, part of the external order of things, presumed to have existed from time immemorial. In practice, of course, some adaptations had to be made over the course of the centuries. Old laws of inheritance were changed by the feudal practice of primogeniture. The system of fines set down in the early codes came to be supplemented by more severe penalties—mutilation or death—for the more serious criminal offenses. But procedures and modes of proof remained inherently irrational and barbarous. The old Teutonic rites of ordeal and compurgation were still a part of everyday legal practice in the twelfth century. It was natural that men of sophisticated intelligence should be dissatisfied with such a system. Moreover, the old rules of law were singularly ill-adapted to cope with problems arising out of the commercial life of the new cities.

This whole background explains the extraordinary enthusiasm for the study of classical Roman law that became a major preoccupation of the medieval schools from about 1100 onward. Some fragments of Roman law had been preserved in Italy and southern France throughout the early medieval centuries, and some elementary teaching in legal formulas and legal argument was given by notaries and professors of rhetoric in cities like Ravenna and Rome. Then, just before 1100, we hear of a master called Irnerius who began to lecture at Bologna on the whole corpus of Roman law as it had been codified by Justinian.* From that time onward, Bologna became the great center of legal studies for the whole medieval world. Irnerius' great achievement was to master the complete body of Roman law and expound it as a unified whole. His surviving work is in the form of glosses

Irnerius.

*See pp. 86–88.

that explain difficult words in the text or relate different parts of the text to one another. This activity was continued by a whole school for glossators. In the middle of the twelfth century, there were four especially famous ones, known as the Four Doctors—Bulgarus, Hugo, Jacobus, and Martinus—who were traditionally regarded as pupils of Irnerius. Their pupils in turn carried the study of Roman law to the major centers of learning throughout the West.

So far as we know, only one complete manuscript of Justinian's codification survived in Italy down to the eleventh century, and some historians have exercised their imagination by marveling at how the possibly chance discovery of this one manuscript transformed the whole history of European law. But this kind of speculation misses the main point. Manuscripts could easily have been obtained from Byzantium if anyone had felt the need for them. The new development around 1100 was the emergence of a society capable of understanding and admiring classical jurisprudence, and putting it to work for its own purposes. In the corpus of Justinian, medieval thinkers found a whole complex body of sophisticated law organized according to rational principles. They also found a strong doctrine of legislative sovereignty—and the changing conditions of the twelfth century were making new legislation a practical necessity. In classical jurisprudence, although certain principles were regarded as immutable, particular laws could be deliberately changed and adapted to meet the changing needs of society. The fact that a law was old did not necessarily prove that it was good. If conditions changed, the law had to be changed. That was what a sovereign legislator was for.

On the subject of the source of sovereignty, the texts of Roman law were not altogether clear. The central idea was that the Roman people had possessed an inherent right to legislate for itself but had transferred that right to the emperors. Some texts suggested, however, that the emperor's power came not from the people but from God. The medieval lawyers explained this contradiction by suggesting that the imperial office was established by God, whereas individual emperors were chosen by a process of election. In general, they were not too interested in the question of whether political power came from above or below, from God or the people. They found it easy to suppose that it came from God *and* the people. The consensus of the community showed that the spirit of God was at work. As one twelfth-century jurist wrote, "In these matters God is the author, we are his instruments."

Particular tenets of Roman law came to be assimilated into all the legal systems of western Europe, the amount varying from place to place—a very great deal in the city-states of Italy, for instance, and relatively little in England. But this assimilation of isolated doctrines does not represent the major impact of Roman law studies in the twelfth and thirteenth centuries. Their greatest effect was to give medieval thinkers a new idea of what a system of law could be, and to inspire them to undertake systematic, ordered codifications of their own legal traditions. Thus the first major work on the laws of England, Glanvill's treatise *On the Laws and Customs of the Realm of England,* written about 1189, referred to the Roman tradition of written law and proudly declared, "It will not seem absurd to call the laws of England 'laws' too even though they are not written." This work was followed toward the middle of the thirteenth century by a much more extensive treatise on English common law composed by the royal judge Henry Bracton, which included a good deal of Roman constitutional law. Other compilations were made for various regions of France and Germany, and about 1265 King Alfonso X the Wise of Castile produced the *Siete Partidas*, another compilation that was influenced heavily by Roman law principles. Roman law reintroduced into Western thought the idea of the state, of government as a public authority endowed with powers of legislation. In feudal practice, the exercise of governmental functions had become essentially a private perquisite, a property right that was received along with other rights of property in a fief. The classical jurists may have been uncertain whether public authority came from God or the people, but they were quite clear that it did not come from possession of landed estates. Again, early medieval kings had worked entirely within the framework of Teutonic or feudal custom. From the thirteenth century onward, they began deliberately to make new laws with full awareness that they were actually legislating and without any pretense that they were merely interpreting or restating old customs.

Before any of the new codifications of secular law appeared, the first systematic application of Roman law principles to concrete problems of administration had already been undertaken in the church. The Investiture Contest had aroused a great interest in ancient church law, and several important collections of canons were made in the eleventh century, but none was universally accepted as authoritative. There simply did not exist any uniform code of law for the whole western church. Marriage law in France was different from marriage law in Italy, for instance. This situation was remedied by a monk of Bologna called Gratian who, about 1140, produced a massive compilation of canonical texts that became known as the *Decretum.* Although it was obviously influenced by the example of Justinian's codification, the first version of the *Decretum* did not contain any direct borrowings from Roman law. On the contrary, Gratian's intention was to show that the canons of the church could form a structure of jurisprudence just as complete in their own sphere as the laws of Justinian were in theirs. Gratian not only provided a far more ample collection of authorities than his predecessors; he also linked the texts together with a critical commentary, in the spirit of Peter Abelard, showing how apparent conflicts between them could be resolved. (Gratian's own title for his work was *A Concord of Discordant Canons.*) The work had great success and was soon universally accepted as an authoritative statement of the law of the church.

Both Roman and canonical jurisprudence emphasized classical and early Christian concepts of natural law; from this time on they held a central place in medieval law and political theory. A text of Justinian's Digest defined natural law as "what is always just and equitable." This reflects the Stoic doctrine that certain principles of justice are inherent in the very nature of things and that they can be discerned by human reason. Gratian added a Christian dimension to the discussion in the opening words of his Decretum:

> The human race is ruled in two ways, by natural law and by human practices. Natural law is what is contained in the Old Testament and the Gospel, whereby each person is commanded to do to others what he wishes to be done to himself and is forbidden to do to others what he does not wish done to himself. (See Matthew 7:12.)

Natural law thus laid down broad principles of conduct. Human law was created to apply the principles of natural law in particular cases and to supplement them with all the numerous additional regulations needed to define legal relationships between person and person, and between ruler and community.

Gratian's texts strongly emphasized the role of the pope as supreme legislator and judge. Several of the pontiffs of this period, especially Alexander III, were themselves great canon lawyers, and they took advantage of the powers claimed for the papacy in the texts of the *Decretum* to promulgate much new legislation and to establish the papal curia as an effective high court of appeal for cases from all over western Christendom. Cases appealed to the papacy from remote parts of Europe were usually investigated by papal delegates. Thus, if two monasteries in England were disputing some inheritance that was to be divided between them and appealed to the papacy, the pope would appoint two prelates in England—perhaps two bishops—to act as his judges-delegate. The prelates would examine the case, hear witnesses, collect evidence, and send a transcript of their findings to Rome. The pope would then promulgate a definitive sentence on the basis of their reports.

This was an important stage in the growth of papal power. The theoretical claims of the twelfth-century lawyer popes were not significantly different from those of their predecessors. What was new was that the popes began to create an adequate administrative machinery to give practical effect to those claims. From this time onward, the old papal claim to primacy of jurisdiction became translated into effective supervision over the more important affairs of all the western churches.

The canon law that the popes administered dealt of course with all matters touching the clergy and church property, but the laity were members of the church too, and canon law also regulated many aspects of their lives. Cases involving marriage or dowries, probate of wills, enforcement of contracts that rested on good faith, disputes about oaths and vows (which could be very important in a feudal society), the provision of poor relief and the supervision of education, the suppression of heresy and usury—all these were matters to be regulated by church law. Procedure in church courts was essentially similar to that laid down in Roman law. Judges received written depositions of evidence and interrogated witnesses when they saw fit. There was a regular hierarchy of appeals from lower courts to higher ones, with an overriding right of appeal to the pope from all levels of the system. We have said that Roman jurisprudence reintroduced the ideas of public law and the state into the medieval world. But those ideas were first exemplified in the structure of the medieval church. As the great legal historian Maitland wrote, "In the Middle Ages the church was a state."

By the end of the twelfth century, important schools of canonists had grown up at Paris and Oxford as well as at Bologna. These "Decretists" devoted themselves to interpreting the old texts assembled by Gratian and to reconciling those texts with the new legislation promulgated by contemporary popes. Canon law can hardly seem an exciting subject to modern students, but it was a fascinating field of study to men of the twelfth century and attracted some of the best minds of the age. They were not concerned simply with the mechanical application of old rules to particular cases, but with the creative task of formulating a whole new unified system of jurisprudence in an area where none had existed before. An enormous literature of canonistic glosses and treatises survives from the twelfth century. Most of this writing dealt with the sort of ecclesiastical and quasi-ecclesiastical subjects mentioned above. But in considering the constitutional law of the church, the canonists were led to write extensively on topics that we should describe as matters of political theory. And there were two such topics on which their writing was so influential for the whole future of medieval thought as to need some consideration here—the problem of church-state relations and the problem of sovereignty.

Several texts in Gratian's *Decretum* raised the issue of church and state for the commentators, but two of them were particularly important. The first was a quotation expounding Pope Gelasius' views on priestly authority and royal power. The second was a description of Pope Zachary's part in bringing about the deposition of the Frankish king Childeric.* In the years around 1200, two rival schools of thought developed, which offered differing interpretations of these texts. The most eminent spokesman of the moderate "dualist" viewpoint was Huguccio of Pisa, who published a great *Summa* on the *Decretum* in 1188. Closely following the thought of Gelasius, Huguccio wrote that God had established the imperial and papal dignities and had assigned to each its proper sphere of action. The emperor's power was not derived from the pope but from the princes and people who elected him. Papal coronation of an emperor conferred only a titular dignity, not the substance of power. When old texts spoke of the pope deposing kings or emperors, they meant only that a pope could ratify the action of secular princes if they determined to rid themselves of a ruler who had become a tyrant.

All these views of Huguccio were rejected by a leading canonist of the next generation named Alanus, an Englishman who made a great reputation as a law professor at Bologna in the first years of the thirteenth century. Alanus wrote that, if Christian society formed one

*See pp. 132–133.

united body, it must have one single head—"otherwise it would be a monster." This head could only be the pope. It followed that the pope possessed both "swords" of spiritual and temporal power. All legitimate political authority was derived from the pope. If necessary, he could, by his own inherent authority, depose an emperor or any other ruler. Both viewpoints, that of Huguccio and that of Alanus, continued to find champions all through the Middle Ages, but the views of Alanus became more fashionable at the papal curia and were more commonly accepted by the later canonists.

The issue of sovereignty, the problem of defining a ruler's rights in relation to the community he goverened, arose for canonists in the course of their reflections on the nature of the pope's power over the church. They were eager to establish in the church a central authority powerful enough to sweep away the mass of harmful customs that had grown up over the centuries, and they found the Roman law doctrine of sovereignty ideally adapted to define such power. Accordingly, they took over all the "absolutist" phrases of Roman law and enthusiastically applied them to the office of the pope. The word "pope" was simply substituted for "prince" in texts like these: "What the prince wills has the force of law"; "The prince is not bound by the laws"; "The prince has all the laws in the shrine of his breast." The pope was presented, in a strictly juridical sense, as an ecclesiastical emperor, a legislator whose will was law and a judge from whom there could be no appeal.

Having reached this point, however, the canonists went on to consider a problem that the classical jurists had hardly touched on at all. What was to be done if a pope abused all these great powers? The canonists where Christians. They believed that all people possessed free will, and the pope, however exalted his position, was after all only a person. He might choose to sin; he might be corrupted by power; he might fall into error. The texts of the *Decretum* in fact mentioned several cases of ancient popes who were alleged to have sinned and erred. The thought that the whole church might be dragged down and corrupted by such a pontiff was intolerable to the canonists. They all agreed that in the worst imaginable case—if a pope actually became a heretic—he must somehow be removed from the papal throne. Some held that a pope who became a notorious sinner was also to be deposed. There was much discussion on how such a deposition could be brought about but no agreed solution.*

Sinful Pope?

The problem posed by a criminal pope was not just one of procedure. If what the pope willed *was* law, then how could any act of his be criminal? If the pope was the supreme judge in matters of faith, how could any pronouncement of his be challenged as heretical? One could say, of course, that the pope was bound by God's laws, but that hardly solved the problem if the pope was the sole interpreter of divine law. The canonists found a way out of this dilemma by blending their Roman law doctrines of sovereignty with patristic ideas on the nature of the church. They believed that although any individual might fail, the whole community of the church—the "congregation

*Sources, no. 58

of the faithful"—could never fail or err. They further maintained that a general council represented the congregation of the faithful and that, accordingly, the council too could not err. Hence even a pope was bound by the statutes of general councils, at least in great matters "touching the faith and the general well-being of the Church."

The canonists felt able to uphold this position while simultaneously calling the pope "supreme legislator" and "supreme judge," because in their theory, the pope was himself the head of a general council. The pope was, to be sure, the supreme legislator in the church; but he could legislate in various ways, and some forms of legislation took precedence over others. The statutes of a council reflecting the consensus of the whole church could be regarded as papal legislation in its highest, most authoritative form. They could therefore bind the pope himself, considered as a solitary individual, and future popes too. Such ideas were generally accepted by the end of the twelfth century.

This complicated chapter of canonical thought is important in medieval history because it so precisely anticipated the later doctrine of parliamentary kingship in the secular sphere, the idea that sovereignty inhered in a "king-in-Parliament." Indeed, virtually all the "political theory" of the later Middle Ages was simply an expression in more general terms of juridical doctrines that were first formulated by twelfth-century lawyers. In later chapters, we shall see how the technical doctrines of the jurists were woven into sophisticated theories of constitutional government during the late medieval period.

READING SUGGESTIONS

* *B. Tierny,* Sources *and* Readings, *Vol. I, nos. 42–44, 57; Vol. II, nos. 16–18, 21.*

The general climate of twelfth-century culture is brilliantly discussed in * R. W. Southern, *The Making of the Middle Ages,* cited in Chapter VII, and in his * *Medieval Humanism* (New York, 1970). The best general survey is R. L. Benson and G. Constable (eds.), *Renaissance and Renewal in the Twelfth Century* (Cambridge, MA, 1982). Two older outstanding works are * C. H. Haskins, *The Renaissance of the Twelfth Century* (Cambridge, MA, 1927), and H. O. Taylor, *The Medieval Mind,* 2 vols., 4th ed. (New York, 1925). M. Clagett *et al.* (eds.), *Twelfth-Century Europe and the Foundations of Modern Society* (Madison, WI, 1961) is a useful collection of essays. Two recent interpretive works are * C. N. L. Brooke, *The Twelfth Century Renaissance* (New York, 1969), and * C. Morris, *The Discovery of the Individual, 1060–1200* (London, 1972). The best study of twelfth-century monasticism is D. Knowles, *The Monastic Order in England* (Cambridge, 1940). * J. Leclercq, *The Love of Learning and the Desire for God* (New York, 1961) provides a good introduction to monastic culture. On St. Bernard of Clairvaux, see W. Williams, *Saint Bernard of Clairvaux* (Manchester, England, 1935); B. S. James, *Saint Bernard of Clairvaux* (London, 1957); E. Gilson, *The Mystical Theology of St. Bernard* (London, 1950). For Bernard's writings, see his *Works,* S. J. Eales (trans.), 5 vols. (London, 1953). On women's spirituality, see * C. Bynum, *Jesus as Mother* (Berkeley and Los Angeles, 1982) and * *Holy Feast and Holy Fast: The Religious Significance of Food to Medieval Women* (Berkeley and Los Angeles, 1987).

The philosophical developments of the twelfth century are discussed in all the standard histories of medieval thought. The most comprehensive one-volume survey is E. Gilson, *History of Christian Philosophy in the Middle Ages* (New York, 1955). Good, shorter works are * F. C. Copleston, *Medieval Philosophy* (London, 1952); * G. Leff, *Medieval Thought* (Harmondsworth, England, 1950); * D. Knowles, *The Evolution of Medieval Thought* (Baltimore, 1962). H. M. Carré, *Realists and Nominalists* (Oxford, England, 1946) is a more specialized study. See also M.-D. Chenu, *Nature, Man and Society in the Twelfth Century* (Chicago, 1968), and * B. Smalley, *The Study of the Bible in the Middle Ages* (Oxford, England, 1941). On Abelard's influence, see L. Grane, *Peter Abelard* (New York, 1970), and D. E. Luscombe, *The School of Peter Abelard* (Cambridge, England, 1969). The story of Heloise and Abelard is finely told in H. O. Taylor's book cited above, and in * E. Gilson, *Heloise and Abelard* (Chicago, 1951). For source material, see Abelard's * *Historia Calamitatum,* J. T. Muckle (trans.) (Toronto, 1954), and *Letters of Heloise and Abelard,* C. K. Scott-Moncrieff (trans.) (New York, 1942). On Anselm, see R. W. Southern, *St. Anselm and His Biographer* (Cambridge, England, 1963). Anselm's *Proslogion* has been translated by S. N. Deane (Chicago, 1935). On the growth of literacy and its far-reaching significance see * B. Stock, *The Implications of Literacy* (Princeton, NJ, 1983).

Two excellent, brief introductions to medieval canon law and Roman law respectively, are S. Kuttner, *Harmony from Dissonance: An Interpretation of Medieval Canon Law* (Latrobe, PA, 1960), and P. Vinogradoff, *Roman Law in Medieval Europe,* 2nd ed. (Oxford, England, 1929). The political theories of the twelfth-century canonists are discussed in W. Ullmann, *Medieval Papalism* (London, 1949), and B. Tierney, *Foundations of the Conciliar Theory* (Cambridge, England, 1955). On Gratian in particular, see S. Chodorow, *Christian Political Theory and Church Politics in the Mid-Twelfth Century* (Berkeley, 1972). On the law of marriage and sexual relations, see J. A. Brundage, *Law, Sex, and Christian Society in Medieval Europe* (Chicago, 1987) and, on the law of war, F. H. Russell, *The Just War in the Middle Ages* (Cambridge, England, 1975).

chapter

XV

The Feudal Monarchies: Empire and Papacy

The revival of law in the twelfth century was not just a matter of academic theory. In several of the major kingdoms of Europe, more orderly and effective systems of government were built up during this period. Different monarchs faced different problems and reacted in different ways. The English kings supplemented their rights as feudal lords by introducing nonfeudal forms of royal jurisdiction that greatly strengthened their authority. In France the most important development was a great increase in the extent of the royal demesne. A new dynasty in Germany tried to build a basis for a strong monarchy by reasserting imperial claims in Lombardy, but this led to a new round of disputes with the papacy. By the end of the century, the English and French monarchies were considerably strengthened; the future of Italy and Germany, however, remained highly uncertain.

46. *England: Normans and Plantagenets*

When William the Conqueror died, he left the duchy of Normandy to his eldest son, Robert, and the English throne to his second son, William (1087–1100).* His third and youngest son, Henry, got a few Norman estates to support him. William II, called Rufus, was a thoroughly unpleasant person, arbitrary, greedy, and probably sexually perverted. His greed led him to exploit every possible source of royal revenue to the utmost, especially the feudal rights that could produce cash. When a baron died, the king made the heir pay as high a relief as he could possibly raise. When a baron wanted permission to marry his daughter, he was obliged to pay a large fee. If a baron died leaving an unmarried daughter, the king sold her to the highest bidder. In at least one case, Rufus collected an aid from the rear-vassals of a barony when the baron died. William II was obliged to face several baronial revolts, but they were not, at least entirely, the result of his

*See Appendix, Table 4, for genealogical chart.

misuse of his rights as a suzerain. His brother Robert felt that he should have had England as well as Normandy and was continually stirring up trouble in England. William repaid this with interest by invading Normandy, which was already in a state of complete confusion under Robert's amiable but ineffective rule. Eventually, Robert mortgaged Normandy to Rufus and departed on the First Crusade.*

One day in 1100, while William Rufus was hunting, one of his noble companions allegedly mistook him for a deer and—perhaps by accident—fatally wounded him with an arrow. The king's brother Henry, who was not far away, resisted his inclination to hasten to the scene and instead promptly secured the royal treasury in Winchester castle. Henry took no action against the man who had slain his brother—in fact, the family of this man, the great house of Clare, became the most powerful in England during Henry's reign.

Henry obtained the English throne because he was on the spot; his claim was not as good as, or at least no better than, that of his brother Robert. Under the circumstances, he felt obliged to conciliate the barons who accepted him as king. On the day of his coronation, he issued a solemn charter in which he promised to put an end to the abuses established by his brother. This document is of great importance as an admission by Henry that he was bound by the law and as a definition of some points in that law. As a practical matter it was of little value, for Henry never allowed the promises contained in it to hamper his practices. He continued his brother's policy with even more enthusiasm.

King Henry I (1100–1135) was a vigorous and effective ruler and a competent captain. When the barons revolted, partly because of Robert's intrigues and partly out of resentment at Henry's firm rule, he crushed the risings and exiled the rebels. Then Henry invaded Normandy and after a long struggle captured his brother and consigned him to an English castle. While the continuous interference of Louis VI (1108–1137) of France in the affairs of Normandy kept Henry from giving the duchy anything that one might call peace and order, he ruled its turbulent lords far more effectively than had Duke Robert. England was a model of peace and quiet under his heavy hand.

Henry I increased the power of the royal government in England by developing devices used by his father and brother and by inventing some of his own. William I and William II had insisted that the pleas of the crown, the more serious criminal cases, be heard by special royal judges. At times they sent out judges for this purpose, but usually they simply ordered the local sheriff to hear them as a royal justice. Henry I established royal justices as a regular part of his administration and sent them throughout England to hear the pleas of the crown. William Rufus had begun replacing the barons who held office as sheriffs with men of lower rank who would be more dependent on the crown, and Henry completed this process. His sheriffs and justices were for the most part men who owed whatever they had to his favor instead of barons with ample independent resources.

An important part of the work of Henry and his officials was the

*See pp. 257–258.

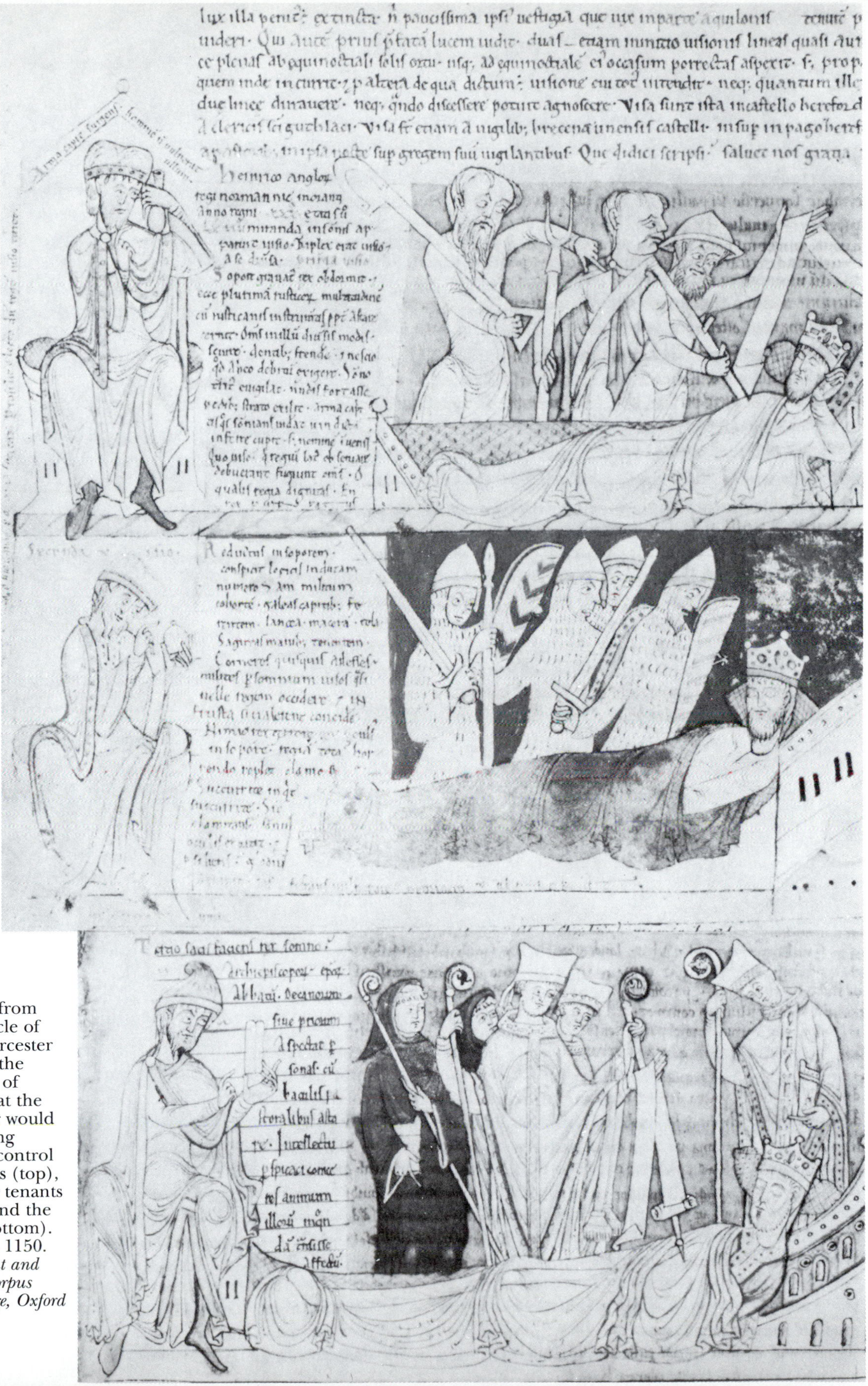

iniatures from
e Chronicle of
hn of Worcester
ustrating the
ghtmares of
enry I: that the
yal power would
ot be strong
ough to control
e peasants (top),
e military tenants
niddle), and the
hurch (bottom).
nglish, ca. 1150.
*e President and
llows of Corpus
risti Colege, Oxford*

development of an effective financial administration. His predecessors had kept a reserve of money in a strong castle, but all current funds were kept in a chest in the king's chamber under the care of his chamberlains. Henry detached three chamberlains from his court and established them at Winchester as permanent financial officials. Before long, one had taken the title of *treasurer*, and the other two were known as *chamberlains of the exchequer*.

Henry's treasurer worked out a system for keeping account of the royal revenue. Twice a year the sheriffs of England appeared before a body of royal officials called the *barons of the exchequer* to render their accounts. Each sheriff owed a definite rent, or "farm," for his county, from which he could subtract sums he paid out by royal command. The sheriff presented to the exchequer the orders authorizing him to pay out money, and the barons balanced his account. He also accounted for any special sources of revenue in his hands, such as baronies in the king's custody because of minor heirs. The sheriff brought with him all the people in his county who owed the king money to answer for their debts. Thus, when the accounting was complete, the barons knew what the king's revenue had been and, more important, what he was still owed. A record of this accounting called the Pipe Roll was drawn up. We have one such record from the reign of Henry I and a continuous series from the beginning of the reign of Henry II.

One of Henry's contemporary biographers said with unconcealed admiration that he took seriously the divine command to populate the earth and was most successful at it. Unfortunately, however, only two of his extremely numerous offspring were legitimate—a son, William, and a daughter, Matilda. While William was still a young man, he and a group of young nobles, all gloriously drunk, embarked on a ship with an equally drunken captain and crew. A storm came up and the ship was lost with all aboard. Thus Henry was left without a male heir. He compelled the prelates and barons of England to swear allegiance to his daughter Matilda, widow of the Holy Roman Emperor Henry V and wife of Geoffrey, count of Anjou.

Henry's only other living close relatives were Thibaut, count of Blois, and his brother Stephen, both sons of Henry's sister. When Henry I died, Stephen, who was count of Boulogne by Henry's gift, hastened to England to claim the crown. The lords of England had sworn to accept Matilda, but they had no enthusiasm for her. No one believed that a woman could rule England effectively, and the barons had a strong suspicion that Geoffrey of Anjou, a feudal brigand of the first order, would rule it too effectively for their taste. Stephen was known as a gentle, kindly man, and the barons chose him as king. Count Thibaut made a few protests at having his younger brother placed ahead of him, but he was too busy with his enormous possessions in France to do anything about it. Matilda and Geoffrey, on the other hand, prepared for war. While Geoffrey invaded Normandy, Matilda crossed to England, rallied her supporters, and waged war on King Stephen.

The Angevin Empire and France, 1189

A glance at the size of the English king's holdings on the Continent is sufficient to make clear the nature of the constant dispute and intrigue between the English and the French rulers: the English king controlled a territory far more vast than that of the French king, whose vassal he technically was.

The entire reign of Stephen (1135–1154) was occupied by bitter civil war between the two parties.* It was the perfect opportunity for the barons. Each lord could sell his allegiance at a high price in lands and privileges and then sell it again if the other side bid higher. Thus a powerful baron of Essex, Geoffrey de Mandeville, by shifting dexterously from one side to the other, acquired the title earl of Essex, extensive royal demesnes as fiefs, the services of a number of minor tenants-in-chief, permission to build a number of castles and to tear down one belonging to the bishop of London that annoyed him, the hereditary command of the Tower of London, the hereditary office of sheriff and royal justice in London and Middlesex and Essex and Hertfordshire, and similar concessions for his relatives. In short, Geoffrey became to all practical purposes absolute master of four shires, including the city of London.

While few barons did quite so well as Geoffrey, most of them gained something. They became sheriffs of their counties and constables of the royal castles. They obtained for themselves royal demesnes and the services of minor tenants-in-chief. All over England new baronial strongholds sprang up. And while the great barons consolidated their power and became practically independent of the crown, lesser men gathered bodies of solders, seized some castle as a base, and unmercifully plundered the countryside. The war finally ended when Stephen came to an agreement with Matilda's son, Henry. Stephen was to remain king as long as he lived, but then the crown would pass to Henry. When Henry duly became king as Henry II in 1154, he was already by hereditary right count of Anjou and duke of Normandy. Through his marriage to the heiress Eleanor, he had also become duke of Aquitaine. Thus he ruled a vast complex of territories—often called the Angevin Empire—that stretched from the Scottish border to the Pyrenees. He was potentially the strongest ruler in western Europe.

In England, however, Henry found the royal power at its lowest point since the conquest. The barons had extorted from Stephen and Matilda lands from the royal demesne, the homage and service of minor barons, and numerous hereditary offices. They had taken advantage of the civil war to fill their lands with strong castles. Moreover, Henry himself, when he was waging war against Stephen, bought baronial support with reckless promises of lands and privileges. If the barons had retained what they gained under Stephen and Matilda and if Henry had kept his promises, the English monarchy would have been seriously weakened for a long time. Fortunately for his dynasty, Henry was not troubled by many scruples. He made almost no pretense of keeping his own promises. Moreover, he calmly ignored many of the grants of his immediate predecessor. He and Stephen had agreed that illegal castles, those built without the king's leave, should be destroyed. Henry was inclined to consider any castle that seemed dangerous to be illegal and either razed it or took it into his own hands. In the case of hereditary offices, Henry usually ignored the claimants and appointed his own men. Within a few years of his acces-

*Sources, no. 56

sion, he had recovered most of the ground lost by the monarchy during the troubled reign of Stephen.

Henry promptly set to work to increase the royal power in every possible direction. Like the Norman kings, he was determined to make the most of his rights as feudal suzerain of the English barons. Feudal custom required a vassal to seek his lord's leave before giving his daughter in marriage, and the Norman kings had aways sold their permission at a good price—a very dubious procedure that Henry I had solemnly promised to abandon. Henry II improved on his grandfather's abuse of his rights. He obliged the barons to obtain his permission to marry their sons and charged a fee for granting it. When a baron whose title to his lands was not open to question was succeeded by his son, Henry usually felt obliged to accept what was considered the correct relief, £100, but if there was any cloud on the title or the heir was not a son, he demanded all he thought he could collect. He also devoted particular attention to increasing the value of the military service owed him by his vassals.

William the Conqueror had established the English military system in the belief that the five thousand-odd knights his vassals owed him were barely enough to defend the realm from Saxon revolts, raids by Welsh and Scots, and Viking invasions. All this had changed by the time of Henry II. No one was quite sure who was a Saxon and who was a Norman, and certainly there was no question of a Saxon revolt. The Scandinavian kingdoms were no longer dangerous, and the Welsh and Scots could be handled effectively by the barons of the border shires. It was on the Continent that Henry needed troops. There he was engaged in a long series of wars with Louis VII of France and his allies of the house of Blois.

The feudal levy of England, however, was of little use in Normandy. It was impossible to transport and supply five thousand knights. Moreover, the feudal levy was bound to serve only for a limited term, and it could barely cross the Channel before its term expired. Henry tried several devices to solve this. He asked for part of the service due for a longer term. But the most convenient solution was to allow his vassals to pay a sum of money for every knight owed and to use this money to hire troops. The only objection to this system was that it often enabled the barons to profit more than the king from a call to service. Most barons had enfeoffed more knights than they owed the king. Thus, when Henry took a *scutage,* a payment by shields, the baron collected more than he paid. The earl of Norfolk owed 60 knights to the host, but he had enfeoffed 162. If the king levied scutage at one mark per fee, the earl paid 60 marks and kept 102 for himself. In 1166 Henry held a great inquest to discover how many knights his barons had enfeoffed and used the results to demand that they pay scutage on the entire number. The barons objected, and eventually the question was compromised: they were to pay on all fees created before the death of Henry I but not on later enfeoffments. This resulted in a large gain for the crown.

During the reign of Stephen, royal control over the church had been weakened. Henry attempted to reassert the royal power in this sphere too, but here he ran into difficulties. In 1164 he promulgated the Constitutions of Clarendon, a restatement, with some modifications, of the powers that Henry I had exercised. Bishops were to do homage to the king before their consecrations (which gave the king at least a veto power in episcopal appointments); no appeals were to be made from the English church to the papacy except by permission of the king; clerics accused of criminal offenses were first to be degraded from their clerical status by an ecclesiastical court and then punished by a royal court. The archbishop of Canterbury, Thomas à Becket, first acquiesced in these rules but then denounced them as uncanonical, objecting particularly to the last point. Becket held that to both degrade a cleric and then subject him to a secular penalty was to punish him twice for the same offense. It was in the course of this dispute that the concept of "double jeopardy" came into English law.

Thomas à Becket had been the king's servant. The son of a London merchant, he was educated in the household of the archbishop of Canterbury and became an archdeacon. Then he entered the royal administration and rose to become the king's chancellor. Henry II found him a brilliant administrator and faithful friend. When the archbishopric of Canterbury became vacant in 1162, Becket was appointed to the office through the king's influence. So far it was a typical medieval success story. But as archbishop, Thomas underwent a sudden transformation. He adopted a life of ostentatious piety and began to fight the king tooth and nail on every issue involving the rights of the church. When he denounced the Constitutions of Clarendon, the king drove him into exile. There was a half-hearted reconciliation in 1170, and Thomas returned to Canterbury, but immediately he stirred up a new quarrel by excommunicating prelates who had supported the king during his exile. In a moment of exasperation, Henry said that he would like to be rid of such a "troublesome priest." Four knights took the king at his word and rode to Canterbury, where they murdered Thomas before the high altar of his cathedral. This act of sacrilege produced a wave of feeling against the king, and he had to compromise all the outstanding issues with the papacy. Henry retained the right to receive the homage of bishops but conceded the right of appeal from English ecclesiastical courts to the papal curia. The system of centralized papal jurisdiction was growing up at just this time and, because of Henry's defeat, the English church became fully subject to Roman canon law.

The chief contribution of Henry II to the development of the English monarchy was to extend the jurisdiction of the royal courts. Henry I had sent his judges through his realm to hear the pleas of the crown. Henry II set to work to increase their business. The only way a criminal case could be brought into court was by an *appeal*, or formal accusation, by the injured party or one of the injured's friends or relatives. Under this system, many criminals went unpunished. If a person who was slain had no friends or relatives, no one would bring an appeal. If the suspected criminal was a powerful person, it might

A thirteenth-century miniature shows the murder of the archbishop Thomas à Becket in the cathedral at Canterbury, the climax of his quarrel with the king, Henry II. From the Carrow Psalter and Hours. *The Walters Art Gallery, Baltimore*

having prosecution initiated by the government. He ordered that twelve men from every hundred (a subdivision of the county) and four from each township should appear before either his justices or the sheriff and state on oath whether anyone in their district was suspected of committing murder, robbery, or theft since the beginning of his reign. If they said someone was suspected, the individual was to be arrested and brought before the king's justices. There the accused was to be tried by the ordeal of water—that is, after certain religious formalities, the individual was bound hand and foot and thrown into a pool, on the theory that water duly blessed would reject a guilty person, who thus would float. An innocent person would be accepted by the water and sink. Henry seems not to have had too much faith in the efficacy of this test. If an individual was proved innocent but the twelve jurors still said they suspected a crime, the accused was to go into exile. This device was the ancestor of our *jury of presentment,* or *grand jury.* It brought many more criminal cases into court and improved public order. Moreover, as the crown confiscated all the property of convicted criminals, it materially increased the royal revenue.

In the realm of civil law, Henry had equally ingenious ideas. His first step was to place possession of property under the protection of his courts. By the law of the day, the rightful owner of the land could forcibly eject an occupant without fear of punishment. Hence, if a powerful lord claimed a piece of land and ejected its occupant, he could enjoy the property while his opponent attempted to establish ownership. Henry decreed that if anyone ejected the occupant of land by force and without a court order, the injured party could complain to the chancellor. That official would issue an order to the sheriff to collect twelve men to appear before the king's justices to swear whether or not the dispossessed man had been ejected by force and without legal sanction. If the jury said he had been so ejected, he was replaced in possession, and the man who had seized the land was heavily fined. If the jury said he had not been so ejected, the complainant was fined for bringing a false charge. Thus possession was protected, and the king collected a fine no matter how the case came out. Cases of this kind were called *possessory assizes,* the assize being the twelve men who gave the decision.*

The invention of the grand jury and the possessory assize greatly increased the business of the royal courts without infringing on the jurisdictions of the barons. They were new procedures that had never existed before. But another of Henry's devices was not so innocuous. Disputes regarding the ownership of land were heard in a feudal court if both parties were vassals of the same lord and in the county court if they held of different lords. The only method of trial was by battle. The plaintiff could not fight himself; he had to supply a vassal who believed his claim to be just. Presumably, however, he could choose the best warrior available. Trial by battle was obviously a hazardous affair and was unlikely to appeal to a man in possession who felt sure that his case was just. King Henry provided an alternative procedure. The defendant could decline to accept the challenge to battle and could seek an order, or *writ,* from the chancery ordering the sheriff to gather twenty-four knights who would state on oath which party had the better right to the land. This procedure was called the *grand assize.* Through it the royal courts took business away from both feudal and popular courts.

*Sources, no. 70

In addition to taking cases from the feudal courts by means of the grand assize, the king interfered even more directly in their business. Litigants in a feudal court who felt that they had been treated unjustly could procure writs transferring their cases to a royal court. Thus, if a widow believed that her husband's heir had not given her an adequate dower and the lord's court did not support her position, she could obtain a writ commanding the heir to assign her the dower she claimed or explain to the king's judges why he was unwilling to do so. Such writs could be used in almost any case to bring it before the royal justices.

These legal innovations of Henry II were the essential beginnings of the *common law.* Common law meant law that was applied throughout the realm—that was common to all people and all regions. Each popular and feudal court had its own customary law, but the royal justices enforced the king's law wherever they went. Under Henry I the royal judges had used common law to decide the pleas of the crown, but this was only a small fragment of the total judicial business of the realm. As the jurisdiction of the royal courts was expanded by Henry II, however, more and more cases came or could be brought before his justices. A feudal court that knew that a case could be removed from it by a royal court was likely to try to decide the case by the common law. Thus this law gradually supplanted its rivals, and for about a century the common law expanded with great rapidity. Whenever a royal judge heard of an injury that seemed to need redress, he was inclined to invent a writ that would bring it into his court. This process was only stopped in the thirteenth century, when the barons insisted that the king and his judges stop making new law in this way without the consent of the baronage. From that time onward, major changes in the law were commonly made by a *statute* issued by the king in Parliament.*

Before leaving the subject of the beginnings of the common law, it seems worthwhile to discuss briefly the origins of the petty, or trial, jury. There was a long tradition in Anglo-Norman government of using a body of sworn men to testify to facts; Domesday Book was based on information obtained by this means. Henry's judges began to use a jury of twelve men in a special way. When juries of presentment said that they suspected a person of committing crimes, but those individuals felt certain that they were innocent and that their neighbors knew them to be so, he could ask the judges to call a "jury of life and member" to state whether or not they were guilty instead of subjecting them to the ordeal. This device was particularly valuable to a person who had been accused by private individuals out of spite. But the defendant had to ask for this method of trial: they could not be compelled to place their fate in the hands of a jury. The ordeal by water was still the only legal means of trial.

In 1215, however, the Fourth Lateran Council condemned ordeal and forbade the clergy to participate in it. As ordeal was a "judgment of God," it was senseless without the aid of a priest. Thus the judges of England suddenly found themselves without any way of trying criminals. They did their best to persuade every accused person to ask for

*See pp. 406–409.

a jury trial. For a while, they simply had to release those who refused. Then they invented an ingenious scheme. People who refused to ask for a jury trial, could not be convicted; instead, they were stripped, tied to a stone floor with a board on their body, and heavy stones were placed on the board until they was crushed to death. The threat of this *peine fort et dur* was enough to persuade most defendants to ask for a jury trial. Hence the petty jury became the normal means of trying criminal cases.

The government of Henry II was not popular with his barons. They resented his efforts to increase their feudal services and to take cases away from their courts. They looked back longingly to their independence under Stephen. At the same time, Henry had alienated his eldest son, Henry. King Henry could not help remembering the confusion brought to England by the disputed succession at the death of Henry I, and he wanted to be sure that there was no question about his successor. Hence he used the Capetian device of having his eldest son crowned as associate king. But while he gave young Henry a royal title, he did not give him lands or castles or even a regular revenue. This displeased the prince, and he entered into a conspiracy with his father-in-law, Louis VII of France, and the dissident barons of England and Normandy. The result was a great baronial revolt combined with invasions of Normandy by Louis and of England by the king of Scotland. This was the supreme test of King Henry's administration, and that administration stood it well. Supported by a few loyal barons, the king's servants defended his realm successfully, and the revolt was suppressed. Henry forgave his son, but several barons spent long years in prison, and all the rebels saw their castles razed to the ground. The English crown was to have no more trouble with its barons until a new generation faced King John.

47. *France: From Philip I to Philip Augustus*

When Philip I (1060–1108) came to the throne of France, the Capetian house had reached a low point in its fortunes. Philip, as we saw, succeeded in checking the shrinkage of the royal demesne and even added to it.* But Philip was far from being a powerful monarch. Especially in his later years, when he grew enormously fat and lethargic, he proved incapable of asserting effective authority over even the petty lords of the royal demesne, let alone over the great vassals of the surrounding fiefs. He was a man of entertaining if far from estimable character, but not really a very effective king.

The successor to Philip, his son Louis VI (1108–1137), was also a great mountain of a man, but one imbued with restless, unflagging energy. He immediately set about the task of reducing to obedience the petty lords of the Ile de France. It was a long, slow, painful struggle, but Louis was an able and determined king. He was also a man of much better moral repute than his father, and he enjoyed the warm

*See pp. 199–200.

support of the church. Above all, he relied on the help of Suger, abbot of the great monastery of St. Denis near Paris. Suger proved to be a very loyal and effective servant of the French monarchy. In 1125 Louis entrusted to him the direction of the whole "civilian" side of the government, thus greatly diminishing the power of the old household offices. Suger built up an expanded staff of competent clerks, the nucleus from which the future French royal bureaucracy would grow, and provided a more efficient administration than had ever existed before. After Louis' death, Suger wrote a biography of the king, which can be seen as a very effective kind of royalist propaganda. It combined a vigorous account of Louis' incessant campaigning with a skillful presentation of Suger's own ideal of kingship—an ideal of strong royal government dedicated to the protection of the church and the upholding of order and justice.*

Louis followed a regular procedure in disciplining his vassals. He first summoned a lord to court to answer for some act of violence, giving him a safe-conduct to return to his castle after his hearing. Naturally, if the baron were condemned by the court, he defied the king as soon as he reached home and broke into open revolt. Louis would then have him excommunicated and march against him at the head of his own troops and those of the church lands. Several times Louis was defeated in the field, and often he failed to take a strong castle, but eventually he was successful. The two most troublesome of his vassals, Hugh de Puiset and Thomas de Marly, saw their castles torn down and their fiefs seized. The other lords hastened to submit to the king. From that time on, the barons of the Ile de France headed by the lords of Montmorency were loyal servitors of the Capetian kings. It was among them that Louis' successors found their constables and marshals to lead their troops to battle.

Louis' efforts to subdue the vassals of the royal demesne were hampered by the fact that he spent most of his reign in a series of bitter wars against a formidable coalition of feudal princes—Henry I (1100–1135), duke of Normandy and king of England, and his nephew Thibaut, count of Blois. While Louis was able to hold his own by persuading the court of Anjou to attack his foes in the rear and by stirring up Henry's Norman vassals to revolt, the most he could achieve was a stalemate. He did, however, begin to make the royal authority felt in the great fiefs. When he learned that the count of Clermont, a vassal of the duke of Aquitaine, was besieging the bishop of Clermont in the episcopal city of Clermont-Ferrand, he gathered an army and hastened to raise the siege. This so astonished the duke that he did homage to Louis and fully acknowledged his feudal obligations. Then, when the count of Flanders was murdered, Louis occupied the country, punished the criminals, and installed a count of his own choice. Although his count was eventually rejected by the Flemings, Louis had asserted his authority as suzerain. Again, in 1124, when Henry V of Germany planned an invasion of France, Louis called out the feudal host of the realm and actually obtained substantial contingents from nearly all the great feudatories of northern

*Sources, no. 55

France. Faced by this show of force, Henry V abandoned his invasion. Perhaps the best sign of Louis' prestige was that when the duke of Aquitaine felt that his death was near, he entrusted his daughter and heiress, Eleanor, to the king.

At the death of Louis VI, the foundations of the Capetian monarchy were firmly established. With no resources beyond those of his predecessors, he had brought the royal demesne firmly under his control and had made his authority felt in at least two of the great fiefs. On these foundations his successors were to build a powerful state.

His last act was to arrange the marriage of his eldest son Louis to Eleanor, duchess of Aquitaine. At first glance, this vast duchy extending from the southern borders of Brittany, Anjou, and Touraine to the Pyrenees, and from the shores of the Bay of Biscay to the frontier of the kingdom of Arles, would seem to be an immensely valuable acquisition. Actually, however, it was more a source of weakness than of strength to the Capetian monarchy. The dukes of Aquitaine effectively controlled only a few small districts around their chief towns such as Poitiers, Bordeaux, and Bayonne. The rest of the duchy was held by powerful and turbulent barons who paid little heed to their duke. Eleanor's son, Richard Plantagenet, was to show that an able warrior willing to live in the saddle at the head of his troops and permanently reside in the duchy could curb the barons to some extent and exercise real authority in the great fief, but a gentle, pious duke residing in Paris was utterly helpless. Louis' rule of Aquitaine was never more than a formality. The Capetian house would have profited far more from a small barony with one or two strong castles in the vicinity of Paris.

Eleanor and Louis were personally incompatible. Louis VII (1137–1180) was a gentle, serious, devout prince, whose chief interest lay in protecting the church. Eleanor's grandfather had been the troubadour William IX of Aquitaine, and she was thoroughly imbued with the ideas of the cult of courtly love. Even if one discounts most of the contemporary tales about her way of life, one is still forced to the conclusion that she was far from prudish. According to the rumor of the day, Eleanor had intimate relations with her uncle Raymond, prince of Antioch, and with the seneschal of France, Geoffrey Plantagenet, count of Anjou. The first of these affairs was considered especially shocking as it took place during a crusade.* But although Eleanor's frivolity probably troubled her husband, there was a far more serious reason for a breach between them. Eleanor bore Louis two daughters but no son, and the future of the Capetian house depended on a male heir. Whatever the exact reasons may have been, Louis and Eleanor agreed to separate, and early in 1152 an assembly of French bishops declared the marriage annulled on the grounds of consanguinity. A few months later Eleanor became the bride of Henry, duke of Normandy and count of Anjou.

Although the loss of the nominal rule over Aquitaine was not a serious blow to the Capetian house, the possession of that duchy by the master of Normandy and Anjou was extremely dangerous, and

*See p. 265.

the menace became more acute two years later when Henry became king of England. Louis fully realized this, but there was little he could do. He declared the marriage illegal, since it had been arranged without his consent as feudal suzerain, and waged war against Henry, but this did not trouble the young duke unduly.

The second marriage of Louis VII, with a princess of Castile, produced only daughters, and in 1164 he took a third wife, Adèle of Blois, sister of Henry the Liberal, count of Champagne; of Thibaut, count of Blois; and of William of Blois, archbishop of Reims. As Louis' two daughters by Eleanor of Aquitaine, Marie and Alix, married the counts of Champagne and Blois at about this same time, a firm alliance was formed between the king and house of Blois, which had formerly been bitterly hostile to him and his father. To gain the support of this mighty feudal dynasty against the even more powerful Henry Plantagenet was clearly sound politics, but the weak king was soon being governed by his strong-willed brothers-in-law. For a time it looked as if France would be divided between the dukes of Normandy and the counts of Champagne.

Despite his essential weakness Louis struggled manfully to maintain the position of his dynasty. He followed his father's policy of increasing the prestige of the monarchy by defending the church against predatory lords. Although he was no match for Henry II on the field of battle, he injured him when he could by intrigue. Thus he supported Henry's foe, Archbishop Thomas à Becket, and lent both aid and encouragement to the great baronial revolt led by Henry's three eldest sons. But Louis could make little progress. Henry suppressed the revolt and tightened his grip even more firmly on his vast lands—England, Normandy, Brittany, Maine, Anjou, and Aquitaine. Louis VII slipped into his dotage under the rule of the house of Blois.

By Adèle of Blois, Louis VII had a son whom he named Philip.* When he reached the age of fifteen, Philip decided to break the hold of the house of Blois on his aged father and his kingdom. To gain support for removing his uncles from power, he married the niece of Philip of Alsace, count of Flanders, and sought an understanding with Henry II. Successful in these ventures, he obtained effective control of the realm a year before his father's death in 1180, which made him king in name as well as in fact.

Despite the fact that he had come into power with the aid of Henry II, Philip II Augustus (1180–1223) realized that his chief aim had to be the defeat of the Plantagenet power. The French monarchy could never be very strong while the kings of England held Normandy, Maine, Anjou, and Aquitaine. Moreover, Henry was not satisfied with what he had; he made several attempts to absorb the county of Toulouse and conducted negotiations with the counts of Maurrienne in Savoy. At first Philip could only follow his father's policy of intrigue. He stirred up Henry's sons against him and aided them in their revolts. When Henry died in 1189, both his surviving sons, Richard and John, were in alliance with Philip. But once on the throne of England, Richard (1189–1199) proved fully as formidable a foe as his father,

*See Appendix, Table 2, for chart of Capetian kings.

and Philip could only wait hopefully. Early in 1190 Richard and Philip departed together on the Third Crusade. They fought a brief war in Sicily and quarreled continually throughout the expedition, until in July 1191 Philip announced his decision to leave Palestine and return home. His excuse was poor health, but his motive was probably political. The count of Flanders had died, and Philip was anxious to secure his wife's share of the inheritance. Moreover, with Richard in Palestine there might well be an opportunity to seize some of his lands.

Shortly after Philip arrived in France, he presented to the seneschal of Normandy a document that purported to be a treaty agreed to by Richard in Sicily that gave Philip a large slice of Normandy. When the seneschal refused to recognize the treaty without direct orders from Richard, Philip summoned his barons to attack Normandy. But as a crusader, Richard and his lands were under papal protection, and the barons refused to move. Philip then turned to intrigue once more—an alliance with Richard's brother John. Philip would aid John to become king of England in return for John's surrender of the Continental fiefs of his house. Richard soon heard rumors of this plot and hastened back from Palestine. He landed at the head of the Adriatic Sea and tried to make his way in disguise through the territory of his foe, the duke of Austria, but he was recognized and captured. The impecunious duke soon sold him to the emperor Henry VI. Philip immediately offered Henry a large sum to keep his prisoner in confinement, and Henry, who hated Richard, was inclined to comply. Richard, however, was well served. His emissaries bribed the princes of Germany to demand his release, and in 1194 he was freed for an enormous ransom. Once more Philip was foiled and could only try to hold his own in a long, drawn-out war with his doughty antagonist—by far the ablest soldier of the day. When in 1199 Richard was slain in a quarrel with a petty Poitevin baron, Philip had made no headway whatever in his attempt to reduce the Plantagenet power.

King Philip found Richard's successor, John I (1199–1216), a less difficult opponent. While John was a competent captain and able administrator, he lacked the personal qualities of Richard and could not hold the confidence and loyalty of his barons. Moreover, there was a rival claimant to the English crown—John's nephew Arthur, duke of Brittany and count of Anjou, son of his elder brother Geoffrey. Philip made his preparations carefully. He courted the friendship of Arthur and built up a reserve of money for a war chest while he waited for John to give him a good opportunity. This John soon supplied by marrying the fiancée of one of his vassals, Hugh de Lusignan, count of La Marche in Poitou. The outraged count of La Marche appealed to Philip's court. As John refused to appear when summoned, he was condemned to lose his fiefs held of the French crown. Philip then formed an alliance with Arthur, loaned him some troops, and attacked Normandy, while Arthur invaded Poitou. Arthur laid seige to the castle of Mirabeau where his grandmother, the aged Queen Eleanor, was living and there he was surprised and captured by John. Arthur promptly disappeared into John's castle of Falaise and was never seen again. While it seems likely that John had him murdered, there is no absolute proof that he did. But Arthur's Breton and Angevin vassals immediately demanded the release of their lord, and when it was refused they went over to King Philip.

Philip had a reserve of money and no scruples about how he used it. When he could buy the constable of a castle, he did so. When he could not use bribery, he brought up his mercenary troops. John lacked both money and the confidence of his men. Philip captured the royal fortresses and great towns of Normandy one by one. Then he went into Touraine and successfully besieged the strongholds of Chinon and Loches. By the end of 1205, he was master of Normandy, Maine, Anjou, and Touraine and had received the submission of most of the barons of Poitou. John refused to accept his defeat as final. He went to work in England to raise funds for the recovery of his lands in France and built up a series of alliances with his nephew Otto IV (1208–1215), the Holy Roman Emperor,* the princes of the Rhine valley, and any French vassals who were open to bribes. In 1214 this great coalition struck. John invaded Anjou, while Otto and his army marched on Paris from the north. Philip met Otto at Bouvines in northern France, and completely crushed him. This great battle ended for over a century any danger that the English would recover Normandy, Maine, or Anjou. Poitou remained a border region. Its turbulent barons were in time of war the friends of anyone in Poitou with an army; and in time of peace, with whatever lord was farthest away and least likely to trouble them. Only in the coastal region of Aquitaine and in Gascony and Guienne did the English king retain a firm hold.

The conquest of Normandy, Maine, Anjou, and Touraine was a major step in the development of the Capetian monarchy. Normandy alone yielded a revenue as large as that of the entire royal demesne before the conquest. And about half of Philip's revenue before the acquisition of these lands came from the county of Artois, which he had obtained as his first wife's share of the possessions of her uncle, the Count of Flanders. Thus Philip II quadrupled the revenue of the French crown and made the monarchy far more powerful than any of its great vassals.

These additions to the royal demesne made the rather primitive organization of the Capetian monarchy entirely inadequate. Philip created two new classes of administrative officials—*baillis* and *seneschals*. Each of these officers was entrusted with the government of a fairly large district; Normandy was divided into five *bailiwicks*. The *baillis* administered justice and collected the king's revenues, in return for a regular salary. They also acted as royal agents in handling the king's relations with the vassals of the demesne. As a rule, they were moved frequently from district to district, in order that they might not develop a community of interests with the people they governed. Moreover, the *baillis* were drawn from the middle class, owed their position to the king's favor, and hence were devoted to his interests. The seneschals ruled bailiwicks that lay near hostile territory and so

*See p. 344.

required a strong military force. They were barons or knights who could command the king's troops and conduct the necessary local campaigns. Otherwise their functions were the same as those of the *baillis*. Both *baillis* and seneschals had agents who aided them in governing their bailiwicks, and these rapidly increased in number to form a rather formidable bureaucracy.

48. *Empire and Papacy*

Before his death in 1125, the last monarch of the Salian line, the emperor Henry V (1106–1125), turned over his personal lands to his nephew Frederick of Hohenstaufen, duke of Swabia, and designated him as his heir.* But Frederick and his father had been firm supporters of the Salian kings against the princes and the papacy. Under the leadership of archbishop of Mainz, these two parties combined to pass over Frederick and to elect as king Lothair of Supplinburg, duke of Saxony. Being essentially the creature of the papacy and the princes, Lothair (1125–1137) was a mere figurehead as king and emperor. Moreover, throughout his reign he was obliged to wage a bitter war with Frederick of Hohenstaufen, who had refused to recognize his election. Lothair married his daughter and heiress to Henry the Proud, duke of Bavaria, the head of the Welf family, who thus became his apparent heir. The papacy and the princes, however, considered the master of both Saxony and Bavaria fully as dangerous as the duke of Swabia. They wanted a weak king. Hence they turned their eyes toward the rival house of Hohenstaufen. They chose not its chief but his younger brother, who was elected king as Conrad III (1137–1152). This, of course, simply increased the tempo of the civil war between the houses of Welf and Hohenstaufen, and Conrad's reign was a period of almost complete anarchy.

The princes of Germany preferred a weak king, but they did not want continual internal confusion. For one thing, they needed a period of peace to consolidate the gains they had made at the expense of the Salian house. Then too, anarchy favored the mass of petty lords whose castles now covered the land and who had become a serious menace to princely authority. Hence, when Conrad died in 1152, the princes were ready for a king who could maintain order. They chose Frederick of Hohenstaufen, called Barbarossa, of Swabia, the son of Lothair's bitter foe. It seemed an ideal choice. Frederick was head of the house of Hohenstaufen, nephew of Conrad, and great-grandson of Henry IV. He was also the first cousin of the new chief of the house of Welf, Henry the Lion, duke of Saxony and Bavaria. And whether or not the princes knew it, Frederick was in addition a statesman of the first rank who was fully the peer of Henry II of England and Philip II Augustus of France.

When Frederick I (1152–1190) came to the throne, the royal demesne of the Salian kings was sadly depleted. Moreover, during the

*See Appendix, Table 5, for genealogical chart. See also p. 241.

reigns of Lothair and Conrad, the princes of Germany had made great progress in establishing themselves as semi-independent rulers. The only firm basis of power that Frederick possessed in Germany was his own family lands in the duchy of Swabia. (The title of duke of Swabia was conferred on Conrad III's son, another Frederick.) The new king had two obvious choices. He could set to work to recover the Salian demesnes, especially those in Franconia and southern Saxony, and attempt to reduce the power of the princes. That would certainly involve war with his cousin Henry the Lion, who coveted Goslar and the district dependent on it. The other was to adopt the policy that had always tempted Swabian dukes—expansion into the kingdoms of Burgundy and Italy. If he could build a strong administration and collect an ample revenue in those regions, he might well be strong enough to discipline the unruly German princes. It was this second alternative that Frederick chose. He gave Goslar to Henry the Lion. At the same time he made Austria into a duchy to balance Henry's power in Bavaria and strengthened the hands of Henry's rival in the north, Albrecht, called the Bear, another scion of the house of Billung. Thus, having pacified and created competition for Henry the Lion, Frederick left Germany to the princes. He took their homage and insisted on their recognizing their feudal obligations to him as their suzerain, but he also gave them a free hand in curbing the lesser lords, who were obliged to become their vassals. Germany had at last become a feudal state. The great issue still to be settled was whether the German king would succeed in making feudalism the basis of a powerful monarchy as the Norman kings of England had done, or whether the princes would become virtually independent rulers. Frederick made his own intentions clear in 1158 when he insisted that, in all feudal oaths of allegiance, the overriding allegiance to the king had to be acknowledged.

In 1156 Frederick married Beatrice of Burgundy and in her name took possession of that kingdom. The next step in his program was the restoration of the imperial authority in Lombardy. Since the reign of Henry IV,* a great political revolution had taken place in that district. The nobles and merchants of the cities had deprived the bishops of their political authority and had established self-governing communes. As the bishops had also been counts and in that capacity the emperor's agents, many of the powers taken over by the communes were imperial ones. The Lombard communes were engaged in bitter rivalries among themselves, and the country was burdened with continual wars. Milan, the most powerful of the cities, had established an extensive hegemony, but her position was being fiercely contested by a group of cities led by Cremona. Hence the cities were in no position to resist the imperial authority effectively. Frederick marched into Lombardy and claimed the rights of the Lombard crown. He had no desire to restore the bishops, but he insisted that he have a voice in choosing the officials of the communes, that these officials recognize that they were his agents, and that he receive a regular revenue. Moreover, he insisted that the authority of these town officials be confined

*See p. 282.

within the city walls and that imperial officials exercise the emperor's rights in the countryside.

Frederick's invasion of Italy almost inevitably led to trouble with the papacy. The popes were determined to maintain the independence they had won during the Investiture Contest and feared a revival of imperial power in Italy. Frederick had been crowned emperor by Pope Adrian IV (1154–1159) in 1154. The popes had no objections to conferring the imperial title so long as it remained merely an empty dignity, but a "Roman" emperor who intended really to rule in Italy could hardly avoid claiming sovereignty over Rome itself, where the popes reigned as temporal lords. Adrian's response to this threat was to insinuate that any rights Federick acquired as emperor were held from the pope as his superior. In 1157 Adrian sent two legates to an imperial diet at Besançon with a letter that referred to the empire as a "benefice" conferred by the pope. The medieval Latin word *beneficium* could mean simply a benefit, but it could also have the technical sense of a fief. The emperor's chancellor, Rainald of Dassel, in translating the pope's letter to the assembled nobles, chose to interpret the word in the second sense. The pope's letter thus apparently claimed that the empire was a fief held from the pope as feudal overlord. Frederick furiously rejected this claim, and the pope was obliged to withdraw it (declaring that he had never intended any such meaning).*

In 1159 Adrian IV died and a majority of the cardinals elected as his successor Alexander III. Alexander was known as an intransigent anti-imperialist; moreover, he had been one of the two legates who had infuriated the emperor at Besançon. Frederick refused to recognize the election and appointed an antipope. Thus, at the time when he was seeking to establish his authority in Lombardy, he became involved in a bitter feud with the papacy. Outside of Lombardy, three men dominated Italy—Frederick's uncle Welf VI, lord of Tuscany and Spoleto; William I, king of Sicily; and the pope. The king of Sicily was opposed to any growth of imperial power in Italy, and the pope was Frederick's enemy. Hence, when Milan rose in revolt, they formed an alliance with her against Frederick. But for the moment, the emperor was too strong and enjoyed the support of Welf VI. In 1162 Milan was captured and largely destroyed. Frederick filled Lombardy with wild German knights, who ruled with a heavy hand. Soon these imperial agents, under the command of Rainald of Dassel, had roused all the communes to desperation. They put aside their quarrels and in 1167 combined in a general federation, the Lombard League. When, after years of skirmishing, Frederick moved to suppress them in 1176, they routed his army at the great battle of Legnano. After this, Frederick negotiated a truce with the cities and made his peace with the papacy, recognizing Alexander III as pope in 1177.

Frederick's defeat at Legnano was to a great extent the result of troubles in Germany. Henry the Lion and his princely allies had refused to send their troops to his aid. Shortly after Frederick's defeat of Milan in 1162, Welf VI of Tuscany had gone over to the papal party,

*Sources, no. 57

and this naturally did not improve relations between the houses of Welf and Hohenstaufen. At the beginning of his reign, as we saw, Frederick had conferred Goslar on Henry the Lion, but in 1168 he moved to recover the old Salian demesnes in the north and deprived Henry of this important citadel. When Frederick asked Henry's aid against the Lombard League, the duke offered to give it in return for Goslar, but Frederick refused to agree. After Legnano, the emperor returned to Germany determined to crush his foe. Soon he had his opportunity. Henry the Lion was ambitious and arrogant. He seized church property and engaged in a fierce quarrel with a group of bishops. Frederick summoned him to court as his vassal and deprived him of all his fiefs. Henry the Lion retired to the court of his father-in-law, Henry II of England, and Frederick was master of Germany. The duchy of Saxony was split in half, and the western part, Westphalia, was given to the archbishop of Cologne, while the eastern section went to Bernard of Anhalt. Bavaria was given to Otto of Wittelsbach, one of Frederick's most faithful supporters.

Having secured his position in Germany, Frederick returned to Italy, but this time he used diplomacy rather than war. In 1183 he made a final settlement with the Lombard League. The communes were left independent, but their officials recognized that they were imperial agents and the cities paid a large annual sum for the exercise of imperial jurisdiction. Moreover, the league promised to aid Frederick in establishing his power in Tuscany and Spoleto, which he had seized from the disloyal Welf VI. The emperor's next step was to reach an agreement with Sicily. Frederick's son and heir, Henry, was married to Constance, a daughter of King Roger II and aunt of the then king, William II.* Tuscany, Spoleto, and Ancona were divided into administrative districts and placed in the charge of German counts. These officials exercised jurisdiction and collected extensive revenues. Since the few large cities of Tuscany, such as Florence, were left outside this system as free communes, Frederick's policy met with no effective resistance. However, some of his lands in central Italy were also claimed by the papacy, and this led to further difficulties between the Hohenstaufen family and the popes.

Frederick Barbarossa had established a new empire, one essentially different from that which had been ruled by the Saxon and Salian emperors. They had aimed at a strong, centralized German kingdom with imperial appendages in Burgundy and Italy. Under Frederick, Germany was a feudal monarchy, and the bulk of his revenues came from outside Germany—from Burgundy, Lombardy, Tuscany, Spoleto, and Ancona. The centers of his political authority were Swabia and central Italy. In addition to laying the material foundations for his imperial regime, Frederick had attempted to give it a sound theoretical basis. After the fall of the Salian line, the triumphant popes had continually asserted that the emperor could not exert imperial authority until he had been crowned by the pope. The revival of the study of Roman law enabled Frederick and his advisers to see very clearly that the Roman emperors had been themselves vice-regents of

*See p. 254.

God on earth and independent of any other authority. Frederick announced that Charlemagne and Otto I had been emperors by right of conquest and as such had enjoyed the full privileges of the Roman emperors. He was Otto's rightful successor. He also took steps to emphasize the sacred character of the imperial office. Charlemagne was canonized in 1165—unfortunately by an antipope, so that he did not for long enjoy that status. Frederick was the first monarch to use the term "holy empire." Also at this time some imperial theorists argued that, by right, the emperor should rule over all Christendom even though, de facto, rulers like the kings of France and England conducted themselves as independent monarchs.

When Frederick Barbarossa died in 1190, the future pattern of German government remained undetermined. There, as we have said, Frederick ruled as a feudal king. Outside his own duchy of Swabia and a few royal demesnes such as Goslar, he ruled simply as a suzerain of the princes. But, in the legal process against Henry the Lion, he had shown that feudal obligations could be enforced by a strong king even against the greatest of vassals. There were, moreover, forces in Germany that would have supported an attempt to revive the royal power there. The towns were growing rapidly in wealth and size, and they were openly hostile to the princes and in favor of a strong monarchy. On the other hand, in return for the princes' support against Henry the Lion, Frederick had had to accept the principle that fiefs which escheated to the crown would be granted out again within a year and a day. It was impossible, therefore, for the German kings to expand their demesne lands in the way that French rulers were doing. Again, a royal authority resting on bases as far apart as Tuscany and Swabia could not be very solid, and imperial claims in Italy were a constant source of conflicts with the papacy. Everything depended on the policies of Frederick's successors. If they had avoided antagonizing the popes and systematically used the revenues drawn from central Italy to build their power in Germany, the future history of that land might have been very different.

In fact, the reign of Frederick's successor saw a decided shift away from concentration on German affairs and toward further involvement in Italy. Frederick Barbarossa was drowned in 1190 crossing a river in Asia Minor while leading the vanguard of the Third Crusade. His son, Henry VI (1190–1197) had already been crowned king of Germany and so was assured of the succession. The new emperor at once found himself faced with a great temptation—the crown of Sicily. King William II of Sicily (1166–1189) had died without children to succeed him, and his aunt Constance, the wife of Henry VI, had a good claim to the throne. The Sicilians had no enthusiasm for being ruled by a German prince, but a strong party favored Constance. Sicily became the focal point of Henry's ambitions.

Henry paid little attention to his German kingdom. He visited it long enough to take the captive Richard I of England from the duke of Austria and to arrange for and collect the first installments of his ransom.* He also obliged Richard to do homage to him and gave him

*See p. 336.

The Empire of Frederick Barbarossa

Germany becomes a feudal state: under Frederick I, the emperor, his power based in his own duchy of Swabia and in northern Italy, was suzerain of the German princes. But because successive emperors were preoccupied with Italian affairs, the princes were left to rule their territories and their vassals, the lesser nobles, with a free hand.

the purely titular dignity of king of Burgundy. Perhaps he hoped that these arrangements would put an end to English support of the house of Welf. If such was the case, he was disappointed. Then, in 1194, Henry moved south and invaded Sicily. Soon he was completely in possession of the Norman kingdom and had placed German officials in its key administrative posts. He was then at the height of his power, master of a truly impressive empire comprising Germany, Burgundy, all Italy, and Sicily.

With the Norman kingdom, Henry took over the dreams of extensive Mediterranean conquests that had long possessed its kings. No sooner was the emperor secure on the Sicilian throne than he began to plan a conquest of Greece and a crusade to Palestine. But before embarking on these adventures he needed to come to an agreement with the pope and the German princes. The future integrity of the vast state he had constructed depended on the election as king of Germany of the heir to the Sicilian crown, Henry's young son Frederick. Henry succeeded in persuading the princes to accept Frederick as the next king of Germany. Then he turned to the pope. He offered him a large annual income from all the churches of the empire in return for the lands in central Italy claimed by the papacy. But the specter of one man ruling all Italy except Rome and its immediate vicinity was too terrifying for the pope, and he declined to accept the terms. The negotiations were interrupted by a fierce Sicilian revolt. Henry suppressed it savagely but died almost immediately afterward, leaving his dream of a great Mediterranean empire unfulfilled.

It looked at first as if Henry's untimely death would do no great harm. The German officials who ruled in Sicily and Italy held their places with firm hands. Henry's younger brother Philip of Hohenstaufen hurried to Germany and was accepted as regent for his young nephew Frederick. But this opportunity was too good to be passed over by the house of Welf. Henry the Lion was dead, but his second son, Otto, was living at the English court. (He was married to Henry II's daughter Matilda.) King Richard supplied him with plenty of money and sent him into Germany to seek his fortune. By generous use of pounds sterling, Otto rapidly gathered a party of princes and was elected king of Germany in 1198. This moved the supporters of Philip of Hohenstaufen to urge him to take the crown—advice which he promptly followed. Thus, at the end of the twelfth century, Germany had rival kings and was again involved in civil war.

READING SUGGESTIONS

* *B. Tierney,* Sources *and* Readings, *vol. I, nos. 54–56.*

The political developments of the twelfth century are described in the works of Brooke, Sayles, Fawtier, Petit-Dutaillis, Barraclough, and Thompson already cited in Chapter IX. See also H. L. Poole, *From Domesday Book to Magna Carta,* 2nd ed. (Oxford, England, 1965); J. E. A. Jolliffe, *Angevin Government* (London, 1955), and for a large-scale selection of source material,

D. C. Douglas and G. W. Greenaway (eds.), *English Historical Documents,* vol. II (New York, 1953). The classic work on the origins of English common law is F. Pollock and F. W. Maitland, *History of English Law,* 2 vols., 2nd ed. (Cambridge, England, 1898).* A. Kelly's biography, *Eleanor of Aquitaine and the Four Kings* (Cambridge, MA, 1950) brings to life many details of English and French history. The standard life of Henry II is W. L. Warren, *Henry II* (Berkeley, 1973). The best approach to Thomas à Becket's complex personality is D. Knowles, *Archbishop Thomas Beckett: A Character Study* (London, 1949). On Norman Sicily, see J. J. C. Norwich, *The Kingdom in the Sun, 1130–1194* (London, 1970). The struggle between Frederick Barbarossa and the papacy is described in the contemporary chronicle of Otto of Freising, * *The Deeds of Frederick Barbarossa,* C. C. Mierow (trans.) (New York, 1953). On the theory of empire, see R. Folz, *The Concept of Empire in Western Europe* (London, 1969). For biographies of leading figures in the conflict, see P. Munz, *Frederick Barbarossa* (Ithaca, NY, 1969); M. Pacaut, *Frederick Barbarossa* (New York, 1970); K. Jordan, *Henry the Lion* (New York, 1986); and M. W. Baldwin, *Alexander III and the Twelfth Century* (New York, 1968). A classic work, now available in translation, is K. Hampe, *The German Empire under the Salian and Hohenstaufen Emperors* (Oxford, England, 1973). See also * H. Fuhrmann, *Germany in the High Middle Ages, c. 1050–1200* (Cambridge, England, 1986).

THE HARVEST OF MEDIEVAL CIVILIZATION

chapter

XVI

Papal Power and Religious Dissent

The thirteenth century was an age of outstanding achievement for western Europe in many diverse areas of human activity—in religious organization, law, philosophy, architecture, art, and literature. The century opened with the pontificate of Innocent III (1198–1216), who is commonly regarded as the greatest of all the medieval popes, both in ability and in achievement. Under him and his immediate successors, the medieval church reached the apex of its spiritual, intellectual, and temporal power. The papal monarchy perfected its organization and expanded its authority over both ecclesiastical and secular affairs. The integration, development, and application of the canon law continued steadily, culminating in the *Decretals* of Pope Gregory IX (1234). When the ardor of the old monastic orders cooled with the passage of time, vigorous, fresh spiritual leadership was provided by new "mendicant," or begging, orders.

But, as medieval civilization grew more mature, it also grew more inflexible. The thirteenth century was an age of heresy, sometimes rooted in popular favor, and of fierce repression directed against the heretics. As the leaders of the church strove to build a more perfect Christian society they grew less tolerant of those who questioned the church's authority. Moreover, as the power of the lay monarchs grew, their impatience with papal dictation became more dangerous. The century was marked by the long, fierce struggle between the papacy and the emperors and by bitter skirmishes with other monarchs. Fortunately for the church, the close alliance between spiritual and political opposition, between heretics and lay princes, that was to mark the Reformation never became more than a vague threat in the thirteenth century; for the time being, the church triumphed over its foes.

49. *The Pontificate of Innocent III*

In 1198 the College of Cardinals elevated to the papal throne Lothario di Segni. This thirty-seven-year-old scion of a powerful noble house was well prepared for high office in the church. Before entering the service of the papal curia, he had studied theology at Paris and canon law at Bologna. He had a thorough command of both subjects and possessed a serene, incisive, orderly mind. Some historians maintain that he accepted the whole, full-blown theory of papal theocracy, as developed by canonists like Alanus,* and deliberately aimed to put the theory into practice. Others see him as more pragmatic. All agree that he sought to maximize the political power of the papacy. But the great distinction of Innocent III is that, although he was active in politics, he was not merely a politician. He devoted constant attention to the moral reform of the church and to improving its internal administration. There seems no reason, moreover, to attribute his activity in temporal politics to mere selfish ambition. Innocent had no sympathy with medieval dreams of a universal Christian commonwealth united under the emperor. He saw very clearly that the reality of power lay with the separate national states that were emerging. But he thought that the peace and tranquillity of the Christian world could still be maintained if only the princes of Europe could be brought to acknowledge the pope as a supreme judge and arbiter set over them all.†

The dispute between Otto of Brunswick and Philip of Hohenstaufen gave Innocent an opportunity to intervene in the affairs of the empire at the very beginning of his reign. Innocent's predecessor had been Celestine III (1191–1198), a feeble octogenarian quite incapable of resisting the encroachments of Henry VI, and Henry died in possession of a large part of the Patrimony of St. Peter. He also, of course, held the kingdom of Sicily, which was a papal fief. In the year 1197–1198, the situation changed dramatically. Henry left only the infant Frederick as his heir, while Celestine was succeeded by the superlatively competent Innocent. The new pope was determined to recover the papal lands and to separate Sicily from the empire. In 1200 he explained to a consistory of cardinals that, while the princes of Germany had the right to nominate a king, the pope had the duty of examining the candidate's suitability before crowning him emperor. According to Innocent, this meant that, in case of a disputed election, the pope could decide which of the candidates was most suitable.

Acting on this principle, Innocent at first supported the Welf, Otto, against Philip of Hohenstaufen, while taking the young Frederick under his protection and upholding his right to the hereditary crown of Sicily. Otto was not very bright and at first had little real support, but in 1208 Philip was murdered by a private enemy and Otto quickly obtained control of Germany. In 1209 he was solemnly crowned emperor by the pope. But Innocent was soon disillusioned about his ally. Although he had promised to give the papacy the lands it claimed, he made no move to do so. Worse yet, he gathered his forces for an invasion of Sicily. Innocent promptly excommunicated him and declared him deprived of the imperial title. Innocent next brought forward as his favored candidate the young prince Frederick, after ex-

*See pp. 317–318.

†Sources, no. 59

tracting from him a solemn promise that, once he received the imperial title, he would give up Sicily. With Innocent's support, Frederick made himself master of Germany. (He was greatly assisted by Philip Augustus' defeat of Otto at the battle of Bouvines in 1214.)* After Innocent's death, Frederick outmaneuvered his successor and managed to keep both Sicily and Germany, but as long as Innocent lived, his imperial policy seemed highly successful. In the eleventh century, emperors had been choosing popes at their own will. Now the pope was choosing emperors.

Besides intervening in the affairs of the empire, Innocent became involved in disputes with other rulers of Christian lands. In France he inherited a controversy over the domestic affairs of the French king. In 1193 Philip had married a Danish princess, Ingeborg, partly for a large marriage portion in cash and partly in the hope that the Danish fleet might aid him in an attack on England. But he had barely seen his new queen when he felt an overwhelming personal distaste for her. Two years later he persuaded a group of French prelates to annul the marriage on the usual ground of consanguinity. As there was no blood relationship between them, the decision was a triumph of political power rather than of ecclesiastical justice. Ingeborg and her Danish relatives appealed to Rome, and the aged Pope Celestine III declared the annulment void. Philip cheerfully ignored the pope's pronouncement and in 1196 married Agnes, daughter of the duke of Meran, a south Bavarian lord. Innocent III was not the man to allow a king to defy the papacy in a matter so clearly in its sphere. A legate was sent to persuade Philip to give way and, if he refused, to lay an *interdict* on France. (This involved a suspension of virtually all the public services of the church.) As the king refused to yield, the interdict was imposed in January 1200. Philip was not anxious to risk the weakening of his influence in France through the resentment caused by an interdict. Moreover, in July Agnes died, and the king's interest in the question became less acute. He submitted, and the interdict was removed in September. But Philip had simply agreed that his annulment was void; he had reserved the right to reopen the case, and he promptly did so. Not until 1213, when Philip had sound political reasons for an accord with Innocent, was Ingeborg formally restored to her position as queen of France.

Innocent had a variety of quarrels with King John of England. The most important of them—a long and bitter dispute—concerned the appointment of an archbishop of Canterbury. When Archbishop Hubert Walter died in 1205, the king was determined to replace him with one of his favorites, John de Grey, bishop of Norwich. As soon as he heard of Hubert's death, the king hastened to Canterbury and made the monks who formed the cathedral chapter agree not to take any action toward electing an archbishop until December. Presumably, John wanted this time to prepare the way for his favorite. But at least part of the chapter met secretly, elected their own subprior, and sent him off to Rome to seek confirmation of his election from the pope. He was instructed not to reveal his election until he reached Rome.

*See p. 337.

Unfortunately, the subprior could not keep a secret, and soon John learned that he was calling himself archbishop-elect. The king went to Canterbury in a fine fury, and the terrified monks denied the earlier election and obediently chose John de Grey, who in turn set out for Rome to seek confirmation of his election. Thus Innocent was faced with a double election. He heard both stories and annulled both elections. The election of the subprior was obviously dubious as it was held by only part of the chapter, in secret, and without the king's permission. But once any election was appealed to Rome, no other could be held until the pope made a decision, and hence John de Grey's election was invalid. Innocent then directed all the interested parties to send delegates to Rome with power to act.

When the delegation from the chapter arrived, it was called into the pope's presence and ordered to elect an archbishop. The delegation split evenly between John de Grey and the subprior. Innocent then suggested the election of Stephen Langton, a canon of York, a noted theologian, and a cardinal. The monks accepted this idea and unanimously chose Stephen. When John's representatives were asked to give the royal assent, they stated that they had been authorized to give it only to John de Grey. The pope then wrote to John announcing the election and asking him to accept Stephen. To this the king replied in violent terms that Stephen was personally objectionable and chosen without his assent. He also sent agents to Canterbury who expelled the monks and seized the property of the Christ Church abbey for the king.

In June 1207, Innocent consecrated Stephen Langton as archbishop of Canterbury and gave him the *pallium*. He thus challenged King John directly. The result was a long and complicated struggle, which can only be outlined here. In March 1208, England was placed under interdict, and in November 1209, John was excommunicated. It seems likely, though it cannot be proved, that late in 1212 Innocent issued letters deposing John and ordering Philip Augustus of France to drive him from his realm. During all this time there were continual negotiations between the two parties. At first John insisted he would never accept Stephen, but by 1208 he had weakened a little. He would accept Stephen if the pope would agree that the affair would not constitute a precedent and that in the future no election of an archbishop of Canterbury would be valid without the king's assent. This was John's avowed position during the rest of the controversy. Innocent was unwilling to grant John's demands in full, and the king was in no hurry to have the quarrel settled. When the interdict was declared, he seized all the property of the church and the clergy, and as long as the struggle lasted, vast revenues streamed into his coffers. Neither interdict nor excommunication bothered him in the slightest degree, however much they might trouble his people. Finally, in 1213, when Philip Augustus was mustering a host to invade England, John gave way in style. He accepted Langton and promised to repay the money extorted from the church. Then he surrendered his kingdom to the pope and received it back as a fief to be held from the papacy.

On the central issue in this famous controversy, both Innocent and John were defending reasonable positions. It was the pope's duty to see that worthy men received high church offices. Stephen Langton was fully qualified for the post of archbishop of Canterbury. He was an Englishman, a distinguished scholar, and an able and devoted ecclesiastical statesman. His rival John de Grey was a pure courtier and civil servant. On the other hand, no king could agree that he had no control over the choice of the primate of his realm. The archbishop of Canterbury was an important political personage and the holder of a very large barony. The king had to insist that he be acceptable to him. On the basis on which the quarrel started, Innocent won a resounding victory: John accepted Stephen without conditions. Moreover, he greatly added to the prestige of the papacy by becoming its vassal. But by 1213 John's needs had changed. His barons were restive, and he felt the need of support against them. Here John came out ahead. Innocent firmly supported him against the barons, and when Langton, who sympathized with the barons, hesitated to enforce the pope's orders against them, he was suspended from office.* And John never repaid any major part of the money he had taken from the church. In short, this quarrel had an unusually happy ending; both sides won.

These three great controversies show clearly the power wielded by Innocent III. He twice chose an emperor, he forced Philip Augustus to receive Ingeborg as queen, and he obliged John to submit. Thus he won major struggles involving the heads of the three chief states of western Europe. There were similar victories in lesser states. The king of Aragon became a papal vassal, and the pope obliged the king of Portugal to recognize his predecessor's homage to the Holy See. The king of Castile was forced to give up his wife because of too close blood relationship, and he also became Innocent's vassal. While this vassalage to the papacy had little practical effect, it increased the prestige of the pope and to some extent his revenues, as each vassal monarch was expected to pay an annual tribute.

To be sure, even Innocent III had his setbacks. He never succeeded in launching a successful crusade against the infidels in the Holy Land, although he declared that this was one of the principal objectives of his pontificate. In 1204 he tried unsuccessfully to stop the fighting between Philip of France and John of England. He likewise failed in an attempt to intervene in a succession dispute in Norway, where King Sverre defied the pope with impunity. But these failures were outweighed by his great achievements. Throughout his reign, Innocent III was the leader of Christendom to a greater degree than any previous pontiff had been.

In the sphere of ecclesiastical reform, Innocent's most lasting work was achieved in a great general council of the church (the Fourth Lateran Council) that met at Rome in 1215.† It was a most impressive

*See pp. 397–398.

†Sources, no. 60.

Detail of a fresco by Giotto, *The Dream of Innocent III,* showing Innocent dreaming that Francis of Assisi and his followers would be the support on which the Church, beset by controversy and in need of reform, could be restored. Upper church of S. Francesco, Assisi. *Alinari–Art Reference Bureau*

assembly attended by more than four hundred bishops, eight hundred abbots, and representatives of all the great princes of Europe. The council enacted a great body of reform legislation. A lengthy dogmatic decree restated the essentials of the Catholic faith in order to refute various contemporary heresies. The doctrine of transubstantiation in the eucharist was solemnly defined (that is, that the "substance" of bread and wine changed to the body and blood of Christ when consecrated by a priest). Catholics were required to confess their sins to a priest at least once a year. Priests were forbidden to participate in judicial ordeals, so that from this time onward secular court had to devise more rational methods of reaching verdicts. To avoid prolonged vacancies in bishoprics, it was decreed that, if a cathedral chapter failed to elect within three months, the archbishop could step in and name a new pontiff. In every province of the church, an episcopal council was to meet once a year at which the assembled bishops could admonish any backsliders in their group. Detailed regulations were laid down concerning the moral life of the clergy. They were to be celibate and sober. They were not to gamble, hunt, engage in trade, frequent taverns, or wear bright, ornate clothes. They were not to hold more than one benefice with "cure of souls" (that is, with pastoral responsibilities). One canon of the council laid down a principle that would have vastly benefited the medieval church if it had ever been adequately enforced: better a few good priests than many bad ones, the canon declared.

The exercise of authority over powerful secular princes and the leadership of a great general council were activities possible only for a very strong pope. The general development of the organization, resources, and power of the papal monarchy, however, was a continuous affair and cannot be effectively discussed in terms of individual pontiffs. Great popes made important innovations, but lesser ones with able servants did equally well. Hence we must turn from the intriguing personality of Pope Innocent to follow topically some of the broad features of the development of the church and the papacy during this period.

Throughout the twelfth and thirteenth centuries, the activities of the papal curia and its agents expanded enormously. The system of papal delegates was used more and more extensively. If one wishes to carry an appeal to the papal court, all that was absolutely necessary was to send a letter to the pope outlining the case. Usually the appellor sent an agent to Rome, and if the agent were not himself an expert in canon law, he hired local legal talent to press his case. Gifts to members of the papal court were considered very useful, if not necessary. By the thirteenth century, the volume of cases carried to Rome and heard by judges-delegate was extremely large. They ranged from the attempt of a petty knight to get rid of his wife to the resounding quarrels between Duke Peter of Dreux and the bishops of Brittany. It was this system of comparatively easy appeal to Rome that made the canon law truly universal. It also kept the pope in close touch with the problems involved in the internal organization of the church and in its relations with the lay world. On the other hand, the growth of centralized jurisdiction in the church had disadvantages that soon gave rise to a chorus of protests. Papal justice was expensive. Moreover, as cases multiplied it became impossible to handle them all expeditiously. Easy access to Rome meant that many trivial cases, which could have been settled locally, were taken to the papal curia, where the litigants often found themselves involved in endless delays.

During this same period, the use of papal legates was greatly increased. Legatine commissions were sometimes given to local prelates. Thus, when Richard I of England went on the crusade, his justiciar Archbishop Hubert Walter, who was to rule England in his absence, was granted legatine authority. In fact, the continuous rivalry of the archbishops of York and Canterbury made it impossible for anyone but a legate to hold a council of the whole English church. But legatine commissions to local prelates were simply a means of granting extra authority where it seemed needed. It was the members of the papal court acting as legates who carried the pope's influence into every corner of Europe. Wherever the pope felt the need of an agent with wide powers, he dispatched a legate. A legate was sent from Rome to England to accept John's submission and another to lift the interdict and reconcile the English king with his clergy. When John died in 1216, leaving young Henry III under age, the pope ordered his legate to safeguard the interests of his youthful vassal. Actually, the legate and the regent, William Marshal, earl of Pembroke, ruled England jointly for several years. When Blanche of Castile was regent of France for her minor son, Louis IX, the pope sent a legate to support her. Then legates were appointed to guide such major papal enterprises as the suppression of the Albigensian heretics and the crusades. By using legates the pope could lessen the effect of the chief hindrance to his government—the vast extent of Christendom.

This tremendous extension of papal activity required corresponding development of the central administration at Rome. Perhaps the most important branch of the papal court was the chancery. Except for the comparatively rare occasions when a legate or *nuncio* was sent from Rome, the pope's commands, decisions, pleas and exhortations had to be conveyed in writing. Important letters must have been dictated by the pope himself, while routine letters were composed by his officials. As precision of statement was of enormous importance, this work required a skilled staff. It was also necessary to develop set forms and formulas to make successful forgery more difficult, for forgery of documents was a favorite medieval pastime. Every king and even most barons had established forms for important documents, and every charter carried a list of those who witnessed its issuance. Forging charters of local magnates was rather hazardous, as these witnesses could be consulted, and many men knew the proper forms. But the cardinals who witnessed papal letters were a long way off, and the forms of the papal chancery were less widely known. Hence forging papal letters was a very common practice. One obvious way to discourage forgery and also to give the pope a record of his and his predecessor's actions was to keep a register of letters sent out. These registers became very full and highly developed under Innocent III and his successors. The papal chancery developed earlier and more rapidly than those of the lay monarchies of western Europe, and the monarchies used it for a model to a great extent.

The enlarged personnel and increased activity of the papal administration raised its cost, and the popes were continually trying to find new sources of revenue and to improve the yield of the old. As lord of the Patrimony of St. Peter, the states of the church, the pope had revenues similar to these of other temporal lords. Demesne manors and towns paid annual rents. There were tolls on bridges, sales taxes at fairs, and the profits of justice. Most of the feudal vassals of the pope paid an annual rent in addition to other services. When Innocent III recovered the papal lands that had been usurped by Frederick I and Henry VI, he organized the entire Patrimony and greatly increased the revenue drawn from it.

The early popes had several sources of income outside their own lands. Beginning in the ninth century, various monastic foundations asked for and received papal protection against lay or ecclesiastical lords. These houses were taken under the permanent protection of the pope and paid an annual sum for the privilege. As these rents were usually small, the total income from this source was not great. Certain countries paid the papacy an annual tax called Peter's Pence—in theory every hearth in these lands paid a penny a year. This tax was established in England by the tenth century and is supposed to have been extended to Denmark by King Canute. An English cardinal serving as legate in Norway and Sweden in the twelfth century probably established it in those countries. It was also paid in Poland. In England, at least, most of the tax was pocketed by the local collectors, and the pope received the very modest sum of £200. Innocent III tried vigorously to remedy this situation but was unable to make any progress. Another resource was the tribute paid by kings and princes who became vassals of the papacy. By the end of the thirteenth century, Portugal, Castile, Aragon, Sicily, and England owed annual tribute. The English tribute was a thousand marks—a very substantial sum. The kings did not pay their tribute very regularly, however, and this source of revenue was essentially unreliable.

From at least the eleventh century, the popes occasionally asked gifts from the prelates of Christendom as a whole or of a particular region. These levies were called *sudsidies* and consisted in theory of voluntary grants of lump sums. Actually, of course, they were no more purely voluntary than the "gracious aids" collected by secular princes from their vassals. Although subsidies were sought only when there was some special need for funds, most any papal requirement was considered an adequate excuse for such a levy.

In addition, in the thirteenth century, popes began to collect income taxes from the clergy. These had their origin, as did several other sources of papal revenue, in measures taken to finance crusades. Before the Third Crusade, both Henry II and Philip Augustus levied income taxes in their kingdoms on both clergy and laity, with the pope's consent, to pay the costs of the expedition to recapture Jerusalem from Saladin. In 1199 Innocent III levied an income tax to finance his crusading plans. In 1228 the pope demanded a tenth of the income of the clergy to pay the costs of a war against Frederick II. From that time on, such taxes were levied whenever the pope needed large sums for any purpose that he could claim was of importance to the church. Actually, he did not succeed in getting any very large proportion of the money collected. Kings did not like to have the resources of their realms drained off by the pope, and who usually had to give the local ruler a large share of the proceeds in order to secure permission for the levy.

50. *Albigensians and Waldensians*

The same era that saw the papacy and the church at the height of their power brought new threats to their position. The most dangerous menace to the institutional structure of the medieval church came from ideas that were deeply rooted in the ideals and teachings of Christianity itself. Christ had preached against the dangers of worldly wealth. A camel could go through the eye of a needle as easily as a rich man could enter heaven. The apostles were commanded to take no thought for the morrow. In the early, enthusiastic, and persecuted Christian community, property had been held in common. The idea that poverty was absolutely necessary to the ideal Christian life was a fundamental concept in monasticism. No monk or nun could own anything; all property belonged to the community as a whole. But, in spite of all this, the wealth of the church had steadily increased, and the way of life of the higher clergy had grown more and more luxurious. As we have seen, their property not only drew them away from apostolic poverty but also involved them deeply in temporal affairs. Pope Paschal had seen the problem clearly and had advocated the abandonment of all property not absolutely necessary for the support of the clergy and the cult. In the twelfth century, many earnest Christians were profoundly disturbed at the striking contrast between the wealth and luxury of the clergy and the apostolic ideal of poverty.

Most such people remained loyal to the church and tried to live an apostolic life within it. But, growing up outside the mainstream of medieval Christian life, were groups of enthusiasts whose zeal led them to reject the entire structure of the established church. There were innumerable groups of these dissidents, all emphasizing poverty and asceticism but differing from one another in their particular religious teachings. Very broadly they can be divided into two categories. Some, although they considered themselves Christians, rejected various fundamental doctrines of traditional Christian orthodoxy; others accepted the basic teachings of traditional Christianity but held that the church of their own day was no longer faithful to those teachings and so had lost its authority. The principal representatives of these movements in the twelfth century were the Cathari and the Waldensians. (The word "Cathari" means "the pure." The Cathari were also called Albigensians from the French town of Albi, which was a center of their religion. The Waldensians were named after their founder, Peter Waldo.)

The basic doctrine of the Cathari was a theological dualism. According to the Old Testament, "In the beginning God created heaven and earth." But according to the Cathari, the good God, the God of light, created only the world of the spirit. It was Satan, the prince of darkness, who created the material world. Spirit was intrinsically good; matter was intrinsically evil. The soul was good; the body was evil. The whole world was a battleground between the forces of light and darkness, spirit and matter. The purpose of human life was to free the soul from the entanglement of the body so that it could enter the kingdom of light after death.

These beliefs were in many ways incompatible with orthodox Christianity. It was impossible for God to become incarnate in the body of a man if material bodies were intrinsically evil. According to the Cathari, therefore, Christ was not God but an emissary of God, and he did not become man but only took on the appearance of a man. Again, to the Cathari, sacraments that claimed to confer divine grace through material elements—the water of baptism, the bread and wine of the Eucharist—were inherently blasphemous. The Cathari also condemned marriage since it led to the production of children and so entrapped more spiritual souls in evil, material bodies.

These beliefs have obvious resemblances to the Oriental religion of Manicheanism, taught by the prophet Mani in the third century after Christ. Catholic theologians of the twelfth century were quite familiar with the doctrines of Manicheanism because St. Augustine had written books against them.* When, therefore, the twelfth-century theologians encountered dualist beliefs among their own contemporaries, they promptly labeled the dissidents as Manicheans. Modern historians have been unable to decide whether there was indeed a continuous Manichean tradition that "surfaced" in Europe during the twelfth century or whether the Cathari emerged as a spontaneous reaction to the abuses of the established church. It is certain that the western Cathari were influenced by missionaries from the Bogomils, a dualist sect that had grown up in Bulgaria and had spread through the Byzantine empire during the tenth and eleventh centuries. The problem is that we are unable to trace the connections—if they existed—between the Bogomils and the original Manicheans. The Bogomils were divided into two groups, both of which had adherents in western Europe. They can be described as "moderate dualists" and "absolute dualists." Both groups held that Satan had created the material world and that it was intrinsically evil. But the former group maintained that Satan himself was a rebellious son of God. The latter group taught that at the very beginning of things there had existed two coequal creative principles, one good and one evil. The doctrine of the absolute dualists is obviously more alien to orthodox Christianity, more strictly Manichean.

But the same practical consequences followed from either form of the dualist doctrine. Since all material things were produced by Satan, the perfect life, according to the teachings of the Cathari, was extremely ascetic. Its devotees had to be absolutely celibate and could eat no animal food. The problem of how a sect with these principles could survive was solved by having two classes—the *perfecti* and the *credentes*. The *perfecti* were bound to lead the ideal life of rigid asceti-

*See p. 51.

cism. They constituted the priestly class. They were inducted into this grade in a ceremony called the *consolamentum,* which was conducted by two *perfecti.* The *credentes* (that is, believers) could live much as they liked. They could follow any career, have families, and eat meat. Their only essential obligations were to renounce allegiance to the established Christian church and to receive the *consolamentum* before they died. This ceremony, which wiped away all previous sins, was usually performed when one of the *credentes* was approaching death. Indeed, there was a feeling that the best course was to commit suicide after the ceremony to avoid the danger of sinning again.

Since a large part of our knowledge of the beliefs of the Cathari comes from the writings of their Christian enemies, the best-known features of their doctrine are those that directly opposed the teachings of the church.* For example, they believed in reincarnation rather than eternal damnation for sinners. A soul was obliged to live again and again in human bodies until it achieved salvation. Also, as we have seen, the Cathari denied the central Christian doctrine of the incarnation and rejected the sacraments of the church. Their condemnation of marriage was particularly obnoxious in the eyes of their opponents, for it was not so much sexual activity in itself that the Cathari objected to as the production of children—a precise reversal of the moral teaching of the medieval church. Hence the Cathari were often accused of "unnatural" sex practices. Finally, the Cathari absolutely refused to take an oath of any sort. Their rejection of important articles of the Christian faith was enough to make them the foes of the church and of all devout laymen. But their refusal to take oaths made them particularly dangerous in an age when the cohesion of society depended so largely on the oaths binding one person to another.

The chief appeal of the Cathari lay in the ascetic life led by the *perfecti.* While some of their foes charged the *perfecti* with carrying their asceticism to absurd lengths, such as testing their devotion to celibacy by sleeping naked with women, in general even their persecutors admitted that they adhered rigidly to their strict way of life. Thus they offered a striking contrast to the Catholic clergy who lived in luxury and whose moral conduct was not always above reproach. In fact, it is fairly clear that the regions in which the Cathari flourished were those in which the Catholic clergy were especially negligent. Pious Christians, particularly the poor and lowly, observed this contrast between the two priestly classes and were strongly drawn toward the Cathari. It may be that the extreme freedom allowed the *credentes* was attractive to many people. Especially in the light-hearted land of southern France, the idea of living as one pleased and then achieving salvation through a deathbed ceremony could have been very alluring. It may also be that the moral laxity of the *credentes* has been greatly exaggerated by their orthodox opponents.

During the course of the twelfth century, there appeared other bands of men, apart from the Cathari, who preached and practiced apostolic poverty and lived lives of extreme asceticism. The most

*Sources, no. 63

noted of their leaders was Peter Waldo, a prosperous merchant of Lyons. In 1173 he happened to hear a wandering minstrel recount the story of St. Alexis, the son of a wealthy Roman noble who gave up his position and his inheritance to live in poverty and celibacy as a wandering beggar supported by alms. The tale made a profound impression on Peter Waldo, and that night he decided to emulate St. Alexis. He told his wife to choose between his personal and real property to keep for her support. When she chose the real estate, Peter began to give away his personal property. First he repaid all the usury he had taken. Then he made generous gifts to several worthy causes. The remainder of his money he simply distributed to the poor of Lyons. Once rid of his property, he proceeded to beg his bread from door to door. This hurt his wife's pride, and she appealed to the archbishop of Lyons. Peter was ordered not to beg from anyone but his wife. Still, he had begun his life of poverty.*

As soon as he began to follow the apostolic way of life, Peter Waldo wanted to learn its precise nature from the original source—the Bible. Since he could not read Latin, he persuaded two priests to translate parts of the New Testament for him. Armed with these, he began to preach his conception of the way of life taught by Christ. Soon others joined him and went about the countryside preaching. Now the church's interpretation of the Bible had been slowly constructed over many centuries. Naturally, unlettered men who read the text might reach rather different results. In 1178 word reached the archbishop of Lyons that Peter and his followers were making grave mistakes in their preaching. According to canon law, no one could preach without a license from his bishop, but this rule had not been enforced very vigorously. The archbishop, however, used it to silence Peter and his followers: they were to stop preaching in public. In 1179 Peter journeyed to Rome to appeal to the papacy. The pope, Alexander III, approved the Waldensians' plan of living in poverty, but he forbade them to preach without the permission of their bishop.

But because their study of the New Testament had convinced them that preaching was a necessary part of the apostolic life, Peter Waldo and his followers ignored the pope's prohibition. They preached with new vigor over a steadily widening area. In 1181 the pope condemned them as heretics along with the Cathari, and in the same year a new archbishop of Lyons expelled them from his diocese. They then spread over the neighboring regions and became especially strong in southern France, where they competed for converts with the local Cathari.

The basic purpose of the followers of Peter Waldo, who were called variously the Poor Men of Lyons and Waldensians, was to live the perfect Christian life as taught by Christ. For some years they went no further and made no attacks on the church or its doctrine. Only when they were finally condemned as heretics and persecution began did they take the offensive against their enemies. They then declared that, since the teachings of Christ could be read in the New Testament, nothing else was needed for salvation. The church and its sacraments

*Sources, no. 62

were completely useless. As their ideas developed further, they were inclined to state that they were the true successors of the apostles because they lived the apostolic life. The Catholic prelates who did not strictly follow Christ's teachings were no true successors to his apostles. It seems likely that their condemnation as heretics in 1181 was basically unjust; they were at that time simply disobedient enthusiasts. But soon they became actual heretics and attackers of the very foundations of Catholic doctrine.

When Pope Innocent III ascended the papal throne it seemed that the entire south of France might be lost to the Albigensian heretics. Innocent was determined to deal with the situation. At first he tried peaceful means. Preachers were sent into the region under the leadership of the abbot of Citeaux, several prelates, and a legate, Peter de Castelnau. The preachers made no progress, and the legate could not persuade the great lords to take an interest in the problem. The chief potentate of the land, Raymond VI, count of Toulouse, was a luxury-loving prince who was well supplied with concubines and almost totally indifferent to religion. While he went through the forms required of a good Catholic and was generous to monastic foundations, he was well disposed toward the heretics and absolutely refused to take any action against them. His vassal Raymond Roger, viscount of Béziers and Carcassone, had the same point of view. The count of Foix was even more impartial. He, too, was a formal Catholic, but his wife and one of his sisters were Waldensians, while another sister was an Albigensian.

By 1204 Innocent III was discouraged and listened to the advice of those who believed that only force could crush the heretics. As the count of Toulouse refused to supply this force it had to come from elsewhere. Innocent appealed to Philip Augustus to lead an army against the heretics, but the French king was much too completely occupied with his war against John of England to consider other ventures. The appeal was repeated in 1205 and 1207, with equal lack of success. Meanwhile, a crisis had arisen in the south. In 1207 the legate Peter de Castelnau excommunicated the count of Toulouse. In the following year the legate was murdered by one of the count's squires. While there was no evidence that Count Raymond had ordered the slaying, the church was naturally inclined to hold him responsible. Innocent III immediately confirmed the count's excommunication and released his subjects from their oaths of fealty to him. The pope also renewed his appeal to Philip.

Philip Augustus was faced with a difficult decision. He was at the moment not actively fighting John and could spare troops. But to attack the lands of a vassal without adequate provocation was a clear violation of feudal custom and might well alarm the other great lords of France. And Philip had no desire to see the principle that excommunication was sufficient cause for dispossession established. In short, the French king was no devotee of the church who was willing to take risks for her sake, and a crusade against the count of Toulouse seemed an unwise enterprise politically. Philip, however, had no objection if his vassals wanted to attack Toulouse as crusaders. Innocent had to be satisfied with what he could get. He preached the crusade, and an army of knights gathered in northern France. Under the general command of the new legate Arnold Amalric, the crusading army moved south in the early summer of 1209.

In July the crusaders appeared before the town of Béziers, a rich place that contained many heretics. On July 21 the town was taken by assault and the entire population massacred. As the crusaders were carrying the walls, someone suggested to the legate that many good Catholics lived in Béziers, but his only reply was "Kill all! Kill all, for God will know his own." Seven thousand people were slaughtered in a single church in which they had taken refuge. The frightful fate of Béziers had the intended effect; it struck terror into the hearts of the people of the region. Raymond Roger surrendered Carcassonne, an almost impregnable stronghold, and himself became a prisoner on the promise of good treatment.

The legate was rewarded with the archepiscopal See of Narbonne and soon left the host. His place as leader was taken by Simon de Montfort, lord of Montfort l'Amaury and titular earl of Leicester in England. In the struggle between the Capetians and the Plantagenets, Simon had supported Philip Augustus and hence had kept his barony of Montfort l'Amaury, but he had never been able to get possession of his rich English earldom of Leicester. He was thus a minor baron. But he was a man of boundless ambition, blind devotion to the church, and great military capacity. Soon after the surrender of Carcassonne, its lord, the viscount Raymond Roger, disappeared in the crusaders' prison. The leaders of the host promptly elected Simon viscount of Béziers and Carcassonne. He then proceeded to reduce one by one the strongholds of the county of Toulouse. These conquests were, of course, accompanied by an enthusiastic slaughter of heretics or at least of those suspected of being heretics.

In 1213, King Peter of Aragon, who claimed suzerainty over parts of Languedoc, tried to intervene. Peter was known as a cheerful, reckless knight who loved tournaments and pretty women. Simon had captured one of his couriers bearing a letter to a lady of the region, saying that the king's expedition was undertaken solely for love of her. Simon asked his men what need there could be to fear a man who declared war on God to please a wanton and proceeded to inflict a resounding defeat on Peter at the battle of Muret.

Simon's success, however, was short-lived. In 1218 the city of Toulouse rose in revolt and Simon was killed in attempting to recapture it. His son Amaury took over the county, but he was unable to hold his own and surrendered the fief to the French crown. Eventually King Louis IX (1226–1270) granted the county to Raymund VII, son of the previous count. But to win the royal grant Raymund had to marry his daughter and heiress to the king's brother Alphonse, count of Poitou. At Alphonse's death, both Poitou and Toulouse were added to the royal demesne. Thus an indirect result of the Albigensian Crusade was a great expansion of royal power into the south of France.

The Albigensian crusade also served the purpose it had been intended for. The power of the nobles of southern France who had protected the heretics was destroyed, and the heretics were left at the mercy of the church. All that was needed for their extermination was an effective ecclesiastical organization to discover them and bring them to trial. This was supplied by the gradual development of the Inquisition.

51. *Heresy and Inquisition*

Our word "heresy" comes from a Greek word meaning "choice." Nowadays it may seem self-evident that people should be free to chose their own religion. And even the medieval church recognized this principle when it prohibited the forced conversion of infidels and Jews. But in the Middle Ages, if a person was already a Christian and then chose to reject the church's teaching, that was seen as an attack on the fundamental values of the whole society. To medieval people heresy was a sort of treason, not just an error but a crime.

Under the canon law of the twelfth century, there were two ways of bringing a case into an ecclesiastical court: accusation by the head of the court, usually an archdeacon, or accusation by a private individual. This system did not work well where heretics were numerous. The archdeacons were too busy to do much heretic-hunting, and private individuals either sympathized with the heretics or feared their vengeance. In most parts of Europe heresy was also a crime against secular law; but secular procedures were inadequate too. The only way to establish guilt was by the old rites of compurgation and ordeal. Sometimes lynch mobs attacked suspected heretics and murdered them without waiting for the uncertain results of legal proceedings.

To the popes it seemed that new measures were needed to deal with the situation. In 1184 Pope Lucius III commanded each bishop to visit twice a year any of his parishes where heresy had been reported; he was to put on trial any persons denounced to him during the visitations. Innocent III severely increased the penalties against heretics by defining heresy as equivalent to the crime of treason in Roman law. Innocent also sent legates like Peter de Castelnau to southern France. While their original purpose was to win over the heretics by argument, they also had the power to arrest and try them. Then Pope Gregory IX (1227–1241) began the practice of commissioning members of the new orders of friars, Franciscans and Dominicans, as papal judges or inquisitors, charged with the task of seeking out heretics in assigned regions. By the middle of the thirteenth century groups of such inquisitors were at work throughout the church. They derived their powers directly from the pope and were, for all practical purposes, exempt from local ecclesiastical authority. They provided a formidable new way of combating heresy. Their purpose was twofold—to save the souls of the heretics and to prevent them from corrupting others.

Improbable as it may seem from the standpoint of modern jurisprudence, the procedures of the Inquisition were intended to provide a fair and rational mode of trial for persons suspected of heresy, something better than the old-fashioned ordeal of random mob violence. When an inquisitor arrived at a city he would first preach a public sermon condemning heresy and urging all Christians to denounce anyone suspected of being a heretic. The inquisitor then took evidence from the accusers and set it down in writing. It was understood that an innocent person might be falsely and maliciously denounced, so when the suspect was summoned for interrogation he was allowed to name any enemies who, he thought, might have accused him. The testimony of any person so named was discarded. But the suspect was not allowed to know who his actual accusers were or to confront them in court. This policy was considered necessary to protect informers against retaliation by friends or family of the accused.

The interrogation of the accused, conducted in secret, aimed at securing a confession of guilt and an expression of repentance.* In medieval law, confession was considered the most certain proof of guilt. Witnesses might lie or be mistaken, evidence might be falsified, but the word of the accused himself seemed indisputable. Confession was supposed to be voluntary, but, following the rule of Roman law and the practice of many medieval secular courts, the inquisitors were allowed to use torture on recalcitrant subjects. According to their rules of procedure, torture could be applied only once, and a confession made under torture had to be repeated voluntarily on a later occasion. But the rule could be evaded by "continuing" rather than "repeating" the torture. If the suspect finally confessed and repented he was assigned a penance. This might consist of fasting, flogging, wearing a distinctive badge, going on pilgrimage, or imprisonment. Also a heretic's property was usually confiscated. If a heretic refused to repent, or did accept a penance and then relapsed into heresy, he was handed over to the secular government for punishment with a recommendation that he be treated with mercy. But, for heretics, "mercy" usually meant burning at the stake and the inquisitors knew this very well.

From the point of view of modern ideas of justice and humanity, the Inquisition was cruel and unjust. But we live in an age when the belief that there is but one clear and certain path to salvation is not generally accepted. Few people see religious diversity as a danger to society. But medieval society was held together by shared religious values. Medieval people saw heresy as a threat to their whole way of life; it was like a communicable disease that destroyed men's souls. For the sake of the common good it had to be eradicated. Some inquisitors may have allowed greed and vengefulness, or even politics, to influence their actions. But the purpose of the Inquisition was honest, and its leaders usually devout, if rather fanatical. What makes the Inquisition hard to defend is its hypocrisy—its violations of its own

*Sources, no. 64

rules and principles in regard to torture, voluntary confession and surrender to the secular government. The church was not adhering to its own conception of right. In short, the honest historian can only call the Inquisition evil, even if they succeed in convincing themselves that it was an understandable evil in the light of its environment.

52. *Franciscans and Dominicans*

Repression was not the only response of the medieval church to the perceived threat of heresy. The same religious impulse that turned some people into heretics brought into being two new religious orders of friars, the Franciscans and Dominicans, that were to play a large part in strengthening the fabric of the church. So far we have mentioned these friars only as inquisitors. But only a small fraction of them were engaged in that activity; their main work was to win back heretics and increase the zeal of Christians by preaching and teaching and personal example. The best of the friars rivalled the Cathari *perfecti* in asceticism and the Waldensians in devotion to apostolic poverty. They showed how it was possible to live an evangelical life within the established church. Although Pope Innocent III launched the Albigensian Crusade against the heretics of France, he knew that the problems of the church could not be solved by force alone, and he vigorously encouraged the formation of the new orders.

The origin and early development of the Franciscans are almost exactly parallel to those of the Waldensians. St. Francis (1182–1226) was the son of a prosperous merchant of Assisi. He was a lively young man who liked to sing the songs of courtly love and fight in the perpetual local wars between Assisi and her neighbors. Captured in one of these affairs, he was put in prison and became ill. This seems to have turned his mind to more serious matters. One day in 1206 when he was praying in the dilapidated little church of St. Damian outside Assisi, he heard a voice that seemed to speak from the painted crucifix above the altar saying to him, "Francis, go build my church." Francis took the command very literally. He helped himself to some goods from his father's shop, sold them, and gave the proceeds to the priest for the repair of his church. His father, Peter Bernadone, showed a lack of appreciation for this idea and for a time imprisoned his son. Francis escaped and put himself under the protection of the local bishop. Then, in a dramatic scene, he repudiated his father and all his wealth. Stripping himself naked, Francis declared:

> Hitherto I have called Peter Bernadone father. . . . Now I return to him his money and also the clothes I wore which are his. From now on I will say "Our Father who art in heaven" and not father Peter Bernadone.

For a time he went around repairing churches with his own hands.

It was a time of confusion and uncertaintly. Francis felt sure he was summoned to some kind of divine service but did not know what his precise vocation was to be. Then one day in church he heard a priest reading from the Gospel of St. Matthew: "As you go, preach the message, 'The kingdom of Heaven is at hand. . . . Freely you have received, freely give. Do not keep gold or silver or money in your girdles, nor wallet for your journey, nor two tunics, nor sandals, nor staffs. . . .' " Francis had a moment of sudden insight. "This is it," he cried. "This I will do with all my heart." From that time on, he began to wander about preaching repentance and the virtue of the apostolic life. Each day he tried to earn by labor enough food to keep himself alive. If work could not be found, he accepted alms. He did not take money and refused more food than he needed for the day. Francis was a man of extraordinarily attractive character—joyous, simple, filled with spontaneous sympathy for the afflictions of other people. People loved him and were inspired by him. Soon he had a little band of followers, for whom he drew up a simple set of rules. The essential difference between this rule and ordinary monastic ones was the absolute poverty insisted on by Francis. Monks had always taken a vow of personal poverty, but the monastic houses of which they were members could become enormously wealthy. Francis insisted that his friars should own no property of any kind whatsoever, either individually or in common. They were to live by their own manual labor and by begging. They were absolutely prohibited from owning money or even touching it. The friars were not to withdraw from the world into monastic houses but to live among the people, wandering the roads preaching and helping the poor. Francis devoted himself especially to the care of lepers.

Francis felt a rare affinity for nature in all its forms—birds, animals, flowers, sun, and wind. Innumerable anecdotes grew up about his love of wild creatures and his ability to control them. This side of Francis' personality has given rise to a lamentable amount of sentimental prose in modern times, and it is commonly remembered only as an amiable eccentricity. But this is to miss much of the point of the saint's career. The heresies that most seriously threatened the church in his day taught that material creation was intrinsically evil. Learned men could present arguments seeking to refute this doctrine on the intellectual level, but Francis provided a refutation for ordinary simple people on the deepest level of emotional experience. He saw a world that was radiant with beauty because God had made it good, and he had the grace of personality and the literary skill to transmit this vision to others. His *Canticle of the Sun,* in which he called on all creatures to praise God as their creator, is one of the first masterpieces of Italian vernacular poetry.*

Francis did not intend his friars to be bound by detailed regulations. Every day was to be lived spontaneously and freely. The first "rule" that he put together was simply a collection of Gospel precepts emphasizing the duty of evangelical preaching and the virtue of poverty. In 1210 Francis went to Rome to ask Innocent III to approve this

*Sources, no. 65

A man enters the religious life and casts away the demon of worldly desires and preoccupations in a parallel to the Gospel story of Christ casting out devils. Roundel from a *Bible moralisée.* French, late 13th century, Ms. Harl. 1527, fol. 33r. *Reproduced by permission of the British Library Board*

unusual rule. This was a critical point in the history of the Franciscans. They were in much the same position as were the Waldensians when Peter Waldo approached the pope. An essential difference, the thing that made possible the growth of the Franciscans as a great order within the Catholic church, was that Francis felt a special devotion to those aspects of the church that contemporary heretics most commonly rejected—the priesthood and the eucharistic sacrament. All the same, the pope was gravely troubled. The rule seemed impossibly vague. Why could not Francis and his followers quietly join an existing monastic order? But one of the cardinals pointed out that the church could hardly in logic refuse to approve the way of life preached by

Christ. Innocent himself may have remembered the case of the Waldensians and feared to create a new band of heretics. In the end, he had the wisdom to see that there was some very special quality in the ragged preacher from Assisi with his troublesome request. He gave verbal approval to the rule and permission to preach.

The Franciscans increased very rapidly. Their headquarters was a group of huts clustered about the church of the Portiuncula in Assisi, but they wandered all over Italy. In 1217 missions were sent out across the Alps and to Tunis and Syria. In 1219 larger groups departed for France, Germany, Hungary, and Spain. These first Franciscan missionaries had a difficult time as they were generally taken to be heretics because of their way of life. Francis himself accompanied the crusading host to Damietta, made his way to the court of the sultan of Egypt, and preached before him. Then he went on to Palestine. In 1220, however, disturbing news called him back to Italy; his followers were showing inclinations toward changing the rule.

There were self-contradictions in Francis' formulation of his ideal that made some kind of change inevitable. Francis distrusted organization; but only a very small group can exist without any, and Francis permitted his order to expand without check. Moreoever, there was no ordered novitiate to provide training for the flood of new recruits. The initial rule of 1210 worked perfectly for the first tiny group of enthusiasts whom Francis could personally guide and counsel. It was quite inadequate for an order of thousands spread all through the Christian world. From the beginning Francis had stressed the virtue of absolute obedience as a mark of humility, but he had not established any regular system of government. The friars did not know exactly whom they were supposed to obey. Again, although Francis wanted the friars to preach as orthodox Catholics, he did not want them to study in the theology schools. But if they were to maintain the Catholic position against heretical objections, they needed theological training, and this might require permanent houses to live in and access to books. Finally, Francis was determined that his followers should not have privileges and spiritual authority. They were to convert by preaching and example. They were not to obtain letters from Rome exempting them from the power of local bishops. But the lands of stiff-necked, worldly bishops, the ones who would most probably refuse the friars permission to preach, were precisely the regions where evangelical preaching was most needed.

Francis was distressed by the breakdown of the early simplicity and withdrew from active government of the order after his return to Italy in 1220. He devoted himself to writing a new rule, but the first draft was criticized as still too vague by the leading friars. In 1223 Francis produced a second version, which was approved by the papacy and became the permanent, official rule of the Franciscans. It reaffirmed the obligation of absolute poverty but imposed a regular hierarchy of government on the order. Finally, when he was dying, Francis dictated a Testament restating his own ideals of poverty, simplicity, and humility.*

*Sources, no. 65

After Francis died in 1226, a series of changes was made. A papal bull of 1230 decreed that a local friend of the friars could hold property and receive gifts of money on behalf of the order. The local Franciscan superior could apply to him for funds in case of necessity. In 1245 another papal bull changed the wording of the regulation. The local superior could apply for purposes of "convenience." This bull of 1245 also transferred to the papacy the legal ownership of all buildings occupied by the order. From the 1220s onward, Franciscans were regularly studying in the universities. In 1254 Pope Alexander IV conceded to them an all-embracing privilege permitting them to preach and hear confessions in any diocese without the permission of the bishop. This was modified in 1300. The final rule was that the friars required a license from the bishop to hear confessions, but each bishop was obligated to grant a specific number of licenses in proportion to the population of his diocese. Modern historians disagree on the question of whether all these changes were necessary and justified. Some see them as inevitable adaptions; others, as corruptions of a noble ideal. For the most part, the changes were requested by the Franciscans themselves and were approved by the great majority of the order. But there were always some radicals who resented all adaptations and compromises as betrayals of the ideal of St. Francis. These "Spiritual Franciscans" were among the most eloquent and bitter critics of the papacy in the latter Middle Ages.*

St. Dominic and the Dominicans

The founder of the second great order of mendicant friars, St. Dominic (1170–1221), was a very different figure from St. Francis. He was an intellectual with a great gift for administration and legislation. Dominic was born in Castile and became a priest there. In 1205 he and his bishop appeared before Innocent III with the request that they be sent as missionaries to the Tartars in Asia. Innocent decided that there was more pressing work to be done close at hand and sent him instead to preach to the Albigensians in southern France. There they decided that the best way to combat heresy was to have learned men who led the apostolic life convince the heretics that they were wrong. Dominic determined to found an order that would carry out this idea. He went to the Fourth Lateran Council in 1215 and asked the pope's permission to organize an order of friars dedicated to preaching. As the council had just passed legislation forbidding the establishment of new orders, the pope suggested that Dominic adopt the rule of St. Augustine, which was so vague that it could be used for almost any type of ecclesiastical organization. Thus was founded the order of Dominican friars, called the Black Friars in contrast to the Franciscans, who were known as the Grey Friars.

adopted St. Augustine's rule.

Although the Dominican rule required its followers to live in poverty, this virtue was not stressed as it was by St. Francis. The latter's emphasis on manual labor and such services as caring for lepers had no place in St. Dominic's plan. The primary function of his order was to preach, and for this purpose his friars had to be well trained in theology. The Dominicans established schools at different levels to educate their members. After two years in a *stadium artium,* or school

*See p. 486.

of arts, the friar passed to a *stadium naturalium,* or school of nature, where he stayed for three years before going to the highest school, the *studium theologiae.* The most important of the schools of theology were called "general" because they drew students from the whole order and were usually connected with a university.

The Dominican rule had two peculiarities. The first was the great emphasis on intellectual study; according to the rule, everything was to be subordinated to this requirement. The second special characteristic was that it provided a sophisticated and elaborate structure of representative government for the order. The Dominicans were divided into provinces, each governed by a provincial prior, while the order as a whole was governed by a master-general. These excecutive officers were elected by the members of the order (as was usual in the older orders). But, in addition, each major officer had a council of friars whose consent was necessary for acts of legislation. The provincial council was composed of the heads of all the houses in the province together with an elected delegate from each house. For the general chapter of the whole order, a three-year cycle was established. One year all the provincial priors met together; then for two successive years, elected delegates from each province met without the priors. Legislation for the order had to be enacted by three successive chapters. All officers were elected for fixed terms of years except the master-general. He was chosen for life, but there was provision for him to be deposed by a general chapter in case of misconduct.

In addition to the Dominicans and Franciscans, a number of other mendicant orders, most of which were both small and short-lived, were created in the thirteenth century. Only two of these became of lasting importance. In 1155 a French priest founded an order of hermits on Mount Carmel. About 1238 they migrated from Palestine to Cyprus, Sicily, and southern France. In 1241 they appeared in England. In 1247 this rule was revised with the aid of two Dominicans. They ceased to be hermits and began to live in communities, were permitted to have their houses in towns, could beg, preach, and hear confessions. The Council of Lyons in 1274 recognized them as a regular mendicant order. They were called Carmelite or White Friars, and their purpose and functions were similar to those of the Dominicans. The other order, called the Friars Hermits of the Order of St. Augustine or Austin Friars, was a combination of several groups of Italian hermits and friars into one order. In 1274 the Council of Lyons recognized the Austin Friars as a mendicant order.

The mendicant friars were an extremely important element in the church. Perhaps their most important service during the thirteenth century was the defense of the spiritual and intellectual supremacy of the church from the heretics. But besides combating heresy in Christian regions, the friars sent far-ranging missions to other lands. During the middle years of the thirteenth century, a Mongol people from central Asia conquered Babylonia and threatened Syria, Palestine, and Egypt. It occurred to both the pope and Louis IX of France that the Mongols might be persuaded to ally with the Christians against the Muslims. Each of these potentates sent a Franciscan to the court of the Great Khan at Karakorum. They were well received by the Khan, a broad-minded pagan who was inclined to prefer Christianity to Mohammedanism. As the Mongols were routed in a series of battles by the sultans of Egypt, the plans for an alliance never bore fruit, but the friars acquired a firm base in the Mongol Empire. A group of Franciscans penetrated to China, and their mission was active there until the overthrow of the Mongol emperors in 1368. John of Monte Corvino labored in China from 1289 to 1328 and became archbishop of Pekin. The Dominicans were also active in Asia. In 1318 the pope divided that vast region between them, entrusting all missionary activities in northern Asia to the Franciscans and in Armenia, Persia, and India to the Dominicans.

Less spactacular, but fully as important as the special functions performed by the friars, was their day-by-day work throughout western Europe. The Fourth Lateran Council had decreed that every Christian should confess at least once a year, but the parish priests were inadequate both in numbers and in learning to carry out this legislation. The friars wandered about the countryside hearing confessions and preaching. They also performed other priestly functions such as the burying of the dead. Although there is little doubt that they served a useful purpose in this way, they naturally incurred the jealousy of the local clergy. There were continuous undignified quarrels about donations and fees. Moreover, the position of the friars was obviously open to abuse. Sinners naturally were inclined to confess to a wandering friar who knew nothing of their past and would be gone the next day, rather than to a parish priest who was all too well informed about them. And the friars were tempted to give light penance in return for fat donations. While the friars still begged from door to door in their wanderings, they lived in comfort, even in luxury, in their houses. One has only to read Chaucer's *Canterbury Tales* to get a vivid account of the charges aimed at the friars in the late fourteenth century.* In the universities, the friars quarreled with the secular clergy just as enthusiastically as they did in the countryside, and only the steady support of the papacy enabled them to hold their own in these institutions. Everywhere the secular clergy felt that the gifts and fees of the faithful were inadequate to support both them and the friars. At the same time, the rapid development of the penitential system was very largely the work of the friars. The official handbook for confessors that was approved by the papacy in the middle of the thirteenth century was the work of Raymond de Penafort, a Dominican. And any survey of the intellectual history of the time will show the important part played in the universities by the friars.

The partiality of the papacy for the friars is not difficult to understand. Despite the vast increase of the pope's authority over the church as a whole, his control of the local clergy was still limited, but the friars formed a large, highly organized army directly subject to his command. While each order held representative general chapters, the executive authority in each rested in a single man, and he was

*Sources, no. 101

immediately responsible to the pope. Thus the mendicant orders added significantly to the strength of the papal monarchy.

53. *The Jews in a Christian Society*

During the twelfth and thirteenth centuries, when standards of life were improving for many people, the Jewish communities of medieval Europe experienced a time of turmoil and trial.* On one level, Jewish scholarship made its own contribution to the intellectual renaissance of the twelfth century. Narbonne, in southern France, was a vigorous center of Talmudic learning; Jewish philosophy flourished in Spain, especially in the work of Moses Maimonides (1135–1204), who shaped a major synthesis of Judaic and Greek thought; and, in northern France, the great Rashi (Solomon ben Isaac) of Troyes (1040–1105) was only the first in a long line of brilliant northern rabbis. But this was also a time of increasingly harsh pressure on the Jewish people, culminating in their expulsion from much of western Europe.

The official attitude of Christian authorities to the Jews had been formed in the early centuries of the church, especially in the writings of St. Augustine. Augustine taught that, although the Jewish people had erred grievously at the time of Christ, still it was God's will that some of them should always survive. They existed to give witness to the historical reality of the Old Law and the prophecies of the Old Testament. Pagans could not argue that the Christians had just made up the prophecies of a coming Messiah so long as Jews existed to give independent witness to the words of the prophets. In Augustine's view a remnant of the Jewish people would survive until the end of time; then their final conversion would herald the second coming of Christ. The acceptance of this theology meant that the medieval Catholic church always upheld a policy of toleration for Judaism—grudging toleration perhaps, but still a recognition that Jews had a right to practice their own religion and be free from forced conversion. Pope Gregory I (590–604) defined this policy in a series of letters which, in the twelfth century, were assimilated into the growing canon law of the church. "Just as the Jews ought not to be allowed more than the law concedes," he wrote, "so too they ought not to suffer harm as regards the things that the law does concede to them." From the early twelfth century onward it became customary for the Jewish community of Rome to request, and the pope to grant, a confirmation of Jewish privileges at the beginning of each new pontificate.

Athough the policy of formal toleration was never abandoned, a harsher note was struck in a decree of Innocent III's Fourth Lateran Council. This law declared:

*Sources, no. 61

> It sometimes happens that through error Christians have relations with the women of Jews or Saracens, and Jews and Saracens with

> Christian women. Therefore . . . we decree that Jews and Saracens of both sexes . . . shall be distinguished from other people by the character of their dress.

It is not clear how far this was intended as a deliberate act of humiliation. In medieval times it was customary for different classes of people to wear different styles of clothes, and Innocent's declared aim of discouraging sexual relations between Christians and Jews was as much favored by the rabbis as by the pope. Enforcement of the law varied in different parts of Europe, but secular authorities commonly interpreted it as requiring all Jews to wear a distinctive badget sewn on an outer garment. This was clearly perceived as a mark of social degradation and Jews tried to resist or evade the regulation whenever they could.

The distinctive badge symbolized the status of the Jews in medieval society. They formed a small, alien minority in a dominantly Christian world. This situation had existed ever since the Roman Empire became Christian in the fourth century. At that time communities of Jews were scattered throughout the Mediterranean world. They survived the barbarian invasions and, in the eleventh century, there were still flourishing Jewish populations in Spain and southern France and Italy. In these Mediterranean regions Jews commonly worked at the same trades and crafts as their Christian neighbors. Some of them were rich merchants, some poor peddlers, some farmers, some craftsmen. In Spain Jewish physicians were especially renowned and Jews served as administrators for Spanish Christian kings.

Jewish settlement in northern France and Germany increased during the tenth and eleventh centuries with the revival of commerce. (In England, Jews immigrated in significant numbers only after the Norman Conquest of 1066.) In these northern regions Jewish economic activity was more restricted than in the south. The guild system in the cities and the feudal system in the countryside worked to exclude Jews from most trades and from landholding. To enter a guild or acquire a fief one had to take an oath—a Christian oath of course—from which Jews were barred. The Jews were increasingly driven to moneylending as the only occupation open to them.

We have seen that church law prohibited usury among Christians.* Similarly Jewish law forbade Jews to take interest from their own people. But they were allowed to charge interest on loans to outsiders. So Jewish moneylenders became an important source of funds for spendthrift Christian nobles and hard-pressed governments as well as for merchants needing venture capital. When a bishop was about to embark on a building operation, or a knight planned to go on crusade, or a noble wanted to indulge in some personal extravagance, he would often turn to a Jewish moneylender for a loan. Interest charges were high. A standard rate was "two pence on the pound per week" which works out at an annual rate of about 43 percent. When the interest was compounded, negligent debtors would soon find themselves faced with impossible sums to repay and would forfeit the

*See p. 287.

lands or goods they had pledged as security for their loans. Such transactions led to increasing animosity against the Jews; but the loans were very profitable for the lenders. When Aaron of Lincoln died without any direct heirs in 1136, the king confiscated all his wealth and it was so huge that a special department of the English treasury, the "Exchequer of Aaron," was set up to administer the estate.

While the church extended religious toleration to the Jews, they were entirely dependent on secular rulers for physical protection and for help in collecting their debts. The ruler, either a king or a local feudal lord in a decentralized country like France, protected "his" Jews only in order to exploit them financially. The Jews had no rights against the ruler; their legal status was like that of serfs. An English law book of the twelfth century declared simply, "The Jews and all their goods belong to the king." In France Jews who left their lords' territories without permission could be pursued and brought back like runaway serfs. In Sicily and Germany, Jews were formally designated as "serfs of the royal chamber." Since the Jews had no rights against the king, he could tax them at will. In England, besides arbitrary tallages, the king regularly took 10 percent of all debts collected by the Jews and a third of the estate when a Jew died. In a way, the situation was one of mutual advantage. The Jews needed protection; the king needed money. But the practical outcome was that the Jews served as a conduit through which money exacted from the Christian population by usury was channeled into the coffers of the king. This was convenient for the king but it contributed to the growing resentment against the Jews.

Still, so long as they enjoyed effective protection, Jewish communities could survive and prosper in medieval society. There were no formal ghettos, but Jews usually lived together in their own quarter of a city. In such a setting, the personal life of Jews centered around their homes and their social lives around the synagogue. Wealthy Jews often built themselves substantial stone houses. There they could find a refuge from the Christian world outside and follow the observances of their religion undisturbed. The festivals of Christianity were usually celebrated in church or outdoors or at a feast in the lord's hall but the great feasts of the Jewish year—Passover, Sukkoth, Hanukkah, Purim—were home feasts, celebrated in a family group as well as in the synagogue. The Jewish law accepted in western Europe enjoined strict monogamy, so a Jewish household would consist of a husband, his wife and children, and domestic servants who might well be Christians. Laws forbidding Christians to work in Jewish homes were enacted over and over again by the medieval church but repeated protests against this "abuse" indicate that the laws were not well obeyed. In rabbinical documents too there are references to Christian servants of Jews, e.g., in discussions about whether such domestics could be allowed to do any work on the sabbath. (One carefully observant rabbi, we are told, used to lock his stove on Friday nights and keep the key so as to prevent his overhelpful Christian maidservant from lighting a fire for him on Saturday.) There might also be a young son-in-law in the household. Jewish girls were sometimes given in marriage while they were still minors and to men only a few years older. The young couple might then live in the bride's home until they could afford to set up their own household. The boys of the family were carefully educated, usually from age five to thirteen, by teachers who received their support from the community or from private fees. The boys first learned to write Hebrew letters, then progressed to reading the scriptures. There was no such formal education for girls, but some Jewish women were literate and a few were known for their learning. A rabbinical opinion held that, while it was wrong to spend time teaching girls, there was no reason why they should not learn on their own, if they felt so inclined.

According to the letter of the law Jews were allowed to maintain old synagogues but not to erect new ones. The law was not enforced, however, and wherever a Jewish community became established a synagogue was built for daily prayer and sabbath observances. Pope Innocent III once complained to the king of France that a new synagogue in the city of Sens had been built higher than the local church; he urged the king to check such presumption. The Jewish community centered on the synagogue formed a largely self-governing enclave in a medieval city, with an elected council to handle community affairs. The council would apportion taxes, distribute poor relief, and administer the local ordinances that the community adopted to regulate its everyday life. Christian authorities usually allowed the Jews to have their own court to hear disputes and punish offenses against Jewish law.

Jews could live happily enough in a Christian society provided that the rights which the church granted to them in theory were respected in practice. In fact, though, from about 1100 onward, Jewish communities suffered increasing harassment. The First Crusade of 1096 was a watershed in Jewish history. Some of the crusaders, inflamed with hatred against the Saracen enemies of Christ whom they were going to fight in the Holy Land, decided that the Jews were enemies of Christianity too. A French chonicler described the reaction of the crusaders at Rouen. They said to one another:

> We desire to fight the enemies of God in the East, but we have under our eyes the Jews, a race more hostile to God than all the others. We are doing this whole thing backwards.

Then they turned on the Jews and massacred them. So far as France is concerned, this was an isolated episode, but as the crusaders moved eastward through Germany the massacres were repeated in city after city—at Trier, Worms, Mainz, Cologne—and then in other Rhineland cities. Altogether several thousand Jews were murdered. And after these outrages, every new Crusade brought new attacks on Jewish communities. Popes deplored the assaults and bishops sometimes tried to protect the Jews of their cities, but outbreaks of violence occurred all the same.

From the mid-twelfth century onward, animosity against the Jews was increased by slanders charging them with murders of Christian children. The first such story comes from Norwich in England. In 1144 the body of a boy was found there on the day before Good Friday. A rumor spread that the Jews had kidnapped the boy, tortured him, and crucified him in a contemptuous re-enactment of the crucifixion of Christ. The local authorities did not believe the story and protected the Jews; but the child was buried with great honor in the cathedral and widely revered as a martyr-saint. Soon many similar incidents were reported from other places in England and then from cities in Europe. Along with the charges of ritual murder, stories of host desecration began to circulate. The Jews were said to procure a host—the consecrated bread of the Eucharist that Christians believed had become the body of Christ—in order to defile it. On the face of it such accusations were absurd. Orthodox Jews obviously would not believe in the Christian doctrine of transubstantiation. But the popular acceptance of such stories is evidence of a changing attitude toward the Jewish people. Many Christians were coming to think that the Jews really knew that Christian teaching was true but refused to assent to it out of stubborn malice.

Historians have argued at great length about whether the increase in popular antagonism toward the Jews was based more on economic or more on religious grounds. But often the two motivations cannot be clearly separated; they came together in an ugly mixture of resentment, hate, and bigotry. This is well illustrated by an episode that occurred at York in northern England. In March 1189, while Richard I was preparing to go on the Third Crusade, a group of knights assembled there. Among them, according to the chronicler William of Newburgh, there were a number of "conspirators" who owed debts to the Jews. One night the conspirators broke into the home of Benedict, a rich Jew who had recently died, murdered his widow and children, and looted the house. This was the signal for an outbreak of anti-Jewish rioting in the city. The Jews—probably about 150 of them—took refuge in the keep of the royal castle. There they were besieged by a mob of knights and townsfolk. At this point a fanatical hermit appeared who roused the mob to a frenzy of hatred by his preaching; the religious fury increased when the hermit was killed by a stone thrown down from the royal keep. It was now Friday, the eve of Passover. The Jews saw that they could not hold out any longer and resolved on an act of self-immolation. They set fire to the building; then their rabbi, Yomtob of Joigny, killed his wife and children. The other men likewise killed their families and then one another. By morning only a handful of Jews were left. When they emerged from the ruins of the castle, begging for mercy and offering to accept conversion, they were massacred. Then a group of knights hastened to the cathedral where the records of Jewish debts were stored, compelled the custodian to hand them over, and made a bonfire of the documents on the floor of the church. After all this some of the knights contentedly set out on their crusade.

In spite of such tragedies, the Jewish population of Europe seems to have increased in the twelfth century. Even at York a Jewish community was reestablished in a few years. But during the thirteenth century the position of the Jews became more and more insecure. In the 1230s there was a new development. A Jewish convert to Christianity, Nicholas Donin, made the pope aware for the first time of the Talmud, the mass of law, ritual, and folklore that guided Jewish life. Donin argued that the Jews had abandoned the religion of Moses for a new Talmudic religion. So they were no longer faithful even to the role Christians assigned to them as keepers of the Old Law. The pope commanded that the Talmud be publicly burned. Moreover the new orders of friars regarded it as part of their divinely ordained task to convert the Jews by preaching and public disputations. When they were rebuffed, they blamed the Jews for refusing to accept the evident truths of Christianity.

A final development that undermined the position of the Jews was a great increase in Christian banking and moneylending. Some Christians had always evaded the canon law against usury but, from the thirteenth century onward, the canonists themselves began to recognize that some compensation for making a loan might be justified. In earlier times the Jews had occupied a necessary niche in an economy that was short of fluid capital. Now they were no longer needed. The Christian moneylenders were hated too; but the Jews were doubly hated on account of their religion. In 1290 King Edward I expelled them all from the kingdom of England. They did not return until 1656. King Philip IV of France confiscated all the property of the Jews and similarly banished them in 1306. Intolerance of Jews spread to Germany in the late Middle Ages; after that the northern Jews found their principal refuge in Poland. In Spain a large Jewish population survived until 1492. Then, when the Christian rulers Ferdinand and Isabella had conquered the last Moorish province of Grenada, they expelled all the Muslims and Jews who would not accept conversion to Christianity. Exceptionally, in Italy, Jewish communities continued to flourish throughout the Middle Ages. The Jews were never expelled from Rome and the Jewish community there has maintained a continuous existence for some 2000 years.

READING SUGGESTIONS

* *B. Tierney,* Sources *and* Readings, *vol. I, nos. 58–64; vol. II, nos. 24.*

The best biography of Innocent III is H. Tillmann, *Pope Innocent III* (New York, 1980). S. R. Packard, *Europe and the Church Under Innocent III,* and L. Elliott-Binns, *Innocent III* (London, 1931) are both introductory sketches. C. Edwards, *Innocent III: Church Defender* (Baton Rouge, LA, 1951) gives some idea of the range of the pope's activities, and * J. M. Powell (ed.), *Innocent III: Vicar of Christ or Lord of the World* (Boston, 1963) presents useful translated extracts from the works of several European scholars. On Innocent's idea of papal power, see J. Watt, *The Theory of Papal Monarchy in the Thirteenth Century*

(New York, 1965). See also C. R. Cheney and W. H. Semple (eds.), *Selected Letters of Pope Innocent III Concerning England* (Edinburgh, 1953) and K. Pennington, *Pope and Bishops: The Papal Monarchy in the Twelfth and Thirteenth Centuries* (Philadelphia, 1984).

On the emergence of heretical movements see * R. I. Moore, *The Origins of European Dissent* (New York, 1977) and J. B. Russell, *Dissent and Reform,* cited in Chapter X. The best introduction to medieval Catharism is W. L. Wakefield and A. P. Evans, *Heresies of the High Middle Ages* (New York, 1969). See also W. L. Wakefield, *Heresy, Crusade, and Inquisition in Southern France, 1100–1250* (Berkeley and Los Angeles, 1974) and S. Runciman, *The Medieval Manichee* (Cambridge, England, 1955). C. H. Lea, *A History of the Inquisition,* 3 vols. (New York, 1888) has never been surpassed as a full-scale indictment of the Inquisition. More lenient interpretations are offered by E. Vacandard, *The Inquisition* (New York, 1918); A. L. Maycock, *The Inquisition* (London, 1927); and A. C. Shannon, *The Popes and Heresy in the Thirteenth Century* (New York, 1955). For a recent overall account see * E. Peters, *The Inquisition* (Berkeley and Los Angeles, 1989); * R. I. Moore tries to explain the growth of intolerance in *The Formation of a Persecuting Society* (Oxford, England, 1987). See also J. Boswell, *Christianity, Social Tolerance and Homosexuality* (Chicago, 1980).

On aspects of popular religion see * R. and C. Brooke, *Popular Religion and the Middle Ages* (London, 1984); B. Hamilton, *Religion in the Medieval West* (London, 1986); and * P. Geary, *Furta Sacra: The Theft of Relics in the Central Middle Ages* (Princeton, 1978).

On the new mendicant orders see R. Brooke, *The Coming of the Friars* (New York, 1975). The two outstanding works on St. Dominic are P. Mandonnet, *St. Dominic and His Work* (London, 1944), and M.-H. Vicaire, *St. Dominic and His Times* (New York, 1964). On the development of the order, see W. A. Hinnebusch, *History of the Dominican Order,* vol. I (Staten Island, NY, 1966), and G. R. Galbraith, *The Constitution of the Dominican Order* (Manchester, England, 1925). And, for source material, see F. C. Lehner, *Saint Dominic: Biographical Documents* (Washington, DC, 1964). The best works among the numerous biographies of St. Francis are P. Sabatier, *The Life of St. Francis of Assisi* (New York, 1894); Father Cuthbert, *St. Francis of Assisi* (London, 1925); and O. Engelbert, *Saint Francis of Assisi,* 2nd rev. English ed. (Chicago, 1966), which contains an exceptionally rich bibliography. On the Franciscan order and its problems, see J. Moorman, *A History of the Franciscan Order* (Oxford, England, 1968); R. Brooke, *Early Franciscan Government* (Cambridge, England, 1959); M. D. Lambert, *Franciscan Poverty* (London, 1961); and D. Burr, *Olivi and Franciscan Poverty* (Philadelphia, 1989). M. A. Habig (ed.), *St. Francis of Assisi: English Omnibus of Sources for the Life of St. Francis,* 4th ed. (Chicago, 1983) is a splendid collection of translated sources with critical introductions.

On relations between Christian Europe and the Far East, see A. Moule, *Christians in China Before the Year 1553* (London, 1930); * M. Prawdin, *The Mongol Empire* (New York, 1950); and * D. Morgan, *Mongols* (Oxford, England, 1986). The most famous narrative, of course, is * *The Travels of Marco Polo,* R. E. Latham (trans.) (Harmondsworth, England, 1958).

There is a large literature on medieval Jewish history. The most detailed account is S. Baron, *A Social and Religious History of the Jews,* 2nd ed., 13 vols. (New York, 1952–1967). Shorter works are * C. Roth, *A History of the Jews,* rev. ed. (New York, 1961) and * E. A. Synam, *The Popes and the Jews in the*

Middle Ages (New York, 1965). Among the works that explore medieval origins of modern antisemitism are * J. Trachtenberg, *The Devil and the Jew: The Medieval Conception of the Jew and Its Relation to Modern Anti-Semitism* (New York, 1966); * J. Cohen, *The Friars and the Jews* (Ithaca, NY, 1982); R. Chazan, *Daggers of Faith: Thirteenth-Century Christian Missionizing and the Jewish Response* (Berkeley and Los Angeles, 1988); G. Langmuir, *History, Religion, and Antisemitism* (Berkeley and Los Angeles, 1990) and *Toward a Definition of Antisemitism* (Berkeley and Los Angeles, 1991); and * R. Po-chia Hsiah, *The Myth of Ritual Murder* (New Haven, CN, 1988).

chapter

XVII

The Development of Medieval Government

In the thirteenth century, not only the papacy but also the secular monarchies in various parts of Europe were gaining in strength. (The one great exception was the German Empire.) The effects of the revival of trade, the development of towns, and the reappearance of an exchange economy profoundly influenced governmental institutions. Kings had money revenues obtained in part at least by taxation and could hire officials and soldiers. No longer did their activities depend on the services rendered by their feudal vassals. The political scene was complicated by the appearance of the middle class with its own desires, ambitions, and social and economic interests. The comparatively simple world of kings, nobles, and peasants, all of whom lived from the produce of the land, was no more.

During this period the three great states of western Europe—England, France, and the Empire—took on the general political complexion and developed the political institutions that were to mark them for at least half a millennium. Students of eighteenth-century Europe who glanced at the institutions of the region in the eleventh century would see little that was familiar, but a similar survey in 1300 would reveal the seeds of the institutions of their own day. The course of development in these three states during the thirteenth century was not consistent. The monarchy that had been strongest in the eleventh century, the Empire, became far the weakest, while the weakest, Capetian France, grew into the most powerful. It is a period of growth, of change, and of great political activity.

54. *The Hohenstaufen Empire*

The emperor Frederick II (1215–1250), whom Pope Innocent III helped to the imperial throne, proved to be one of the most dangerous enemies of the papacy. Frederick was half Sicilian in blood and more so in taste. He found Germany a cold, damp, gloomy country with altogether too many swamps and forests. Although he stayed in his northern kingdom until 1220, he did so only to organize it so that it would need the least possible attention, and after his departure, he returned only for brief visits. In his organization of his German realm, Frederick followed his father's general policy with much more consistency—one might say with abandon.* He gave the princes practically everything they asked for. Their fiefs were made fully hereditary, and they were given complete powers of jurisdiction. The king promised not to build fortresses or levy taxes in the lands of the princes without their consent. He even delivered over to them the last firm bulwark of the royal power, the German towns. Needless to say, this method of handling the princes was successful only in one sense: it kept them quiet. Once they had gained everything they wanted from Frederick, they took no interest in his fortunes and cheerfully refused to aid him in his Italian campaigns.

Frederick II was a remarkable man who captured the imagination of his own contemporaries and has exercised the same charm over later writers.† He was highly educated and highly intelligent, a poet and a patron of poets. He had been brought up in the Sicilian court, which was deeply imbued with Muslim culture. He was rumored to have a harem filled with Muslim beauties. While his antagonism to the church may have been exaggerated, he was certainly far less devout than most monarchs of his day. The priestly, even the papal, office filled him with little awe, and he had not the slightest objection to entering into friendly relations with Muslim princes. In short, he was exactly the type of monarch that would not be thought well of by the popes no matter what realm he ruled. When in 1220 he left Germany, determined to build Italy into a centralized state dominated by the Norman kingdom of Sicily, he became almost at once a deadly foe of the papacy.

Innocent III's successor, Honorius III (1216–1227), was a mild-mannered pontiff. Frederick gained his favor by undertaking to go on crusade and by promising to restore territories claimed by the Roman church that had been in imperial hands since the days of Frederick Barbarossa. Won over by these promises, which Frederick of course had no intention of keeping, Honorius made the blunder of crowning Federick emperor without first compelling him to relinquish Sicily. Frederick then turned all his energies to consolidating his power in his Sicilian kingdom and in central Italy. In the latter region, the German officials of his father and grandfather were replaced by Sicilians who were still less popular. Even the meek Honorius was losing patience with Frederick II toward the end of his pontificate. The next pope, Gregory IX (1227–1241), was a fiery zealot, determined to defend every jot and tittle of the papal claims, and he promptly excommunicated Frederick on the ground that the emperor had broken his oath to go on crusade.

To the pope's exasperation, Frederick then did set off for the Holy Land without troubling to be reconciled to the church. The ensuing

*See pp. 342–344.

†Sources, no 69

NORWAY
SWEDEN
Stockholm
Kalmar
Novgorod
Moscow
ESTONIA
Riga
CURLAND
TEUTONIC ORDER
LITHUANIA
RUSSIA
BALTIC SEA
SCOTLAND
Edinburgh
IRELAND
IRISH PALE
Dublin
York
Lincoln
WALES
ENGLAND
Oxford
Cambridge
London
Thames R.
Winchester
Canterbury
NORTH SEA
DENMARK
Copenhagen
Danzig
Lubeck
Hamburg
Bremen
SAXONY
POLAND
Kiev
Dnieper R.
MONGOL EMPIRE
ATLANTIC OCEAN
Bruges
Ghent
FLANDERS
Cologne
Mainz
Elbe R.
BOHEMIA
Prague
Vistula R.
Reims
Paris
BRITTANY
NORMANDY
Orleans
Seine R.
HOLY ROMAN EMPIRE
Rhine R.
AUSTRIA
Vienna
FRANCE
Poitiers
Limoges
Besancon
HUNGARY
BLACK SEA
Bordeaux
Garonne R.
AQUITAINE
Rhone R.
Milan
LOMBARDY
Venice
Genoa
Bologna
Danube R.
Leon
Avignon
PROVENCE
Pisa
Florence
Zara
Tarnovo
NAVARRE
Toulouse
Marseilles
TUSCANY
ADRIATIC SEA
SERBIA
BULGARIA
Constantinople
PORTUGAL
CASTILE
ARAGON
Madrid
Assisi
Nicea
EMPIRE OF NICEA
SULTINATE OF RUM
Toledo
Barcelona
CORSICA
Rome
PAPAL STATES
Lisbon
Tagus R.
Naples
Bari
Valencia
SARDINIA
LATIN EMPIRE OF CONSTANTINOPLE
AEGEAN SEA
Cordoba
BALEARICS
KINGDOM OF THE TWO SICILIES
Guadalquivir R.
Granada
GRANADA
Palermo
SICILY
Athens
MEDITERRANEAN SEA
CYPRUS
Tunis
AFRICA
TUNISIA
CRETE

crusade was a weird affair. When Frederick arrived in Jerusalem, he was fiercely denounced by the patriarch as an excommunicate. This did not, however, trouble Frederick. He marched his army about Palestine, all the while carrying on negotiations with the sultan of Egypt, who held Jerusalem. Eventually, the sultan got tired of the proceedings and came to terms. Frederick was to receive Jerusalem, Bethlehem, Nazareth, and a few other towns—in short, the Holy City and a wide corridor leading to it. Both Christians and Muslims were to have freedom of religion in Jerusalem, and Frederick promised not to aid any crusade against the sultan or his lands. This treaty horrified the patriarch. No sooner had Frederick entered Jerusalem than it was placed under an interdict. Soon Frederick learned that a papal army was invading his Italian lands. Frederick hurried home, and the magnificent comedy came to an end. It must be pointed out, however, that Frederick had gained more than any other recent crusader. He had recovered Jerusalem.

Back in Italy, Frederick easily defeated the papal forces and compelled Gregory to make peace in 1230. The following year was one of decisive importance in Frederick's reign. In Sicily he summoned a great council at Melfi that promulgated a new code of law for the kingdom. It strongly emphasized the king's absolute authority as supreme legislator and judge, severely curtailed the privileges of feudal nobility and townsfolk alike, and assigned all major civil and criminal cases to royal courts. Sicily was divided into eleven provinces, each governed by an imperially appointed justiciar (for criminal matters) and chamberlain (for civil affairs). These local officials were in turn supervised by a central government staffed by bureaucrats. The system has sometimes been regarded as a first prototype of the modern absolutist state. It had a progressive aspect, however. Frederick was interested in fostering commerce, and he reduced customs duties. Other taxes were high, but they fell fairly on all classes. Occasional representative assemblies were summoned at which delegates from the cities joined with nobles and prelates in advising the king.

In the same year that the Constitution of Melfi were promulgated, Frederick held a Diet at Ravenna where he announced his intention of imposing a similar regime on the cities of Lombardy. Also in this same year he promulgated a *Constitution in Favor of the Princes* for Germany, which conceded to each prince virtually sovereign rights in his own territory. Frederick's intention was clear. Italy was to become a highly disciplined monarchy; Germany could go its own way as a remote, outlying, and relatively unimportant province of the empire.*

The most difficult part of the program proved to be the subjugation of Lombardy. Soon the Lombard League that had fought Frederick Barbarossa† was re-created with papal encouragement. In 1239 the pope excommunicated Frederick again, and when Gregory died in 1241, the emperor was preparing an attack on Rome itself. The next pope, Celestine IV, lived only a couple of weeks after his election but his successor, Innocent IV (1243–1254), was another very powerful pontiff. Innocent was a great canon lawyer and a hard, implacable,

*Sources, no. 67

†See pp. 339–341.

tenacious fighter. At the beginning of his reign, he escaped from Rome and established the papal curia across the Alps at Lyons, which was safely out of Frederick's reach. There Innocent summoned a general council that declared the emperor excommunicated (once again!) and also deposed him from the imperial dignity. Unlike Innocent III, Innocent IV permitted the political exigencies of his reign to take precedence over every other consideration and used his powers as pope primarily to raise revenues from all over the church (often by dubious means) in order to finance the continuing war in Italy.

Innocent IV also did his best to persuade the princes of Europe to intervene. As Henry III of England had nothing to intervene with and St. Louis of France, though a pious and devout monarch, had little sympathy with the more extreme claims of the papacy, this last effort came to nothing. For his part, Frederick sent flamboyant letters to his fellow sovereigns denouncing the worldly pretensions of the Roman curia and announcing his intention of reducing the church in his own territories to a becoming state of apostolic poverty. The conventionally minded Catholic monarchs of the day found the proposal interesting but a little extreme. Neither side, in fact, could enlist effective foreign allies. The issue had to be fought out between the emperor on the one hand and the Lombard cities, supported by papal money, on the other. Frederick won many individual battles but he could never finally win the war. His resources in men and money were not sufficient to defeat the forces of the league in the field and then reduce the walled towns one by one.

The emperor died in 1250 with Lombardy still unsubdued, and his death marked for all practical purposes the end of the house of Hohenstaufen. Federick's son, Conrad, was recognized as king in Germany, but he was a mere figurehead. His position in Sicily was stronger, but he died in 1254 before he could consolidate his power there.* After Conrad's death, the imperial electors in Germany split into two factions, each of which chose a foreign prince as emperor. The two would-be emperors were King Alfonso X of Castile and Richard of Cornwall, a brother of King Henry III of England. Both of them had to bribe the German princes handsomely, and neither was able to establish any effective authority in Germany, an entirely satisfactory situation from the point of view of the German princes. Finally, in 1273, the electors agreed to choose as king Rudolph, count of Hapsburg, a petty lord who won the pope's support by renouncing all imperial claims over the papal states. Although Rudolph (1273–1291) used his position very effectively to lay the foundation for the future greatness of his house by marrying his son to the heiress of Austria, he did nothing to increase the authority of the German crown. In fact, there was but little that could be done. The princes of Germany had become masters of the realm, and they had no intention of permitting a revival of effective royal authority. Essentially, Germany was no longer a single state but a loose alliance of princes under the vague suzerainty of an elected king.

*See p. 388–390.

While Frederick II was devoting his whole energy to skirmishing in

Italy, two events were taking place on the borders of his German kingdom that influenced the history of eastern Europe for centuries to come. The first was the expansion of the Teutonic Knights into Prussia. The order had been founded to defend the Holy Land, but, in the early thirteenth century, its members began to find a more rewarding field of operation among the pagan Slavs beyond the German borders. Frederick II granted East Prussia to the master-general of the order, Hermann von Salza, in 1226. In 1231 the Teutonic Knights crossed the Vistula and occupied the lands to the east in a series of campaigns extending over the next thirty years. The pagan inhabitants were converted at the point of the sword or driven off the land and replaced by German settlers. During the second half of the thirteenth century, Prussia became predominantly German and Christian.

The other major event in the East was a devastating invasion by a horde of Mongols—the first such threat to Europe since Otto the Great had broken the power of the Magyars in 955. In 1237 a great Mongol army usually known as the Golden Horde, under the command of Batu (1224–1256), grandson of Genghis Khan (1206–1227), swept over the steppes of southern Russia. The nomadic peoples of the steppes as well as the Russian princes were defeated and subjugated. The Mongols moved on to overrun Hungary and Poland after destroying the armies of the king of Hungary and the combined forces of Poland and the Teutonic Knights. While his troops were plundering the eastern shores of the Adriatic Sea, Batu learned of the death of his uncle, the Great Khan, and immediately hastened to Central Asia to take part in the contest for the succession. His army retired to the Russian steppes, where they established a Mongol state. Many historians have assumed that, if Batu had not been interrupted, he could easily have overrun the countries of western Europe; and that might have been the end of Western civilization. In fact, the Mongols were not invincible. The Egyptians defeated them several times, and the armies of western Europe might have done so too. It was a fortunate accident that spared Europe the test. Although the Mongols withdrew from Hungary and Poland, however, they continued to dominate the Slavs of southern Russia. For two centuries, the Russian state originally established by the Viking adventurers of the tenth century remained under Tartar rule.

55. *The Mediterranean: Spain and Sicily*

During the thirteenth century, Castile and Aragon emerged as the two most powerful Spanish kingdoms. León was permanently united with Castile after 1230, and Barcelona with Aragon from 1137 onward. (Portugal remained independent. The little kingdom of Navarre was inherited by Count Theobald of Champagne in 1234 and subsequently fell under French influence.) The Spanish kingdoms all displayed a restless energy and vitality at this time. There was constitutional experimentation, commercial expansion, and considerable cultural achievement. The one thing that was always lacking in medieval Spain was political stability.

Conditions varied from kingdom to kingdom. Within each kingdom, too, there were important differences between the old Christian lands and the territories newly conquered from the Muslims. Spain participated in the general growth of urban life that characterized the twelfth century and, by the end of the century, many Spanish towns, especially in the north, had acquired privileges by royal charter. In 1188 a new development was recorded. Delegates from the cities of León were invited to attend the *Cortes*, the council of king and nobility that deliberated on the fiscal and legal affairs of the kingdom. Within half a century, similar assemblies, which included urban delegates, had been summoned in all the Spanish kingdoms. It seems that these early Spanish *Cortes* were not yet fully fledged representative assemblies since the delegations from the cities did not have full power to bind their communities by their decisions. This full power (*plena potestas*) was an essential characteristic of later medieval (and modern) representative assemblies.* But the fact that urban delegations were present in Spanish deliberative bodies at such an early date at any rate indicates the growing importance of the towns and the bourgeoisie.

Urban life was less developed in the southern territories. Muslim Andalusia, before its conquest by Castile, had been a land of thriving cities, but after the conquest most of their inhabitants were expelled. Much of the central region of Castile was given over to a grazing economy. Huge herds of half-wild cattle and sheep roamed the land. The country was divided into great ranches, which were granted to the military orders or to lay nobles who had participated in the Reconquista. Centuries later this pattern of ranching was transferred to Spanish Mexico, which included modern Texas.

The Muslim territory of Valencia, occupied by Aragon, was a well-irrigated land with many small farms. Here Muslim peasants continued to work the land after the conquest, paying heavy rents to Christian lords. On the greater agricultural estates, slave labor was commonly used. In all the newly conquered territories, the power of the religious orders and the problems of controlling large Muslim populations hindered any development of constitutional government.

A major result of the Reconquista was that it made possible the growth of a brilliant cosmopolitan culture to which Islamic, Jewish, and Christian traditions all contributed. Alfonso X of Castile (1252–1284), a great patron of learning, liked to call himself "King of the Three Religions." Under his rule, Toledo flourished as a thriving center of intellectual life. The greatest age of original creative thought among the Jews and Muslims of Spain had been in the eleventh and twelfth centuries; but the thirteenth century produced major works of synthesis. Jewish scholars translated a great body of Islamic philosophy into Castilian. They also produced an important set of astronomical tables, which were dedicated to the king and so are

*See pp. 405–406.

known as the Alfonsine Tables. Alfonso's jurists produced a major work of legal codification, called *Las Siete Partidas,* that combined Castilian law with substantial borrowings from Roman and canonical jurisprudence.

Unfortunately, Alfonso was far less successful as a statesman than as a patron of culture. In political affairs, he was always ambitious but usually inept. During the long interregnum in Germany after the fall of the Hohenstaufen dynasty, he was one of the two leading candidates for the imperial throne. (The king's mother, Beatrice, was a granddaughter of Frederick Barbarossa.) Alfonso not only failed in this bid; he did not even succeed in keeping the peace in his own kingdom of Castile. When his eldest son, Ferdinand, died in 1275, Alfonso (following the principles of Roman law) maintained that Ferdinand's infant son was the proper heir to the throne. The Castilian nobility, however, preferred the claims of Sancho, Ferdinand's younger brother. Civil war broke out, and eventually Sancho succeeded as King Sancho IV (1284–1295). But no clearcut law of succession was established, and the later political history of Castile consisted mainly of a tangle of succession disputes and civil wars in which factions of nobles supported rival candidates for the throne or struggled to control the council of regency during the occasional minorities.

In the neighboring kingdom of Aragon, political life was complicated by the practice of dividing a king's possessions among his sons. Thus, when James I (1213–1276) completed the conquest of Majorca, he bestowed it as an independent kingdom on his younger son, while his elder son, Peter, inherited the mainland territories. Also, deep-rooted tensions persisted between the people of the old kingdom of Aragon and those of Catalonia (the region around Barcelona). Old Aragon was a land power; its people were principally concerned with the internal affairs of the Spanish peninsula. The Catalans were seafarers, interested in spreading a network of commerce and influence throughout the Mediterranean world. The kings of Aragon shared the ambitions of their Catalan subjects. They were usually happy to placate the nobles and cities of old Aragon with grants of privileges in order to be allowed a free hand in overseas ventures. Hence, although Aragon had its share of succession disputes and civil wars, its political history was dominated by a greater theme—the quest of its kings for a great Mediterranean empire. James I's conquest of Majorca was only a first step. By the end of the thirteenth century, Sicily, Sardinia, and Corsica had passed under Aragonese rule. Meanwhile, Barcelona had grown into one of the great trading cities of the medieval world, rivaling Venice and Genoa in its wealth and power.

In Italy the principal political problem that emerged after the death of Frederick II was the disposition of the crown of Sicily. Pope Innocent IV would have liked simply to annex the kingdom of Sicily to the Papal States. When a revolt against the imperial government broke out in Naples immediately after Frederick's death, the pope eagerly supported it; but Frederick's son Conrad succeeded in suppressing

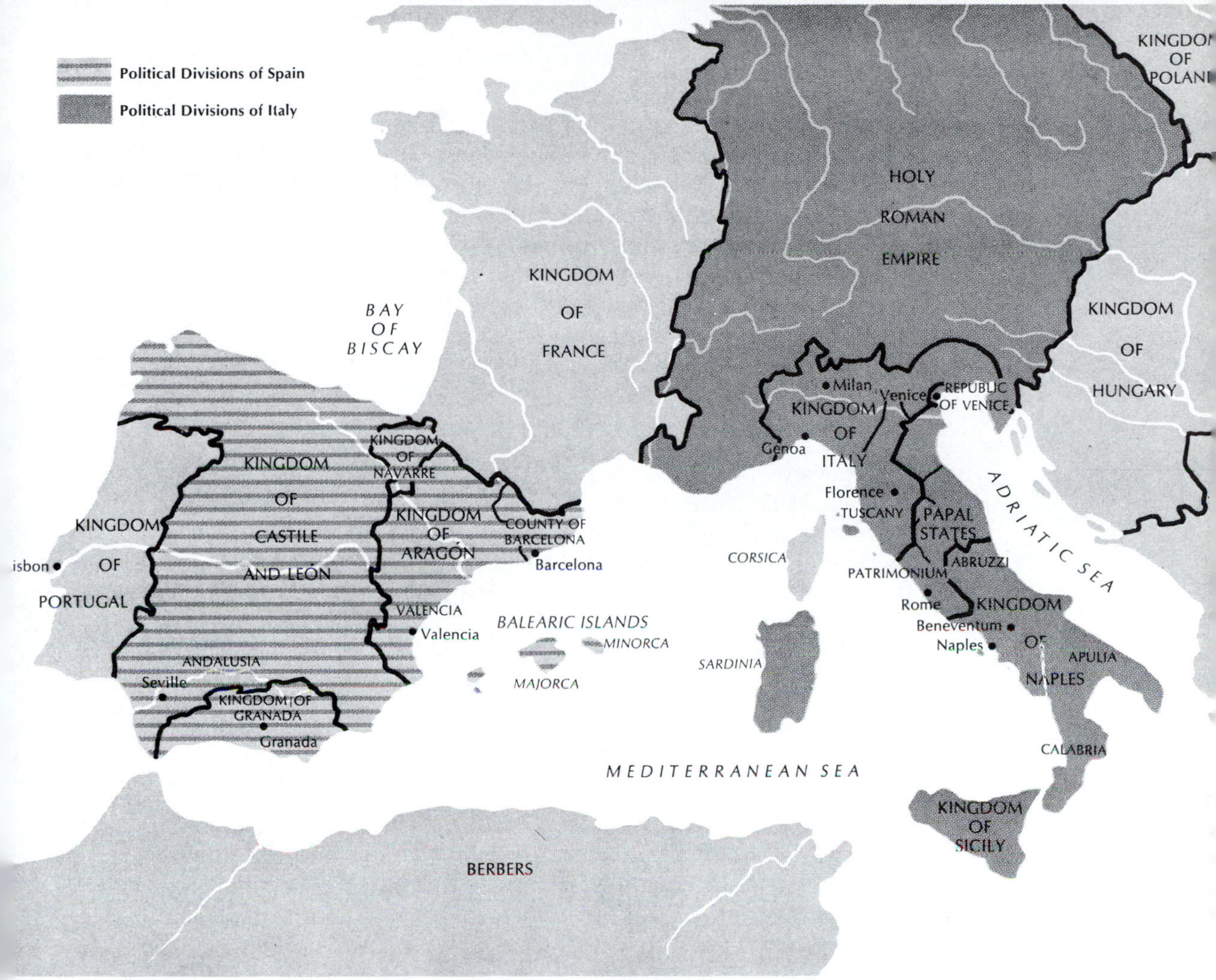

Spain and Italy, ca. 1300

the rebellion. Then, when Conrad died in 1254, his half brother, Manfred, seized power in Sicily. Manfred was an illegitimate son of Frederick II, and he ruled officially as regent for Conrad's infant son, Conradin, the legitimate heir to the throne. Manfred was a popular and able ruler. Soon the pope realized that, in order to dislodge him, he would have to grant the kingdom of Sicily to some foreign prince strong enough to conquer it with his own resources. Innocent IV first turned to King Henry III of England, who sought the throne of Sicily for his younger son, Edmund Crouchback. The popes obtained subsidies from Henry to finance campaigns against Manfred, but in 1258 Manfred won a decisive victory. In that same year, the English barons made it plain that they would no longer provide financial support for their king's Mediterranean venture. The papacy next turned to France and offered the crown of Sicily to Charles of Anjou, brother of King Louis IX. In 1266 Charles invaded Sicily, defeated and killed Manfred at the battle of Beneventum, and established himself as king.

One last attempt was made to reassert the Hohenstaufen power in Sicily. The young prince Conradin led a German army into south Italy in 1268. But Conradin—the last of the Hohenstaufens—was defeated, captured, and publicly executed. Charles was left as undisputed king of Sicily until 1282, when a rebellion and subsequent Aragonese invasion challenged his power there.

In the north of Italy, the collapse of imperial power left the greater cities free to pursue their own political and economic objectives as virtually independent units. Dozens of autonomous city-states existed, but a few of the greater ones were rising to positions of dominating influence. Genoa won a great victory over her old enemy Pisa in 1284 and emerged as the dominant maritime state in that region. Florence affirmed her leadership in Tuscany as head of a new Tuscan League of cities, and in 1293 adopted a new republican constitution; this did not, however, end the faction-fighting that characterized Florentine politics. Milan, the dominant city of the Lombard plain, fell under the control of the Visconti family. Venice, the capital of a great commercial empire, provided a rare example of stable republican government.* If we take an overall view of the whole peninsula, Italy—like Spain—presented a picture of great economic vitality but considerable political confusion in the second half of the thirteenth century.

56. *France: The Growth of Royal Power*

In its political development, France provides a contrast with Germany and Italy. In France there was a persistent increase in royal power throughout the thirteenth century. Philip II Augustus (1180–1223) had laid firm foundations for the growth of a strong monarchy, and the next four generations of Capetian kings continued this development. The royal demesne was steadily expanded. Marriage alliances brought the county of Toulouse and the great fief of Champagne into the possession of the crown. If the kings had kept possession of all the lands that had come into their hands, the royal demesne would have embraced more than half of France by the early years of the fourteenth century; this did not happen because of a policy revived by Philip Augustus' son, Louis VIII (1223–1226)—that of giving *appanages* to the king's younger sons.

The problem of how to provide for the king's younger sons was a perplexing one in all feudal monarchies. Even if the royal revenue permitted the payment of allowances in money, no high-spirited prince would be satisfied with such a solution. He wanted his own manors and vassals and the independence that came with the possession of a fief. The early Capetians had been fortunate in having small families. They had regularly endowed their younger sons from the royal demesne, but the lack of sons had limited the results of this practice. Louis VIII was simply following the customs of his time when he created fiefs for his younger sons—but he had three of them to

*See pp. 542–545.

provide for. Robert was given the county of Artois; Alphonse, the county of Poitou; and Charles, Anjou and Maine. Thus Louis's own inheritance from his mother and about half the land taken from John of England by Philip Augustus passed out of the direct control of the crown.

At first glance, this policy of creating *appanages* appears most unwise, and many historians have so regarded it. Actually, it was probably necessary at the time. The royal demesne of Philip Augustus and Louis VIII was too large to handle through the available administrative organization. By granting lands in *appanage,* the king supplied a lord who could govern effectively and upon whose loyalty he could rely. But this policy weakened the crown in the long run. A king's brothers would usually be loyal to him, their sons might feel equally bound to his son, but the tie between second cousins in the next generation was too vague to have much force. By 1328 only four of the great ancient fiefs survived—Flanders, Brittany, Burgundy, and Aquitaine—but the granting of *appanages* had created a new group of feudal princes. In the thirteenth century, however, the long-range results of this policy were not apparent. For the time being, the holders of *appanages* were entirely loyal to the crown, and the king's power seemed greater than ever before.

As we have seen in an earlier chapter, the development of towns, the revival of commerce, and the reappearance of an exchange economy had increased the power of the greater princes. The master of rich towns and flourishing fairs enjoyed a revenue in money with which he could hire officials devoted to his interests and soldiers ready to obey his commands. This worked to the advantage of the kings, too. Philip Augustus and his successors made use of their revenues in money to hire middle-class officials and mercenary soldiers; no longer could a petty baron of the demesne hope to defy the king.

But the other feudal princes were developing their power in the same manner. Hence it was extremely fortunate for the Capetian kings that so many great fiefs came into the hands of the crown during this period. When one speaks of the increase of the royal power at the expense of the nobles during the thirteenth century, one refers primarily to the royal demesne. The power of the monarchy grew throughout this period, partly because the kings learned to govern their demesne more effectively but mainly because—in spite of the creation of the *appanages*—the demesne itself became far greater in extent than it had been in the twelfth century. Louis VI (1108–1137) had exercised effective control only in the region around Paris. Louis IX (1226–1270) commanded a great array of territories stretching from the North Sea to the Mediterranean. The two principal stages in the growth of the royal demesne were the conquest of John's northern fiefs by Philip Augustus and the acquisition of extensive territories in the south as a long-range result of the Albigensian Crusade.

Throughout the middle years of the thirteenth century, this enhanced royal power was wielded by the greatest of medieval French kings. Louis IX—later canonized as St. Louis—was the closest ap-

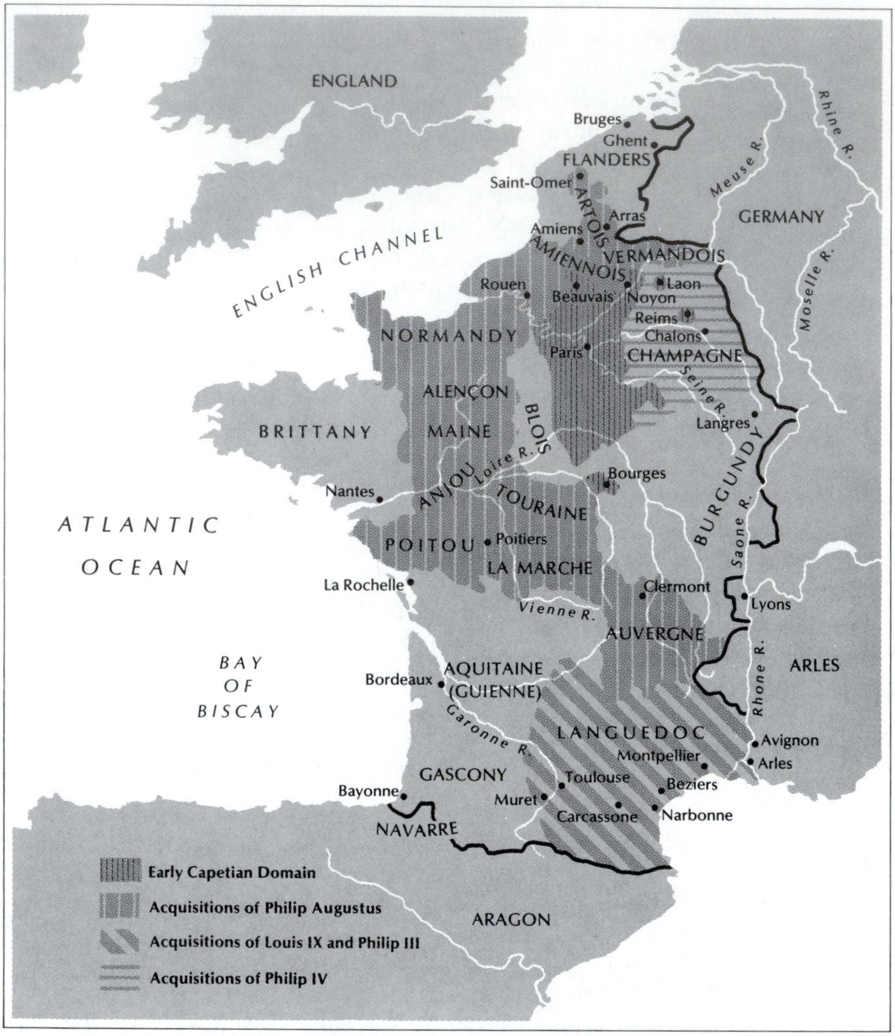

The French Royal Demesne, ca. 1300

In the twelfth and thirteenth centuries, the French kings steadily expanded the area of the royal demesne at the expense of the English kings and their own French vassals; they developed as well the system of centralized administration that gave them effective control over the areas they ruled. Compare this map with the earlier one of the area controlled by Philip I two hundred years before.

proximation to an ideal feudal king that the Middle Ages ever produced. He was brave, generous, deeply pious, and universally respected. Very few medieval kings could have said, as Louis did, ''I sleep alone, perfectly safe, because nobody bears me a grudge.'' Louis' biographer, Joinville, tells many stories of the king's devotion to his people and of his even-handed justice. Sometimes he would hold court informally under a great oak tree in the forest of Vincennes and redress any wrongs that were brought to his attention. He was as anxious to give other people their rights as he was to insist on his own. Instead of attempting to drive Henry III from Gascony, he made peace with him. Henry was to surrender his claim to Normandy, Maine, Anjou, and Poitou in return for Louis' recognition of his claim to hold Gascony as a vassal of the French crown. When his barons protested that this was an unnecessary concession to the English king, Louis replied, "It is fitting that there should be peace between us." Once a man who had been enfeoffed by Louis' father was asked to prove his right to his fief. He presented a badly torn charter, which Louis' officers urged him not to accept. But the king could recognize his father's seal on the damaged document, and he insisted on honoring it.*

When Louis came to the throne, the land was ringing with complaints about the extortions and injustices of the royal *baillis.* Louis regarded the proper exercise of royal power as a religious duty, and he would not tolerate abuses by his own servants. His solution was to send out *enquêteurs,* traveling representatives of the king, who were given authority to investigate the conduct of local officials and redress grievances. Louis also encouraged the vassals of feudal princes outside the royal demesne to appeal to his court if they felt that they had been unjustly treated by their lords. A right of appeal to the king as overlord had always existed in theory, but it had been little exercised in practice. Under Louis—a king who was widely esteemed and had the power to enforce his sentences—such appeals became more common.

Important changes were made in the organization of the royal court in order to cope with the increasing load of cases. In the reigns of Louis VII and Philip Augustus, cases had been heard by members of the royal household, barons, prelates, and knights, aided by a few clerks with special knowledge of the law. This court wandered about with the king and was in fact simply part of his household. In the reign of Louis IX, the business of the king's court increased so much that it had to stay in one place and sit fairly continually. A permanent royal court holding regular sessions in the city of Paris became established. The barons and prelates took part in the proceedings only when the importance of the litigants required their presence. When a case involved a great lord, his equals, or his "peers," participated in the deliberations of the court, but the great mass of routine cases was disposed of by a permanent staff of professional jurists. In the reign of Louis IX, this central royal court became known as the *parlement* of Paris.

Louis was firm in upholding the rights of the crown in relation to the barons. As a pious and devout man, he detested feudal warfare. He first hedged it about with restrictions. Before starting a war, a noble had to defy his enemy well in advance. He also had to notify his foe's relatives and ask them if they planned to take part in the war. If one party asked for a truce, the other had to grant it. In short, the waging of private war was made so complicated that it was very little fun. Later in his reign, Louis forbade private war entirely and even prohibited his nobles from riding round at the head of armed bands. Louis was able to discipline his barons to a degree that would have

*Sources, no 66

been resented and resisted if it had been attempted by a lesser man. Under his rule and that of his son and grandson, France was more orderly than it was to be again for several centuries.

Louis had some of the faults of his age as well as its virtues. He hated heretics and was intolerant of Jews. The only form of warfare that he really approved of was crusading against the infidel. This enthusiasm for crusading led to the only major setbacks of Louis' career. In 1244 the city of Jerusalem, recovered for the Latin kingdom by Frederick II's eccentric crusade of 1227, was recaptured by a horde of Turks allied to the sultan of Egypt. All attempts to retake it failed. In 1249 Louis took the cross and collected a great host. His plan was to strike at Egypt as the center of the Muslim power. Damietta was captured, and the army started its march through the delta of the Nile but soon became hopelessly confused among the many branches of the river. Then they were attacked and completely defeated by the Egyptian troops. Louis was captured, with most of his noble followers. The king eventually obtained his freedom by paying a large ransom and spent four years in Palestine, but all he accomplished was to build a few fortresses. Louis IX launched another crusade in 1270 together with his brother, Charles of Anjou; but Louis died shortly after landing in Tunis, and without his leadership the crusade quickly collapsed.

Louis' successors, Philip III (1270–1285) and Philip IV (1285–1314), maintained his policies in France. Their officials continued to infringe on the jurisdiction of the nobles, and private war was sternly suppressed. The *parlement* of Paris acquired a more complicated organization. By the time of Philip IV, it was divided into three sections. The *chambre des plaids* actually heard and decided cases. The *chambre des requêts* received complaints and determined whether or not they should be heard. The *chambre des enquêtes* conducted judicial investigations.

There were also important developments in the handling of royal finances. The central financial administration of Philip Augustus had consisted of an annual audit of the accounts of the *baillis* and provosts held in the house of the Templars in Paris by members of that order acting as royal agents. The Temple also served as a storehouse for the king's reserve treasure. When Philip conquered John's fiefs, he took over intact the complicated and efficient financial system established by the Angevin kings. In all probability, he and his successors used this system as a model for the improvement of their own administration. The first step was to appoint a group of household officers and royal clerks to conduct the annual audit. Philip IV, however, found that there was too much business for a group of dignitaries who could only devote a short time to the task and created a permanent financial body, the *chambre des comptes*. Philip also moved the treasury from the Temple to his castle of the Louvre and appointed officials to receive and pay out his moneys.

In addition to the men who managed his finances and dealt out justice in his court, the king had a group of councilors to give him advice. These men took a special oath to give the best advice they could. Thus the functions that had been performed by the king's household under the early Capetians became divided among three bodies—the council, the *chambre des comptes,* and *parlement.* This does not mean that the personnel of these groups was completely distinct; an important servant of the crown might have a place on all of them. But in general, the royal administration was carried on by specialists who were professionals as well. It is important to notice that the growth of the central administration added to the bureaucracy. When one considers the members of the central administration and the *baillis* and seneschals with their numerous subordinates, it is clear that a large number of men were living on the king's pay.

Every feudal lord had his *curia,* the assembly of all his vassals, and the Capetian kings were no exception to this rule. This body met at certain times, such as Christmas and Easter, and whenever the king needed advice on a question too important for his permanent councillors, e.g., legislation that affected the interests of the great vassals. As long as the king of France was essentially only a feudal suzerain, the assembly of his vassals could give him whatever advice he needed. But as the Capetians developed their functions as kings, as distinct from those they exercised as feudal overlords, they felt the need of contact with other groups of their subjects. Thus the towns supplied an important part of the financial and military resources of the realm, and the good will of their inhabitants was extremely important to the king. Moreover, as general taxation began to take the place of purely feudal revenues, the lesser nobles who might not be direct vassals of the king acquired an interest in royal policy. The kings soon found that it was easier to collect taxes and enforce legislation that had been agreed to by those whom it involved. Hence the crown sought from time to time the advice of various groups that were not represented in the *curia.* Then in 1302 Philip IV found himself engaged in a life and death struggle with the papacy and felt the need for the support of his people as a whole. He therefore summoned the Church, the nobility, and the towns to send representatives to meet in the first *Estates General.**

This body vigorously supported the king's policy and enabled him to face his foes at the head of a united people. Philip and his successors continued to summon this new body when any emergency arose. It was found particularly useful when the king needed money or when he desired legislation that went against established custom. In short, the power of a feudal monarch was limited by custom and tradition. Only when supported by his people through their representatives could he change or transgress custom in important matters without meeting at least passive resistance. Thus the *Estates General* was established because it was useful to the king and strengthened his power. With its approval, he could do things that he could not do otherwise. It was only later that the idea appeared that the *Estates General* could also control the king by refusing its approval.

Philip II Augustus, Louis IX, and the men who served them worked to increase the royal power, but they operated within the limits set by

*See p. 489.

custom. They aspired to make the Capetian state a strong feudal monarchy. Philip IV, on the other hand, had at his court a group of men who thought of the royal power in quite different terms. Trained in Roman law, they were inclined to think of the king as God's agent on earth, appointed to rule the realm with absolute power. It was his duty to rule for the benefit of the country as a whole, but only he could decide what was beneficial. These ideas were absorbed to a considerable extent by the bureaucracy as a whole. This body of royal servants developed very exalted ideas of the power not so much of the king as an individual as of the crown as an institution. Moreover, they were inclined to think of themselves as the crown—that is, as the royal government. Thus, under Philip IV, one finds both the seeds of absolute monarchy and of an all-powerful breaucracy.

57. *England: The Development of Limited Monarchy*

In England, as in France, the authority of the royal government increased during the thirteenth century, but here new forms of opposition to the exercise of arbitrary power grew up. The sons of Henry II, Richard (1189–1199) and John (1199–1216), aimed to continue their father's policy of building up the royal power. They demanded heavy reliefs, made as much money as possible out of the military service due them, and sold heiresses to the highest bidder. They continued to extend the jurisdiction of the royal courts and the common law. Richard was an attractive man but a negligent monarch. He was handsome, frank, open, and generous. A patron of poets, he wrote passable poetry himself. As the leader of a crusade, he was usually in favor with the church. Moreover, he was by far the ablest soldier of his day. But during a reign of ten years, he spent less than a year in England. War was his one delight, and his only interest in England was a source of funds for his crusade and his bitter wars with Philip Augustus. Except for a few who plotted with John and Philip while Richard was in prison in Germany, Richard had no trouble with his barons. They liked him personally and feared wholeheartedly the weight of his sword.

John was a striking contrast to his brother: he was an able king and a thoroughly unpleasant man. He worked hard at the business of government, sitting in person in his courts and at the exchequer and devising ways to improve his administration. He saw a problem that had not greatly troubled his casual brother. The towns of England were growing, trade was flourishing, and the market for agricultural products was increasing rapidly. The merchants of the towns and the members of the feudal class who drew their income from agriculture were rapidly increasing in wealth. But the revenues of the crown were largely fixed and increased very little. John was determined to have his share of the new wealth. To some extent he could do this by demanding scutage more frequently, insisting on high reliefs, and charging enormous sums for favors granted by the crown. But he also tried novel devices. Henry II had levied an income and property tax to finance a crusade, and Richard had done the same to pay his ransom. John levied such a tax to raise a war chest. He also tried collecting customs duties. Convinced that the fixed sums paid by the sheriffs for the counties were grossly inadequate, he removed the sheriffs and replaced them with custodians who received a salary and paid into the exchequer all the money they collected. In short, John was an efficient monarch who strove to increase his power and revenue. As this increase was bound to be at the expense of his barons, his policy was deeply resented.

John lacked the one thing most necessary to the prestige of a medieval king, a reputation as a valiant fighter. While he conducted successful campaigns in Scotland, Wales, and Ireland, his Continental ventures were complete failures. He lost Normandy to Philip Augustus, and his great effort to crush the French king with the aid of the emperor Otto IV ended in humiliating defeat.* Justly or not, his people called him John Softsword. He had at the same time a quality that no medieval king could afford—an inability to forgive. The best baron was turbulent and unruly. A king had to expect that during his reign he would quarrel at least once with every baron. Richard either crushed his foe completely or forgave him equally completely. John pretended to forgive but never again trusted the man he forgave. As a result, by the end of his reign, he trusted no baron and no baron trusted him.

This mutual distrust was made more acute by John's love of devious methods. Thus, when John believed that a baron would soon ask him for a castle he thought he had a right to, the king would tell his constables not to deliver the castle to anyone unless the order to do so contained a countersign such as "I take you by your big toe." Then, when the baron asked for a castle, John would cheerfully give him letters ordering its delivery to him and would even commiserate with him on the obstinacy of the constable who refused to obey. Finally, John was extremely lustful and cruel. He seduced the wives and daughters of his vassals. He pretty certainly ordered the murder of his nephew Arthur, and the wife and son of a baron who was out of favor were starved to death in a royal castle.

Throughout John's reign, individual barons or small groups with personal grievances against the king had plotted against him. When he returned defeated from his Continental campaign in the autumn of 1214, all his baronial foes joined together against him and held a great meeting to organize a revolt. With them met Stephen Langton, archbishop of Canterbury. Stephen had no reason to love John. The king had refused to accept him as archbishop and had kept him in exile for seven years. He had driven Stephen's relatives from the realm. But Stephen was one of the great men of his age. He had been professor of theology at Paris and a cardinal in the papal court. He believed that, just as the church was ruled by canon law, there should be a law to govern lay society—a law that king, barons, and people

*See p. 337.

had to obey. He urged the barons to relegate their private grievances to the background and to draw up a general plan of reform that would appeal to all the barons of the land.

Early in the spring of 1215, the barons rose in armed revolt. John could not decide what to do. At one moment he was offering to negotiate and at the next summoning troops from Gascony. Finally, with the aid of the citizens, who thoroughly hated John, the rebels occupied London. Protected by its walls, they were in a very strong military position, and John gave way. The barons met the king in the Thames River meadows near Windsor at a place called Runnymede and presented a written schedule of reforms—the so-called "Articles of the Barons." John agreed to accept the demands and had his seal affixed to the schedule. Then the expert royal clerks went to work to draw up the formal charter that would embody these reforms. This document we know as Magna Carta.*

The provisions of Magna Carta fall naturally into four groups. One of these comprises only one article, dealing with the relations between church and state. John promised the church her full rights. Then there were fifteen chapters concerning the feudal relations between the king and his vassals. John promised not to demand more than £100 for the relief for a barony or £5 for a knight's fee. He also agreed not to levy a scutage or a special aid without the consent of an assembly of all tenants-in-chief of the crown. Thirty-five chapters dealt with the procedures and practices of the royal government For instance, John promised not to try to get more revenue from the sheriffs but to accept the customary "farms," or rents, for the counties. Another chapter provided that civil cases between subjects of the king in which he had no interest would not be tried before the court that wandered about with him but in regular sessions held at Westminster. These three divisions of Magna Carta comprised the reform program of the barons. The fourth was intended to satisfy their personal desires. The barons were promised their just rights, and a committee of twenty-five elected by them was to see that they got them.

Most of the provisions of Magna Carta were of purely temporary significance. There were, however, two notable exceptions. The promise by John that, except for the three recognized occasions—the knighting of the king's eldest son, the marriage of his eldest daughter, or the payment of his ransom if he were captured—he would not levy an aid without the consent of a council composed of all his tenants-in-chief was not included in later reissues of the charter. The kings observed it in practice, however, and it became the basis for parliamentary control of taxation. Then, chapter thirty-nine stated: "No free man shall be arrested, or imprisoned, or deprived of his property, or outlawed, or exiled, or in any way destroyed nor shall we go against him or send against him unless by legal judgment of his peers or by the law of the land." This famous passage forms the basis of the Anglo-American conception of personal freedom. The government can take no action against an individual without going through the proper legal procedures—what we call "due process of law." And this prom-

*Sources, no. 71

ise was not limited to barons or knights but applied to every freeman. It is true that in 1215 well under half the population of England was free, but as time went on and freedom spread, these rights spread with it.

Despite the importance of this clause protecting all freemen from arbitrary actions of the government, the significance of Magna Carta does not lie in its precise provisions. By issuing Magna Carta, John admitted that he was subject to the law. This was of extreme importance. While one can argue that the feudal relationship was essentially a mutual contract and that all feudal suzerains were subject to feudal custom, the charter of liberties of Henry I and Magna Carta are the earliest explicit recognitions of this fact. The generations that followed John fully realized this. Whenever the barons of England felt that the king was getting too autocratic but had difficulty in finding specific abuses to accuse him of, they simply demanded that he confirm Magna Carta. By so doing he recognized the supremacy of the law of the land. Thus Magna Carta served as a perpetual reminder to English kings that they were "limited monarchs."

John's son, Henry III (1216–1272), was an exceedingly weak monarch. Throughout his reign, he was governed by friends and favorites whom he chose with little discretion. For the most part, they were foreign adventurers—relatives of him and his wife. After John's death, his queen, Isabelle, married Hugh de Lusignan, count of La Marche. Her younger sons came over to seek their fortunes at the court of their half-brother. Henry himself married Eleanor, daughter of the count of Provence, and her impecunious uncles sought soft berths in England. These relatives obtained offices and lands and also tempted Henry into costly foreign ventures. Then Henry was a pious man who could not resist the pleas of the pope, who was engaged in his bitter struggle with the emperor Frederick II of Hohenstaufen.* The pope persuaded Henry to allow him to raise large sums of money in England, and he involved the foolish king in a wild scheme to conquer Sicily for his second son—a project that came to nothing. Hence, throughout his reign, Henry needed money, and when he got it, he had neither the will power nor the wisdom to spend it well. The barons resented his favor to his foreign relatives, his subservience to the pope, and his careless extravagance. Moreover, like many weak individuals, Henry could be hasty, capricious, and arbitrary when aroused, and he frequently violated what his barons considered their rights.

Our chief interest in Henry's reign lies in the efforts of the barons to control the king for the benefit of the realm and themselves. Early in the reign, the barons confined their opposition to attempts to get the king to spend his money wisely and efficiently. When this appeared to be hopeless, they started to refuse to grant him special aids. In 1258, exasperated by the King's expensive and unsuccessful Sicilian policy, they took stronger measures under the leadership of Simon de Montfort, earl of Leicester (a son of the Simon de Montfort who led the Albigensian Crusade). They forced the king to accept a baronial justiciar to head his government and baronial control of the

*See pp. 384–386 and 389.

royal administration. This was too much for Henry, and he attempted to crush his foes. This effort ended in his defeat and capture. For several years, Simon de Montfort and his allies ruled England in Henry's name. Simon dreamed of an England governed by the feudal class working as a whole for the good of the realm, but once the victory was won, he could not hold his baronial allies together. They quarreled fiercely over the spoils and resented every attempt to limit their rapacity. Henry's son Edward took advantage of this situation to negotiate with Simon's foes, escape from custody, and gather an army about him. Edward was a man of first-rate capacity both as a soldier and as a statesmen. Moving with incredible rapidity, he surprised Simon's sons, who were marching to their father's aid, and dispersed their army. He then met and crushed Simon's forces at the great battle of Evesham. Simon was killed and his party completely destroyed.

Edward I (1272–1307) proved a formidable monarch. He ruled effectively and generally retained the support of the nobles and other leading men of the realm by consulting them in frequent councils. One of the first tasks that faced him was to recover the ground that the crown had lost during the civil wars of his father's reign. The barons had used this period of confusion to usurp privileges of all sorts—especially rights of jurisdiction. They had forbidden the sheriffs to enter their lands and had taken over their functions. They had stopped their tenants from attending the hundred courts and obliged them to carry their cases to their private courts. Edward decided to recover the royal rights usurped during the civil war and to prevent future usurpations. He ordered every lord who claimed any privilege that was legally a *franchise,* or grant from the crown, to appear before his judges and prove his right to it. The lord must either show a royal charter or prove that he had enjoyed the privilege in King Richard's reign. Actually, Edward did not deprive many lords of their franchises; he usually took a round sum of money for confirming a usurpation. But once a lord had listed the franchises he claimed, he could not claim new ones without a royal grant to support his position. Thus the usurpation of public rights by private individuals was stopped.

Another measure of Edward's stopped the growth of the feudal hierarchy and started its slow decline. By the second half of the thirteenth century, continued subinfeudation had made the feudal system incredibly complex. There could be six or seven lords between the man who actually held a piece of land in demesne and the king. This made it almost impossible to enforce feudal obligations. Edward checked this process of subinfeudation by a statute called *quia emptores.* Before this time a fief could not legally be sold. It could only be granted out as a fief to a subtenant. So, if a man wanted to acquire feudal land, he handed over a sum of money and then held the land as a fief from the original lord. Edward's statute allowed land to be bought and sold but provided that the buyer should hold it, not from the seller, but from the seller's superior lord. Thus, if Baron X held a fief from the king and sold it, then Baron X ceased to be lord of the fief and the buyer held it directly from the king. This effectively stopped the progress of subinfeudation. While there were lords and vassals until the actual abolition of the feudal system in 1660, more and more of them came to hold directly from the crown.

By Edward's reign, the English administration had become definitely divided into specialized bodies. We have seen how the exchequer was established under Henry I and how the royal courts became important under Henry II.* Although the exchequer and the *curia regis* had different functions, they shared the same personnel. The king was surrounded by a group of household officers and servants who acted as barons of the exchequer, as judges, and as councilors as the occasion might require. As time went on, however, each of these branches became specialized. There were four barons of the exchequer, who supervised accounts and decided cases dealing with the king's revenue. The deputy of the chancellor, who sealed the orders summoning debtors to pay the money they owed, became an independent officer, the *chancellor of the exchequer.* Then two distinct royal courts appeared. The *court of common pleas,* consisting of four judges, heard all civil cases between subjects. The *court of king's bench* heard all cases, whether civil or criminal, that were of interest to the king. Finally, there was a group of sworn councilors who advised the king. Another most important development of this period was the growth of the English Parliament, discussed in the following section (Representative Government: Ideas and Institutions).

During the reign of Edward, two steps were taken toward uniting all Britain in one realm. One of these was completely successful, but the other was abortive. Ever since the Norman conquest, the barons and knights of England had been waging war against the Welsh and extending their lands at the latter's expense. As early as the reign of Henry I, the lowlands of southern Wales and the rich river valleys running westward from England into Wales had been held by Norman lords. But the Welsh had held their own in their mountain fastnesses, and from time to time broke out to attack their foes. Again and again English kings led armies of knights into Wales. These armies marched along the valleys while the Welsh sat calmly on the hills out of their reach. During the civil wars of the reign of Henry III, the Welsh had aided the Montfortian party. When he came to the throne Edward was determined to crush them once and for all. He called out the feudal levy of England to move into Wales from the south and the east to drive the Welsh into their most remote hills. Then he summoned bands of infantry collected in the western shires to blockade them there. All around the central mass of mountains, he constructed a line of great castles strongly garrisoned. Before long the Welsh were forced to submit, and Wales was divided into shires. While there were to be many Welsh risings, never again were they for long free from English rule.

In 1290 the death of Margaret, the last of the elder line of the Scots royal house, gave Edward an opportunity to extend his influence to the north. There were some dozen claimants to the Scots throne, and Edward I was asked to decide who was the rightful heir. His legal

*See pp. 323–324 and 330.

experts debated long and earnestly and finally awarded the throne to John Baliol, an English noble who was descended through a female line from the brother of a Scots king. John was obliged to do homage to Edward for the kingdom of Scotland. But when the English king attempted to make his suzerainty a reality by interfering in the government of Scotland, the Scots rose and drove Baliol out. Edward invaded Scotland and soon occupied the country. A revolt led by Sir William Wallace, a Scots patriot, was crushed and Wallace hanged. Soon, however, the Scots found another leader in Robert Bruce, also an English noble, whose grandfather had been Baliol's chief rival for the crown. While Edward was busy elsewhere, Bruce made considerable headway against his troops. Edward learned of the rising and moved north to suppress it, but he died on the Scots border. This gave Robert Bruce a breathing spell. By the time Edward II (1307–1327) was ready to act against him, he had reduced all but one of the English fortresses in Scotland. Edward marched with a great many to relieve this stronghold, Stirling castle. By a small brook called Bannockburn, he was met and utterly defeated by Bruce and his army. Scotland became once more an independent state under the rule of Robert Bruce.

58. *Representative Government: Ideas and Institutions*

The most important development in English government during the reign of Edward I—the rise of Parliament—can best be understood as part of a general European movement of the thirteenth century. The growth of representative government was not a peculiarly English phenomenon. Spain, Sicily, and Hungary were developing representative assemblies at about the same time. The Scandinavian countries had similar institutions in the fourteenth century. So did the various principalities of Germany. The French *Estates General* met for the first time in 1302. The general councils of the Church were conceived of as representative bodies at least from the time of the Fourth Lateran Council of 1215. Thus the convoking of representative assemblies to participate in shaping governmental decisions became a common practice in the later Middle Ages. On the other hand, it is a highly exceptional phenomenon in the history of human government as a whole. None of the great Oriental civilizations developed such a system. There was nothing quite like it in classical Greece or Rome. The problem of why such an unusual—and evidently important—development in the art of government should have taken place in medieval Europe and not in other civilizations has been widely debated among modern historians, but so far no agreed answer has been found. It is fairly easy to understand why medieval kings never became absolute, theocratic monarchs on the Oriental model. The unruliness of the feudal barons and the persistent tensions between church and state were sufficient to prevent that development. It is more difficult to define the positive factors that stimulated the growth of representative government during the Middle Ages.

Two major lines of explanation have been put forward. The great English Whig historians of the nineteenth century were inclined to believe that the parliamentary institutions of their own day represented an ideal form of government. They believed that the innate love of liberty diffused among the primitive Teutonic tribesmen of the early Middle Ages provided the indispensable raw material from which such institutions had grown. The actual emergence of representative assemblies and their rise to a position of dominance in the state were due to the strivings of great statesmen who, through long centuries of arduous struggle, had been inspired by the ideal of parliamentary constitutionalism and had striven to embody that ideal in concrete institutions. In particular, the English Parliament came to exist in the years around 1300 because of "The defining genius, the political wisdom and the honesty of Edward I."

This interpretation is usually dismissed nowadays as obviously anachronistic because it attributes modern motives to medieval individuals. A more fashionable approach argues that institutions are not shaped by abstract ideas and ideals but by conflicts and adjustments of interests among individuals and pressure groups. Rulers seek power, which is morally neutral in itself. Governments need money. Subjects object to taxation. And this is the real stuff of politics. Thus no one in the Middle Ages conceived of an ideal of modern constitutional government and then tried to shape institutions to fit the ideal. Medieval kings summoned representative assemblies quite simply because they found it administratively convenient to do so.

Many modern historians seem to find this second set of arguments satisfyingly tough-minded and realistic. The arguments are all valid, of course; but, unfortunately, they are also mostly irrelevant. People have always been swayed by self-interest. Rulers have always wanted to increase their power. Governments always need more money. But these circumstances have not normally led to the growth of representative insitutions of government. That development took place only in medieval Europe. Calling attention to the features that are common to all political regimes does not begin to account for the peculiar features of the medieval system. The real problem is to explain why medieval kings—unlike other rulers—did in fact find it "administratively convenient" to summon representative assemblies. Any adequate explanation must involve some consideration of the underlying medieval ideas and presuppositions about society and government. But if historians are to avoid anachronistic arguments, they have to explain how the relevant presuppositions grew out of the structure of medieval society itself, not out of some fancied anticipation of modern ideals.

Medieval rulers evidently acted from a variety of motives in calling representative assemblies into existence. When the emperor Frederick II summoned the Council of Melfi, his intention was to exact a recognition of his own sovereignty and to enact a code of legislation.

The French *Estates General* was first convoked to mobilize national opinion in support of the king's ecclesiastical policies. In England, the need of the king to gain consent to taxation was an important factor in the summoning of Parliaments. General councils of the church were concerned with reform legislation, with defining the orthodox faith, and with matters of high ecclesiastical politics. But always there was a presupposition that certain major innovative measures could be carried through effectively only by the very highest authority in a given society—and that that authority inhered in a monarch surrounded by an assembly which adequately represented the society as a whole. No such presupposition existed in the ancient Roman Empire, or in Byzantium, or in the states of Islam.

To understand how such a way of thinking grew up in the first place, we must recall the unusual combination of influences—Christian, Roman, and Teutonic—that went into the making of medieval civilization. The underlying idea of the sovereignty of a representative assembly was first formulated by the church lawyers of the twelfth century in their discussions on general councils as embodying the consensus of the Christian community. The Dominicans had further shown how such ideas could be woven into the fabric of a complex system of representative government.* But medieval kings were under no compulsion to imitate such ecclesiastical patterns, and they would never have undertaken similar experiments of their own unless such experiments promised immediate practical advantages. In fact, they proved very useful indeed. A major problem for medieval kings was the need to make new laws and raise new taxes (a need which grew out of the changing structure of society itself) in the face of an obstinate resistance to all deliberate innovation on the part of their subjects. In the early eleventh century, the idea of a king consciously abolishing old laws and making new ones was hardly conceivable. After the revival of Roman law and the growth of canon law, it became evident that legislative innovation could be justified by Roman theories of sovereignty. Moreover, a knowledge of such theories was not confined to scholars in the universities. The bureaucracies of medieval kings were largely staffed by men with legal training. (A recent investigation of the careers of sixty-one middle-ranking administrators in the government of Edward I of England revealed that a majority of them had studied either Roman law or canon law or both.) Such men were convinced that their kings could legislate. But attempts to make new law could be thwarted in practice by the popular, ingrained conviction, rooted in feudal and manorial custom, and going back ultimately to Teutonic folkways, which held that law was not a command imposed from above but a spontaneous outgrowth of the whole life of the community.

Faced with this problem, secular lawyers began to discuss the questions raised earlier by the canonists about the right relationship between ruler and community.† They often concluded that a ruler could indeed enact laws but that major measures required the counsel and consent of the whole "community of the realm." This view was ex-

*See p. 371.

†See pp. 318–319.

pressed very clearly by the greatest English jurist of the thirteenth century, Henry Bracton. Bracton was not a theorist writing for other theorists but a royal judge who played an active role in the reorganization of English government in the years around 1260. He declared repeatedly that the king had no equal or superior in the realm of England. He knew the Roman law maxim "What the Prince wills has the force of law," and applied it to the English king. Yet he also wrote that the king was "under the law." The apparent paradox was explained by Bracton's definition of law. The king's will made law, but not the king's will alone:

> Whatever is justly defined and approved by the counsel and consent of the magnates and the common agreement of the realm, with the authority of the prince or king preceeding—that has the force of law.

Once established, such laws could not be changed except by the common consent of those who had promulgated them.

Bracton had a clear idea that law should be shaped by the community of the realm, but he still thought of the political community as constituted solely by the feudal baronage. By the second half of the thirteenth century, however, the merchants of the cities and the country knights were evidently an important part of the national community. Their cooperation could be useful in securing the acceptance of new laws and new taxes. But if they were to be drawn into a central assembly, new procedures were needed. The feudal barons could all attend in person; large-scale communities had to be represented.

Even before the thirteenth century, there were many precedents in different lands for rulers consulting with nominees of local groups. Kings often summoned groups of merchants from the cities to advise them on fiscal matters, and in England particularly, there was a tradition of chosen spokespeople acting on behalf of rural communities. As early as 1086 a jury was summoned from each village to give information to the compilers of Domesday Book. In 1213 King John summoned four knights from each county "to discuss the affairs of the realm." Often knights were chosen in county courts to "bear the record" of the court to the king's judges at Westminster.

All these practices help to explain the later growth of representative assemblies. And yet there is an enormous gap between sending messengers to report on local affairs and electing representatives empowered to bind communities by their decisions. The idea of representation in this full, legal sense seems to have come from ecclesiastical law. Much of the day-to-day business of a professional canonist dealt with litigation between ecclesiastical corporations like monasteries and cathedral chapters, which had to plead in court through designated representatives. Hence a sophisticated jurisprudence about the delegation of authority by corporate bodies grew up at just about the same time that the need to summon representatives from large communities was becoming apparent in the political sphere. The key

Philip IV the Fair presiding over a *parlement*, ca. 1322. Nobles and churchmen sit to the right and left below the king; above the two groups are their coats of arms. Miniature from *Actes du Procès de Robert d'Artois*, Ms. French 18437, fol. 2r. *Bibliothèque Nationale, Paris*

phrases in the canonists' discussions were the technical terms *full power (plena potestas)* and *full authority (plena auctoritas)*. A community was irrevocably bound by the acts of a representative when it appointed him with a mandate of *plena potestas* or *plena auctoritas*. By the early thirteenth century, the phrases were being used in writs of summons to secular assemblies as well as in ecclesiastical documents. The first use of *plena potestas* in this way in England came in 1283, and it was regularly used in writs of summons to Parliament from 1294 onward. The formula adopted in 1294 continued to be used in England with only minor variations until 1872. Similar formulas are found in the summonses to many Continental assemblies.

We can now consider in more detail against this general background of medieval ideas and practices the growth of the English Parliament in particular. Parliament provides the best example for illustrating the development of medieval representative government for two reasons. An unusually large body of documents survives in England, from which we can trace the development of parliamentary institutions in some detail. Moreover, the English Parliament was the most sturdy and enduring of the medieval assemblies. The vitality of Parliament made possible the survival of the medieval tradition of representative government beyond the Middle Ages until it could take a new lease on life in the modern world.

The word *parliamentum* was coined in the thirteenth century. At first it did not refer to a particular institution but could be used to describe any "parley," or discussion, between two or more persons. In the 1240s the word began to be applied to meetings of the English Great Council, occasions when the king, together with his judges, advisers, and principal officers of state, met with the great barons and prelates of the land. The original Parliament thus did not contain elected representatives, but the barons no longer thought of themselves simply as individuals acting each for himself. They realized that they formed a corporate group with the duty of acting for the whole realm. In the reform movement of 1258, the barons often referred to themselves as "the community of the realm."

In 1265 Simon de Montfort summoned two knights from every shire and two burgesses from every borough to meet with the prelates and barons. This was the first time that elected representatives attended an English Parliament. Simon's purpose was to gain the support of the knights and townspeople at a time when his baronial supporters were inclined to desert him. Since Simon was denounced as a traitor and defeated and killed the following year, his action obviously did not constitute a binding precedent for the future. However, the next king, Edward I, made a practice of holding Parliaments regularly and of summoning representatives to them occasionally. There was, for instance, a great assembly in 1275 with representatives in attendance that enacted legislation and granted the king substantial new taxes. The prelates and the barons each received a personal letter summoning him to the meeting. Representatives were summoned through letters addressed to the sheriffs commanding them to have elections held in the county court and in every borough of the county.

All the motives that stimulated medieval kings to summon representative assemblies influenced the policy of Edward I. He had much legislation to enact. He became engaged in great wars for which he had to stir up national support. Moreover, the wars were expensive and he needed frequent grants of taxes. Taxation in medieval England was of two general types. Aids based on the knight's fee or on income were levied on the rural population, and tallage was collected from the royal demesne, which included most towns. Magna Carta had laid down that consent was needed for the aids. It was not technically needed for tallages, but ever since the time of Henry II, tallage had been levied on the towns by means of bargains with the taxpayers. The king's agents would go to a town and negotiate for a grant of tallage. Edward found that the process was simplified by summoning representatives of the towns to a general meeting to agree to a tax. Toward the end of his reign, as Edward became hard-pressed for revenue, he summoned representatives to his Parliaments more and more frequently.

In 1295 he held a particularly full assembly which, for no apparent reason, is usually called the Model Parliament. Representatives of the countries, cities, and boroughs and of the lower clergy met with the secular and ecclesiastical lords. This meeting did not, in fact, form a model for future Parliaments, because the representatives of the lower clergy ceased to attend Parliament in the fourteenth century and made grants of taxes in their own separate assembly of Convocation. A more important Parliament met in 1297. By then Edward had become involved in a hopelessly expensive tangle of wars. He angered the merchants and nobles in 1296 by seeking to impose new custom duties without consent, and the following year the leaders of Parliament insisted on a reissue of Magna Carta with an explicit emphasis on the right of consent to taxation. There is an interesting change of language in this so-called *Confirmatio* of 1297.* It is addressed to the "Archbishops, bishops, abbots, priors, . . . earls, barons, . . . and the whole community of the land." Forty years earlier, the prelates and barons had thought that they *were* the community of the land. From this time onward, it was taken for granted in England that elected representatives had a legal right of consent to taxation.

Besides granting taxes, deliberating about politics, and enacting laws, the Parliaments of Edward I also transacted a great deal of routine judicial business. A session of Parliament provided a very convenient opportunity for individuals and communities to petition the king for redress of their grievances. The right to petition was valued and very extensively employed. Some historians have even maintained that Parliament was "essentially" a court of judicature and that all its other activities were "inessential." But this seems an exaggeration. It is proper to insist that Parliament was in a sense a court. Medieval people themselves came to call it "the High Court of Parliament." But the phrase is meaningful only if we remember that, in the Middle Ages, the word *court* could designate an assembly capable of handling any judicial, legislative, financial, and administrative business that was brought before it. The exercise of royal jurisdiction in Parliament was a source of strength to the institution and was rather unusual. In France, for instance, the judicial *parlement* and the representative *Estates General* always remained quite separate from one another. Another unusual feature of Parliament was the separate representation of the lower feudal nobility through elected "knights of the shire." In other countries, members of the lesser aristocracy were often considered to be represented by the heads of their families who sat in the estate of nobility. The English system made possible the eventual emergence of a powerful House of Commons.

We should not exaggerate the importance of the Commons in the

*Sources, no. 72

reign of Edward I. It was enormously important for the future that representatives were from time to time incorporated into meetings of Parliament. But, when Edward died in 1307, everything was still in a state of flux. Although Edward had summoned Parliament often because he found it useful to do so, there was no constitutional obligation on his successors to continue the pratice. The ultimate structure and composition of Parliament remained undetermined. An assembly that everyone would recognize as a Parliament could still meet at the beginnings of the fourteenth century without any elected representatives (though the practice of including them was becoming more and more common). When the representatives did attend, they played a very subordinate role in the proceedings. Virtually the only duty they carried out was to consent to taxation, and often, when they had fulfilled this function, they were summarily dismissed, while the prelates and barons stayed on to discuss high matters of state. Always the initiative lay with the king and the great lords. But still, when we have made all the necessary reservations, it remains true that the English Parliament, one of the most influential political institutions in the history of the Western world, had begun to grow into a real organ of government by the end of the thirteenth century.

READING SUGGESTIONS

* *B. Tierney,* Sources *and* Readings, *vol. I, nos. 66–72; vol. II, nos. 25–28.*

For the thirteenth-century Empire the works of Barraclough and Thompson, cited in Chapter IX, should be supplemented by E. Kantorowicz, *Frederick II* (London, 1931); G. Masson, *Frederick II of Hohenstaufen* (London, 1957); and C. C. Bayley, *The Formation of the German College of Electors in the Thirteenth Century* (Toronto, 1949). On Italy, see J. Larner, *The Lords of Romagna* (Ithaca, NY, 1965); W. F. Butler, *The Lombard Communes* (New York, 1966); and D. P. Waley, *The Papal State in the Thirteenth Century* (London, 1961). The works of Callaghan, Merriman, and Jackson, cited in Chapter XI, should be consulted for Spain. See also J. L. Schneidman, *The Rise of the Catalan Empire, 1200–1350* (New York, 1970). On France, besides Fawtier and Petit-Dutaillis, cited in Chapter IX, see J. R. Strayer and C. H. Taylor, *Studies in Early French Taxation* (Cambridge, MA, 1939), and C. T. Wood, *The French Appanages and the Capetian Monarchy* (Cambridge, MA, 1966). The best introduction by far to the reign of Louis IX is Joinville's *History of St. Louis,* J. Evans (trans.) (Oxford, England, 1938), or R. Hague (New York, 1955). See also M. W. Labarge, *Saint Louis* (London, 1968). Sayles' *Medieval Foundations,* cited in Chapter IX, covers thirteenth-century England. A more detailed account is F. M. Powicke, *The Thirteenth Century* (Oxford, England, 1953). There are three good biographies of King John: * S. Painter, *The Reign of King John* (Baltimore, 1949); W. L. Warren, *King John* (London, 1961); and J. Appleby, *John, King of England* (New York, 1958). A good modern work on Magna Carta with references to the extensive earlier literature is J. C. Holt, *Magna Carta* (Cambridge, England, 1965). Differing views on Stephen Langton's role are presented in F. M. Powicke, *Stephen Langton,* and in H. G Richardson and G. O. Sayles, *The Governance of Medieval England* (Edinburgh, 1963). On the baronial reform, see R. F. Treharne, *The Baronial*

Plan of Reform (Manchester, England, 1932), and C. Bémont, *Simon de Montfort* (Oxford, England, 1930). On Edward I, see L. F. Salzmann, *Edward I* (London, 1968). For source material, see C. Stephenson and F. G. Marcham, *Sources of English Constitutional History* (New York, 1937).

The theory of representative government is discussed in several works on medieval political thought. The most detailed is the Carlyles' work, cited in the Introduction. Good one-volume surveys are * O. von Gierke, *Political Theories of the Middle Ages* (Cambridge, England, 1900); C. H. McIlwain, *Growth of Political Thought in the West* (New York, 1932); * J. B. Morrall, *Political Thought in Medieval Times* (London, 1960); * W. Vilmann, *A History of Political Thought: The Middle Ages* (Baltimore, 1965); * J. R Strayer, *On the Medieval Origins of the Modern State* (Princeton, NJ, 1970); and A. P. Monahan, *Consent, Coercion and Limit: The Medieval Origins of Parliamentary Democracy* (Toronto, 1987). * T. N. Bisson, *Medieval Representative Institutions* (Hinsdale, IL, 1973) is a useful collection of essays. More specialized are F. Kern, *Kingship and Law* (Oxford, England, 1939); E. Kantorowicz, *The King's Two Bodies* (Princeton, 1957); G. Post, *Studies in Medieval Legal Thought* (Princeton, 1964); A. Black, *Guilds and Civil Society in European Political Thought* (Ithaca, NY, 1984); M. Wilks, *The Problem of Sovereignty in the Later Middle Ages* (Cambridge, England, 1963); and B. Tierney, *Religion, Law, and the Growth of Constitutional Thought* (Cambridge, England, 1982). E. Lewis, *Medieval Political Ideas,* 2 vols. (New York, 1954) provides a good selection of translated source material. For representative institutions in particular regions, see A. Marongiu, *Medieval Parliaments: A Comparative Study* (London, 1968), which deals mostly with Italy; T. N. Bisson, *Assemblies and Representation in Languedoc* (Princeton, 1964); J. F. O'Callaghan, *The Cortes of Castile-Leon, 1188–1350* (Philadelphia, 1988); and M. V. Clarke, *Medieval Representation and Consent* (London, 1936). The labyrinthine literature on the English Parliament is well summarized in * G. L. Haskins, *Growth of English Representative Government* (Philadelphia, 1948), and P. Spufford, *Origins of the English Parliament* (London, 1967).

chapter

XVIII

The World of Thought

A characteristic intellectual activity of the thirteenth century was the creation of works of synthesis that sought to present all the detailed knowledge in a given field as a harmonious whole. On the highest level, works like the *Summa Theologiae* of Thomas Aquinas drew materials from half a dozen fields that we should regard as separate disciplines—for example, philosophy, theology, law, psychology, physics—and sought to integrate them into unified systems of knowledge. The most important educational institutions in which such work was carried on were the medieval universities. Thirteenth-century philosophy is often called "scholastic" because it was developed in the schools by individuals who earned their living as teachers. During this period, the greatest advances in knowledge were often found in works intended to be used as university textbooks. Of course, an opus like the *Summa Theologiae* was no mean textbook.

Before considering the universities, we should note that medieval education cannot be described solely in terms of academic institutions. Every baronial household was a school for young nobles. The baron saw that the sons of his vassals and relatives who had been entrusted to him were given the training required to make them good knights. When a young man was formally dubbed a knight, he graduated from school and was ready to take his place in society. The baron's wife supervised the education of the girls and prepared them for marriage. In the towns the apprentice system of the guilds performed a similar function. The apprentices lived in their masters' house and learned the trade under their supervision. Apprentices passed their final examinations when they completed their "masterpiece" and were formally admitted to the guild as a master craftsman. The same system carried over into the academic world. Students of the liberal arts were, in effect, apprentices of an established master. When they had completed the necessary studies and given evidence of the necessary proficiency, they in turn became masters. In this case they were "Masters of Arts."

59. *The First Universities*

The university as we know it today—a community of scholars and students offering regular courses of study leading to recognized degrees—had its origins in the late twelfth and early thirteenth centuries. The word *universitas* meant basically "all" in a collective sense and could be used for any group of people cooperating for a common end. It was freely used for the members of a guild. One finds it applied to the barons of England and even the English people as a whole. The universities were essentially educational guilds. In northern Europe they were guilds of masters, while in Italy and southern Europe they were student guilds. In both cases they were formed to protect their members and to further their common educational interests. As masters or students could form such cooperative organizations without specific permission from a prince and without attracting the attention of contemporary chroniclers, no foundation date can be set for the three oldest universities, Bologna, Paris, and Oxford. As a rule, one can only say when they received some form of official recognition. Later universities were established by princes, and hence their foundation dates can be easily determined.

Masters of rhetoric taught continuously in Italy during the early Middle Ages. Naturally, these were most numerous in the more important towns. Bologna was particularly noted for the effective teaching of the art of expression, and a number of important works on rhetoric were produced by its masters. Then, in the eleventh century, Italian lawyers began to become discontented with the simple manuals of Roman law that they were using and sought a deeper knowledge of their subject. This enthusiasm was increased with the rediscovery of the *Corpus Juris Civilis* of Justinian. As we have seen, Italian students were soon exploring the entire body of Roman law, and the chief center of these studies was Bologna. Late in the eleventh century, there are references to a master named Pepo, who was famous as a teacher at Bologna. But the real founder of Bologna's reputation as a center of legal studies was Irnerius, who was apparently the first to use a comprehensive knowledge of the Roman law in commentaries on the legal codes actually in use. Gratian, whom we have already discussed as the organizer and codifier of the canon law, worked at Bologna in the middle of the twelfth century. As medical studies had already spread through Italy from the famous medical school at Salerno, Bologna in the late twelfth century had at least four curriculums: rhetoric, civil law, canon law, and medicine.

The fame of the schools of Bologna drew students from all over western Europe, who flocked there to study under the various masters. As individuals, these students could not protect themselves from being overcharged by landlords and shopkeepers as well as by the masters, and they soon founded two guilds for mutual protection. The students from outside Italy formed the Ultramontane guild, or *nation,* while the Italians composed the Cismontane. Each nation was headed by an elected *rector.* Soon the masters teaching the different subjects formed guilds of their own, but the student guilds were dominant in all questions except the requirements for degrees. The masters, or professors, were obliged to swear obedience to the rectors, had to obtain their permission to leave town, and were fined for beginning a lecture late or for continuing it too long. At first the masters subsisted entirely on student fees. Later, salaried chairs were established in the various subjects.

The University of Paris was formed by masters attracted to the French capital by the fame of the cathedral school of Notre Dame. The chancellor, who was the official of the chapter entrusted with the supervision of the school and with the authority to issue licenses to teach, permitted qualified masters to conduct lectures in houses near the cathedral on the Ile de la Cité. Actually, the only connection between these masters and the cathedral school proper was that they obtained their licenses from the chancellor and could be deprived of them by him. Each master rented a suitable room, gave his lectures, and collected fees from his students, but the chancellor gave the students their licenses to teach and their degrees. When William of Champeaux and Peter Abelard held their controversy on the nature of universals, they were both masters teaching under the shelter of Notre Dame.

There was bound to be friction between the chancellor and the masters, especially when the latter included such independent spirits as Abelard. On a hill on the left bank of the Seine directly opposite the Ile de la Cité stood the monastery of St. Geneviève. Its site is now occupied by the Pantheon, which is decorated with murals depicting St. Geneviève's life and good works. Masters who quarreled with the chancellor often moved over the river to teach under the protection of the abbot. As time went on, the land about this monastery and the slope leading down to the Seine became the site of the schools of Paris, and the Ile de la Cité was largely deserted by the masters. There today the University of Paris still stands, in the midst of the Latin quarter.

By the close of the twelfth century, the masters teaching at Paris had formed a guild, or university. In 1200 a charter of Philip II Augustus granting privileges to the masters and students of Paris mentions the university, and within ten years a university official called a *proctor* is referred to. By 1219 the masters of arts had divided themselves into four nations, each headed by a proctor: France, Normandy, Picardy, and England. About the middle of the thirteenth century, there appeared an elected head of all the masters of arts called the rector. The masters of theology, canon law, and medicine formed separate faculties headed by deans. The rector was in theory simply the head of the faculty of arts, but since this was much the largest, he claimed to be the chief officer of the university and, after a long and bitter struggle with the dean of the faculty of theology, was recognized as such.

In England the town of Oxford was centrally located geographically and, during the first half of the twelfth century, wandering masters from Paris and even Bologna occasionally lectured there. The more or less continuous hostilities between Henry II and Louis VII of France made the position of the English scholars at Paris rather difficult, and in 1167 Henry ordered them all to come home. This may well have marked the establishment of Oxford as a large-scale center of schools, though the fact has never been proved. Certainly by 1185 Giraldus Cambrensis read one of his works before a large assembly of masters and students, and by 1209 a perhaps overenthusiastic chronicler estimated the number of students in Oxford at 3,000. In 1214 one first hears of the head of the university called the chancellor. For a time, the masters were divided into two nations, a northern and a southern, headed by proctors; but before the end of the thirteenth century, the nations were abolished, although the two proctors remained as university officials. Unlike Paris, the superior faculties at Oxford had no deans and little separate organization. The chancellor and proctors were the officials of the university as a whole, and most of the functions of government were carried out in general assemblies of all the masters.

The origins of Cambridge are extremely obscure, but it seems clear that it was founded by migrants from Oxford and Paris. As the early universities had no buildings but simply rented the facilities they needed it was easy for the masters and students to move. Several times emigrations from Oxford resulted from quarrels with the town or with the royal government, and some of the migrants seem to have settled at Cambridge. In 1230 the students of Paris had a truly magnificent quarrel with the Queen Regent, Blanche of Castile, and the papal legate who was assisting her in governing the realm for her infant son. Spouting scurrilous poems about the relations between the queen and the legate, the members of the university left Paris *en masse.* Many went to Angers, then held by Blanche's bitter baronial foe, Peter of Dreux, duke of Brittany, but others went to Cambridge.

In the thirteenth, fourteenth, and fifteenth centuries, many universities were founded. In 1222 a migration from Bologna started a university at Padua. In 1224 Frederick II established at Naples the first university to be created by princely command. Six years later, the pope founded one at Toulouse to aid in the suppression of the Albigensian heretics. At the end of the thirteenth century, universities were also established in Spain and Portugal. During the fourteenth century, seven were founded in Italy, four in France, and five in Germany. In the fifteenth century, there were seven new establishments in France and a number of others in Italy and Germany.

Although the universities of Paris, Oxford, and Cambridge differed in many ways, their major characteristics were essentially the same and can be discussed in general terms. Each of the universities conducted a long struggle to become independent of both ecclesiastical and lay authorities. As all the masters and students wore the clerical tonsure and were in orders, they were theoretically exempt from arrest or punishment by the secular government. Actually, the heads of the

Amaury de Bène teaching at the University of Paris, detail of a minature from the *Chroniques de France ou de St. Denis,* French, early 14th century, Ms. Roy. 16 G. VI, fol. 368v. *Reproduced by permission of the British Library Board*

universities obtained for themselves extensive secular authority. The ways in which they attained this end were much the same. A student would commit some offense—tear a wine shop to pieces or rape a woman. The townsmen and their officials would try to arrest the student. Then there would be a riot, sometimes on a grand scale. On one occasion, the students of Oxford were besieged for several days by an armed mob. Since the students were also armed, the contest was bitter and was only brought to an end by the arrival of the royal troops. After a riot, the university officials would appeal to the king, and he nearly always solved the dispute by giving the head of the university increased secular power. If the king hesitated, the university could usually rely on papal support. In the end, the university always won. The chancellor of Oxford won full jurisdiction over the masters, the students, and their servants. All quarrels over the price of food and lodging between students and townfolk came before him. The rector of the university of Paris also had jurisdiction over all who depended on him. In addition, he had supervision of the guilds that supplied things specially needed by the university, such as booksellers, ink makers, and paper sellers.

When the university of Paris first appeared, the granting of degrees and licenses to teach was in the hands of the chancellor of the chapter of Notre Dame, and the bishop of Paris had ecclesiastical jurisdiction over the masters and students. After a long, fierce struggle involving many appeals to the pope, the powers of bishop and chancellor were reduced to pure formalities. The bishop delegated his jurisdiction to the rector, and although the chancellor continued to give licenses, he was forbidden to refuse them to anyone presented to him by the faculties. Oxford was even more successful. The bishop of Lincoln lived a long way from Oxford, and his local representative, the archdeacon of Oxford, was no match for the chancellor of the university, an official chosen by the masters. Soon the chancellor had complete ecclesiastical jurisdiction over the masters and students.

In order to be admitted to a university, a student was expected to prove his ability to read and write Latin, but the examinations were very casual, and many students were poorly prepared. It was to improve this situation that William of Wykeham founded Winchester College as a preparatory school for New College in Oxford. Once admitted, the student started work on grammar, rhetoric, and logic (the *trivium*). The master would read the text of a work such as the *Institutes* of Priscian with comments made on the text by his more noted predecessors, and then add his own comments. This process was described as "hearing" a book. At Paris, when a student had heard two books on grammar and five on logic, he became a bachelor of arts. He was then a sort of apprentice teacher and could instruct others aspiring for that degree. He was also required to study the other "liberal arts"—arithmetic, geometry, music, and astronomy (the *quadrivium*). Five or six years of such work led to a master of arts degree. In addition to hearing books, the student was expected to read a few. At Oxford a candidate for a degree had to provide a certain number of masters to swear that he had heard and read the required works.*

After qualifying as a master of arts, a student could either leave the university, begin to teach the liberal arts, or embark on the lengthy course of study leading to a degree in law, medicine, or theology. Law was taught by the method described above—the reading of texts and commentaries by the master, who added his own comments, which he hoped would in time be used by his successors. In medicine the students heard two types of works, those on theory and those on practice. There was no actual practice in our sense and, of course, no laboratories. The most esteemed curriculum was theology, and to obtain the doctor's degree was a real achievement. A master of arts spent four years listening to lectures on the Bible and two more hearing discourses on Peter Lombard's *Book of Sentences* to become a bachelor of divinity. He then studied six more years, which were also chiefly devoted to the Bible and the *Sentences*, to receive his license to teach theology. It usually required another year to be formally accepted as a doctor and installed in the doctor's chair. During most of these years of study, the student took part in many "disputations," or public debates, on points of theology. Participation in a certain number of these was required for the degree. He also, as a rule, had to preach a number of sermons. Although theology was revered as the "queen of the sciences," very few medieval scholars survived this grueling course of study. Medieval theologians were always complaining that most students preferred the more lucrative professions of law and medicine.

*Sources, no. 77

The intellectual vitality of the universities was maintained by a constant influx of new materials into the curriculum. Among the seven liberal arts, the *quadrivium* was transformed by new forms of mathematical study. Euclid's *Geometry* was translated into Latin before the middle of the twelfth century, and the Arabic sciences of trigonometry, algebra, and arithmetic, with our familiar "arabic" numerals (derived originally from India), became known in the second half of the century. Work in the *trivium* became essentially a study of Aristotelian philosophy after the translations discussed in the next section had been made. The medical doctors used translations of Galen and Hippocrates made toward the end of the twelfth century. The theologians had to cope with new dogmatic decrees issued by popes and general councils. Canon law was constantly growing and changing as more and more new ecclesiastical legislation was promulgated. The decrees of popes and councils in the century after Gratian were gathered together in an authoritative codification known as the *Decretals*, which was promulgated by Pope Gregory IX in 1234. The principal work of the academic canonists in the mid-thirteenth century was to expound and interpret this collection. The greatest commentaries on the *Decretals* were written by Hostiensis (ca. 1200–1271), who finished his career as cardinal-bishop of Ostia, and by Sinibaldo de Fieschi (ca. 1200–1254), who became Pope Innocent IV. Subsequent collections of decretals, promulgated in 1298 and 1317, completed the official *Corpus Juris Canonici*. The *corpus* of ancient Roman law could not grow in the same way, of course (though jurists solemnly appended the decrees of medieval emperors to the legislation of Justinian), but toward the end of the thirteenth century, the study of civil law found a new orientation. Instead of simply trying to explicate the old texts of Justinian, the jurists concentrated rather on adapting Roman law doctrines so as to make them serve the needs of their own society more effectively. The greatest figure in this school of "post-glossators" was Bartolus of Sassoferato (1313–1357).

In the second half of the thirteenth century, a number of pious and benevolent men and women began to be troubled by the plight of the poor student. Lodging and meals were expensive, and many could not afford them. These benefactors founded houses where poor students could be fed and lodged either for nothing or for very low fees. In order to ensure some degree of good behavior in these houses, there was usually a provision for the support of one or more masters to live with the students. When a student wanted help in his studies, he sought the aid of one of these masters resident in his house. Thus came into being the colleges that play so important a part in the history of these three universities. One of the first colleges at Paris was founded by Robert de Sorbon, confessor of Louis IX, in 1258, and the Sorbonne is still famous. By 1500 there were some sixty colleges at Paris. In 1264 Walter of Merton, bishop of Rochester, founded Merton College at Oxford, and at about the same time John Baliol, a great lord of northern England, established Baliol College. The first college at Cambridge was Peterhouse, founded in 1284. The colleges were well endowed with lands and rents. Often the endowment included the right of presentation to a number of churches, which could be bestowed on masters who had taken priestly orders. In the later Middle Ages, university lectures became less important, and the colleges took over most of the work of instruction.

The students of the Middle Ages were not unlike those of today.* Some studied and some did not. Many drank and wenched. Most were in perpetual need of money. We have some of the handbooks containing model letters for the use of students. Many of these letters are examples of different excuses for obtaining money from parents, relatives, or patrons, but others show how to invite a girl to supper. As the Middle Ages was a time of violence, both masters and students were inclined to be turbulent. A German master who had slain several of his colleagues was finally dismissed for stabbing one to death in a faculty meeting. A professor at Oxford was charged with getting his students to kill a priest who had offended him. The Oxford rules forbade students to bring bows and arrows to class. Bloody riots between students and townspeople were fairly frequent. Robberies and burglaries by students were all too common. It is important to notice, however, that it was not too difficult to acquire the status of a student and that it was a tempting cloak for individuals who were essentially criminals. The students were exempt from the secular authorities, and the ecclesiastical courts were notoriously mild. In Paris of the fifteenth century, the worst criminal section of the city lay just behind the university, and many of its inhabitants masqueraded as students.

Despite its many and obvious defects, the university performed signal services for medieval civilization. It supported scholars and supplied an environment conducive to learning. Most of the eminent scholars of the later Middle Ages were attached to a university. Then, the various faculties served as authorities on their respective subjects: a pope once apologized for deciding a theological point without consulting the faculty of theology at Paris. The graduates of the universities staffed the learned professions. The masters of arts who did not continue to teach in the universities became the masters of schools or administrators. The doctors of civil law either practiced in the lands where Roman law was used or became the servants of secular princes. The canon lawyers always carried on the enormous business of the ecclesiastical courts. The doctorate of thoelogy led either to a professorship or to preferment in the church. In short, it seems most unlikely that the general development of civilization that marked the later Middle Ages could have taken place without the universities.

60. Muslim and Jewish Thought: The Recovery of Aristotle

We have mentioned that a number of works of Greek science first appeared in Latin translations during the twelfth century. By far the most important result of this work of translation was the introduction

*Sources, no. 78

into Western thought of the whole *corpus* of Aristotelian writings. The content and structure of thirteenth-century scholastic philosophy grew out of attempts to assimilate Aristotelian thought into a framework of Christian doctrine. Hence we need to understand how this problem first arose for medieval thinkers.

After the fall of the Roman Empire, the only works of Aristotle that continued to be known in the West were the elementary logical treatises translated by Boethius.* Excellent Greek manuscripts of Aristotle's works survived in Byzantium, but they did not inspire any creative tradition of philosophical thinking there. The situation was different in the Mohammedan world. The Arabs found schools of Greek philosophy well established in the lands of Hellenistic culture that they conquered. They absorbed the learning of those schools, made it their own, and developed it extensively. And it was primarily through contacts with the Arab world that western Christians eventually recovered the whole heritage of Greek philosophy.

In the period from 750 to 900, all of Aristotle's works were translated into Arabic, some directly from the Greek, some from Syriac versions. A number of Neoplatonic works were similarly translated and mistakenly attributed to Aristotle. From the tenth to the twelfth centuries, a series of great thinkers in the Islamic world, both Jews and Arabs, strove to interpret these works and to harmonize their doctrines with the monotheistic religions of Judaism and Islam. This was by no means easy. Aristotle's philosophy presented a deterministic universe that had existed from all eternity. It seemed to exclude both an initial creation through a personal God and subsequent interventions of divine providence in human history. Again, Aristotle's teaching raised difficulties about the immortality of the soul. In his philosophy—as in Plato's—all substances consisted of matter and form, but for Aristotle, the forms did not exist separately in a realm of their own. The human mind new them only as inhering in matter. (Peter Abelard, without knowing of Aristotle's metaphysics, reached an essentially similar solution to the problem of universals.†) For Aristotle, the soul was the form of the person. It was hard to explain, then, how the soul could exist separately after the death of the body. Plato had plainly taught the immortality of the soul. Aristotle's teaching was at best ambiguous.

Among the Arabic and Jewish philosophers, there were four of especial importance for the Western scholars of the thirteenth century. These were Avicebron (Solomon Ibn Gabirol, 1021–1070), Maimonides (Moses ben Maimun, 1135–1204), Avicenna (Ibn Sina, 980–1037), and Averroës (Ibn Rushd, 1126–1198). Avicebron's distinctive contribution was a doctrine called "hylomorphism," which became a subject of burning controversy at Paris two centuries after its author had died. The doctrine held that spiritual substances, for example, the human soul, consisted of matter and form as did corporeal bodies (though with a different kind of "spiritual matter"). By this theory, it was easy to understand how the soul could exist separately from the body after death but almost impossible to explain how

*See p. 80.
†See p. 309.

soul and body could ever be united to form a single person. Maimonides was a profoundly learned Talmudic scholar who labored to reconcile Aristotle with the religion of the Old Testament. He produced proofs for the existence of God similar to those of Thomas Aquinas but also introduced allegorical interpretations of Scriptural texts that aroused the suspicions of more conservative rabbis. Avicenna taught a Neoplatonic doctrine of emanation as the source of all being. From a single divine source a creative intelligence emanated, from this a lesser intelligence, and so on down a chain terminating in the material world. This doctrine was hardly compatible with the Old Testament account of creation accepted by Mohammed.

The last of the great Arabic philosophers, Averroës, set himself to present the pure doctrine of Aristotle without any compromise or corruptions. He strongly emphasized the eternity of the world, that is, the doctrine that the universe never had a beginning in time. He also denied the immortality of the individual soul. For Averroës, there was only one single active intellect which operated in separate human beings. Individuals simply passed away; only the universal intellect persisted. These doctrines obviously contradicted the Koran. Averroës declared therefore that the Koran expressed only such approximations to truth as common people could grasp. For the philosopher, there was a higher order of truth to be attained by pure reason. These views were violently attacked by orthodox Mohammedans, and at the end of his life Averroës was disgraced and exiled.

Christian authors first came to know Aristotle's works from Arabic rather than Byzantine sources presumably because, among the Arabs, they encountered a vigorous living tradition of Aristotelian philosophy. Certainly, nearly all the twelfth-century translations of Aristotle into Latin came from areas where Christians and Mohammedans lived side by side. A few were made in Sicily, but the greatest center for translations was Toledo in Spain. This had several results. The works of Aristotle came to the West equipped with Jewish and Arabic commentaries; Neoplatonic treatises mistakenly attributed to Aristotle by Arabic scholars were included in the *corpus* of his works; and finally, many textual problems arose because the original Greek works had been translated so many times—often from Greek into Syriac, from Syriac into Arabic, and then from Arabic into Latin. This difficulty was overcome in the middle of the thirteenth century when William of Moerbeke produced a series of very literal translations from the original Greek texts.

The first new works of Aristotle to become known in the West were his advanced logical treatises. When Peter Abelard died in 1142, he knew only the "Old Logic" (the works translated by Boethius). By 1160, the rest of Aristotle's logical works, known as the "New Logic," were being used at Paris. In the second half of the twelfth century, the whole range of Aristotle's scientific works was translated, principally by Dominic Gundisalvi and Gerard of Cremona, who worked under the patronage of Archbishop Raymond of Toledo. From this time on, Aristotle became famous in the Western world not only as the founder of a philosophical system but as a great teacher in every field of knowledge. Western scholars found in his works not only a new logic and a new metaphysics but new theories of ethics, psychology and politics, new physics, astronomy, meteorology, and zoology. Dante called Aristotle simply "the master of those who know."

61. *Medieval Science and Technology*

So far as medieval science was concerned, Aristotle's enormous prestige had a rather stultifying effect at first. Aristotle taught that natural science should be based on extensive observations, followed by reflection leading to scientific generalizations. But instead of using this excellent method, thirteenth-century thinkers were content for the most part to assimilate Aristotle's results and pass them on unchanged and uncriticized. It was not that medieval people were incapable of observing nature or uninterested in doing so. Thirteenth-century sculpture and painting, and many practical treatises like the emperor Frederick II's work on falconry, give abundant evidence of detailed observation in the natural world. Medical doctors were practicing dissection of corpses at Salerno and Bologna in the thirteenth century. Albertus Magnus, the master of Thomas Aquinas, added first-hand information about the flora and fauna of his native Germany in commenting on Aristotle's biological works. But there was no real attempt to criticize Aristotle's scientific presuppositions or his conclusions in the light of the newly collected evidence.

Hence, at the end of the thirteenth century, an educated person's picture of the physical universe was essentially similar to that of the ancient Greeks. Educated individuals accepted the classical theory that the earth was composed of four elements—earth, water, air, and fire. They understood that the earth was spherical but supposed that it was fixed at the midpoint of the universe. The basest matter, earth, formed the center; then there was a layer of water; then one of air; and finally came the finest element, fire. In the northern hemisphere, the force of the stars drew the earth above the water in some places. Beyond the earth, the universe consisted of a series of concentric, crystalline spheres in which the moon, sun, and planets were set like jewels. Last of all came the outermost sphere of the fixed stars. In Aristotle's universe, every substance tended to fulfill its natural potentialities and in doing so to reach a state of rest. This applied to living creatures as well as inanimate matter. Thus the investigation of human nature could lead to a science of rational ethics that would show people how to attain a state of peace and felicity. Among inanimate objects the intrinsic nature of things determined the way in which they moved. Heavy, "earthy" things belonged naturally to the lower sphere of earth and so tended to fall; flames, on the other hand, tended to rise to the higher sphere of fire. If any object was moving in a direction other than its "natural" one, a force was being applied to it. The

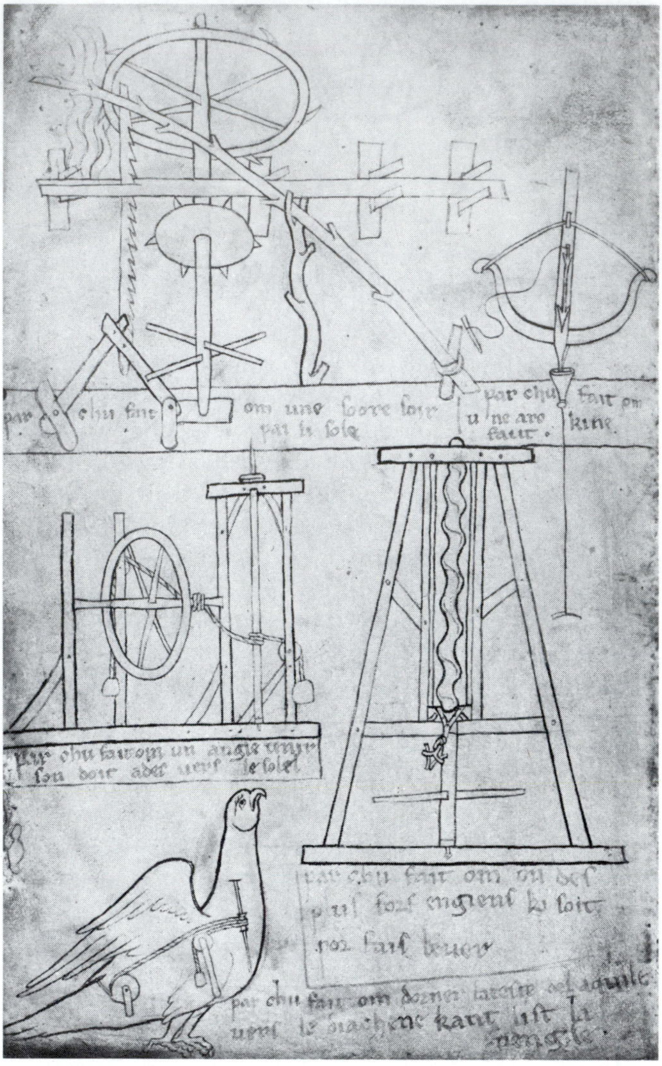

A page from the album of Villard de Honnecourt showing several designs for machines: a water-powered saw (top left); "a crossbow that cannot miss" (top right); a device to keep a statue rotating with the sun (middle, left); a weight-lifting device (middle, right); and a mechanical eagle (bottom). Ms. Fr. 19093, fol. 22V. *Bibliothèque Nationale, Paris*

force that drove the heavenly spheres was a mysterious "prime mover" which caused the sphere of the fixed stars to rotate, and this in turn imparted motion to the lower spheres. The Arabic Neoplatonists varied the scheme by inventing for each sphere a guiding intelligence that presided over the sphere and caused it to move. This idea was widely accepted in the Middle Ages. Also some medieval thinkers knew of the more complex Ptolemaic system of eccentrically rotating circles that had been devised to explain the irregular movements of the planets.

But attempts to go beyond Aristotle's account of the physical world usually led only to the pseudosciences of astrology and alchemy. The pervasive belief in astrology at least kept alive an interest in astronomical observation and in the construction of tables predicting the movements of heavenly bodies. Such work was facilitated by the introduction into Europe of Arabic mathematics and of instruments like the astrolabe. The alchemists, starting out from the common belief that all substances were made up of earth, air, fire, and water, hoped to achieve the transmutation of elements by combining different substances and subjecting them to various processes of heating and cooling. They can be credited with devising useful pieces of chemical apparatus and with introducing valuable new processes in the field of distillation. Although they never learned how to make gold, they did learn how to make brandy, which was something. However, their efforts were fundamentally misdirected. All their significant results were achieved by serendipity.

Thirteenth-century people achieved far more striking advances in practical technology than in pure science, advances that were stimulated more by the needs of real life than by the abstruse experiments of the alchemists. Humble but extremely useful implements like the spinning wheel and the wheelbarrow came into use. Treadles were used for the first time to operate lathes and looms. The magnetic compass was introduced from China. Spectacles for reading were invented. Water wheels were used to drive increasingly elaborate chains of gearing, which in turn operated sawmills or bellows for iron-smelting forges. Windmills came into use on a large scale. Some medieval writers were fascinated by the idea of perpetual motion that came to the West from India, and occasionally they speculated on the possibility of constructing magnetically driven engines that would run forever. Medieval engineers did actually harness the force of gravity in a new way by constructing, around 1300, the first weight-driven mechanical clocks that incorporated an adequate escapement device. These clocks were perhaps the most sophisticated and complex mechanisms that any society had created up to this time.

Although Aristotle's whole picture of the physical world was not significantly changed during the thirteenth century and there was far more obvious progress in applied technology than in theoretical science, some advances were made in the sphere of scientific methodology. The most important figure in this field was the Englishman Robert Grosseteste (1168–1253). He was chancellor of Oxford University in 1215 and volunteered to become the teacher of the first ragged band of Franciscans who arrived at Oxford in 1224. Through this work, he became the founder of a whole school of English Franciscan philosophy. In 1235 Grosseteste was elected bishop of Lincoln, and in that capacity, as one of the great prelates of England, he played a major role in the affairs of church and state for nearly twenty years.

As a philosopher, his principal characteristic was an insistence on first-hand knowledge and first-hand observation. Students of theology, he held, should know the actual text of the Bible in Greek and Hebrew; students of philosophy should learn to read Aristotle in Greek; students of nature should directly observe natural phenomena. Grosseteste himself was particularly fascinated by the science of optics. In both Neoplatonic and Christian texts, "light" was used as a symbol for divinity, and to a medieval person such symbolism was

Nicole Oresme at work; next to the desk stands an armillary sphere, a medieval device used to teach astronomy. Enlarged miniature from Oresme's translation of Aristotle's *De coelo et mundo,* French 14th century, Ms. French 565, fol. Ir. *Bibliothèque Nationale, Paris*

not just a literary device. It implied rather some kind of meaningful relationship between real light and St. John's "true light that enlightens every man" (John, 1:9). Grosseteste was convinced that a complete knowledge of the behavior of actual physical light would lead to a deeper understanding of the whole nature of the universe. This led him to his first major contribution to scientific methodology. The radiation of light could best be represented geometrically, and through his interest in such work Grosseteste came to insist on the mathematical expression of physical laws as a necessary part of the natural philosopher's task. His own most striking achievement was a sophisticated mathematical explanation of the formation of the rainbow. Grosseteste's other important contribution to scientific methodology was his development of the principle of experimental falsification of hypotheses. Everyone understood that a natural philosopher ought first to observe the phenomena of nature and then formulate a hypothesis to account for the observed facts. Grosseteste went a step further. Normally, several hypotheses would account for the same set of facts. It was necessary, therefore, to eliminate false hypotheses by deliberately seeking further evidence that would invalidate them or propositions logically derived from them. This procedure became the basis of the modern experimental method.

Nowadays, Grosseteste's follower, the Franciscan friar Roger Bacon (1220–1292), is better known than Grosseteste himself, but he was a much lesser thinker. Bacon was essentially a brilliant and imaginative critic. He argued that the progress of human knowledge was being impeded by excessive regard for ancient authorities, by popular prejudice, and by the reluctance of philosophers to admit their own ignorance. He advocated a thoroughgoing use of "experimental science" in the investigation of natural phenomena. He foresaw the invention of flying machines, submarines, and mechanically driven ships. All this is admirable, no doubt, but there is little evidence that Bacon ever conducted any meaningful original experiments, and he certainly discovered no new scientific laws.

The first major break with Aristotelian physics came in the work of two Paris philosophers of the fourteenth century, Jean Buridan (ca. 1300–1370) and Nicole Oresme (ca. 1330–1382), who both criticized Aristotle's law of motion. Aristotle held that if a body was in motion, it must be moving because a force was continuously acting on it. But what force could be said to act on a spear once it left the thrower's hand? Aristotle replied that the initial movement created a disturbance in the atmosphere. Air rushed in behind the spear to fill the space created by the first movement. This pushed the spear further forward, creating a new disturbance—and so on. But this explanation seemed inconsistent with the actual behavior of moving bodies. Medieval critics argued that, according to Aristotle's theory, a spear sharply pointed at both ends would not move through the air at all or would move only very slowly (for there would be almost no surface at the back for the air to press on). But this was observably not the case. Moreover, when a power source was disengaged from a mill wheel, the wheel continued to spin for a time before coming to rest. And this continuing circular motion was quite inexplicable by Aristotle's theory. Buridan proposed, therefore, that when a force was applied to a body to set it in motion, the body acquired an *impetus* which kept it in motion until it was stopped by a countervailing force, for example, friction. In a void, a moving body would continue to move indefinitely.

Buridan's younger colleague Nicole Oresme investigated particularly the behavior of falling bodies and formulated correctly for the first time the law of uniform acceleration. Buridan and Oresme both saw that the theory of impetus could be applied to heavenly bodies as well as earthly ones. It was not necessary to suppose that any force was continually acting on them to keep them in motion. Once the spheres had been given an initial impetus, they would continue to move indefinitely in the void of space. Oresme even compared the universe to a gigantic clock originally set in motion by God. He further noted that the whole theory of rotating heavenly spheres was an unproved hypothesis. The observed phenomena could be accounted for equally well by assuming that the earth rotated.*

These were the first major steps in scientific thought away from the Aristotelian world-picture and toward the "scientific revolution" of the sixteenth and seventeenth centuries. Nowadays there is perhaps a tendency to exaggerate the importance of medieval scientific discoveries in reaction against an earlier school of thought that dismissed them as utterly negligible. In fact, medieval achievement in physical science was less than in most other fields. There was only a thin trickle of original creative work; but that is because, in the fourteenth century, we are so close to the source of the whole modern scientific tradition.

62. *Philosophy and Theology: Thomas Aquinas*

Religion was a dominant theme of medieval culture. Hence the problems that Aristotle's philosophy posed in the sphere of theology seemed to medieval thinkers much more important than those to which it gave rise in the field of natural science. The theological problems attracted much more attention among medieval scholars. Such problems arose for several reasons. To begin with, Aristotle's philosophy was more materialistic, less mystical, than Plato's. Then, the works of the early church fathers were saturated in Neoplatonism, and any departure from their philosophical presuppositions seemed dangerous. Added to this, the new translations of Aristotle came mostly from Mohammedan and Jewish sources and so were naturally suspect. Finally, Aristotle taught (or was held to teach) a number of doctrines that flatly contradicted the Christian faith, for example, the eternity of the universe and the mortality of the individual soul. To be a Platonist and a Christian was not too difficult. That required only a little faith. To be an Aristotelian and a Christian required considerable ingenuity too. And yet Aristotle's conclusions had been arrived at by purely rational analysis conducted by the most eminent of philosophers. (Aristotle's prestige stood so high that medieval writers commonly referred to him simply as "the Philosopher.") If reason contradicted faith, what then? This was the central problem for thirteenth-century thinkers.

The Christian philosophy of the thirteenth century was only the latest in a series of attempts to cope with the problems of faith and reason that arose when religious revelation and Aristotelian thought were studied side by side. Mohammedan and Jewish scholars had already confronted the issue, as we have seen, but they had not been able to deal with it satisfactorily. The fundamentalist Mohammedan religious leaders successfully denounced Averroës, and the scandal caused by his heterodoxy aroused a fanatical antiintellectualism that cut short the whole tradition of rational philosophy among the Arabs.

*Sources, no. 79

Maimonides fared little better with the rabbis. For the most part, they rejected his attempts to bridge the gap between reason and faith and retreated into a cocoon of Talmudic erudition. The first reaction in the West to the dangers of the new Aristotle was again simply repressive. In 1210 a local church council decreed, under pain of excommunication, that no books of Aristotle on natural science were to be studied at Paris. In 1231 Pope Gregory IX modified this ruling. He had been informed, he wrote, that the condemned works of Aristotle contained useful as well as useless material, and accordingly, he set up a commission to examine the controversial works. The commission was to exclude all that was erroneous from them. Meanwhile, they continued to be banned. There is no record of the commission ever having carried out its task, but in 1255 all of Aristotle's scientific works (unexpurgated) were included in the syllabus of studies for the degree of Master of Arts at Paris. In 1263 Pope Urban IV renewed the ban of 1231. No one at Paris seems to have taken the slightest notice. Aristotle's science was too fascinating and too important to be abandoned at a word of command, even when the command came from the pope. The issues it raised had to be settled by hard thinking and hard debate if they were ever to be settled at all.

In the middle years of the thirteenth century, three distinct schools of thought emerged at Paris. The most conservative thinkers, the Augustinians, sought to preserve the pure doctrine of St. Augustine from contamination by "pagan" thought. This attitude was common among the Franciscans, and its greatest exponent was St. Bonaventura (1217–1274), who became minister-general of the Franciscan order in 1257. The name Augustinian is not to be taken too literally. All the thinkers of the mid-thirteenth century were influenced by the flood of translations from Arabic and Greek, and all the major scholastic systems of thought were syntheses of Aristotelian, Neoplatonic, and Christian doctrines. Bonaventura, for instance, warmly defended the doctrine of hylomorphism (the view that the soul was composed of matter and form). He thought that this theory was necessary to safeguard the Christian teaching of the soul's immortality, and he was convinced that it had been taught by Augustine. In fact, the doctrine was invented by the Jewish thinker Avicebron in the eleventh century.

Although all the philosophical systems of the thirteenth century derived from common sources, there were marked differences of emphasis among them. The Augustinians emphasized intuitive knowledge and goodness of will as necessary means to the attainment of truth. Bonaventura was skeptical about the ability of the human mind to attain truth by the exercise of its own natural faculties. He thought that divine illumination was needed too. He believed, like all the thinkers of his generation, that the physical universe known to sense experience was the handiwork of God and so could reveal something of the divine nature to humans. "The world of creatures is like a book in which the Creator is reflected," he wrote—a good Franciscan sentiment. However, St. Bonaventura did not think, any more than St. Francis had, that elaborate argumentation was necessary to establish the existence of God from the existence of the created world. He repeated approvingly St. Anselm's argument that the presence of an idea of God in the mind proved that God actually existed,* but Bonaventura hardly thought such proofs necessary at all. The mind unenlightened by divine illumination could not grasp truth with certitude in any case; the enlightened mind had only to glance at its own intuitions or at the external world of nature to be convinced of God's reality.† Along with these convictions went an attitude that was inclined to reject summarily on theological grounds any philosophical propositions that seemed contrary to faith and that regarded the refutation of such arguments on the philosophical level as a matter of secondary importance. For the Augustinians, more than for most medieval philosophers, philosophy was merely "the handmaid of theology"; and they intended to keep the servant wench in her proper place.

At the opposite pole from the Augustinians stood the group known as Latin Averroists, whose principal spokesman was Siger of Brabant (ca. 1240–1284). They accepted the commentaries of Averroës as true interpretations of Aristotle's doctrines and Aristotle's doctrines, in turn, as irrefutable conclusions of human reason. Thus they believed as philosophers that the universe had never had a beginning in time and that individual souls were absorbed into a single "active intellect" after death. But as Christians they were bound to believe that God had created the universe out of nothing and that individual human souls were immortal. Siger and his followers therefore maintained a doctrine usually called the theory of "double truth." They held, that is, that the conclusions of philosophy and of theology could be in conflict with one another and yet both sets of conclusions be valid. Actually, Siger never used the word *truth (veritas)* to describe the conclusions of reason. He reserved that word for the divinely revealed truths of faith. His arguments may have been just a way of professing a skepticism about religion without laying himself open to a charge of heresy. More probably, he was a sincere believer who held that, given the limitations of the human intellect, certain paradoxes were insoluble. Whatever Siger's precise beliefs, his view that the central doctrines of the church were contradicted by human reason seemed highly disruptive to conservative theologians.

In between the Augustians and the Averroists stood St. Thomas Aquinas (1225–1274), who is nowadays usually regarded as the greatest thinker of the Middle Ages. He was the son of a southern Italian baron, the Count of Aquino, and was related to the ruling Hohenstaufen family. (Thomas Aquinas was a second cousin of the emperor Frederick II.) He studied at the University of Naples, then joined the Dominican order in 1244, and worked under Albertus Magnus at Paris and Cologne. Albertus was a scholar of encyclopedic learning and the first in the Western schools who really mastered the whole *corpus* of Aristotle's works. After studying with him, Thomas began to lecture at Paris in 1252. From 1259 to 1268 he was in attendance at the papal

*See p. 308.

†Sources, no. 79

court. In 1268, at the height of his powers, he returned to Paris and there he completed his famous *Summa Theologiae.*

Considering that he died before he was fifty, Thomas left an enormous body of writing. His works fill thirty-two large volumes in a modern printed edition. He wrote commentaries on various books of the Old and New Testaments and also on the works of Aristotle. Besides this, there were numerous short treatises on disputed points and, finally, the two works on which his fame chiefly rests, the *Summa Contra Gentiles* and the *Summa Theologiae.* The first was a treatise on "natural religion," that is, on those tenets of religion that could be established by the human reason; the second accepted the doctrines of Christianity as divinely revealed truths and wove them into a vast synthesis dealing with the whole nature of the universe and the human place in it.

The *Summa Theologiae* is the supreme example of the "dialectical" method of arguing through the juxtaposition of opposing texts that Peter Abelard had pioneered in the twelfth century. The work is divided into Questions, each covering some broad field of inquiry. The Questions are subdivided into Articles, each posing a specific question. Thus the first Question is "Concerning sacred doctrine, what it is and what it extends to"; and the first Article is "Whether besides philosophy any further doctrine is required?" Thomas' treatment of the problem provides a good illustration of his method. He first posed objections from the Old Testament and from Aristotle suggesting that rational philosophy provided all the knowledge that man needed on earth. Then, in opposition to this view, he cited a text of St. Paul, "All Scripture inspired of God is profitable. . . ." At this point Thomas presented his own conclusion. Divine revelation was necessary for humans because certain truths essential to salvation could not be attained by human reason. Then, last of all, he answered the initial objections. All subsequent Articles were discussed in exactly the same fashion. The *Summa* contained more than six hundred Articles and, in discussing them, Aquinas raised and answered some ten thousand objections.

The first Article set the tone of the whole work. Aquinas believed that there were truths of reason and truths of faith, but, unlike the Averroists, he was serenely convinced that the two kinds of truth could never conflict with one another. He accepted the whole Aristotelian theory of knowledge—that the human mind, reflecting on sense experience, could attain to truth about the natural universe. But he added that there were supernatural truths as well, which people could know only because God, out of his grace, had chosen to reveal them. For instance, unaided reason could attain to the knowledge that God exists, but only divine revelation could tell a person that God was a Trinity of three Persons. Similarly, the incarnation of God in Christ or the presence of Christ in the eucharist could only be known as truths of faith and not by rational demonstration. For Aquinas, however, supernatural truth did not contradict natural knowledge but complemented and perfected it. His most characteristic saying was, "Grace does not destroy nature but perfects it." Supernatural truth and natural truth together made an all-embracing unity that a Christian philosopher could confidently explore.

Aquinas accepted almost the whole of Aristotelian science, but where Aristotle explicitly contradicted Christian doctrine, he argued against "the Philosopher." Aquinas did not simply invoke the superior authority of divine revelation in such cases but sought to refute Aristotle on his own ground, that is, by rational philosophical arguments. Thus he argued on philosophical grounds that Aristotle had never conclusively proved the universe had existed from all eternity. Aquinas himself thought it was impossible for human reason to establish whether the universe did or did not have a beginning in time. In other matters, Aquinas demonstrated that Aristotle had never held views that were attributed to him. He showed, for instance, that the doctrine of emanation which was derived from Avicenna (but often attributed to Aristotle) was quite alien to the Philosopher's thought. Likewise, he showed that the doctrine of the unity of the active intellect was an invention of Averroës and was not stated explicitly in Aristotle's own writings. Aquinas held, with Aristotle, that the soul was a pure form, but he insisted that this view was compatible with the Christian doctrine of immortality.

Thomas Aquinas was probably as much of a rationalist as it is possible for a Christian to be. He strongly emphasized the infinite divine reason in all his work, and he saw human reason as a link between the world of nature and the pure spiritual being of God. Reason could contemplate either external nature or the inner nature of humanity itself. Aquinas' most famous arguments about external nature are those that sought to demonstrate five ways to prove the existence of God. When St. Anselm had wanted to prove the existence of God, he started out, in Platonic fashion, from the idea of God in the mind. St. Thomas, as a good Aristotelian, started out from the facts of sense experience. The fact that things are seen to be moved implies the existence of a First Mover, he argued; and, likewise, the fact that things are seen to be caused implies the existence of a First Cause. In his third argument, Thomas pointed out that all the objects present to sense experience are transitory and changing. They can exist or not exist. They do not carry in themselves any cause of their own existence. But, Thomas argued, for things to exist at all something must exist necessarily. God was this entity whose intrinsic nature it was to exist, to be the ground of all other being. (Thomas used the word "essence" to describe the essential quality of anything, that which determined its intrinsic nature, and in his technical language, the essence of God was precisely existence.) Fourth, Thomas argued, we discern different grades of perfection in things, and this implies an absolute standard of perfection which can exist only in God. Finally, we can observe orderly sequences of events in nature that are not the result of mere random accident (for example, the growth of a plant from a seed); and this, for Thomas, implied the existence of a Supreme Intelligence governing the universe. As with Anselm's argument, these "proofs" have been discussed by philosophers all down the centuries and are still being discussed.*

In reflecting on human nature, Aquinas sought to adapt Aristotle's ethics and politics to serve the needs of a Christian society. He cheerfully accepted Aristotle's view that a proper end of humanity was to attain a state of earthly felicity and that a rational system of ethics could lead people to this end. But for Thomas, this was only one end of humanity, and a lesser end. The higher end was "beatitude," the contemplation of God. Aristotle had held up the intellectual life as the best way of achieving felicity. Thomas agreed, but added that the supreme end of the intellect was to know God. This end would only be fully achieved in the next world, and salvation in the afterlife required not only the practice of Aristotle's natural virtues but also that of the Christian virtues of faith and charity.

In the sphere of political theory, Aquinas' influence was very considerable. Ever since the days of Augustine, theologians had commonly assumed that the state existed only because humans had fallen into sin. In this view, the coercive power of princes was imposed on people by God partly as a remedy and partly as a punishment for sin. Aquinas, closely following Aristotle, maintained, on the contrary, that the state was natural to humanity. People had many potentialities for achieving good (intellectual, material, and moral), which could be achieved only in a society among other people. But whenever such a society existed, government was necessary, for common interests arose which required a commonly acknowledged authority to protect them. The proper form of state authority was a matter to be decided by rational reflection on the nature and needs of humanity. As usual, Aquinas' Christianity led him to go a step beyond Aristotle. If humanity's sole end had been to live a life of natural felicity on earth, the state would have provided a completely sufficient society for all human needs. But because he also had a supernatural destiny, a life with God in the next world, the Church was necessary too to guide them to this other end.

Apart from insisting, characteristically, on reason as the necessary foundation for law and indicating a preference for limited monarchy (which was a quite conventional viewpoint in the late thirteenth century), Aquinas did not elaborate a political theory of his own. Likewise, his views on the right relationship between church and state were ambiguous because he never treated the question in detail. But his teaching on the natural origin of the state formed the basis for several later theories of church-state separation and of constitutional government. The classical idea that the state was a natural society had been familiar to students of Roman law for more than a century, but they had not developed the doctrine significantly, and it remained outside the mainstream of theological and philosophical thought. Aquinas' vigorous reassertion of Aristotle's teaching made possible for the first time in many centuries the study of political theory as an important department of natural philosophy—not just as a branch of law or

*Sources, no. 79

theology. This was important, for subsequent thinkers did not merely repeat Greek ideas about the state; rather, they tended to generalize into universal political principles rules of law that had grown up in their own society. By the early fourteenth century, ideas like the right of consent to government, the subordination of government to law, and the validity of majority decisions were being defended in sophisticated works of political philosophy.

In studying the work of Thomas Aquinas, we encounter a thinker with a serene and powerful intelligence addressing himself vigorously to all the great problems of his age. It is not hard to understand why, long after the Middle Ages, his thought was accepted as the official philosophy of the Roman Catholic church. But, just for that reason, it is important to realize that in his own day Aquinas was a highly controversial figure. His critics thought that he emphasized reason too much at the expense of simple faith. Conservative church figures regarded him as a bold and dangerous radical. In the thirteenth century, Aquinas was not the acknowledged leader of Christian thought but only the founder of one particular philosophical system, which took its place among several competing ones.

Thirteenth-century people can be credited with many great achievements in the world of thought—the founding of universities, the creation of subtle theologies and sophisticated systems of law, the beginnings of a new scientific methodology. But none of them, not even Thomas Aquinas, achieved the end they most sought—a harmonious, fully satisfying synthesis of all available knowledge. At any rate, they did not succeed in creating a synthesis that satisfied medieval thinkers themselves.*

*See pp. 472 and 494–497.

READING SUGGESTIONS

* *B. Tierney,* Sources *and* Readings, *vol. I, nos. 76–78; vol. II, no. 32.*

The standard history of medieval universities is H. Rashdall, *The Universities of Europe in the Middle Ages,* rev. ed., 3 vols. (Oxford, England, 1936). Briefer introductions are * C. H. Haskins, *The Rise of the Universities* (New York, 1923); * H. Wieruszowski, *The Medieval University* (New York, 1966); * G. Leff, *Paris and Oxford Universities in the Thirteenth and Fourteenth Centuries* (New York, 1968); and * (J. W. Baldwin, *The Scholastic Culture of the Middle Ages, 1000–1300* (Lexington, MA, 1971). See also P. Kibre, *The Nations in the Medieval Universities* (Cambridge, MA, 1948). L. Thorndike, *University Records and Life in the Middle Ages* (New York, 1949) provides an excellent collection of source material.

On philosophical developments in this period, see the general histories of medieval thought cited in Chapter XII. See also D. E. Sharp, *Franciscan Philosophy at Oxford* (Oxford, England, 1930); F. J. Roensch, *The Early Thomistic School* (Dubuque, IA, 1964); and * I. Husik, *A History of Medieval Jewish Philosophy* (New York, 1958). The position of the Averroists is discussed in * E. Gilson, *Reason and Revelation in the Middle Ages* (New York, 1938). On Bonaventura, see E. Bettoni, *Saint Bonaventure* (Notre Dame, IN, 1964); E. Gilson, *The Philosophy of St. Bonaventura* (New York, 1938); and J. de Vinck (trans.), *The Works of Bonaventure* (Paterson, NJ, 1960———). Five volumes have so far appeared. The best introductions to Thomas Aquinas are E. Gilson, *The Philosophy of Aquinas,* 2nd ed. (Cambridge, England, 1939) and M. D. Chenu, *Toward Understanding St. Thomas* (Chicago, 1964). Other good studies are M. Grabmann, *Thomas Aquinas* (New York, 1928); * J. Maritain, *Saint Thomas Aquinas* (London, 1931); and * F. C. Coplestone, *Aquinas,* 2 vols. (New York, 1945). Smaller collections of excerpts are * V. J. Bourke (ed.), *The Pocket Aquinas* (New York, 1960); * R. P. Goodwin (ed.), *Selected Writings of St. Thomas Aquinas* (Indianapolis, 1964); and * D. Bigongiari (ed.), *Political Ideas of St. Thomas Aquinas* (New York, 1963).

On medieval science there are two older large-scale surveys by L. Thorndike, cited in the Introduction, and G. Sarton, *Introduction to the History of Science,* 3 vols. (Baltimore, 1927–1947). Two excellent introductions are * A. C. Crombie, *Medieval and Early Modern Science,* rev. ed. (New York, 1959) and * R. C. Dales, *The Scientific Achievement of the Middle Ages* (Philadelphia, 1973). For more specialized studies, see N. G. Siraisi, *Medieval and Early Renaissance Medicine* (Chicago, 1990); A. C. Crombie, *Robert Grosseteste and the Origins of Experimental Science* (Oxford, England, 1953); M. Clagett, *The Science of Mechanics in the Middle Ages* (Philadelphia, 1958); J. A. Weisheipl, *The Development of Physical Theory in the Middle Ages* (London, 1959); and E. Grant, *Physical Science in the Middle Ages* (New York, 1971). On Roger Bacon, see S. E. Easton, *Roger Bacon* (Oxford, England, 1952), and the translation of the *Opus Maius* by R. B. Burke (Philadelphia, 1928). Good works on technology are C. Singer *et al.* (eds.), *A History of Technology,* vol. II (Oxford, England, 1956); * A. P. Usher, *A History of Mechanical Inventions,* 2nd ed. (Cambridge, MA, 1954); * J. Gimpel, *The Medieval Machine* (New York, 1976); G. Ovitt, *The Restoration of Perfection: Labor and Technology in Medieval Culture* (New Brunswick, NJ, 1987); and, for a stimulating introduction, * L. White, *Medieval Technology and Social Change* (Oxford, England, 1962). On Arabic texts see R. Walzer, *Greek into Arabic* (Oxford, England, 1962) and F. E. Peters, *Aristotle and the Arabs* (New York, 1968).

chapter

XIX

Architecture, Art, and Literature

An eleventh-century chronicler wrote that, during his lifetime, Europe had become covered with "a white robe of churches." Yet he had seen only the beginning of an extraordinary outburst of building activity that was to continue throughout the medieval period. Religious architecture was the dominant art form of the Middle Ages, and the Gothic cathedral, developed in the twelfth century and perfected in the thirteenth, was the greatest esthetic achievement of medieval civilization. The age of the cathedral builders also saw the production of outstanding works of Latin and vernacular literature. By the end of the thirteenth century, an impressive and richly creative civilization had emerged from the chaos of the early medieval period. In this chapter, we shall describe some of the major achievements of the Middle Ages in art and literature and try to convey something of the spirit that informed them.

63. *Romanesque Culture: Architecture and Liturgy*

During the era of medieval history that we might designate as Romanesque—from the time of Charlemagne to the mid-twelfth century—two outstanding developments occurred in the sphere of religious culture. The first was the emergence of Romanesque architecture, and the second was a rich elaboration of the liturgical worship of the Western church.

In appraising medieval achievements in architecture, an important consideration to be borne in mind is the sheer volume of fine work that was produced. Hundreds of great cathedrals and abbeys survive from the Middle Ages along with thousands of parish churches. For an "underdeveloped," "preindustrial" society, the sheer number of projects that was undertaken is impressive. Moreover, the greater buildings were huge in size. John Harvey has pointed out that, for

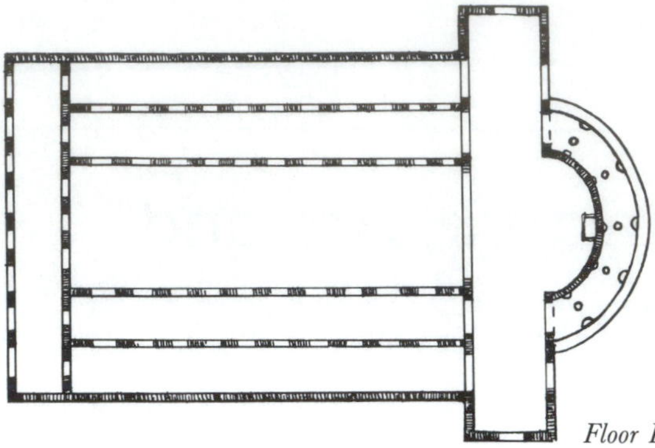

Floor Plan of a Basilica

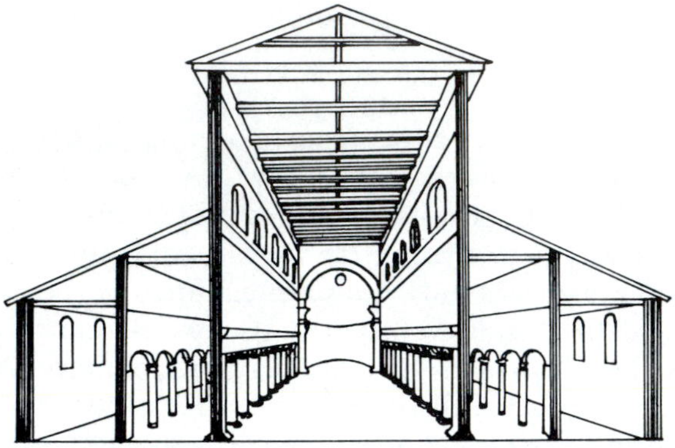

Clerestory (Basilica)

seven centuries after the age of Constantine, no buildings were erected in western Europe that were at all comparable in scale to the great classical basilicas. The central hall of the Basilica of Constantine at Rome, for instance, measured 265 by 83 feet. The most impressive building erected in the West in the half-millennium after the fall of Rome was the church of Charlemagne at Aachen (ca. 800). It is an octagonal domed structure, not without a certain grandeur, but in actual size it is only some 50 feet across. By contrast, the great hall of William Rufus at Westminster built in 1097–1099 measured 238 feet by 83 feet, and many of the great churches of the next century were far larger than that. This question of size is important because building on a massive scale raised problems of construction which helped to stimulate the architectural experiments that led to Gothic design.

In the late years of the Roman Empire, the Christian churches of Italy were usually simple *basilicas*—rectangular buildings with flat wooden roofs. The interior consisted of a *nave* and one or more aisles separated by rows of columns. Decoration was largely in the form of beautiful marble and mosaics. The *apse* at the east end where the altar was placed was usually covered by a semidome. Sometimes a *transept* at right angles to the nave separated the apse from the rest of the church and gave an appropriately symbolical cruciform shape to the whole building. The roof over the nave could be raised above the aisles by poising it on two interior walls running the whole length of the building. The walls were supported by round arches joining the columns that ran down each side of the nave, and the portions of the walls that projected above the aisles to form a *clerestory* were pierced with windows to light the building. A surviving church of this kind is St. Paul's-Outside-the-Walls at Rome.

This basilica style continued to be dominant in Italy well into the Middle Ages. Its only serious rival was the Byzantine domed architecture found especially at Ravenna. A few great medieval churches were built in the Byzantine manner, notably St. Mark's in Venice, but when large-scale building operations began in the north in the tenth and eleventh centuries, the designers preferred to continue the Roman tradition. The assimilation of Roman elements into medieval architecture is analogous to the assimilation of Roman law into medieval jurisprudence. In both cases, genuinely classical motifs were revived, but they were given a changed significance by people of a different civilization and eventually were built into edifices—of stone or of thought—different from any that the ancient Romans had imagined.

The early *Romanesque* churches resembled the ancient basilicas in their basic shape. There was typically a long nave flanked by aisles, a clerestory, a transept at right angles to the nave, and sometimes an extension of the nave, called a *choir,* beyond the transept. At the east end of the church was a rounded aspe, commonly surrounded by an *ambulatory.* The great innovation of the Romanesque builders was their replacement of the flat wooden roofs of the classical basilicas by round stone vaults. (Such vaults were not unknown to the Romans. It was their use on a massive scale that gave rise to the new features of Romanesque.) The wooden roofs were a perpetual fire hazard, and

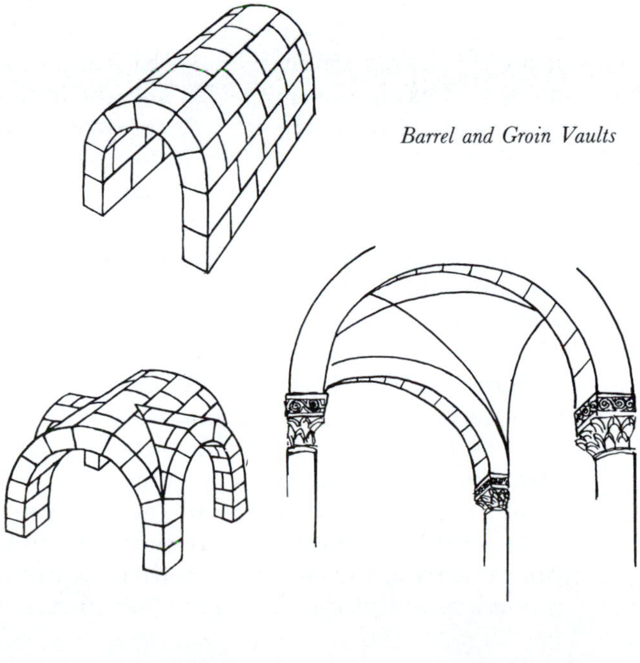

Barrel and Groin Vaults

this no doubt helped to stimulate alternative types of construction, especially since many of the Romanesque churches were built to replace structures burned down by the Vikings. But the building of vast stone vaults raised such difficult problems of construction that the whole endeavor cannot be attributed simply to utilitarian motives. Romanesque builders evidently found the old-fashioned flat roofs, which had no organic connection with the walls or round arches of the clerestory, to be esthetically unsatisfying. Perhaps too their religious susceptibilities were offended by the use of an intrinsically impermanent method of construction in churches dedicated to an eternal God.

The simplest form of Romanesque roofing was the *barrel vault,* a long tunnel of stone running over the nave, sometimes strengthened by transverse arches joining pairs of pillars on opposite sides of the nave. Its great weight had to be supported by massive walls with no windows or virtually none. Where two barrel vaults intersected, as at the transept, a *groin vault,* or *cross vault,* was produced. A groin vault enclosed a square or rectangular space; in the final form of Romanesque architecture, each rectangle created by the lines of pillars running along the nave was treated as a separate "bay" and roofed with a cross vault. The thrust of the cross vault was concentrated mainly at its corners, and if the wall was strengthened with buttressing at these points, other sections of the walls could be pierced with windows. The great abbey church of Vézelay provides a splendid example of this style.

In all forms of Romanesque building, however, the stone roofs were enormously heavy and required massive walls and piers to support them. Even at Vézelay the windows were narrow, and in most churches they were mere slits, so that Romanesque interiors are dark and gloomy. The buildings have an air of mystery and of magnificent solidity. They have been called "fortresses of God," and the phrase is more than a metaphor. The age of Romanesque architecture was also an age of castle building. The massive walls and slit windows characteristic of tenth- and eleventh-century building in general served a highly practical purpose in military architecture.

The Romanesque builders broke with the tradition of the Roman basilica again in their very extensive use of ornamental sculpture, especially on the exteriors of their churches. The great entrance portals and especially the semicircular *tympana* above them were carved with figures of humans and animals portraying scenes from the Bible. The figures were intended as symbols, not portraits, and they were wholly subordinated to the requirements of architectural design. A favorite theme for the tympanum was Christ in majesty surrounded by the saints. Another favorite motif was the four living creatures mentioned in the Apocalypse—the man, the lion, the ox, and the eagle—which were taken to represent the four evangelists—Matthew, Mark, Luke, and John. A dove could mean the church; a lamb, Christ; a lily, purity; a rose, the blood of martyrs; a nettle, the forces of evil. Romanesque sculpture was a grave hieratic art, with simplified forms that gave the same impression of solidity and mass as the round vaults of the interiors. It was a kind of expressionism in stone. It made no attempt at naturalism but powerfully conveyed religious emotion.

The liturgical worship that was carried on in the great Romanesque churches matched the architecture and sculpture in its solemnity and rich symbolism. Here again we find old forms assimilated into new structures. St. Benedict, following the practice observed in the ancient Roman basilicas, had laid down that his monks were to meet together seven times a day for corporate prayer and the chanting of psalms. From the late sixth century onward, Benedictine monks carried the observance of this "Divine Office" to northern Europe. Also, the celebration of the seven "canonical hours" spread from monasteries to cathedrals and other major churches in the north. The Divine Office, together with the daily mass and the rituals for administering sacraments, constituted the liturgy, the solemn public worship of the medieval Church. Many local variations in practice had grown up by the eighth century. To check this fragmentation, King Pepin introduced the rites of the church of Rome into Gaul shortly after the Franco-papal alliance of 752, and Charlemagne commanded repeatedly that the Roman usages be observed in all the churches of his realm. From this time onward, Roman forms of ritual were commonly followed in western Europe, though there was never complete uniformity in the Middle Ages. (For instance, England retained the "Rite of Sarum," and Milan, the "Ambrosian Rite.") Moreover, the Roman rite itself did not remain static. In the great cathedrals and monasteries of northern Europe, the Roman liturgy underwent modifications that, in the mid-tenth century (the age of Otto the Great), began to react back and to influence the ritual practices of Rome itself.

The ninth and tenth centuries were an era of major development and of systematization. Charlemagne's friend Alcuin took the lead in producing corrected editions of the liturgical texts and in encouraging their diffusion. His disciple Amalarius of Metz wrote an allegorical commentary on the whole corpus of Roman liturgy. During this same period, the initial core of liturgical material was embellished with numerous additions—newly composed hymns, offices of the Blessed Virgin, prayers for the dead, commemorations of saints. The great abbey of Cluny was especially fertile in devising such supplementary prayers.

The process of growth and change continued throughout the Middle Ages and, indeed, it still continues in modern times. But by the eleventh century the basic structure of the medieval liturgy had been created. The Divine Office and the mass formed an intricate cycle of daily prayer, and the prayers for each day were linked to each other so as to form a coherent pattern extending over a whole year. The Church's "liturgical year" centered around the three great feasts of Easter, Pentecost, and Christmas; the prayers for any given day were related primarily to these sacred feasts. But the daily round of worship was also related to the changing seasons of the secular year. At Christmas medieval people worshiped Christ as a new "light" come to illuminate the world. But in pagan times the date of Christmas had been a feast of the winter solstice, marking a time when the darkest day of the year had passed and the sun was beginning to return to the northern hemisphere. Easter was the feast of the Resurrection and, in preparing for it, people recalled the saying of Christ, "Unless a grain of wheat falls into the ground and dies it remains alone; but if it dies it brings forth much fruit." This was interpreted, of course, as referring to the death and burial and resurrection of Christ. But Easter was also a spring festival when the grain that had been sown in the preceding autumn was beginning to sprout and to fill the fields with visible signs of new life. In many such ways, the prayers of the liturgy gave a ritual significance to the changing round of seasonal activities.

The early development of liturgical music is currently a matter of complex argumentation among specialists. Perhaps the first Christian songs were derived from the chants of the Jewish synagogue, but no manuscripts survive from which such a development can be traced. The same is true of the early forms of Gregorian chant, which grew up from the sixth century onward. (It is so-called in honor of Pope Gregory the Great, though there is no clear evidence that he contributed anything to the development of the style.) We do have manuscripts from the ninth century marked with musical notation and by then hundreds of liturgical melodies existed and new ones were constantly being composed. The Gregorian chant recorded in these earliest manuscripts had probably been formed from a fusion of Roman and Gallic elements. The melodies were all "monophonic"; that is, all the singers in a choir chanted the same tune, and if they were accompanied by an organ (as was often the case), it carried the same melody also. For this reason, Gregorian chant is often called "plain chant." It is music of great simplicity and great dignity.

Plain chant continued to be sung by monastic choirs throughout the Middle Ages, but from the tenth century on (and probably from an earlier period), it was supplemented by polyphonic compositions. The earliest musical works written in a form of modern staff notation were by Guido of Arezzo (ca. 992–1050), and his writings also describe the simpler forms of counterpoint. By the thirteenth century there were systems of notation that correctly indicated the rhythm of the music as well as the pitch of the notes.

The creativity of medieval musicians and the development of an adequate system of notation, first as a mnemonic device, then as a way of preserving musical texts—something unknown in the ancient world—made possible the growth of a whole new musical language, an aesthetic achievement comparable to that of the great cathedrals themselves.

When music was studied academically in the schools as one of the seven liberal arts, it was conceived of as a kind of mathematics of number and proportion; musical harmonies were treated as expressions of the intrinsic order and harmony of the whole universe. Students of these higher mysteries were sometimes disdainful of the ordinary practitioners who produced real, sensuous music, something one could actually hear and sing and play. Guido of Arezzo compared a cantor disparagingly with a true musical scholar:

> *Nam qui facit quod non sapit*
> *diffinitur bestia*
>
> Who does what he does not understand
> deserves to be called a beast

But it was the practical musicians, cantors and choirmasters in the churches, minstrels and troubadours in the secular world, who built up the great heritage of medieval music. In the twelfth and thirteenth centuries liturgical chant became increasingly complex, with a great growth of polyphonic compositions. Motets from thirteenth century France used three melodic lines, sometimes with different words sung to the different melodies. Secular music was mostly monophonic until the thirteenth century; then troubadours borrowed the motet form for their love songs, sometimes attaching light-hearted words to originally sacred melodies. The organ continued to be used in church music, the employment of other instruments in church being frowned on by the authorities as unduly frivolous. But the troubadours often accompanied their songs with harps, woodwinds, lutes, and guitars (which they played with a bow, another importation from Muslim Spain). From the thirteenth century on there are musical texts written for instruments alone, probably to accompany dancing.

The epoch of the twelfth and thirteenth centuries, when church music was growing more complex and sophisticated, was also the period when the relatively simple structures of the Romanesque were giving way to the increasingly elaborate innovations of the new Gothic style.

64. *The Gothic Cathedral*

The great church at Vézelay achieved all that could be achieved within the limits of Romanesque techniques of construction. Yet medieval builders remained unsatisfied. They wanted their churches to soar still higher, and they wanted to open them up and fill them with light. Then about the middle of the twelfth century, a series of architectural innovations led to the new *Gothic* style, in which medieval esthetic and religious impulses found their most mature expression. The basic technical innovations were the *ribbed vault* and the *pointed arch* that was its logical accompaniment. In the first experiments with the new system of vaulting, semicircular ribs were erected on each side of a square or rectangular bay and also on the diagonals connecting the corners. It was a question of simply adding to the familiar groin vault two diagonal ribs. This sturdy framework strengthened the vault, and the relatively small triangular segments created by the ribs could be filled in with light slabs of stone in place of the heavy masonry of the Romanesque roofs.

The obvious difficulty created by a simple rib vault was that the diagonal arches, since they were erected on longer base lines, rose to a greater height than the other four. The effect was visually displeasing, and the resulting vaults did not achieve the maximum possible stability, as medieval builders soon discovered by trial and error. Their solution was to develop the use of the pointed arch. Romanesque builders had sometimes used the pointed arch too, but only as a decorative motif borrowed from Muslim architecture. Now it became a key element in the developing techniques of Gothic construction. If the arches on the sides of a square or rectangle were pointed, they could be raised to the exact height of the intersection of the diagonals. This innovation opened up all kinds of exciting possibilities. The pointed arches produced a more vertical, less lateral, thrust than round ones, and this, together with the lighter stonework of the roofs, enabled the builders to raise their vaults higher and to poise them on less heavy pillars. As the clerestories soared above the naves, a problem arose of buttressing them at the point of stress where the ribs transmitted the weight of the roof to the pillars. This was solved by the final technical innovation of the Gothic style, the *flying buttress.* Heavy piers of stone were constructed outside the building. Arches sprang from the summits of these piers, flying over the low roofs of the aisles to support the ribs of the nave vaults at the points of stress. (Other arches could be sprung from lower points on the piers to support the aisle walls.) The whole weight of the cathedral then rested on an intricate structure of ribs, arches, and pillars. The walls practically ceased to be load-bearing surfaces. They could be opened up with windows at the will of the designer. In some late medieval churches, like Kings College Chapel at Cambridge, the walls were almost replaced by screens of stained glass.

The use of architectural innovations for practical purposes of construction did not in itself produce a Gothic church. The nave of Durham cathedral, completed as early as 1104, has a ribbed vault in the

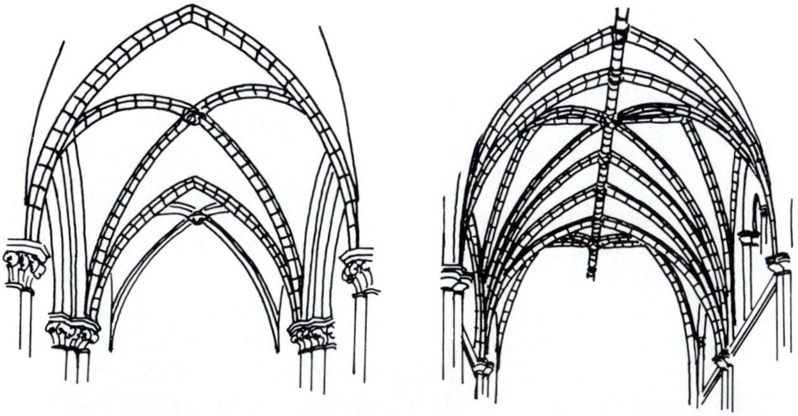

Gothic Ribbed Vault

The groin-vaulted Romanesque nave (later the choir) of the abbey church of La Madeleine at Vézelay in Burgundy ca. 1104–1130 (the apse beyond is from a later period). *Marburg—Art Reference Bureau*

The Gothic nave of Cologne Cathedral, begun in 1248. *Marburg—Art Reference Bureau*

Romanesque cathedral sculpture, the Last Judgment, carved by Giselbertus before 1135. Tympanum of the west doorway, Cathedral of Saint-Lazare at Autun. *Jean Roubier*

Gothic cathedral sculpture, figures on the central portal of the north transept, Chartres Cathedral, ca. 1200. From the left, Melchisedec, Abraham and Isaac, Moses, Samuel, King David. *Marburg—Art Reference Bureau*

A late Gothic sculpture of a smiling Virgin and Child. French, polychromed oak, h. 15⅞ in., Gift of J. Pierpont Morgan. *The Metropolitan Museum of Art, New York*

A deeply carved Romanesque sculpture, the prophet Isaiah from the stone abutment of the doorway of the church at Souillac, ca. 1120. *Bulloz—Art Reference Bureau*

The west facade of Reims, begun in 1211. Sculptured figures whose lines follow that of the structure itself emphasize the soaring, upward striving effect. *Photographie Giraudon/Art Resource*

Late Gothic stone tracery in the French *flamboyant* style; a rose window surrounded by a wheel of fortune, the south transept of Amiens Cathedral, ca. 1500. *Marburg—Art Reference Bureau*

The interior of the upper chapel at Ste. Chapelle, Paris, built between 1243 and 1248, shows the walls to be almost screens of magnificent stained glass. *Giraudon*

Flying Buttress

Gothic manner, yet the whole structure is Romanesque in its total effect—a building of thick walls, massive piers, and narrow windows. Gothic architecture came into existence when people began deliberately to explore the esthetic possibilities inherent in the new techniques of construction. The first such attempt was made in the building of the abbey church of St. Denis near Paris, constructed under the patronage of the great abbot Suger between 1140 and 1150. Pointed arches were used throughout the choir and nave, and the consequent possibility of increasing the size of the windows was deliberately exploited. A whole school of workers in stained glass was formed at St. Denis in the 1140s, and its members carried their art to many other centers. They achieved extraordinarily brilliant effects by staining small pieces of glass in glowing primary colors. The glass was then set in thin lead frames shaped to form pictures which were used to illustrate religious themes—the life of Christ, or some Biblical episode, or the legend of a saint. Such windows filled the whole building with colored light. This was no chance achievement. Suger, like many medieval individuals, was fascinated by Neoplatonic light mysticism. He thought that a church built for the worship of Christ, "the true light," should itself be radiant, and he deliberately aimed at an effect of luminosity. When the splendid choir of his church was completed, he wrote with evident satisfaction, "The entire sanctuary is pervaded by a wonderful and continuous light."

The new style of St. Denis was quickly imitated and developed in other churches of the Ile de France. It was carried to England by William of Sens, who undertook the rebuilding of Canterbury cathedral in 1175. During the thirteenth century, Gothic building spread all over the Christian world, though the Italians were never really at home with the northern style and never produced the same esthetic effects as the French designers. (They preferred to retain large wall surfaces that could be painted with frescoes instead of expanding the window space of their churches.) In Spain a distinctive style emerged, in which the basic forms of Romanesque and Gothic architecture, borrowed from the Christian north, were varied by the ornamental brickwork, ceramics, and colorful tile floors of Muslim craftsmen.

By the middle of the thirteenth century, French Gothic architecture had reached a harmonious perfection in cathedrals like those of Paris, Reims, Amiens, and Chartres. The visual impression produced by a cathedral in the mature Gothic style is very different from that of a Romanesque church. The Gothic building is a thing of soaring grace. In place of massive solidity, there is an air of delicate poise and balance. The two essential innovations, the extensive use of stained glass and the extensive use of ribbed vaulting, gave rise to a whole new set of esthetic values. Where the Romanesque church was dark, the Gothic church was flooded with colored light. Moreover, Gothic architecture was "functional" in a quite new way. That is, the esthetic effect of a building was created by the structural members themselves, by the ribs and arches and buttresses that actually held it up. There was no attempt to hide this structural framework. The beauty of the building inhered precisely in the elegance of the constructional techniques that were employed.

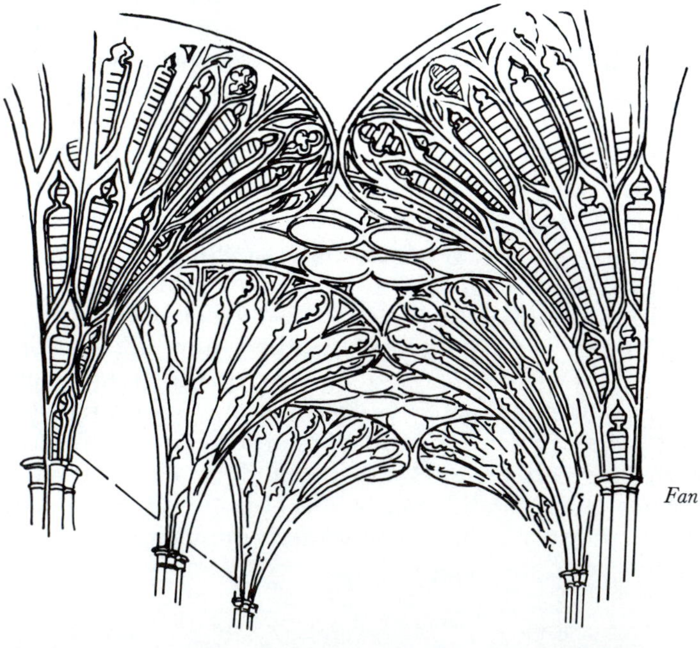

Fan Vault Flamboyant

This had a further corollary. Whereas Romanesque architecture and art (like classical art) emphasized volume and mass, the esthetic values of the Gothic style were essentially linear. A Gothic cathedral was full of elaborate tracery. The lines of the roof ribs were carried down the whole length of the supporting pillars to give an elegant fluted effect. Additional lines of ribbing were added to the vaults, at first perhaps to strengthen them, but soon for purely decorative effect. The technique was carried to its ultimate conclusion in the English fan vaults of the late Middle Ages. Stone tracery, growing always more elaborate, was erected in the window spaces to frame the colored glass. (The flame-like shape of such tracery gave rise to the term *flamboyant* to describe a highly ornamental school of late Gothic architecture.) During the course of the thirteenth century, the beautiful sinuous Gothic line which had appeared first as an architectural motif came to dominate all forms of visual art—sculpture, drawing, painting, and tapestry. Even handwriting became Gothic in the thirteenth century.

Modern critics often admire most of all the earliest Gothic buildings where the "functionalism" of the style stands out in stark simplicity. Medieval puritans like Bernard of Clairvaux felt the same way, and some of the very best examples of the early, more austere style are found in Cistercian churches like the one that survives at Pontigny. But for the most part, medieval designers did not think that functional beauty was marred by decorative art. Their great facades—as at Reims, for instance—were covered with a riot of sculpture. This was not purely decorative but also served a didactic purpose. Most medieval people were illiterate and needed visual images as well as sermons to help them understand their religion. Suger himself emphasized the point when he wrote, "Our earthbound minds can apprehend the Truth only by means of representations."

The themes and symbols of Gothic sculpture remained much the same as those of Romanesque art, but the style changed. Human figures became more lifelike and often seem to have been portraits of real persons. Flowers and animals were carved with a new naturalism. Botanists can recognize dozens of actual plants among the carved Gothic foliage—arum, fern, clover, columbine, ivy, and many more. Along with the familiar animals of the farm and countryside, Gothic sculptors carved Eastern beasts—lions, elephants, camels—and also strange, mythical monsters—dragons, basilisks, griffins, unicorns. In emphasizing the inherent logic of Gothic construction, we should not neglect the element of sheer fantasy in Gothic decoration. Of course, nearly all the plants and animals portrayed had some symbolic religious significance, but secular scenes and symbols were also carved in the great cathedrals, representations of the seven liberal arts and scenes depicting the agricultural labors of each month in the year.

The Gothic cathedral was a microcosm of the whole world of medieval humanity. Its carvings and stained glass both portrayed their activities and symbolized their faith. Its proportions were based on mathematical ratios, derived ultimately from the ancient school of

Pythagoras, which were thought to express the inherent harmony of the universe. And for medieval people, the universe that was symbolized in their cathedrals was itself a divine artifact. The physical world was God's thought made concrete. Hence the whole of material creation was a symbol of divine truth—a truth that the rational intellect could partly comprehend but could not completely grasp. Where reason ended there was room for a leap into faith—or into beauty. A twelfth-century man wrote, "If all that God hath willed is fair, then all that which hath a temporal fairness is, as it were, an image of the eternal beauty."

Endless analogies have been drawn between the cathedral and other major achievements of medieval civilization, like the great scholastic *Summae.* Gothic cathedrals have been compared to medieval music in their use of mathematical proportion and to the finest works of medieval literature in their encyclopedic content and complexity of structure. It cannot be denied that such resemblances exist, and it may be useful to insist on them, provided that they do not mislead us about the actual facts of medieval building operations. There used to be a vague idea that, when a great church was to be built, a pious bishop gathered his people around him (or an abbot his monks), and they laid one stone on another until somehow a Gothic cathedral crystallized out of the prevailing religious instinct of the times. This is absurd, of course. As the art historian Emile Mâle observed, "Instinct never made anything come up out of the ground." Medieval cathedrals were designed by hard-headed professional builders called master-masons, who both drew the plans for the churches and supervised the actual construction work. The best of them were great architects, but it would never have occurred to them to imitate a scholastic *Summa* in stone. Labor for the cathedrals was provided by highly skilled stonemasons and other craftsmen, who were organized into guilds and paid a daily wage for their work. They too were not given to reading the *Summa Theologiae.*

The resemblances that undoubtedly do exist between Gothic cathedrals and other achievements of medieval civilization must be explained by an underlying attitude of mind that was common to many medieval people. Everywhere one encounters a will to subordinate intricate masses of detail to an overall unity of design. This attitude is found in philosophy, theology, law, and literature as well as in architecture. And behind all these activities there was, of course, a common religious faith. The cathedrals emerged as fitting symbols of medieval Christianity because they were built to satisfy patrons—individuals or whole communities—whose sensibilities had been shaped by medieval religion. And yet the underlying religious impulse does not in itself fully explain the actual form of Gothic architecture. After all, the culture of Byzantium was deeply Christian too, but its architects never produced anything remotely like a Gothic cathedral. The greatest works of art cannot be explained in wholly rational terms, and no doubt there will always be an element of mystery about the emergence of Gothic architecture; but, as is so often the case when dealing with medieval culture, we can at least see that the essential process taking place involved an interaction of Christian and classical motifs with a distinctly northern sensibility.

Romanesque building grew from adaptations of late classical forms made by people who wanted to honor their Christian God by building massive churches in stone. The ribbed vault was then introduced probably for reasons of structural efficiency. But—so far as structural techniques are concerned—there was no necessary logical progression leading from the ribbed vaults of, say, Romanesque Durham to the intricate decorative tracery of Gothic Gloucester. The ancient Romans knew how to build a ribbed vault and apparently found the structure totally uninteresting from an esthetic point of view. But the lines of the diagonal and transverse ribs suggested to northern people, with their ancient traditions of abstract linear art, the possibility of esthetic effects that the Mediterranean world had never dreamed of. The emergence of Gothic becomes intelligible only when we remember the intricate linear patterns of early Germanic and Celtic art.*

A similar argument applies to the great diaphanous walls of colored glass that light up medieval cathedrals. Here again there was a felicitous blending of classical symbolism and northern sensibility. The image of light as a symbol for divinity was both classical and early Christian, but such symbolism aroused an emotional intensity that could inspire a whole new art form only among people who were starved for real light in the long northern winters. It is strange that the medieval period used to be called the "Dark Ages." In science, in art, in liturgical symbolism, the whole civilization was fascinated by light.

65. *Latin Literature*

All medieval scholars had to study Latin, the language of the church and the medium of instruction in the schools. They learned it from the old grammars of Priscian and Donatus and, after 1199, from the *Doctrinale* of Alexander de Villedieu, a popular textbook written in verse for easy memorizing. Medieval thinkers learned Latin as few of us do nowadays. For them it was not a dead language: they spoke Latin fluently. They could think in Latin, debate in Latin, make jokes in Latin and, above all, write poetry in Latin.

Every medieval century has left a legacy of Latin verses, but in this sphere, as in various others, the greatest burst of creative activity came in the late eleventh and twelfth centuries. The foremost center of literary studies was Chartres, and the Englishman John of Salisbury, who learned his own elegant Latin style there, has left an account of the manner of teaching at the beginning of the twelfth century:

> Evening drill, which was called declension, was packed with so much grammar that one who gave a whole year to it would have at his command, unless unusually dull, a method of speaking and writing.

*See p. 116.

But it was not all grammar and drill. Bernard of Chartres (the master whose teaching John was describing) also introduced his students to the poets and orators of antiquity and taught them how to write with similar eloquence. His pupils "wrote prose and poetry daily and trained themselves by mutual comparison." (While Bernard was chancellor of Chartres, the west front of the cathedral was under construction—and Donatus and Cicero were carved there along with the prophets and apostles.) Some students of ancient literature learned to write poetry in classical meters. Most of it was mere pastiche, but there were occasional exceptions. Hildebert of Lavardin (ca. 1055–1133) wrote stately verses that are grave and serene in spirit and so good in technique that they have been mistaken for genuine classical poems.

The vast bulk of Latin verse was, however, written in a different style. Classical meter was based on long and short vowels. Medieval poets discovered a new way of using the old language; they wrote in rhymed verse and in stressed accentual rhythms. Many great hymns were written in this fashion, and the one commonly regarded as the finest of them all illustrates the technique to perfection. In the following pattern of stresses, "blow follows blow like a hammer on an anvil."*

Dies irae, dies illa
Solvet saeclum in favilla
Teste David cum Sybilla

The day of wrath, that dreadful day
Shall the whole world in ashes lay
As David and the Sybils say

Most medieval verse did not move on this exalted level. There was a vast froth of drinking songs and love songs, nature songs and songs on the joys of youth, all filled with life and gaiety.† These secular lyrics are called *Goliardic* poetry after Golias, the Old Testament Goliath, whose name was often used in the Middle Ages to mean the devil. Then Goliards were vagabond students who identified themselves with a mythical "Order of Vagabonds" under the patronage of Golias. The Goliardic verse was written by such students or, more often perhaps, by older men who still remembered what it was like to have been a student. One such is known simply as the Archpoet. He was a hanger-on in the household of Rainald of Dassel, archbishop of Cologne and chancellor to the emperor Frederick Barbarossa. (We have encountered Rainald in another context at Barbarossa's Diet of Bensançon.)‡ The chancellor was an austere man, but he evidently found the Archpoet's rhyming irresistible. The whole Goliardic spirit is captured in the Archpoet's *Confession*, where he overtly rejected all the standards of respectable society and praised the pleasures of love and wine. One stanza§ is especially famous:

*Anon., *The Seven Great Hymns of the Western Church*, 7th ed., New York, 1868

†Sources, no. 52

‡See p. 340.

§J.A. Symonds, *Wine, Women and Song*, London, 1884.

In the public-house to die
   Is my resolution;
Let wine to my lips be nigh
   At life's dissolution:
That will make the angels cry,
   With glad elocution,
"Grant this toper, God on high,
   Grace and absolution!"

Toward the end of the thirteenth century a group of monks at the Bavarian abbey of Benedictbeuern copied out a collection of earlier songs and poems. The manuscript happily survives and preserves for us a whole range of secular Latin lyrics on the most diverse themes.* There was another fine drinking song:

Potatores exquisiti
Licet sitis sine siti
Et bibatis expediti
Et syphorum inobliti . . .

To you consummate drinkers,
Though little be your drought
Good speed be to your tankards
And send the wine about . . .

love poems with an ache of longing in them:

Si me dignetur quam desidero
Felicitate Jovem supero . . .

If she whom I desire would stoop to love me,
I should look down on Jove . . .

poems in praise of springtime and youth:

Nunc ergo canunt juvenes
Nunc cantum promunt Volucres . . .

Now go the young men singing
And singing every bird . . .

But along with all this more than half pagan poetry, there was a serious protest that the true charity of Christ was disappearing from "Rome's high places."

Dic Christi veritas,
Dic cara raritas,
Dic rara caritas,
Ubi nunc habitas?

*Subsequent Latin poems and translations in this section reprinted from Helen Waddell, *Medieval Latin Lyrics,* 1929, by permission of the publisher, W.C. Constable, London.

O truth of Christ,
O most dear rarity,
O most rare charity,
Where dwell'st thou now?

Protest literature formed a large part of the whole Goliardic corpus of writing. It usually took the form of satire and parody, which was often in prose. *The Gospel According to Mark(s) of Silver,* for instance, mocked the corruption of the papal curia in pseudo-Biblical language and ended with a well-bribed pope instructing his cardinals, "Even as I receive, so receive ye also." All this was rather hard on the popes. The Roman church was, in fact, much better conducted in the twelfth century than in the preceding period—but no doubt people had come to expect much more of it.

Historical writing formed another important branch of medieval Latin literature. From a very early period, many monasteries kept a record of events of interest to the house in the form of annals. Before the twelfth century, almost all of these were narrow in range and slight in bulk. They would record the death of an abbot and the election of his successor, changes in important abbey officers, gifts to the house, important events in the lives of neighboring lords—especially if they had been donors of the house—and occasionally some more remote event such as the death of a king or pope. They are historical sources but hardly history in themselves. Although most of the monastic annals continued throughout the Middle Ages to follow this rather primitive model, at times real historians were entrusted with their composition, and they became true histories. Early in the twelfth century, a Norman monk named Orderic Vitalis wrote a *Historia Ecclesiastica.* Basically, it was the annals of his own monastery, but Orderic had a genuine historical enthusiasm and no objection to diverging from his theme. Whenever he mentioned a Norman noble house, he was inclined to give an account of its history. He devoted a great deal of space to the activities of the Norman dukes. The result was a vast, if rather confused, history of Normandy in the eleventh and early twelfth centuries. Other French historians were stimulated by the crusading movement, and two major accounts of the First Crusade were composed in Latin by Guibert of Nogent and Fulbert of Chartres. Later chroniclers of the crusades more commonly wrote in French.

In Germany the twelfth-century Cistercian abbot Otto of Freising attempted to compose a whole philosophy of history on Augustinian principles in a work called *The Two Cities.* He also wrote an account of his own times in *The Deeds of Frederick Barbarossa.* Many other medieval historians tried to survey the whole history of the human race from the creation to their own day. The earlier sections were put together from the Bible and from whatever classical histories or earlier medieval chronicles the historian had at hand. This introductory material was freely copied from one chronicle to another. Such works begin to acquire independent historical value at the point where the author starts to record the events of his own time.

Of all the medieval countries, England was the greatest center of historical writing. As early as the ninth century, Alfred the Great directed a number of monasteries to keep annals, and these, known today as the Anglo-Saxon Chronicle, provide a good outline of English history down to the twelfth century. Also, in the twelfth century, many abbeys, for example Canterbury, Worcester, Durham, and Bury St. Edmunds, produced distinguished historians. Perhaps the greatest of them was William of Malmesbury, whose *History of the Kings of England* is a considerable work of literature, marked by great narrative skill and a sober judgment of events. By the end of the twelfth century, most major historians are found working outside the monasteries, although the abbey of St. Albans provides an exception. Two of the best-known chroniclers of the Middle Ages wrote there in the thirteenth century. They were Roger of Wendover and Matthew Paris, who described the great events of their day with matchless color and vigor.

The medieval chroniclers lacked one motive that is dominant among modern historians: the desire to penetrate deeply into the characteristic forms of life and thought of past ages. They thought of Julius Caesar as a feudal king with a retinue of feudal knights. They envisaged Alexander as living in a medieval castle, dressed in medieval armor. On the other hand, they displayed a sound historical instinct in their desire to record and evaluate the events of the recent past. They often seem to modern critics unduly credulous in recounting improbable stories at second hand, and since the monastic chroniclers were servants of God and writing for his glory, they could rarely resist a miracle or the opportunity to point a moral. Their works have to be used with caution, but they provide the basic framework of our knowledge of medieval history.

There were relatively few autobiographies or biographies of secular figures. Peter Abelard's *Historia Calamitatum* is quite exceptional. The abbot Suger, who was important in the development of medieval architecture as the builder of St. Denis and in the development of the French state as a minister of Louis VI, was also a notable writer. His *Life of Louis VI* provides a vivid picture of the condition of the French royal demesne at the beginning of the twelfth century. Many works that are not formal biographies contain details about the lives and personalities of important figures. The chronicle of Jocelyn of Brakelond, for instance, provides a vivid character sketch of a great medieval prelate in its portrayal of Abbot Samson of Bury St. Edmunds. While there were few secular biographies, there were innumerable medieval *Lives* of saints. The saints played an extremely important part in popular religion, and accounts of their lives were of wide interest to the people of the day. As a rule, the life of a saint was written and rewritten many times and grew fuller and more detailed each time. These accounts are, of course, filled with miraculous events. They are of great value to the student of medieval beliefs and religious ideas.

The Middle Ages produced many other kinds of writing in Latin.

There were many devotional works. Then there were treatises on various practical subjects. In the thirteenth century, an Englishman named Walter of Henley wrote a treatise on agriculture. The treasurer of England, Richard Fitz Neal, wrote a work describing the procedures of the English exchequer. A number of scholars wrote works on the proper training of the young. These were usually intended to guide the education of princes and nobles. Books were also produced on the chief noble sports—hunting and tourneying. Finally, the Middle Ages were well supplied with anecdotists. The greatest of them was John of Salisbury, who, after his first studies at Chartres, spent several years at the papal curia and wrote a lively account of his experiences there. He also wrote a work of political theory, the *Policraticus,* which was famous in the later Middle Ages for its defense of tyrannicide. In another book called the *Metalogicon,* John reminisced about his days as a student and criticized the educational tendencies of the mid-twelfth century. He deplored the increasing concentration of formal logic, which he saw as mere sterile word-spinning, for he feared that such vanities would drive out all the sound, humanistic, literary studies that had formed his own mind. John had the good fortune to end his days as bishop of Chartres, the city that he had first known as a young student and that was still a stronghold of humanism at the end of the twelfth century.

66. *Vernacular Literature to Dante*

John of Salisbury was wrong in supposing that the new philosophical studies would be merely sterile, but he was right in seeing that the schools were turning away from the study of Latin literature as a major preoccupation. Indeed (if we except a few great hymns), the ability—and the desire—to produce creative works of imaginative literature in Latin hardly outlived the twelfth century. Even before then, much of the most significant literature had been written in vernacular tongues. The poets who wrote in Latin produced many brilliant short lyrics, but the only long, complex works of medieval literature that are comparable in esthetic achievement to the great Gothic cathedrals were composed in Germanic or Romance languages.

The earliest of these works that survive are of German origin. The early Germans were accustomed to composing songs celebrating the deeds of heroic warriors to be sung at feasts and other festive occasions. Charlemagne is said to have ordered a collection of such songs to be made, but if his order was carried out, the collection has been lost. We have only a few fragments of what may have been an extensive literature. By far the most important of these early works is the Anglo-Saxon epic poem *Beowulf.* This seems to be a combination of several songs composed in the Danish peninsula in heathen times, told and retold, and finally reduced to writing after the conversion of the Anglo-Saxons. The central theme of the story is the heroic deeds of

Beowulf, who slays two savage monsters and a fire-breathing dragon but is slain himself in the last adventure. This poem is a masterpiece of literature and gives the reader a feeling that in it he has the true spirit of the early German culture. Except for one or two fragments, *Beowulf* is our only surviving example of the Anglo-Saxon epic. It is also in its present form the oldest extant piece of Germanic vernacular literature.

There is, however, a considerable amount of early German literature that survives in comparatively late manuscripts. The oldest of these is the *Hildebrandslied,* a tale of the times of Attila the Hun, which may well have been a song of Charlemagne's time that has come down to us in an eleventh-century manuscript. The cycle of the *Nibelungenlied* is composed of stories that originated in the early German times, but the form in which it has survived dates from the thirteenth century. These entrancing mixtures of heroism and magic form an important part of the literary heritage of western Europe. Then the Vikings who plundered the coasts of Europe and colonized the wild islands of the North Atlantic and even the American coast composed long *sagas* about their adventures. Here again, our earliest manuscripts come from the twelfth century, but many of the stories deal with earlier times. No one who has not read some of this literature can understand the great achievements of these wild adventurers. In fact, it is in the sagas that we can best see the Germanic characteristics—love of freedom, impatience with restraint, reckless bravery, lavish generosity—that formed so important a part of upper-class ethics in the Middle Ages. The military chivalry of later times can only be comprehended through a knowledge of the Germanic warriors.

Beowulf was but a small part of Anglo-Saxon literature. There were two great religious poets, Caedmon and Cynewulf, and many lesser masters of that craft. We have already noted that King Alfred translated into Anglo-Saxon a varied series of works—the *Pastoral Care* of Gregory the Great, the history of Orosius, Bede's *Ecclesiastical History,* and Boethius' *Consolation of Philosophy.* In Anglo-Saxon England, Latin was reserved for the works of high ecclesiastics writing on purely religious subjects. The chronicles, official documents, royal decrees, tales of battles and noble deeds, and even popular religious works were in the vernacular. Thus England had a written language and flourishing literature of its own at a time when Latin ruled supreme in the rest of western Europe. Only after the Norman conquest did Anglo-Saxon slowly wither away, to reappear in the fourteenth century as Middle English.

Toward the close of the eleventh century, vernacular literature began to appear in France. The people of this kingdom spoke two different Romance languages—the *langue d'oil* in the north, and the *langue d'oc* in the south, which took their names from the different pronunciation of the word "yes." The earliest literature in the *langue d'oc* was lyric poetry that had love as its chief theme. The origins of this poetry are obscure. It seems clear that a certain amount of popular poetry had survived in southern France from Roman times, and this may well have served as the original model. Then, across the Pyrenees in Spain, there flourished lyrical love poetry among the Arabs. There is some evidence that verse forms, if not ideas, came from this source. At any rate, in the last years of the eleventh century, poets in southern France began composing love poetry in the *langue d'oc*.*

This idea caught the interest of the greatest feudal prince of the region, William IX, count of Poitou and duke of Aquitaine. Duke William began to write poetry. One of his best lyrics describes his emotions on setting out for the Holy Land.

Since now I have a mind to sing
I'll make a song of that which saddens me,
That no more in Poitou or Limousin,
Shall I love's servant be.

William's patronage was enough to make the new art popular. Soon there were many poets between the Alps and the Pyrenees. They were called *troubadours.* Some troubadours were men of high rank like Duke William, and many were of knightly birth, but others were simply talented poets who wanted to make a living. The basic idea of troubadour poetry was the beneficial effects of admiration for a worthy woman. By loving a noble lady, a man became a better knight and a better poet. This love could be quite distant and still yield its benefits:

Most sad, most joyous shall I go away,
Let me have seen her for a single day,
My love afar.

The first troubadours were imaginative artists, but soon this poetry became extremely conventional. All ladies were blond with pure white skin. Their lovers had no interest in food and drink; they did not notice either hot or cold. Their minds were wholly absorbed in love for their ladies. If a lover served his lady long and faithfully and wrote many poems in her honor, she might reward him with a smile, a kiss, or even a more intimate favor. As these ladies were always married, scholars have wondered whether this poetry was an adjunct to adultery. The answer seems fairly simple. When the poet was a great lord, he undoubtedly expected and often obtained the ultimate reward. Certainly, Duke William of Aquitaine was no distant admirer of fair ladies. But when the poet was a humble knight praising the wife of a great baron, he confined his love to admiration, if he had any normal discretion. And as the dignity of the lady gave prestige to her lovers, great noblewomen were the usual subjects of the troubadour poems. Troubadour poetry reached its height in imagery, freshness, and vigor about the middle of the twelfth century. While it survived another hundred years, it grew steadily more conventional and less spontaneous. The fearful Albigensian crusade ravaged the troubadour country, and destroyed much of the carefree spirit that had animated its poems.

*Sources, no. 51

The fashion for writing poetry and the interest in love was carried into northern France by Eleanor, duchess of Aquitaine, when she became the wife of King Louis VII. Eleanor was the granddaughter of the earliest troubadour, Duke William IX, and also the patroness of many poets. When Eleanor's marriage to Louis was annulled and she became queen of England, her court remained for some years a center of literature and courtly love. Her imprisonment in Winchester castle for encouraging the revolt of her sons was mourned by many troubadours. Eleanor's place as chief patroness of courtly love was taken by her two daughters, Marie, countess of Champagne, and Alix, countess of Blois. Marie's court at Troyes became the literary capital of France, and her grandson, Thibaut IV, count of Champagne, was the most prolific and one of the most talented lyric poets of the thirteenth century. Writing poetry became as fashionable in the north as it had been in the south. Eleanor's son, King Richard I of England, was an enthusiastic though not very adept poet. During the first half of the thirteenth century, northern France produced a dozen or so noble devotees of lyric love poetry. Moreover, the fashion spread to Italy and Germany, where Walther von der Vogelweide (d. 1228) wrote beautiful love songs as well as much satiric verse.* (While the *minnesingers* of Germany flourished for a comparatively short time, the troubadour tradition continued in Italy until the Renaissance. Meanwhile, in both France and Germany the writing of poetry had been taken over by the burghers of the great towns and continued among them into the fourteenth century.

When the troubadour ideas were transplanted to the north, the word *love* took on a rather different meaning. To the troubadours, distant admiration and faithful service to a lady could bring the benefits bestowed by love, but when the northern writers spoke of love, they meant sexual relations. While the noble lady might be put on a pedestal, this was purely as a matter of form, and there was never any doubt what the poet expected from her. This change may have been a result of the fact that the men of the north were less civilized and cruder than those of the south, but it may also have come from the source to which they turned for new ideas about love. When the people of the twelfth century wanted information, they turned naturally to some ancient authority. The devotees of courtly love soon found such a work—Ovid's *Ars Amoris.*

Ovid wrote about a society in which very few women were bound in permanent matrimony—the wives of the most exalted senators with religious duties in the Roman cult. Most husbands and wives could separate by mutual consent, and many couples never bothered with any formal legal connection. The women of Ovid were either lightly bound wives or completely unfettered adventuresses. And there was nothing courtly or romantic about love in Ovid; it was purely and completely sensual. But the courtly lovers managed to ignore his cruder ideas and draw from his book ideas and conceits about the nature of love. Chrétien de Troyes, who served the Countess Marie of Champagne, translated the *Ars Amoris.* Another member of Marie's house-

*Sources no. 51

hold, Andrew the Chaplain, drew freely on it in composing a handbook of courtly love that he called *De Amore.* Andrew presented his work—perhaps satirically—as a guide to all who might want to be engaged in courtly love. He carefully defined love, showed who was eligible to practice it, invented a code of the laws of love, and supplied sample conversations as aids to efficient seduction. Then, in case his reader didn't believe in courtly love, his last section was a bitter diatribe against women.*

While lyric poetry was developing in southern France, another type of French literature appeared—the *chanson de geste.* These *chansons* were products of the late eleventh and twelfth centuries, though the authors drew on earlier legends for their material. Although there are incidents in the *chansons* that are historic, they have been modified so much that the songs are of no use to the historian as records of actual fact. Thus, after one of Charlemagne's campaigns in Spain, his rear guard was attacked and severely mauled by the Basques in a narrow mountain pass in the Pyrenees. In the *Song of Roland* the rear guard is attacked by Saracens in a broad valley.

The *chansons de geste* were clearly composed primarily for the entertainment of the feudal male. Their chief elements were the two subjects in which he was most interested—fighting and feudal politics. The first part of the finest of these poems, the *Chanson de Roland,* consists of a political contest at Charlemagne's court between Roland and Ganelon. Then there came the great battle in which Roland and his companions slew untold thousands of Saracens.† Although in some of the *chansons* feudal warfare between Christians replaced the fighting against Saracens, the general ingredients were the same. Women had little place in these poems. Occasionally, we see a mother sending her sons to war or a wife being brutally beaten by her husband. Then here and there appear charming princesses, Christian or Muslim, burning with enthusiasm to join some knight in his bed. Muslim princesses had one great advantage—they had to be converted and baptized, and the latter ceremony involved undressing them and describing their charms in detail. Only in a few late *chanson* are there feeble glimmerings of the ideas of courtly love. The lyric poems were written to please women, but the *chansons de geste* were definitely for men's taste.

By the middle of the twelfth century, there was an active demand for stories. The nobles and their courts wanted to be entertained during the long evenings, and the wandering minstrel who had good tales to recite could be sure of a generous reward. The *trouvères,* as the composers of these stories were called, used any material they could find. Legends from Roman literature were popular. Thus a *trouvère* based a romance on the story of Aeneas. With all the formalities of courtly love, Aeneas loved and left Dido and finally won Lavinia. But the chief source of tales for the writers of twelfth-century France was the folklore of Wales.

Toward the middle of the twelfth century, an English clerk named Geoffrey of Monmouth wrote (in Latin) a *History of the Kings of Britain.*

*Sources, no. 54

†Sources, no. 50

Geoffrey told how the Trojan Brutus came to Britain and became its king. He then recited a history of the kingdom to the coming of the Anglo-Saxons. Among his kings was a heroic warrior named Arthur, who vigorously fought the foes of his realm. Geoffrey's contemporaries had no hesitation in saying that his work was wholly imaginary, and many modern scholars share this view. Geoffrey himself said he got his material from an old Welsh book. Now there was undoubtedly a large mass of Welsh folklore—tales of giants and fairies, or brave heroes and fair ladies—much of which came to be interwoven into later versions of the Arthurian legend. The controversy as to whether Geoffrey invented King Arthur or found him in Welsh tales is too complicated to go into at length. On the whole, there seems to be adequate evidence that the Welsh did have such a hero and that Geoffrey got his ideas from them. Be that as it may, Geoffrey's book was immensely popular, and about 1155 a French version of it was produced by the Norman Wace. From then onward, King Arthur and his knights were seized upon as a marvelous subject for stories. Moreover, the *trouvères* dipped deeply into Welsh folklore and came up with many tales not used by Geoffrey.

Perhaps the most noted user of this new material was Marie of Champagne's favorite writer, Chrétien de Troyes. He took Welsh stories and wrote into them the ideas of courtly love. When he needed a little variety, he had no objection to using classical material. One of his stories, "Cliges," is laid half at Arthur's court and half in Constantinople. All the chief Arthurian heroes received attention from Chrétien. He wrote a "Tristran" that is lost, a "Lancelot," and a "Percival." The "Lancelot" is a pure work of courtly love. Lancelot, the best of Arthur's knights, gave up everything a knight should hold dear for love. He committed the serious feudal crime of adultery with his lord's wife, Queen Guinevere. He allowed himself to be carried in a hangman's cart. He resisted the wiles of all other ladies. He was the perfect courtly lover. Actually, Chrétien had his doubts about Lancelot and is careful to say that the Countess Marie gave him the material and told him how to use it. Later he wrote of Percival, the Christian knight, who resisted all ladies. Chrétien de Troyes was a master storyteller, and his tales still make excellent reading. A contemporary of Chrétien, Marie de France, wrote short narrative poems, or lays, that were an adroit mixture of Welsh legend, courtly love, and the life she saw about her. Her verve and charm make her works also acceptable to the modern reader.

The Arthurian material was immensely popular and was used by many writers. By the thirteenth century, the stories about King Arthur and his knights had been developed into an extensive series culminating in the finding of the Holy Grail. Here again French examples inspired German writers. Wolfram von Eisenbach's *Parzifal* (ca. 1220) is the greatest of all the Grail Romances. As time went on, the tales grew longer and more numerous. In the fifteenth century, an English knight, Sir Thomas Malory, drew from them the material for his *Morte d'Arthur.* This magnificent collection of Arthurian tales, written with great verve and enthusiasm, has inspired English writers ever since that time—including, in wildly different ways, Alfred Lord Tennyson, Mark Twain, T. S. Eliot, and the creators of the musical play *Camelot.* It is an important part of our literary heritage.

Another interesting type of French literature were the *fabliaux*—short stories often based on Aesop's fables. These tales were likely to be coarse in their wit and were clearly intended to amuse not too delicate audiences. While some scholars have assumed that they were intended primarily for the bourgeois taste, there is little doubt that they were fully appreciated in castle halls. Marie de France, whose *Lais* depicted the noble life, was the author of a famous collection of *fabliaux* that cannot be said to be notable for their delicacy.

There was a similar earthy flavor in much of the drama that constituted an important branch of medieval vernacular literature in all the major languages. By the thirteenth century, three types of plays were commonly performed: mystery plays based on the Bible, miracle plays derived from saints' lives, and morality plays in which the actors appeared as personified virtues and vices—Wisdom, Folly, Anger, Lust, and so on. The plays were occasionally acted in old Roman theaters or, more commonly, on wooden stages with crude scenery, which were erected in the city squares. In England plays were mounted on wagons that could be dragged through a city, stopping at several points to repeat the performance for different audiences. The greater cycles of mystery plays, like the Lincoln plays, presented the whole story of humanity's fall and redemption in dozens of scenes based on the Old and New Testaments. Often the guilds of a city would each undertake to produce a particular scene, choosing an appropriate one wherever possible. The carpenters might enact the building of Noah's ark; the wine merchants, the marriage at Cana; and the bakers, the feeding of the five thousand.

Coarse and comical episodes were woven even into plays dealing with the most solemn themes, but this only shows to what an extent religion was part and parcel of everyday life in the Middle Ages. Some of the incidents may seem disconcerting to modern religious sensibilities. The Devil often appeared as a comical figure to be mocked at; more surprisingly, St. Joseph was sometimes portrayed unsympathetically. Apparently, medieval people could not help seeing something ridiculous in a man who had been cuckolded—even by God. In the Lincoln plays, Joseph appeared as a cross-grained curmudgeon who was rude and discourteous to his wife as they journeyed toward Bethlehem. Mary asked him to climb a cherry tree to bring her some fruit. He refused surlily and spat out:

> Let him get you cherries that got you with child!

But at those words the cherry tree miraculously bowed down to Mary and offered her its fruit—no doubt to the great delight of the spectators.

From the late twelfth century onward, we find major historical and biographical works written in French. The first such work was Wace's *Roman de Rou,* a rather uninspiring verse history of the dukes of Normandy. A much greater work was the account of the Fourth Crusade and the conquest of Constantinople composed by Geoffrey de Villehardouin (d. 1213). Villehardouin was a layman who had taken part in the crusade that he described. A little later, about 1255, an anonymous author wrote a biography in French of the great English baron, William Marshal. This historian was far more sophisticated than most of his contemporaries. He distinguishes carefully between what he knows and what he feels is uncertain. Often he cites his sources. Several times he admits that his informants differ and that he does not know just what happened. In everything directly relevant to the career of his hero, he is extremely accurate. Toward the end of the thirteenth century, John, lord of Joinville, dictated one of the most famous biographies of the Middle Ages, the *History of St. Louis.* He provides a splendid portrait of a great king, and his eye for homely detail and lively style make his book interesting reading today, as it was in his own time.*

In Spain the great epic poem of the Cid was composed in Castilian about 1140. In the next century, King Alfonso X (1252–1284) organized the writing of a great history of Castile in the vernacular—the *Grande e Generale Estoria.*

Italian vernacular poetry developed more slowly than French, though the *Canticle of the Sun* by St. Francis of Assisi provides a masterpiece from the early thirteenth century. The most famous of Italian poets was Dante Alighieri (1265–1321), and his *Divine Comedy* is commonly reckoned the greatest literary achievement of the whole Middle Ages. Dante took the familiar idea of medieval chivalry that devotion to a lady ennobled a knight and turned it into an allegory of divine love. His early writing tells how he fell in love with a young Florentine girl, Beatrice, who died when the poet was twenty-five. After a period of despair, he turned to the study of philosophy, and in 1308 he wrote *The Banquet,* an exposition in Italian of Aristotelian ethics. Meanwhile, Dante had been exiled from his native city of Florence for supporting a political faction that opposed the Italian policies of the pope. This experience made him a bitter critic of the papacy and strongly proimperial in his political sympathies. In a treatise called *On Monarchy,* he argued in favor of a universal world state presided over by the emperor.

Dante's masterpiece, the *Divine Comedy,* was written in the last years of his life. It is a vision of the whole Christian universe and the place of man in it, reflecting the views of contemporary theologians and philosophers and expressed with incomparable insight and literary skill. The poem tells of a journey by the author through the regions of hell, purgatory, and paradise. At every level Dante describes encounters with a great variety of persons—historical figures, characters from medieval legends, well-known personalities of his own day. (Dante reserved a special place in hell for his old enemy, Pope Boniface VIII.†) The work has often been described as a literary counter-

*Sources, no. 66

†Sources, no. 82

part of Thomas Aquinas' *Summa Theologiae.* In the *Summa* one finds, brought together in one great treatise, all the accepted ideas of the age about the spiritual and physical world and the virtues and vices of humanity. Dante's *Divine Comedy* is a similar work of art. There, in heaven, purgatory, or hell, are found the people who represent every phase of human life, each in his or her proper place according to the tenets of the faith. For some temperaments, Dante's will always seem the more perfect synthesis in that the complexities of human thought and behavior can be seen more clearly and fully through individual men and women than in abstract discussions of virtues and vices. Thus one might study the *Summa Theologiae* long and hard before learning the Church's opinion of courtly literature; but when Francesca tells Dante how reading about Lancelot brought her and Paolo to sin, this relationship stands forth clear and precise. And the warrior baron and troubadour Bertran de Born suffers in hell not for robbing merchants or devastating the countryside but for alienating young Prince Henry from his father King Henry II of England.

Dante's characters have symbolic significance, but they are also real persons who discourse on history and religion and (often bitingly) on the contemporary affairs of Dante's world. The exposition moves always on the two levels of realism and allegory. For the first part of the journey through hell and purgatory, the poet's guide was the pagan Vergil. But for the ascent into heaven, the guide was Beatrice. The lost love of Dante's youth reemerged in his greatest work as an allegorical figure symbolizing the divine light of Christian revelation. At the conclusion of the *Paradiso,* Beatrice leads Dante to the threshold of the highest sphere of heaven, and the whole work ends as the poet enters the presence of God with a vision of the divine love that Dante saw pervading the entire universe:

> The Love that sways the sun and other stars

Dante's poetry, like the great cathedrals and the scholastic *Summae,* may serve to remind us once again that the Christian faith was a central theme of medieval culture.

READING SUGGESTIONS

* *B. Tierney,* Sources *and* Readings, *vol. I, nos. 49–53, 81; vol. II, no. 31.*

Many beautifully illustrated works on medieval art are available. Among the most important studies are H. Focillon, *The Art of the West in the Middle Ages,* 2 vols. (London, England, 1963); W. R. Lethaby, *Medieval Art,* rev. ed. (London, England, 1949), E. W Anthony, *Romanesque Frescoes* (Princeton, 1951); A. N. Grabar and C. Nordenfalk, *Romanesque Painting from the Eleventh to the Thirteenth Centuries* (Lausanne, 1958); P. Deschamps, *French Sculpture of the Romanesque Period* (Paris, France, 1930); M. Aubert, *French Sculpture at the Beginning of the Gothic Period* (Paris, France, 1929); H. Arnold, *Stained Glass of the Middle Ages* (London, England, 1939). On architecture, see K. J. Conant, *Early Medieval Church Architecture* (Baltimore, 1942); A. W. Clapham, *Romanesque Architecture in Western Europe* (Oxford, England, 1936); P. Frankl, *Gothic Architecture* (Harmondsworth, 1962); T. G. Jackson, *Gothic Architecture,* 2 vols. (Cambridge, 1915). The standard work on iconography is * E. Mâle, *The Gothic Image: Religious Art in France of the Thirteenth Century* (London, England, 1913).

For building techniques, see * T. Bowie (ed.), *The Sketchbook of Villard de Honnecourt* (Bloomington, Ind., 1968); * J. Gimpel, *The Cathedral Builders* (New York, 1961); and J. F. Fitchen, *The Construction of the Gothic Cathedrals* (New York, 1961). The following works deal with the relationships between art and architecture and the background of medieval society and culture; * H. Adams, *Mont-Saint-Michel and Chartres* (Washington, 1904), an old classic; * A. Hauser, *The Social History of Art,* vol. I (New York, 1957); * O. von Simson, *The Gothic Cathedral* (New York, 1956); * E. Panofsky, *Gothic Architecture and Scholasticism* (Latrobe, Pa., 1951); * J. Harvey, *The Gothic World, 1100–1600* (London, England, 1950). Suger's description of the church of St. Denis is translated by E. Panofsky, *Abbot Suger on the Abbey Church of St. Denis* (Princeton, 1946).

For Latin literature, see E. J. E. Raby, *A History of Secular Latin Poetry,* 2nd ed. (Oxford, England, 1957); *A History of Christian Latin Poetry,* 2nd ed. (Oxford, England, 1953); * E. Curtius, *European Literature and the Latin Middle Ages* (New York, 1953). H. Waddell provides a lively introduction to the Goliards in * *The Wandering Scholars* (London, England, 1934), and sensitive translations of their verse in * *Mediaeval Latin Lyrics* (London, England, 1933). Another collection of translations is J. A. Symonds, *Wine, Women and Song* (London, England, 1925). Most of the English chronicles mentioned above are translated in the *Bohn Antiquarian Library.* For chronicles of the Crusades, see Chapter XI. The best introduction to liturgical literature and music is W. Apel, *Gregorian Chant* (Bloomington, Ind., 1958). See also G. Reese, *Music in the Middle Ages* (New York, 1940). Several records of Gregorian chant are available, and the Benediktbeuern songs mentioned in the text have also been recorded under the title *Carmina Burana.*

The works of R. W. Southern and H. O. Taylor cited in Chapters VII and XIII are valuable for vernacular literature. An excellent introduction to medieval Romance is * C. S. Lewis, *The Allegory of Love* (Oxford, England, 1938). For a different approach, see A. J. Denomy, *The Heresy of Courtly Love* (New York, 1947). W. Kerr, *Epic and Romance* (Oxford, England, 1908) is still valuable. Standard works on particular countries are A. W. Ward and A. R. Waller, *The Cambridge History of English Literature,* vol. I (Cambridge, 1907); U. T. Holmes, *A History of Old French Literature,* 2nd ed. (London, England, 1948); E. H. Wilkins, *A History of Italian Literature* (Cambridge, Mass., 1954); J. G Robertson, *A History of German Literature,* 2nd ed. (London, England, 1947). A brief introduction to the complicated world of Dante studies is T. G. Bergin, *Dante* (New York, 1965). Other valuable studies are K. Vossler, *Medieval Culture: An Introduction to Dante and His Times,* 2 vols. (New York, 1929); E. Gilson, *Dante the Philosopher* (New York, 1949); A. P. d'Entréves, *Dante as a Political Thinker* (London, England, 1952). On drama, see K. Young, *The Drama of the Medieval Church* (Oxford, England, 1933), and H. Craig, *English Religious Drama of the Middle Ages* (Oxford, England, 1955). Among the numerous translations from medieval vernacular literature, the following are available in paperback editions: * D. Wright, *Beowulf* (Harmondsworth, England, 1957); * C. K. Scott-Moncrieff, *The Song of Roland* (London, 1920); * L. B. Simpson, *The Poem of the Cid* (Berkeley, 1957);

* R. S. and L. H. Loomis, *Medieval Romances* (New York, 1957) [contains Perceval, Tristan, Aucassin and Nicolette, Sir Gawain, etc.]; * D. Sayers and B. Reynolds *The Comedy of Dante Alighieri* (Harmondsworth, England, 1949–1962). Many varieties of medieval literature are presented in C. W. Jones, *Medieval Literature in Translation* (New York, 1950).

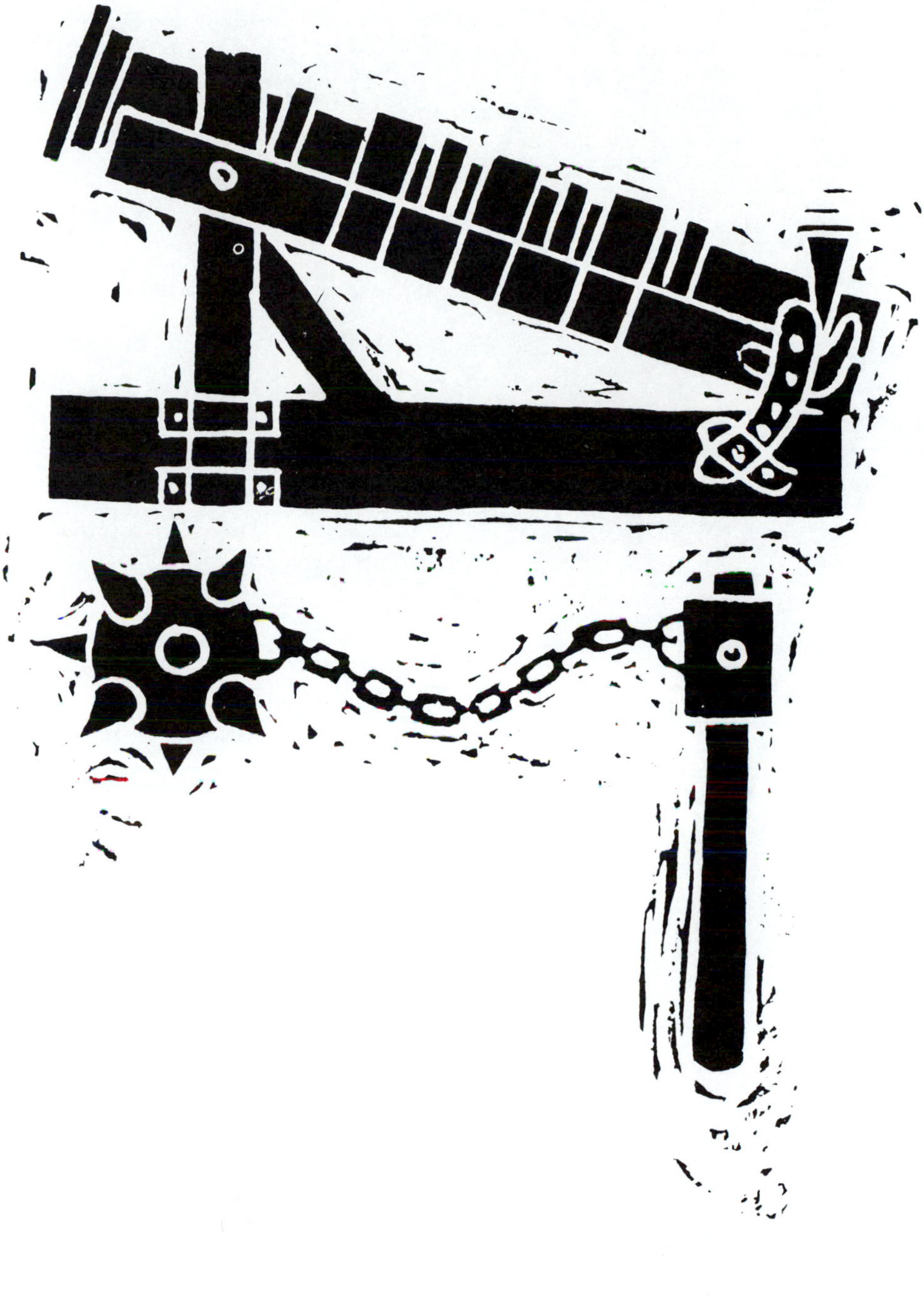

THE MEDIEVAL WORLD IN CRISIS

chapter

XX

An Age of Adversity

The fourteenth century was an age of rapid change, much of it changed for the worse. There were new wars, an unprecedented plague, rebellions, famine, schism in the church. Because of such developments, the late medieval period has often been called an age of disintegration or presented as merely the gloomy twilight of a "waning" civilization. But this is very much an oversimplification. The people of the fourteenth and fifteenth centuries showed creative vigor in many fields. They produced brilliant new works of art and literature, new movements of philosophical and scientific thought, the first systematic theories of representative government, the English House of Commons, the whole political framework of early modern Europe. Some medieval institutions and ideas were indeed decaying, but others found a new vitality as they adapted themselves to the changing circumstances of a new era. By the end of the period, Western civilization was again entering on an age of expansion; but it was no longer the same civilization as that of the thirteenth century. The late medieval period was an age of extreme complexity precisely because it was an age of transition. In the following chapters, we shall consider some of the forces that disrupted the apparently stable civilization of the thirteenth century.

67. *Problems of Medieval Civilization: Intellectual, Social, Economic, and Political*

In 1275 a medieval man and woman might reasonably have hoped that their society was on the way to creating a serene civilization that could endure for centuries. The upsurge of religious vitality that began in the eleventh century had transformed the structure of society and had inspired both profound philosophies and beautiful works of art. The dualist heresies of the twelfth century had been represssed, and the papacy was universally accepted as head of a common Christian religion. The struggle of empire and papacy had come to an end, and the empire had found a new head in Rudolph of Hapsburg. Europe was prosperous. The great nations of the Western world were at peace with one another and an optimist might have supposed that the basic political problems of the age had been solved so that no occasion need arise for major wars in the future.

All this appearance of tranquillity was an illusion. The achievements of the thirteenth century were splendid, but they were not stable. The very works that are most commonly cited as examples of a "medieval synthesis" were filled with sharp tensions. Thomas Aquinas' *Summa* contained elements of Greek philosophy and of Christian doctrine that later thinkers often regarded as intrinsically incompatible with one another. Dante, the greatest of Catholic poets, was bitterly hostile to the popes of his own day. The Gothic cathedral was no symbol of a static civilization but a dynamic affair of thrusts and counterthrusts.

In every sphere of medieval life and thought—intellectual, economic, political, and religious—forces making for radical change existed at the end of the thirteenth century. In intellectual life, the dominant fact was the failure of Thomas Aquinas' synthesis to command general assent. The bishop of Paris condemned a long list of Averroistic propositions in 1277, and among them were doctrines that Thomas had defended and incorporated into his own system of thought. The Dominicans succeeded in having the Thomistic theses rehabilitated and they came to regard Thomas as the official doctor of their order, but outside the Dominican community his philosophy was not widely accepted. The Franciscans, for instance, preferred to follow Bonaventura* or Duns Scotus (ca. 1266–1308). (Scotus propounded a more "realist" solution to the problem of universals than Thomas Aquinas and laid a greater stress on the will as against the reason.) At first the differences among the leaders of thought were technical disagreements within a common framework of accepted ideas; but the greatest logician of the fourteenth century, William of Ockham (ca. 1285–1349), produced a radically destructive critique of the whole preceding tradition of medieval philosophy and introduced a new mood of skepticism into the university world. His work is discussed below.†

Another set of problems for thirteenth-century people arose from the changing structure of society, above all from the growing obsolescence of feudal institutions. The growth of an exchange economy based on money transactions altered greatly the relationship between lord and vassal. With a money revenue, a lord could hire soldiers to fight for him and officials to administer his affairs. Instead of a feudal levy that went home at the end of forty days, a lord could have troops who would serve as long as they were paid. Moreover, by engaging as officers men of the middle class, a lord could procure agents who would put his interests first. A seneschal who was a vassal always had in mind the point of view of his fellow vassals; a middle-class seneschal

*See p. 427.
†See pp. 496–497.

had no such sympathies. There was also a tendency to commute feudal services into money payments. The lord would accept a sum of money from a vassal instead of requiring his service in the host, and with the money he would hire a soldier. Bit by bit the relations between lord and vassals became less personal and more purely financial. By the end of the thirteenth century, tenure by knight service was largely a rather expensive way to hold land.

In one sense all these changes might be regarded as signs of progress. The difficulty was that the whole coherence of medieval society, at least in northern Europe, had depended on an implicit acceptance of feudal values. During the twelfth and thirteenth centuries, the structure of society changed radically, but no alternative set of values came to be generally accepted by the dominant feudal nobility. Hence feudal forms continued to dominate many areas of medieval life, even though they were becoming increasingly out of tune with social realities. Kingdoms were inherited like pieces of feudal property and acquired by judicious marriage alliances long after medieval jurists had developed Roman law theories of public authority and of popular consent as the basis of sovereignty. Customary land law continued to be riddled with anachronistic feudal regulations. Great nobles continued to play chivalrous, feudal games, though if they actually went to war, they were liable to be shot down by a mercenary archer. There was a great lag in the adjustment of social ideas to changing realities.

In the economic sphere too major difficulties arose. Some of the abundant natural resources of early medieval Europe were becoming exhausted. Agricultural production ceased to grow; output of silver and other metals fell off as the mines which had penetrated to deep strata became exposed to flooding. The commercial expansion which had lasted through the twelfth and thirteenth centuries came to a halt.

All the achievements of medieval civilization that we have described in earlier chapters had rested on the basis of a steadily expanding agrarian economy. The steady growth of wealth facilitated the accumulation of capital to finance trade. It also made practical the creation of sophisticated and expensive structures of government without too grievous pressure on the subject populations. In a declining economy, interrelated strains began to appear in every sphere of medieval life. The growth of a network of commerce and international finance had made the different regions of Europe more economically dependent on one another; but this interdependence created vulnerability in time of stress. In the 1340s the two greatest financial houses of Florence, the Peruzzi and the Bardi, went bankrupt, bringing ruin to many of their depositors. The Florentine banks collapsed because King Edward III of England defaulted on enormous loans they had made to him; Edward in turn had accumulated huge debts because he wanted to finance a war with France.

Political conditions as well as economic ones worsened toward the end of the thirteenth century. The relative tranquillity that existed in the 1270s did not last. England and France had remained at peace in the middle years of the century only because Henry III was a feeble king and Louis IX was a magnanimous one who did not choose to take advantage of his vassal's weakness. The holding of a French province by English kings would provide plenty of opportunities for conflict under future rulers, and these conflicts led eventually to the devastating Hundred Years' War.

Moreoever, although the fact did not become apparent at once, Innocent IV's destruction of the Hohenstaufen power in Italy created a state of instability throughout the Mediterranean region. The fragmentation of the empire had removed a threat to the papacy, but it also weakened the strength of the Western world as a whole. By the end of the thirteenth century, western Christian society was no longer capable of holding the conquests of the twelfth century and still less capable of further expansion. As we have seen, it was merely a matter of chance that Germany did not suffer a major Mongol invasion in 1242.* It was also a matter of luck that there were no other major incursions from Central Asia during the rest of the Middle Ages. In the eastern Mediterranean, on the other hand, the Saracens continued to launch frequent attacks and a steady erosion of the Western positions took place there.

The Latin kingdom of Jerusalem, confined to a few fortress cities on the coast after the unsuccessful crusade of St. Louis in 1249, could not long endure. That it lasted as long as it did was largely the result of the coming of the Mongols who took Bagdad in 1258. For a few years the Mongols kept the Egyptians occupied. Then in 1260 the sultan of Egypt routed the Mongols and was ready to turn against the Latin states. One by one the fortresses fell, until in 1291 the last strongholds of the Latin kingdom were reduced. The long and valiant defense of Acre in 1291 gave most of the Christians time to escape to Cyprus. The Templar forces in Palestine died defending their castle in Acre, but a strong body of Hospitalers withdrew to Cyprus. Some years later they transferred their headquarters to Rhodes, where they remained as a vigorous and belligerent outpost of western Christendom until they were overwhelmed by the Ottoman Turks under Suleiman the Magnificant in 1522 and forced to retreat to Malta.

The Byzantine Empire, which had been an invaluable bulwark against Islamic attacks all through the early centuries, had been reduced to a shambles of feuding principalities by the Fourth Crusade. In 1259 a Greek general named Michael Palaeologus (1259–1282) seized the kingdom of Nicea and took the title of emperor. In 1261 he succeeded in reoccupying Constantinople so that once again there was a Byzantine Empire based on the ancient capital city. But it was a sadly truncated state. The emperor controlled only the city itself and its immediate environs, the lands around Nicea in Asia Minor, and a part of Thessalonica. Michael was unable to inspire any great revival of Byzantine power. He and his successors, who ruled Byzantium until its fall in 1453, devoted themselves to endless feuds and intrigues against the Venetians and the Frankish duchies. Meanwhile, a new Mohammedan foe, the Ottoman Turks, began to attack the eastern

*See p. 386.

provinces of the empire. No pope or king or emperor of the later Middle Ages ever succeeded in organizing an effective crusade against them. Political idealism seems to have died with St. Louis.

68. *Population and Climate*

Many of the problems of fourteenth-century civilization arose out of the inherent tensions of medieval society and out of the deliberate choices of medieval people. If it were the business of a historian to award praise and blame, we could "blame" individual rulers for many of the things that went wrong in the later Middle Ages. But, in addition to all such self-made troubles, fourteenth-century society had to cope with a long-range demographic problem and then to endure one of the greatest natural calamities of all Western history—the Black Death. These were major factors in the developing crisis of the medieval world.

Although the situation varied from region to region, two broad generalizations can be made about conditions in early fourteenth-century Europe. The region was becoming saturated with population; and, at the same time, the climate was gradually changing for the worse.

Between 1000 and 1300 the population of western Europe increased by a factor of about 2.5—probably, for example, from about two million to five million in England, six million to fourteen million in France, four million to eleven million in Germany, and about the same in Italy. Such figures are very rough estimates, but the gross increase is evident enough. Obviously we cannot say that Europe was overpopulated in an absolute sense; the same region came to support many more people from the eighteenth century onward; but Europe in 1300 was very fully populated in relation to the existing technology and patterns of soil exploitation. The clearest indication of this is that the curve of demographic expansion flattened in the late thirteenth century and then turned downward.

During the period of growth, population had generally increased more rapidly in rural areas; city populations barely reproduced themselves, and were maintained or increased by immigration from the surrounding countryside. Rural overpopulation in the early fourteenth century is suggested by a continuing migration from the countryside to the cities, even after gross population had ceased to increase. Here and there precise figures survive. For instance, Lübeck in north Germany (with a population of ten to fifteen thousand) gained about 180 new families a year from immigration in the first half of the fourteenth century. Such migration could indicate a healthy reallocation of labor resources so long as urban industry and commerce were flourishing. But, in fact, during the fourteenth century we encounter in various parts of Europe increasing complaints of poverty in the cities as well as of vagabondage in the countryside.

In 1330 the chronicler Villani recorded with dismay that Florence had a population of seventeen thousand paupers. At the other end of Europe, the little agricultural village of Broughton in eastern England provides another kind of statistic. A recent investigation shows that the community lost eighteen percent of its population between 1288 and 1340, and that the loss can be accounted for largely by emigration. It would be optimistic to suppose that all who left their native village found equal or better opportunities elsewhere.

English manorial records provide extensive information about the relationship of population to reserves of land. Where comparisons can be made between surveys of the same estates carried out in the twelfth century and in the thirteenth century, they indicate a persistent decline in the size of peasant holdings. It is usually estimated that a holding of ten or fifteen acres was the minimum that could provide adequate subsistence for a typical family. But, by the end of the thirteenth century, about fifty percent of English peasants had holdings of ten acres or less. In one large sampling of about 13,500 holdings, over a third were only two acres or less. These figures do not prove, as is sometimes suggested, that half the population of England lived in a state of permanent destitution, on the very edge of starvation. Peasants with a holding too small to support their families by subsistence agriculture had always augmented their income in various ways—by practicing a craft perhaps or, most commonly, by working part-time for a richer neighbor. But the figures do suggest that the demographic growth of preceding centuries had reached a limit. Moreover, the agricultural expansion had led to the working of much marginal land. Around 1300 there were signs of significant declines in productivity and of abandonment of land that had become too poor to be worked profitably. Large-scale reclamation of fertile wasteland petered out in England in the late thirteenth century, presumably because such land was no longer available. Some small-scale assarting still went on here and there,* but it was probably more than offset by the marginal land that went out of cultivation. Population stagnated or declined.

Evidence of population saturation comes also from other parts of Europe. Twenty-three villages of the county of Beaumont-le-Roger in Normandy had a population of over a hundred thousand in 1313—not much different from that of the present day. In this region, land prices increased steadily from 1204 to 1270 but remained steady or declined from 1270 to 1313, suggesting a leveling off of population around 1300. The rich archives of Italy tell a similar story. The density of rural population around the Tuscan city of San Gemigniano in 1300 again approached twentieth-century levels. Shortage of land around Pistoia is indicated by very high rents; typically peasants had to pay more than half their annual income to landlords (and heavy city taxes on top of that). The population of this region was about thirty-four thousand in 1244, but a hundred years later it had declined by nearly a quarter. Rents reached their highest rate in the period 1250–1275.

*See p. 192.

Before considering further the implications of these demographic trends, we need to look at another factor influencing agrarian production, a gradual change in climatic conditions during the fourteenth century. Climatologists can investigate long-range changes in past weather conditions from many kinds of data. Fossilized pollen grains show the types of vegetation prevalent at different times and, especially in marginal areas, this can provide good evidence of climatic conditions. The study of tree rings ("dendrochronology" to its practitioners) provides indications of changes in precipitation, and advances and retreats of glaciers show evidence of changes in temperature. These kinds of data can be supplemented by information from medieval written sources—references to particularly wet or dry seasons, dates of harvests, distribution of vineyards. From all the available information a fairly clear picture emerges. The time of maximum medieval expansion from about 1000 to 1300 was a period of favorable weather conditions for farming in northern Europe—a "climatic optimum." But toward 1300 a cyclical change set in and the weather became significantly colder and wetter. There was a further fall in average temperature around 1550 and colder weather persisted until the nineteenth century. During the past century the climate has become generally warmer again.

Climatic conditions alone do not determine the course of history; the important question is how people cope with them. (The period of adverse conditions known as the "little ice age" in Europe, from the sixteenth century to the nineteenth, was one of extraordinary vitality and expansion.) Still, over a long period of time, the climatic changes of the late Middle Ages did put additional pressures on medieval society, especially in northern Europe. In mountainous regions the tree line crept lower as fields at higher altitudes were abandoned, and in Scandinavia the area of land capable of producing grain diminished. Drift ice made voyaging in the north Atlantic more difficult. The sea route to Greenland became unnavigable, and the Christian Viking settlement there ceased to exist; its last survivors were apparently absorbed into the primitive Eskimo population of the region. Herrings, which provided a major source of food in northern Europe, almost disappeared from the Baltic. Disastrous floods occurred in the polders of Holland. In England, which had had a substantial wine industry in the thirteenth century, grapes went out of cultivation. (In recent years, after the warming trend of the twentieth century, grapes have again been grown commercially in England.)

Such changes occurred very slowly. The change in average temperatures from the twelfth century to the fifteenth was about 1 to 1.5°C. This would be imperceptible to a human being over the course of a lifetime; but a difference of only 1° can influence the length of the summer growing season and the distribution of vegetation. The normal fluctuations from year to year were much more noticeable than the long-term trend; the possibility of a bad season had always existed; but, as the climate slowly worsened, the chance that a very bad year would occur marginally increased.

The worst possibilities were realized in 1313–1317, a time of widespread famine and epidemics throughout Europe. In 1315, rain began to fall heavily in May and it continued throughout the summer and autumn.* Peasants and their lords, seeing that a disaster was impending, tried to avert it by organized prayer. The Archbishop of Canterbury ordered his clergy to make solemn processions, ringing bells, carrying relics, and chanting litanies. A French writer described similar processions of lay folk, walking barefoot or altogether naked. "Many, even the women were naked . . . and they devoutly carried bodies of saints and other relics to be adored." On this occasion the prayers were not answered. Everywhere the harvest failed and hunger set in. (In September of this hideous year, while the grain rotted in the fields, the king of France decided to have a little war with the count of Flanders; fortunately his troops bogged down in the deep mud and withdrew without causing much additional distress.) The real catastrophe came in 1316, when the harvest failed again. During the following winter many people died from starvation and from the diseases that afflict a starving population. There were many ugly rumors of cannibalism. English chroniclers wrote of parents eating their own children, Irish writers told stories of corpses disinterred from graveyards, and Polish ones of criminals' bodies snatched from the gibbets to be devoured.

It is hard to make a coherent pattern out of all the numerous fragments of information we possess regarding conditions at the beginning of the fourteenth century. Some scholars are tempted to see the bad years of 1315–1317 as a definitive turning point in the social and economic history of medieval Europe; others point out that famine years occurred in every period of medieval history, that conditions had returned to normal by 1320, and that slow climatic change would have taken much longer to display any appreciable effect. As regards conditions in early fourteenth-century England, for instance, estimates vary from "starving and overpopulated" (M. M. Postan) to "a prosperous country in all but the worst years" (J. C. Russell). In evaluating such judgments one should bear in mind that, even in "prosperous" times, a medieval peasant expected only a subsistence standard of living, and that the possibility of the "worst years" occurring increased during the fourteenth century.†

Similar difficulties arise in evaluating the demographic evidence. Certainly there was some pressure of population on resources, and certainly population began to decline slightly after a long period of steady increase. But it is not clear how far the decline was due to a lower birth rate and how far to a higher death rate. It is possible that medieval people were generally maintaining their standard of living and adjusting sensibly to population pressures by marrying a little later and having slightly smaller families. Many historians, however, think that material conditions of life worsened and that the calamity of the Black Death fell on a population made unusually vulnerable by widespread malnutrition.

*Sources, nos. 82, 83

†Sources, no. 98

69. *The Black Death*

The Black Death—or plague—is primarily a disease of rodents, which can be transmitted to humans by fleas parasitic on infected rats. The flea ingests plague bacilli from the rat and then regurgitates them into the skin of the person it bites. The symptoms of the sickness that ensues are high temperature, aching limbs, and—most typically—great swellings *(buboes)* of the lymph nodes. The disease in this form, bubonic plague, is not necessarily fatal, though it can have devastating effects on populations already weakened by malnutrition. There are two subvarieties of plague which are nearly always fatal: septicaemic plague, in which the bloodstream is infected, and pneumonic plague, in which the bacillus attacks the lungs and the symptoms are similar to those of pneumonia. Pneumonic plague is, moreover, highly infectious. The accounts of the Black Death suggest that this form of the disease was widespread in the fourteenth-century epidemic.

Only once before had the plague visited Europe, in the sixth century when it swept through Justinian's empire. The epidemic of 1347–1350 originated in China; Europeans first encountered it in the Black Sea ports that were terminuses for the caravan routes to the Far East. From the Crimea, merchants carried the plague to Constantinople, then to Genoa, Sicily, and Venice. All Italy was ravaged during 1347. Toward the end of that year, the plague reached the French Mediterranean port of Marseilles and quickly spread to the papal city of Avignon, where it wiped out half the College of Cardinals in a few weeks. During 1348 the plague swept through France and, in the autumn, was carried to England. It raged in the British Isles all through 1349. In 1350 the disease spread throughout northern Europe from Iceland to Russia.

The loss of life was catastrophic. Medieval accounts tell of half the populations of infected cities being killed by plague. Although we have to allow for exaggeration and bear in mind that some places escaped the plague altogether, it seems likely that nearly a third of the total population of Europe was wiped out. But this was not the whole story. Plague remained endemic in Europe for centuries after the Black Death and, in the fifty years after the first outbreak, there were several major epidemics. By 1400 the population of Europe was reduced by a third to a half compared with preplague figures. Apparently, the decline ceased in the first half of the fifteenth century and, in the second half of the century, the population began slowly to increase again. Not until the seventeenth century, however, was Europe as densely populated as it had been in the thirteenth. The last outbreak of the plague in England was the famous Great Plague of London in 1665; the last in Europe occurred at Marseilles in 1720. Such epidemics were not ended by any improvements in hygiene or medicine. One explanation for their cessation is that the black rats which had carried the plague were replaced by a different species of brown rats during the eighteenth century. And, naturally, over the course of many generations, immunity to the plague would build up among those who survived.

Contemporary accounts of the plague portray a variety of reactions to it. Some priests stayed with their flocks to care for them. Some people turned to prayer and died with dignity. Some adopted a philosophy of "eat, drink, and be merry for tomorrow we die." But the more common picture is one of general panic and demoralization. Those who could fled from the infected cities; fathers deserted their families; no one could be found to nurse the sick; the dead could not be decently buried.* The horror of the situation was increased by the fact that, of course, no one understood it. People argued whether the plague was a work of the devil or a punishment of God. The Faculty of Medicine at the University of Paris declared that the epidemic of 1348 was caused by the unusual planetary conjunction of Saturn, Jupiter, and Mars in the sign of Aquarius, which had occurred in 1345. This planetary conjunction caused hot, moist conditions, which in turn caused the earth to exhale poisonous vapors. Belief that the plague was due to some kind of poisoning was widespread. All over Europe unpopular individuals and groups were accused of willfully spreading the plague by poisoning water sources. Most of all suspicion

A *danse macabre:* skeletons dance with figures representing the various levels of society. Section of a wall painting in the abbey church, La Chaise-Dieu, Haute Loire, ca. 1460. *Photographie Giraudon/Art Resource*

*Sources, no. 84

fastened on the Jews, the inevitable victims of Christian hysteria in the Middle Ages. There were hideous massacres of Jews in German cities when the plague spread there in 1348. Pope Clement VI issued a sensible declaration pointing out that Jews suffered as much as other people from the plague and therefore could not be held responsible for it, but this did not prevent further massacres in 1349.

The church as a whole suffered from a great loss of clergy. They could not easily be replaced, and the standards required for ordination were lowered in the next generation. The corporate life of many monastic communities was shattered. There were also bizarre outbreaks of religious mania, such as that of the Flagellants. The Flagellants believed that the plague was a judgment of God on sinful humanity and that only extraordinary measures could save people from its ravages. Bands of men and women gathered together and traveled about the country flogging one another. They preached the belief that anyone who subjected himself or herself to this for thirty-three days would be completely cleansed from all their sins. At first people looked on the Flagellants with sympathy. The feeling that inspired them was generally shared, and their method seemed in conformity with the basic asceticism that formed an important element in Christianity. But soon both secular and lay authorities grew alarmed at the

wandering mobs. This alarm was increased when the marchers developed inclinations toward killing Jews and even members of the clergy who opposed them. In October 1349, the Flagellants were solemnly condemned by the pope, and all authorities ordered to suppress them. As in the case of other heretics, the intention outstripped the means, and the Flagellants remained a continual if sporadic problem well into the fifteenth century.

It is not surprising that some of the first reactions to the Black Death were marked by a sort of pathological irrationality. But, in the long run, the plague did not produce any sudden change in the direction of medieval history. Rather, it magnified the destructive effect of various tensions that already existed in early fourteenth-century society. We next have to consider some of the problems that were emerging in the spheres of religious life and international politics.

READING SUGGESTIONS

* *B. Tierney,* Sources *and* Readings, *vol. I, 83–84, 96; vol. II, 32–33 & 35.*

On population see J. C. Russell, *Late Ancient and Medieval Population* (Philadelphia, 1958) and *The Control of Late Ancient and Medieval Population* (Philadelphia, 1985); and on climate R. Claiborne, *Climate, Man, and History* (New York; 1970) and * E. Le Roy Ladurie, *Times of Feast, Times of Famine* (New York, 1971). A work of fundamental importance for late medieval demography is D. Herlihy and C. Klapisch-Zuber, *Tuscans and Their Families: A Study of the Florentine Catasto of 1427* (New Haven, 1985). Differing assessments of peasant conditions in the early fourteenth century are given by M. M. Postan, *The Medieval Economy and Society* (Berkeley, 1972) and D. Herlihy, *Medieval and Renaissance Pistoia* (New Haven, 1967). See also * C. Dyer, *Standards of Living in the Later Middle Ages* (Cambridge, England, 1989). On the Black Death, see J. Nohl, *The Black Death* (London, 1961), a compilation from contemporary sources; * P. Ziegler, *the Black Death* (New York, 1969); H. Zinsser, *Rats, Lice, and History* (New York, 1957); * W. H. McNeill, *Plagues and People* (New York, 1976); * P. Aries, *Western Attitudes Towards Death* (Baltimore, 1975); and * M. Meiss, *Painting in Florence and Siena After the Black Death* (New York, 1964).

chapter

XXI

The Failure of Papal Leadership

During the thirteenth century the medieval papacy reached the apogee of its power and influence. The popes emerged as victors from their struggle with the Hohenstaufen emperors. For a time there seemed a possibility of realizing the dream of the greatest medieval pontiffs—to make of Europe a Christian commonwealth united under papal leadership. But, in the years around 1300, it became apparent that the popes had overestimated their power in the political sphere. The next two centuries were filled with mounting criticism of papal rule and of the whole established structure of church institutions.

70. The Popes and Medieval Politics

Toward the end of the thirteenth century, while the Turks were steadily encroaching on Christian territory in the eastern Mediterranean, all the great Christian rulers of the region—including the popes—were devoting their attention to a quite different problem, a power struggle for the island of Sicily. Charles of Anjou, Louis IX's brother, had been installed there with the support of the papacy in 1266. This arrangement exasperated King Peter III of Aragon, who had married a daughter of Manfred, illegitimate son of Frederick II, and thought that this gave him a good claim to the Sicilian crown. Moreover, Charles of Anjou was not content with Sicily. He revived Henry VI's grandiose dreams of conquest in the eastern Mediterranean and formed an alliance with Venice aimed at the conquest of the Byzantine Empire. This naturally aroused the hostility of Michael Palaeologus.

There was one final element in the situation that was to prove of decisive importance. When the popes were busily hawking the crown of Sicily around Europe, it never occurred to them to consult the wishes of the Sicilian people themselves; this, as it turned out, was an unfortunate oversight. Sicily was like a volcano where all the suppressed tensions of Mediterranean politics were ready to erupt. The Sicilians hated their cold-blooded French king; they hated the insolent foreign soldiers he brought with him; they hated the taxes he imposed on them to pay for the further wars that he planned. Both Peter of Aragon and Michael Palaeologus sent agents to stir up discontent, and an elaborate web of conspiracy spread over the Mediterranean world from Barcelona to Constantinople. On Easter Monday, 1282, at the hour of Vespers, the population of Palermo suddenly turned on the French garrison there and massacred it. This was a signal for other massacres of the French all over the island of Sicily. Charles of Anjou began to gather an army on the Italian mainland to crush the rebels, who promptly offered the Sicilian crown to Peter of Aragon. Peter landed in Sicily with a strong army in August 1282. The ensuing War of the Sicilian Vespers dragged on for twenty years. In the end, the house of Aragon retained the island of Sicily, and the house of Anjou kept the mainland territories of southern Italy with the title, "king of Naples."

For the stability of medieval civilization as a whole, the worst feature of the war was the intimate involvement of the papacy. Pope Martin IV (1281–1285) was a Frenchman and a former servant of the French crown. He promptly excommunicated Peter of Aragon, preached a crusade against him, declared that his kingdom was forfeit, and bestowed the crown of Aragon on a French prince. Philip III of France launched a crusade into Aragon to enforce the papal sentence, but it was an unsuccessful expedition and Philip died in the course of it.

To many contemporaries, the pope's support of such a "crusade" seemed a gross abuse of the spiritual power of the Roman church. And, among all the disruptive factors that were present in medieval civilization at the end of the thirteenth century, perhaps the most important of all was a failure of the papacy to command general support for its policies and to provide adequate spiritual leadership for the church. Medieval civilization at its best was profoundly Christian in inspiration. As we have seen, its art, literature, and institutions were all rooted in a common religious belief. If that belief crumbled away, the whole society might crumble. And the medieval form of Christianity very plainly required a papacy that could serve as a center of unity for the whole church and popes who could be regarded, without too gross a strain on people's credulity, as vicars of Christ on earth. From the late thirteenth century onward, the Roman church proved less and less capable of playing its traditional role. It was not simply that the church was intricately involved in the social and political affairs of the age. Such involvement had become a part of the tradition of western Christianity and, at best, it could be a force for good in checking the power of tyrants or stimulating the reform of corrupt institutions. The problem was that, in the eyes of many contemporaries, the thirteenth-century popes seemed to aim increasingly at dominating Christian society rather than serving it.

The growing preoccupation with worldly power that undermined

The organization of medieval society is vividly shown in this detail of a fresco painted to glorify the Dominican order. Pope and emperor sit in the center; at their feet is the Christian community (lambs) guarded by spotted dogs (the Dominicans). Next to the pope are his subordinates, the cardinal, archbishop, and abbot; below them are representatives of all levels of ecclesiastical society. Next to the emperor are the king and the count palatinate; below them, all the levels of secular society. Detail of the *Allegory of the Dominican Order, the Church Militant* by Andrea de Firenze, 1355. Spanish Chapel, Sta. Maria Novella, Florence. *Alinari—Art Reference Bureau*

the moral prestige of the papacy was perhaps an inevitable consequence of the policies that Innocent III had adopted at the beginning of the thirteenth century. Innocent wanted to make the papacy a sort of supreme tribunal standing above the petty affairs of the nations and impartially judging their disputes. It is doubtful whether in the best of circumstances any line of pontiffs could have played such an exalted role for long. Even Innocent himself did not wholly succeed. But, in any case, there was a fatal flaw in the whole grand program. The pope was not only a spiritual leader, standing above the nations as head of the church, but also the temporal lord of a little Italian principality. There was a constant temptation to use the universal spiritual powers of the Holy See to advance the pope's interest as a petty Italian prince. This became evident in Innocent IV's campaign against the emperor Frederick II; but Innocent could claim with some plausibility—even though he did not succeed in convincing St. Louis IX—that Frederick's schemes in Italy threatened the very existence of the papacy and so had to be resisted at all costs. In the case of Pope Martin's "crusade" against Peter of Aragon, there could be no such pretense. Nothing was involved except a power struggle between two Catholic princes. For diplomatic reasons, the pope, in his capacity as lord of an Italian principality, found it convenient to side with one of these princes against the other. Martin tried to use the spiritual powers of the papacy to defeat the prince he opposed, and he failed because people refused to believe that there could be anything divinely inspired about such papal meddling in temporal affairs.

The popes also compromised the credibility of their position by favoring more and more exalted theories of universal papal sovereignty just at the time when they were becoming more and more obsessed with local Italian politics. The philosopher Giles of Rome (d. 1316) declared that the pope, as vicar of God, was so truly the lord of the whole world that all legitimate rights of government and rights of property were derived from him and were revocable at his will. Such ideas become commonplace among the papal apologists of the fourteenth century. They were blankly unacceptable to the princes of Europe.

The temporal claims of the papacy were also rejected by the more radical Franciscans, who saw in them a complete negation of the ideals of poverty and humility that St. Francis had preached. The criticisms of these "Spiritual Franciscans" (a small minority of the whole order) acquired a new edge in the second half of the thirteenth century. The most extreme of them began then to revive the teachings of Joachim of Flora, a Calabrian mystic who had lived in the generation before St. Francis. Joachim held a highly individual view of Christian history. He thought that, just as there were three persons in God—Father, Son, and Holy Spirit—so there would be three ages in the history of humanity. The age of the Father was the era of the Old Testament; the age of the Son was the era of the New Testament (in which medieval people were still living); the age of the Holy Spirit lay in the future. In the existing second age, institutions of the law and government were necessary, Joachim conceded, but in the coming third age people would live in a happy simple Christian anarchy guided by the direct promptings of the Holy Spirit. In Joachim's system, each age had a great world figure as its inaugurator. Thus Moses inaugurated the first age, and Christ the second. The most radical Franciscans began to see St. Francis as the inaugurator of the third age and themselves as prophets of the new gospel. Exponents of such views were persecuted by the papacy at the beginning of the fourteenth century, and a few were burned as heretics.

The Spiritual Franciscans are often presented as the true heirs to the spirit of St. Francis, and perhaps the best of them were. Others displayed a self-opinionated fanaticism in asserting their highly eccentric beliefs that was far removed from the humility of Francis himself. Nonetheless, they exercised a considerable influence. Along with all the rational criticisms of papal abuses, there grew up in the later Middle Ages a mood of apocalyptic misgiving about the whole existing structure of ecclesiastical institutions.

Even more dangerous for the organized church than such radical movements of protest was a gradual secularization of society as a whole. The secular spirit that had long been strong in literature increased its hold. Commercial activities were playing an increasingly important part in the world. Most important of all was the rapid development of the secular point of view in politics. This has frequently been attributed to the spreading knowledge of Roman law and of Aristotelian philosophy that pictured the dominance of the secular state; and certainly there was a very significant development of what one might call "statism," whether or not the lawyers and philosophers were responsible for it. The general appearance of assemblies of estates show clearly that princes and peoples were beginning to think of themselves as political units with definite interests. The common welfare of the state gradually became far more important in their eyes than the interests of Christendom as a whole. Philip Augustus would have been aghast at the suggestion that he would be justified in destroying the papacy if the interests of France demanded such a step, but such an idea might not have seriously disturbed Philip IV and would have seemed quite natural to Charles VII. This feeling that the welfare of the secular state was humanity's first concern had profound effects within the church organization. Many, perhaps most, prelates of the fourteenth and fifteenth centuries believed that their primary duty was to their prince.

71. Conflicts of Church and State, 1295–1350

The growing power of secular kings and the diminishing influence of the popes became apparent in a series of clashes between church and state that began in 1296. In previous conflicts, the popes had either emerged victorious or at least had achieved honorable compromises. At the beginning of the fourteenth century, for the first time, the papacy suffered a total and humiliating defeat at the hands of a secular monarch. The victorious king was Philip IV of France.

In 1285, when both King Philip III and Pope Martin IV died, the French monarchy was considered one of the chief bulwarks of papal authority. But as young Philip IV (1285–1314) strove to extricate the remnants of his father's crusading army from its unfortunate invasion of Catalonia, he may well have felt some resentment toward the papacy for having encouraged the expedition. Philip was a man of virtuous life and conventional piety, but he was cold, calculating, and ruthless, and imbued with determination to increase the royal power. He surrounded himself with men trained in the civil law who believed in the supremacy of the secular state. Although the ideas of Peter Dubois, who advocated the seizure by the secular princes of all the property and temporal authority of the church and the support of the clergy by regular salaries from the secular government, were probably more advanced than those of most of Philip's entourage, they show clearly the general trend of thought at his court. Moreover, the men who served Philip had no shadow of a scruple about the means by which they achieved their ends. They believed that sufficiently outrageous and numerous false accusations made with overwhelming energy and confidence could destroy any opponent. And judicious use of torture could always produce witnesses to support the most fantastic charges.

Philip IV quarreled mildly with Honorius IV (1285–1287) and Nicholas IV (1288–1292), but no serious crisis arose. Then, in July 1294, the ten cardinals who composed the college met to elect a successor to Nicholas IV. Two mighty Roman noble families dominated the College of Cardinals—the Orsini and the Colonna. While the representatives of these two houses struggled for victory in the conclave, their adherents waged bloody battles in the streets of Rome. Finally, after months of deadlock, one of the cardinals thought of a brilliant and novel compromise. A revered hermit who dwelt on a mountain in the kingdom of Naples was elected pope and in a state of decided bemusement took the name of Celestine V. Before the worthy but completely innocent pontiff escaped from the clutches of his natural lord, Charles II of Anjou, king of Naples, he had created twelve new cardinals, of whom eight were Frenchmen and four Neapolitans. Both pope and cardinals soon discovered that a saint was out of place on St. Peter's throne, and within a year Celestine had resigned. He had been encouraged, if not forced, into this decision by the most vigorous of the cardinals, Benedict Gaetani, and in December 1294 Benedict became pope as Boniface VIII (1294–1303).

Scion of a minor noble family, the aged Boniface was an able administrator and canon lawyer, but he was haughty, overbearing, vain, and incredibly ambitious. While it seems most improbable that he had any large percentage of the vices credited to him by his enemies, his personal morals were clearly not above reproach. He was determined to exalt his own position and that of his great office, but he was almost equally interested in expanding the fortune of his family. His vanity led him to distribute statuettes of himself, and under the influence of his overbearing bad temper he once kicked an envoy to his court. Far more serious, however, were his efforts to provide for his family at the expense of other noble houses—particularly the Colonna. Early in his reign, he gave his nephew money from the papal treasury to buy a valuable estate. The Colonna, who had wanted the estate themselves, raided the convoy carrying the purchase money and stored the treasure in one of their strongholds. Boniface promptly preached a crusade against the Colonna, captured their castles, gave their lands to his relatives, and exiled or imprisoned the members of the house. By these means, he supplied himself with many bitter enemies among the Roman nobility, and thus weakened at home, he heedlessly plunged into conflict with the two dominant monarchs of western Europe.

In 1295 Philip IV of France and Edward I (1272–1307) of England were preparing for war over the duchy of Gascony, and both of them wanted to raise funds by taxing their clergy. In 1296 Boniface issued the bull *Clericis Laicos,* which forbade the clergy of any state to pay taxes to the prince without the consent of the pope. It was a direct challenge to the sovereignty of national kings in their own realms. Philip replied by placing a ban on the export of gold and silver from his realm, thus cutting off the flow of money from France to the papal court. Although Boniface held on through the winter, he was greatly embarrassed, not only by the loss of revenue but also by the rebellion of the Colonna cardinals who were still unsubdued. Early in 1297 the Colonnas were joined by several influential leaders of the Spiritual Franciscans at their fortress of Longhezza, and from there a series of manifestoes was issued denouncing Boniface as a usurper. The argument advanced was that a pope could not lawfully abdicate; therefore Celestine's resignation of the papacy was unlawful and Boniface's election correspondingly invalid. In the spring of 1297 the French king indicated that he was inclined to support this position and, under this new threat, Boniface gave way completely. He declared that, whenever a state of emergency involving the defense of the French realm arose, the king could tax his clergy at will; and Boniface's bull explicitly delcared that it was for the king—not the pope—to decide when such a state of emergency existed. To demonstrate even more completely his affection for the French monarchy, Boniface canonized Louis IX in 1297.

The harmony between Philip and Boniface did not last for long. In 1301 a bishop of southern France, a certain Bernard Saisset, incurred Philip's enmity, and the king set his lawyers to work to destroy him. They drew up a magnificent list of charges, including heresy, blasphemy, and treason; put the bishop on trial before a royal court; and imprisoned him in Paris. Then Philip wrote to Boniface asking him to approve these actions. Although one of the charges against Saisset declared that he had "called our most holy father Boniface the devil incarnate," the pope saw that the issues involved were purely political and that the independence of the whole French episcopate was at stake. He declined to support the king and, after a vigorous exchange of recriminations, issued a bull that reasserted the doctrine of *Clericis Laicos.* It was on this occasion that Philip sought the support of his people by summoning the French *Estates General* for the first time. The king's ministers addressed the assembly and declared that Boniface was a heretic and criminal who deserved to be removed from the papacy. Boniface replied that he would depose the king of France "like a servant" if such action became necessary. Boniface also promulgated the famous bull *Unam Sanctam,* which expressed in its most extreme form the doctrine of papal supremacy over kings.* It was studded with phrases like these: "The temporal authority ought to be

*Sources, no. 80

subject to the spiritual power." "If the earthly power errs it shall be judged by the spiritual power." "The spiritual power excels any earthly one in dignity and nobility." In 1303 Boniface decided to act on these principles by excommunicating Philip. Despite support from his people, Philip was unwilling to face this most terrible of ecclesiastical weapons. He resolved to strike first.

One of Philip's servitors was a peculiarly fascinating personage named William de Nogaret, who was a past master at the art of drawing up accusations and then providing witnesses to support them. When the king suspected that the bishop of Troyes, who was in charge of the revenues of the county of Champagne, was a thief, he sent Nogaret into action. Nogaret charged and proved to his own and the king's satisfaction that the bishop had conspired with a witch to kill the queen by sticking pins in an image of her and had committed various other horrible crimes. When one of Nogaret's agents was asked if a witness was testifying entirely voluntarily, he assured the court that he was. All the agent had done to encourage him was to strip him naked, daub honey on him, and hang him over a beehive. It was to this ingenious and devoted servant that Philip entrusted the task of suppressing Pope Boniface. Nogaret started with his usual list of accusations. Boniface was a heretic and a sorcerer deeply steeped in black magic. He had poisoned a number of high ecclesiastics. Perhaps the most delightful item in the long list of charges was the statement that Boniface kept mistresses to conceal the fact that he was a sodomite. Then, having built up his justification, Nogaret set off for Italy in company with one of Boniface's most implacable foes, Sciara Colonna. In the vicinity of Rome they gathered a band consisting of partisans of the Colonna family, well mixed with ordinary brigands, and marched to Anagni, where Boniface was staying. On September 7, 1303, the desperadoes attacked the town and captured the aged pontiff. Although the nobles of the countryside soon forced Nogaret to release the pope, the shock and humiliation were too much for Boniface, and he died soon after.

The new pope, Benedict XI (1303–1304), found himself in a most embarrassing position. He had been a servant and friend of Boniface, and no pope worthy of the name could allow the crime committed at Anagni to go completely unpunished. Yet Benedict was a cautious man and had no desire to cross swords with Philip IV. Hence he attempted an ingenious solution. All the censures heaped on the French king by Boniface were revoked, but he was directed to punish Nogaret. Pope Benedict died before he found out whether or not this pusillanimous maneuver was going to be effective.

In June 1305, the College of Cardinals elected to the papal office Bertrand de Got, archbishop of Bordeaux. While there is no definite evidence that Philip was responsible for Bertrand's election, it seems very likely that he was. The French cardinals formed a powerful minority in the college. Although they were not numerous enough to choose one of their own number, they could strongly influence the election. The archbishop of Bordeaux was a subject of Philip's foe

One in a series of frescoes located in the Church of San Francesco, Siena. The artist, Lorenzetti, depicts Boniface VIII receiving the novice Lodovico. *Alinari—Art Resource*

Edward I and so was not branded as a Frenchman in the eyes of the Italian cardinals. A contemporary chronicle asserts that Philip and Bertrand met and that the archbishop made various promises in return for Philip's support. Although it seems clear from the royal itinerary that this meeting never took place, it is possible that a similar agreement was reached by negotiation through envoys.

The new pope took the title of Clement V (1305–1314). When he learned of his election, Clement summoned the cardinals to meet him at Lyons, and there he was consecrated and enthroned. He then took up his residence in the city of Avignon on the east bank of the Rhone. Avignon was the seat of the county of Venaissin, a part of the kingdom of Burgundy belonging to the counts of Provence. It was thus in the territory of the Holy Roman Empire, but it depended on the princes of the house of Anjou, and Philip's lands lay just across the Rhone. Without actually being in France, the pope was completely subject to French influence. Of the twenty-eight cardinals created by Clements, twenty-five were Frenchmen. The papacy had conquered the Hohenstaufens, but it had itself been captured by the Capetians. A

French pope, surrounded by French cardinals, lived in a French-speaking city on the French frontier.

No sooner was Clement seated on the papal throne than Nogaret began to insist that his conduct toward Boniface should be declared justified. The pope pleaded to be spared this supreme humiliation and managed to defer action for some six years, but eventually he was obliged to open an inquest into Boniface's behavior and allow Nogaret to present his case. As one would expect, the case was a good one and well supported by witnesses. The fact that only a few points here and there were true did not trouble Nogaret. He cheerfully demanded that Boniface's bones should be disinterred and publicly burned. Finally, a compromise was reached. The pope withdrew all ecclesiastical censures leveled against Philip or any of his servants in connection with the affair and declared that the king had acted in a praiseworthy and just manner. Thus Clement was spared the actual formal condemnation of his predecessor.

While the affair of Pope Boniface was hanging fire at the papal court, Philip IV and his servants were engaged in an equally honorable enterprise. When Acre fell to the Muslims in 1291, most of the Templars in Palestine perished in its defense. The remnants of the order, those who had not been in the Holy Land and a few who had escaped from other Palestinian strongholds, retired to live on their extensive estates scattered over western Europe. Naturally the impecunious princes of the day cast greedy eyes on the rich properties no longer serving the purpose for which they had been given. But Philip was not the man to admit that his motive was pure greed; he had to find a better reason. Once more his experts went to work. They declared that the order had abandoned its old rule and adopted one full of blasphemous heresies. When a knight was initiated, he was obliged to deny Christ and to perform obscene rites before statues of the devil. The order reeked with the most horrible vices. Philip was profoundly shocked. Every Templar in France was arrested, and the houses of the order were thoroughly searched. Edward I and other princes were informed of the crimes of which the Templars were suspected and were urged to take action against them. Edward arrested the leaders of the order in England and waited to see what would come next.

The search of the houses of the Templars was not very fruitful, but Philip's agents went to work with their instruments of torture on the imprisoned Templars and soon obtained ample confirmation of all their charges. Then, bursting with pride, they notified Pope Clement of the horrible scandal they had uncovered. The pope promptly sent commissioners to hear the evidence and report their findings to a council. But once the Templars found themselves before a reasonably impartial body, they immediately repudiated their confessions. This gravely alarmed Philip. The situation required drastic action. At Philip's command, the archbishop of Sens condemned some fifty Templars, who were promptly burned as heretics by the secular power. This removed some troublesome witnesses and dissuaded others from changing their testimony. Finally, the affair was brought before a general council assembled at Vienne. Once more poor Clement was forced to issue a strange decision. The order was not condemned, but it was ordered dissolved, and Philip was congratulated for his zeal. The French king held the property of the Templars for some years and then turned it over to the Hospitalers with a generous bill for the expenses he had incurred in seizing and managing it. Edward I seized the Temple's property, milked it, and handed it over to the Hospital, but he did not bother the Templars themselves.

After all these defeats and humiliations for the papacy, it is astonishing that Clement's successor, Pope John XXII (1316–1334), had the confidence to plunge into yet another conflict of church and state, this time with the emperor Lewis of Germany. We saw how, after the long interregnum in the empire, Rudolph of Hapsburg was elected in 1273.* He was succeeded by his son Albert I (1298–1308). Then in 1308 the imperial throne passed to Henry VII (1308–1313) of the house of Luxemburg. From this time onward, the imperial throne was almost invariably held by a Hapsburg or a Luxemburg, but in the election of 1314 five of the seven prince-electors chose Lewis of Bavaria, head of the Wittelsbach house that continued to rule Bavaria down to the twentieth century. Two of the electors, however, preferred a Hampsburg candidate and civil war broke out between the rival claimants.

In 1317 John XXII decided to take umbrage at the fact that he had not been appealed to as a superior judge to settle the dispute, and he unilaterally declared the imperial throne vacant. Lewis ignored this decree, defeated his rival in Germany, and then invaded Italy. In 1328 he occupied Rome for a few months. There he had himself acclaimed emperor by the Roman people and crowned by one of their representatives. The man who crowned Lewis, Sciara Colonna, was the same person who had led the assault on Boniface at Anagni twenty-five years before. Meanwhile, John XXII fumed and fretted powerlessly at Avignon. In 1338 the prince-electors of Germany issued a solemn declaration that the imperial dignity was held directly from God, not from the pope, and that no papal approval or confirmation was necessary in the process of electing an emperor. It was a final rejection of the claims of Innocent III. Lewis continued to reign (not very effectively, to be sure) until his death in 1347.

John XXII was an almost unbelievably cantankerous old man; at the height of his conflict with Lewis, he became involved in a squabble with the whole Franciscan order. The Franciscans cherished the belief that they alone followed Christ perfectly since they lived in absolute poverty, owning no goods either individually or in common. This claim tended to exasperate all the other orders in the church and their members often pointed out that, according to the words of Scripture, Christ and the apostles had shared a common purse. The Franciscans replied that on certain occasions Christ might have "condescended" to give an example for imperfect Christians to follow but that still they alone followed a perfect way of life. To their critics, it seemed that the Franciscans were claiming to be more perfect than

*See p. 385.

Christ himself. In 1323 John XXII decided to end the whole unseemly squabble, and he did so in the most offensive fashion possible from the Franciscan point of view. The pope solemnly defined as heretical the doctrine that Christ and the apostles had never owned anything, individually or in common. After a period of dismayed protest, the main body of Franciscans reluctantly accepted the pope's decision, but the minister-general of the order, Michael of Cesena, deserted the pope and fled to the protection of Lewis, taking with him a few other irreconcilables. Among them was the English Franciscan philosopher William of Ockham, who was to prove the most influential thinker of the fourteenth century. These men became ardent propagandists for Lewis and very effective oppenents of the contemporary popes.

72. *Critics of the Papacy: Secularists and Mystics*

The conflicts of church and state that occurred during the first half of the fourteenth century are noteworthy not only for their immediate political effects but also for the controversial literature they inspired. Several major works of political theory were produced at this time, which defended the autonomy of the secular state against papal claims to world monarchy and also attacked the doctrine of absolute papal sovereignty even in ecclesiastical affairs. Thus the growing secularism of the later Middle Ages did not remain merely a vague mood. It found highly articulate exponents. Apart from William of Ockham, the two most important of them were John of Paris and Marsilius of Padua. The works of these men remained influential for the rest of the medieval period.*

John of Paris (ca. 1250–1306), a French Dominican and follower of Thomas Aquinas, wrote his treatise *On Papal and Royal Power* about 1302 during the conflict between Boniface VIII and Philip IV the Fair. Secular government, he wrote, derived its authority from the natural inclination of people to live together in communities. There had been kings before there were popes. Hence the royal power was obviously not derived from the papacy and popes had no authority to depose kings. At the most, by excommunicating an evil king, a pope might encourage his subjects to depose him. When Christ established the papacy, he did not confer on it any temporal power or wealth and, insofar as the popes possessed anything of this kind, it had come to them through the grant of secular princes. The papacy, considered as an institution, did possess by divine right a supreme jurisdiction in purely spiritual affairs, John conceded; but if an individual pope showed himself unworthy of his office by abusing his powers, he could be deposed by a general council or by the cardinals acting on behalf of the whole church.

*Sources, no. 81

John of Paris tried to maintain a balanced dualism in his treatment of church and state. Marsilius of Padua (ca. 1275–1342), who became

William of Ockham, whose brilliant, critical intelligence was a dominant influence in the cultural life of the Middle Ages, depicted in a late medieval drawing. Ms. 464/571. *Gonville and Caius College, Cambridge*

rector of the University of Paris in 1313, propounded a much more radical doctrine. His work, *The Defender of the Peace,* persistently stressed the principle of popular consent as the basis of all legitimate government, though Marsilius was not a democrat in the modern sense since he gave more weight to the opinions of important men than to those of common citizens. In considering the structure of the state, Marsilius wrote that the only body which could licitly make law or appoint executive officers of government was the whole community. The clergy was merely one constituent part of the community and were bound by all its laws. The same principle was then extended to church government. The only body competent to enact ecclesiastical law was the whole body of believers or their representatives in a general council. Marsilius' great innovation was to deny that the papacy had ever been established by divine authority. For him, the papacy was simply an executive office established by the Christian community and liable to abolition by the community if that ever seemed desirable. Throughout the latter part of his work, Marsilius assumed that all the powers inherent in the community could in practice be exercised by the secular ruler whom they designated (it was Marsilius who stage-managed Lewis' acclamation by the "Roman people" in 1328). Hence his work tended to favor a system of radical secularism.

The third of our trio of thinkers, William of Ockham (ca. 1285–1349), was also an extreme radical but in a different way. He was not only a political theorist but a philosopher of great subtlety and power who attacked the whole thought world of thirteenth-century scholasticism. Ockham propounded a new and extreme form of philosophic nominalism. All universal ideas, all general concepts, were mere names, he argued. The only realities the mind could know where the specific individual objects that presented themselves to sense experience. A logician could juggle with concepts, but these exercises had no demonstrable connection with external reality. Hence the mind could not demonstrate the truth of any general proposition about the external world. One could not, for instance, by pure reason establish the truth of the proposition, "God exists." Ockham was certainly a Christian believer, but he held that "truths of faith" were exactly what the phrase implied. That is, he thought that the basic truths of religion were known solely by intuitive faith. The mind could not rise from the contemplation of individual natural objects to an understanding of supernatural truths. These ideas negated all the intellectual tendencies of the preceding two centuries. They rendered meaningless not only Abelard's "By enquiring we come to the truth," but Anselm's "Faith seeking understanding," and Aquinas' "Grace perfects nature."*

In Ockham's voluminous polemical writings on behalf of Lewis of Bavaria, his thought was dominated by an unshakable conviction that John XXII and his immediate successors in the papacy were heretics because of their teaching on Franciscan poverty. Hence he revived and developed in intricate detail the old canonistic arguments about the possibility of deposing a heretical pope. Ockham went far beyond the canonists, however, in asserting that no institution of church government, not even a general council, could define with certain truth the faith of the church. After all, Ockham was defending a "truth" about Franciscan poverty that virtually all the church had rejected, including most of the Franciscans themselves. He argued, therefore, that the old doctrine which maintained that the whole church could not err meant only that somewhere within the church, in some unspecified individuals, the true faith would always survive, even when popes and councils were denying the truth. This view has obvious affinities with some types of later Protestant thought. Ockham's theology of the church was never widely accepted during the Middle Ages, but his nominalist philosophy quickly became dominant in the University of Paris and exercised a pervasive—some would say corrosive—influence on the whole climate of late medieval thought. Ockham's philosophy probably had a stimulating effect in the field of physical science by encouraging the observation of specific, concrete phenomena. Certainly, in the sphere of religion, it led to a distintegration of

*See pp. 308, 311, and 429.

the synthesis between reason and faith that the great scholastic philosophers had worked to achieve.

In spite of the growth of secularist philosophies of the state, the fourteenth century as a whole was not an age of wordly cynicism about religion. In some ways, life might have been easier for the popes if it had been. On the contrary, Europe was pullulating with new forms of religious vitality and with new religious movements that were often hostile, in varying degrees, to the established regime of papal church government. Such movements, usually inspired by leaders who claimed to have received personal mystical revelations, were especially strong in Germany and the Low Countries. Mysticism had, of course, always been an important element in Christianity. Mystical experience lay at the heart of the religious life of men like Bernard of Clairvaux and Francis of Assisi. The individuals who could move the masses, the enthusiastic reformers and successful preachers, were almost certain to be motivated by deeply felt personal religious experiences. But mysticism could easily slip across the line into heresy. The person who thought in terms of direct union with God through ecstatic contemplation was all too likely to forget the established intermediary, the church.

Among the most noted mystics of the fourteenth century were two Dominicans: Eckhart, who lived from 1260 to 1327, and his disciple Tauler, whose life spanned the period 1290 to 1361. Both found their inspiration in Neoplatonism, and both taught ideas that verged on heresy. In fact, a number of Eckhart's teachings were condemned as heretical in the year of his death. These elements of heresy grew out of the pantheistic tendencies in Neoplatonism, where divinity was thought of as all-pervasive. But the two Dominicans did not draw from this belief the heretical conclusion that there was no need for the church and its sacraments. Indeed, the Sacraments played an important part in their thought. Tauler became the leader of a group called the "Friends of God," composed of laypeople and ecclesiastics who hoped to reform the church from within by enthusiastically living and preaching the Christian life. Despite their own orthodoxy, the followers of Eckhart and Tauler played a part in paving the way for Martin Luther by their emphasis on personal religious experience and their dissatisfaction with mere ecclesiastical formalism.

Women mystics from many lands enriched the life of the church in the late Middle Ages. In England, Julian of Norwich (1342–c. 1420) wrote her *Revelations of Divine Love,* a direct, personal account of a series of fifteen visions of Christ in which she was assured of God's love for all of humankind. Another English visionary, Margery Kempe (c. 1393–c. 1439), married and had fourteen children; then she left her husband, apparently with his whole-hearted consent—according to her own account she was not an easy woman to live with. Margery next traveled to the Holy Land and various European shrines. Back in England she was accused of heresy but acquitted. Toward the end of her life she dictated a vivid account of her travels and mystical experiences, sometimes called the first woman's autobiography.

Bridget of Sweden (1302–1372) also had a large family (eight children) before turning to a life of religious devotion, this time after the death of her husband. She then founded a new religious order, the Bridgettines, at the monastery of Valdstena in Sweden. As the order grew, each house of nuns had a community of monks associated with it, with monks and nuns all living under the rule of the abbess. In 1349 Bridget journeyed to Rome and lived the rest of her life there. Her letters from this period often complain of abuses in the conduct of ecclesiastical affairs; she was especially concerned that the pope should end the residence of the papal curia at Avignon and return to Rome.

When Bridget died in 1373 this cause was taken up by a still more remarkable woman, Catherine of Siena (1347–1380). Born the twenty-third child of a Sienese cloth dyer, Catherine exasperated her family by refusing to marry. Instead she gave herself to a life of rigorous asceticism and prayer, marked by frequent ecstasies and visions. Catherine felt called, not only to live a life of personal devotion, but also to correct all the evident ills in the life of the church. In one of her visions Christ told her that this was not only a task for men but that he would also send "women, unlearned and weak" to help in the work. Catherine responded by dictating a series of extraordinary letters addressed to the great public figures of the day including the pope. Some were pure spiritual exhortation, others rebuked moral failings, still others were concerned with specific political issues.* In 1376 Catherine traveled to Avignon. There, face to face with Pope Gregory XI, she denounced the "stench" of corruption in the papal court and urged the pope to return to his See of Rome. Within a few months the pope complied; he left Avignon and in 1377 entered Rome. But perhaps it is not always expedient for saints to intervene in public affairs. The return of the papal court to Rome led almost at once to a disastrous schism in the church.†

All these mystics remained devoted to the Roman church even when they attacked its abuses. (Catherine called the pope "sweet Christ on earth.") But other exponents of popular mysticism taught doctrines that were frankly heretical. Probably the most widespread and dangerous of these groups was the Brethren of the Free Spirit. (The more formal theological heresies of Wyclif and Huss, which became prominent around 1400, will be discussed in a later chapter.) The Brethren of the Free Spirit were essentially pantheists who believed that God was in everything and that all living things reverted to God at death. Hence there could be neither hell nor purgatory, and the conception of sin was impossible. All that people did was inspired by God. They believed that all property should be held in common and that work was unnecessary. While the more elevated members of this sect led an extremely austere life, avoiding all worldly interests and passions, the doctrine of the nonexistence of sin was an encouragement to looser behavior on the part of the less devout. Obviously, the beliefs of the Brethren were dangerous to both the church and the orthodox Christian faith. They were regarded as pe-

*Sources, no. 90

†See pp. 538–541.

culiarly obnoxious heretics and were vigorously persecuted by whatever machinery was available.

In their efforts to suppress the Brethren of the Free Spirit, the ecclesiastical authorities were gravely hampered by the difficulty of distinguishing between them and various other radical but orthodox groups. In the thirteenth century, the Low Countries had been the nursery of many informal religious communities, especially of women. A group of women would gather together, lead a common life, and support themselves by work or begging. Although they promised chastity and obedience while they lived in the community, they retained their private property and could leave the community at will. Such women were commonly called *Beguines.* They were greatly favored by the counts of Flanders and other great lords of the region, and in the fourteenth century, the idea spread through Germany. Soon there were similar communities of men known as *Beghards.* Most of the Beguines and Beghards lived in these settled communities, but many began wandering about as beggars. The Brethren of the Free Spirit and other heretical sects were inclined to call themselves *Beghards* and to be so known by the people in general. This caused endless confusion. Several popes drew the line clearly between those living in settled communities and those wandering about. The former were to be protected; the latter, suppressed.

The most important orthodox movement of lay piety in the fourteenth century was the Brotherhood of the Common Life, founded in Holland by Gerard Groote (1340–1384). Groote and his first followers were not priests and did not take formal religious vows but lived in small groups, practicing works of charity and meeting together for prayer. From this circle came one of the great classics of devotional literature of the later Middle Ages, *The Imitation of Christ,* attributed to Thomas à Kempis. Gerard Groote, although a university master himself, urged his friends to turn away from recondite speculations about fine points of doctrine and to cultivate a simple piety of the heart. The ideals of the Brotherhood outlasted the Middle Ages and influenced both Erasmus and Luther in the sixteenth century.

Evidently the story of religion in the fourteenth century is not simply one of decay. The great failure of the papacy was its inability to canalize all the abundant religious energy that existed in a constructive fashion. As the popes became increasingly preoccupied with the worldly details of ecclesiastical administration, they lost the capacity for dealing sympathetically with all the more fervid, evangelical movements of Christian thought that kept welling up outside the official ecclesiastical establishment. But such movements of popular enthusiasm, though often embarrassing for professional clerical administrators, are essential to the continuing vitality of a religious faith. In the early thirteenth century, Innocent III had the courage and faith to launch a Francis of Assisi on the world, apparently quite convinced that a movement devoted to preaching simple gospel truths to simple people could not conflict with the aims of the institutional church over which he presided. Fourteenth-century popes looked with suspicion on every new kind of religious thought or religious sentiment. For a time, the Roman church seemed to have lost the inner reservoir of spiritual power that in the past had enabled it to reform itself when necessary and to direct the reform of other churches.

READING SUGGESTIONS

* *B. Tierney,* Sources *and* Readings, *vol. I, nos. 79–81, 89.*

On the political developments in the Mediterranean region, see * S. Runciman, *The Sicilian Vespers: A History of the Mediterranean World in the Thirteenth Century* (Cambridge, England, 1958). The conflict between Boniface VIII and Philip IV is discussed in T. S. R. Boase, *Boniface VIII* (London, England, 1933), and A. C. Flick, *the Decline of the Middle Church,* 2 vols. (New York, 1930). See also J. R. Strayer, *The Reign of Philip the Fair* (Princeton, NJ, 1980). The general histories of political theory already cited in Chapter XVI deal with the doctrines involved in the church-state conflicts of this period. For theories of papal authority, see M. J. Wilks, *The Problem of Sovereignty in the Later Middle Ages* (Cambridge, England, 1963), and B. Tierney, *Origins of Papal Infallibility* 2nd ed., (Leiden, 1988); and for particular thinkers, C. R. S. Harris, *Duns Scotus,* 2 vols. (Oxford, England, 1927); E. Bettoni, *Duns Scotus* (Washington, DC, 1961); * A. Gewirth, *Marsilius of Padua,* 2 vols. (New York, 1951–1956), which includes a translation of the *Defensor Pacis;* M. M. Adams, William Ockham, 2 vols. (Notre Dame, IN, 1987); A. S. McGrade, *The Political Thought of William of Ockham* (Cambridge, England, 1974); and P. Boehner, *Collected Articles on Ockham* (New York, 1958). Boehner argues that Ockham was much more of a moderate than is generally supposed.

The religious orders of the late Middle Ages are discussed in the classic work of D. Knowles, *The Religious Orders in England,* 3 vols. (Cambridge, England, 1948–1959), and less sympathetically in G. G. Coulton, *Five Centuries of Religion,* 4 vols. (Cambridge, England, 1923–1950). On the Spiritual Franciscans and Joachism, see D. Douie, *the Nature and Effect of the Heresy of the Fraticelli* (Manchester, England, 1932), and G. Leff, *Heresy in the Late Middle Ages* (Manchester, England, 1967); M. Reeves, *The Influence of Prophecy in the Later Middle Ages* (Oxford, England, 1969); and D. West (ed.), *Joachim of Fiore in Christian Thought,* 2 vols. (New York, 1975). E. McDonnell, *The Beguines and Beghards in Medieval Culture* (New Brunswick, NJ, 1954) is a detailed study. On mysticism, see * F. Underhill, *Mysticism,* 14th ed. (London, 1944); J. M. Clarke, *The Great German Mystics: Eckhart, Tauler and Suso* (Oxford, England, 1949); F. Tobin, *Meister Eckhart: Thought and Language* (Philadelphia, 1986). On Groote and his circle, see A. Hyma, *The Brethren of the Common Life* (Grand Rapids, MI, 1950), and T. van Zijl, *Gerard Groote: Ascetic and Reformer* (Washington, DC, 1963). Good translations are R. C. Petry, *Late Mediaeval Mysticism* (Philadelphia, 1957); * R. B. Blakeney, *Meister Eckhart* (New York, 1941); * L. Sherley-Price, *the Imitation of Christ* (Harmondsworth, England, 1952); and * B. A. Windeatt, *the Book of Margery Kempe* (New York, 1985). On Margery Kempe see also K. Lochrie, *From Body to Book. Margery Kempe: Gender and Medieval Mysticism* (Philadephia, 1991). The best introductions to Catherine of Siena are * S. Noffke, *Catherine of Siena, The Dialog* (New York, 1980) and *The Letters of St. Catherine of Siena* (Binghamton, NY, 1988).

chapter

XXII

The Hundred Years' War: Fourteenth-Century Campaigns

The struggle between England and France that historians have chosen to designate as the Hundred Years' War was not really one war but several, a long series of campaigns broken by occasional interludes of truce and peace. In the course of these campaigns, all the inherent violence of a feudal society which the church had never more than half tamed flared out in a savagely destructive fashion. French towns and villages suffered appalling ravages so that kings and nobles could indulge their ineradicable taste for honor and loot. In the history of feudal warfare and feudal institutions, the Hundred Year's War marked a period of transition. The conflict grew out of a feudal dispute, and the leading participants often behaved toward one another according to the approved code of knightly chivalry; but feudal levies proved inadequate for the campaigns, and both sides relied heavily on hired mercenaries. The great set battles were not won by mounted knights but by yeoman archers. Eventually, the war inspired a mood of nationalism in France that helped the French monarchy to overcome feudal particularism. While it was going on, this contest monopolized a major part of the human and material resources of the two states and was deeply intertwined in the general politics of western Europe. Hence a knowledge of the Hundred Year's War forms a necessary background for understanding the whole political, social, and economic history of the later Middle Ages.

73. The Background

By the Treaty of Pairs in 1259, King Henry III (1216–1272) had abandoned his claims to Normandy, Maine, Anjou, Touraine, and Poitou, while Louis IX (1226–1270) of France recognized his right to hold as a fief from the French crown the fragment of the duchy of Aquitaine that was still in the English king's possession, mainly the duchy of Gascony.*

In the days when the Capetian kings had no authority within the great fiefs held of the crown, there had been no basic difficulty involved in having a foreign sovereign hold one of those fiefs. But by the second half of the thirteenth century, the French kings had reduced the independence of their great vassals. Their most effective weapon in this process was the accepting of appeals from the courts of the vassals to the king's court in Paris—that is, to the *parlement* of Paris. The hearing of such appeals involved sending royal officials into the fiefs to sequester goods under litigation and to enforce decisions. This annoyed all the great vassals, but it was peculiarly exasperating to the English king, who was the peer of the Capetian monarch. Bitter quarrels burst out between the seneschal of Gascony and the royal officials, and often these quarrels involved their royal masters. In 1294 and again in 1324 the French king seized the duchy of Gascony on the ground that its duke was a contumacious vassal. While each of these disputes was finally settled by negotiation and the duchy restored to the king of England, they left angry memories. Moreover, the king of France began to feel certain that he could confiscate the duchy whenever it seemed convenient, and his English rival continually suspected him of planning to do so. Finally, the Capetians never kept their promise of 1259. Alphonse of Poitou died childless, but the English king never obtained the promised lands. In short, the French and English monarchs were always quarreling over questions concerning Gascony, and at any time this could lead to open war.

While the duchy of Gascony was the major cause of friction between the two kings, there were other irritants. In the thirteenth and fourteenth centuries, the terms "pirate" and "seaman" were almost synonymous. No shipmaster could easily resist the temptation to plunder a vessel weaker than his own. Year in and year out, the seamen of France and England preyed on each other with rare enthusiasm. This piracy was more or less legalized by "letters of reprisal." When an English seaman was robbed by a French mariner, he could go to the chancery and obtain royal letters authorizing him to take the same amount of property from the next French person he met. The same process was used in France. Obviously, before long most shipmasters would be equipped with letters of reprisal. When they wanted to be at peace, the two kings calmly ignored the continual bickering of their seamen even when it resulted in large-scale naval engagements, but when they were contemplating hostilities the complaints of the seamen were a very convenient excuse.

Carcassonne. The walled city of Carcassonne was extensively restored in the nineteenth century. Today it presents much the same appearance as in the Middle Ages. The suburbs in the foreground could be sacrificed in time of siege while the residents found safety within the city walls. *Eric Shaal, Life Magazine © Time Warner, Inc.*

Another fruitful source of discord between France and England was the complicated political situation in the county of Flanders. In the early fourteenth century, the artisans of the towns grew restive under the political and economic domination of the rich merchants. This led to frequent riots and revolts. As the count of Flanders was unable to handle the situation, the French king was inclined to intervene. Flanders was the chief market for English wool, and the export duties

*See pp. 392–393.

on wool formed an important part of the revenue of the king of England. Hence the latter was most unwilling to have the king of France in effective control of Flanders so that he could at will disrupt the wool trade. Since the king of France was inclined to support the rich merchants, the English king sympathized with the artisans.

The relationship between the kings of France and England was further complicated in 1328 when Edward III became a potential claimant to the French throne.* In 1316 Louis X (1314–1316) of France threw his realm into consternation by dying, leaving a daughter and a pregnant widow. While the country eagerly waited to see if the Capetians still kept their ability to produce male heirs, the late king's brother Philip took over the government as regent. In due time the queen bore a son, but he died almost immediately. Thus France was faced with a question that had never before plagued it—could a woman succeed to the throne? According to the general feudal custom of the time, a daughter could succeed to her father's fief, and many argued that the same rule should apply to the crown. Others maintained that kingship was a peculiarly sacred dignity to which no woman could aspire. The quarrel was bitter and fiercely argued; but, as one might expect, the claimant in actual control won, and Philip (1315–1322) was crowned king of France as Philip V. Louis' daughter, Jeanne, married her cousin Philip, count of Evreux, and received the little kingdom of Navarre as an inheritance from her grandmother. Later she bore a son, Charles of Navarre, who was to play a major role in the intrigues of the next generation.

When Philip died in 1322, leaving only daughters, there was no serious debate, and his brother Charles (1322–1328) succeeded him without question. But Charles IV also failed to produce a son, and at his death in 1328 the senior branch of the Capetian house was extinct in the male line. Now a new question arose. Even if a woman could not wear the crown, might she not transmit it to her son? If one believed that the French crown could be neither worn nor transmitted by a female, the heir to the vacant throne was Philip, count of Valois, son of a younger brother of Philip IV. But, if a woman could transmit the crown to her son, there was a closer relative with a better claim. Isabelle, daughter of Philip IV and sister of the last three kings, had married Edward II of England, and her son was Edward III of England.† It seemed now that Edward III might also be the rightful king of France. (Jeanne's son, Charles of Navarre, was not born until 1332, and he was never a serious contender for the throne.) Philip of Valois was, in fact, generally accepted as king. Isabelle protested his accession, but she could do nothing more, and young Edward felt unable even to protest. In 1329 he went to France and did homage to Philip VI for his duchy of Gascony, and thus he seemed to recognize Philip as king of France.

In 1330, at the age of eighteen, Edward III (1327–1377) arrested his mother, who had been acting as regent, and took the government of England into his own hands. Edward was quite unlike any of his recent predecessors; perhaps he resembled most closely his great-

*To understand the succession dispute described above, see the genealogy given in Appendix, Table 2.

†See pp. 522–523

grandiuncle Richard I. He was a strong-willed and firm-handed ruler who could handle the turbulent baronage of the realm. While he knew how to choose able men to conduct his administration, he had little personal interest in the details of government. He loved luxurious living and pretty ladies. He also had a burning desire for glory and prestige, and like most nobles of his day, he believed that these were to be gained chiefly by military exploits. Fortunately, under the circumstances, he was an excellent captain and tactician who could inspire his soldiers and handle them ably on the field of battle. He had too little grasp of reality to be a competent strategist. Here one finds him in striking contrast to his grandfather Edward I. When Edward I went to war, he had a practical aim that he felt sure he could accomplish, and he carefully planned and carried out the necessary operations. Edward III was always aiming at something that was far beyond his capacities and resources. Although he was usually practical in details and did not allow the whimsies of chivalry to carry him too far, he was essentially a crowned knight and a thoroughly chivalrous monarch. As such, he had no objection to squandering the human and financial resources of England to seek honor and glory for himself.

Philip VI (1328–1350) of France had his rival's weaknesses in even more exaggerated form, a few extra ones of his own, and no good qualities to compensate for them. Before he ascended the throne, Philip's love of pomp, luxurious living, and such knightly sports as tournaments had kept him continually deep in debt. As king, he indulged his expensive tastes to his heart's content. Like Edward, he sought prestige and glory as a warrior, but unlike the English king, he had no ability to lead soldiers and no comprehension of tactics. He was proud, easily offended, and almost pathologically suspicious of everyone. Philip was the ideal chivalrous monarch, and not very bright.

Clearly enough, almost any provocation could bring two such monarchs as Edward III and Philip VI to war. This provocation was supplied by that perennial bone of contention, the duchy of Gascony. The lawyers of Philip's court decided in 1330 that the homage performed by Edward III in 1329 had been improper; it had been simple and not liege homage. As Edward refused to remedy this defect, a diplomatic controversy developed. Meanwhile, there was a new burst of appeals to the *parlement* of Paris from Gascony. Edward was at war with the Scots, and Philip encouraged French knights to aid the Scots against him. The English king's protests were blandly ignored. Finally, Philip decided that the time had come to drive the English from Gascony, and in 1337 he declared the duchy confiscated. Edward's answer was prompt. He declared war on Philip, "so-called king of France." While Edward did not immediately assume himself the title of king of England and France, he had clearly shown his intention to do so. He was no man to play around with limited objectives.

From the point of view of total resources, there was no comparison between France and England; any contest between them would be a struggle of a pygmy against a giant. England had about 3.5 million inhabitants, while the lands that recognized the rule of Philip VI contained some 16 million people, of whom about 12 million lived in the royal demesne. France was also a highly productive and prosperous land with a high standard of living. But in the fourteenth century, total resources had little bearing on the military power of a country: the question was who controlled the resources and whether they could be used effectively. In an age when transportation was costly and difficult, an efficient system of supply was almost out of the question, and armies in general expected to live off the country. Thus they could not be very large, no matter how many soldiers were theoretically available. Then, warfare required soldiers who were trained and equipped, and obviously their ratio to the total population could vary greatly. France still relied on its mounted nobility supported by town militia and a few mercenary crossbowmen, while England had developed an effective peasant or at least yeoman infantry. It seems likely that the total number of men capable of effective military service was not utterly different in the two countries. Finally, wars cost money, and here it seems fairly clear that the resources of the two kings were about equal. In fact, it is quite possible that the revenue of Edward III was a little larger than that of his enemy.

The French army of 1337 differed little from those of the twelfth and thirteenth centuries. Its basic element was the levy of heavily armed noble horsemen who followed their lords to battle. The armor of the knight was somewhat heavier than it had been in the past. Visored helmets were usual, pieces of plate metal protected exposed spots, and the horses wore armor as well. As this equipment was extremely expensive, only the richer lords possessed it, and other nobles served in lighter armor. They were, as a rule, called *squires*, or *mounted sergeants*. The only essential difference between the heavy cavalry of 1337 and the feudal levy of the thirteenth century was that it was paid for its services; but as each great lord received the money to pay the vassals who followed him, the discipline of the army was little improved. In addition to the cavalry, there was the militia of the towns, consisting of infantry armed with pikes. When the cavalry was patient enough to allow the infantry to arrive on the field, something that happened but rarely, these troops were reasonably useful in battle. The only troops in the French army equipped with missile weapons were mercenary crossbowmen, who were usually foreigners. The Genoese were particularly noted for their skill with this weapon and were frequently employed, but because such regular professional soldiers were expensive, their numbers were usually very small.

The English army had come a long way since the days of John and Henry III. When Edward I was planning the conquest of Wales, he realized that he needed infantry to follow the Welsh into their mountain fastnesses.* For this purpose he levied large numbers of men from the western shires and paid them for their service. Later, when he conquered Scotland, he used the same device. Thus there was built up in England a body of men who had military experience and who

*See p. 401.

were willing to fight for pay. At the beginning, almost all these infantrymen were armed with the pike, but as time went on many of them adopted a new and highly effective weapon—the *longbow.* The longbow was apparently invented by the southern Welsh. During the Welsh wars, it was taken over by some of the English infantry, and soon every shire was well supplied with men who were adept in its use. Some six feet long, this great bow had rather better range and striking power than the crossbow. If the range were not too great, it could pierce chain mail. But its great advantage was its speed of fire. A good longbowman could shoot ten or twelve arrows a minute as against the two bolts of the most expert crossbowman.

Edward I had little enthusiasm for the clumsy, undisciplined feudal levy with its short term of service, and he called it only when he needed a large body of heavy calvary for a special purpose. As a rule, he relied on paid companies. An experienced and able soldier, usually a knight, was given a sum of money to raise a company. He hired a

The English-held castle of Mortagne near Bordeaux under siege by the French in 1377. The besiegers use both bow and arrow and a kind of primitive gun. Miniature from Jean de Waverin's *Chronique d'Angleterre,* Flemish, late 15th century. Ms. Roy. 14.E.IV, fol. 23r. *Reproduced by permission of the British Library Board*

few other knights or squires to serve as officers. Then he sent men out to recruit archers and pikemen. A company thus consisted of a few mounted men and a fair-sized body of infantry—perhaps a hundred men in all. The very great lords, earls, and powerful barons were expected to serve without pay for as long as they were needed, and each of these brought with him a small retinue of horsemen. This supplied a small body of heavy cavalry. In addition to these troops, when war was being conducted in France, the English king relied heavily on his Gascons. The nobility of the duchy furnished a body of heavy cavalry similar to that of the French army, and Gascony could always supply a fair number of crossbowmen.

In addition to developing a new weapon, the English had learned how to use it tactically. John Giffard of Brimpsfield, marching to relieve a castle besieged by the Welsh, had found a strong body of enemy spearmen ensconced on a rise of ground blocking his path. Giffard put his bowmen between his horsemen so that the Welsh could not attack them. Then the archers rained arrows on the Welsh formation until it wavered and gaps appeared in its ranks. At that point, his cavalry charged and cut the enemy to pieces. Similar tactics were later used to defeat the spearmen of the Scots Highlands who followed William Wallace. On another occasion, a fairly small force of knights accompanied by a strong body of pikemen and archers found themselves faced by the entire feudal levy of Scotland. The knights dismounted and fought with the pikemen. The archers were thrown in front and on the flanks of this line of pikes. The whole formation took its position on the top of a hill. The Scots horsemen also dismounted and with their pikemen formed a solid mass that marched slowly up the hill. But from both in front and on the flank English arrows rained on their ranks. When they reached the English infantry, the archers drew off to one side and continued to shoot at the Scots, who eventually broke and fled. These two tactical devices, one offensive and one defensive, were to be the English army's chief reliance throughout the Hundred Years' War.

74. *The Conquests of Edward III*

King Edward made his preparations carefully. While he gathered his army, his agents, well supplied with money, were active among the princes of Germany building up a coalition against France. Lewis of Wittelsbach (1314–1347), duke of Bavaria and Holy Roman Emperor, was persuaded to create Edward vicar of the empire in the lower Rhine valley and thus give him theoretical authority over the princes he subsidized. The English king crossed in 1338, too late to do anything but hold love-fests with his allies. In 1339 he was back again with his army, and Philip mustered his host. The two kings moved back and forth around the country, but neither felt strong enough to risk a pitched battle, and each satisfied his pride by offering the other battle under impossible conditions. There were a few marvelous adventures. One day a small group of English knights rode gaily in the early evening into the town where the heir to the French throne, John, duke of Normandy, was comfortably camped. Their modest purpose was to kidnap the duke. They got into the room where he was dining but decided that there were too many troops about. Soon they found a less well-guarded dinner party and captured a group of French nobles, but as they were escorting them out of town the alarm was raised. The English promptly released their prisoners on parole and made their way safely out of town. In due time, their prisoners, like true knights, surrendered to them in their headquarters in Brabant and were profitably ransomed. The campaign of 1339 was fully as useless as that of the year before; the two armies never came to grips. By the end of the season, Edward has used up all his money, had pawned one of his crowns to the archbishop of Treves, and owed every banker who would lend him funds. As soon as the English king's money began to run out, the enthusiasm of the German princes cooled. By 1341 the emperor and his vassals had come to terms with France, and Edward's only friends in the region were the artisans of Flanders. As Philip had also used up all his available cash, it looked as if the war would die quietly with little harm done.

But at this point another conflict broke out, this time over a disputed succession to the duchy of Brittany. Edward supported one candidate, John of Montfort, Philip another, Charles of Blois. English garrisons occupied many of the castles of Brittany and fought over the countryside with the garrisons that held for Charles. On one occasion, someone had the idea of settling the matter by a battle of thirty champions. The champions met and dutifully carved each other up, but as no one could agree as to which side won, the war just went on.

While English and French captains were fighting in Brittany, Philip's forces were attempting without much success to conquer the duchy of Gascony. Early in the summer of 1346, Edward mustered an army to go to the assistance of his troops in the duchy. But when he set sail, contrary winds blew him back on the coast of Cornwall, to his great annoyance. He then announced that he would go where the wind wanted him to and on July 11 landed at La Hogue in Normandy. On July 20 he took and plundered the prosperous city of Caen, but soon after he heard that Philip was mustering all the forces of France at Paris in order to crush him. As Edward had only about nine thousand men, he decided to go home. In this plan, however, he reckoned without his seamen. They had gotten bored waiting for him, and when Edward arrived on the coast be found that the fleet had gone home and that he was stranded in France. He had only one hope—to get to Flanders and find refuge with his allies there until a new fleet could be mustered to take his army home. The English army promptly marched to the Seine and tried to find a crossing, but Philip had moved all boats to the north bank, and the bridges were either destroyed or strongly held. Finally, they found a weak force holding the bridge at Poissy and succeeded in crossing the river. The next obstacle was the Somme. Here Edward by good luck found a ford that was usable at low tide and got across just before the advance guard of the French army came up. But the king knew that the chase was over. His army was tired, and his infantry could not move as fast as the French cavalry that was pursuing them. On August 26 he halted near the village of Crécy in the county of Ponthieu and drew up his army in battle array.

Edward chose a fairly strong position on a hill just to the north of the forest of Crécy. His right flank was protected by a stream that ran along the edge of the forest, but his left was covered only by the rising ground and a tiny village. The army was drawn up in three "battles," or divisions, each of which consisted of a solid core of dismounted knights and pikemen with archers on each flank. Two of these battles formed the front line, while the third was held in reserve to the rear. Edward himself climbed to the top of a windmill just to the rear of his right flank, from which he could watch the whole battlefield. While Edward was arraying his host, the French army left Abbeville on the Somme and started north on the road that passed to the west of the forest of Crécy. Philip had no idea where the English were, but he assumed that they were still hastening toward Flanders. As he rode north, however, he received word that his enemies were north of the forest near the road that passed to the east of it, and he immediately ordered his forces to move across to the other road. He also sent scouts out to discover what Edward was doing. The scouts soon found the English position and returned to inform Philip of the situation. The leader of the scouting party was a soldier of experience and intelligence. He pointed out to the king that the French army was scattered in utter disorder along the road from Abbeville, that the day was rapidly passing, and that the only sensible course was to halt some distance from the English position and wait until the next day to attack it. Amazingly enough, this sound idea penetrated the chivalrous haze that shrouded the king's mind, and he sent orders to his vanguard under his brother the count of Alençon to halt where it was.

When the order to halt reached Alençon, it was late in the afternoon and he had just come in sight of the enemy. He obeyed his royal brother's command and stopped his advance, but the divisions behind him all tried to press as far forward as possible and so threw the situation into incredible confusion. When Philip himself arrived on the scene, the sight of the enemy and the eagerness of his knights quickly overcame his judgment, and he ordered Alençon to attack. Alençon had with him the only troops in the French army who were armed with missile weapons—a strong bank of Genoese crossbowmen. He sent them forward to drive off the English archers covering Edward's left flank, while he followed close behind with his heavy cavalry. Unfortunately, the English longbows slightly outranged the crossbows, and the English had the additional advantage of shooting downhill. The Genoese wavered under the rain of arrows. This deeply annoyed the impatient Alençon, and he ordered his cavalry to charge, despite the fact that the Genoese were between them and the enemy.

The result was, of course, complete confusion. The horsemen and crossbowmen became hopelessly entangled on the lower slopes of the hill, while the English archers poured their arrows into the struggling mass of men. Soon Alençon's whole division was destroyed.*

While Alençon's attack was in progress, the other French troops who had arrived on the field managed to form a line and prepare for a charge. As soon as they were ready, they pressed forward against the enemy. Among them rode John of Luxemburg, king of Bohemia, who despite his royal title was actually a mercenary captain in Philip's pay. John was blind, and his knights took the bridle of his horse to lead him into battle. As the French rode up the hill, the English archers poured arrows upon them, killing many horses and wounding some knights. The few horsemen who reached the line of English spears were easily killed or captured. John of Luxemburg died in the midst of his faithful knights. This was the last attack that was made with any semblance of order. After its failure, every French division as it arrived on the field charged up the hill at the English position, and each was routed in the same way. The English archers firing from the flanks always reduced the charging force to a number that the pikemen could handle without too much difficulty. There were some fifteen or sixteen separate assaults, of which the last was made about midnight. Then the exhausted English lay down on their arms where they stood, while the remnants of the French host fled toward the south. Early the next morning, the earl of Salisbury marched out with an English force and cut to pieces the infantry of the French towns that was marching toward the battlefield, apparently unaware that the battle was over.

As he counted his prisoners and the bodies on the field of Crécy, Edward realized that he had won a great victory, but it was difficult to think of any way to exploit it. Although northern France lay open before him, he dared not attempt an invasion with his small and extremely tired army. The most useful course seemed to be to capture a port on the coast that could serve as a permanent beachhead for future invasions. With this in mind, he laid siege to the port of Calais. Edward built a complete string of fortifications around the landward side of the town facing both toward Calais and toward the inland roads by which a relieving army would have to approach. As many as thirty thousand troops were used in these works at one time or another, but it seems most unlikely that more than ten to fifteen thousand were ever there at one time. After some months, it occurred to Edward that he was doing little more than annoying the garrison of Calais. Although he had blocked all entrance from the land, the town was being adequately supplied by sea. The English king then brought up a fleet and blockaded the sea side as well. Once this was done, the garrison was lost if it was not relieved in a reasonable time. Late in July 1347, Philip mustered an army and marched to Calais, but he dared not attack Edward's force behind its strong fortifications. On August 2 he called on the English king to behave like a true knight and come out to fight in the open. But the practical side of Edward's mind was able

*Sources, no. 85.

to resist his chivalrous inclinations, and he refused. Philip retired in disgust, and Calais surrendered on August 4. At first Edward was determined to slaughter all the inhabitants, but he agreed to be content with hanging the mayor and a few prominent citizens and eventually was persuaded by his queen to spare them as well. He did, however, deport a fair part of the population and replace them with English colonists. He then strengthened the fortifications of the town and placed in it a powerful garrison. Calais was to remain an impregnable English fortress until 1558.

Philip VI died in 1350 and was succeeded by his son John (1350–1364), who was called for no reason any historian has been able to fathom "the Good." John was more stupid than his father and even more thoroughly imbued with chivalric ideas. He was incurably suspicious and saw treason in everything. Although usually weak and vacillating, he was capable of bursts of decisive energy in which he was likely to be brutal and savage. His only redeeming features were his reckless personal courage and his rather quixotic conception of knightly honor. As a king he was utterly worthless. Soon after he came to the throne, he raised up a new and dangerous enemy to plague his house, Charles of Navarre. Charles was the son of the royal princess Jeanne and was both count of Evreux and king of Navarre.* He was usually known as "the Bad," a name which raises no problems for historians. King John had a favorite, a Spanish prince whom he had made constable of France and who was heartily hated by the French nobility. Charles the Bad lured the constable into an ambush and murdered him. By way of revenge, the king invaded a hall where Charles was dining and had all his companions slaughtered before his eyes. Charles himself was cast into prison for a time. Charles' kingdom of Navarre was a long way off and could give little trouble, but his Norman lands bristled with strong castles that were thrown open to English troops.

A series of truces interspersed with small-scale hostilities followed the capture of Calais, and major operations were not undertaken until 1355. In that year Edward, prince of Wales, known from the color of his armor as the Black Prince, marched from Gascony into southern France at the head of a small but highly mobile army. His archers were supplied with horses so that they could keep up with the English knights and the Gascon nobles. Young Edward plundered and burned the entire length of the county of Toulouse; he boasted that he had burned five hundred places, including the suburbs of Carcassonne and Narbonne. The French commander in the region saw his own lands ravaged without daring to offer battle or even come near enough to annoy the English army. Early in December, the Black Prince returned to Bordeaux laden with booty. This was the sort of expedition the English were particularly fond of. The army marched through the open country stealing everything of value and burning the unfortified towns and villages. No attempt was made to attack fortified places, and every effort was made to avoid battle with anything like an equal force. It was great fun and highly profitable.

*See p. 504.

There is some reason for thinking that, during the spring of 1356, the English conceived what was for them an astonishingly complex idea, two coordinated invasions of France. The most powerful of the English barons, Edward's second cousin Henry, duke of Lancaster, was to cross to Brittany with a small force, gather the English companies that were already in that duchy, invade Normandy, and eventually move south toward the Loire. The Black Prince would march north from Gascony to meet Henry near the Loire. If there really was such a comprehensive strategic plan, it was carried out with characteristic incompetence. Duke Henry landed in Brittany in mid-June and invaded Normandy, but early in July he learned that John was approaching at the head of his army. As Lancaster had but a tiny force, he hastily withdrew into Brittany, while John vainly besieged one of the four Norman fortresses he had captured. The Black Prince on his side did not start from Gascony until the middle of August. He marched in leisurely fashion through Périgord, the Limousin, and Berry, plundering and burning as he moved. About the first of September, he reached the Loire, but since the river was in flood and the French had removed all the boats to the northern bank, he could not cross the stream. While this mischance prevented him from joining Duke Henry in Brittany, it probably did not worry the Black Prince. The Loire valley was rich and prosperous, and it had never been really thoroughly plundered. Young Edward did a good, complete job, and then on September 11 he started back toward Bordeaux with a long train of wagons loaded with plunder.

When John learned of the Black Prince's expedition, he determined to march against him. As most of the French host had gone home after Lancaster's retirement, it took some time to reassemble, but shortly before the English left the Loire valley for the south, the French crossed the river and moved to cut them off. The Black Prince had no desire for battle. His army was small and tired from a long campaign, besides being heavily laden with booty. But John felt that he had the English at his mercy and was unwilling to offer any terms the Black Prince would consider. Forced to give battle, the prince took up his position on slightly rising ground southeast of the town of Poitiers. His left flank was protected by a deep ravine containing a small river, while his right was covered to some extent by the outskirts of a thick wood. The front of the position was guarded by hedges and thickets except where a small road crossed it. The army was formed in the usual three battles of dismounted cavalry, pikemen, and archers. Early in the morning of the day of battle, one of the three divisions fell back to begin the retreat and was hastily recalled when the prince saw that the French were going to attack before he could retire.

John and his advisers had been thinking deeply. They saw that the battleground was strewn with thickets and hedges and hence far from ideal for a cavalry charge. They also remembered that at Crécy the English knights had fought on foot and had won. The obvious answer seemed to be to dismount his knights. What the king forgot was that a march of a mile or so across rough country would be incredibly exhausting for heavily armed men used to fighting on horseback. The English knights who had fought on foot at Crécy had stayed in one place on the defensive. The French knights dismounted and arrayed themselves in three massive divisions. The crossbowmen were carefully placed behind the men-at-arms so that there would be no danger of their getting into action and depriving the gentlemen of the glory of victory. But John did have one ingenious ideal—to send a body of cavalry down the road to punch a gap in the English line for the main divisions to exploit. This force of three hundred picked knights was commanded by the marshal of France, John of Clermont, who incidentally had advised against an attack on the English position, had been called a coward for his pains, and was determined to show his courage.

The idea was a good one, and a large mass of cavalry charging down the road might well have broken the English line, but three hundred were far too few for the purpose. Fired on from both sides by the English archers, most of the knights never reached the line, and those who did were easily captured. Then the first French division under the command of the king's eldest son, the Dauphin Charles, advanced against the English. This was a powerful body, and, despite their exhaustion after their long march, the knights fought vigorously. Prince Edward was forced to throw in his reserve division in order to rout them. But routed they were, and the remnants fled in disorder. The second division of the French host was under the command of John's younger brother, Philip, duke of Orleans. Orleans and his captains took a long look at the fleeing remnants of his nephew's troops and decided they preferred some other neighborhood. Without striking a blow, the whole division fled from the field. This left only the third division, commanded by the king in person. With two-thirds of his army dispersed, the day was obviously lost. Any sensible monarch would have saved himself and the men he led. But John was a knight who would not flinch before the enemy, and he led his division against the English line. Once more the battle was sharp and furious, but the English soon gained the day. John's household knights were killed around him, and he and his youngest son Philip were captured. The battle was over. In addition to the booty loaded on his wagons, the Black Prince now had the king of France, his son, an archbishop, thirteen counts, five viscounts, sixteen men of baronial rank, and many lesser captives.

After the bloody battle there was an interlude of story-book chivalry. The Black Prince gave a banquet for King John and waited at his table, saying that he was not worthy to sit at dinner with so great a lord. Then he told the king that all the English had agreed to award him the "prize and chaplet" as the most valiant knight on the field of battle. So in a way the affair ended happily for everyone. King John was delighted with the honor he had won. The Black Prince contentedly marched back to Bordeaux with his booty.*

*Sources no. 85

The Battle of Poitiers brought to an end the first phase of the Hundred Years' War. The next step was to make a peace treaty by which the French king would be released. Meanwhile, the dauphin, who took over the government in his father's absence, was kept occupied by a rising of the bourgeoisie of Paris, a revolt of the peasants in the country north of Paris, and a war with Charles the Bad of Navarre.*

John was treated with extreme courtesy by the Black Prince in Bordeaux and by his father in London. Edward allowed his captive to live in royal state—at his own expense. The other noble prisoners were allowed to go where they pleased within the island realm to the considerable perturbation of English noblemen with handsome wives. In 1359 a treaty of peace was agreed to by King John. He was to pay a vast ransom of four million crowns. Gascony was to be extended to include the entire ancient duchy of Aquitaine, and Edward was to have in addition Touraine, Anjou, Maine, Normandy, the suzerainty over Brittany, and a block of territory surrounding Calais. He was to surrender his claim to be king of France, and John was to renounce all rights as a feudal suzerain over Edward's French lands. It is doubtful that anyone expected this treaty to go into force. The dauphin treated it as a pleasant joke, and he and the Black Prince began serious negotiations. The result was the Treaty of Brétigny, later confirmed by the two monarchs at Calais. The ransom was reduced to three million crowns. Edward was to have the ancient lands of the duchy of Aquitaine, the county of Ponthieu, and a small territory surrounding Calais. When all the territorial changes had been carried out and the ransom paid, Edward and John were at the same moment to renounce their respective claims to the throne of France and the suzerainty over the English lands in France. This masterpiece of an arrangement was probably concocted in the subtle brain of the very keen young man who was soon to be king of France. He had no desire to see the French crown renounce its right to valuable lands in return for Edward giving up a vague claim, and he felt fairly certain it would never happen under this treaty.

75. *The French Recovery*

There was never the slightest chance that the Treaty of Brétigny would be carried out. The French government could not possibly raise three million crowns. Moreover, the territorial adjustments were highly difficult. No two people agreed exactly on the boundaries of the districts mentioned in the treaty, and this could lead to years of pleasant negotiation. Many castles in Normandy and Maine were held by English captains, while the parts of Aquitaine to be given Edward were in the hands of French nobles. The French lords had no desire to become vassals of Edward and made as many delays as possible, but the real difficulty lay with the English captains. They were comfortably seated in strong fortresses ruling the countryside, and they had no intention of giving up their positions just because they were ordered to.

*See pp. 532–533.

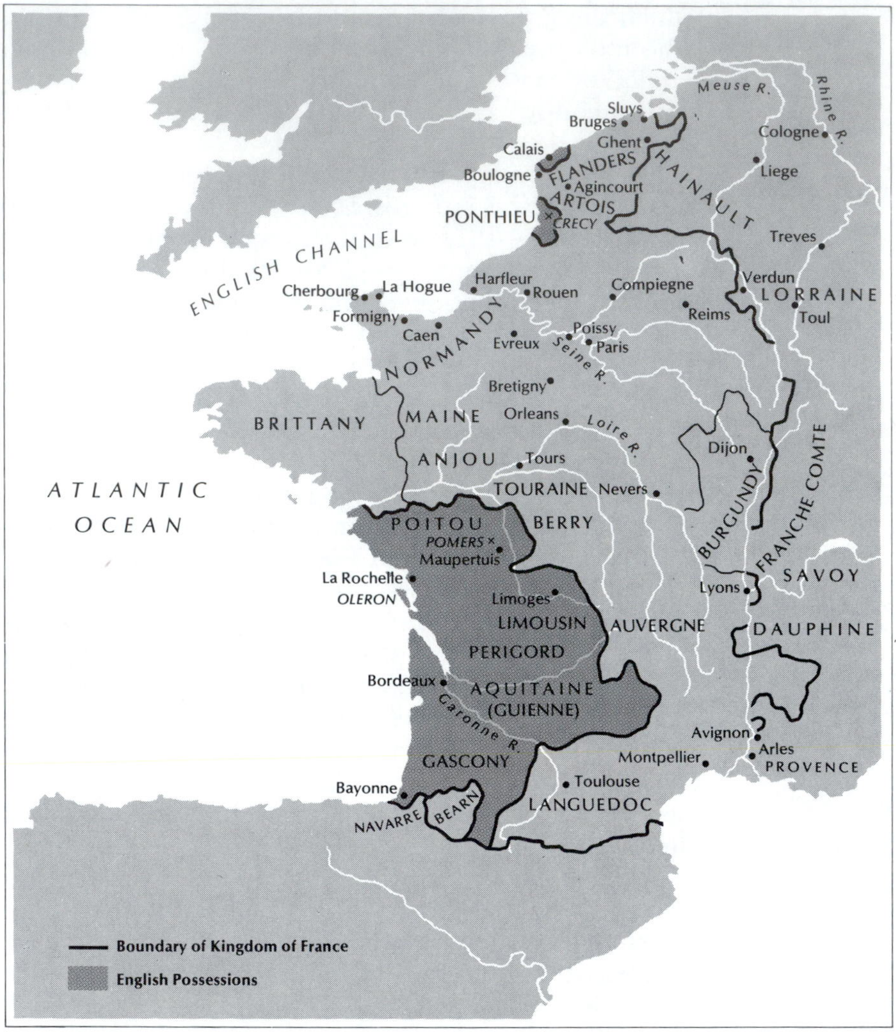

The Hundred Years' War, 1360

The division of territories agreed upon at the end of the first major phase of the war, brought to a close by the defeat of the French at Poitiers in 1356, was never actually effected: under the astute leadership of Charles V, the French steadily recovered lands from the English by avoiding open battles and concentrating on reducing the English fortresses one by one.

Although only four hundred thousand crowns of the three-million-crown ransom had been paid when the Treaty of Brétigny was ratified at Calais, Edward accepted it as a first installment and released his royal captive. The king's brother, two of his sons, and many of the greatest nobles of France remained in England as hostages for the payment of the ransom. The dauphin had been making heroic efforts to raise the money for the ransom and had sold his sister to the duke of Milan for a fine round sum, but when the amiable and chivalrous king arrived in Paris, he promptly spent the money in a series of festivities to celebrate his liberation. As France could not at once support John and collect money for his ransom, the gathering of the ransom made slow progress. Then came a stroke of good fortune for France. John's second son, Louis, duke of Anjou, was a hostage for his father. He was living in Calais and had full freedom to wander about the countryside at will. Just before Poitiers, he had married a charming woman, and she was living in one of his castles not far from Calais. Temptation was too strong for young Louis' honor. One day he simply left Calais and went to join his bride. To the shocked protests of his father and brother, he turned a deaf ear. John, a thoroughly chivalrous gentleman, saw only one possible course; he surrendered himself once more as a prisoner. In 1364 he died in London.

The new king of France, Charles V (1364–1380), was a far different man from his father and grandfather. They had been large, handsome, and stupid; he was small, homely, and highly intelligent. He had no love for battles; his experience at Poitiers was enough to satisfy him for the rest of his life. Instead, he worked diligently with his ministers and spent his spare time reading political theory. But he knew how to choose men, both soldiers and civilians, and how to use them to the limits of their talents. In the sixteen years of his reign, he recovered what his father and grandfather had lost.

Charles V fully recognized his obligation to go through the forms of carrying out the Treaty of Brétigny. The negotiations about the territorial settlements went on, although at a leisurely pace, and he continued to collect money for the ransom. In 1366 a new agreement was reached under which Charles promised to maintain a regular schedule of payments. In return, Edward released the hostages of royal blood. As a matter of fact, Charles actually paid four hundred thousand crowns. In short, Charles was a man who wanted his position to be absolutely correct. He fully intended to recommence the war and regain what had been lost, but he was resolved to do so with complete propriety. Fortunately, he had little trouble finding an excuse. The Black Prince, who was ruling Aquitaine for his father, was an efficient, strict, and severe administrator. His taxes were high, he collected them firmly, and he insisted on prompt obedience to his commands. The people of the provinces added to Gascony by the Treaty of Brétigny were used to the heavy-handed agents of the French crown and were not troubled by the Black Prince and his officers, but the nobles of Gascony were accustomed to easygoing and powerless officers whom they could defy with impunity. Soon two of the chief barons of Gascony lodged appeals with the *parlement* of Paris. In 1369 the Black Prince was summoned to Paris to answer the appeals but refused to go. He was then declared contumacious and condemned to forfeit Aquitaine. In 1370 he invaded the French king's territory; besieged the city of Limoges; and, after the usual chivalrous games during the course of the siege, carried out an atrocious massacre of the civilian population.* The war was on again.

The war that raged for the next five years was a weird affair. The English used their favorite device of large-scale plundering expedi-

*Sources, no. 85

tions. Thus in 1373 the third son of Edward III, John of Ghent, landed with an army at Calais, marched down through Champagne and on to Bordeaux. He ravaged the open country and burned any unfortified places he passed. When he reached a castle or walled town, he paused to have a few enjoyable little skirmishes with the knights of the garrison but made no attempt to take the stronghold. As he moved through the hills of central France, food grew scarce for both men and horses, and by the time the army reached Bordeaux, it was completely exhausted. Under the direction of the canny Charles V, the French carefully kept out of battles. A few French knights would place themselves in the fortresses along the English route to participate in the entertaining little skirmishes. Sometimes, if the expedition showed signs of exhaustion while still in French territory, small French forces would move in to harass its march, but no attempt was made to stop these excursions by pitched battles. The peasants of the French countryside suffered desperately, but there was no way in which Edward could win a decisive victory so long as the French refused to give battle.

While the English were proudly and futilely marching across the land, Charles' captains were systematically reducing their fortresses by any means that came to hand. The actual work was done by a varied group of captains of whom the most famous, both in his own day and in the pages of history, was Bertran Duguesclin. This petty Breton nobleman was a man of courage, personal prowess, and considerable competence as a leader of small bands. He was hopelessly ineffective in large-scale engagements and could nearly always manage to lose a pitched battle, but he was a genius at ambushes, surprises, and sudden unexpected assaults on castles.

When the war was renewed, King Charles made Duguesclin constable of France and turned him loose on the English. His first exploit was to harass an English force that had marched from Calais through the Ile de France on its way to Brittany. So skillfully did Duguesclin operate that he succeeded in cutting off and destroying a fair part of the English army. But his true forte was the taking of castles. If possible, he would bribe someone within to open a gate late at night. He was not above sending fair ladies of easy virtue into a castle to seduce the garrison and, when the time came, let him in. Often he would simply rush suddenly on the castle in the dead of night, and his men would scale the walls before the garrison knew what was happening.

Duguesclin was not the only captain engaged in this good work. One of the most successful was Louis, duke of Bourbon, a prince of the blood royal and one of the greatest lords of France. One of Duke Louis' exploits shows particularly clearly the nature of much of this warfare. He was operating on the borders of Poitou at the head of a strong company, almost a small army, consisting largely of his own retainers and vassals. He decided to attack a castle that was held for the Black Prince by an English garrison commanded by a squire. The duke first attempted to take the place by assault, but it was too strong and too well defended. He then settled down to mining. The garrison soon guessed what was going on and started a countermine. One day as the duke was sitting in his tent, one of his men came to tell him that the two mines had met. He immediately ordered his herald to inquire whether any noble knight in the castle would like to meet a noble French knight in the mine. The captain replied that the garrison lacked knights, but a noble squire would be delighted to fight in the mine.

This satisfied the duke, and arming himself from head to foot, he descended into the mine to meet the English captain. The mine was so low and narrow that one could neither raise a weapon nor move one's arms far from one's sides. Fighting consisted of the two men poking swords at one another. As it was impossible for knights in armor to hurt each other in this way, it was a thoroughly enjoyable affair. The duke got so excited that he shouted his war cry, and the squire recognized it and asked if he were really fighting the duke of Bourbon. When he learned what a great honor had been done him by being allowed to fight so noble a prince, he offered to surrender the castle if Bourbon would dub him a knight. The duke agreed but asked that the surrender be put off till the next day. It would be selfish of them to deny their followers the pleasure of fighting in the mine. So all that day, two by two, French and English poked at each other in the mine. Next morning the castle surrendered, the duke dubbed the squire, they exchanged gifts, and everyone went his way. The biographer of Duke Louis assures us that everyone who heard of this affair was filled with admiration for the courtesy of the two participants. The duke of Bourbon was a chivalrous gentleman, beloved by both knights and ladies. His biographer suggests that Edward III released him from captivity in England at the request of his nobles who feared for the virtue of their wives. It is worth noticing, however, that he got the castle.

The French armies were quickly successful. Edward III was growing old, the Black Prince was in wretched health and had few more years to live, and their captains seemed no match for Duguesclin and his colleagues. One by one the English fortresses fell, until the capture of La Réole in 1374 reduced the duchy of Gascony to the coastal region between the mouth of the Garonne and the Pyrenees. By avoiding battles and systematically taking the enemy strongholds—and thus the land dependent on them—Charles V had recovered rather more than his ancestors had lost.

Unfortunately, the defeat of the English did not free France from the horrors of war. When a medieval monarch no longer had need of his hired troops, he stopped paying them. He felt no responsibility whatever for seeing that they got home. Moreover, many of the captains and men who served Edward and his sons were not Englishmen but adventurers from many lands who fought for pay and booty. When their pay stopped, they proceeded to live off the countryside, wandering about and plundering at will. Freed from what little discipline their noble generals had been able to impose, they became fiendishly cruel marauders. These "free companies," as they were called at first, became a serious menace in the interval of peace after the Treaty of Brétigny. The renewal of the war kept them busy for a while, but when hostilities slackened after 1374 they became unemployed once more. While they ordinarily avoided fortified places, they would at times storm a small castle or town and were not above holding noble ladies for ransom. Attempts were made to send them off into other lands, but France was good plundering, and they usually refused to move. When the nobles of a region grew desperate and marched against them, the companies usually won. Several times they defeated royal armies in pitched battles. Duguesclin's last battle was fought against them; he won the battle but was killed in it. These companies were to be the bane of France for over a century.

The Black Prince died in 1376; Edward III, in 1377; and Charles V, in 1380. There was at first no formal peace between the two hostile states, but in this period internal troubles in the two kingdoms kept their rulers busy at home. A twenty-year truce concluded in 1396 brought to an end the fourteenth-century phase of the Hundred Years' War. We shall next turn to the internal development of England, France, and the other major European powers during this same period.

READING SUGGESTIONS

* *B. Tierney,* Sources *and* Readings, *vol. I, no. 84; vol. II, no. 36.*

All general histories of England and France deal with the Hundred Years' War. Good general surveys are K. Fowler. *The Hundred Years' War* (New York, 1971); * E. Perroy, *The Hundred Years' War* (London, 1951); and * C. Allmand, *The Hundred Years' War* (Cambridge, England, 1988). On the diplomatic background, see H. Lucas, *The Low Countries and the Hundred Years' War* (Ann Arbor, MI, 1929), and on particular campaigns, A. H. Burne, *The Crécy War* (London, 1955); H. J. Hewitt, *The Black Prince's Expedition of 1355–1357* (Manchester, England, 1958); and R. Russell, *The English Intervention in Spain and Portugal in the Time of Edward III and Richard II* (New York, 1955). A convenient translation of Froissart's *Chronicle* is that of * C. W. Dunn (New York, 1961).

chapter

XXIII

Late Medieval Politics: A Century of Schisms

In considering the development of government during the fourteenth century, we find a similar story repeated over and over. Everywhere, larger, more complex government machines were growing up, staffed increasingly by well-trained, professional bureaucrats. But, throughout the century, disputes arose about the proper functions of government and above all about who had the right to control these developing governmental institutions. Finally, in the years around 1400, a series of major conflicts broke out, which produced simultaneously a state of schism in the church and of civil war in several of the leading states of Europe.

Each of these conflicts had its own immediate cause, but the situation as a whole can be understood only when all are seen as aspects of a general crisis of loyalty that threatened the whole foundation of medieval government. Everywhere there was a breakdown of traditional allegiances. In the secular sphere, feudal loyalties had decayed and national loyalties were not yet strong enough to provide an adequate substitute. In the church, the position of the pope as the indubitable, personal representative of Christ on earth had been called into question by the propaganda of secularist philosophers and of religious radicals. Factions of princes and nobility in various lands seized every opportunity that arose to grasp power for themselves without any regard for the interests of the state. Similarly, the "princes of the church," the cardinals, did not hesitate to attack the pope when they felt it would serve their own interests to do so.

By the end of the fourteenth century, it had become apparent that no universal consensus existed about the characteristics which made political power legitimate. In both church and state, attempts were made to establish a clear-cut basis for legitimacy in the principle of popular consent expressed through representative assemblies. Such attempts were only partially successful at the time, though they established extremely important precedents for the future. Once again we are faced with a highly complex situation arising from the fact that the fourteenth century was not only an age of decay but also an era of transition.

76. *England and the Last Plantagenets*

The monarchy of the Plantagenet kings of England founded by Henry II reached its height under Edward I (1272–1307).* Edward made the most of the ancient feudal sources of royal revenue as well as property taxes and customs duties. In war he used the feudal levy as well as drafts of infantry and paid companies. His government was conducted by a highly efficient bureaucracy of royal servants who were completely subject to his will. No officer of state was in a position to hamper the king's personal authority. The most important institution in the bureaucracy was the body of sworn councilors who advised the king and conducted the routine business of government. This group of royal servants decided major questions of policy and drew up legislation. It was the dominant force in Parliament. The barons were ruled with an iron hand. By highly dubious methods several of the great baronies were brought into the hands of members of the royal house. In short, Edward was a strong, efficient, and high-handed ruler, whose policies were certain to bring a reaction against his methods of government.

The reaction began to appear toward the end of Edward I's reign in the resistance of Parliament to royal demands for taxation.† It was plainly expressed at the coronation of Edward's son, Edward II (1307–1327), when a fresh clause was added to the traditional coronation oath, and the new king was required to swear that he would faithfully observe "the just laws and customs that the community of the realm shall have chosen"‡ Moreover, in taking the customary oath of loyalty, the barons explicitly declared that their allegiance was owed primarily to the crown of England, not to the person of the king. It was the same distinction between person and office that we have encountered in the antipapal writings of the early fourteenth century.

Edward II, it turned out, was a striking contrast to his father. Ineffective, weak, and vacillating, he was always under the thumb of some stronger character—his queen, Isabelle of France; his Gascon favorite, Peter Gaveston; or the English Dispenser family. In the early years of his reign, he was obliged to accept the tutelage of a coalition of barons led by his cousin Thomas, earl of Lancaster. The primary object of these barons, commonly called the Lords Ordainers, was to limit the king's control over the royal administration. Although the Lords Ordainers claimed that they acted in the common interest, they were in fact greedy and self-seeking. Like earlier coalitions of the same sort, this alliance eventually fell to pieces. Thomas of Lancaster murdered Peter Gaveston and was in turn defeated and executed by Edward. In 1322 a statute was promulgated declaring that all matters concerning the state of the kingdom were to be decided by the king in Parliament,

*See Appendix, Tables 4 and 6, for genealogy of the English kings.

†See pp. 400–402.

‡Sources, no 73.

with the consent of the prelates and nobles and of the community of the realm. But, in fact, the realm was governed for the next few years in the king's name by the haughty and rapacious Dispensers. In 1326 Queen Isabelle and her lover, Roger Mortimer, overthrew them and forced the feeble king to abdicate in favor of his son. Edward II was soon brutally murdered by his custodians. For a few years, the young king, Edward III, watched the disgraceful spectacle of his mother and Mortimer plundering England, but when they executed his favorite uncle, Edward lost patience. Gathering a band of knights, he seized the queen and her lover. Mortimer was executed, and Isabelle was confined to a royal manor.

Although Edward III (1327–1377) devoted so much of his personal attention to campaigning in France, his long reign—only three monarchs in England's history occupied the throne for so many years—was a period of immense importance in the development of English political institutions. There were two basic questions at issue. The first of these was whether the royal government should be conducted by men who were simply the king's servants, bound to accept his will without question, or whether its more vital functions should be performed by officers of state responsible to Parliament, that is, to the faction of aristocracy dominant in Parliament at any given time. The second major question was how the institutional structure of Parliament itself would develop. Edward was inclined to set up an administration of royal servants like that of his grandfather. The barons wanted the great officers of state to be answerable to the magnates in Parliament and insisted that there should be a strong baronial element in the king's council. Once, in a moment when he desperately needed funds, Edward agreed to permit baronial control of his ministers, but he promptly revoked his promise. Throughout his reign, he appointed his own officials as he saw fit, but he did accept the fact that the great officers of state had a responsibility beyond the mere execution of his will. Late in his reign, when advancing years had enfeebled him, the barons were able to enforce this conception of ministerial responsibility. Several royal servants were convicted of improper acts by the magnates in Parliament. Thus the principle was advanced that, while it was extremely difficult to force the king to obey the law, his ministers could be punished for carrying out illegal commands. This was the beginning of the practice known as *impeachment*—trial of an officer of state by the Lords in Parliament at the request of the Commons.

Although to the people of the fourteenth century the all-important issue was the control of the royal government that ruled England from day to day, week to week, month to month, and year to year, historians are inclined to be more interested in the development of Parliament because of its later importance. The reign of Edward III was peculiarly propitious for the growth of parliamentary institutions and functions. Although the king was unwilling to have the barons control his administration, Edward was basically not much interested in the internal government of England. He was a soldier who was chiefly preoccupied with his wars in France. In general, he was willing to make almost any concession in return for the vast sums of money needed for his military operations. At the same time, his military success made him a national hero, and his open, genial, easy manners brought him the affection of his people. Hence the process of parliamentary development that might have led to bitter quarrels under another monarch was essentially amiable.

During Edward's reign, the composition and organization of Parliament began to assume the form that was to last until today. One of the most significant developments was in the nature of the Great Council, soon to become the House of Lords. Magna Carta had defined this body as an assembly of tenants-in-chief, those who held fiefs directly from the king. But by the middle of the thirteenth century, feudalism was little more than a series of forms. Tenure had no real meaning, and power was no longer determined by the number of knightly vassals a man had. Importance in the realm was largely the result of a combination of personal qualities and money income. Henry III summoned men who were not tenurial barons to the Great Council, and Edward I paid little attention to tenurial qualifications. He summoned the men who seemed to him to be important. In the reign of Edward III, it began to be customary to summon the son of a man who had sat in the Great Council. Although the right of the heir to succeed to a seat in the council was not firmly established in custom until the fifteenth century, it became the usual practice during Edward's reign. Thus the parliamentary peerage of England began to take definite form. This peerage was personal. Once a man had been summoned to a Parliament, his heirs were presumed to be entitled to be summoned whether or not they possessed any particular estates.

This same period saw a gradual reduction in the ecclesiastical element in Parliament. Abbots and priors found attendance burdensome and did their best to avoid it. During the reigns of Edward II and Edward III, individual prelates were continually claiming exemption on the ground that they did not hold by barony. While some of these requests were refused, many more were granted, and the crown accepted the doctrine that only prelates holding by barony were subject to summons. A limited list of abbots and priors liable to summons was established, but its composition had little to do with tenure. It seems to have been based primarily on the wealth and importance of the house. The only definite principle that seems to have been in operation was the exemption of orders like the Cistercian that clearly held their possessions in free alms. The representatives of the lower clergy also disappeared from Parliament. When the king wanted money from the clergy, he negotiated with separate ecclesiastical assemblies, and hence the presence of the clergy in Parliament was unnecessary and might involve them unduly in secular affairs. By the end of Edward's reign, the ecclesiastics sitting in Parliament were reduced to twenty-one bishops and twenty-seven abbots and priors. Usually this was enough to provide an ecclesiastical majority in the House of Lords.

As we have seen, throughout the reign of Edward I, the term "parliament" could be applied to a meeting of the king's council with the magnates; but, under his son and grandson, the presence of the representatives of the shires and towns became more and more frequent. When such a full Parliament met in solemn conclave, the whole body sat together—king, council, magnates, and representatives. But the lords of the Great Council dealt with many affairs that were beyond the competence of the representatives and hence held many sessions by themselves. The knights of the shires and the burghers also met separately to debate issues in advance of the general meetings. As these two groups had one thing in common—they were both outside the Great Council—they frequently met together to decide their policy. Soon one finds them referred to collectively as "the commons." Gradually, in this way, the two houses of Parliament came into being. The magnates of the Great Council became the House of Lords, and the representatives of the shires and towns, the House of Commons. The first record of the Commons meeting in their own chamber as an organized group, separate from the Lords, dates from 1341.

Before the reign of Edward III, the Commons had little actual share in the work of Parliament except for voting grants of taxes. Under Edward II, they approved the ordinances made by the Lords Ordainers and participated in accepting the abdication of the king, but all initiative lay in the hands of the council and the magnates. There was, however, one means by which the Commons could take the initiative—they could draw up petitions and present them to the Lords. If the Lords approved them, they would be transmitted to the king and council. This device was used rarely under Edward II, but in the reign of Edward III it became the usual way of creating new legislation. When the Commons felt there was a need for a new law, they would draw up a petition and send it to the Lords. If passed by them and accepted by the king, it became a statute. But the Commons had in this period no way of controlling the eventual form of legislation. Lords, council, and king could change it much as they pleased before issuing it. Nevertheless, it became customary for most legislation to be initiated in the Commons and for all grants of money to have their origin there.

Edward's continual need of money to wage his war in France gave Parliament many opportunities to increase its authority. On only a few occasions was it expressly stated that grants would be made in return for concessions, but it was generally understood that this would be the case. Edward promised to levy no direct taxes without the approval of Parliament. Later he admitted that body's right to control customs duties. He even permitted parliamentary committees to supervise the expenditure of the money granted, by auditing accounts. Moreover, he frequently consulted Parliament about important questions of policy, such as the making of truces. In short, in his reign Parliament as a whole, Lords and Commons, became an integral part of the English government. When in Edward's old age his administration fell into disorder, everyone assumed that it was the business of Parliament to bring about a reform. The result was the impeachment of corrupt and inefficient officials.

In the reign of Edward III, there were also important developments in the administration of justice. The House of Lords emerged clearly as the supreme court of the realm by the end of the fourteenth century. In the case of a peer accused of felony or treason, it was the court of original jurisdiction. It also heard appeals from the decisions of the courts of common law. Meanwhile, a new court, that of the chancellor, had taken definite form. According to the accepted theory, it was the king's duty to see that justice was done. If injustice was found that had no remedy in the law, the king should devise some means of remedying it. The chancellor, as the custodian of the king's conscience, was expected to perform this function. Thus, a person failing to carry out a contract, the individual could be sued at common law and compelled to pay a penalty, but the individual could not be forced to carry out the contract. The chancellor's court could oblige him to do this. The common law covered only written agreements and took no notice of oral arrangements, but the chancellor, judged according to "equity" rather than common law, would enforce oral agreements if they were properly established.

Perhaps the most important judicial development of Edward's reign was the establishment of the *justices of the peace.* As early as the time of Edward I, officials called *keepers of the peace* has been established in every county to supervise the sheriff and coroners in the performance of their duties. Soon they were given the authority to receive indictments and order the arrest of the persons indicted. In 1329 they were given the power to try those accused of felony, and so became justices of the peace. In 1388 it was provided that all the justices of a county should meet in the county seat four times a year to try cases and transact other business. Thus were established the Quarter Sessions that have been so important a part of the English judicial system. The justices were appointed by the king from the ranks of the nobles and lesser landholders. Bit by bit they gathered into their hands the police court jurisdiction that had once belonged to the popular and franchise courts. Soon the hundred courts disappeared, and the county court became merely a tribunal for insignificant civil cases. The justices of the peace became the chief power in local government. Although they were appointed by the crown and were royal officials, they were unpaid, and their primary loyalty was to their class in society.

For most of his reign Edward III dominated England because he was an able ruler who pursued a successful foreign policy. Under his grandson, Richard II (1377–1399), aristocratic factionalism led to a series of bitter political crises, culminating in the deposition of the king. When Edward III died in 1377, his eldest son, the Black Prince, was already dead and the latter's heir, Richard, was only nine years old. The government was entrusted to a council of regency dominated by the king's uncles, John of Ghent and Thomas of Gloucester. The most powerful figure at first was John of Ghent, duke of Lancaster (Shakespeare's John of Gaunt), an energetic and ambitious, though not very successful, soldier. He had acquired vast estates through his marriage to the heiress of the duchy of Lancaster and became the leader of a powerful faction of nobility, but he was not well liked by the country at large.

The first years of young Richard's reign were ones of violent discontent that culminated in the Peasants' Rebellion of 1381.* Then, when Richard prepared to take control of his own government in 1386, his uncle, Thomas of Gloucester, attempted a coup d'état. Thomas was in a position to do this because his powerful brother John of Ghent was away in Spain fighting an unsuccessful campaign for the crown of Castile. (John had married a Spanish princess as his second wife.) Thomas and his faction, called the Lords Appellant, dominated a Parliament held in 1386 and opened an attack on the king's closest friends and servants. Richard obtained from the judges of England a declaration that the king alone could determine what business was to be conducted in Parliament, that the king's ministers were responsible to him alone, and that he could dismiss Parliament at will. But Thomas of Gloucester could command more military support than Richard, and the king had to endure the humiliation of seeing his most faithful friends executed as traitors.

In 1389 John of Ghent came back to England and thus restored a sort of balance of power. Richard was allowed to assume control of the government, ruling in cooperation with his two uncles, and for several years things went quietly. Richard used these years to build up a basis of personal power. He filled the bureaucracy with servants completely obedient to him. He also created peerages for many of his favorites and appointed some of them members of his council. Thus he secured firm control of the council and a strong party in the House of Lords. As the sheriffs conducted the elections for knights of the shire and a majority of the boroughs were royal, a king could always pack the House of Commons if he took sufficient trouble; but the English kings had as a rule been either too conscientious or too lazy to do so. Richard went at it with energy and produced a well-packed Parliament. Then, suddenly, in 1397, he denounced Thomas of Gloucester and the Lords Appellant who had humiliated him ten years before. All those who had participated in the coalition against Richard were arrested, convicted by the packed House of Lords, and either executed or exiled. Richard then made it plain that he proposed to rule as an absolute monarch in the future. Parliament was persuaded to delegate its powers to a committee chosen by the king and to make an unprecedented grant of taxes on wool to Richard for the rest of his life. By these maneuvers, the king had apparently emancipated himself from all parliamentary control. No doubt Richard felt that he was simply realizing in practice the legal conception of monarchical power that his judges had obligingly defined for him in 1386.

If the interpretation of the law of England made by the judges was allowed to stand, the English king would have practically absolute power. In making this claim, Richard went too far. The English barons

*See pp. 554–557.

and people were used to quarreling more or less amiably with their monarchs over what limits should be set to the royal authority, but they had no intention of even considering the doctrine that there should be no such limits. Moreover, Richard showed all too clearly how he intended to use his power. All the shires of England were declared guilty of offenses against the crown and heavily fined. Some years before this, Richard had exiled Henry of Lancaster, son of John of Ghent, but had promised that he should receive his great inheritance when his father died. Instead, when John died, Richard seized all his vast lands. In short, Richard made it clear that he intended to be absolute in practice as well as in theory. The result was a baronial revolt led by Henry of Lancaster. Richard's favorites whom he had created peers could vote his way in council and Parliament, but they lacked the resources to be of much use in a civil war. Soon the king found himself deserted and was obliged to surrender to his adversary.

The problem now arose of how to dispose of the crown of England. Richard's enemies were determined to remove him from the throne and were in a position to compel him to abdicate, but many of them were not content with this procedure and wanted to establish the principle that a king could legally be deposed. Moreover, while the legitimate heir to the throne was the infant Edmund Mortimer, descendant of John of Ghent's elder brother Lionel, Henry of Lancaster was determined to have the crown for himself. He accordingly fabricated a fantastic hereditary claim—that his ancestor Edmund of Lancaster had been in reality the eldest son of King Henry III so that Edward I and his descendants were all usurpers. This was a highly convenient piece of fiction, but, unfortunately, no one could be persuaded to take it seriously.

The transfer of the crown was finally stage-managed in a fashion designed to please as many people as possible. Writs of summons to a Parliament were issued in the name of King Richard; but when the assembly came together in Westminster Hall, the archbishop of Canterbury announced that the king had already abdicated, and the members saw that the royal throne stood conspicuously vacant with a cloth of gold draped over it. The assembled estates enthusiastically accepted the abdication but declared that Richard ought also to be deposed for his crimes. A decree of deposition was read which was likewise accepted. At this point, Henry of Lancaster rose and claimed the crown of England, asserting that he was of the blood royal, being descended from Henry III, and that his victory showed that God favored his cause.

> In the name of Fadir, Son, and Holy Gost, I, Henry of Lancaster chalenge this rewme of Yngland and the corone with all the membres and the appurtenances, als I that am disendit be right lyne of the blode comyng fro the gude lorde Kyng Henry Therde, and thorghe that ryght that God of his grace hath sent me, with the helpe of my kyn and of my frendes, to recover it—the whiche rewme was in poynt to be undone for defaut of governance and undoyng of the gode lawes.

Richard II of England, a portrait by an unknown artist of the French school, ca. 1395. Detail from the Wilton Diptych. *Reproduced by the courtesy of the Trustees, The National Gallery, London*

The assembly assented to this claim and the archbishop of Canterbury conducted Henry to the vacant royal throne. From this point on, the account of the proceedings recorded in the Rolls of Parliament refers to Henry as "king."*

Henry IV (1399–1413) was a competent captain and a conscientious and able ruler, but the circumstances surrounding his accession made it almost inevitable that his reign would be a troubled one. He owed the throne primarily to the support of a group of great barons headed by Henry Percy, earl of Northumberland, the master of northeastern England. These lords expected grants and favors in return for their support. When these were not forthcoming with satisfactory speed, they were ready for another rising. Henry was barely seated on the throne when a group of barons revolted to restore Richard II. Henry promptly arranged the murder of the deposed monarch, but this did not halt the trouble. Throughout his reign, he was faced with a series of baronial revolts. Meanwhile, the Welsh, who had long pined for freedom from the English yoke, had found a leader in Owen Glendower. Owen raised the standard of rebellion in Wales and formed alliances with the disaffected barons. The revolts all failed and the Welsh were suppressed, but these victories required all Henry's limited resources.

Parliament did not neglect to take advantage of Henry's troubles. As it had made him king, it could presumably depose him and give the crown to another. Moreover, because the continual rebellions kept Henry in need of money, he had to make frequent requests for grants. Henry accepted as a matter of course the control over taxation and legislation that Parliament had acquired under Edward III. Henry was also obliged to confirm the privileges claimed by Parliament—that no action could be taken against a member for remarks made in Parliament and that no member could be arrested while on the way to a session, during the session, or while going home afterward. Finally, a statute of the Lancastrian period forbade the king or council to alter the wording of legislation after it was passed by Parliament.

The decree that had deposed Richard II was carefully modeled on the terminology of the sentence enacted against Emperor Frederick II at the Council of Lyons in 1245.† The underlying theory seems to have been that if a general council of all Europe could depose an emperor, then evidently a national council could depose a king. Certainly, a new precedent had been established in England: a national assembly had chosen a king who was not the legal heir to the throne. This was to lead to a tangle of civil wars in the fifteenth century—the War of the Roses.

77. *France under the House of Valois*

The French government in the reign of Philip IV (1285–1314) was in many ways similar to that of England under Edward I (1272–1307).

*Sources, no. 93

†See p. 385.

Philip had a council much like Edward's. His *chambre des comptes* exercised the functions of the English exchequer, and his *parlement*, those of the three central courts. The *Estates General* contained the same basic elements as the English Parliament and was used by the crown in much the same way. Philip's *baillis* and seneschals were not very different from Edward's sheriffs. Both kings drew their revenues from a mixture of feudal and manorial dues and general taxes. There were, however, important differences between the two realms. The French bureaucracy was very much larger than the English. On the other hand, France was far less unified than England. The king's government ruled the royal demesne and had little to do with the lands of the princes. But, even within the demesne, the provinces had different customs and interests, and there was a good deal of local patriotism. Under Philip's sons, many of these provinces secured charters guaranteeing them special privileges. The king of France could not rule his demesne as a unit, to say nothing of his whole kingdom.

These differences become more obvious if one compares the France of Philip VI (1328–1350) with the England of Edward III (1327–1377). The French bureaucracy was growing fast and had become immense. One example will suffice. In 1340 the *parlement* of Paris had 167 members as against the 12 judges of the English central courts. Moreover, provincial particularism was even stronger than before. The *Estates General* rarely represented the whole realm but only the north, or Languedoil, while the southern provinces acted through a separate assembly, the estates of Languedoc. In addition, there were provincial estates. When the king needed money, he sought it as he saw fit from the *Estates General*, the estates of Languedoc, or the provincial estates. Often he made a series of bargains with the various provinces. In short, in the period when the English Parliament was becoming an established part of English government through active cooperation with Edward III, the *Estates General* was simply one of many bodies the French king could consult when he needed money.

The regular revenues of Philip VI from his royal demesne just about covered the peacetime cost of the government. Whenever he contemplated waging war, he had to seek additional funds. The chief reliance of the French government in the form of a general tax was a levy on sales, which varied in amount from time to time and from province to province. Then, in 1343, there appeared the *gabelle*, or salt tax. Finally, there was a hearth tax, which was originally called a *fouage*, and later a *taille*. Despite frequent levies of these various taxes, the government never had enough money to cover its military expenses and was obliged to resort to all sorts of special devices. The most obvious was to borrow money, and this was done on a large scale. Far more serious in its effect on the economy of the country was the crown's proclivity for changing the metal content of the money. The system was both ingenious and tempting. The coinage would be depreciated so that the king could pay his obligations in cheap money. Then when he was about to collect a tax, he would reform the money so that his income would be in good coins. Between 1337 and 1350, the money was changed twenty-four times. Although there seems to be no way to determine how much the government actually profited from these maneuvers, there is no question about their harmful effect on the country. When a merchant made a contract, he never could be sure in what sort of coin payment would be made.

Throughout the reign of Philip VI and the first years of that of John the Good (1350–1364), the bourgeoisie grew more and more restive. The sales taxes bore heavily on them, and they were the source of most of the loans procured by the crown. They also suffered severely from the frequent alterations of the money; in fact, that was probably their chief grievance. As the armies of France met defeat after defeat, the bourgeoisie had less and less enthusiasm for paying to support the war. They felt that the nobles, who were entirely exempt from the hearth tax, were running the war at their expense and running it very badly. This discontent was brought to a climax by the battle of Poitiers. The king had conducted the battle with magnificent incompetence and then had followed his chivalric ideas with no regard for his obligations to his people in staying on the field after all hope of victory was gone. He had been captured, and enormous sums would be needed to ransom him. The nobility as a whole had not even shown chivalrous bravery. The entire second division under the duke of Orleans had fled from the field without striking a blow. The good people of the towns, especially the inhabitants of Paris, were thoroughly exasperated. Moreover, they had a leader, Etienne Marcel, provost of the merchants of Paris. The office of provost of the merchants was essentially that of mayor of the merchant settlement on the right bank of the Seine, and its holder was a powerful figure, with all the powers of government except high justice. Etienne Marcel belonged to one of the great merchant families of Paris that had supplied many officials to the royal government. Marcel was an able, honest man with genuine sympathy for the plight of the lower classes as well as the bourgeoisie. His chief fault was a lack of good judgment in choosing allies.

As the Dauphin Charles desperately needed money to pay his troops and prepare to ransom his father, he was obliged to summon a meeting of the *Estates General* immediately after the battle of Poitiers. New taxes were granted, but under the leadership of Marcel and a few others, the members of the third estate insisted on imposing conditions on the government. The Grande Ordonnance of 1357 provided that the king's principal ministers be nominated by the *Estates General*. Moreover the *Estates General* were to meet frequently, whether summoned by the king or not. Their approval was needed for new taxes. Officers of the *Estates General* would collect and disburse any taxes granted. No important political move such as the conclusion of a truce or peace should be made without their consent. The money could not be altered without their approval. The expenses of the government were to be greatly reduced, and all grants made from the royal demesne since the time of Philip IV were to be revoked. This last was a point very dear to the middle classes. The royal demesne was the crown's natural source of revenue, and it was wrong for the king to diminish it by making gifts to nobles from it.

Marcel and his friends in the *Estates General* made one serious mistake: they demanded the release from prison of Charles the Bad, king of Navarre and count of Evreux.* Charles was a powerful figure in the Paris region because of his lands and castles along the border between the Ile de France and Normandy. Moreover, he was greedy, ambitious, and had all the prejudices and beliefs of the noble in an unusually violent form. As soon as he was free, he went to war with the dauphin and increased the general confusion. Meanwhile, the people of Paris grew more and more impatient. Paper reforms were all very well, but they wanted some sort of definite action, and they slowly pressed Marcel toward open violence. One day a mob headed by Marcel broke into the dauphin's house and murdered two high government officials in his presence. Up to that time, the dauphin had hoped to come to terms with the reformers, but this assault on his household moved him to leave Paris and set up a rival government at Compiègne.

At this point, to complicate the situation still more, a savage peasant rebellion broke out in the region north of Paris.† When Marcel learned of this he made another error of judgment by forming an alliance with the rebels. Probably he felt that he needed help wherever he could find it. But his relations with the peasants deeply disturbed the conservative elements among his supporters in Paris. One night, as he made the rounds of the guard posts on the walls, he was murdered, and the city was delivered to the dauphin.

Etienne Marcel and his supporters were responsible for the only serious attempt to establish a system of representative government for France; they wanted to make the *Estates General* an integral and effective part of the administration. Although the rapidity of their failure was largely the result of Marcel's inability to control his Parisian followers, it seems unlikely that their effort could have had any permanent result. The nobles had little or no interest in the reform plan; it was essentially a movement conducted by the third estate which was the weakest of the elements that made up the *Estates General.* Moreover the dauphin, who became king, Charles V, proved to be a strong and able monarch, and the circumstances of the Hundred Years' War favored such strong kingship. Devastated by a foreign invader, the French people were more interested in effective royal leadership than in constitutional experimentation.

Just as Charles V (1364–1380) found effective captains to recover the lands conquered by the English, so he appointed able men of middle-class origin to head his civil government. The country as a whole was so well pleased to be under a strong government which kept order at home and conducted the war successfully that there was little inclination on anyone's part to question the king's authority. Because of this, Charles was able to establish taxation on a regular and semipermanent basis. As his entire reign was devoted to war against the English and the free companies, he was always in need of money. He persuaded the *Estates General* to vote him taxes without

*See p. 504.
†See pp. 551–554.

setting a fixed time limit to the grant. Then he simply continued to collect them without bothering to ask the *Estates'* approval. While Charles clearly doubted the propriety of this policy and on his deathbed asked his son to discontinue it, he did make the country accustomed to regular taxation levied at the king's will. So, while Parliament was increasing its control over taxation in England, France chose a path that could lead to absolute monarchy.

At the end of Charles' reign the principal threat to the growing power of the French crown was the rise of the new house of Burgundy. When the ancient line of dukes became extinct, Charles gave the duchy to his brother Philip, known as "the Bold" for his conduct at Poitiers. Then, by marrying the heiress of Flanders and acquiring her lands also, Philip built up a really formidable aggregation of territory. When Charles V died in 1380, his son Charles VI (1380–1422) was a minor. A council of regency was formed, dominated by Philip. But when the young king was old enough to take over the government himself, he restored his father's ministers who had been removed by the princes and showered lands and offices on his younger brother Louis, duke of Orleans. A great feud that split the royal house of France for more than a generation subsequently opened up between the house of Orleans and the house of Burgundy.

In England the great governmental crisis of 1399 arose because Richard II tried to rule as an absolute monarch. The faction-fighting in France began for precisely the opposite reason. In 1392 Charles VI became insane and so incapable of ruling at all. The duke of Burgundy was made regent. From this time onward until his death in 1422, Charles had brief periods of sanity in which he took over his royal duties to some extent but actually simply followed the advice of his brother Orleans. Thus, when Charles was insane, Burgundy ruled, and when he was sane, Orleans was in power. Needless to say, the government was in perpetual chaos while these two princes struggled with one another. Both used their periods of power to benefit themselves, for example, by such measures as exempting their own lands from taxation. Although the routine functions of government were carried on as always by professional civil servants, all was confusion at the top.

In 1404 Philip of Burgundy died and was succeeded by his son John, an able, ambitious, and completely ruthless prince. Duke John soon decided to get rid of his rival. One evening in 1407 as Louis of Orleans was on his way home through the streets of Paris, he was set upon and murdered by a band in the employ of the duke of Burgundy. This act of violence split France into two hostile parties. The new young duke of Orleans, Charles, and his father-in-law, the count of Armagnac, became bitter and implacable foes of the Burgundian duke. Duke John boasted of his crime and maintained that he had simply rid France of a dangerous tyrant. He obliged the poor mad king, his family, and the court to listen to a long sermon on the virtue of tyrannicide delivered by one of his clerical partisans. The result was a murderous civil war. In general, the nobles favored the Orleanist party while the towns, especially Paris, preferred the Burgundians.

The only attempt during this period to regulate the affairs of France through a representative assembly came in 1413 when the *Estates General* was summoned to Paris. The *Estates* had been summoned to cope with a financial crisis, but its leaders demanded changes in the organization of government and drew up a scheme of reform. At this point, the Paris mob took a hand in affairs. Under the leadership of one Simon Caboche, an unruly crowd made a series of attacks on leaders of the Armagnac party and assassinated some of them. They demanded also that the scheme of government reform already drawn up should be put into effect. The reforms were then promulgated in a document known as the Cabochian Ordinance.

It is an extremely interesting document. Its authors took it for granted that the government should be conducted by a bureaucracy of royal servants. Although they could conceive of this bureaucracy controlling the king if he did something harmful to the crown, such as alienating too much of the royal demesne, they had no thought of giving anybody else any control over the government. Their only interest was to try to make that government honest and effective. Their method was to have all important decisions made not by one man but by a committee or council. Practically every officer was supplied with a council to advise him. The members of these councils, as well as the officials, were to be elected by the traditional governing bodies of the bureaucracy, the *parlement* and the *chambres des comptes.* It was, of course, a grandly impractical plan, which fortunately was never tried, but it shows how far apart the political ideas of France and England had grown.

Later in 1413 the Armagnacs drove the Burgundians out of Paris, and civil war between the two factions continued throughout 1414. In 1415, when Henry V renewed the English attack on France, the country seemed hopelessly divided against itself.

78. The Papacy: Centralization and Schism

For seventy-two years after the election of Clement V,* the seat of the papacy remained at Avignon. The popes often announced their intention of returning to Rome at a propitious time, but central Italy was in a state of turmoil, and the propitious time never seemed to come. In the 1330s the popes began to build the vast palace that still stands on the bank of the Rhone, and many of the cardinals took up residence in the luxurious suburb of Villeneuve on the French side of the river.

The poet Petrarch coined the phrase "Babylonian Captivity" to describe this period of papal history, implying that the popes were held in exile as prisoners of the French monarchy. Like many other

*See pp. 490–491.

contemporaries, Petrarch inveighed against the luxury and worldliness of the papal court, describing Avignon elegantly as "the sewer of the world." But Petrarch was a disappointed man. He had hoped to be given a bishopric as a fitting tribute to his literary gifts and was offered instead only a clerkship in the papal bureaucracy, which he indignantly refused. In fact, the more colorful charges made by contemporaries against the Avignon popes seemed to be mostly untrue. The popes were all Frenchmen, but after Clement V, they tried hard to pursue an independent line in international diplomacy. They were not saints, but they were able and reasonably upright administrators. The main trouble with them was that they found it hard to conceive of the Roman church as anything other than an administrative machine.

The setbacks of the early fourteenth century and the mounting criticisms of secularist philosophers and mystical theologians did not destroy the papacy as a major force in the medieval world. But they threw it on the defensive. The clash with Philip IV the Fair of France showed that popes could no longer impose their wills on secular monarchs as Innocent III had done. Instead, they turned their attention to building up a more effective structure of government and taxation within the ecclesiastical sphere. Under the Avignon popes, the papal bureaucracy became the most sophisticated engine of government the medieval world had ever known. At the head of the system stood the pope with his college of cardinals. This body was the highest judicial, executive, and legislative organ in the church. (No general council was summoned between 1309 and 1408.) In theory, the pope alone was the supreme, sovereign head of the Church; in practice, however, he relied on the cardinals to supervise the machinery of ecclesiastical administration, and the cardinals at this time were becoming very zealous in defense of their own privileges. This became especially clear in an agreement known as the Election Capitulations of 1352. Before voting for a new pope, each of the cardinals took an oath that, if he were the one elected, he would respect a whole array of privileges claimed by the Sacred College. No cardinal would be appointed or deposed without the approval of the college; the cardinals were to receive half the papal revenues; their consent would be required for appointments to high offices in the curia. The pope who was actually elected on this occasion, Innocent VI (1342–1362), declared that the pact was contrary to canon law and not binding, but similar "capitulations" were often made at subsequent elections.

Below the consistory of pope and cardinals were four major departments of Church government. The *Roman rota* dealt with routine judicial work. The *chancery*, divided now into seven subdepartments, prepared and recorded the vast papal correspondence. Its output consisted mostly of stereotyped form letters granting favors to petitioners or initiating legal processes. The *papal penitentiary* supervised dispensations (for example, in marriage cases) and the granting of pardons from papal excommunications or interdicts. Most important of all was the financial department, the *papal chamber*, directed by a *camerarius* who was the most powerful official in the whole structure. He was assisted by a treasurer and a group of highly trained clerks. They kept careful records of all the sources of papal revenue and audited the accounts of the local collectors. Before the fourteenth century, these local collectors were usually either prelates of the region or legates sent to collect a particular levy. Later, permanent collectors were appointed to handle all the various types of revenue in their districts.

The absence of the popes from Rome deprived them almost entirely of the revenues of the papal states, and the frequent wars that broke out in central Italy were very expensive. Hence the popes needed new sources of income. They succeeded in vastly expanding the papal revenues from Christendom as a whole, but the methods by which they did so aroused fierce criticism. One lucrative sideline was the sale of indulgences. According to the doctrine of the Church, truly repentant sinners who confessed and were absolved was relieved of the menace of hell, but a blemish remained on their soul that had to be removed either by stays in purgatory or by performing acts pleasing to God—by penance. Penance could take a wide variety of forms, such as prayers, fasts, and pilgrimages. The number of days of purgatory that the sinner was relieved of varied with the severity of the penance. Penitents received *indulgences* when they were permitted to perform some act of piety like contributing money to a charitable cause instead of doing penance. (According to the accepted doctrine, when the pope granted an indulgence, he was drawing on a "treasury of good works" accumulated by the saints and martyrs of the past.) A *plenary* indulgence provided complete relief from purgatory for sins duly repented of and confessed. During the fourteenth century, such indulgences came to be more and more frequently granted and more and more flagrantly sold for hard cash. The papal "pardoners" who hawked them around Europe were favorite targets for satirists in the later Middle Ages.

Much more important as a source of revenue for the popes was a vast patronage machine built up under the Avignon regime. This was founded on the principle, first anunciated by Pope Clement IV in 1265, that the pope in theory had the right to appoint to any ecclesiastical office anywhere in Christendom. Clement IV presented this as if it were a well-established doctrine. In reality, it was a considerable innovation, but Clement proposed actually to exercise his right only in the case of persons who died while visiting the papal court, and the pope's right of appointment in these particular cases was already a matter of accepted custom. Hence the novel principle went unchallenged and the Avignon popes were able to extend it almost indefinitely. The procedure was to define more and more classes of benefices that were "reserved" to the papacy. That is, a cleric could be appointed to them only by papal "provision." This principle was extended, for example, to all bishoprics and abbacies, to all benefices vacated by deposition or by the pope's transferring the incumbent to a new position, to all benefices left vacant by the death of a cardinal or curial official.

The point of all this from the papacy's point of view was that the system was immensely profitable, for every prelate who received his office by papal provision paid heavy taxes to the curia. It may seem surprising that lay rulers permitted such a growth of papal patronage. The point is that the popes were careful not to encroach on the rights of lay patrons. The benefices they claimed would normally have been filled by clerical electors or bishops or ecclesiastical corporations like monasteries. Even so, there was a strong reaction in England against the papal claims, expressed in the Statute of Provisors (1351) and the Statute of Praemunire (1353). The first forbade all papal provisions in England, and the second, all appeals to the papal curia. But these acts were never enforced, and there was never any serious intention of enforcing them. They were intended only to strengthen the king's hand in his dealings with the pope. In practice, in England and elsewhere, the popes won kings over to the support of the provision system simply by sharing the loot with them. Kings received a substantial portion of all papal taxes collected in their kingdoms. Where they had appointed bishops de facto they continued to do so, simply submitting the appropriate names to the pope for his automatic approval.

The system of papal provisions has been defended on the ground that the popes appointed better-qualified men to ecclesiastical benefices than local patrons were likely to do. It is true that universities regularly submitted lists of scholars to the curia and that many graduates received papal provisions as a result. But there was little serious attempt to use the system to improve the pastoral work of the church. It was fundamentally a revenue-raising operation. The worst feature of the system was that it encouraged pluralism and absenteeism. The pope provided for the cardinals and for a host of curial officials by bestowing on them ecclesiastical benefices scattered all over Europe. The duties of the benefices were performed by vicars, usually meagerly paid. A cardinal might be bishop of half a dozen cities and never set foot in any one of them. Kings found the system useful too. They all had clerical servants for whom salaries had to be found, and a convenient solution was to present periodic lists to Avignon with a demand for papal provisions. Again, such appointees did not reside in their churches. A major weakness of the late medieval church was the slackening of effective pastoral activity caused by this toleration of widespread absenteeism.

The system of centralized administration that the Avignon popes had built up fell apart in the crisis of the Great Schism, which broke out in 1378. The schism did not have its origin in any external movement hostile to the papacy but in the internal tensions that had grown up in the papal curia itself. It came about like this. After several false starts, the curia finally returned from Avignon to Rome in 1377. Pope Gregory XI (1370–1378) died at Rome in the following year, and at once disorders broke out in the city. The Romans were afraid that the French cardinals who dominated the Sacred College would once again choose a French pope and that he would return to Avignon. Mobs of Romans, reinforced by thousands of peasants from the surrounding countryside, filled the streets shouting "We want a Roman" and, sometimes, "We want a Roman or at least an Italian." The cardinals went into conclave on the evening of April 7. During the first night, contrary to the rules governing papal elections, they were forced to receive the political leaders of the Roman wards, who told them that their safety could not be guaranteed if they elected a Frenchman. Early on the morning of April 8, the cardinals went to mass in St. Peter's. They could still hear the mob shouting outside. Very quickly after the mass they decided to elect an Italian prelate named Bartholomew Prignani. Before he could be brought to the Vatican to accept the election, a mob of Romans burst into the conclave and the terrified cardinals scattered through the city. When news spread that the cardinals had in fact chosen an Italian, the city became calm again. The cardinals were able to meet with Bartholomew Prignani on April 9, and he duly accepted election as pope, taking the title Urban VI (1378–1389). The great feast of Easter came in the next week. The cardinals took part in all the public liturgies, repeatedly acknowledging Urban as pope, and he was duly crowned on Easter Sunday.

Bartholomew Prignani had been vice-chancellor of the Roman church and archbishop of Bari. He was a distinguished, high-ranking curial administrator. But he had not belonged to the ruling group of cardinals. They had been accustomed to giving him orders. And perhaps they expected to continue to do so after the election. If so, they made a major blunder. The personality of the new pope seemed to change immediately after his election. He announced his intention of thoroughly reforming the papal curia, which was no doubt a worthy objective; but Urban's only method of reform was to turn with explosive rage on the cardinals. He repeatedly denounced and rebuked them. He called one a liar, one a fool, one a traitor. And he threatened to create enough Italian cardinals to end forever the French dominance of the Sacred College.

In the summer of 1378 the cardinals withdrew from the heat of Rome to the hill city of Anagni. On August 2 they issued a manifesto declaring that the election of April 8 was invalid since it had been made under duress and calling on Urban VI to give up the papacy. When he refused, they denounced him as a usurper. Then, on September 20, the cardinals held a second conclave and elected another pope, a Frenchman who called himself Clement VII. Clement returned to Avignon, Urban remained in Rome, and the peoples of Europe aligned themselves behind one or other of the rival pontiffs. France was for Clement; England for Urban; Spain for Clement, Germany for Urban; Scotland for Clement; Scandinavia for Urban. Most of Italy supported Urban, but Naples and Sicily chose Clement. For nearly forty years, there were two lines of popes. Clement VII (1378–1394) was succeeded at Avignon by Benedict XIII (1394–1417). Urban VI (1378–1389) was succeeded by Boniface IX (1389–1404), Innocent VII (1404–1406), and Gregory XII (1406–1415).

Only by a conscious effort of the imagination can a modern person comprehend the consternation created in western Europe by the Great Schism. The pope was—or should have been—far more than the administrative head of the church: as the successor to St. Peter, he was in a sense the church's very foundation and the chosen custodian of the Christian way of life. In his hands were the symbolic keys to heaven and hell, the terrible power to bind and loose. Moreover, as each of the two popes claimed to be the only true one, each one was inclined to appoint to every ecclesiastical office under papal control. Not only did people not know who was the rightful pope, but they could not even be sure who was the rightful bishop of a diocese. This was especially true in regions where war was raging. When the English occupied a French diocese, a bishop acknowledging the Roman pope was likely to replace the one recognizing the pope at Avignon. Although the division of territory between the two popes did not absolutely follow political lines, there was a strong inclination in that direction. The friends of France were likely to accept the Avignon pope, and her foes, the Roman. England was one of the Roman pope's firmest adherents, while Scotland stood equally fervently for his rival. Thus the church and Christendom itself were rent asunder.

It is impossible for a modern historian to know who was the real pope during the Great Schism. It may be that Urban was invalidly elected in 1378 as the cardinals claimed; it may be that the cardinals unanimously lied about the matter. It is also possible that the election was valid in form but the candidate mad, in which case he was ineligible to become pope. Urban certainly acted with irrational violence from the beginning of his reign. It seems clear at least that, in the days immediately after the coronation of Urban, the cardinals intended to abide by their choice, whatever the precise circumstances of the election had been. They denounced Urban only after they discovered that they had elected a pope who was, from their point of view, quite intolerable. The constitutional law of the church provided no clear-cut procedure for resolving the impasse, and at first the Avignon popes hoped to settle the issue by force. French armies invaded Italy in 1382 and 1390, but neither expedition achieved any success.

In 1394 the University of Paris declared that the proper solution was for both popes to abdicate, and from this time the idea grew up that, if either pope refused to abdicate when his rival was willing to do so, he would be guilty of wilfully prolonging the schism and that this would be equivalent to heresy (for it was an article of faith that there should be "*one* holy Catholic church"). All attempts to bring about a simultaneous abdication of the two popes failed, however, because neither of them had the faintest intention of resigning. Each hoped that he could trick the other into abdicating and then claim to be the one remaining pope. In 1398 the French government and church, exasperated by the prevarications of Benedict XIII, withdrew allegiance from him without, however, recognizing his rival. The French obedience to Benedict was restored in 1403 but withdrawn again in 1408. By that time the English and Germans were also growing impatient with their pope, Gregory XII of the Roman line.

From the beginning of the dispute it had been argued that, ideally, a general council ought to meet to heal the schism. The problem was that, according to canon law, only the pope could summon a general council—and to decide who was pope was precisely the issue at stake. As early as 1381 a Paris theologian, Conrad of Gelnhausen, suggested that in times of grievous emergency it was not necessary to respect the letter of the law. Rather, the higher principle of equity should be invoked. He concluded that if a general council could be assembled by any means, it would be competent to settle all the outstanding issues. This idea found more and more supporters when all other ways of ending the schism had proved ineffective. Finally, in 1408, a majority of the cardinals from both obediences deserted their respective popes and summoned a general council on their own initiative. The council duly met at Pisa in 1409. It was well attended and promptly proceeded to dispose of the rival popes. The procedure was rather similar to that used in the deposition of Richard II of England. Both pontiffs were declared to have already forfeited their claims to the papacy because of their crimes of schism and heresy, and then, to make doubly sure, the council enacted sentences of deposition against them. The united cardinals then elected a new pope, Alexander V. Unfortunately, since neither of the other two popes would accept the decrees of deposition and both retained influential supporters, the net result of the Council of Pisa was to produce three popes instead of two.

79. *Remnants of Empire: Italy and Germany*

In discussing England, France, and the papacy, we have considered three monarchical systems that seemed in danger of disintegrating in the years around 1400. The medieval Empire presents a rather different picture. There the process of disintegration had begun earlier and gone much further. Northern Italy was torn by wars between the city-states and faction-fighting within them. Also, the pattern of schism that we have seen in other monarchies appeared in the imperial office at the beginning of the fifteenth century. In the year 1410, when there were three would-be pontiffs claiming the papal throne, there were also three rival German princes, each claiming to be the true emperor.

Italy was composed of a number of independent states. Indeed, the process that we have called the "disintegration" of the Empire can be seen from another point of view as a consolidation of new territorial units. Throughout the whole period, the kingdom of Sicily was ruled by princes of the house of Aragon—a cadet line until 1409, when the king of Aragon inherited Sicily.* The kingdom of Naples

*See Appendix, Tables 9 and 10.

continued in the possession of the descendants of Charles of Anjou until the death of Joanna II in 1435. Then Alfonso V, king of Aragon and Sicily, took possession of the kingdom (though the house of Anjou continued to claim it). To the north of Naples lay the papal states. This region fell into near anarchy after the popes withdrew to Avignon, but a measure of order was restored by a very able legate, Gil Albornoz, in the period 1353–1363.

Northern Italy was a land of small independent city-states, characterized by enormous cultural vitality but endless political turmoil. The cities were still mostly ruled by free communes at the end of the thirteenth century, but were usually divided by internal strife. Two major developments occurred in the fourteenth century—the emergence in many places of *signore* (''lords'' or, more plainly, tyrants), and the building of regional states, which took shape as a few major cities subjugated their weaker neighbors. In the wars that accompanied these conquests all parties relied on bands of hired mercenaries. The same ''free companies'' that fought in the Hundred Years' War often found employment in Italy during the interludes of peace between England and France. And, as in France, they roamed the countryside, living by brigandage and blackmail, when they were not engaged in formal campaigns.

Tyrannies were accepted in many Italian cities—Venice is the striking exception—because of a desperately felt need for some power, however harsh, that could provide internal order and protection from external enemies. The new regimes had no roots in ancient hereditary right or traditional law. They were sometimes given a veneer of legitimacy by the purchase of a title from the emperor, still nominal overlord of the region. But in reality they were created by force and cunning, and often maintained by unscrupulous abuses of power. Stories of treacheries and cruelties among the Italian despots of this era have become legendary. In fact, as one might expect, patterns of conduct varied from place to place and from person to person. The Este family of Ferrara began savagely enough—Dante put one of them in a river of blood in Hell as a tyrant and murderer—but they developed into reasonably benevolent despots, supporting an urbane, courtly culture with its own distinctively elegant style of painting. Can Grande della Scala enhanced his prestige at Verona by patronizing poets and scholars. On the other hand, Giovanni Maria Visconti of Milan liked to display his power by having people who offended him devoured by packs of hunting dogs. The greatest of the tyrants were ''statesmen'' in a literal sense—men who knew how to build a state and then maintain it by any necessary means. Their experience, crystallized later in Machiavelli's work, *The Prince*, has never ceased to fascinate some of those who wield power—and those who theorize about it.

Each of the northern Italian cities has its own history. We can illustrate the general tendencies by considering briefly the most powerful ones—Milan, Venice, and Florence. Milan provides the classic example of an Italian tyranny. Situated in the center of the fertile Lombard plain at a juncture of several trade routes, the city distinguished itself in the twelfth and thirteenth centuries as the principal center of opposition to imperial rule in Italy. Although the Milanese won that battle, they were unable to achieve a stable, free form of government for themselves subsequently. The underlying problem was persistent conflict between the nobles, with rich estates in the countryside, and the merchant oligarchy of the city. The problem was resolved by the acceptance of the Visconti as absolute rulers. At the beginning of the fourteenth century Matteo Visconti—a leader of the noble faction—was elected to rule the city with the resounding title "Captain of the People." His powers included the right to make and enforce laws, to levy taxes, and to declare war. Matteo succeeded in passing on all this authority to his son before he died in 1322, and from then until 1447 the Visconti ruled as hereditary lords of Milan. (They were succeeded by the Sforza family.) The greatest of the Visconti, Giangaleazzo (1385–1402), extended Milanese power over all Lombardy and thrust southward into Tuscany and the Papal States. He also married a French princess and bought the title of duke from the emperor Wenceslas. For a time it seemed that Giangaleazzo might go even further and make himself king of all northern Italy. The possibility ended with Giangaleazzo's death in 1402 and the accession of his psychopathic son, Giovanni Maria.

Venice, the center of a vast network of commerce extending from the eastern Mediterranean to northern Europe, was exceptional among the Italian cities in that it retained a republican form of government into modern times. Before the fourteenth century, the city had never possessed substantial mainland territories, so it had no feudal class of nobility with roots in the countryside. The only nobles of Venice were merchant-princes. A constitution, adopted in 1297, excluded from the ruling Grand Council all but about two hundred of the richest families. Then, having avoided the extremes of despotism and popular government, the oligarchy succeeded in maintaining its power undisturbed for centuries. The conduct of Venetian government has been compared to that of a vast commercial corporation in which the leading families functioned as shareholders and directors; at any rate it gave Venice an unusual level of internal peace and prosperity in the late medieval period. After the death of Giangaleazzo Visconti, the Venetians—alarmed by his conquests—expanded into west Lombardy and for the first time built up a substantial territorial empire.

In Florence yet another pattern of government developed. Here a facade of republican institutions was maintained, but real authority fell into the hands of one dominant family, the Medici. Florentine class structure was complex. A powerful group of nobles (*grandi*) existed, but they were legally barred from holding political office. The citizens were divided into rich merchant-industrialists (*popolo grasso*) and small independent craftsmen or shopkeepers (*popolo minuto*). Below these was a large body of hired workmen without political rights. (The wealth of Florence was built on a textile industry that required many such workers.) The struggle for power was usually between

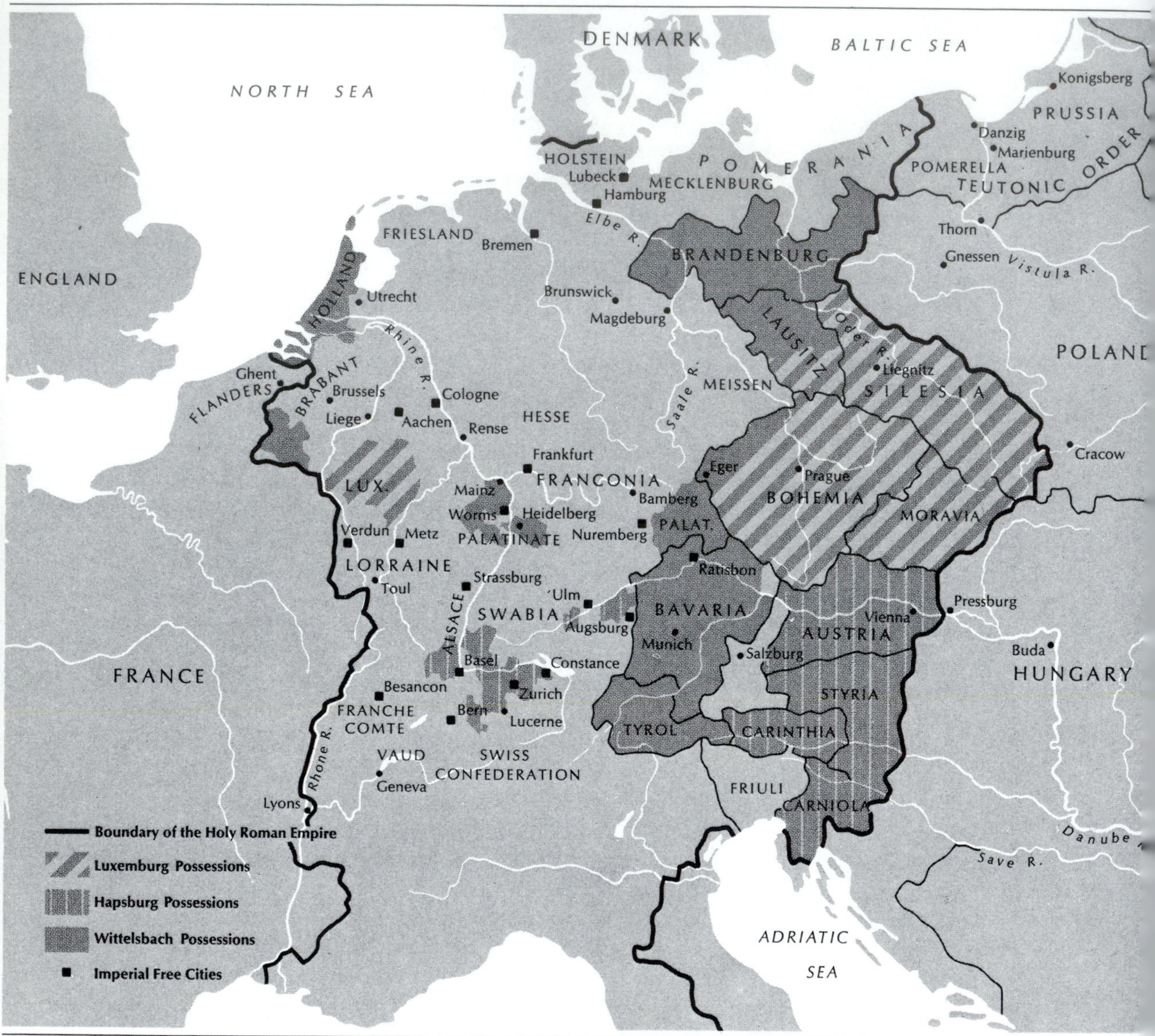

Germany, ca. 1356

Under the emperor Charles IV of Luxemburg, the proclamation of the Golden Bull made legal the form that the Medieval Empire had already assumed: the emperor was to be chosen by seven princes, called the electors, whose lands could not thereafter be divided. The electors were the archbishops of Mainz, Trier, and Cologne; the count palatinate of the Rhine; the duke of Saxony; the Margrave of Brandenburg; and the king of Bohemia.

guilds representing the *popolo grasso* and the *popolo minuto* except for a brief period from 1378 to 1381 when the common workmen seized power. After the movement collapsed the merchant oligarchy became dominant.

The constitution of Florence, originally established in the Ordinances of Justice of 1293, gave the highest power to a group of elected "priors" and a "gonfaloniere of justice"; but it also provided for several other elected officers and a variety of councils and committees with vague and overlapping powers. The system could hardly work smoothly without a power behind the scenes, some organization or person able to control appointments to the various governing bodies and so ensure that they did not constantly work at cross-purposes. In the first half of the fifteenth century this role was gradually assumed by Cosimo de Medici. An enormously wealthy merchant and banker, he acquired power, not by assuming an imposing title like Duke or Prince, but more in the manner of an old-fashioned city boss of the modern era. He built up a network of patronage by judiciously dispensing favors and bribes until, from 1434 onward, he was the effective ruler of the city. His authority was accepted without any need for the terrorism that often accompanied the rise of tyrants, probably because it was perceived as necessary to maintain the existing order of society. Cosimo's Medici successors ruled more overtly as signore of Florence.

Although Florence became only nominally a republic it produced a rich and influential literature on the virtues of republican liberty. The threat of conquest by the Visconti of Milan around 1400 stimulated a patriotic reaction in Florence. Florentine intellectuals liked to see their city as a successor to the tradition of the ancient Roman republic and as a defender of liberty against Milanese tyranny. Coluccio Salutati wrote, "The Florentine people are defenders of the liberty of all peoples." In the writings of Salutati and his friends the medieval tradition of civic freedom was clothed in a new classical rhetoric; their "civic humanism" significantly influenced early modern political theory. Still, Salutati's words cannot be taken too literally. Florence showed little regard for the liberty of its neighbors when she became strong enough to dominate them. By 1400 the Florentines had extended their power over the once independent little city-states of Tuscany. After the defeat and subjugation of the rival city of Pisa in 1406, Florence emerged as a third major territorial state along with Milan and Venice.

The German emperors played little part in the affairs of Italy during this period except to grant the occasional title of nobility. During the fourteenth and fifteenth centuries, Germany had become a conglomeration of practically independent states. There were some sixteen hundred such units, ranging in size and importance from the duchies of Austria, Bavaria, and Saxony; the Margravate of Brandenburg; and the County Palatine of the Rhine to small free cities and the territories of petty imperial knights. No German state was powerful enough to exercise even temporary hegemony over the others. If the emperor was to have any real authority, he had to draw it from outside Germany. Throughout this period, the imperial power usually rested on the possession of either Bohemia or Hungary, or both.

The last German emperor whose reign we considered was Lewis the Bavarian (1314–1347) of the house of Wittelsbach.* After him the imperial crown was held by the Luxemburg family for nearly a century. (It finally passed to the Hapsburgs in 1440.) The Luxemburgs

*See p. 493. See also Appendix, Table 8

were of Rhineland origin, but in 1308 the emperor Henry VII of Luxemburg married his son to the heiress of Bohemia, and it was as kings of Bohemia that the Luxemburgs played a major role in German politics for the rest of the Middle Ages. Henry of Luxemburg's son was John, the blind king of Bohemia who fell at Crécy (1346). Then, in 1347, John's son, Charles, king of Bohemia, defeated and deposed Lewis the Bavarian and became emperor as Charles IV (1346–1378).

The form that the Empire had taken of its own accord was formalized by this emperor in 1356 by the publication of the famous Golden Bull. Seven princes—the archbishops of Mainz, Trier, and Cologne; the count palatine of the Rhine; the duke of Saxony; the margrave of Brandenburg; and the king of Bohemia—were designated as *electors* who had the legal power to choose the "king of the Romans" (this was the official title of the German king before his coronation as emperor). When an emperor died, they were to meet at once in the city of Frankfurt and elect a new ruler by majority vote. Any elector who did not attend or send a proxy forfeited his right to participate in that election. The electoral dignity was to be hereditary in the male line, except in Bohemia where the crown was elective, and no electoral state could be divided among heirs. The electors were given almost all the rights of sovereign princes. Moreover, the bull suggested that they should serve as a supervisory committee over Germany as a whole. The Golden Bull made disputed imperial elections less likely and also settled the legal form of the Empire for the rest of its existence. The bull made no reference to any right of the papacy to confirm the imperial election or take any part in it. According to the prevailing theory, the electoral college constituted a representative body that acted on behalf of all the princes and peoples of the Empire in choosing its head.*

In the second half of the fourteenth century, not only was Germany divided into many principalities, but the individual principalities themselves seemed to be disintegrating into a state of near anarchy. In Germany, more than anywhere else perhaps, we find a lack of any universally accepted principles of legitimacy and right order in government. The kingship was an elective dignity—but each prince was a feudal lord who regarded his principality as his own private property, held by hereditary right. The subjects of a prince were often conscious of forming a political unity with rights to be defended against princes who were frequently aliens, imposed on them by some accident of inheritance. Hence there was incessant feuding between the princes and the various leagues and associations formed by their citizens. The foremost opponents of princely power were autonomous leagues of cities like the Hanseatic League of northern Germany, which conducted its own foreign policy with virtually no regard for the princes in whose territories the individual cities were situated. From time to time, leagues of knights were formed to defend the interests of the lower feudal nobility. But the most typical tendency, in Germany as elsewhere, was for citizens, knights, and clergy to coalesce into assemblies of estates.

*Sources, no. 92

In Germany, however, the princes were not effective heads and leaders of the estates as the English king was head of Parliament or the pope of a general council in normal times. The estates claimed the right to assemble of their own volition without any summons from the prince. Their function was solely to protect the subjects' rights, especially property rights, against princely encroachments. They were not so much interested in asserting a constructive right of consent to taxation as an obstructive power to prevent any new taxes at all.

These circumstances help to explain the "schism" in the Empire at the beginning of the fifteenth century. Charles IV died in 1378 and left two sons, Wenceslas and Sigismund. Wenceslas received the crown of Bohemia and was elected "king of the Romans," while Sigismund married the heiress of Hungary and became king of that land. Wenceslas, it turned out, was a drunkard and a fool, and he became increasingly unpopular as his reign wore on. His vacillating policy helped to prolong a particularly destructive war between a league of Swabian cities and the local nobility, and his attempts to intervene in the papal schism were ineffective. In 1398 he met with Charles VI of France in an attempt to formulate a common policy toward the rival popes, but nothing constructive came of the meeting. (The story goes that Wenceslas was sober only in the mornings, while Charles was sane only in the afternoons, so that difficulties of communication inevitably arose between the two monarchs.) In 1400 four of the seven electors became exasperated by Wenceslas' conduct and decided to get rid of him. There was no precedent for such a move, but the electors, acting very much like the English barons the year before, drew up a list of charges against the king, declared him deposed, and elected a successor. The prince they chose was Rupert of the Palatinate, who died in 1410. The electors then split between two rival candidates of the House of Luxemburg, Wenceslas' brother, Sigismund of Hungary, and his cousin, Jobst of Moravia. One faction elected Sigismund; the other, Jobst. Since Wenceslas had never agreed to relinquish the crown, there were three would-be emperors at this point. Fortunately, Jobst died in 1411. Wenceslas and Sigismund then reached an agreement whereby Wenceslas continued to rule in Bohemia while Sigismund kept the royal title of the Empire. And when Wenceslas died in 1419, Sigismund inherited the throne of Bohemia too.

The political developments of the fourteenth and early fifteenth centuries were highly paradoxical. Some historians interpret the age as one of constructive institutional growth, while others see it as an era of political disintegration—and both groups are right. Except in Germany (which came closest to sheer anarchy), governments everywhere grew more powerful but, at the same time, more unstable. Bureaucracies expanded, but the right to direct their activities, the right to wield supreme power in the state, was everywhere disputed. Assemblies of estates struggled with kings; general councils with popes. Rival princes in many lands fought one another. In the years around 1400, there were two claimants to the throne of England; two aristocratic factions contended for control of the government in France; three would-be popes fulminated against each other; and three German princes fought for the phantom dignity of the imperial title. In our last chapter on medieval political history, we shall see how the disruptive tendencies of the fourteenth century were overcome at the end of the Middle Ages. Before turning to that theme, however, we need to consider the crises in social, economic, and intellectual life that accompanied the political stresses of the fourteenth century.

READING SUGGESTIONS

* *B. Tierney,* Sources *and* Readings, *vol. I, nos. 91, 92.*

Political developments of the fourteenth century are described in D. Hay, *Europe in the Fourteenth and Fifteenth Centuries* (London, 1966), and D. Waley, *Later Medieval Europe* (New York, 1964). J. R. Hale *et al.* (eds.), *Europe in the Later Middle Ages* (Evanston, IL, 1965) contains essays dealing with the politics of the major European states. On England, see M. McKisack, *The Fourteenth Century* (London, 1959), and for a briefer introduction, * A. R. Myers, *England in the Late Middle Ages* (Harmondsworth, England, 1952). On institutional developments, see B. Wilkinson, *Constitutional History of England,* 3 vols. (London, 1948–1958), with translated documents; F. Thompson, *A Short History of Parliament* (Minneapolis, 1953); J. F. Willard *et al.*, *The English Government at Work, 1327–1336,* 3 vols. (Cambridge, MA, 1940–1950); G. W. S. Barrow, *Robert Bruce and the Community of the Realm of Scotland* (London, 1964); A. Steel, *Richard II* (Cambridge, England, 1941); and R. H. Jones, *The Royal Policy of Richard II* (New York, 1968). Two collections of essays by H. Cam deal mainly with the late medieval period. They are *Liberties and Communities of Medieval England* (Cambridge, England, 1944), and *Law-Finders and Law-Makers in Medieval England* (New York, 1963).

On French institutions, see F. Pegues, *The Lawyers of the Last Capetians* (Princeton, 1962); P. S. Lewis, *Later Medieval France: The Polity* (New York, 1967); J. H. Shennan, *The Parlement of Paris* (Ithaca, NY, 1968); R. Vaughan, *Philip the Bold* (London, 1962) and *John the Fearless* (London, 1966). The outstanding work on the fourteenth-century papacy is * G. Mollat, *The Popes at Avignon,* 9th ed. (London, 1963). See also Y. Renouard, *The Avignon Papacy, 1305–1403* (London, 1970) and W. Ullmann, *The Origins of the Great Schism* (London, 1948). On papal administration, see G. Barraclough, *Papal Provisions* (Oxford, England, 1935), and on the financial system, W. E. Lunt, *Financial Relations of the Papacy with England,* 2 vols. (Cambridge, MA, 1939–1962). Lunt's *Papal Revenues in the Middle Ages* (New York, 1934) presents translated documents.

chapter

XXIV

Society, Economy, and Culture

The economic and cultural life of the late medieval world was full of complexities and contrasts. The Black Death reversed the demographic situation of the early fourteenth century, leaving Europe again relatively underpopulated. The immediate effect of the plague was to cause almost intolerable distress. The next half-century was a time or turmoil marked by peasant rebellions in various parts of Europe. But the new conditions created by the plague gave rise to unprecedented opportunities for some of the survivors. The art and literature of the age reflect both the disasters that occurred and the vitality that enabled Western society to survive them. In these spheres the late medieval period was not only an age of adversity but also one of great achievement.

80. Rural Life and Peasant Revolts

Always in the Middle Ages, below the world of kings and lords and ladies, below the class of rich merchants and the intellectual elite of the universities—the people who mostly fill the pages of the history books—there stood the mass of rural peasants. They formed by far the greater part of the population. Their labor supported the whole superstructure of medieval civilization.

For centuries the peasants accepted their harsh conditions of life as something intrinsic in the nature of things, unchanging and unchangeable. Medieval village societies were inherently conservative. When peasants did complain it was nearly always in the name of the "good old law" or "good old custom" that guaranteed them some minimal security of life and stability of land tenure. But during the fourteenth century events took a radically different turn; peasant rebellions broke out in many parts of western Europe.

The rebellions were evidently related to the stressful conditions of an age marked by famine, war, and plague; but it is not clear whether they were caused more by increased misery or by rising expectations. Sometimes ethnic tensions were involved. In Flanders, Flemish-speaking peasants and artisans resented a French aristocracy, and in Bohemia a Czech population was dominated by a German nobility. In Spain, anti-Jewish riots sometimes turned into broader movements of social protest. Peasant rebellions did not break out in the times of most acute distress, e.g., during the famine years of 1315–1317 or at the onset of the Black Death in 1347–1348. Even to rebel requires a certain physical vitality.

What finally drove medieval peasants to rise in revolt was not just growing exasperation with old grievances but always some new circumstance, some new law, some new exaction. Most typically the grievance was some form of increased taxation needed to finance the endless wars of the fourteenth century, wars that were entertaining for the knights but often devastating for the peasants. The first great rebellion of the century, the rising of maritime Flanders in 1325, was sparked by an unpopular new tax levied by the count. The peasants, joined by the cities of Ypres and Bruges, held out for three years and were defeated only when the king of France sent an army against them.

Most of the fourteenth-century rebellions broke out in the years after the Black Death. The plague brought new calamities but also new opportunities. Its most obvious effect in the countryside was to produce a severe shortage of labor. Landlords halted the process of emancipating serfs, which had made great headway in the preceding centuries, and rigorously exacted the old burdensome labor services from their tenants. Laborers tried to take advantage of the situation by demanding higher pay. (Often a peasant family could survive only because one or more members worked as hired laborers for richer neighbors.) But governments responded with laws that fixed wages at the old levels. The French government enacted such repressive measures for the countryside around Paris. In Castille King Pedro I (known as Pedro the Cruel) prescribed whipping for laborers and fines for artisans who demanded higher pay. But the most ample evidence of governmental attempts to control wages comes from England. There the Statute of Laborers (1351) fixed all wages at the level that had prevailed in 1346; anyone who benefitted from a higher wage had to pay a fine equal to twice the wage received. Special commissions of judges were appointed to enforce the law at first, and then local justices of the peace took up the task. In the county of Essex, during the years 1377–1379, seventy percent of indictments before the justices were for infringements of the Statute of Laborers. The English Peasants' Rebellion broke out in Essex in 1381.

The Black Death broke the old cake of custom that had led most peasants to take their hard, monotonous lives for granted as something intrinsically unchangeable. Traditional farming arrangements in villages all over Europe must have been thrown into chaos by the sudden extinction of many families, the failure of heirs in others, the unprecedented surplus of land. Peasants in many countries seem to have resolved that, since conditions evidently had to change and were visibly changing, they should be made to change for the better.

Now, for the first time, we hear of outbreaks of religious fervor among the common people that aimed not just at preparing people for the next world, but at establishing a sort of democratic, egalitarian heaven in this one. In England the wandering preacher John Ball harangued the villagers in phrases like these, recorded by the chronicler Froissart:

> Oh good people, things do not go well in England and they will not go well until everything is held in common and there are no more serfs or lords. . . . Why should we be kept thus in bondage? We are all come from one father and one mother, Adam and Eve. How can they say or prove that they are greater lords than we are except that they make us work for what they spend?

When the peasants' hopes for a better life were frustrated by the repressive measures of governments or landlords, they rose in violent rebellions all over Europe.

Two of the best documented risings of the fourteenth century are the French Jacquerie of 1358 and the English rebellion of 1381. They can serve to illustrate two types of peasant protest. The first is usually seen as an aimless, incoherent outbreak, a savage reaction against unendurable conditions; the second was a relatively disciplined movement aiming at specific reforms. Its leader Wat Tyler, declared, "We come not as thieves and robbers; we come seeking social justice."

To understand the French outbreak we must recall the political chaos in northern France after the battle of Poitiers (1356). King John had been captured and was in exile in England. Etienne Marcel, the merchant leader, had seized power in Paris but he quarreled with the Dauphin Charles, the heir to the throne. Charles established a rival government at Compiègne outside Paris with the support of most of the local nobility. Finally Charles the Bad, another member of the royal family, commanded an independent army and could throw his support to whichever side offered him the greater reward.* Eventually it was this Charles the Bad who turned his forces against the peasants and crushed their revolt.

The peasants of the countryside around Paris suffered desperately from the unsettled conditions. The government demanded heavy taxes from them to pay for the recent war; but for the peasants the war had not ended. Although there were no formal campaigns in the two years after Poitiers, bands of mercenary soldiers from both sides roamed the countryside, looting and burning the villages. Over and over again the peasants saw their fields laid waste and their homes destroyed. The local nobles, humiliated and demoralized by their defeat, did nothing to stop the brigandage. Rather they added to the peasants' distress with new exactions. When a lord was captured, for instance, his peasants had to contribute to his ransom. Besides, the

*See pp. 532–533.

English had discovered a very convenient device for raising money. They would capture a castle and sell it back to the owner at a high price. To the noble it seemed far less trouble to collect from his peasants the money to buy back the castle than to defend it adequately in the first place.

The rage and hatred of the peasants first broke out at the village of St. Leu about twenty-five miles north of Paris on May 28, 1358. A mob of villagers attacked a group of soldiers and succeeded in killing four knights and five squires. Then, excited by their success, they roused the neighboring villages. A band of peasants marched off to a nearby manor house where they murdered the lord and all his family, after first raping the man's wife and daughter. It was as though the whole region had been waiting for a signal. The rebellion spread from village to village and then to the neighboring provinces. Everywhere the peasants declared that the nobles were traitors who deserved to die. Their anger was never directed against the absent king whose incompetent rule had caused much of the trouble. Some of the rebel banners even carried the royal emblem, the *fleur-de-lis.* Medieval peasants nearly always maintained a touching faith that kings were sent by God to do justice to all and especially to defend the small people against the great. Peasant rage was reserved for the local nobles whose oppressive conduct they knew all too well from first-hand experience.

Contemporary chroniclers tell of savage atrocities committed against the knights and their families. Froissart wrote, "I dare not recount the horrible deeds that they did to ladies and damsels." (He then went on at once to recount a particularly ugly example.*) We do not know how many such incidents actually occurred; a small number of cases could have furnished the chroniclers with their materials. Besides, all the chronicles agree that the nobles panicked at the outbreak of the rebellion and fled to safe districts, leaving their houses empty and unguarded. Probably the peasants took their revenge mostly by looting and destroying unoccupied chateaux.

After a few days an army of several thousand rebels assembled under a leader called Guillaume Carle. Realizing that he needed allies, Carle approached Etienne Marcel in Paris. There was really no common bond between bourgeois merchants and enraged peasants except that, for the moment, they had a common enemy in the nobles around Paris. Marcel agreed to an alliance and sent out bands from the city to cooperate with the Jacquerie in attacking some of the noble strongholds. One such expedition moved to attack the city of Meaux where the wife of the Dauphin and many other noble ladies together with their children had taken refuge. They were in a fortified market area of the city approached by a bridge over the River Marne. When the rebels arrived at the city the townsfolk opened the gates and welcomed them with food and wine. Then the peasants began their assult on the ladies' stronghold. It proved to be a turning point in the history of the Jacquerie.

*Sources, no. 86

Two noblemen from the south of France, the Captal of Buch and the Count of Foix, bored by the peace after the battle of Poitiers, had gone off for an interlude of crusading with the Teutonic knights in eastern Germany. Returning home through France they heard of the plight of the ladies at Meaux. Although the two southern gentlemen owed different allegiances in the war between France and England, they were happy to cooperate in the knightly adventure that now offered itself. They rushed their troops to Meaux and entered the fortified area just before the army of rebels arrived at the city. On the morning of June 7 the peasants swarmed on to the bridge leading to the stronghold, expecting, presumably, to engage in a brief skirmish and then to enjoy the usual aftermath of rape and murder. Suddenly the gates of the fortification were thrown open. The Captal and the Count, mounted on their warhorses, charged out at the head of their troops and drove the rebels from the bridge, cutting them down with swords and tumbling their bodies into the river. Then the knights pressed on to attack the main body of rebels. Soon they drove them out of the city, and pursued them through the countryside, "striking them down like beasts" according to Froissart. Then, after a pleasant day of peasant hunting, the knights returned to the admiration of the rescued ladies. They also remembered to burn down the disloyal city of Meaux.

In fourteenth-century warfare disciplined infantry could sometimes withstand a charge of feudal cavalry. But a mob of untrained, ill-armed peasants had no chance against mailed warriors equipped with lances, swords, and axes. The final battle of the uprising took place on June 10. Charles the Bad, persuaded by the other nobles to deploy his forces against the rebels, faced the peasant army under Guillaume Carle near Clermont. To make sure that nothing went wrong, he first invited Carle to join him for negotiations; but when the rebel leader was in his power, Charles promptly imprisoned him and later had him killed. Knightly rules of courtesy did not apply to peasant rebels. Deprived of their leader, the peasants crumbled before Charles' attack; then his mounted knights harassed them through the countryside killing all they could find. This was the end of the Jacquerie. The whole affair had lasted just two weeks. During the following two weeks bands of knights roamed through the affected regions burning villages and massacring peasants at will, sometimes decorating the trees with their hanging bodies.

Some modern scholars have doubted whether the Jacquerie was really just an aimless outburst of peasant anger and even whether it can properly be called a "peasant rebellion" at all. Certainly others besides peasants took part in it. Some towns like Senlis and Beauvais, and Meaux as we have seen, opened their gates to the rebels. Also, the royal pardons that were granted after the rebellion had been suppressed often mentioned small tradespeople, craftsmen, petty officials, and even priests, but seldom poor peasants. It may be, though, that such evidence gives a distorted impression. Many of the common peasants who took part in the rising never received pardons—they were not spared, they were slaughtered. Besides, Jacques was the common nickname for French peasants (from the short tunic or jacket, *jacque*, that they wore) and there seems no reason why contemporaries should have chosen to call the rebellion a Jacquerie if they had not seen it as primarily a peasants' rising. Still it is clear that a movement that began with peasant outrages was soon joined by people of other nonnoble classes.

Another disputed point concerns the relationship between the Jacquerie and the bourgeois movement of Etienne Marcel. The rebels were eager to kill the gentry and destroy their castles. Marcel wanted to prevent the rural nobility from attaining a position of commanding power while he sought allies in the towns. The confluence of interests has led some scholars to suggest that Marcel instigated the whole affair. But there is no really convincing evidence of this. Probably, on this point, the older interpretation is substantially true. The Jacquerie was an unplanned explosion of class hatred against a noble caste that exploited the common people but failed to protect them. Etienne Marcel tried for a few days—unsuccessfully—to manipulate the movement to his own advantage. The rebels themselves had no coherent objectives or plan of reform. When a group of them were asked why they were rebelling, they said they did not know, except that other people were doing it and they wanted to kill all the gentry.

The English Peasants' Rebellion of 1381 was in some ways a milder affair than the Jacquerie; but for two days it came close to toppling the government of England. The king at the time was Richard II, a boy of fourteen. Government was conducted by a council of regency, dominated by the king's uncle, John of Ghent, Duke of Lancaster. The rebels' anger this time was not directed at first against the whole class of nobility, though the rebels came to demand radical social change, but more specifically against the agents of an unpopular government who were denounced as traitors to the king. The rebels always professed the utmost loyalty to the young king himself. They had a password used to identify friends. "With whom hold you?" The proper answer was, "With King Richard and the true commons."

The fundamental causes of unrest in England included all the dislocations of rural life that followed the Black Death, especially the widespread resentment against the Statute of Laborers and against the harsh enforcement of villein services. But the immediate event that triggered the rebellion was the imposition of a new tax to finance the ongoing war in France. The usual way of raising revenue in England was by a tax on movable property. This was reasonably fair; the rich paid more than the poor. But in 1377 the government levied a new *poll*, or head tax. Still the amount demanded was low and the tax was collected without incident. Then, in 1380, another poll tax was imposed, this time at the very heavy rate of 12 pennies from every man and woman over the age of fifteen. The new levy was perceived as grossly unjust; a poor peasant and his wife owed as much as the lord and lady of the manor. Collection of the tax proved difficult. According to the evidence of the tax rolls, the population of England mysteriously declined by a third between 1377 and 1380; in fact, of course, the poll tax was being widely evaded. The response of the government was to send special commissions of inquiry into the counties to seek out evaders and enforce payment. Sometimes they were so rough and aggressive that their behavior gave rise to rumors, at least, of gross misconduct. The chronicler Henry Knighton asserted that some commissioners went about examining girls to see if they were virgins and taxing them as adults if they were not.

Overt resistance began on May 31 with an attack on tax commissioners by the people of Fobbing, a village in the county of Essex, just north of the River Thames. Within a few days the rebellion spread throughout Essex and then to the county of Kent on the other side of the Thames. This was not just a rising of the poorest of the poor. Among the rebels there were many common villeins, but also substantial farmers, sympathizers from the towns, and many rural craftsmen. The leader who emerged to head the rebellion was a man of Kent, Wat Tyler. We know almost nothing of his earlier life; according to some sources he came originally from Essex and Froissart wrote that he had been a soldier in the French wars.

On June 7 the Kentish rebels took the king's castle at Rochester and on June 10 entered the city of Canterbury, with no resistance from the townsfolk. It happened that the archbishop of Canterbury, Simon Sudbury, was also the king's chancellor, the head of the royal administration. When the rebels broke into the cathedral, they shouted at the frightened monks that they would soon need a new archbishop since the present one was going to be killed as a traitor (as indeed he was a few days later). The rebels also seized the sheriff and burned all his financial and judicial records. About this time they released from the archbishop's prison the radical preacher, John Ball, who accompanied them and preached to them during the following days. Meanwhile, in Essex, similar events were taking place. There the rebels looted the house of the sheriff and destroyed properties controlled by Sir Robert Hales, who was the king's treasurer and a particularly unpopular official.

On June 10 the rebel armies from Kent and Essex, apparently acting in concert, marched on the city of London. By June 12 Wat Tyler and his followers from Kent were encamped south of the city while the Essex contingent massed at Mile End, just north of the Thames. On June 13 the citizens of London opened the gates of the capital and both armies poured into the city. They plundered the houses of royal officials and burned down the palace of the archbishop of Canterbury at Lambeth, destroying all the chancery records that were kept there. The palace of the Duke of Lancaster on the Strand made a particularly splendid bonfire; the conflagration was luckily helped by the explosion of some barrels of gunpowder stored in the cellar.

Meanwhile, in the tower of London, young King Richard faced divided counsels. A force of several hundred archers and soldiers was available for use against the rebels, and the mayor of London, William Walworth, urged an immediate attack. Others were afraid that the soldiers would be overwhelmed. Finally, Richard decided to negotiate. On the next morning, June 14, he rode out to Mile End and met with the Essex rebels. There are various accounts of the demands that the peasants put forward on this occasion, but clearly the one of fundamental importance to them was the abolition of serfdom. English peasants wanted to be free. And those taking part in the uprising who were already free, the craftworkers and more prosperous farmers, wanted to be assured that there could be no reimposition of the old servile status. King Richard agreed—or pretended to agree—to the rebels' demands, and a staff of clerks drew up charters of freedom and pardon for all the people of Essex. Most of them, well-satisfied, began to return to their villages.

This was not the end of the trouble, though. In the king's absence, Wat Tyler and his followers entered the tower of London, captured Simon Sudbury and Robert Hales, and beheaded the two "traitors." A third intended victim succeeded in escaping; this was Henry, son of the Duke of Lancaster, who lived to become King Henry IV.

More murders and looting took place on June 14. According to an official record of the City of London, "there was hardly a street in the City in which there were not bodies lying." But the rebel forces were becoming less formidable by this time. Most of the Essex men had gone home. Of those in the city, many, we are told, were too drunk to be of use. Amid all the turmoil and bloodshed, there was always something carnivalesque about medieval uprisings; when peasants came upon stores of rich food and fine wine they typically feasted and got drunk.

The final confrontation came on June 15.* King Richard agreed to meet with Wat Tyler and the rebels at Smithfield, just outside the walls of London. The demands presented there were more radical than those put forward at Mile End the day before. The rebels now demanded that the property of the church should be confiscated and divided among the laity, and that there should be no lord in England except the king and "no law but the law of Winchester." The Statute of Winchester (1285) had laid down that every man should keep arms in his house so that he could assist in keeping the peace when called upon. The rebel leaders seem to have envisaged an abolition of the whole feudal and seigneurial system; instead, England would be ruled by a remote and benevolent monarch, while local affairs would be effectively controlled by a peasant militia. Such changes could never have been granted by the king. In the event, they were not even seriously discussed. Wat Tyler, as spokesman for the rebels, rode over to the king's party and began to present his demands in an insolent and aggressive fashion. Then a scuffle broke out that has never been adequately explained. Apparently Tyler threatened one of the king's squires with a dagger. Mayor Walworth, who had all along wanted to use force against the peasants, promptly drew his sword and killed the rebel leader. It was a moment of sudden danger. But King Richard saved the situation. He rode over to the rebel army, cried out to the peasants that he was their true leader, and urged them to follow him. Frightened and confused, they allowed themselves to be led away from the city, with the king riding at their head. Meanwhile Walworth called

*Sources, no. 87

out the professional soldiers who had been held in reserve, and they surrounded the retreating rebel army. The peasants were not attacked but allowed to disperse peacefully to their homes.

During the following weeks sporadic local risings continued in Essex and also broke out in other parts of England; but the threat to the capital and the government ended on June 15. On July 2 Richard revoked all the letters of pardon and charters of liberty that he had granted. Later in the summer some two hundred persons identified as leaders of the rebellion were brought to trial and executed, including the preacher John Ball. However, there were no indiscriminate mass reprisals against the peasants such as occurred after the French Jacquerie.

None of the peasant rebellions was immediately successful but, in the end, the continued shortage of agricultural labor in relation to the land available for cultivation brought about changes that could not be achieved suddenly by violence. The process sometimes called "the distintegration of the manor," which had begun as early as the twelfth century, gained a new momentum in the fourteenth.* In the long run, it proved impossible, or at best highly inefficient, to exact labor services from a deeply reluctant and depleted peasantry. Lords found it more profitable to accept money rents and to acknowledge the personal freedom of their tenants. The lords' own demesne lands were either rented out or worked by hired labor. Except in eastern Europe, serfdom was disappearing by the end of the fifteenth century, although in some regions—especially France—the lords retained the financial perquisites of their old seigneurial jurisdiction in the form of various tolls, fees, and dues. The whole intricate structure of manorial customs and services was slowly replaced by a system of contracts based on cash. The change did not invariably work to the advantage of the peasants. On the whole, it favored those who retained substantial holdings of land, but landless laborers were exposed to all the vagaries of changing economic conditions in a time of great instability. Probably their ancestors had been better off, scratching a living from a small holding within the integrated community of an old-fashioned manor.

81. Cities and Commerce

The one certain truth a historian can set down about economic conditions in the century after the Black Death is that we do not fully understand them. Even with all the wealth of statistics currently available, economists cannot completely explain the pattern of modern booms and slumps. For the fourteenth century, we have only fragmentary statistics, and there are no disasters comparable to the Black Death in modern history to provide reliable analogies. Almost no uniformly valid generalizations can be made on the basis of the surviving

*See p. 288.

evidence—mainly medieval chronicles, tax rolls, customs receipts, and account books.

Fifty years ago, historians often presented the period from 1250 to 1450 as an age of steadily increasing wealth, aggressive mercantile activity, and rising prosperity. How else could a dynamic, modern civilization have arisen from the static, feudal world of the Middle Ages? This interpretation simply ignored the basic demographic facts of life in the fourteenth century. Then medieval historians, well aware of the economic vitality of the twelfth century and of the disastrous setbacks of the fourteenth, began to present the whole late medieval period as a time of unmitigated economic decay. This interpretation has not proved very satisfactory either. In fact, the evidence is confusing because the situation was confused. Different cities, different industries, and different individuals were all affected differently by the plague and the Hundred Years' War. Bruges decayed and Antwerp flourished. English exports of cloth greatly increased and English imports of wine greatly diminished. Many people grew poorer; a few became enormously rich. Moreover, the short-term effects of the plague were often different from the long-range ones.

In the sphere of urban life and commercial activity, the immediate effect of the Black Death was to create an oversupply of goods and a sharp drop in overall demand. The well-established, wealthy bourgeoisie reacted to the difficult circumstances in the same way as the landlords in the countryside. They tried to hold on to what they had and to keep the lower orders in their places by enacting restrictive guild regulations and city ordinances. In the twelfth century, all industrious young apprentices could look forward to becoming masters after they had completed their training. By the late fourteenth century, in many guilds only the sons of masters or the fortunate young men who married their daughters had any chance of becoming masters themselves. Another effect of the restrictive practices was to exclude women from the guilds. There were far fewer women guild members at the close of the Middle Ages than in the twelfth and thirteenth centuries.

An important feature of urban life in the fourteenth century was the growth of a large class of proletarian laborers, living at the mercy of the masters and forbidden to form organizations to defend their own interests. Such workers often bitterly resented their position, and there were many city riots comparable in violence to the peasants' rebellions. As early as 1302 the artisans of Bruges rebelled against the French-dominated city government. Later in the fourteenth century, there were urban rebellions in every part of Europe; for example, the people of Thessalonica revolted in 1341; those of Ghent, in 1381; those of Rouen, in 1382. All these risings were quickly crushed, but in 1378 the common workers of Florence, the Ciompi, seized control of the city and held power for three years before their movement was suppressed in 1381.

If the fourteenth century produced a larger class of proletarian laborers, it also produced new aggregations of capitalist wealth. Most historians agree that, in the century after 1350, there was a severe decline in the total volume of trade. Obviously, a much smaller population would tend to produce and exchange fewer goods. It is not so clear that there was a fall in per capita production or consumption, and it is certain that some regions and some industries prospered greatly in spite of the general decline. In England, for instance, a highly profitable cloth-manufacturing industry grew up, based on a new technique which used the power of water mills in the process of fulling. England had exported wool to the cloth industry of Flanders on a large scale ever since the twelfth century, but the circumstances of the Hundred Years' War disrupted this mutually advantageous trade. For Flanders the change was all loss. England gained by developing a new export trade in manufactured cloth which proved much more profitable than the old trade in raw wool. Substantial fortunes were made in England in the cloth trade, and evidence of them survives in the splendid fifteenth-century "wool churches," which were built by pious millionaires to thank God for their newly acquired wealth.

Many other changes in patterns of trade occurred at this time. In Germany a league of northern cities—the Hanseatic League—which had grown into existence in the thirteenth century organized itself into a close political alliance in the mid-fourteenth century. In 1370 this Hanseatic League, centered on Lübeck, won a victory over Denmark and acquired a monopoly of trade in the Baltic. The league maintained trading posts in all the commercial centers of the north, for instance, in London, Bruges, Bergen, and Novgorod. During this same period, the fairs of Champagne were declining in importance. This was partly a result of the fact that Champagne came into the possession of the kings of France, who charged higher booth rents and sales taxes than the traffic would bear. There were, however, rival routes appearing. The Venetians began to send galleys by sea to England and Flanders. These were great heavily armed ships, owned and equipped by the Venetian government, in which the merchants rented space. The Hanseatic cities meanwhile helped to develop an alternative overland route from Italy. From Venice and Genoa merchants carried their goods over the Alpine passes to Ulm and Augsburg and on to the north. The Hanseatic towns then distributed them along the coasts of the northern seas. The route up the Rhone was not entirely deserted, but it terminated at Lyons. There was held a great fair, which to some extent replaced those once held in Champagne. Another major change occurred in the trade routes to the Far East. The Mongol Empire, which had been established a century earlier, began to disintegrate in the 1360s. The resulting chaos in Central Asia meant that Western caravans could no longer follow the long overland route to China. The fact did not, however, put an end to trade between East and West. The Venetians continued to obtain Oriental spices through Beirut and Alexandria.

Although so many changes took place, there was never a collapse of the whole structure of international commerce at any point in the fourteenth and fifteenth centuries. At the end of the Middle Ages, one could still buy Oriental pepper in Prussia, English wool in Florence, and the sweet wines of Cyprus in England. The peristence of the fabric of international trade is strikingly illustrated in the surviving records of an Italian merchant, Francesco Datini (1335–1410), who left a vast archive of some three hundred thousand documents that recorded his highly profitable trading transactions conducted through a network of agents stretching from London to the eastern Mediterranean.

Datini's records also illustrate another aspect of late medieval commerce. The difficulties of doing business profitably in a shrinking market stimulated more rational and scientific techniques of business management. The Datini transactions, for instance, were recorded in meticulous double-entry bookkeeping. Not all merchants could adapt successfully to the demands of the new conditions, and there were great variations of wealth within the merchant class. During the thirteenth century, in a climate of general prosperity, most reasonably competent traders could expect to grow moderately wealthy. In the more harshly competitive conditions of the fifteenth century, the wealth of the merchant class as a whole was probably less than in the earlier period, but the most successful entrepreneurs built up enormous fortunes.*

In the later Middle Ages merchants often had more capital than they could use effectively in their business and were searching for ways to invest it. Many bought land. In the great Italian cities, it was possible to buy government bonds. As a rule, the merchant who put money into lands or bonds soon gave up mercantile activity to live on his income. But a few mercantile houses, or rather partnerships, used their money in what we would call banking operations. Probably the most successful as well as the best known of these partnerships was the house of Medici. The Medici (who later emerged as rulers of Florence) started as merchants dealing in anything that might show a profit but particularly in textiles. They bought raw wool, distributed it to Florentine spinners, bought the thread from the spinners to pass on to the weavers, and finally bought the finished cloth and sold it on the world markets. They thus employed what we call the "putting-out system." The Medici financed large-scale production of cloth and sold the product. At first they used their capital in regular commercial ventures, but in the 1390s a Medici bank was established in Rome. It grew to be the largest in Europe, with branches in the major commercial centers both north and south of the Alps. Banking became the dominant activity of the Medici, with the textile business continued as a profitable sideline. The Fuggers of Augsburg built up a similar financial empire in Germany. Again, their fortune was created originally by dealings in textiles, though in this case the commodity involved was linen rather than wool.

Governments as well as merchant families often commanded greater resources in the fourteenth century than in the earlier Middle Ages. The institutional developments of the preceding period had

*Sources, no. 99, 100

created more effective machinery for tax gathering, and fourteenth-century kings needed large revenues to finance their expensive wars. Often they turned to the great merchant companies for loans. This was a risky business from the merchants' point of view. Government debts might be repudiated or left unpaid without formal repudiation. Major bankruptcies, like those of the Florentine banks in the 1340s, could ensue. But, in the later Middle Ages, governments and merchant-bankers learned to cooperate more successfully. The real advantage that lenders could derive from such transactions lay in the trading privileges that governments were able to grant, and a most important feature of economic life in the later Middle Ages was a growing interdependence between governments and merchant companies. The Medici made loans to secular princes and, in the early fifteenth century, became the principal financiers of the papacy. The Fugger family in Germany provided the financial support that enabled Charles IV to obtain the imperial crown in 1346. Jacques Coeur, an enormously wealthy merchant of Bourges, financed the last French campaigns of the Hundred Years' War. In England the government decreed that all English wool had to be shipped to a designated Continental port, called the "staple" port, and that this shipping could only be done by merchants who were members of the "Company of the Staple." Thus the king secured the monopoly of the export of wool for a group of his subjects. When he wanted to borrow money, he borrowed from them. The staple was first located at Bruges. Later, when the English captured Calais, it was moved to that port. This increasing cooperation between government and business was highly important for the future. Eventually, it made possible the great pioneering voyages of exploration that opened up new worlds to European traders at the end of the Middle Ages.

If we take the longest view, it can be argued that the depopulation of Europe by the Black Death created the possibility of a new era of expansion, once the disruptive short-term effects of the disaster had been overcome. Once again a population comparable to that of 1100 had the resources of all western Europe to exploit. But the situation was not quite the same as it had been three centuries before. In the later Middle Ages, men had at their disposal substantial capital resources that in the earlier period had had to be created out of current income. Above all, they possessed an accumulated capital of technological and commercial skills. For instance, seafarers were helped by two technical innovations of the thirteenth century, the pivoted magnetic compass and the hinged rudder, which came into general use in the later Middle Ages. These devices greatly enhanced the possibility of making long ocean voyages with some degree of security. When a new expansion began, it could go further than the advance of the twelfth century.

82. *Art and Literature*

When we study the economic life of the later Middle Ages, we find a kaleidoscope of conflicting facts. There is abundant evidence both of decay and of renewal. When we turn to the art and literature of the period, we encounter a similar situation. The people of the later Middle Ages produced much morbid and degenerate work but also splendid creative achievements, which were filled with vitality and new forms of sensitivity. It is as though the widespread disasters that drove some people to despair stimulated in others a vivid exhilaration at the very fact of being alive, at the fact of having survived. The mood of the fifteenth century was brilliantly caught in the title of a modern book on the period by Alberto Tenenti, *The Awareness of Death and the Love of Life* (*Il senso dello morte e l'amore della vita nel Rinascimento*).

We might expect to find that an age which had experienced the great plague would be obsessed with the image of death in all its gross physical detail, and there is abundant evidence of this in contemporary art. Medieval sculptors commonly carved a representation of a dead man on his tomb, and hundreds of such figures from the thirteenth century survive in churches all over Europe. The prelates and knights and ladies lie, garbed in their best clothes, with calm composed faces, resting serenely with their God after the storms of life. Around 1400 the fashion changed. When Cardinal Lagrange died in 1402, the figure carved on his tomb at Avignon was that of a half-decayed corpse. This mode of presentation became common in the fifteenth century. Sometimes loathsome creatures, worms and toads and snails, were shown burrowing into the body, eating the rotting flesh.

People were appalled not only by the omnipresent fact of death but by the fear of unspeakable torments in the next world. The church did not encourage Christians to think they were likely to go straight to heaven without paying for the privilege. Without an indulgence, those who were dying could at best expect years of agony in purgatory—and there were many preachers who would cheerfully inform them that the pains of purgatory surpassed anything that could be experienced on earth. The Last Judgment had always been an important theme of Christian art, but in Romanesque sculpture the scene was dominated by a figure of Christ in majesty. Most fifteenth-century presentations of the scene concentrated on the horrors of hell. Numerous wall paintings were executed, sometimes in humble parish churches, which showed the naked figures of the damned being dragged off to hideous tortures by grotesque demons.

Around 1400, moreover, a new theme became popular in European art, the *danse macabre*, the Dance of Death. Its origin was a thirteenth-century tale about three nobles who, one day as they rode in the country, were accosted by three skeletons. After some talk the nobles asked who the skeletons were and learned that they were their own future selves. Only in the later Middle Ages did the story really grip

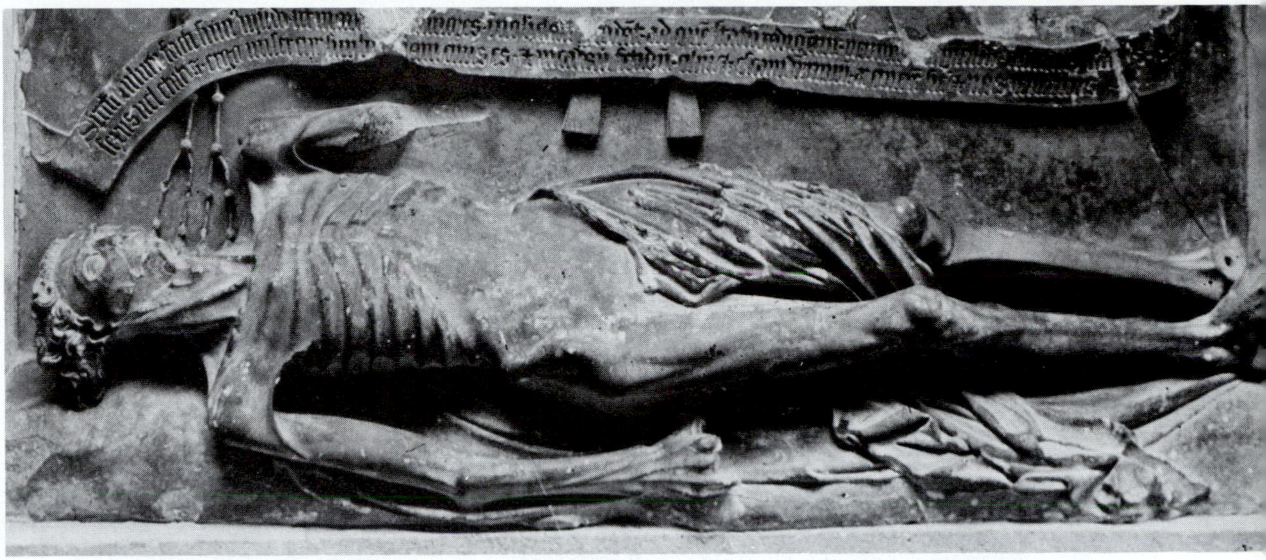

The tomb of Jean, cardinal de Lagrange, who died in 1402. In his will he directed that his skeleton be buried at Avignon and his flesh, at Amiens. Musée Calvet, Avignon. *Marburg—Art Reference Bureau*

men's imagination. Then the scene of skeletons—or corpses—mixing with living people was portrayed over and over again. It was painted on the walls of churches from Sweden to Sicily, and it appeared in the form of woodcut illustrations in some of the earliest printed books.

It might seem that we have here the perfect symbolism for a dying civilization, the image of death everywhere dominant. But the same generation that produced these morbid horrors also created a new style of painting filled with life and light. This style, called "International Gothic," was apparently formed at Avignon through the interaction of French and Italian painters there. Paris became its great center; from there it radiated out to England, to the Netherlands, to Germany, and back to Italy. The new style was characterized by a delicately gracious Gothic line, bold, brilliant colors, and a profusion of exquisitely observed decorative detail. It influenced the northern Italian painters Pisanello and Gentile da Fabriano, but most of all in Italy the style took root in the school of Siena. The series of panels on the life of St. Francis by the Sienese painter Sassetta (1392–1447) provides a fine example of Italian painting in this late Gothic manner.

One of these panels of Sassetta is to be seen at the Musée Condé in Chantilly—and, as it happens, this same museum also has the work that is often regarded as the finest example of late Gothic painting executed north of the Alps: an illuminated manuscript known as *Les Très Riches Heurs du Duc de Berry.* This is a prayer book, a Book of Hours, prepared at the beginning of the fifteenth century for the duke of Berry, brother of the French king, and painted mainly by the Flemish artist Pol de Limbourg. One section of the manuscript contains a calendar with a full-page painting representing each of the twelve months of the year. The pictures are filled with gaiety, love of life, delight in natural beauty. The picture for April, for instance, shows

A page from the *Très Riches Heures du Duc de Berry*, by Pol de Limbourg. The month of June. Peasant girls are mowing hay in the meadows outside Paris. In the background the spire of Ste. Chapelle can be seen. Musée Condé, Chantilly. *Giraudon*

courtly lovers exchanging rings in a meadow, while elegant young ladies in long flowing dresses gather the first spring flowers. The picture for May depicts lords and ladies riding in a May Day procession. For June we are shown peasant girls working in the hay fields outside Paris. In this vision of life, even peasant girls are comely—and very nicely gowned. The sun in these pictures always shines, the sky is azure blue, the grass a vivid green. Yet in another section of the same manuscript, we find the inevitable Dance of Death and a terrifying picture of the damned roasting in hell. There are always these stark contrasts in the later Middle Ages. It was not a merely senescent age, but it was not a simple one either.

Apart from "International Gothic," two other great schools of painting grew up during the early fifteenth century, in the Netherlands and in Florence. We shall only mention them here since any adequate account of their development would carry us far beyond the limits of strictly medieval history. Jan van Eyck (ca. 1385–1440), the first great painter in the new northern style, retained the Gothic technique of meticulously rendered detail, but combined it with a skillful use of perspective to achieve effects of far greater realism than his predecessors. In his paintings of interiors, it is as though we look through an open window to see in depth the whole living reality within. This was not yet "secular" art. The carefully observed objects that filled van Eyck's paintings virtually all had a symbolic significance for fifteenth-century observers, but the symbols were presented as parts of a completely realistic portrayal of the world. Jan van Eyck's painting is a final statement of the medieval conviction that the real world itself was a symbol of a divine order of things.

Florentine painting made more of a break with the medieval tradition, although chronologically its origins lie deep in the Middle Ages. The first great founder of the school was Giotto (1266–1337), who turned away from the formal hieratic Byzantine style that was dominant in the Italy of his day to produce paintings alive with a new kind of naturalism. Giotto's feeling for nature has often been compared to that of St. Francis. He has also been called a Gothic painter, but the phrase is not very meaningful. His work is based rather on a revival of classical values, though they were transformed by the artist's own genius. Giotto's figures were solid, rounded forms, modeled so as to give a feeling of depth. He had a great gift for portraying expressive gestures and for dramatic grouping of figures. These qualities are apparent in his greatest paintings, the narrative cycles of frescoes preserved in the Scrovegni chapel at Padua and in the church of Santa Croce in Florence. Giotto also worked on the famous frescoes of the life of St. Francis in the basilica at Assisi, though specialists argue about how much of the painting to be seen there represents the master's own work. There was no worthy successor to Giotto in fourteenth-century Florence, but in the early fifteenth century, a figure of comparable genius appeared. This was Masaccio (ca. 1400–1428). Masaccio had all of Giotto's dramatic power and combined with it a more scientific understanding of perspective, chiaroscuro, and human anatomy. These two great artists established the tradition of painting that made Florentine art a model for all Italy—and, eventually, for all Europe. So far as the art of painting is concerned, the century after the Black Death was one of the most creative periods in the whole history of the Western world.

There were great achievements in literature too, along with much third-rate imitative work, which merely illustrates how the older tradition of feudal epic and romance was becoming exhausted. We have seen that the feudal ideas that had inspired so much earlier literature were growing increasingly irrelevant to real life in the fourteenth century. Feudal tactics no longer won battles; feudal forms of land tenure were becoming obsolete; feudal loyalties no longer held society together. But the only pattern of honorable conduct that the nobility could understand was the code of chivalry. Chivalry therefore persisted as a social atavism in the later Middle Ages, influencing literature and the ritual of upper-class life long after the society that had given rise to it had been transformed by the advent of a money economy. Eventually, the most sensible ideals of medieval chivalry—personal bravery, courtesy to women, a spirit of service—were assimilated into later ideas of gentlemanly conduct.

But the great nobles of the fourteenth and fifteenth centuries seem to have tried to persuade themselves that chivalrous ideals were still alive and meaningful by exaggerating all their most fanciful aspects. The science of heraldry developed all its arcane ramifications at this time. The tournament became more like a mounted ballet than a mock battle. Orders of chivalry were founded which had no purpose except to provide occasions for feasting and for displays of pomp and ritual. It is symptomatic of the whole situation that the order of the Knights of the Temple, which had been founded in a mood of high Christian heroism, was dissolved in 1311; and the Order of the Garter, which had no Christian or heroic purpose at all, was founded in 1344. (It was a nineteenth-century prime minister who said that he liked the Garter because it had "no damned merit" about it, but the sentiment would have held good for the fourteenth century too.) It was an age of fantastic vows, most of which presumably went unfulfilled. In 1465, for instance, Duke Philip of Burgundy held a magnificent feast to celebrate his taking the vows of a crusader. All the details of the feast, including the various half-crazy oaths that were taken by the assembled courtiers, were recorded at length in an admiring and tedious poem. The duke never went crusading.

Evidently, in such a climate, the old-fashioned chivalrous literature could not continue to flourish indefinitely. The surprising thing perhaps is that it remained fashionable for so long. A few new *chansons de geste* were produced and old ones remade, usually by lengthening them. Four knights composed the *Cent Ballades* on the conventional themes of courtly love. Christine de Pisan (1364–1430), next to Marie de France the greatest female writer of the Middle Ages, composed the *Book of the Duke of True Lovers.* Christine followed the usual conventions to a certain point and then stopped; her ladies kept their

In a late fifteenth-century miniature, Pope Gregory the Great leads a mournful procession in prayer, seeking an end to the plague. Even as they pray a monk succumbs to the disease. From the *Très Riches Heures du Duc de Berry.* Musée Condé Chantilly. *Photographie Giraudon*

virtue. Christine also argued, unusually for her age, that women were just as intelligent as men and that, if their achievements were less striking, it was because they were required to stay at home and "run the household."* Duke Philip the Good of Burgundy was fascinated by chivalric ideas. His court produced remodeled *chansons de geste* and two biographies of perfect knights. Late chivalry in its more exaggerated form can be seen to perfection in these two works—*The Book of the Deeds of Jacques de Lalaing* and *Le Petit Jehan de Saintré.* In such works, the ideas of chivalry developed in the twelfth and thirteenth centuries were carried to ridiculous lengths. Chivalrous tales were becoming more and more works of fantasy. But fantasy could still produce an occasional masterpiece like the English *Sir Gawayne and the Grene Knight* (ca. 1370).

In general, the most interesting works of the later Middle Ages are by authors who deliberately turned away from the conventional ideas of courtly romance. As early as the latter part of the thirteenth century, Jean de Meung, in his *Roman de la Rose,* satirized the ideas of courtly love and many other traditional conceptions. A later satire, the *Fifteen Joys of Marriage,* was a fierce, if amusing, diatribe against women in general. Another work, one that is hard to classify—*Les Cent*

*Sources, no. 91

Nouvelles—tended in the same general direction. This was a collection of stories, usually of amorous adventures, supposed to have been told at the court of Duke Philip the Good. They can be taken as a reaction against courtly love or as a new sort of *fabliaux.* They certainly showed clearly that, by the fifteenth century, love could be dealt with in literature without using the courtly conventions.

Italy produced three truly great literary figures in the fourteenth century—Dante, Petrarch, and Boccaccio. We have already discussed Dante. Petrarch was a very different genius. He was brought up in the troubadour tradition, and much of his poetry followed its conventions, but it did so with rare freshness and delicate vigor. He was also fascinated by classical literature and has been called the first of the humanists. Boccaccio also began his career in the tradition of courtly love, but soon left it behind. The work of which he was most proud was a vast *Genealogy of the Gods,* a rather ponderous Latin monument of classical erudition. But his fame rests on his *Decameron.* This is a collection of short stories of many types drawn from a wide variety of sources. A large proportion of them deal with the perennially entertaining sins of adultery and fornication. In a good many of the tales, the participants in these forbidden delights are members of the regular or secular clergy. Boccaccio was a master storyteller and has been called the father of the modern short story.

Fourteenth-century England produced two great poets in William Langland (ca. 1332–1400) and Geoffrey Chaucer (ca. 1340–1400). Langland's *Piers Plowman* is the only major work of medieval literature written from the standpoint of the poor village priest and of the peasants among whom he lived. His poem is a series of "visions" of life in England, filled with reproaches against the abuses of the times, especially abuses in the church:

See there a pardoner preaching like a priest
A papal bull he brought sealed by the bishop . . .
If the bishop were holy and worth both his ears
He would not send his seal to deceive the people
But against the bishop your pardoner preacheth not
For the parson and the pardoner share the sermon-silver
Which the parish poor would get if the pardoner were away,

Geoffrey Chaucer was one of the world's great poets. While his purpose was less ambitious and less elevated than Dante's, he was his peer in poetic insight and literary skill. Chaucer is chiefly known for his *Canterbury Tales.* The pilgrims as described in the prologue give us a marvelous survey of the society of the age, from the noble knight to the rude miller, from the gentle abbess to the poor parish priest. Then the tales illustrate almost every medieval genre and satisfy every taste. There is knightly romance and courtly love. There are sophisticated satires like Boccaccio's. There are crude coarse tales. The weaknesses, vices, and foibles of the various social groups are clearly brought forth. The "Parson's Tale" is essentially a guide to confessors. In short, the

Canterbury Tales are a marvelous medley of all the threads of late medieval literature and the society that produced it. But more important is Chaucer's genius for haunting beauty of expression and precise, clear, forceful exposition. Also, Chaucer had an imaginative, original mind. No tale is quite what you would expect it to be. No character is simple, and no story is treated purely conventionally. Chaucer wrote many other works, some of which are of considerable interest, and all of which show in varying degree his genius. He could take an essentially silly tale like that of *Troilus and Criseyde* and turn it into a moving, if not entirely credible, love story. No one who hopes to understand the Middle Ages should fail to read Chaucer.*

The lyric tradition had never disappeared in France. Throughout the fourteenth century, there were lyric poets, but none of them could be called distinguished. In the fifteenth century, three poets—Alan Chartier; Charles, duke of Orleans; and François Villon—revived the French lyric. Chartier was a writer of fairly conventional love poetry, but he is even better known for his patriotic verse stirring up the French against their English foes. He can be said to share with Joan of Arc the credit for arousing the spirit of France. Charles of Orleans wrote charming love poems. Villon was one of the greatest of medieval poets, and his fame is still strong.† His verses provide a vivid picture of the seamier side of life in Paris in mid-fifteenth century. He was a failed scholar of the university, always at the same time poverty-stricken and luxury-loving, a sensualist, a rogue, a petty criminal. But he himself knew exactly what he was and portrayed himself and his world in poems distinguished by a hard clarity and utter lack of sentimentality. His verses were filled with sardonic, ribald wit but also, behind everything else, with a sort of despairing faith. Villon was twice condemned to death and twice reprieved. When he wrote his own epitaph, he saw himself as a hanged criminal. We do not know what his real end was, but his verses could stand as an epitaph for a whole civilization:

Men, brother men, that after us yet live
Let not your hearts too hard against us be;
For if some pity of us poor men you give
The sooner shall God take of you pity.

READING SUGGESTIONS

* *B. Tierney,* Sources *and* Readings, *vol. I, nos, 85–88, 91, 96–97, 99–102; vol. II, no. 34, 36.*

The general works on art, literature, and economic history already cited in earlier chapters should again be consulted (see Chapters VIII, XII, XVIII).

On late medieval commerce, see R. A. De Roover, *The Medici Bank* (New York, 1948), and *Money, Banking and Credit in Medieval Bruges* (Cambridge, MA, 1948); E. Powell, *The Wool Trade in English History* (New York, 1941); and * R. Lopez and I. Raymond, *Medieaval Trade in the Mediterranean World* (New York, 1955), with translated documents. For the merchant class, see A. B.

*Sources, no. 101

†Sources, no. 102

Kerr, *Jacques Coeur* (New York, 1928); I. Origo, *The Merchant of Prato* (New York, 1957); and S. Thrupp, *The Merchant Class of Medieval London* (Chicago, 1948). On late medieval feudalism, see B. Lyon, *From Fief to Indenture* (Cambridge, MA, 1957) for institutional developments, and O. Cartellieri, *The Court of Burgundy* (New York, 1929) for the practice of chivalry. * H. Pirenne, *Early Democracies in the Low Countries* (Paris, 1910) deals with social conflicts in the cities, and * N. Cohn, *The Pursuit of the Millennium* (London, 1957) considers the relationship between religious and social radicalism. M. Mollat considers changing attitudes toward the poor in * *The Poor in the Middle Ages* (New Haven, CT, 1986). On women's roles see * M. Howell, *Women, Production and Patriarchy in Late Medieval Cities* (Chicago, 1986).

On popular rebellions see M. Mollat and P. Wolff, *The Popular Revolutions of the Late Middle Ages* (London, 1972); S. Fourquin, *The Anatomy of Popular Rebellion in the Middle Ages* (New York, 1978); * R. B. Dobson, *The Peasants' Revolt of 1381* (New York, 1970); * R. H. Hilton, *Bondmen Made Free* (London, 1977); * R. H. Hilton and T. Ashton, *The English Rising of 1381* (Cambridge, England, 1984); and M. Mullett, *Popular Culture and Popular Protest in Late Medieval and Early Modern Europe* (London, 1987).

* H. A. Miskimin, *The Economy of Early Renaissance Europe, 1300–1460* (Englewood Cliffs, NJ, 1969) provides a survey of economic history.

Two fine introductions to the culture of the late medieval period are * J. Huizinga, *The Waning of the Middle Ages* (London, 1924) and G. Duby, *Foundations of a New Humanism, 1280–1440* (Cleveland, 1966). E. P. Cheyney, *The Dawn of a New Era* (New York, 1936) provides an excellent, more conventional survey. For general works on the Italian Renaissance, see Chapter XXV. On the schools of painting discussed in the text, see * B. Berenson, *Italian Painters of the Renaissance*, rev. ed. (New York, 1957); * M. Meiss, *Giotto and Assisi* (New York, 1960), and * *Painting in Florence and Siena after the Black Death* (Princeton, 1951); E. Panofsky, *Early Netherlandish Painting* (Cambridge, MA, 1954); and L. Castelfranchi Vegas, *International Gothic Art in Italy* (Leipzig, 1966). See also J. M. Clark, *The Dance of Death* (Glasgow, 1950). Good works on fourteenth-century literature are E. H. Williams, *Studies in the Life and Works of Petrarch* (Cambridge, MA, 1955); E. Hutton, *Giovanni Boccaccio, a Biographical Study* (London, 1910); H. S. Bennett, *Chaucer and the Fifteenth Century* (Oxford, England, 1947); E. F. Chaney, *François Villon in His Environment* (Oxford, England, 1946). For translations of Petrarch, see * T. G. Bergin, *Selected Sonnets, Odes and Letters* (New York, 1966); for Boccaccio, * R. Aldington, *The Decameron* (New York, 1938). Chaucer and Langland, respectively, have been rendered into modern English by * N. Coghill (Harmondsworth, England, 1952) and * J. H. Goodrich (Harmondsworth, England, 1959). For Villon, see the translations of J. Payne (London, 1892), and * N. Cameron (New York, 1966).

FROM MEDIEVAL TO MODERN EUROPE

chapter

XXV

The End of the Hundred Years' War

At the beginning of the fifteenth-century, the medieval world seemed in a state of total disarray. The issues involved in the struggle between England and France had not been settled. The church was in schism. Within every major state, rival factions of nobility contended for control of the government. Yet there were abundant signs of vitality in many spheres of medieval life—in art, literature, technology, economic affairs. The fifteenth century saw a gradual process of reintegration. Problems that had seemed hopelessly intractable were finally resolved, and the recovery of some degree of order made possible a new growth of civilization. One problem that had caused dissension ever since the twelfth century, the claims of English kings to territories in France, was finally settled by the last campaigns of the Hundred Years' War.*

83. *The English Attack on France*

Henry IV of England died in 1413 and was succeeded by his son Henry V (1413–1422). The new king was an able captain and a brave soldier, whose name has gone down in history wreathed in martial glory. Away from the battlefield he was a thoroughly unpleasant person. He was so avid for power that he had tried to depose his father so that he could take his place. He was a cold, heartless bigot with no interest except his own welfare. Henry's love of war, combined with his lust for power and a belief that if he kept the English barons busy in France they would be less likely to revolt at home, led him to reopen the long-suspended war. He had no difficulty finding good excuses. He still claimed the crown of France. Moreover, both parties in that kingdom had asked his aid in their quarrels. But Henry's demands were heavier than either Burgundians or Armagnacs felt able to meet. Henry wanted all Aquitaine, Anjou, Maine, Touraine, and Normandy,

*See Chapter XXII.

with suzerainty over Brittany and Flanders. In August 1415 the English kind landed in Normandy with some two thousand men-at-arms and about six thousand archers and immediately laid siege to the town of Harfleur. The place fell on September 22, but an epidemic of dysentery had gravely reduced both the size and efficiency of his army. Henry decided to go home, but in order to show his contempt for his enemy, he planned to go by way of Calais. Meanwhile, the host of France had been slowly assembling. The duke of Burgundy refused to answer the summons, but many of his nobles headed by one of his brothers joined the army.

Henry's idea of marching to Calais was an extremely reckless one. Disease and the casualties incurred at the siege of Harfleur had reduced his army to some six thousand men. He was so short of supplies that his men were almost starving, and heavy rains had turned the countryside into a sea of mud. When he learned that the French army was marching against him, his men were too weak and exhausted to attempt to flee further, and he was obliged to prepare to fight. Choosing a position where his flanks were covered by the gardens and orchards of two villages, Tramecourt and Agincourt, Henry arrayed his men in the usual three divisions, with the knights and pikemen forming solid blocks flanked by the archers.

The French had learned from Poitiers not to risk either their king or his heir in battle. The nominal commander of the army was the constable, the lord of Albret, but, as he was a comparatively insignificant lord, he could do little with the royal princes such as Orleans and Bourbon. The constable was an old soldier who remembered the methods of Duguesclin. He saw no point in attacking the English position. If the French army placed itself between Henry and Calais, Henry would have to take the offensive. But once more the noble kings had their way. The only course for gentlemen was to fight at once. The tactics of Poitiers were followed almost exactly. A small body of horses was to charge first. Then the cavalry of France were to attack on foot, ranged in three divisions. The crossbowmen were apparently once more placed behind the men-at-arms, so that they were utterly unable to use their weapons.

The plan of battle that made some slight sense at Poitiers was utterly insane at Agincourt. For one thing, armor had been steadily increasing in weight. In the hope of protecting themselves completely from missile weapons, the knights of France and England had adopted massive plate armor. It was extremely difficult for them to walk any distance, and if they fell down it was almost impossible for them to get up without help. Moreover, the rains had reduced the countryside to a quagmire. As at Poitiers, the French cavalry charge was largely stopped by the English archers. While their arrows could not pierce the armor of the knights, they killed the knights' horses and so broke up the charge. Then the French dismounted divisions advanced. By the time these knights had struggled through the mud to the English line, they were much too exhausted to fight. Seeing their plight, Henry ordered his archers to drop their bows and go out to fight the

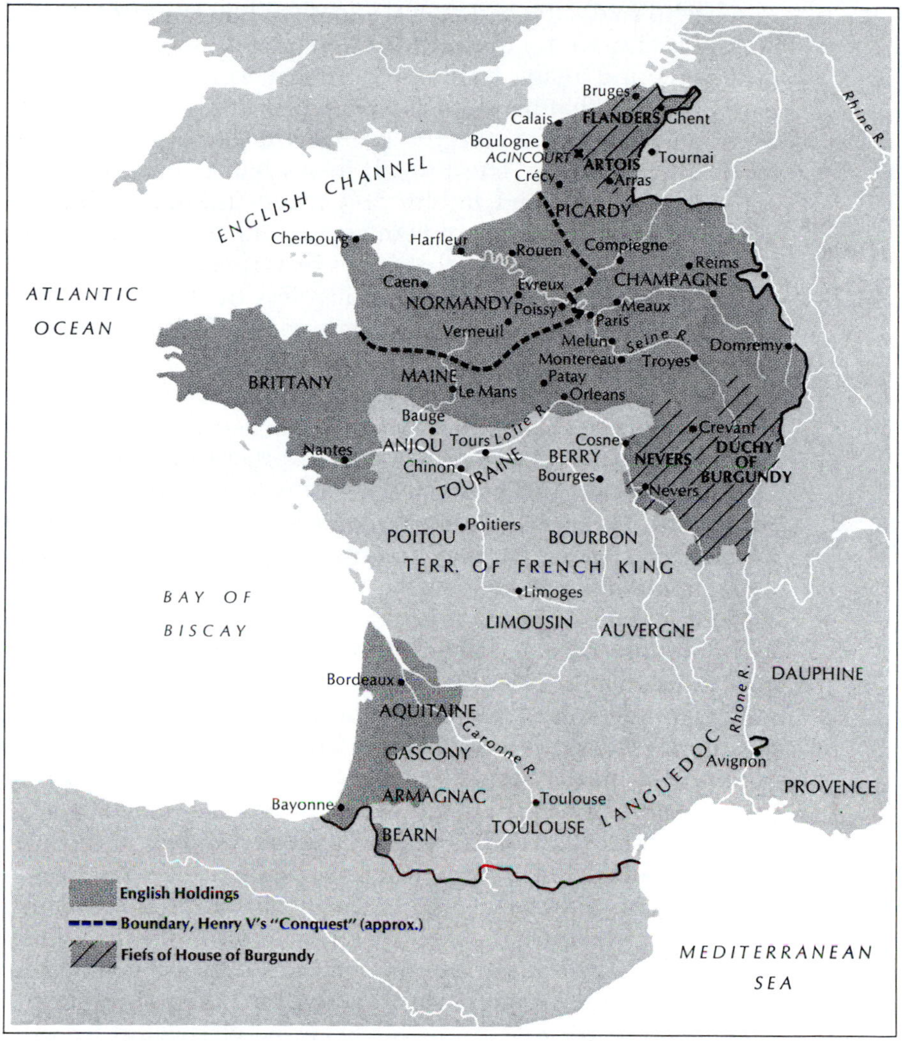

The Hundred Years' War, 1428

The victories of Henry V and his alliance with the duke of Burgundy made the English masters of all northern France. However, the territories they held in 1428 were steadily recovered by the French; by 1450, the English held only Calais and its environs.

French hand to hand. As the tired French knights could hardly raise their arms to use their weapons, they were easily captured or slain. By the time the third French division was ready to attack, Henry had almost as many prisoners as troops.

Then, just as the last French battle moved toward his line, Henry received word that another enemy force was in his rear attacking his camp. Actually, it was only a country squire, the lord of Agincourt, at the head of a group of peasants who had decided to see what plunder he could find in the unguarded camp, but Henry was thoroughly alarmed and ordered his men to kill all their prisoners. No one paid the slightest attention to this command. Most of the prisoners were great nobles whose ransoms meant incredible fortunes to the archers who had captured them, and they had no intention of killing them. Finally, Henry ordered his household knights to conduct the slaughter, and many noble Frenchmen were murdered before the king learned that his fears had been groundless. The lord of Agincourt was not dangerous, and the French third division discreetly retired without attacking. The French losses had been extremely severe—some fifteen hundred nobles and three thousand ordinary men-at-arms. Despite the killing of many prisoners, Henry still had over a thousand captives, including the dukes of Orleans and Bourbon. The English losses were fantastically small—less than a hundred. Their most important casualty was the king's cousin Edward, duke of York. Edward had lived well and easily. The weight of his armor in the hot summer day and the excitement of battle were too much for him, and he died of apoplexy.

The defeat of Agincourt had practically wiped out the Armagnac party, and the duke of Burgundy once more became master of the realm. The remnants of his foes were led by the heir to the throne, the Dauphin Charles. In an attempt to restore peace in the kingdom in the face of the English menace, the dauphin and Duke John had a series of conferences. At one of these conferences, held in the middle of a bridge, an old Orleanist captain finally avenged his duke's death by slaying the duke of Burgundy. The new duke, Philip, called "the Good," promptly made an alliance with Henry V, who was engaged in methodically reducing the strongholds of Normandy. As the Burgundians were masters of Paris and the king, this led in May 1420 to the Treaty of Troyes with Henry V. This treaty declared the Dauphin Charles disinherited for his "horrible and enormous crimes." In fact, as the queen had obligingly stated that he was not really the son of Charles VI, he was referred to as the "so-called Dauphin." Henry V was to marry the king's daughter Catherine and become heir to the French throne. While his father-in-law lived, Henry was to hold Normandy as well as Aquitaine. The duke of Burgundy was guaranteed all the rights and privileges he claimed in his own lands—something very close to complete sovereignty.

During the year 1422, both Charles VI and Henry V died, and in accordance with the Treaty of Troyes the crowns of France and England passed to the latter's son, Henry, who was only a few months old. The infant king's uncles, John, duke of Bedford, and Humphrey, duke of Gloucester, became regents in France and England, respectively. Actually, France was divided into three separate states. The duke of Bedford ruled in the name of his nephew over Normandy, Maine, the Ile de France, and Champagne. Paris and the region to the west were actually held by English garrisons, while Champagne was occupied by Burgundian troops acting as Bedford's allies. The near independence granted the duke of Burgundy by the Treaty of Troyes was made virtually complete by the minority of the king. Bedford was obliged to treat him as a sovereign ally. In theory, the duke of Brittany acknowledged Henry VI, and hence his territory formed part of the English domains; but he was always ready to do what seemed most profitable to him and was a most unreliable vassal. The Loire valley and all France to the south of the Loire River outside of the duchy of Gascony recognized as king the Dauphin Charles, who made his capital at Bourges. A large proportion of the civil servants of the French crown moved to Bourges and from there governed the southern two-thirds of the realm.

The dauphin's position was essentially strong. The English upper classes had little interest in their child monarch's French kingdom and no intention whatever of paying for its maintenance. Bedford had very few English troops and found it extremely difficult to raise the money needed to support them. His efforts to increase taxes in the region he controlled made him less popular and failed to obtain enough money. The duke of Burgundy was interested solely in schemes for increasing his own power in eastern France and the Low Countries. He would promise Bedford troops, but they rarely arrived. Most of the nobles of the lands ruled by Bedford had stayed loyal to the dauphin and followed him to the south. Moreover, most of the captains of the French army had accepted the dauphin. All through Bedford's territory, especially to the east of Paris, were fortresses held by these captains in the name of the dauphin. Thus, along the frontier between Champagne and Lorraine, Robert de Baudricourt, captain of the castle of Vaucouleurs, dominated the countryside. The dauphin's chief disadvantage was his own character. Charles was a sickly, homely, weak-willed, and timid young man, whose oversensitive feelings had been deeply wounded by the Treaty of Troyes—especially by his mother's statement that he was a bastard.

In the year 1428, Bedford found himself faced with a perplexing problem. He wanted to extend his nephew's territories south of the Loire, but the valley of the river was controlled by two great princes, the dukes of Orleans and Anjou, whom he hoped to win over to the cause of Henry VI. Charles, duke of Orleans, had been captured at Agincourt and was a prisoner in England, but the duchy was being vigorously defended by the duchess and the duke's illegitimate half-brother, the count of Dunois, known as the bastard of Orleans. After long consideration, Bedford decided that it was better to offend Orleans than Anjou, and his troops moved into the duchy and laid siege to its fortresses, including the city of Orleans. The English built works to blockade the city and conducted the siege as energetically as their very small numbers would permit. The local militia and a few professional soldiers conducted a rather lackadaisical defense. As time went on, it looked more and more as if the English army would capture the key to the Loire valley. The supporters of the dauphin seemed to lack all spirit and cohesion. They would occasionally ravage Bedford's territory and surprise isolated castles, but they showed no desire to meet English troops in battle. The long succession of defeats suffered by the armies of France seemed to have hopelessly destroyed their confidence.

84. *Joan of Arc and the Victory of France*

Meanwhile, on the eastern border of Champagne, Robert de Baudricourt, captain of Vaucouleurs, was as perplexed as the duke of Bedford but for a quite different reason: a young and very determined peasant girl from the village of Domrémy was bothering him to death. For a century after the county of Champagne had come into the possession of the crown, Domrémy had been part of the royal demesne. Then it had belonged to Louis of Orleans, who had been a kindly prince well loved by his people. While they knew little about the English except that they were in some way responsible for the wars, their villages had recently been plundered by the Burgundians, and they longed for the peaceful days of Duke Louis. In Domrémy lived a simple, completely uneducated, and deeply religious peasant girl named Joan of Arc. Her mind was filled with stories of the saints and with the wrongs done by the English and Burgundians to France and her rightful king. She believed that several of her favorite saints appeared to her and commanded her to raise the siege of Orleans and have the dauphin crowned at Reims. Joan made her way to Vaucouleurs to tell Robert de Baudricourt of her visions and to urge him to send her to the dauphin. Robert was a tough, rather brutal professional soldier and a man of the world. He knew that this was no new phenomenon. There had been a regular epidemic of women with visions. He had no desire to annoy the court with another, and he may have been kindly enough to hate to see a foolish girl get into trouble. But Joan was determined. She won the faith of some of Robert's men, and the captain finally told them that they might take her to Chinon if they were foolish enough to want to.

On February 23, 1429, after safely crossing a countryside held by the English and Burgundians, Joan and her slender escort arrived at Chinon. She is said to have told Charles something that gave him new hope and courage—perhaps she assured him that he was legitimate. But the dauphin was suspicious of women with visions, and he ordered his clerks to examine Joan. They found her to be what she was, an ignorant young girl filled with belief in her mission and fully confident that she was obeying the commands of God. There was a rough and ready test for witchcraft, and the examiners decided to use it and abide by the result. As witches have regular intercourse with the devil, a virgin could not be a witch. Hence, when a committee of noble matrons certified to Joan's virginity, the clerks assured Charles that she was not a witch. Since nothing could make his troops fight worse, Charles saw no reason for refusing Joan a chance, especially as she had quickly won the confidence of several of his captains including a prince of the blood, John II, duke of Alençon. Alençon was about to lead a force to carry supplies into Orleans, and Joan went along with him.

The captains who served the dauphin were a mixed crew. There were two great nobles, the duke of Alençon and Arthur, count of

Richmont, constable of France, and brother of the duke of Brittany. Then there were wild and reckless young lords such as Gilles de Rais, later to win immortal ill fame as Bluebeard, and Dunois, the bastard of Orleans. Finally, there were the fierce, brutal, rapacious mercenary captains who served Charles when he paid them and plundered the countryside for their own profit when they were unemployed. All these varied types seem to have been impressed by Joan's simple faith. Still more important, her confidence inspired the soldier themselves and made them believe that perhaps Frenchmen could beat Englishmen. This restoration of confidence was the miracle wrought by Joan of Arc. The garrison of Orleans sallied out, destroyed the English works, and drove off the besieging army. The same fate quickly overtook the English forces besieging the other fortresses of the duchy, and an English army hastening to their assistance was crushed in a pitched battle. In the space of a few weeks, the Loire valley was cleared of the enemy and Bedford's military resources temporarily crippled.

By raising the siege of Orleans, Joan had fulfilled one of the tasks imposed upon her by her visions. The second, the consecration of the dauphin at Reims, was even closer to her heart. Although here and there signs were appearing of what we call national feeling, a belief that there was such a thing as the French people, in the minds of most people France was still simply the land ruled by the king of France. Hence, until the dauphin was crowned, there could be no true France. Joan, with the strong support of the king's chief ecclesiastical counselor, the archbishop of Reims, urged an immediate expedition to the primate's seat. Late in June Charles started the long march, at the head of some twelve thousand men. What had appeared to the timid as a dangerous expedition across hostile territory was in fact a pleasant parade. Bedford was frantically mustering his forces to defend Paris and Normandy, while the Burgundians were completely unprepared for effective action. As Charles moved through the country, the towns opened their gates to him. On July 16 he occupied Reims, and the next day he was duly consecrated in its cathedral. Although the crown and scepter were in the possession of the English and no lay peer of France was present, the sacred oil that created a king was the prime essence of a coronation. The Dauphin Charles had become Charles VII (1422–1461) of France.

Her success did not quench Joan's enthusiasm, and her burning zeal carried the armies of France to the very walls of Paris. But the English garrisons held firm in the great city and a ring of subsidiary fortresses. Meanwhile, the king and court were slipping back into their customary apathy. The campaign in the Loire valley, the march to Reims, and the campaign that followed had drained the treasury. The courtiers hated to see money that could be used for pleasant living wasted in military campaigns. Now that Charles was king, diplomacy seemed to them a more suitable weapon than the sword. If Brittany and Burgundy could be won over, the English cause would be lost. Even the captains were a little tired of Joan's zeal for fighting. To them war was a business, and plundering its most profitable element.

One had to fight battles occasionally, but they were not to be sought too avidly. Hence the campaign ground slowly to a halt. Worse yet, the Burgundians had now mustered their forces and were beginning a counterattack by attempting to reduce the strongholds north of Paris that had long been held by captains in Charles' pay. One of Duke Philip's captains, John of Luxemburg, laid siege to the town of Compiègne. Burning to be in battle once more, Joan hastened there with a few troops to reinforce the garrison. Some days later she led a sortie against the besieging forces. Although they were taken by surprise, the Burgundians rallied quickly and routed Joan's force, which retired toward the gate. Joan, however, refusing to admit defeat, continued to fight at the head of a few devoted followers. The commander of the town, who feared that if he left the gate open too long the Burgundians would rush in, ordered it closed, and Joan and her followers were captured.

It was but natural that the English and Burgundians should have considered Joan the source of all their recent troubles. Her presence had inspired an army that had been able to do no more than defend rather feebly a few strongholds and make occasional plundering raids to win victory after victory. Her fiery enthusiasm had deprived Bedford of several of his best captains and nearly half his territory in France. The modern historian, little given to belief in divine intervention, finds it hard to explain Joan's career and to account for the extraordinary inspiration that a simple peasant girl gave to the royal cause. To ordinary people in that age of faith, Joan's success was clearly supernatural, and whether they believed that it sprang from God or the Devil depended largely on which side they were on. The learned doctors of the University of Paris, whose sympathies were overwhelmingly Burgundian, demanded that Joan be turned over to the Inquisition for prosecution for witchcraft, and it is likely that they fairly represented English and Burgundian opinion. Whether Bedford believed Joan to be a witch or simply an intolerable nuisance is a matter of small moment except to his own conscience. He promptly bought her from the impecunious John of Luxemburg, placed her safely in Rouen castle, and assigned Peter Cauchon, bishop of Beauvais, to conduct her trial.

According to the law of the time, the trial was fair enough as regards the external forms of procedure. The church had the authority to decide whether a person had genuine visions or mere delusions of the devil. But Cauchon was a political bishop, completely under Bedford's thumb. The duke never allowed him to forget that his task was to send Joan to the stake. The essential illegality of the trial lies in the fact that Joan's judges were not impartial. Her guilt was predetermined. Obviously, an English-dominated court could not consider without bias the question of whether Joan's visions were divinely inspired when the main point of the visions was to show that the English king was not the rightful king of France.*

*Sources, no. 94

Fortunately for Bedford's reputation, his calculating cruelty has been overshadowed in the pages of history by Charles' pusillanimity.

Despite his heavy obligations to Joan, Charles did nothing whatever to save her. And there were a number of things he might have done. John of Luxemburg was a thoroughly decent soldier who would have preferred to sell Joan to her friends, but no one made him an adequate offer. Charles had noble English prisoners who could be used to negotiate for exchange. While rescue of Joan by force was probably impossible, a major military effort against the weak English positions might well have obliged Bedford to release Joan in return for a truce. Only when some years later he realized that it was not dignified to owe his crown to a condemned heretic did Charles make any move in Joan's favor. Then a newly convened ecclesiastical court reversed the verdict of 1429. Only in the twentieth century was Joan formally proclaimed a saint.

After Joan's death, the war went on in much the same desultory fashion as before her appearance. Charles lacked the energy and the resources to do anything decisive, and Bedford could merely hold his own against the petty operations of the French captains. It soon became clear that the only course for Charles was to make peace with Burgundy. Duke Philip still remembered bitterly the murder of his father and was too completely the noble knight to turn suddenly against his English allies, but his affection for the latter had for some years been growing cooler. After long negotiations between Charles and Philip, the duke of Burgundy agreed to discuss terms of peace, but he insisted that the conference should include his English allies.

In August 1435 the three parties met at the town of Arras. It soon became clear that peace with England was impossible. Bedford insisted that Henry VI be recognized as king of France and that Charles hold the lands in his possession as Henry's vassal. The English quit the conference on September 1. Then Duke Philip, whose conscience was now at rest, began serious negotiations, and on September 20 the Treaty of Arras was concluded. Philip obtained two counties bordering his Burgundian lands, Macon and Auxerre, and two adjoining Flanders. While Charles lived, he would not do homage for his fiefs held of the French crown. Charles would make public amends for his part in the murder of Duke John.

This reconciliation with Burgundy made possible the final victory of Charles VII, whose claim to the throne was supported by the great mass of the French people. In 1439 an important financial ordinance, approved by an *Estates General,* provided revenues to continue the struggle against the English. Moreover, the king's principal adversary, Bedford, died shortly after the conclusion of the Treaty of Arras. While the men who commanded in France for Henry VI held out for another fifteen years, it must have been fairly clear that their cause was hopeless. One by one the towns and castles held by the English surrendered to Charles' captains. The last battle in the north was fought in 1450 at Formigny in Normandy. A small English force sent to relieve the garrisons being besieged met a French army under the constable of Richmont. The battle had a novel feature. The English took up their favorite position on a hill, but instead of attacking directly, Richmont mounted canon and bombarded them until they broke their formation. Then he easily cut them to pieces. Two years later, the crushing defeat of the earl of Shrewsbury near Bordeaux ended the English rule in Gascony. All that was left to Henry VI of his kingdom of France was the town of Calais and its environs. While all English kings until George III continued to bear the title king of France, it was an entirely empty dignity.

85. *The Art of War in the Late Middle Ages*

The final capitulation of Bordeaux in 1452 ended the Hundred Years' War, but before closing this chapter it seems well to glance briefly at the important changes in military institutions that marked the late Middle Ages. One of the most interesting of these was the gradual increase in the use of gunpowder. Cannon were known in Europe as early as 1324. Edward III possessed a fair number. While the statement of some chroniclers that he used cannon at Crécy is dubious, he certainly had them at the siege of Calais. From that time on, cannon formed a regular part of the military equipment of the states of western Europe. This early artillery was not, however, very effective. The balls of stone and metal were too light and were thrown with too little force to do much harm to stone walls. As the cannon lacked movable mounts, they were of little use in the field except when an army on the defensive wanted to forbid the enemy the use of some narrow passage. The noise of cannon created a certain amount of confusion and consternation, but there is little evidence that during the fourteenth century they did anyone much harm. Captains besieging castles usually found it more effective to use the powder intended for their cannon to make explosions in mines. The smaller firearms, commonly called *ribaulds,* were not much more effective. These were mounted on wheels, usually two or three barrels to a carriage, or a number of them were placed on a cart. They were intended to kill or wound troops, but they took so long to load and fire that they were not much use in battle.

In the fifteenth century, artillery began to be important in the siege and defense of castles and towns. Professional artillerymen appeared who acquired great skill in handling their weapons. While the cannon were still not very effective against the massive stone walls of fortresses, they could batter down gates and thus gain entrance for the besieging troops. A common device in the early fifteenth century was to place a number of cannon in a semicircle so that all bore on a town gate and gradually battered it to pieces. As soon as cannon became common as siege weapons, the owners of castles felt the need of them for defense, but this created serious problems. The recoil of the cannon quickly shook to pieces the walls on which they were mounted. The usual solution was to cut down the outer wall to about a third of its height and increase its thickness so it could support the cannon. Artillery was still of little value in the field except under unusual circumstances. If an army was operating on the defensive, cannon could make the ground directly in front of them untenable, but they could be moved only with great difficulty. Occasionally, they could be used against an army drawn up in a defensive position, as at Formigny. But in a battle where the troops had freedom of movement they could easily get out of the way of the enemy cannon.

The *ribaulds* became more numerous in the fifteenth century but as a rule were not very valuable. Their chief use was from the walls of fortresses against besieging troops. When the emperor Sigismund attempted to suppress the Hussite heretics, he found himself faced with masses of carts on which *ribaulds* were mounted.* His cavalry could not break through the ring of carts and suffered heavily from the *ribaulds*. There are references to the use of a very small *ribauld* carried by individual soldiers—the ancestor of the musket of the sixteenth century. It seems doubtful, however, that they could compete in effectiveness with either the crossbow or the longbow as a missile weapon. They were very slow-firing and magnificently inaccurate. Still, in spite of the shortcomings of these earliest firearms, their introduction at the end of the Middle Ages marked the beginning of a "military revolution" that would transform the art of war in the following centuries. As the accuracy of the guns improved, new tactics were devised to use them more effectively. The Venetian Republic began to replace its crossbowmen with gunners in 1490. The English continued to rely on the longbow until the 1560s; then they too turned to firearms.

It has frequently been claimed that the development of firearms resulted in the abandonment of armor, but actually there seems to have been little connection between the two processes. During the fourteenth century, the increased effectiveness of the crossbow and longbow led the knights to increase the thickness and weight of their armor. By the time of Agincourt, a fully armed cavalryman was completely encased in heavy plate armor, and his horse was similarly equipped. As a result, the knight was helpless on foot and when mounted could only move with ponderous dignity over the most favorable ground. In short, the heavy cavalry became useful only for charges under ideal conditions. By the end of the century, most troops were using lighter armor to increase their mobility. The officers continued to wear the massive plate armor, but even in the heavy cavalry the ordinary soldier began to reduce the weight of his equipment. Certainly, throughout the sixteenth century, armor was an effective protection against the handguns of the day. Only a lucky shot that hit a weak spot could pierce heavy plate armor.

There was one interesting development in tactics in the fifteenth century. The son and successor of Duke Philip of Burgundy, Charles, called the Rash, was an ambitious prince who hoped to build an independent state between France and Germany—to reconstruct the ancient state of Lothair. This involved conquering Lorraine, which lay between his possessions in the Low Countries and Burgundy, and

*See pp. 594–595.

Switzerland, through which ran the passes leading to Italy. This scheme led him into a series of wars with the Swiss. Like the northern Welsh and the Highland Scots, the Swiss were essentially spearmen who fought on foot in massive formation. But they had learned something that other medieval spearmen had not—to move in close formation without breaking their ranks. The Welsh and the Highlanders massed on the defensive could repulse heavy cavalry, but once they tried to move, their ranks opened and gave the horsemen a chance to break in. The Swiss were drilled so that they could march and charge in solid columns. When Duke Charles led his Burgundian cavalry up the narrow Swiss valleys, the Swiss came charging down with a solid mass of pikes and completely routed the horsemen. During the last decades of the fifteenth and the first decades of the sixteenth centuries, the Swiss spearmen were the most valued soldiers of Europe and were hired by all belligerents to aid in their wars.

The reign of Charles VII saw the establishment of the first regular army that western Europe had known since the collapse of the Roman Empire. As the Hundred Years' War drew toward its close, the unemployed companies once more became the scourge of France. All sorts of devices were used in the attempt to get rid of them. Several times they were rented to German princes and led off to new and distant wars, but they preferred France and always wandered back again. Charles conceived the idea of taking some of these companies into his service on a permanent basis and using them to fight his wars and suppress the other companies. In a decree of May 26, 1445, the king announced that he was establishing fifteen *compagnies d'ordonnance.* Each company was to consist of a hundred *lances.* A lance was the usual fifteenth-century term for a fully armed horseman and his attendants. Each lance in the new companies was to contain a fully armed cavalryman, a knife-wielder whose chief purpose was to kill or capture men knocked down by the knight or squire, two archers, a *valet d'armes,* and a page. The last two were noncombatant servants who cared for the man-at-arms. All these were mounted so that they could move together on a march. Thus Charles had a standing army of six thousand men. These companies were commanded by great nobles and were named after these commanders. They were the ancestors of the ancient regiments that formed the nucleus of the later French army.

In order to obtain infantry armed with missile weapons who had some training in their use, Charles organized a body of militia called free archers. Every parish in the royal demesne was to supply a number of men determined by the king's agents. These men were to be equipped by the king, paid a small salary, and exempted from most taxes. In return, they were expected to practice regularly and meet at times for drill and instruction. The king's idea was not received with any great enthusiasm among a peasant population unused to arms, and very few men actually became free archers. There are said to have been eight thousand under Charles and sixteen thousand under his son Louis XI. It seems most unlikely that their drilling was adequate to make them very effective troops. One contemporary suggests that the exemption from taxation tempted the older and more influential villagers and that when the free archers were mustered they turned out to be mostly aged and portly. Certainly this militia never became an important part of the French military system.

The other changes that we have described had effects outside the strictly military sphere. Cavalry continued to be important in warfare down to the twentieth century. But heavily armed and armored cavalrymen were becoming obsolete in the fourteenth century, and the whole original point of the medieval feudal system had been to support such warriors. The use of artillery in siege warfare, the deployment of disciplined infantry, the maintenance of permanent professional armies—all these changes could influence the art of government as well as the art of war by strengthening the power of rulers who learned to use the new techniques effectively.

READING SUGGESTIONS

* *B. Tierney,* Sources *and* Readings, *vol. I, no. 93.*

Besides the works cited in Chapter XXII see * E. F. Jacob, *Henry V and the Invasion of France* (London, 1947); P. S. Lewis, *The Recovery of France in the Fifteenth Century* (New York, 1972); and A. H. Burne, *The Agincourt War* (London, 1955). Outstanding among the numerous books on Joan of Arc are F. Lowell, *Joan of Arc* (Boston, 1897); A. Lang, *The Maid of France,* 3rd ed. (London, 1938); L. Fabre, *Joan of Arc* (New York, 1954); S. Stolpe, *The Maid of Orlèans* (London, 1956); and, for a review of the literature, C. W. Lightbody, *The Judgements of Joan* (Cambridge, MA, 1961). M. Warner, *Joan of Arc, The Image of Female Heroism* (New York, 1981) provides a fresh perspective. However, the best introduction to Joan is the record of her trial, *Trial of Jeanne d'Arc,* W. P. Barrett (trans.) (London, 1931). Other valuable source material is collected in R. Pernoud, *The Retrial of Joan of Arc* (New York, 1955).

On medieval warfare, the standard work is * C. W. C. Oman, *The Art of War in the Middle Ages,* rev. ed. (Ithaca, NY, 1953). Other important studies are J. Beeler, *Warfare in England 1066–1198* (Ithaca, NY, 1966); H. J. Hewitt, *The Organization of War Under Edward III* (Manchester, England, 1966); F. W. Brooks, *The English Naval Forces, 1199–1272* (London, 1962); S. Toy, *Castles: A Short History of Fortification from 1600 B.C. to A.D. 1600* (London, 1939); * P. Contamine, *War in the Middle Ages* (Oxford, England, 1984); and J. F. Verbruggen, *The Art of Warfare in Western Europe during the Middle Ages* (Amsterdam, 1977). G. Parker discusses the transition from medieval methods of warfare in * *The Military Revolution* (Cambridge, England, 1988).

chapter

XXVI

The End of the Great Schism

We have seen that the Council of Pisa tried to end the Great Schism by electing Alexander V as a pope of unity but that this merely produced three "popes" instead of two.* A new assembly, the Council of Constance, met in 1414. Its leaders were determined not only to end the schism but also to remedy all the other major ills of the church. The successes—and failures—of this council decisively shaped the history of the medieval Catholic church in the last century before the Protestant Reformation.

86. The Conciliarists, Wyclif, and Huss

At first it seemed that the Pisan popes might win the support of all Europe. The rulers of England, France, and Germany were all inclined to support them; but unfortunately the second pope of this line, who called himself John XXIII (1410–1415), was a disreputable scoundrel. He was a soldier by profession who rose to become a cardinal through his effectiveness as a civil governor in the Papal States. The cardinals elected him in the hope that he would occupy Rome and pacify central Italy, but he did not succeed even in these military tasks. In 1413 the emperor-elect Sigismund insisted that a new general council be held to seek a final solution to the schism. (Sigismund had been elected "King of the Romans" in 1410 but was not yet crowned emperor.) John XXIII reluctantly convoked a council, which assembled in the city of Constance at the end of 1414.

By this time, the issue facing the church was no longer just how to bring the schism to an end. Intellectuals in universities throughout Europe were urging that the constitutional structure of the church must be changed in such a way as to prevent the outbreak of any similar scandal in the future. The advocates of reform were also determined to bring about the moral regeneration of the church by

*See p. 541.

eliminating all the abuses that had grown up in the past century. Finally, they were anxious to eradicate a new form of heresy which had been spread in England by John Wyclif and in Bohemia by John Huss, a heresy which seemed to threaten the very existence of the church as an ordered institution.

The reformers whose ideas dominated the Council of Constance could be described as moderate constitutionalists. They favored a system of limited monarchy as the ideal pattern of church government. They wanted to unite the church again under a single pope but also to limit the pope's power in the future through frequent meetings of representative general councils. The leading theorists of this "conciliar movement" were drawn from several different nations. Among them were the Frenchmen Pierre d'Ailly (1350–1420) and Jean Gerson (1363–1429), both of whom were doctors of theology at the University of Paris; the Italian jurist Zabarella (1360–1417); and the German Dietrich of Niem (1338–1418). These men all participated actively in the work of the council. Naturally, there were differences of emphasis among them. Pierre d'Ailly wrote as a political theorist, much influenced by the work of William of Ockham. Gerson was essentially interested in moral reform and was prepared to back any system of church government that seemed likely to bring it about. Zabarella was a brilliant canonist who was able to present conciliarism as a coherent structure of constitutional law based on the old texts of the *Decretum*. Dietrich of Niem was a high official of the papal chancery, primarily interested in rooting out the administrative abuses of the curia.

The fundamental idea they all had in common was that the whole church was greater than any single individual within it, even the pope. Christ had promised that he would be with his church until the end of time, that the church could never fail. On the other hand, it seemed clear from contemporary events that the promise of unfailing divine guidance did not apply to the papacy. The conciliarists concluded from this that ultimate ecclesiastical authority resided with the whole Christian community or with a general council representing the community. The papal office was established by Christ, they acknowledged, but it existed to serve the church, and any individual pope might prove unworthy of his divine office. Cardinal Zabarella wrote that the pope was the highest officer in the church "so long as he rules well." If the pope ruled badly it was for the community, acting through a council, to correct him or in the last resort to depose him.

These ideas were by no means new. The novel thing in the fifteenth century was that there was a serious attempt to put them into practice. The conciliar theories were derived in part from the constitutional law of the twelfth-century canonists and in part from the royalist writers of the early fourteenth century like John of Paris. Marsilius of Padua and William of Ockham were influential too in that both of them transmitted in their works, and helped to popularize, a considerable body of earlier criticism of papal absolutism.* But the fifteenth-century conciliarists avoided the more personal and radical views of

*See pp. 318–319, 494–496.

Marsilius and Ockahm themselves, for example, Marsilius' denial of the divine origin of the papacy and Ockham's skepticism about the ability of a general council to represent the church fully.

It is important to distinguish between the ideas of the conciliarists and those of the contemporary reformers Wyclif and Huss. The prelates of the Council of Constance hated Wyclif and they killed Huss. The conciliarists were essentially medieval Catholics who intended to preserve the whole structure of the medieval church. Wyclif and Huss held positions closer to those of sixteenth-century Protestanism and called into question the legitimacy of all existing ecclesiastical institutions.

John Wyclif (ca. 1330–1384), a theologian of Oxford University, first became prominent around 1375 for attacking the wealth and luxury of the church and for maintaining that all church property was held only at the discretion of the secular authorities. At this time, a group of English nobles headed by John of Ghent, duke of Lancaster, were looking with greedy eyes on the possessions of the church and were delighted to find an ecclesiastical supporter. Wyclif was lucky in having the protection of the powerful duke of Lancaster for the rest of his life. His theory of the church grew out of a doctrine of dominion first developed in his writings on church property. True dominion belonged only to God, Wyclif pointed out, while humans acted as God's agents on earth. This was conventional enough, but Wyclif went on to argue that only people who were God's friends could rightfully exercise any form of dominion. Hence a person who fell into sin could not licitly own property or exercise jurisdiction. A sinful priest lost the power to administer sacraments; a sinful bishop possessed no episcopal jurisdiction. These views were associated with a belief in predestination. To Wyclif it was inconceivable that anything could happen that was not actively willed by God. Hence he believed that some people were predestined by their creator to salvation and some to damnation. The pope might well be one of the latter.*

Wyclif's theological views were largely based on the works of St. Augustine. Like Luther and Calvin after him, he found there the emphasis on the absolute power and dominance of God's will that was central in his thought. Yet Wyclif's doctrine that a sinful priest lost the power to administer sacraments was an unconscious revival of the Donatist position that Augustine had fought so hard.† This doctrine, moreover, threw the whole established sacramental system of the church into chaos, for people could never know for certain whether their priests or bishops were sinners. Wyclif accordingly argued that, while sacraments were useful and harmless, they were not really essential to salvation. The church and its rites had little place in a belief founded on the doctrine of predestination. In particular, Wyclif attacked the accepted teaching on the sacrament of the eucharist. He maintained that the bread and wine retained its substance—that is, remained bread and wine—after its consecration by the priest. Christ was present spiritually but not in substance.

Wyclif also maintained that the Christian way of life should be

*Sources, no. 81

†See p. 52.

sought in the Bible itself rather than in the teachings of the church. Hence it was necessary that the Bible should be available to everyone. Under his direction, certain of his followers produced two English translations that were to play an important part in the background of the Reformation. In short, from the point of view of orthodox clerics, Wyclif was clearly an extremely dangerous heretic. His political teachings endangered the property and revenues of the church. His theological views destroyed its spiritual authority. The clergy became a mere convenience unnecessary to salvation. Wyclif's doctrines were condemned by Pope Gregory XI in 1377 and, again, by an English council headed by the archbishop of Canterbury in 1382, but because of the protection of John of Ghent, he was able to live out his life in peace.

Even before Wyclif's death, his followers began preaching his doctrines in the English countryside. Some of these individuals were Oxford scholars, but more were poor priests. Later, laypeople began to wander about spreading Wyclif's teachings throughout the land. The followers of Wyclif were called Lollards, probably after a rather obscure German heretical sect. The preachers who wandered about the countryside, were, of course, violating ecclesiastical law by preaching condemned views and doing so without license, but during the reign of Richard II, the church could do little but arrest and imprison them. They usually cheerfully recanted and equally cheerfully returned to their preaching. When Henry IV came to the throne, Parliament passed a new statute called *De Haeretico Comburendo,* which specified that all who preached Lollardy were to be handed over to the church for trial and, if condemned, were to be burned by the secular authority. To Henry IV, this statute was more or less a formality. Although some Lollards were burned, the statue was not enforced with any great enthusiasm. Henry V, however, persecuted the sect with ruthlessness and vigor. By the end of his reign, open Lollardy had almost completely disappeared, though there is evidence that in various country districts it survived in secret until the Reformation.

Although Wyclif's followers never had any great influence in England and were fairly quickly suppressed, his ideas were extremely potent in the affairs of a distant land. From 1378 to 1419 Wenceslas, eldest son of the emperor Charles IV, ruled the kingdom of Bohemia. His sister Anne was the first wife of King Richard II of England. Many Bohemians followed Anne to England, and some were scholars who studied at the universities. There they soon learned of the teachings of Wyclif, and as early as 1380 some of his works were known in Bohemia. In 1401–1402 a noted Bohemian scholar, Jerome of Prague, brought Wyclif's theological writings over from England to add to the political works that had already arrived. Jerome was an enthusiastic supporter of Wyclif's ideas and soon found allies among other Bohemian scholars.

Charles IV, emperor and king of Bohemia, had been primarily devoted to the interests of his kingdom of Bohemia and hoped to make it the chief state of the Empire. In 1347 he had founded the University of Prague. It soon became a great international center of learning, with its faculty divided into the four traditional nations. Although it was the only university in Bohemia, it was essentially controlled by foreign scholars, since the Czechs formed but one of the four nations. It was among the Czech scholars at the University of Prague that Jerome found the most enthusiastic support for Wyclif's ideas. By 1403 the clergy became alarmed at the rapid spread of the new doctrines, and the archepiscopal chapter submitted forty-five articles drawn from Wyclif's works to the university for an opinion on their orthodoxy. After a fierce debate, they were duly condemned as heretical, but a minority of the Czech scholars opposed this action. Among these dissidents was Master John Huss.

John Huss (1370–1415) was an enthusiast for religious reform. A group of individuals interested in church reform had endowed a church, Bethlehem Chapel in Prague, to serve as a center for the preaching of Christian life. In 1402 Huss was appointed to this church and became an extremely popular preacher. In 1403, as we have seen, Huss was one of the Czech masters who opposed the condemnation of Wyclif's works. Although he was clearly sympathetic to much of Wyclif's teaching and certainly accepted some of it early in his career, as late as 1411 he solemnly denied that he believed in the chief points of Wyclif's doctrines. Huss was a preacher and reformer rather than a theologian and scholar. He used the ideas he needed and apparently did not bother too much about the rest of Wyclif's teaching. Huss certainly agreed with Wyclif's attacks on the wealth and worldliness of the higher clergy and with his emphasis on Scripture as the essential guide to Christian truth. He probably did not accept fully Wyclif's theories on the priesthood and the sacraments. Certainly, Huss' followers laid great emphasis on the central role of the eucharist in Christian life, and one of their principal demands was that the laity as well as the clergy should receive the consecrated wine at communion.

The national feeling of the Czechs had long chafed at the control of their university by the three foreign nations. The controversy over Wyclif's works made this issue more acute. While the majority of the Czech masters did not accept Wyclif's teachings and even forbade their students to read his works, they had no desire to take any action against those who did accept them—especially men like Huss who only adopted Wyclif's ideas in part. It was the German scholars who pressed for active suppression of the heretical ideas.

The crisis in Huss' career came in 1412. The disreputable John XXIII quarreled with the king of Naples and preached a crusade against him. Indulgences were promised to all who would join the expedition or contribute money to it. The giving of indulgences in exchange for money to benefit such a pontiff and such a cause was fiercely resented by all the reformers. Huss in particular preached against indulgences in general and this one in particular; thereupon the university renewed its condemnation of Wyclif's works with particular emphasis on certain of his arguments against indulgences that had been used by Huss. The pope excommunicated Huss and ordered

Bethlehem Chapel to be razed, while King Wenceslas expelled Huss' friends and supporters from the university and from Prague itself. Huss retired to the Bohemian countryside, where he continued his preaching, appealing now to the Czech peasantry in the fields and villages. When the convocation of the Council of Constance was announced, Huss voluntarily declared that he would appear before the council to defend the orthodoxy of his teaching. The emperor-elect Sigismund gave him a safe conduct, and he left Prague for Constance in October 1414.

87. *The Council of Constance*

The Council of Constance was a splendid affair. All the great nations sent representatives: the council was attended by twenty-nine cardinals, nearly two hundred bishops, a hundred abbots, and more than three hundred doctors of theology and canon law. There was also to begin with a pope, if we can count John XXIII. King Sigismund, the emperor-elect, was present too and played a major part in the conduct of the council.

The assembly faced three tasks: to end the schism, to root out heresy, and to reform the church. Pope John, who had summoned the council and was at first accepted as pope by all its members, hoped that the assembled prelates would simply repeat the previous condemnations of his two rivals and confirm him as pope. Nearly half the bishops present at the beginning of the council were Italians, and John could rely on their support. The numerical advantage of the Italians was neutralized, however, by a procedural maneuver. The northern delegations insisted that the council be divided into "nations" in the manner of the medieval universities, with each nation casting one vote. There were at first four nations—Italian, French, English, and German. The Spanish formed a fifth when they joined the council in 1416.

At the beginning of 1415, it became clear that the northern nations were determined to investigate John XXIII's fitness to be pope as well as the claims of his rivals. John at first promised to abdicate but then, on March 20, fled from the council and withdrew his promise, hoping that the council would dissolve in the absence of a legitimate head. After a few days of confusion, Sigismund, supported by Cardinals d'Ailly and Zabarella, succeeded in rallying the members of the assembly. They came together in a general session on March 26 and declared that they would continue to sit as a general council and carry through the reform of the church whether the pope returned or not. It was now necessary for the assembly to promulgate a constitutional statute defining the nature of its own authority and, after ten days of confused debate, the following measure was adopted on April 6. It is usually known as *Haec Sancta* (or *Sacrosancta*).

> This holy synod of Constance . . . declares that, being lawfully assembled in the Holy Spirit, constituting a general council and representing the Catholic Church militant, it has its power directly from Christ and that all persons of whatever rank, state or dignity, even the papal, are bound to obey it in manners relating to the faith, the ending of the schism and the general reform of the church in head and members.

The decree added that popes were similarly bound by the acts of "any other general council, lawfully assembled." *Haec Sancta* has been called a "revolutionary" document. It was certainly a very explicit assertion of the sovereign power of a representative assembly in the church. From this time on, the idea of a sort of divine right inherent in the community was always present in Western thought to balance the divine-right theory of monarchy.*

The council now proceeded swiftly against John XXIII. On May 14, 1415, he was suspended under charges of fornication, adultery, incest, sodomy, and poisoning his predecessor. He was probably guilty of a moderate percentage of these offenses. On May 29 he was solemnly deposed and acquiesced in the sentence. The pontiff of the Roman line, Gregory XII, had by now been abandoned by virtually all his supporters and, under threat of deposition, he offered to abdicate. Gregory insisted to the end that he was true pope. His legate was permitted to read a bull at Constance convoking the prelates as a general council for the second time. Then Gregory resigned on July 4, 1415; his cardinals joined the council at Constance and were accepted as cardinals.

*Sources, no. 96

There was now only one pope left, Benedict XIII of the Avignon line. With his rivals removed, this obstinate and wily old man was more

John Huss being burned at the stake after his condemnation at the Council of Constance. Illustration from *Chronik der Konstance Koncils. Rosgartenmuseum, Konstanz*

determined than ever to cling to his office. He was still recognized by the kings of Castile, Aragon, and Navarre. In the summer of 1415, Sigismund himself traveled to Spain to conduct negotiations with Benedict and his supporters. He could not move the pope, but he persuaded the Spanish kings to desert his cause and send delegates to Constance. Benedict's cardinals also deserted him and joined the council. Finally, on July 26, 1417, Benedict was deposed as a heretic, schismatic, and perjurer. The council then set up an electoral college to choose the next pope. The cardinals (forming one college from all three obediences) and representatives of each of the five nations were to vote in six separate groups; two-thirds of the votes of each group was required for an election. By this procedure, the council chose Cardinal Odo Colonna at the end of 1417, and he took office as Pope Martin V (1417–1431). Benedict XIII never accepted his deposition but retired to a family fortress at Peniscola and appointed new cardinals. They elected yet another pope when Benedict died in 1423, but this Clement VIII, as he called himself, had no significant support anywhere in Europe and he abdicated in 1429. Effectively, the Great Schism was ended by the election of Martin V in 1417.

The Council of Constance thus succeeded admirably in its first task of reuniting the church. It was less effective in its approach to the second problem, that of rooting out heresy. John Huss arrived at the council on November 3, 1414; in spite of Sigismund's promise of safe conduct, he was thrown into prison on November 28. Sigismund made genuine, though not overenergetic, attempts to obtain his release. The council, however, insisted that Sigismund's safe conduct to a heretic was invalid. It is interesting to note that in later years a more determined emperor forced the acceptance of a safe conduct granted to Martin Luther. Immediately after the council had affirmed its own supremacy in matters of faith in the decree *Haec Sancta*, it appointed a commission to examine Huss. He was ordered to state his position on forty-five articles drawn from Wyclif's works and forty-two from his own. He stated that he agreed with some of Wyclif's beliefs and refused to disown his own teachings when the council demanded that he do so. On July 6, 1415, Huss was degraded from the priesthood and turned over to the secular power. Sigismund, to his everlasting shame, had him burned. A year later, Jerome of Prague, who had come to Constance to support Huss, was also burned. Presumably, the prelates at Constance were exasperated by Huss' refusal to recognize the overriding authority of the council during the critical weeks of negotiation with John XXIII and Gregory XII, when the whole future unity of the church seemed to depend on a universal acknowledgment of that authority. But the circumstances do not justify their behavior. Huss was a radical reformer but probably not an obdurate heretic. If his examiners had given him a sympathetic hearing, they might have achieved a reconciliation and prevented much future trouble.

The execution of Huss was not only cruel; it was stupid. Many Bohemians of all classes saw Huss as a beloved preacher who had been martyred by the clergy he sought to reform. He also became a considerable symbol of Czech nationalism. It seems clear that Huss had many friends and supporters, especially among the nobles, who had little interest in the details of his theology. In May 1415, while Huss was in prison awaiting trial, a large assembly of Bohemian nobles wrote to the council in his favor. His death roused them to fury, and in September, five hundred nobles swore they would not recognize any action of the council. For a while the pot simply seethed, but in 1419 a Hussite mob seized Prague and massacred the town council. Sigismund, who had just succeeded his brother Wenceslas as king of Bohemia, marched on Prague and was utterly routed by the rebels. There followed a series of crusades against the Hussites led by Sigismund. Each time the proud chivalry of the Empire was thoroughly routed by the wild peasant armies entrenched behind their gun-laden wagons. The Council of Constance had precipitated this problem. It was left for other councils to solve.

The third task that faced the prelates of Constance was to bring about a general reform of the church. Here again its record was not very impressive. Many reform proposals were debated. It was proposed that local councils be held in all the provinces of Christendom to reform the lives of the diocesan clergy. There were many suggestions for limiting papal indulgences and privileges and for reducing papal taxation. Protests were made against overt simoniacal trafficking in papally filled benefices and against pluralities and absenteeism. But in the end, little was accomplished. The reform of the church became a major topic of discussion at the council after the deposition of Benedict XIII in 1417, but a split quickly developed between the more conservative and the more radical members. The conservatives wanted to elect a pope of unity and let him direct the work of reform. The radicals wanted to take advantage of the fact that the papacy was vacant to enact a sweeping program of reforms before making an election so that the incoming pontiff would be faced by a *fait accompli.* The situation was greatly complicated by animosities that were growing up among the different nations represented at Constance. The Hundred Years' War had begun again in 1415. Sigismund was an ally of the English king. It was hard for the English, French, and Germans to work smoothly together in any conciliar business, and these were the nations that had been most in favor of thoroughgoing reform.

Eventually it was decided that the task of reforming the church could not be completed at Constance, but should be undertaken in a series of future councils. Accordingly, an important constitutional measure, the canon *Frequens,* was enacted. It specified that a new council was to meet in five years, another seven years later, a third ten years after that, and then one every ten years in the future. At the end of each council, the time and place of the next one was to be specified. If the reigning pope failed to convoke a council at the appropriate time, it was to assemble spontaneously. Similarly, if a schism arose, a council was to assemble within a year at the place designated for the next meeting without any papal convocation.*

*Sources, no. 97

In addition to considering the schism, heresy, and reform, the Council of Constance spent a great deal of time on miscellaneous matters. All the ordinary routine business of the papal curia was carried on by it during the session. Then, there were various disputes to settle. The most important one, apart from those we have mentioned, concerned the licitness of tyrannicide. A Burgundian clerk, Jean Petit, had maintained after the murder of Louis of Orleans that to kill a tyrant was a just and virtuous act. The Orleanists wanted the council to declare the doctrine heretical, and to condemn Jean and his ducal master. After long and fierce debate, the council gently hedged. It announced that tyrannicide was unjustifiable, but carefully mentioned no names.

88. *The Victory of the Popes*

The Council of Constance solved the problem of the Great Schism but only by raising new problems concerning the constitutional structure of the church. The fathers of Constance had proclaimed the supremacy of general councils in ecclesiastical government and had provided for the summoning of future councils at regular intervals. If the decrees *Haec Sancta* and *Frequens* had been fulfilled to the letter, the Roman church might have grown into the first great constitutional monarchy of the modern world. Instead, the popes succeeded in destroying the conciliar movement, but only at the price of abandoning reform.

The attitude of Pope Martin V to the decrees of the Council of Constance was ambiguous. The most clear-cut evidence that he did in principle accept all the decisions of the council as valid is provided by the bull *Inter Cunctos*, which he promulgated in 1418. This dealt with the interrogation of suspected Hussite heretics. Among other things, the suspects were required to affirm that they accepted all the decrees of the Council of Constance. The particular decree that the framers of the bull had in mind was, of course, the sentence against Huss. But the council that had condemned Huss in 1415 was exactly the same body that had enacted the decree *Haec Sancta* three months earlier. It was, indeed, by virtue of the authority claimed in *Haec Sancta* that the council had proceeded against Huss. Moreover, the validity of Martin V's own election depended on the validity of the preceding decrees of Constance. It was the council that had ended the schism and authorized the novel form of electoral college which chose Martin.

The pope realized all this and never overtly attacked any of the declarations of the Council of Constance. On the other hand, he displayed a total lack of enthusiasm for the program of constitutional reform that the leaders of the council had envisaged. The first council provided for in the decrees of Constance met at Pavia in 1423 and quickly moved to Siena because of an outbreak of the plague. The members bickered with one another and with the pope, and Martin took advantage of their disagreements to dissolve the council before anything significant had been accomplished. The next council was scheduled to meet at Basel in July 1431. After duly convoking this assembly, Martin died at the beginning of that year. The issue of supremacy in the church was fought out between the Council of Basel and the next pope, Eugenius IV (1431–1447).

The opening sessions of the Council of Basel were dominated by news of a great Hussite victory at the battle of Taussig (August 14, 1431). The council decided to send delegates to offer concessions to the Hussites. Eugenius IV, determined to keep all negotiations with the rebels in his own hands, dissolved the council in December 1431. This set the stage for a final series of confrontations between pope and council. The prelates at Basel—there were very few bishops there, but a large number of lesser clergy including many doctors of theology and canon law—refused to be dismissed, and in 1432 they reenacted the legislation of Constance affirming the principle of conciliar supremacy. The princes of Europe were inclined to support the council, and in 1434 Eugenius suffered a major humiliation: he was compelled to withdraw his bull dissolving the council, to acknowledge that all its sessions had been canonical and to confirm its legislation.

Meanwhile, the council had been negotiating successfully with the Hussites. Ever since the wars in Bohemia began, the Hussites, under two great leaders, Zizka and Procop, had proved unbeatable on the battlefield, but they were becoming badly divided among themselves. Even while Huss was alive, he and his supporters had had rather divergent doctrines. Thus Huss never accepted the teachings of Wyclif as completely as had Jerome of Prague. Once their leader was dead, the Hussites split into a wide variety of different sects. Almost every known heresy and a few new ones soon appeared under the Hussite cloak, and the members of the party ranged from conservative nobles who wanted only the right to have the laity share the wine with the clergy at communion to wild radicals who wanted complete communism. The latter group, known as Taborites, accepted the full Wycliffite doctrine of the church with some added eccentricities of their own. In 1420 the various groups managed to concoct a statement of principles that all agreed on, known as the "Four Articles of Prague," but it represented only the fundamental demands they had in common. People were to preach freely as they wished; the laity were to have the wine; large church estates were to be confiscated; and all sins severely punished. So firm a reputation for moral ardor did the Hussites develop that, when the Council of Basel expected a delegation from them, it ordered all the prostitutes off the streets of the city.

By 1434 the more conservative Hussites had become thoroughly alarmed by the radicals and were yearning for peace. The council agreed to their demand that the laity should receive the consecrated wine and, on this basis, an alliance was formed between moderate Hussite and Catholic nobles in Bohemia. In 1434 they were able to defeat the radicals; in 1436 Sigismund entered Prague and was generally acknowledged as king of Bohemia. After his death in 1437, more fighting broke out leading to the establishment of a moderate Hussite as king. This was George Podiebrad (1458–1471). During his reign, the pope unwisely repudiated the concession of 1434 and so precipitated yet another series of conflicts. Hussites were still fighting Catholics in Bohemia at the end of the fifteenth century. The agreement of 1434, however, brought to an end the most dangerous period of Hussite power and was a triumph for the Council of Basel.

The leaders of the council next turned to the task of reforming the church, but by this time reform had come to mean little more than limiting the powers of the pope almost to the point of abolishing them. This position was far more radical than the original program of Constance and, from this time onward, many of the more moderate conciliarists began to move over to the support of the pope. Among them was Nicholas of Cusa, one of the leading theorists of the conciliar movement in the earlier stages of the Council of Basel. In 1435 the council passed a decree that would have virtually eliminated all the papal revenues from outside the Papal States. Now Eugenius began to fight back again, his position strengthened by a new development. The Byzantine emperor, faced with the rapidly growing power of the Turks, decided that the only hope of obtaining help from western Europe lay in ending the old schism between the Greek and Latin churches. The crucial question was whether the Greeks would choose to negotiate with the pope or with the council. In 1437 the emperor made his decision and sent delegates to the pope in Italy. Eugenius ordered the prelates at Basel to assemble in Ferrara for a new council of unity, and virtually all the bishops obeyed the papal command. The Council of Ferrara (transferred to Florence in 1439) was firmly under papal control from the beginning, and it enacted a decree reaffirming the pope's plenitude of power over the whole church by virtue of his role as Vicar of Christ. The Greek representatives accepted this principle and a decree of union was issued, but as it was never recognized by the Greek church as a whole, it had no real effect.

The minority of ecclesiastics who refused to obey the pope and stayed in session at Basel went through the farce of solemnly deposing Eugenius IV and electing an antipope named Felix V (1439–1449). Few people could have supposed at this time that a small and quite unrepresentative group of radicals calling itself a general council could licitly depose a pope who was at that very moment presiding over a much more full and representative assembly. The existence of the antipope acquired significance only because a number of secular princes used the threat of supporting him to extract concessions from the papacy. In 1438 a council of the French church, dominated by the royal government, adopted the Pragmatic Sanction of Bourges. This forbade the payment of certain taxes to Rome and ended all papal rights to appoint people to benefices in France. Bishops and abbots were to be elected by the chapters. The king and princes would "use benign and well-intentioned solicitation in favor of persons of merit who were zealous for the good of the church and the realm." This passage shows clearly the difference in interests between princes and reformers. The Council of Basel had simply decreed the right of chapters to elect without interference from the papacy, but the reformers had no desire to give the pope's former power to the prince. The Pragmatic Sanction of Bourges made the king the master of the French church. Although the Pragmatic Sanction was repealed by Louis XI, its essential provisions are found in the concordats that later governed the relations between the French kings and the popes. In 1439 the German princes issued the Pragmatic Sanction of Mainz, which enacted similar measures in Germany. It was modified by a concordat between the princes and Pope Nicholas V, arrived at in 1448, by which the pope gave up the right to appoint bishops and abbots in Germany but regained some of the taxes that had been previously abolished.

Having reached this agreement with the pope, the princes no longer had any interest in supporting the antipope Felix V, who abdicated in 1449. This marked the end of the conciliar movement and the victory of the papacy. In the second half of the fifteenth century, the doctrine of papal supremacy was strongly reaffirmed. Perhaps even more important was the fact that the church had most decidedly not been reformed. In fact, the pope who finally triumphed over the Council of Basel, Nicholas V (1447–1455), was a scholarly humanist most noted as a patron of arts and letters—the first Renaissance pope. At his court lived as his librarian Lorenzo Valla, who had proved the Donation of Constantine to be a forgery and who was to advocate such novel ideas as turning all nunneries into what a less broad-minded age would call houses of ill fame.

The conciliar movement never had much chance of succeeding. There was simply not enough urgent will to reform among the worldly and wealthy prelates of the fifteenth century. The conciliarists, moreover, were out of touch with the mood of the times. They wanted to set up an international council to rule the church in an age of growing nationalism. They wanted to establish intricate constitutional restraints on monarchy at a time when most people were looking for strong rulers to curb anarchy. The hostile attitude of the popes to the program of Constance destroyed any possibility of its being realized. The attitude of the princes was also not helpful in the long run. They saw that, if the power of the papacy was reduced, princely control over the various churches might be strengthened. But, unfortunately for the conciliar party, the princes often gave primary concern to immediate diplomatic problems. Whatever the papacy might become in the future, it had been in the past and was still a potent political power. Although a prince might realize that in the long run it was to the interest of his dynasty to reduce the papal power, he might at the moment be desperately anxious to win the support of the reigning pope. Hence, throughout the controversy, the policy of the princes was inconsistent and vacillating. Moreover, few princes had any real sympathy with the constitutional theories of the conciliarists. On one occasion, Pope Eugenius IV wrote to the king of France pointing out that, if the king persisted in supporting subversive movements in the church, he might expect to find similar movements growing up in the state. The argument was apparently convincing when it had had time to sink in, and eventually all the secular princes threw their support to the papacy.

In one sense, the conciliar movement was not a failure. It not only reunited the church; its intellectual leaders also worked out the first detailed, systematic theories of representative government. Their writings form an important chapter in the history of medieval political thought and greatly influenced theories of secular constitutionalism in the sixteenth and seventeenth centuries. But, so far as the task of revivifying the medieval church was concerned, conciliarism certainly failed, and its failure was a tragedy for the Catholic church. If the work of reform that was carried out a century later at the Council of Trent could have been done at Constance and Basel, it is possible that the Protestant Reformation would never have taken place. But in fact, despite the earnest efforts of many church officials, no effective general reform was achieved. Moreover, the secular princes had succeeded to a great extent in setting up national churches largely under their own control and were watching eagerly for any opportunity to make that control more complete. Heresy was rampant in secret in many lands, and openly in Bohemia. At the end of the Middle Ages, the essential foundations for the Reformation were solidly laid.

READING SUGGESTIONS

* *B. Tierney,* Sources *and* Readings, *vol. I, nos. 80, 96–97.*

On the background of the conciliar movement, see E. F. Jacob, *Essays in the Conciliar Epoch,* 3rd ed. (Manchester, England, 1963); B. Tierney, *Foundations of the Conciliar Theory* (Cambridge, England, 1955); * J. N. Figgis, *From Gerson to Grotius,* 2nd ed. (Cambridge, England, 1916); and * A. J. Black, *Monarchy and Community* (Cambridge, England, 1970). Good studies on particular authors are J. B. Morrall, *Gerson and the Great Schism* (Manchester, England, 1961); F. Oakley, *The Political Thought of Pierre d'Ailly* (New Haven, CT, 1964); P. Sigmund, *Nicholas of Cusa* (Cambridge, MA, 1963); and M. Watanabe, *The Political Ideas of Nicholas of Cusa* (Geneva, 1963). On the conciliarists and later political theory see B. Tierney, *Religion, Law, and the Growth of Constitutional Thought, 1150–1650* (Cambridge, England, 1982).

The standard work on Wyclif is H. B. Workman, *John Wyclif,* 2 vols. (Oxford, England, 1926). For good, briefer introductions see K. B. McFarlane, *John Wycliffe and the Beginnings of English Nonconformity* (London, 1952); J. Dahmus, *The Prosecution of John Wyclif* (New Haven, CT, 1952); and * A. J. P. Kenny, *Wyclif* (Oxford, England, 1985). J. A. Robson, *Wyclif and the Oxford Schools* (Cambridge, England, 1961) is more technical. G. Leff, *Heresy in the Later Middle Ages,* vol. II (Manchester, England, 1967) deals with both Wyclif and Huss. Other good works on Huss and the Hussite wars are M. Spinka, *John Hus and the Czech Reform* (Chicago, 1941) and *John Huss: A Biography* (Princeton, 1968); H. Kaminsky, *A History of the Hussite Revolution* (Berkeley, 1967); and F. G. Heymann, *John Zizka and the Hussite Revolution* (Princeton, 1955) and *George of Bohemia* (Princeton, 1965). For theories of the Church among late medieval nominalists, see H. A. Oberman, *The Harvest of Medieval Theology* (Cambridge, MA, 1963).

On the defeat of conciliarism and the restoration of papal power, see J. Gill, *The Council of Florence* (Cambridge, England, 1959) and *Eugenius IV* (Westminster, MD, 1961); D. P. Partner, *The Papal State Under Martin V* (London, 1958); and J. W. Stieber, *Pope Eugenius IV, the Council of Basel, and the Secular and Ecclesiastical Authorities in the Empire* (Leiden, 1978). F. Oakley provides an excellent overview of the whole period in * *The Western Church in the Later Middle Ages* (Ithaca, NY, 1980). The following books contain translated sources: M. Spinka, *Advocates of Reform* (Philadelphia, 1953) and *John Hus at the Council of Constance* (New York, 1961); L. R. Loomis, *The Council of Constance* (New York, 1961); Aeneas Piccolominus (Pope Pius II), *De Gestis Concilii Basiliensis*, D. Hay and W. H. Smith (trans.) (Oxford, England, 1967); and * L. M. D. Crowder, *Unity, Heresy and Reform, 1378–1460* (London, 1977).

chapter

XXVII

The Growth of National Monarchy

During the later Middle Ages, the authority of royal governments increased very greatly. The decay of feudal ideas had vitally changed the relationship between the king and his people and the institutions that gave it effect. The conception of a primarily tenurial relationship running through the feudal hierarchy gradually disappeared. No longer was the king's concern limited largely to the interests and desires of his tenants-in-chief; he was the ruler of all the people who lived in his land and was expected to consider their common welfare. This change in the relationship between the king and the inhabitants of his land brought the beginnings of what the historian calls *nationalism.* The subjects of each king began to feel that they had common interests and were bound together through their ruler. They developed a feeling that this was the way God had intended things to be and would not lightly transfer their allegiance to another ruler. Everywhere people looked to their kings to provide the peace and order that all classes but the feuding nobility longed for.

This strong traditional feeling for a dynasty could be a very potent patriotic force, and it greatly strengthened the power of kings who learned to exploit it. As the sentiment of nationalism developed in the various states of western Europe, the map of the region became more stabilized, and lasting conquests by force more difficult. By the end of the fifteenth century, virtually all the great states of modern Europe had become permanently established political entities.

89. *France and Burgundy*

Charles VII of France (1422–1461) is commonly known as the "Well-served," and rarely has an appellation been more appropriate. Joan of Arc won him his crown, and Richmont and his fellow captains expelled the English from France. His finances were managed by a great merchant, Jacques Coeur, who both augmented the royal revenue and spread the commercial influence of France into the eastern Mediterranean. The wisdom of Charles' ministers brought about the military reforms already mentioned, primarily the establishment of a standing army. They also took advantage of the French people's willingness to provide revenues for the purpose of expelling the English to establish complete royal control of taxation. After Charles' reign, the king no longer felt any need to consult the *Estates General* before levying taxes.

Although Charles' ministers succeeded in increasing the royal authority in his demesne, his lack of any effective control over the princes kept him from being a powerful ruler of all France. The Treaty of Arras gave the duke of Burgundy almost complete independence. Although the royal princes whose lands lay in the interior of the kingdom—the dukes of Anjou, Orleans, and Bourbon—were not quite so autonomous as the duke of Burgundy, Philip the Good, they were pretty much the masters of their own lands. A few great lords, in addition to the royal princes, had almost equal power and independence. The most dangerous of these were the great barons of the south: the count of Foix, who was also king of Navarre; the lord of Albret; and the count of Armagnac. Each of these princes had his own court, his petty bureaucracy, and his private army. They were continually forming alliances for their mutual benefit to plague Charles and his government. Many of these leagues against Charles were headed by his son, the Dauphin Louis. Occasionally one of the weaker princes would go too far. Thus the duke of Alençon and the count of Armagnac lost their lands for making the error of revolting without adequate support from the greater lords.

While the princes who either had sufficient autonomy to levy their own taxes or could at least oblige the king to give them a good share of the royal levies taken from their estates flourished, the lesser nobles were in a difficult position. In the course of the fourteenth century, many of them had leased their productive lands at fixed rents. Hence any inflation seriously reduced their real income. During the Hundred Years' War, variations in prices were largely the result of depreciations of the coinage; once the war was over, however, France quickly recovered its prosperity, and prices rose as in any boom period. Thus only the greatest of the nobles could live in style on the revenues of their estates; others were forced to seek new sources of income. The most natural course was to enter the service of the king or a prince. The king and the duke of Burgundy employed many nobles as soldiers and officials and granted pensions to many others whose support they wanted. Indeed, the idea of a pension from the royal treasury was far from repugnant to the lesser princes. Most of the coalitions against the crown were dissolved by the simple expedient of giving generous annuities to the leaders. In short, if the nobles were to live like nobles, they had to do so at the expense of the general taxpayer, as dependents of the king.

When Charles VII died in 1461, the Dauphin Louis was in exile at the court of his father's bitter enemy Philip the Good. Louis had fled from France after the collapse of one of his conspiracies against the king. From his refuge in Burgundy, he had bribed his father's physician to notify him promptly of any good news about the king's failing health, if not actually to hasten the process. Louis XI (1461–1483) was the most unpleasant and unkingly man ever to occupy the throne of France. He was extremely homely and dressed meanly. When he first entered his realm as king, he noticed some people smiling at his costume and promptly inflicted a crushing fine on the town he was passing through. Although he was very religious, his religion was largely a matter of superstition, leading him to cover his clothes with religious insignia and to bribe all the saints before undertaking an important operation. He had no sense of ordinary decency. When he learned that his daughter was so hopeless a cripple that she could never bear children, he promptly married her to Louis, the heir of the house of Orleans, in order to extinguish that princely line. Louis loved low company. His favorite pastime was sitting in a public tavern drinking and telling dirty stories. He surrounded himself with low-born men, many of whom had criminal records, and made them his most trusted servants and officials. His only noble taste was for hunting, and he spent enormous sums on horses and hunting dogs. He was, however, an effective king. The middle classes who were becoming more and more important admired his simple if crude tastes. His officials, although cruel and unprincipled, served him well—or went quickly to the gallows. Louis was highly intelligent, completely lacking in scruples, and a master of intrigue. All these qualities were of help in dealing with the princes. He had no use whatever for war—bad luck could bring a disastrous defeat. It was just as cheap and far more effective to get one's way by intrigue, well enforced with bribes.

The chief task facing Louis if he wanted to solidify the royal authority was to reduce the power of the princes. Shortly after he ascended the throne, a great coalition calling itself the League of the Public Weal rose in revolt under the leadership of his own brother, the duke of Berry, and the dukes of Burgundy, Bourbon, and Anjou. A great battle was fought, in which both sides retreated as soon as they came together, and victory was claimed by the one that retired the shortest distance. Then the two armies faced each other quietly for some months across a river. Eventually, the "Public Weal" was safeguarded by generous grants of lands and pensions to the princes and their chief followers. Louis was obliged to give Normandy to his brother, thus cutting the royal demesne off from the Channel and connecting the princely estates of Burgundy with those of the duke of Brittany through the lands of their ally. The princes believed that they had won the struggle and reduced Louis to complete impotence. They were very sadly mistaken. The king soon succeeded in sowing seeds of dissension between his brother and the duke of Brittany and before long made the former's position in Normandy so uncomfortable that he gladly accepted Gascony instead and thus became separated from his princely associates. There, in the pleasant lands of the south, he rapidly drank himself to death. Later on Louis persuaded the duke of Anjou to bequeath his lands to the crown and secured the friendship of Bourbon by marrying his daughter to the heir of the duchy.

By far the most dangerous of the princes was the duke of Burgundy. The revenues from the prosperous towns of the Low Countries made him the richest prince of western Europe; only the Republic of Venice could compete with him in this respect. His court was unrivaled for splendor and luxury, and in it were developing the etiquette and complicated ceremonial procedures that were to mark the royal courts of later years. Philip the Good was a patron of arts and letters. Italian craftsmen embellished the Burgundian capital at Dijon, and the best Flemish artists painted the duke and his courtiers. While Philip's personal taste in literature ran chiefly to salacious stories, he was a generous patron of a wide variety of writers. Throughout his life, the duke dreamed of leading the forces of Christendom in a grand crusade to crush the Turkish power, but he never did anything about it except to inaugurate the magnificent chivalric order of the Golden Fleece. Philip had a large and effective army and was served by many of the greatest nobles of France. Fortunately for the French monarchy, he preferred dreaming about crusades to nourishing practical political designs. As long as he was left alone in his estates, he was content to be the most powerful and magnificent of French princes.

In 1467 Duke Philip died and was succeeded by his son Charles, known as the Rash. The new duke was determined to make the most of the political opportunities his father had ignored. If he could add Alsace and Lorraine to his domains, he would have the northern part of the ancient kingdom of Lothair.* Once that was accomplished, the conquest of either the valley of the Rhone or Switzerland would place him at the gates to Italy, and that peninsula was in no state to resist so powerful a prince. But even without Italy, he could have a great state between France and Germany, and diligent diplomacy backed by might should persuade the emperor to grant him the royal title he craved. In short, Charles was not content to remain a French prince but wanted to be king of Lotharingia. Had his plans succeeded, the whole political structure of early modern Europe would have taken a different form. If the French state was not to be gravely weakened, Louis had to defeat the plans of the Burgundian duke.

Louis XI promptly put his skill at intrigue and bribery to work against his formidable foe. His agents stirred up discontent in the lands of Charles and his allies, while generous subsidies flowed to all the duke's enemies. Soon Louis had so many different schemes in motion that he could not keep track of them all. In 1468 he paid a visit to Charles at Peronne, apparently forgetting that his agents were stirring up a revolt against the duke's ally, the bishop of Liège. When the impetuous duke heard that the people of Liège had rebelled with Louis' encouragement, he imprisoned his royal guest. By skillful bribery of Charles' ministers, Louis secured his freedom, but he was obliged to suffer the humiliation of helping Charles to punish Liège.

*See p. 149.

The elegance and splendor of the Burgundian court in the 15th century far surpassed that of the king of France. Here Philip the Good, duke of Burgundy and a famous patron of the arts, receives a copy of the *Chroniques de Hainault* of Jacques de Guise. Miniature from the manuscript, Flemish, 1448. Ms. 9242, fol. lr. *Bibliothèque Royale de Belgique, Brussels*

For a time, the duke's plans continued to go well. Within a few years, he had conquered all Alsace and Lorraine except for a few towns, and although the emperor Frederick III showed no enthusiasm for granting him the royal dignity, he recognized Charles' conquest of the two duchies. Then, in 1476, Charles turned his arms against the Swiss. This was the turning point of his career. In two great battles, the Swiss spearmen routed the chivalry of Burgundy. After these victories, Swiss troops paid by Louis entered the service of the duke of Lorraine and marched to relieve the town of Nancy, which was being besieged by Charles. Louis had also thoughtfully bribed one of Charles' mercenary captains to betray him. As a result, the Burgundians were defeated and the duke slain.

The death of Charles gave Louis a magnificent opportunity, but one that he did not know how to exploit. The heir to the vast Burgundian lands was the duke's daughter, Mary, who was in the custody of the stubborn burghers of Flanders. Whoever married Mary would acquire her lands, but he would have to be acceptable to both Mary and the burghers. As the latter were French in their sympathy, Louis seemed in a strong position. Unfortunately, Louis' son, Charles, the obvious candidate, was a mere baby, and despite the king's urging,

Mary refused to consider him. Although there were several French princes who would have been acceptable, Louis hesitated to let one of them take the place of Charles the Rash. While he pondered his problem, the emperor acted. Maximilian of Hapsburg, son and heir of Frederick III, married Mary and became lord of her lands. All Louis could do was declare the marriage illegal because it lacked his consent and seize the duchy of Burgundy. As Flanders was too strong to occupy, it passed to Maximilian and was lost to France forever.

At the close of the reign of Louis XI, the French monarchy was well on the way to becoming absolute. The government was conducted by a bureaucracy almost completely dependent on the king's will. *Estates General* were no longer summoned since the king could levy taxes as he saw fit. With this revenue, he maintained a standing army to support his authority. Only two princely houses of importance remained in existence, Orleans and Bourbon, and both were allied by marriage to the royal family. While there were a number of secondary houses, such as those of the dukes of Lorraine and Montpensier and the lords of Albret, who could give trouble if they formed an effective coalition, their diverse interests made a dangerous combination unlikely. The nobles of France were to make attempts in the future to dominate the royal government, but their efforts to rival it were at an end.

90. The Hapsburg Empire

The settlement of the Burgundian question influenced the future of Germany as well as that of France in that it marked an important stage in the rise of the house of Hapsburg. After the death of Sigismund in 1437, the German crown passed first to Albert V of Hapsburg (1438–1439) and then to his distant cousin Frederick of Hapsburg (1440–1493). This Frederick III had a long but entirely inglorious and ineffective reign. Apart from arranging the fortunate marriage alliance of his son, Maximilian, he achieved nothing except to retain his title and to perpetuate the Hapsburg dynasty. The process of national consolidation that was so evident in France (and which characterized other fifteenth-century states as well) did not take place in Germany under Frederick III. There was no increase in the power of the imperial government. Indeed, Frederick did not govern anything except his own hereditary duchy of Austria and he even lost that for a time.

On the other hand, consolidation and centralization did take place within the separate principalities. At the end of the fifteenth century, a group of very able rulers succeeded in imposing more disciplined government on several of the most important states of Germany. Prominent among them were Albert Achilles of Brandenburg (1471–1486), Lewis of Bavaria (1450–1479), and Magnus of Mecklenburg (1477–1503). These men all succeeded in establishing the rule that only the prince had a right to convoke the *estates general* of his territories. Also, they were all able to induce their *estates* to make substantial grants of taxation by persuasion or coercion, and they used the taxes to build up more efficient systems of administration. When cities or nobles produced ancient charters exempting them from taxation, the princes successfully invoked the Roman law doctrine of sovereignty, which held that levying taxes was an inherent and inalienable right of the ruler. By such means, the autonomous centralized principalities, which remained the basic political units of Germany down to the nineteenth century, were brought into existence.

Two other political developments—of the greatest importance for later European diplomatic history—need to be mentioned briefly here. At the end of the fifteenth century, Italy became a battleground between France and the Hapsburg empire. Cosimo de Medici had negotiated a treaty in 1455, the Peace of Lodi, which established a rough balance of power among the major Italian states (Venice, Milan, Florence, the papacy, and the kingdom of Naples). In 1495 the balance was disrupted by a dispute between Naples and Milan. Ludovico Sforza of Milan appealed to the French for help; in response King Charles VIII of France (1483–1498) reasserted the old French claim of the house of Anjou to the throne of Naples and invaded Italy. His army of thirty thousand men swept through the peninsula, occupying in turn Florence, Rome, and Naples. Charles soon had to withdraw because of threats to his communication lines in the north, and Ferdinand of Aragon sent Spanish troops to reoccupy Naples. But Charles' campaign had shown the vulnerability of the rich Italian cities. Subsequently Italy was invaded repeatedly by French, Spanish, and Austrian armies. The Italians had lost for centuries any chance of developing as an independent nation.

The other political development which requires notice here was the creation of the Swiss Confederation. Northern Switzerland was originally a part of the duchy of Swabia, and in the fourteenth century the Hapsburgs, who were the most powerful house in Swabia, attempted to extend their authority over that region. In 1291 three cantons, called the Forest Cantons, formed a league for defense against Hapsburg ambitions, and in 1315 they inflicted a crushing defeat on Leopold II, duke of Austria. Other cantons, including those of Lucerne, Zurich, and Bern, joined the other three, and in 1386 the confederation again defeated the Hapsburg forces. The confederation then took the offensive and began to expand its territory at the expense of various petty lords, the counts of Savoy, and the Hapsburgs. In 1477, as we have seen, the Swiss defeated the forces of Charles the Rash and became recognized throughout Europe as a formidable military power. The confederation was ruled by a federal diet, but the cantons retained almost complete independence. While they would usually combine effectively against an outside enemy, they frequently quarreled among themselves and at times resorted to civil war. The strength of the confederation lay not in the effectiveness of its government but in its topography and the military qualities of its inhabitants.

While the various states of the Empire established their own regimes, the Hapsburg family was being drawn into a dominant position in European politics as a result of the Burgundian marriage of 1477. The union of Austria with the wealthy Netherlands made Maximilian (1493–1519) more powerful than any other German prince. Then Maximilian and Mary of Burgundy had a son, Philip, who was married to the heiress of Spain. The child of this marriage, Charles V, inherited a vast complex of territories, including Spain, Sicily, Austria, and the Netherlands. The marriage of 1477 and the ensuing dispute over the division of Burgundy also gave rise to the rivalry between Hapsburg Austria and Valois France that dominated the diplomatic history of early modern Europe.

91. *The Wars of the Roses in England*

England, like France, went through a spell of civil wars in the middle years of the fifteenth century and then emerged with a strong stable monarchy, which was well established before 1500. The immediate cause of the "Wars of the Roses" was the dynastic instability arising from the fact that the legitimate heir to the throne had been passed over in the coup that installed Henry IV as king in 1399.* A deeper reason for the sporadic violence of the mid-fifteenth century was the whole social structure of England, which gave excessive power to a highly irresponsible class of great nobles.

The later Middle Ages saw considerable changes in the social struture of England. At the head of society stood some fifty great families whose position was based on large money incomes. For the most part, these incomes were drawn from ancient franchises, feudal dues, and the rents from extensive landed estates, but some—especially the members of the royal family—had generous annuities from the exchequer. The heads of these houses possessed strong stone castles and could quickly raise small private armies. The armies were procured by what was known as *livery and maintenance.* Livery was a retaining fee paid to a man on condition that he serve the employer in arms when called upon. Maintenance was general support of the lesser man by the greater, especially before the courts. As many of these great men were captains in the French wars, their followers were likely to be experienced soldiers. Livery and maintenance were a perpetual source of disorder. The great men overawed judges and juries, at times by actual threats of violence, to protect their followers. The system has been called "bastard feudalism." It reproduced all the anarchic tendencies of early feudalism without the element of stability involved in permanent land tenures. Moreover, the possessor of a private army was always tempted to use it, not only against his neighbors but even against the government. These great men were either peers or the heads of rising families that would soon attain the peerage.

*See p. 529.

Below this group of peers and rich knights who would soon become peers were the gentry. In theory, the mark of a gentleman was the rightful possession of a coat of arms, but arms were not too difficult to procure for those whose position made them suitable. Perhaps the best definition of a gentleman is one who owned enough land so that he could live in reasonable style on the rents without taking any active part in agricultural production. The gentleman would live in a manor house lightly fortified with moat and stone walls. He would probably be the lord of at least one manor with the right of presentation to a church or two and perhaps the patronage over a small monastic house. He might be a knight, but knighthood had by the fourteenth century become a rather rare dignity, and few gentlemen achieved it. Mostly they were called *armigers* or squires; Chaucer preferred the older term of *franklin.* The parliamentary knights of the shire—who, incidentally, were rarely knights—were chosen from among the more substantial gentry. As a matter of fact, the representatives of the boroughs were likely to be gentlemen from the surrounding countryside. A small rural borough felt that it could best be represented by gentlemen who could hold their own with the knights and even with the lords. Then the justices of the peace were by statute required to be gentlemen. Thus, although no individual gentleman could compete in political authority with a peer, as a class they were extremely powerful. In most respects, their economic and social interests coincided with those of the peers, and the two classes cooperated effectively. There was, however, one highly important matter on which they were inclined to differ: the peer could afford civil war and disorder if it seemed likely to gain him something, but the gentleman, as a rule, wanted peace and order.

It is important to notice that in England the line between burgher and gentleman was not very rigid. The cadets of gentle houses frequently became apprenticed to merchants and themselves eventually acquired mercantile fortunes. Then if a prosperous merchant bought a landed estate, it took only a generation or so for his family to be fully accepted among the gentry. In the vicinity of the woolen manufacturing towns that arose during the fifteenth century, it was difficult to distinguish between gentleman and merchant. The wool merchant bought sheep pasture, and the wool-growing gentleman or his sons entered the wool trade. In short, the laws and ideas that kept the French lesser nobility, the group that corresponded to the English gentry, from any connection with trade did not exist in England. The gentry and merchants in reality formed one middle class between the peers and the mass of the people.

One other class deserves mention—the *yeomen.* The yeoman was either a small freeholder or the tenant of a large farm. He worked himself, but he frequently employed hired labor as well. This class rose rapidly in numbers and importance during the fourteenth and fifteenth centuries. When the manorial lords ceased to cultivate their demesnes, they either divided them into small freeholds or into large tenant farms. These, added to the small freeholds that already existed, created a large yeoman class. Like other English classes, it was far from static. An energetic and successful peasant family could gradually increase its holdings until it attained yeoman status, and prosperous yeomen merged easily into the gentry. In practice, to become a gentleman the yeoman simply had to obtain enough property so that he could live off the rents and acquire, legally or by pure usurpation, a coat of arms. The yeoman freeholder differed from the tenant in only one important particular; he could vote for the knights of the shire. Legislation of the reign of Henry VI limited the franchise to freeholders with an income of forty shillings a year from their freeholds. As forty shillings was a very small sum—many peasant holdings were worth that much—this statute gave the vote to most freeholders. The fact that they supplied the pikemen and archers who served England in its wars was enough to give the yeoman class a position of importance.

In mid-fifteenth century England, there thus existed a powerful class of gentry and substantial groups of merchants and yeomen who were eager to see a permanent state of law and order established so that they could enjoy their peaceful and profitable pursuits without undue molestation. Above them stood a class of hereditary nobles who thoroughly enjoyed fighting and who stood to gain enormous wealth and power if they belonged to a faction that could seize control of the royal government.

Henry IV died in 1413 and was succeeded by his son, Henry V (1413–1422). As this monarch devoted most of his time and energy to the renewal of the war with France, there is little to say about his reign in England. Baronial plots continued, but there was no serious open revolt.

When Henry V died in 1422 his son, Henry VI (1422–1461), was but a few months old. The government was taken over by the young king's uncles. John, duke of Bedford, became regent of France, and Humphrey, duke of Gloucester, lord protector of England. His adventurous and turbulent nature kept England in a state of confusion until he was finally replaced by members of the house of Beaufort. Late in life, John of Ghent had married a lady by whom he had already had several children. They took the name of Beaufort and were legitimized by Parliament but specifically denied any right of succession to the throne. A strong and ambitious clan, the Beauforts dominated the government of young Henry VI. Eventually, they were joined by an equally strong character, Margaret of Anjou, who became Henry's queen.

Henry VI was a gentle, kindly man who was never very bright and who went completely insane when he was about thirty. But, even before he went insane, Henry VI was utterly unable to rule his realm. Constitutionally unable to say "no," Henry gave everyone whatever he asked for, even if he had given it to someone else the day before. Not only were the royal revenues dissipated, but there were lines of men waiting for every office and pension. The king never had any money, and as a result never paid his officials or troops. Such important posts as governor of Calais were held by great lords who paid the garrisons out of their own pockets and ruled as they saw fit, completely ignoring the weak and penniless king. At home the nobles and their armed retainers carried on continual private wars and plundered the country at will. There was only one man in England of any real stature—Richard, duke of York, a descendant of Edward III with a strong claim to be the true king by hereditary right.* When Henry went insane, he was made regent and acknowledged as the heir to the throne if Henry had no son. Unfortunately for the peace of the realm, the mad king produced a son and heir. While there is no evidence that Richard of York had any disloyal intentions or planned any harm to Henry or his son, Queen Margaret suspected him of such plans. With the support of the Beauforts and other nobles, she attacked the duke's lands and drove him from England. But Richard soon returned with an army, and the fierce civil war known in modern times as the Wars of the Roses began. The name was derived from the badges assumed by the two parties—red roses for Lancaster, white roses for York.

For five years the fortunes of war wavered, but in 1460 the royal forces defeated the Yorkists at the battle of Wakefield. Richard of York was killed in battle and one of his sons was murdered in cold blood after he was captured. Ironically enough, the death of Richard was a crushing blow to his Lancastrian foes. He had been a conscientious, amiable man who had only risen in revolt in self-defense. His son and successor, Edward, was very different. He was, for one thing, by far the ablest captain of his day, with a keen eye for strategy as well as tactics. He was also ambitious, selfish, cruel, and extremely able as an administrator. Within a year of his father's death, he had routed the Lancastrians and assumed the crown as Edward IV (1461–1483). But Queen Margaret refused to give up, and the civil war continued until the king finally crushed all his foes in a series of overwhelming victories. Margaret was driven into exile, and her son Edward was slain. Poor King Henry had not played a very glamorous part in the war. One side or the other had led him on to the field of battle, and he stood there in a daze until someone captured him. Eventually Edward imprisoned him in the Tower of London, where he died.

Edward IV died in 1483, leaving two young sons and several daughters. The obvious candidate for regent was his brother, Duke Richard of Gloucester. Richard had served Edward loyally and ably throughout the civil wars and was fully competent to handle the realm until his young nephew came of age. The two years following Edward's death are among the most mysterious in English history. The accounts of the period that have survived were written under the Tudors and were intended to please those highly opinionated monarchs. As the first Tudor won the crown by overthrowing Richard III, their historians looked with little favor on the last of the Plantagenet kings. In fact, they have painted him as a monster of perfidy and cruelty. The clear facts are few. Richard assumed the office of protector of the realm upon his brother's death and apparently began to make arrangements

*See Appendix, Table 6.

for his nephew's coronation. Then suddenly Parliament declared the two young princes illegitimate, and Duke Richard assumed the crown. The princes were lodged in the Tower of London, but one must remember that it was a royal residence as well as a prison. Both of them disappeared shortly after Richard's coronation. The traditional and probably correct story is that Richard had them killed. It is possible that they survived until 1485 and were murdered by the next king, Henry VII.

Richard III was not destined for a long reign. In a castle high in the Breton hills overlooking the Bay of Biscay there languished in prison a young Englishman—Henry Tudor, earl of Richmond. Henry was the grandson of a petty Welsh gentleman, Owen Tudor, who had won the heart and hand of Catherine of France, widow of Henry V. His father was Edmund Tudor, earl of Richmond, and his mother was Margaret Beaufort—the last of that mighty house. It was through his mother that Henry Tudor derived a claim to the throne of England, though, since the Beauforts had been explicitly excluded from the succession, his claim was at best a slim one.* But he was the only possible candidate of the house of Lancaster, and Louis XI of France was heartily tired of the rule of the house of York, which had favored his bitter foe, the duke of Burgundy. In 1484 Henry persuaded the French government to support his claim to the throne of England. The following year Henry landed in Wales with a small force of about two thousand men and advanced into England, picking up support along the way. On August 21, 1485, he fought a decisive battle against the forces of Richard III at Bosworth Field. Richard died fighting fiercely on the field of battle. The victorious Henry Tudor was acknowledged as king by Parliament and made a bow to hereditary right by marrying Elizabeth of York, daughter of Edward IV.

The Wars of the Roses had relatively little effect on England. They were fought by nobles at the head of their bands of armed retainers. In general, the participants were careful not to annoy the population more than was necessary: the site of one skirmish was moved so that it would not injure a wheat field. London and the other great towns calmly ignored the war and closed their gates to the contending forces. While many nobles were killed in battle and others were executed after capture, most of them left heirs to carry on their lines. As the barons had been turbulent and disorderly before the wars started, they could hardly become much worse. It does seem likely, however, that the wars finally ended the patience of the middle class—the country gentlemen and the townspeople. When Henry VII ascended the throne, they were heartily tired of noble anarchy and were ready to support a strong king who could check it—as Henry VII did very effectively.

Henry VII has been called the founder of a "new monarchy" in England, but in fact, the reign of Edward IV had been in some ways a preparation for the reign of his Tudor successor. Under these two strong kings, Parliament fell into the background for a time, and it seemed that representative institutions might wither away in England

*For genealogy, see Appendix, Table 6.

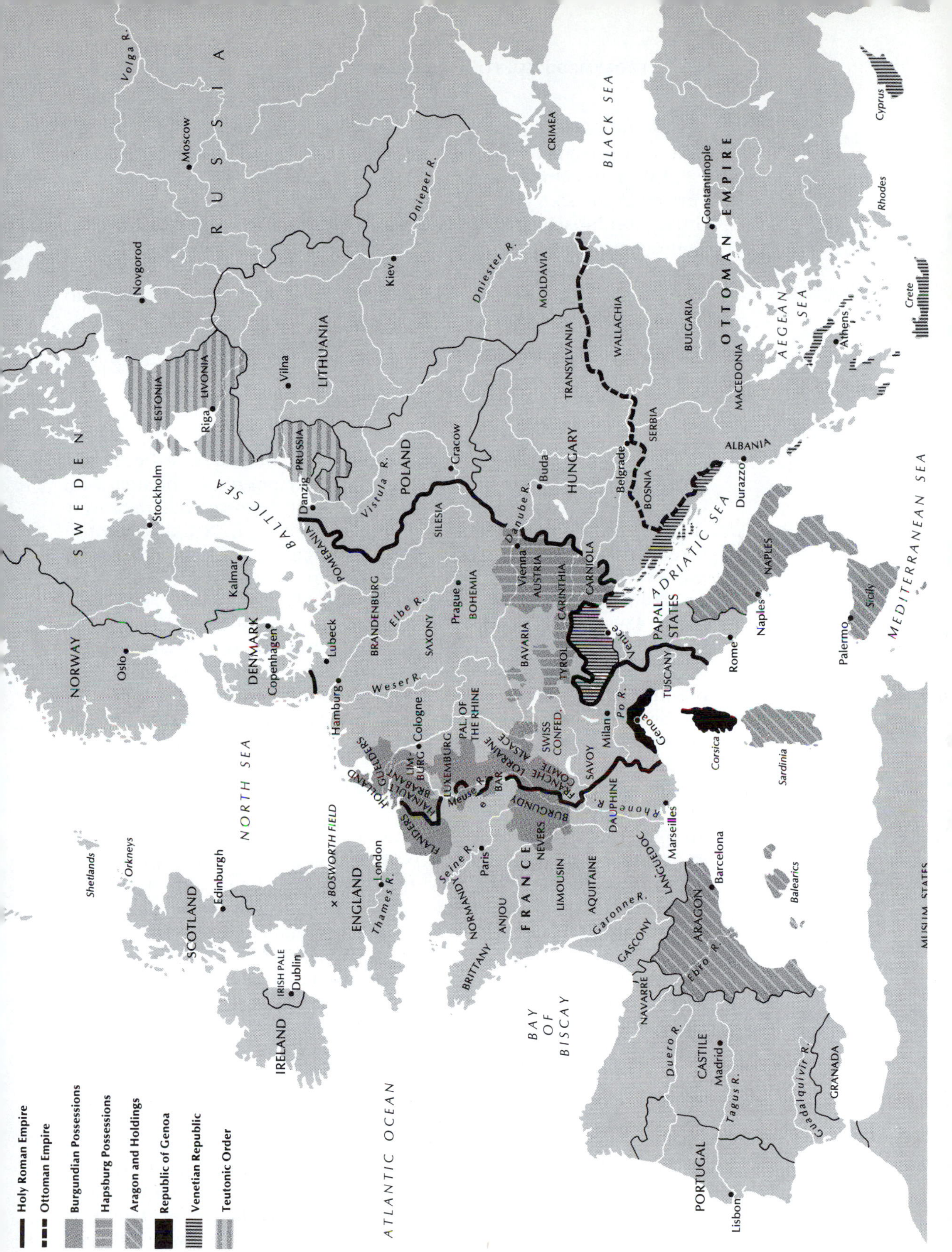

Holy Roman Empire
Ottoman Empire
Burgundian Possessions
Hapsburg Possessions
Aragon and Holdings
Republic of Genoa
Venetian Republic
Teutonic Order
ATLANTIC OCEAN
NORTH SEA
BALTIC SEA
BAY OF BISCAY
BLACK SEA
ADRIATIC SEA
AEGEAN SEA
MEDITERRANEAN SEA
IRELAND
Dublin
IRISH PALE
SCOTLAND
Edinburgh
ENGLAND
London
Thames R.
× BOSWORTH FIELD
Shetlands
Orkneys
NORWAY
Oslo
SWEDEN
Stockholm
Kalmar
DENMARK
Copenhagen
Lubeck
Hamburg
RUSSIA
Moscow
Novgorod
Volga R.
ESTONIA
LIVONIA
Riga
Vilna
LITHUANIA
PRUSSIA
Danzig
POMERANIA
POLAND
Cracow
Vistula R.
Kiev
Dnieper R.
Dniester R.
MOLDAVIA
CRIMEA
BRANDENBURG
SAXONY
SILESIA
BOHEMIA
Prague
Elbe R.
Weser R.
Cologne
PAL. OF THE RHINE
BAVARIA
AUSTRIA
Vienna
Danube R.
HUNGARY
Buda
TRANSYLVANIA
WALLACHIA
CARNIOLA
CARINTHIA
TYROL
Venice
SWISS CONFED.
ALSACE
LORRAINE
FRANCHE COMTE
SAVOY
Milan
Po R.
Genoa
Corsica
Sardinia
TUSCANY
PAPAL STATES
Rome
NAPLES
Naples
Sicily
Palermo
HOLLAND
GUELDERS
BRABANT
LIMBURG
HAINAULT
LUXEMBURG
FLANDERS
Meuse R.
BAR
BURGUNDY
NEVERS
Paris
Seine R.
NORMANDY
BRITTANY
ANJOU
FRANCE
LIMOUSIN
AQUITAINE
DAUPHINE
Rhone R.
Marseilles
LANGUEDOC
GASCONY
Garonne R.
NAVARRE
ARAGON
Ebro R.
Barcelona
Balearics
CASTILE
Madrid
Duero R.
Tagus R.
PORTUGAL
Lisbon
Guadalquivir R.
GRANADA
MUSLIM STATES
Belgrade
SERBIA
BOSNIA
Durazzo
ALBANIA
MACEDONIA
BULGARIA
Athens
Crete
Rhodes
Cyprus
Constantinople
OTTOMAN EMPIRE

as they did in France. But, in fact, during the reigns of the Plantagenet and Lancastrian kings, Parliament had become deeply rooted in English political tradition and had established precedents that were revived in the sixteenth century and were remembered by the foes of Stuart absolutism. And England had never developed the institutions that encouraged such absolutism. The English paid bureaucracy was very small. There was no standing army like that of the French king. If an English king were to rule as an effective monarch, he had to do it by the consent of his people.

92. *The Beginnings of Modern Europe*

Not only in England, France, and the Empire, but also in other lands, forming a great circle around the whole periphery of Christendom, changes were taking place in the fifteenth century that decisively shaped the political system of modern Europe. In Scandinavia the three northern kingdoms of Norway, Denmark, and Sweden had been joined into a single realm by the "Union of Kalmar" (1397). The union was maintained under King Eric (1397–1439) and King Christian (1439–1481) in spite of several rebellions in Sweden. These were not mere outbursts of unruly nobles but national risings that attracted substantial support from burghers and peasants. A successful rebellion in 1467 broke the union. It was temporarily restored in 1497 but finally broken in 1501. From then onward, Sweden remained an independent power; the union between Denmark and Norway, on the other hand, lasted until 1814.

The modern state of Russia with its capital at Moscow also came into existence in the second half of the fifteenth century. After the Mongol invasion of 1237, Russia was divided into several principalities, each under a petty local Russian prince. These princes, in turn, were subject to a Mongol khan to whom they owed a heavy annual tribute. The Grand Duchy of Moscow began to emerge as the leading principality under Ivan I (1328–1341). Ivan persuaded the Mongols to appoint him as sole tribute-collector for all the Russian vassal states, and he and his successors used this position to establish their authority over the other princes. In 1380 a grand duke of Moscow felt strong enough to rebel against the Mongols themselves, but after an initial victory, he was defeated and his rebellion suppressed. During the following century, the Mongols were weakened by a series of civil wars, and just a hundred years after the first rebellion, the Grand Prince Ivan III the Great (1462–1505) succeeded in throwing off the "Tartar yoke" and subjecting all the other Russian princes to his rule. During the rise of the Grand Duchy of Moscow, the metropolitan bishop of Moscow had become the chief prelate of the Russian Orthodox Church, and the church consistently supported the political aims of the grand dukes. In 1472 Ivan III married as his second wife a Byzantine princess, niece of the last emperor to rule in Constantinople. He then abandoned the title of grand prince and called himself *Tsar*, or Caesar. In Ivan's mind he was the successor of the Byzantine emperors, and Moscow had taken the place of Constantinople as the center of Orthodox Christian civilization.

Moscow could become in this fashion the "Third Rome" because the "Second Rome," Byzantium, had finally ceased to exist as a Christian state. For a century before its downfall in 1453 the Byzantine Empire had been losing territory to the Ottoman Turks.* In 1356 a Turkish army crossed to Europe and captured Adrianople. During the next thirty years, the Turks became masters of the Balkans. The Bulgarian state was destroyed, and Serbia lost much of its territory and became a vassal principality. In 1397 the sultan Bayazid (1389–1402) laid siege to Constantinople, and it looked as if the Byzantine Empire had reached its end. But once more fortune favored the ancient state. The great Mongol Khan Timur the Lame, known as Tamerlane, swept into Asia Minor at the head of his horde, and Bayazid hastened to meet him. On July 20, 1402, Timur routed the Turkish army, captured the sultan, and temporarily broke the Ottoman power. For the next fifty years, the sultans were occupied with wars against the kings of Hungary and Poland on land and Venice on the sea. The helpless Byzantine emperor, who held only Constantinople and its immediate environs, could merely watch the struggle. By 1453 the sultan Mohammed II (1451–1481) at last found his hands free for a great attack on Constantinople. On May 29 of that year, the city fell and the last emperor of Byzantium, Constantine XI, died bravely in the fighting. The flow of Byzantine refugees into Italy that accompanied the Turkish conquests helped to stimulate the Greek learning of the Italian Renaissance. The Balkans remained under Turkish rule until the nineteenth century. Constantinople, the modern Istanbul, is still a Turkish city.

If we complete our circuit of the map by glancing at Spain, we find there too a process of decisive change taking place in the second half of the fifteenth century. The reconquest of Moorish territory undertaken by the Christian kings of the twelfth century had ground to a halt with the death of Ferdinand III of Castile in 1252.† Until the end of the Middle Ages, Moorish kings ruled a Mohammedan state, the kingdom of Granada, in southern Spain. Meanwhile, the three major Christian states, Castile, Aragon and Portugal, devoted themselves to endless wars against one another. In all of these kingdoms, there were also frequent rebellions of the great nobility against royal authority, varied by occasional uprisings of peasants. Yet, in spite of all this, the Spanish kingdoms made substantial progress in some spheres. The cities continued to grow in wealth and influence, and a notable development of representative institutions occurred, especially in the Cortes of Aragon. But the medieval kings of Spain were too weak to establish a tradition of orderly, disciplined, effective government. A turning point came with the marriage between Ferdinand of Aragon and Isabella of Castile in 1469. These two rulers began to weld their respective states into a united Spanish kingdom. Like other rulers of

*See p. 474.
†See p. 253.

the time, they were able to appeal successfully to the cities for tax revenues, which gave them sufficient strength to discipline the nobility. They also, in 1482, began a war against the Moorish kingdom of Granada and finally conquered and annexed it in 1492. Portugal remained outside the union of Aragon and Castile and emerged from the Middle Ages an independent state, as she still remains.

Spain and Portugal were not only becoming nations in the second half of the fifteenth century; they were reaching out for a new destiny. The civil wars among the Mongols and the advance of the Ottoman Turks had disrupted the established overland trade route to the Far East so that there was an urgent need to find a viable sea route to the Indies. The Iberian kingdoms with their long Atlantic coastline were ideally placed to lead a new movement of exploration. Prince Henry the Navigator of Portugal (1394–1460) encouraged a series of exploring ventures down the coast of Africa which culminated, after his death, in the discovery of a sea route around the Cape of Good Hope to the East Indies. And Isabella of Spain financed the voyage of Christopher Columbus across the Atlantic.

There is obviously no one particular year which can be designated as "the end of the Middle Ages." We have rather arbitrarily chosen 1475 in the title of this book to mark the midpoint of the half-century of decisive changes that took place between 1450 and 1500. In 1450, according to most reckonings, Europe was still "medieval." By 1500 there were many signs that a new era was beginning. In many lands strong new monarchies had been established. Richard III of England died on Bosworth Field in 1485 and was succeeded by the first of the Tudors; the emperor Frederick III died in 1493; and Louis XI ended his reign in 1483. Richard is often regarded as the last medieval monarch of England, and Frederick was the last Holy Roman Emperor to be crowned in Rome. Although some historians call Louis XI a modern king, and they have sound arguments, his deep piety and the nature of the problems he faced were essentially medieval. The year 1479 saw the birth of modern Spain, with the accession of Ferdinand and Isabella to the thrones of Aragon and Castile. The son of Louis XI, Charles VIII, was soon to start the bitter wars that changed Italian politics by making the peninsula a pawn in the race for power of her great neighboring states. In the East, Constantinople had fallen to the Turks in 1453, and Ivan III, grand duke of Moscow, assumed the title of Tsar in 1472.

Then, these fifty years saw the first great strokes toward the expansion of European interests across the seas. In 1487 Bartolomeu Dias rounded the Cape of Good Hope, and in 1492 Columbus reached the West Indies. In 1497 Vasco de Gama made the first direct sea voyage to the East Indies, and in the same year John Cabot first explored the shores of North America.

In the fields of religion, art, and literature, vital changes were in the air. The technology of the Middle Ages, which had been developing increasingly complex mechanisms ever since the twelfth century, finally produced, in the printing press, an invention that revolutionized the cultural life of Europe. Erasmus was born in 1467, Thomas More in 1478, and Martin Luther in 1483. Copernicus, who is often called the father of modern science, was born in 1473. In Italy the Renaissance was in full bloom—Leonardo da Vinci born in 1452; Pica della Mirandola in 1463; Machiavelli in 1469; Michelangelo in 1475; and Castiglione in 1478.

All this does not mean that there was any sudden break in the threads of history. There was simply an accelerated pace of change. Except for his Italian ambitions, Charles VIII had views little different from his father's, and the coronation of emperors at Rome had become a mere formality long before it ceased. Dias and da Gama were the successors of a long line of explorers who sailed down the African coast. Erasmus and More were influenced by earlier humanists, and Huss had anticipated many of the ideas of Luther. But the seeds that had been steadily growing during the fourteenth and fifteenth centuries bloomed quite suddenly to produce a rather different world—perhaps a better one?

READING SUGGESTIONS

Many of the works on political and institutional history cited in Chapter XXIII are useful for the fifteenth century. In addition, see, for England, E. F. Jacob, *The Fifteenth Century* (Oxford, England, 1961); S. B. Chrimes, *English Constitutional Ideas in the Fifteenth Century* (Cambridge, England, 1936); B. Wilkinson, *Constitutional History of England in the Fifteenth Century* (London, 1964), with documents; and J. R. Lander, *The Wars of the Roses* (London, 1965), a compilation from contemporary chronicles. On France and Burgundy, see P. Champion, *Louis XI* (New York, 1929); J. R. Major, *Representative Institutions in Renaissance France* (Madison, WI, 1960); R. Vaughan, *Philip the Good* (London, 1970), *Charles the Bold* (London, 1973), and *Valois Burgundy* (London, 1975); and C. Beanne, *The Birth of an Ideology: Myths and Symbols of Nation in Late-Medieval France* (Berkely and Los Angeles, 1991).

E. Bonjour *et al.*, *A Short History of Switzerland* (Oxford, England, 1952) is an introductory survey. Two works of F. L. Carsten deal in part with fifteenth-century Germany: *The Origins of Prussia* (Oxford, England, 1954), and *Princes and Parliaments in Germany* (Oxford, England, 1959). See also * F. R. H. Du Boulay, *Germany in the Later Middle Ages* (New York, 1983). The *Memoires* of Commines, A. R. Scoble (trans.) (London, 1855–1856) provides a lively contemporary account of European affairs.

For developments in Scandinavia, see K. Larsen, *A History of Norway* (Princeton, 1948); I. Andersen, *A History of Sweden* (London, 1956); and P. Lauring, *A History of the Kingdom of Denmark* (Copenhagen, 1973). Good studies in eastern Europe are O. Halecki, *A History of Poland* (New York, 1956) and *Borderlands of Civilization: A History of East Central Europe* (New York, 1952). On Russia, see G. Vernadsky, *The Mongols and Russia* (New Haven, CT, 1953), and V. O. Klutchevsky, *History of Russia,* vol. I (London, 1931). S. Runciman, *The Fall of Constantinople* (Cambridge, England, 1965) is a fine account. On the eastern Mediterranean, see also D. R. Nicol, *The Last Centuries of Byzantium, 1261–1453* (London, 1972), and A. S. Atiya, *The Crusade in the Later Middle Ages* (London, 1938). For Spain, R. Merriam, *Rise of the Spanish Empire,* cited in Chapter XI, can be supplemented by * D. W. Lomax, *The Reconquest of Spain* (New York, 1978), and J. N. Hillgarth, *The Spanish*

Kingdoms, 1250–1516, 2 vols. (New York, 1976, 1978). Late medieval exploration is discussed in C. Beazley, *The Dawn of Modern Geography,* rev. ed., 3 vols. (New York, 1949); P. Sykes, *A History of Exploration,* 3rd ed. (New York, 1950); and * B. W. Diffie, *Prelude to Empire* (Lincoln, NE, 1960). F. Fernandez-Armesto, *Before Columbus: Exploration and Colonization from the Mediterranean to the Atlantic, 1229–1492* (Philadelphia, 1987) gives extensive bibliography.

Finally, on the transition from medieval to Renaissance culture, a classic work is * J. Burckhardt, *The Civilization of the Renaissance in Italy* (New York, 1954), first published in 1860. More modern interpretations of the Renaissance can be found in W. K. Ferguson. *The Renaissance in Historical Thought* (Cambridge, MA, 1948); P. O. Kristeller, *Studies in Renaissance Thought and Letters* (Rome, 1956); W. J. Bouwsma, *The Interpretation of Renaissance Humanism* (Washington, DC, 1959); * W. H. Werkmeister (ed.), *Facets of the Renaissance* (Los Angeles, 1959); and D. Hay, *The Italian Renaissance in Its Historical Background* (Cambridge, England, 1961). On the development of printing, see G. P. Winship, *Printing in the Fifteenth Century* (Philadelphia, 1940), and P. Butler, *The Origins of Printing in Europe* (Chicago, 1940).

Epilogue

93. *The Achievement of the Middle Ages*

In evaluating the achievements of the Middle Ages, one can consider them from two different points of view, as we indicated at the outset in the Introduction to this book. We can consider the contributions of medieval people to the later development of Western civilization, or we can estimate the quality of their achievement in terms of their own time and their own objectives. The importance of the medieval period in the general history of Western civilization is evidently very great. In 500 A.D. western Europe was a chaos of barbaric peoples squabbling in the ruins of the Roman Empire; by 1500 A.D. the peoples of that same region had created an advanced society that was poised to embark on the extraordinary adventure of the following age—the Westernization, for better or worse, of almost the whole world.

Innovations of decisive importance for the future occurred in every sphere of life and thought. The political framework of modern Europe was created in the late medieval period. Two great institutional innovations of the Middle Ages still play a prominent role in the present age—the development of the representative assembly as an institution of government and of the university as an institution of learning. The civilization of the modern West could never have grown into existence without both of them. In the sphere of religion, much of the dogma, liturgy, and law of the modern Roman Catholic church was first formulated in the medieval period, while the central ideas of Protestantism grew out of the thought of late medieval teachers like Ockham, Wyclif, and Huss. Also during the medieval centuries there was established a continuing, fruitful tension between church and state, which has persisted as a characteristic feature of Western society. Above all, the medieval church embraced a program of "religious activism," of constant engagement in the affairs of the world. This policy reflected an idea of religious perfection different from the more purely contemplative ideal of most Oriental religions, and it has persisted in modern Catholicism and in various forms of Protestantism.

In technology, medieval individuals displayed extraordinary creativity both in originating new devices and in assimilating and improving the inventions of other civilizations. By the twelfth century, the medieval West had surpassed Byzantium and Islam in the application of mechanical power sources to routine productive processes, and, in the fourteenth century, Europe began to take the lead in technology from China, which until then had possessed the most technologically advanced civilization in the world.

Social ideas have changed radically since the Middle Ages, but here, too, something of the medieval heritage survives. The ideas of individual freedom that marked the members of the feudal class became a strong element in later conceptions of the "rights of man." The cult of romantic love, a strange eccentricity of Western culture, has lived on in literature and has, at least in Anglo-Saxon lands, been widely accepted as a sound basis for the relations between the sexes. Many of the stories invented by medieval writers are still a living part of our literary heritage. The creation of musical notation made possible the whole subsequent development of the art of music in the West.

When one views the achievements of the people of the Middle Ages in terms of their own times, it is again evident that this was one of the great eras of human history. A vast region was reclaimed from bog, forest, and waste and turned into fertile farmland. Methods of agriculture were devised that made this region productive and enabled it to support a large population. This clearing and placing in cultivation of the waste lands of Europe was a tremendous achievement. On this foundation, the people of the Middle Ages built a distinctive civilization.

The feudal, seignorial, and guild systems were essentially novel and were products of great creative imagination. The development of representative institutions of government was a unique achievement. While the complicated hierarchy of the church had been originally modeled on that of the Roman Empire, it was modified by medieval ecclesiastics to suit their needs. The monastic system was almost entirely a creation of the Middle Ages. In the realm of ideas, the period was equally fertile. The basis of Christian theology had been constructed by the Church Fathers under the Late Roman Empire, but the system was completed by the medieval theologians and was supplemented by the canon law. Other fields of thought were woven into the fringes of theology in attempts to create a consistent whole. The greatest works of scholastic theology were magnificent structures created by thinkers of rare ability. In the field of literature, the Middle Ages produced works that have never been surpassed. Dante's *Divine Comedy* and Chaucer's *Canterbury Tales* rank among the great literary productions of all time, and *Beowulf*, the *Chanson de Roland*, and the best of the troubadour lyrics are not far behind them. Finally, the people of the Middle Ages demonstrated astounding creative imagination in the realm of architecture. Despite its name, the Romanesque style was their own, and the Gothic was entirely novel, completely unlike anything that had been seen before. The mere erection of the stone churches of medieval Europe was a stupendous achievement for people with little theoretical knowledge of engineering and slight reserves of labor power.

In the last century of the medieval era, the peoples of Europe had to cope with an unprecedented combination of plague, war, schism, and economic decline, all occurring simultaneously and all interacting with one another. In the face of these disasters, medieval people did not lose their nerve. They did not succumb to a "death wish." Instead, they kept working at their problems, solved them as best they could, and in doing so, brought into existence the institutions of the early modern world. Thus the "time of troubles" of the late Middle Ages did not lead to a disintegration of Western civilization but to a new era of expansion and achievement. Unlike the population of ancient Rome, the peoples of medieval Europe conducted themselves with enough sense and courage to avert the threat of a new Dark Age. That was the greatest achievement of medieval civilization.

Appendix

The Medieval Popes* and Genealogical Tables

Sylvester I, 314–335
Mark, 336
Julius I, 337–352
Liberius, 352–365
Felix II, 355–365
Damasus I, 366–384
Siricius, 384–399
Anastasius I, 399–401
Innocent I, 401–417
Zosimus, 417–418
Boniface I, 418–422
Celestine I, 422–432
Sixtus III, 432–440
Leo I the Great, 440–461
Hilary, 461–468
Simplicius, 468–483
Felix III, 483–492
Gelasius I, 492–496
Anastasius II, 496–498
Symmachus, 498–514
Hormisdas, 514–523
John I, 523–526
Felix IV, 526–530
Boniface II, 530–532
John II, 533–535
Agapitus I, 535–536
Silverius, 536–537
Vigilius, 537–555
Pelagius I, 555–561
John III, 561–574
Benedict I, 575–579
Pelagius II, 579–590
Gregory I the Great, 590–604
Sabinianus, 604–606
Boniface III, 607
Boniface IV, 608–615
Deusdedit, 615–618
Boniface V, 619–625
Honorius I, 625–638
Severinus, 640
John IV, 640–642
Theodore I, 642–649
Martin I, 649–655
Eugenius I, 654–657
Vitalian, 657–672
Adeodatus, 672–676
Donus, 676–678
Agatho, 678–681
Leo II, 682–683
Benedict II, 684–685
John V, 685–686
Conon, 686–687
Sergius I, 687–701
John VI, 701–705
John VII, 705–707
Sisinnius, 708
Constantine, 708–715
Gregory II, 715–731
Gregory III, 731–741
Zacharias, 741–752
Stephen II, 752–757
Paul I, 757–767
Stephen III, 768–772
Adrian I, 772–795
Leo III, 795–816
Stephen IV, 816–817
Paschal I, 817–824
Eugenius II, 824–827
Valentine, 827
Gregory IV, 827–844
Sergius II, 844–847
Leo IV, 847–855
Benedict III, 855–858
Nicholas I the Great, 858–867
Adrian II, 867–872
John VIII, 872–882
Marinus I, 882–884
Adrian III, 884–885
Stephen V, 885–891
Formosus, 891–896
Boniface VI, 896
Stephen VI, 896–897
Romanus, 897
Theodore II, 897
John IX, 898–900
Benedict IV, 900–903
Leo V, 903
Christopher, 903–904
Sergius III, 904–911
Anastasius III, 911–913
Lando, 913–914
John X, 914–928
Leo VI, 928
Stephen VII, 928–931
John XI, 931–935
Leo VII, 936–939
Stephen VIII, 939–942
Marinus II, 942–946
Agapitus II, 946–955
John XII, 955–964
Leo VIII, 963–965

*This list is based on the one given by Angelo Mercato in *Medieval Studies,* IX (1947), 71–80. Permission granted by the Pontifical Institute of Medieval Studies. Names of antipopes are shown in italic.

Benedict V, 964–966
John XIII, 965–972
Benedict VI, 973–974
Boniface VII, 974 and 984–985
Benedict VII, 974–983
John XIV, 983–984
John XV, 985–996
Gregory V, 996–999
John XVI, 997–998
Sylvester II, 999–1003
John XVII, 1003
John XVIII, 1004–1009
Sergius IV, 1009–1012
Benedict VIII, 1012–1024
John XIX, 1024–1032
Benedict IX, 1032–1044
Sylvester III, 1045
Benedict IX, 1045 [for the second time]
Gregory VI, 1045–1046
Clement II, 1046–1047
Benedict IX, 1047–1048 [for the third time]
Damasus II, 1048
Leo IX, 1049–1054
Victor II, 1055–1057
Stephen IX, 1057–1058
Benedict X, 1058–1059
Nicholas II, 1059–1061
Alexander II, 1061–1073
Gregory VII, 1073–1085
Clement III, 1080 and 1084–1100
Victor III, 1086–1087
Urban II, 1088–1099
Paschal II, 1099–1118
Theodoric, 1100
Albert, 1102
Sylvester IV 1105–1111
Gelasius II, 1118–1119
Gregory VIII, 1118–1121
Calixtus II, 1119–1124
Honorius II, 1124–1130
Innocent II, 1130–1143
Anacletus II, 1130–1138
Celestine II, 1143–1144
Lucius II, 1144–1145
Eugenius III, 1145–1153
Anastasius IV, 1153–1154
Adrian IV, 1154–1159
Alexander III, 1159–1181
Victor IV, 1159–1164
Paschal III, 1164–1168
Calixtus III, 1168–1178
Innocent III, 1179–1180
Lucius III, 1181–1185
Urban III, 1185–1187
Gregory VIII, 1187
Clement III, 1187–1191
Celestine III, 1191–1198
Innocent III, 1198–1216
Honorius III, 1216–1227
Gregory IX, 1227–1241
Celestine IV, 1241
Innocent IV, 1243–1254
Alexander IV, 1254–1261
Urban IV, 1261–1264
Clement IV, 1265–1268
Gregory X, 1271–1276
Innocent V, 1276
Adrian V, 1276
John XXI, 1276–1277*
Nicholas III, 1277–1280
Martin IV, 1281–1285
Honorius IV, 1285–1287
Nicholas IV, 1288–1292
Celestine V, 1294
Boniface VIII, 1294–1303
Benedict XI, 1303–1304
Clement V, 1305–1314
John XXII, 1316–1334
Benedict XII, 1334–1342
Clement VI, 1342–1352
Innocent VI, 1352–1362
Urban V, 1362–1370
Gregory XI, 1370–1378
Urban VI, 1378–1389
Clement VII, 1378–1394†
Boniface IX, 1389–1404
Benedict XIII, 1394–1423†
Innocent VII, 1404–1406
Gregory XII, 1406–1415
Alexander V, 1409–1410‡
John XXIII, 1410–1415‡
Martin V, 1417–1431
Clement VIII, 1423–1429
Eugenius IV, 1431–1447
Felix V, 1439–1449
Nicholas V, 1447–1455
Calixtus III, 1455–1458
Pius II, 1458–1464
Paul II, 1464–1471
Sixtus IV, 1471–1484
Innocent VIII, 1484–1492
Alexander VI, 1492–1503

*So-called through an error in enumeration. There was no John XX.

†Of the Avignon line. There is no certainty as to who was true pope during the Great Schism, 1378–1417.

‡Of the Pisan line.

Table 1

The Descendants of Charlemagne

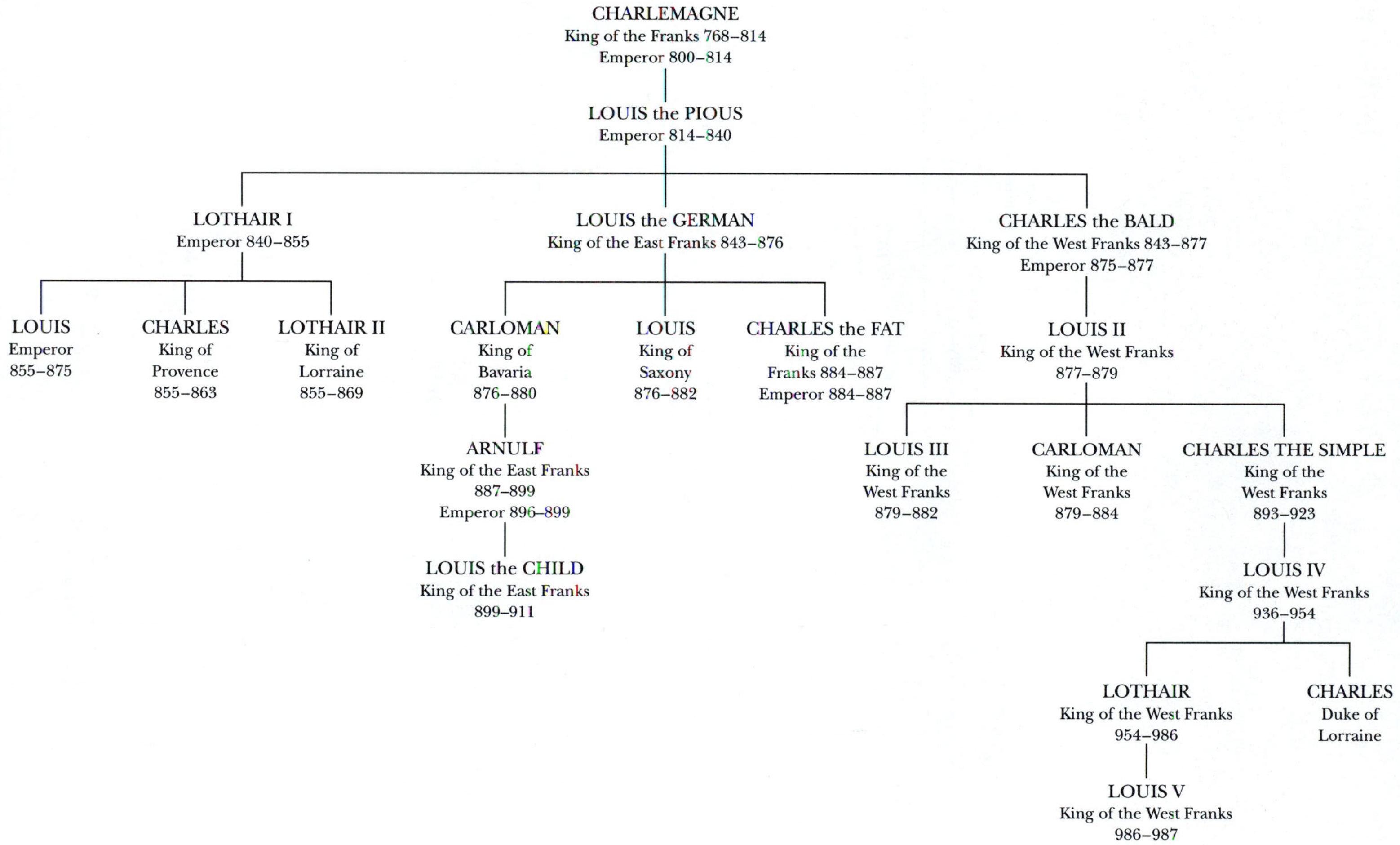
CHARLEMAGNE
King of the Franks 768–814
Emperor 800–814
LOUIS the PIOUS
Emperor 814–840
LOTHAIR I
Emperor 840–855
LOUIS the GERMAN
King of the East Franks 843–876
CHARLES the BALD
King of the West Franks 843–877
Emperor 875–877
LOUIS
Emperor
855–875
CHARLES
King of
Provence
855–863
LOTHAIR II
King of
Lorraine
855–869
CARLOMAN
King of
Bavaria
876–880
LOUIS
King of
Saxony
876–882
CHARLES the FAT
King of the
Franks 884–887
Emperor 884–887
LOUIS II
King of the West Franks
877–879
ARNULF
King of the East Franks
887–899
Emperor 896–899
LOUIS the CHILD
King of the East Franks
899–911
LOUIS III
King of the
West Franks
879–882
CARLOMAN
King of the
West Franks
879–884
CHARLES THE SIMPLE
King of the
West Franks
893–923
LOUIS IV
King of the West Franks
936–954
LOTHAIR
King of the West Franks
954–986
CHARLES
Duke of
Lorraine
LOUIS V
King of the West Franks
986–987

Table 2

The Capetian Kings of the Senior Line

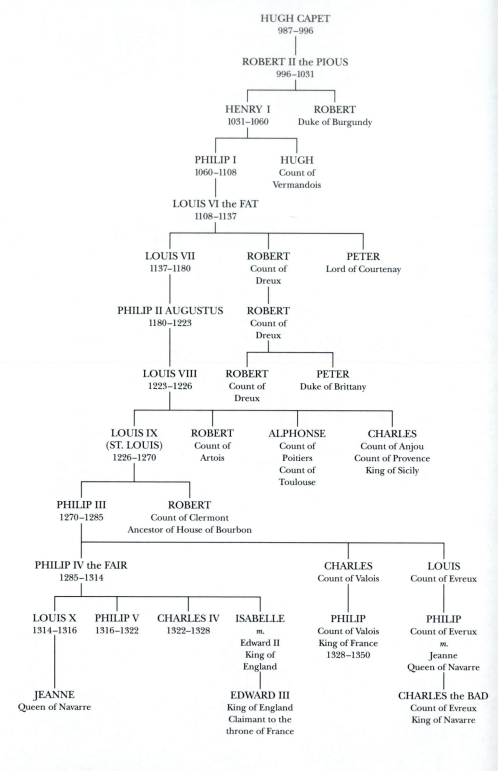

- HUGH CAPET 987–996
  - ROBERT II the PIOUS 996–1031
    - HENRY I 1031–1060
      - PHILIP I 1060–1108
        - LOUIS VI the FAT 1108–1137
          - LOUIS VII 1137–1180
            - PHILIP II AUGUSTUS 1180–1223
              - LOUIS VIII 1223–1226
                - LOUIS IX (ST. LOUIS) 1226–1270
                  - PHILIP III 1270–1285
                    - PHILIP IV the FAIR 1285–1314
                      - LOUIS X 1314–1316
                        - JEANNE Queen of Navarre
                      - PHILIP V 1316–1322
                      - CHARLES IV 1322–1328
                      - ISABELLE *m.* Edward II King of England
                        - EDWARD III King of England Claimant to the throne of France
                    - CHARLES Count of Valois
                      - PHILIP Count of Valois King of France 1328–1350
                    - LOUIS Count of Evreux
                      - PHILIP Count of Everux *m.* Jeanne Queen of Navarre
                        - CHARLES the BAD Count of Evreux King of Navarre
                  - ROBERT Count of Clermont Ancestor of House of Bourbon
                - ROBERT Count of Artois
                - ALPHONSE Count of Poitiers Count of Toulouse
                - CHARLES Count of Anjou Count of Provence King of Sicily
          - ROBERT Count of Dreux
            - ROBERT Count of Dreux
              - ROBERT Count of Dreux
              - PETER Duke of Brittany
          - PETER Lord of Courtenay
      - HUGH Count of Vermandois
    - ROBERT Duke of Burgundy

Table 3
The Saxon and Salian Kings of Germany

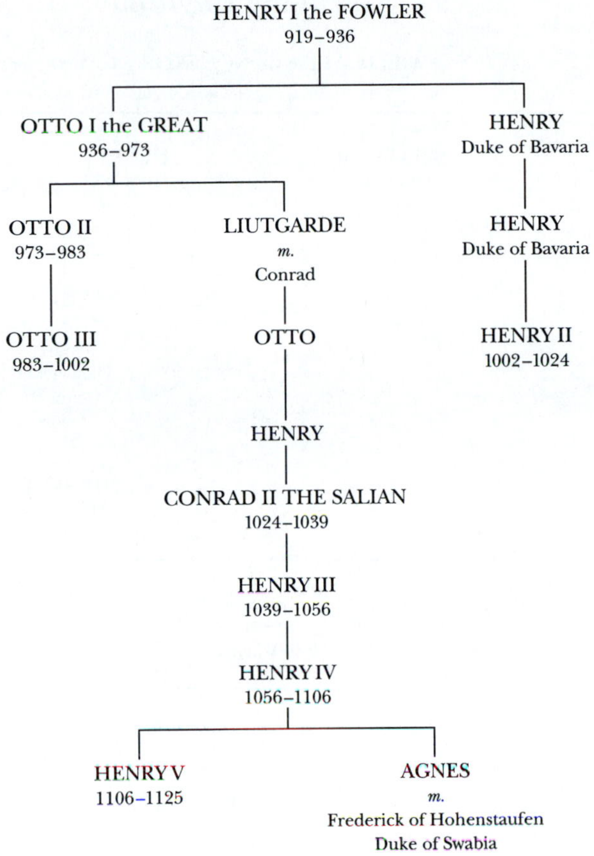

Table 4

The Norman and Early Plantagenet Kings of England

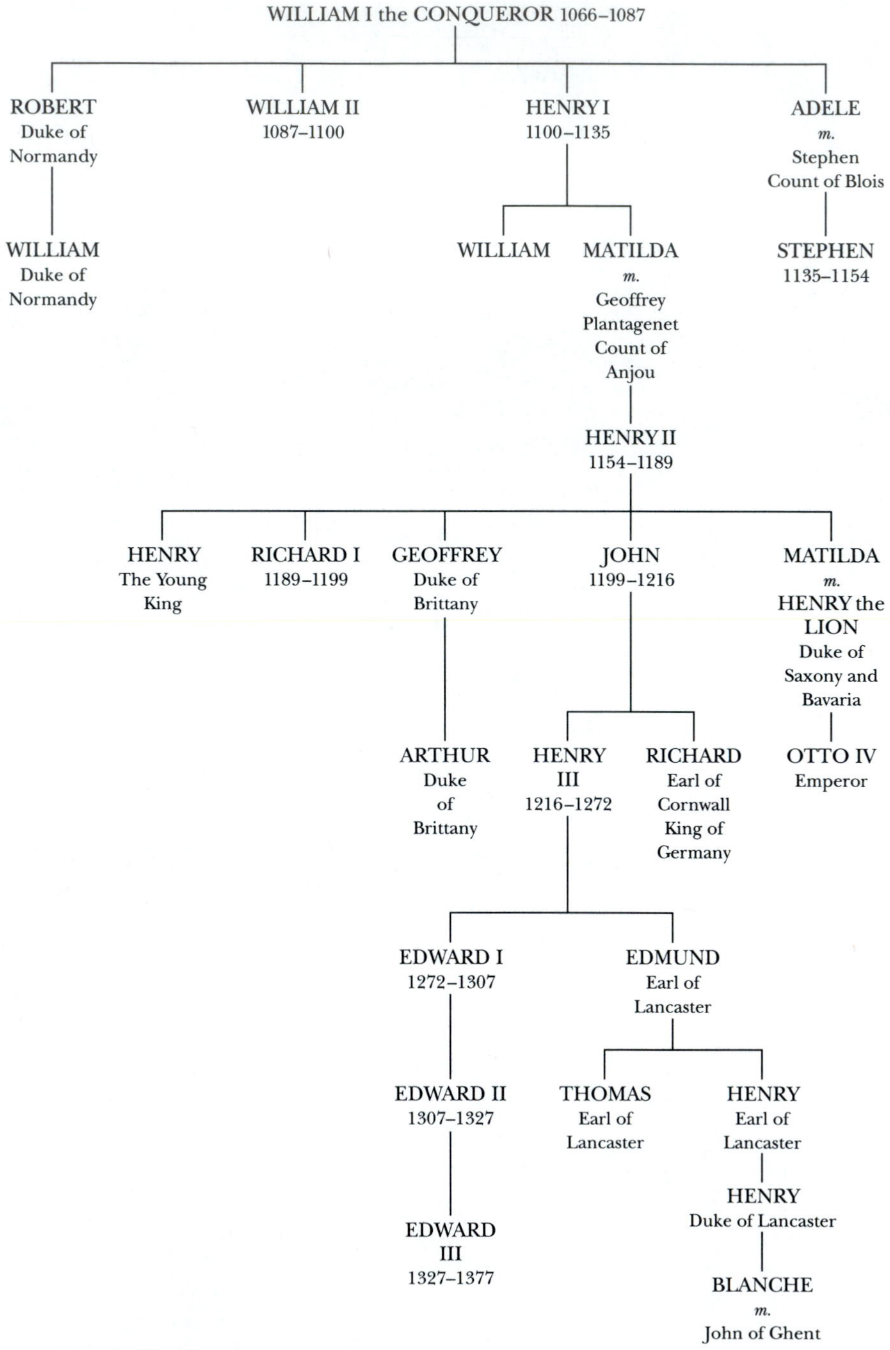
WILLIAM I the CONQUEROR 1066–1087
ROBERT Duke of Normandy
WILLIAM II 1087–1100
HENRY I 1100–1135
ADELE m. Stephen Count of Blois
WILLIAM Duke of Normandy
WILLIAM
MATILDA m. Geoffrey Plantagenet Count of Anjou
STEPHEN 1135–1154
HENRY II 1154–1189
HENRY The Young King
RICHARD I 1189–1199
GEOFFREY Duke of Brittany
JOHN 1199–1216
MATILDA m. HENRY the LION Duke of Saxony and Bavaria
ARTHUR Duke of Brittany
HENRY III 1216–1272
RICHARD Earl of Cornwall King of Germany
OTTO IV Emperor
EDWARD I 1272–1307
EDMUND Earl of Lancaster
EDWARD II 1307–1327
THOMAS Earl of Lancaster
HENRY Earl of Lancaster
HENRY Duke of Lancaster
EDWARD III 1327–1377
BLANCHE m. John of Ghent

Table 5
The Hohenstaufens and Their Rivals

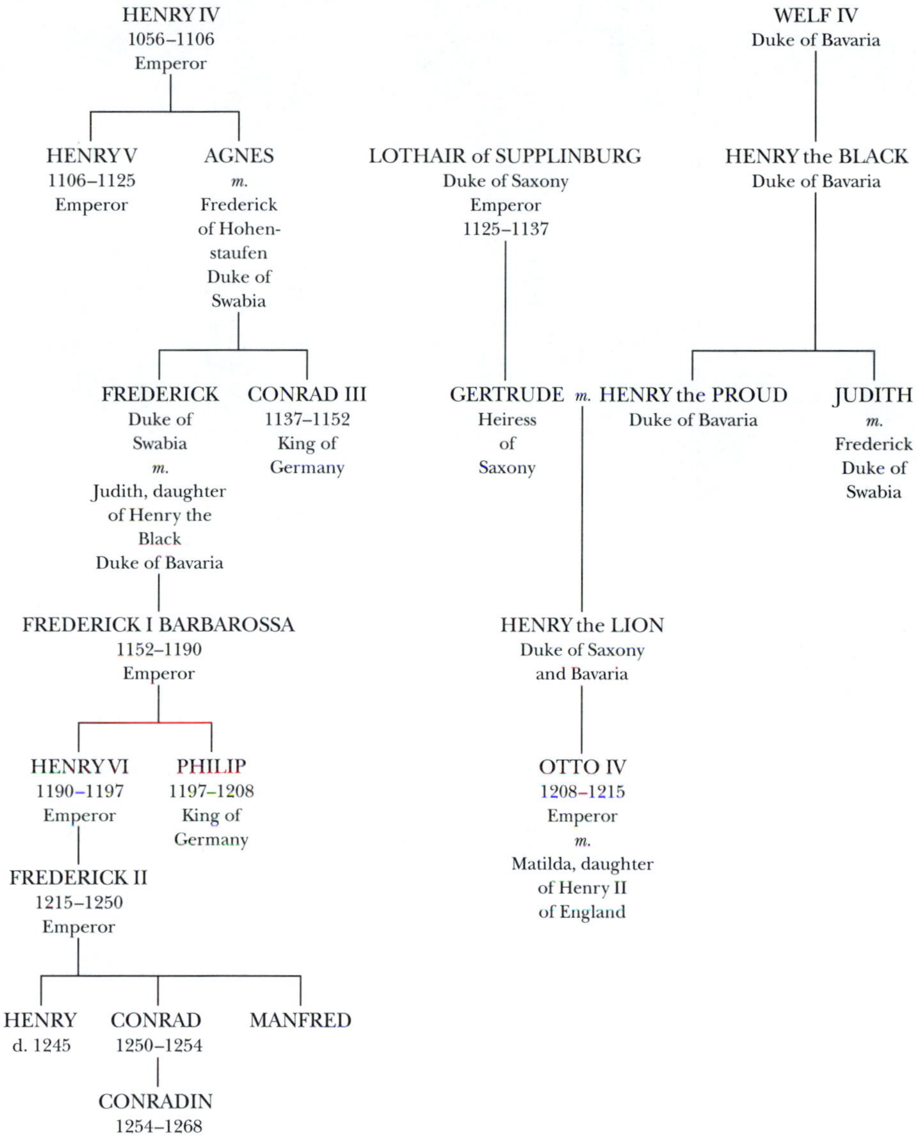
HENRY IV
1056–1106
Emperor
HENRY V
1106–1125
Emperor
AGNES
m.
Frederick of Hohen-staufen
Duke of Swabia
FREDERICK
Duke of Swabia
m.
Judith, daughter of Henry the Black
Duke of Bavaria
CONRAD III
1137–1152
King of Germany
FREDERICK I BARBAROSSA
1152–1190
Emperor
HENRY VI
1190–1197
Emperor
PHILIP
1197–1208
King of Germany
FREDERICK II
1215–1250
Emperor
HENRY
d. 1245
CONRAD
1250–1254
MANFRED
CONRADIN
1254–1268
LOTHAIR of SUPPLINBURG
Duke of Saxony
Emperor
1125–1137
GERTRUDE
Heiress of Saxony
m.
WELF IV
Duke of Bavaria
HENRY the BLACK
Duke of Bavaria
HENRY the PROUD
Duke of Bavaria
JUDITH
m.
Frederick
Duke of Swabia
HENRY the LION
Duke of Saxony and Bavaria
OTTO IV
1208–1215
Emperor
m.
Matilda, daughter of Henry II of England

Table 6
The Later Plantagenet Kings of England

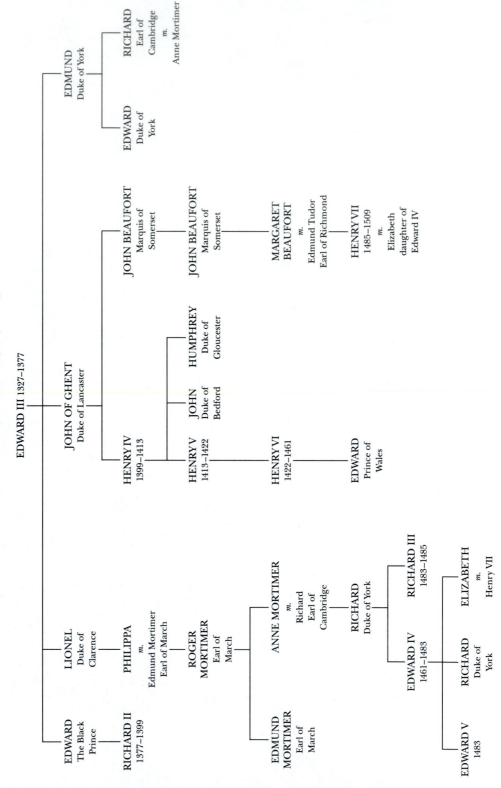

- EDWARD III 1327–1377
  - EDWARD The Black Prince
    - RICHARD II 1377–1399
  - LIONEL Duke of Clarence
    - PHILIPPA *m.* Edmund Mortimer Earl of March
      - ROGER MORTIMER Earl of March
        - EDMUND MORTIMER Earl of March
        - ANNE MORTIMER *m.* Richard Earl of Cambridge
          - RICHARD Duke of York
            - EDWARD IV 1461–1483
              - EDWARD V 1483
              - RICHARD Duke of York
              - ELIZABETH *m.* Henry VII
            - RICHARD III 1483–1485
  - JOHN OF GHENT Duke of Lancaster
    - HENRY IV 1399–1413
      - HENRY V 1413–1422
        - HENRY VI 1422–1461
          - EDWARD Prince of Wales
      - JOHN Duke of Bedford
      - HUMPHREY Duke of Gloucester
    - JOHN BEAUFORT Marquis of Somerset
      - JOHN BEAUFORT Marquis of Somerset
        - MARGARET BEAUFORT *m.* Edmund Tudor Earl of Richmond
          - HENRY VII 1485–1509 *m.* Elizabeth daughter of Edward IV
  - EDMUND Duke of York
    - EDWARD Duke of York
    - RICHARD Earl of Cambridge *m.* Anne Mortimer

Table 7
The Valois Kings of France

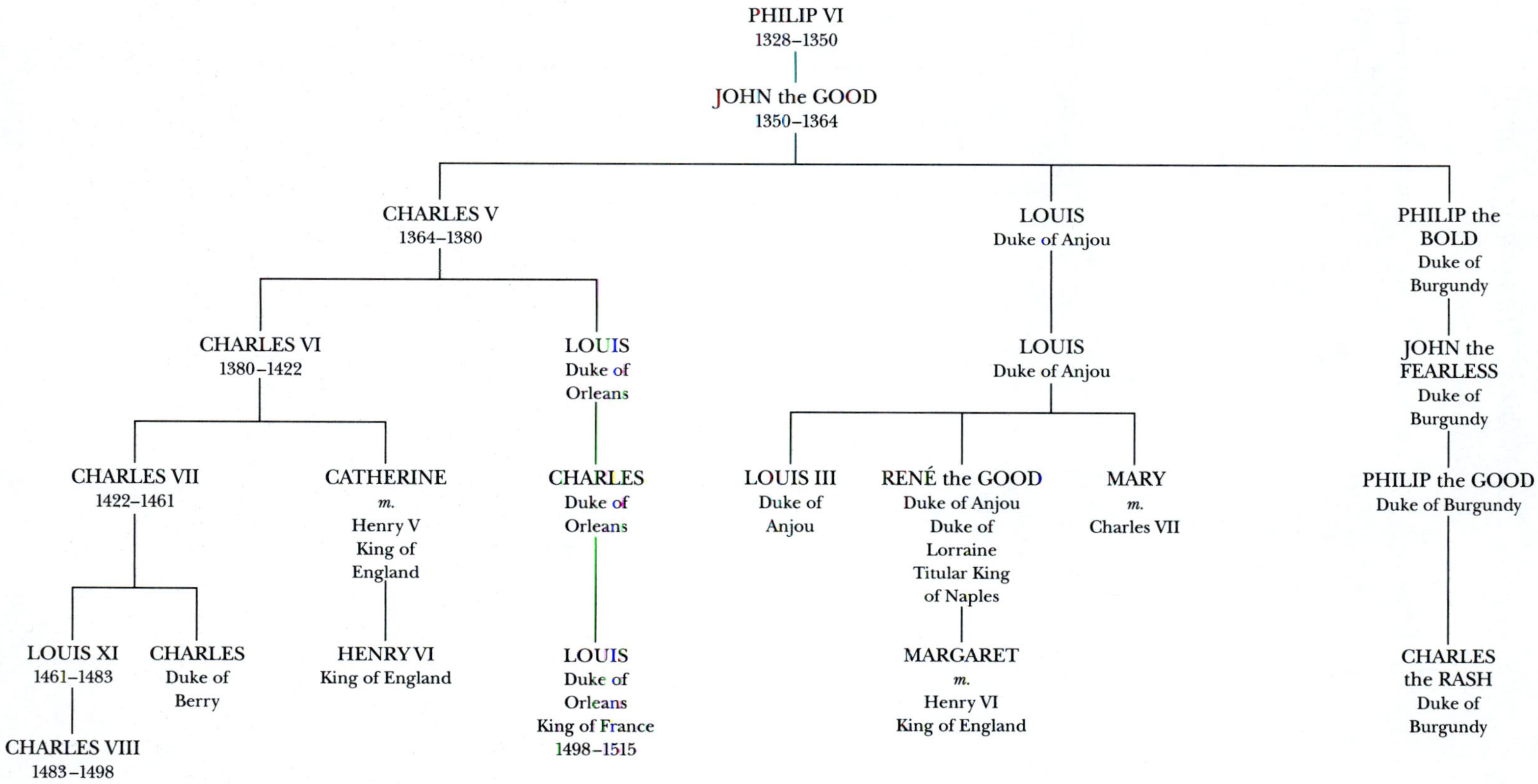
PHILIP VI
1328–1350
JOHN the GOOD
1350–1364
CHARLES V
1364–1380
LOUIS
Duke of Anjou
PHILIP the BOLD
Duke of Burgundy
CHARLES VI
1380–1422
LOUIS
Duke of Orleans
LOUIS
Duke of Anjou
JOHN the FEARLESS
Duke of Burgundy
CHARLES VII
1422–1461
CATHERINE
m.
Henry V
King of England
CHARLES
Duke of Orleans
LOUIS III
Duke of Anjou
RENÉ the GOOD
Duke of Anjou
Duke of Lorraine
Titular King of Naples
MARY
m.
Charles VII
PHILIP the GOOD
Duke of Burgundy
LOUIS XI
1461–1483
CHARLES
Duke of Berry
HENRY VI
King of England
LOUIS
Duke of Orleans
King of France
1498–1515
MARGARET
m.
Henry VI
King of England
CHARLES
the RASH
Duke of Burgundy
CHARLES VIII
1483–1498

Table 8
The Luxemburg, Hapsburg, and Wittelsbach Emperors

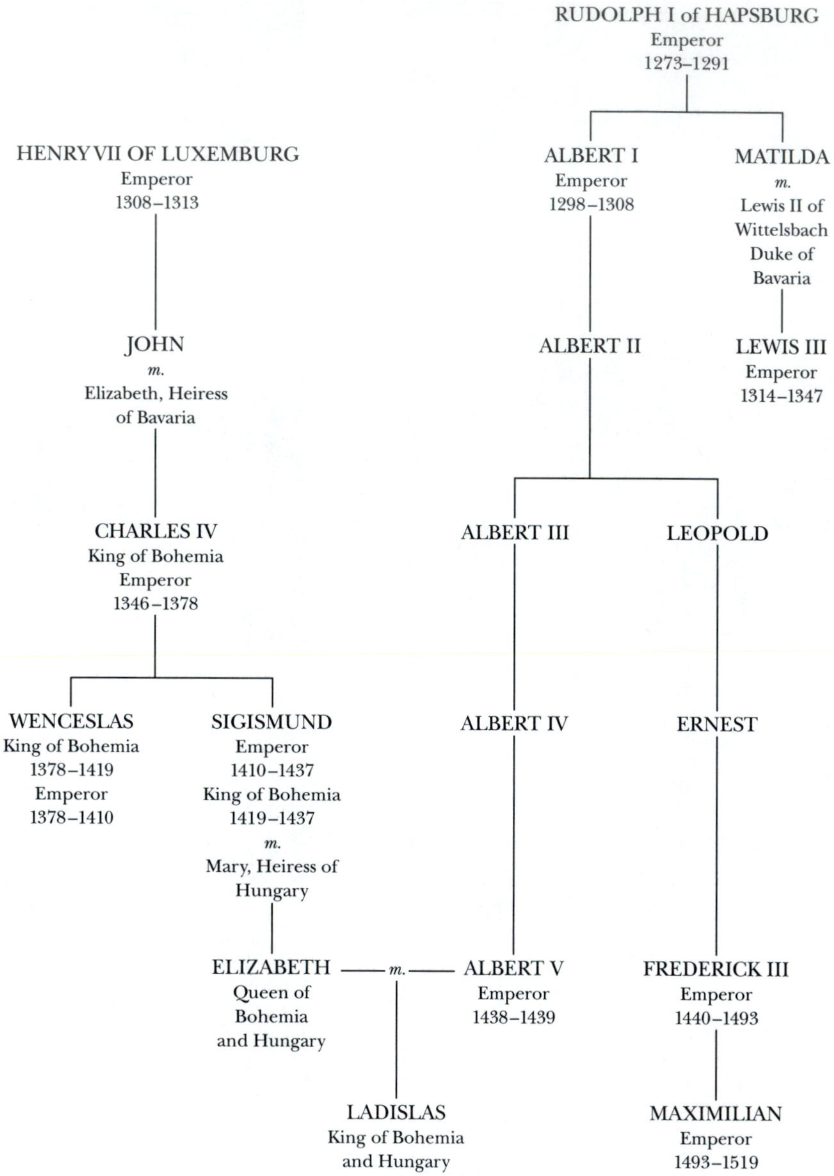
RUDOLPH I of HAPSBURG
Emperor
1273–1291
HENRY VII OF LUXEMBURG
Emperor
1308–1313
ALBERT I
Emperor
1298–1308
MATILDA
m.
Lewis II of Wittelsbach Duke of Bavaria
JOHN
m.
Elizabeth, Heiress of Bavaria
ALBERT II
LEWIS III
Emperor
1314–1347
CHARLES IV
King of Bohemia
Emperor
1346–1378
ALBERT III
LEOPOLD
WENCESLAS
King of Bohemia
1378–1419
Emperor
1378–1410
SIGISMUND
Emperor
1410–1437
King of Bohemia
1419–1437
m.
Mary, Heiress of Hungary
ALBERT IV
ERNEST
ELIZABETH
Queen of Bohemia and Hungary
m.
ALBERT V
Emperor
1438–1439
FREDERICK III
Emperor
1440–1493
LADISLAS
King of Bohemia and Hungary
MAXIMILIAN
Emperor
1493–1519

Table 9

The Spanish Kings from the Tenth to the Thirteenth Centuries

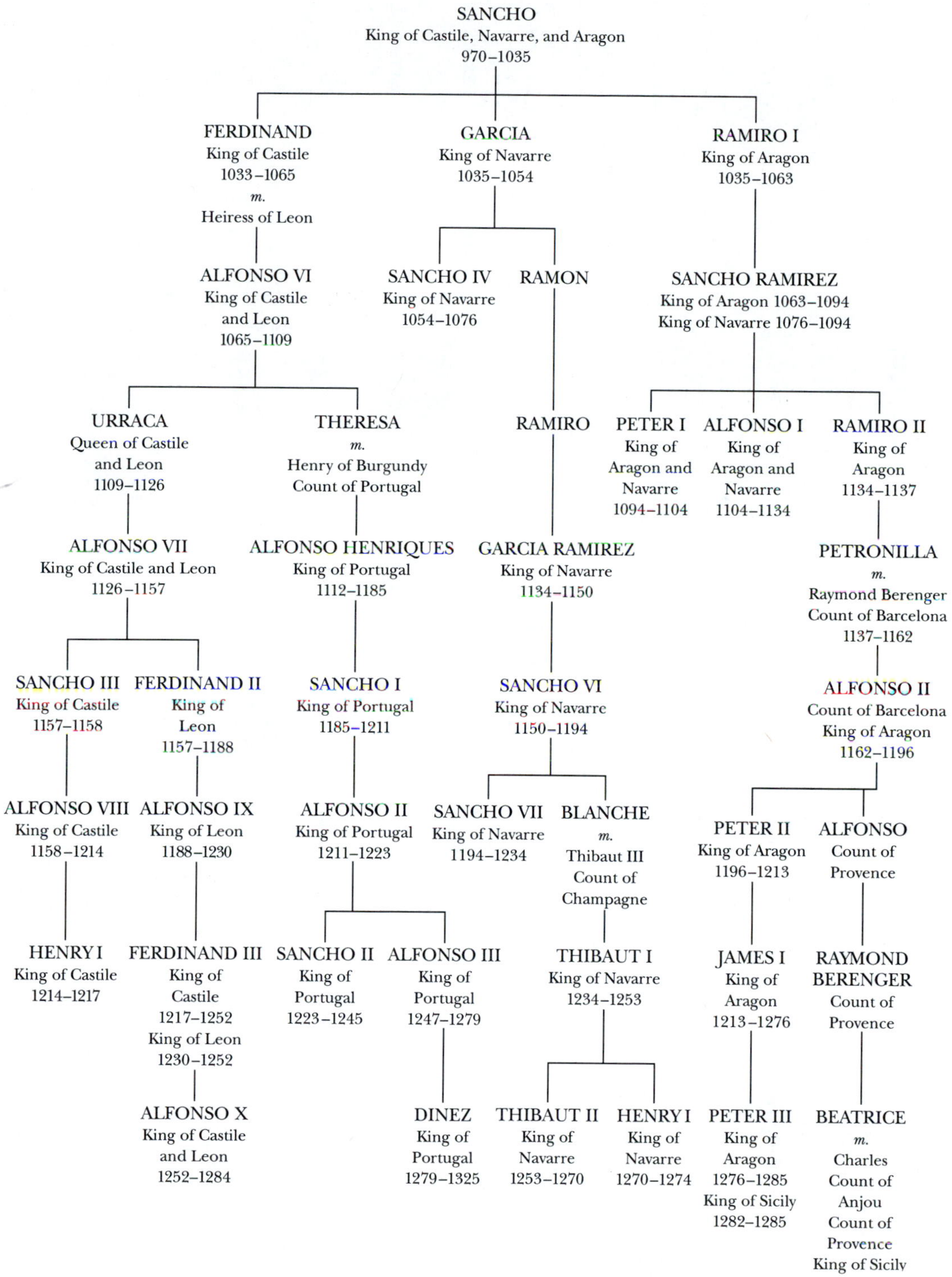

Table 10

The Spanish Kings in the Later Middle Ages

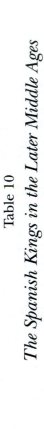

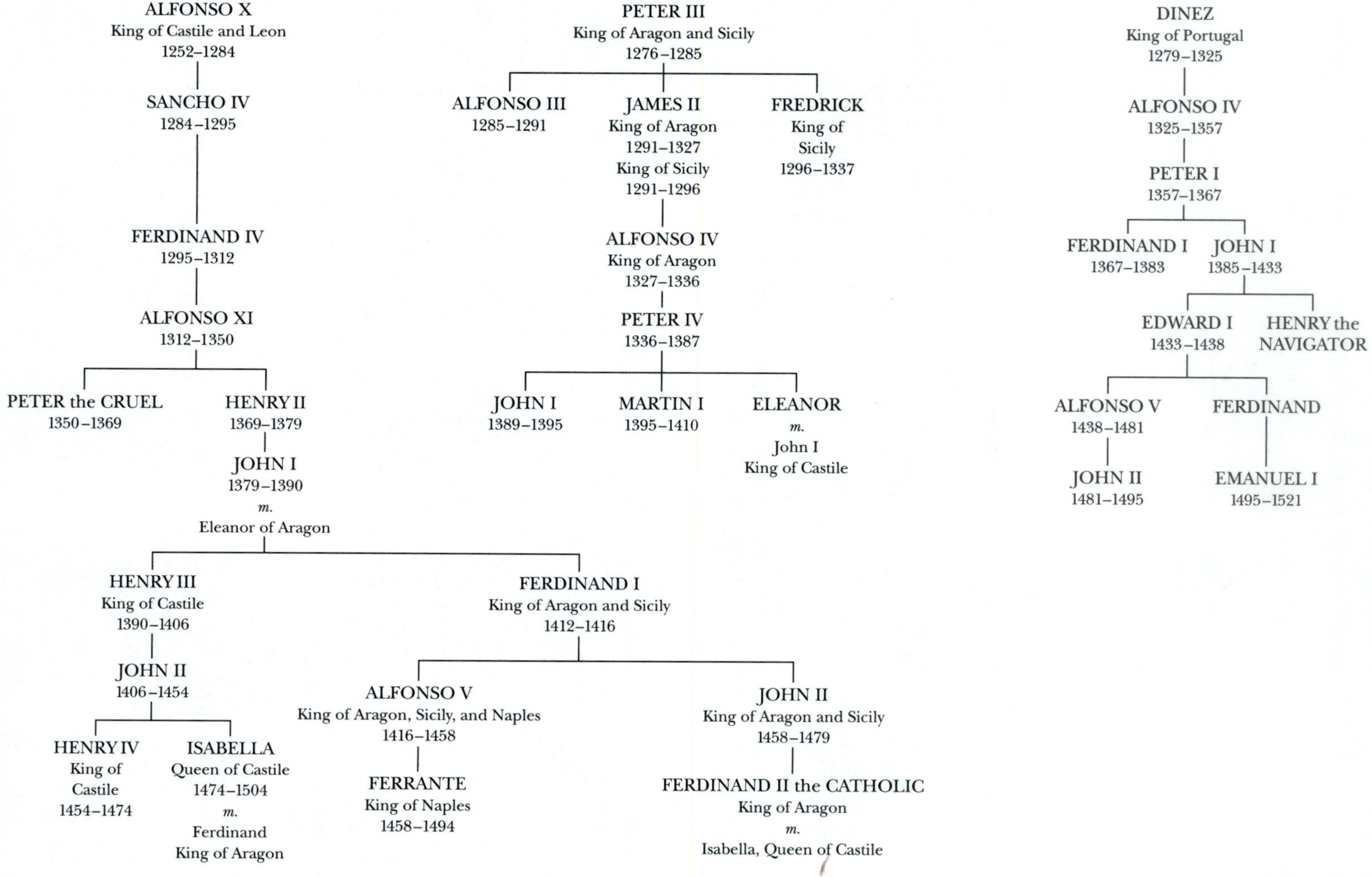

Index

A Note On The Type

The text of this book has been set on the computer in a type-face called "Baskerville," based on the linotype face of the same name. The face is a facsimile reproduction of types cast from molds made for John Baskerville (1706–75) from his designs. John Baskerville's original face was one of the forerunners of the type-style known as "modern face" to printers—a "modern" of the period A.D. 1800.